ANCIENT PHILOSOPHY

Philosophic Classics, Third Edition
Volume I

ANCIENT PHILOSOPHY

FORREST E. BAIRD, EDITOR
Whitworth College

WALTER KAUFMANN
Late, of Princeton University

Prentice Hall, Upper Saddle River, New Jersey 07458

Library of Congress Cataloging-in-Publication Data

Philosophic classics / Forrest E. Baird, editor.—3rd ed.
    p. cm.
    "Walter Kaufmann, late, of Princeton University."
    Includes bibliographical references.
    Contents: v. 1. Ancient philosophy—v. 2. Medieval philosophy—
v. 3. Modern philosophy—v. 4. Nineteenth-century philosophy. 2nd
ed.—v. 5. Twentiety-century philosophy. 2nd ed.
    ISBN 0–13–021314–4 (v. 1).—ISBN 0–13–021315–2 (v. 2).—ISBN
0–13–021316–0 (v. 3).—ISBN 0–13–021533–3 (v. 4).—ISBN
0–13–021534–1 (v. 5)
    1. Philosophy.   I. Baird, Forrest E.   II. Kaufmann, Walter
Arnold.
B21.P39   2000
100—dc21   98–32332
                                               CIP

Editor-in-chief: Charlyce Jones-Owen
Acquisitions editor: Karita France
Editorial assistant: Jennifer Ackerman
Prepress and manufacturing buyer:
  Tricia Kenny
Production liaison: Fran Russello
Editorial/production supervision:
  Bruce Hobart (Pine Tree Composition)
Cover director: Jayne Conte
Cover photo: Exekias. "Achilles and Ajax playing dice." Black figured amphora,
  Attic. Museo Gregoriano Etrusco, Vatican Museums, Vatican State.
  Scala/Art Resource, NY.
Marketing manager: Ilse Wolfe

This book was set in 10/12 Times Roman by Pine Tree Composition, Inc.,
and was printed and bound by R.R. Donnelley & Sons Company.
The cover was printed by Phoenix Color Corp.

Printed in the United States of America

10 9 8 7 6 5 4 3 2 1

ISBN 0-13-021314-4

Prentice-Hall International (UK) Limited, *London*
Prentice-Hall of Australia Pty. Limited, *Sydney*
Prentice-Hall Canada, Inc., *Toronto*
Prentice-Hall Hispanoamericana, S.A., *Mexico*
Prentice-Hall of India Private Limited, *New Dehli*
Prentice-Hall of Japan, Ltd., *Tokyo*
Pearson Education Asia Pte. Ltd., *Singapore*
Editora Prentice-Hall do Brasil, Ltda., *Rio de Janeiro*

This volume is dedicated to

STANLEY R. OBITTS

and

ROBERT N. WENNBERG

Professors of Philosophy
Westmont College

Contents

Preface

The philosophers of ancient Greece have fascinated thinking persons for centuries, and their writings have been one of the key influences on the development of Western civilization. Beginning with the fragmentary statements of the Pre-Socratics, moving to the all-embracing systems of Plato and Aristotle, and culminating in the practical advice of the Hellenistic writers, Greek philosophers have defined the questions and suggested many of the answers for subsequent generations. As the great Greek statesman, Pericles, sagely predicted, "Future ages will wonder at us, as the present age wonders at us now."

This volume in the *Philosophic Classics* series includes the writings of the most important Greek philosophers, along with selections from some of their Roman followers. In choosing texts for this volume, I tried wherever possible to follow three principles: (1) to use complete works or, where more appropriate, complete sections of works (2) in clear translations (3) of texts central to the thinker's philosophy or widely accepted as part of the "canon." To make the works more accessible to students, most footnotes treating textual matters (variant readings, etc.) have been omitted and all Greek words have been transliterated and put in angle brackets. In addition, each thinker is introduced by a brief essay composed of three sections: (1) biographical (a glimpse of the life), (2) philosophical (a résumé of the philosopher's thought), and (3) bibliographical (suggestions for further reading).

For this edition, a number of small changes have been made:

Additions: Thucydides' report of Pericles' *Funeral Oration* and *The Melian Conference* are included as context to give two views of Athens. The portion of Book I from Plato's *Republic* that discusses justice is now included, and I have changed to the Cornford translation. A selection from Aristotle's *Politics* is also now included.

Deletions: To make room for the additions listed above, I cut some of the Democritus fragments and dropped Antiphon altogether. The selections from Aristotle's *Posterior Analytics* and *Physics* have been shortened as has the selection from Lucretius's *On the Nature of Things.*

Those who use this first volume in a one-term course in ancient philosophy will find more material here than can easily fit a normal semester. But this embarrassment of riches gives teachers some choice and, for those who offer the same course year after year, an opportunity to change the menu.

*   *   *

I would like to thank the many people who assisted me in this volume, including the library staff of Whitworth College, especially Hans Bynagle, Gail Fielding, and Jeanette Langston; my colleagues F. Dale Bruner, who made helpful suggestions on all the introductions, and Barbara Filo, who helped select the artwork; Stephen Davis, Claremont McKenna College; Jerry H. Gill, The College of St. Rose; Rex Hollowell, Spokane Falls Community College; Stanley Obitts, Westmont College; and Charles Young, The Claremont College Graduate School, who each read some of the introductions and gave helpful advice; my secretary, Michelle Seefried; and my production editor, Bruce Hobart, my acquisitions editor, Karita France of Prentice Hall; and my former acquisitions editors, Angela Stone and Ted Bolen. I would also like to acknowledge the following reviewers: James W. Allard, Montana State University; David Apolloni, Augsberg College; Robert C. Bennett, El Centro College; Herbert L. Carson, Ferris State University; Helen S. Lang, Trinity College; Scott MacDonald, University of Iowa; Reginald Savage, North Carolina State University; Gregory Schultz, Wisconsin Lutheran College; Stephen Scott, Eastern Washington University; Daniel C. Shartin, Worcester State College; Donald Phillip Verene, Emory University; Robert M. Wieman, Ohio University; and Sarah Worth, Allegheny College.

I am especially thankful to my wife, Joy Lynn Fulton Baird, and to our children, Whitney Jaye, Sydney Tev, and Soren David, who have supported me in this enterprise. Finally, I would like to thank Stanley R. Obitts and Robert N. Wennberg, who first introduced me to the joys of philosophy. It is to them that this volume is dedicated.

Forrest E. Baird
Professor of Philosophy
Whitworth College
Spokane, WA 99251
email: fbaird@whitworth.edu

ANCIENT PHILOSOPHY

Philosophers In This Volume

600 B.C.	500 B.C	400 B.C.	300 B.C.	200 B.C.
Thales		Plato		
Anaximander		Aristotle		
Anaximenes		Pyrrho		
Pythagoras			Epicurus	
Xenophanes			Zeno of Citium	
	Heraclitus		Cleanthes	
	Anaxagoras			
	Protagoras			
	Pericles			
	Sophocles			
	Parmenides			
	Empedocles			
	Herodotus			
	Gorgias			
	Euripides			
	Socrates			
	Zeno of Elea			
	Thucydides			
	Democritus			
	Hippocrates			
	Melissus			
	Aristophanes			
	Ezra			

Other Important Figures

600 B.C.	500 B.C	400 B.C.	300 B.C.	200 B.C.
Zoroaster		Nehemiah		
Lao Tzu		Alexander the Great		
Ezekial		Euclid		
	Buddah			
	Confucius			

A Sampling of Major Events

600 B.C.	500 B.C	400 B.C.	300 B.C.	200 B.C.
Jerusalem falls to Babylonians			Punic Wars and rise of Rome	
Battle of Marathon			Wall of China	
Parthenon built				
Peloponnesian War				

600 B.C.	500 B.C	400 B.C.	300 B.C.	200 B.C.

Lucretius

Epictetus

Marcus Aurelius

Sextus
Empiricus
Plotinus

Julius Caesar

Philo of Alexandria
Jesus
Paul

Justin Martyr
Ptolemy (astronomer)
Clement of Alexandria
Tertullian
Origen

Caesar meets Cleopatra in Egypt
Jerusalem Temple destroyed
Farthest extent of the Roman
Empire
Chinese invent paper

BEFORE
SOCRATES

——◀︎◯▶︎——

Something unusual happened in Greece and the Greek colonies of the Aegean Sea some twenty-five hundred years ago. Whereas the previous great cultures of the Mediterranean had used mythological stories of the gods to explain the operations of the world and of the self, some of the Greeks began to discover new ways of explaining things. Instead of reading their ideas into, or out of, ancient scriptures or poems, they began to use reason, contemplation, and sensory observation to make sense of reality.

The story, as we know it, began with the Greeks living on the coast of Asia Minor (present-day Turkey). These colonists, such as Thales, tried to find the one common element in the diversity of nature. Subsequent thinkers, such as Anaximenes, sought not only to find this one common element, but also to find the process by which one form changes into another. Other thinkers, such as Pythagoras, turned to the nature of form itself rather than the basic stuff that takes on a particular form. These lovers of wisdom, or *philosophers,* came to very different conclusions and often spoke disrespectfully of one another. Some held the universe to be one, while others insisted that it must be many. Some believed that human knowledge was capable of understanding virtually everything about the world, while others thought that it was not possible to have any knowledge at all. But despite all their differences, there is a thread of continuity, a continuing focus: the *human* attempt to understand the world, using *human* reason. This fact distinguishes these philosophers from the great minds that preceded them.

There are excellent reasons for beginning a study of philosophy with these men and then proceeding to Socrates and Plato. This, after all, is how Western

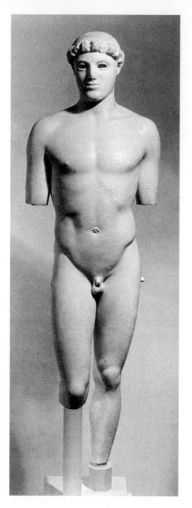

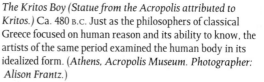

The Kritos Boy (Statue from the Acropolis attributed to Kritos.) Ca. 480 B.C. Just as the philosophers of classical Greece focused on human reason and its ability to know, the artists of the same period examined the human body in its idealized form. (*Athens, Acropolis Museum. Photographer: Alison Frantz.*)

philosophy did begin, and we can still recapture something of the excitement of this new way of thinking as we move from the bald statements of Thales to the all-embracing questions of Socrates, and thence to Plato's efforts to fuse criticism with construction.

If dissatisfaction with facile answers is the starting point of philosophic thought, the fragments of the Pre-Socratics are especially appropriate for a beginning. Not one of their works has survived complete—all we have are scattered quotations and reports from later writers. As a result, Pre-Socratic thought has a mysterious quality. Cryptic passages and forceful aphorisms, whose original context is lost, stimulate the imagination. Instead of looking for "the" answer, one is fascinated by a wealth of possible answers. And in the effort to show why some suggested answers are untenable, one develops critical faculties.

Some fragments may remind readers of archaic statues—heads with broken noses, torsos without heads or arms—pieces so perfect in form that one has no regrets at the loss of the whole and may even believe that the complete work could not have been as fascinating.

For all that, most interest in the Pre-Socratics is motivated by the fact that these thinkers furnish the backdrop for the thought of Socrates, Plato, and Aristotle—this is why one lumps them together as the "Pre-Socratics." But this magnificent succession of thinkers deserves more respect. Though often enigmatic and at times oracular, the Pre-Socratics are distinguished above all by their appeal to reason. And through the appeal to reason, each thinker makes it possible for successors to exercise criticism, to amend, to develop alternatives, to move beyond.

The Pre-Socratics' influence on Plato was so great that a study of their thought is essential to understanding many passages in his dialogues and his intentions; many problems were suggested to him by Heraclitus, the Eleatics, and the Pythagoreans—and, of course, by his originality. Aristotle studied the Pre-Socratics closely and discussed them at length in the first book of his *Metaphysics* (reprinted in this volume). Of the later Greek philosophers, it has often been remarked that the Stoics were particularly influenced by Heraclitus, and the Epicureans by Democritus. Elements of Orphism, an early Greek religious movement, also found their way into the ideas of the Pre-Socratics—most obviously, but by no means only, into Pythagoreanism—and hence into Plato and, later, into Christianity. In fact, a few of the fragments survived only as quotations in the works of early Christian writers.

*   *   *

What follows is only a selection. There is no such thing as a complete roster of the Pre-Socratics. The so-called Sophists were Socrates' contemporaries, but Protagoras and Gorgias were older than he and had acquired reputations before he came along and challenged them; they are included here. After all, his thought developed partly in response to their teaching. Among the older writers, it is arguable who was, and who was not, a philosopher. Various poets, for example, are occasionally included among the Pre-Socratics. Not counting the Sophists, the present selection concentrates on twelve major figures. They might conveniently be arranged into four groups of three: (1) the three great Milesians (Thales, Anaximander, and Anaximenes); (2) the three great independents—figures who came from different places and stood for quite different principles (Pythagoras, Xenophanes, and Heraclitus); (3) the three great Eleatics (Parmenides, Zeno of Elea, and Melissus); and finally (4) the three great pluralists (Empedocles, Anaxagoras, and Democritus). The only major name missing in this list is Leucippus, founder of the atomistic philosophy, who is included with his better-known follower, Democritus.

If we were to offer all the fragments of the twelve figures, we would have to include such unhelpful items as the following, each given in its entirety: "The joint connects two things"; "as when fig juice binds white milk"; "having kneaded together barley-meal with water" (Empedocles, fragments 32, 33, 34). Instead, the following selections were chosen to give an idea of each thinker's main teachings, as far as possible in his own words, and to provide some sense of his way of thinking and feeling. In short, the selections should give us the essence of thinkers who still have the power to astonish students across roughly twenty-five hundred years.

*   *   *

For a discussion of the primary sources, see the "Sources of the Fragments" section on page 47. For a comprehensive work on the Pre-Socratics, see Volumes I and II of W.K.C. Guthrie's authoritative *The History of Greek Philosophy,* six volumes (Cambridge: Cambridge University Press, 1962–1981). John Burnet, *Early Greek Philosophy* (1892; reprinted New York: Meridian, 1960); John Mansley Robinson, *An Introduction to Early Greek Philosophy* (Boston: Houghton Mifflin, 1968); Jonathan Barnes, *The Pre-Socratic Philosophers* (London: Routledge & Kegan Paul, 1982); and Edward Hussey, *The Presocratics* (Indianapolis, IN: Hackett, 1995) are standard secondary sources, while the relevant sections of W.T. Jones, *The Classical Mind* (New York: Harcourt, Brace & World, 1969); Frederick Copleston, *A History of Philosophy: Volume I, Greece & Rome, Part I* (Garden City, NY: Doubleday, 1962); Friedo Ricken, *Philosophy of the Ancients,* translated by Eric Watkins (Notre Dame, IN: University of Notre Dame Press, 1991); and J.V. Luce, *An Introduction to Greek Philosophy* (New York: Thames and Hudson, 1992) provide basic introductions. Robert S. Brumbaugh, *The Philosophers of Greece* (Albany, NY: SUNY Press, 1981), is an accessible introduction with pictures, charts, and maps. Francis MacDonald Cornford, *Principium Sapientiae: The Origins of Greek Philosophical Thought* (Cambridge: Cambridge University Press, 1952), and Werner Jaeger, *The Theology of the Early Greek Philosophers* (Oxford: Clarendon Press, 1947) are both classic works that discuss the movement from mythology to philosophy. For collections of essays, see David J. Furley and R.E. Allen, eds., *Studies in Presocratic Philosophy,* two volumes (New York: Humanities Press, 1970–1975); A.P.D. Mourelatos, ed., *The Pre-Socratics* (Princeton, NJ: Princeton University Press, 1993); Gregory Vlastos, ed., *Studies in Greek Philosophy, Volume I: The Presocratics* (Princeton, NJ: Princeton University Press, 1995); and Terence Irwin, ed., *Philosophy Before Socrates* (Hamden, CT: Garland Publishing, 1995).

In addition to the general sources listed here, the individual articles in Paul Edwards, ed., *The Encyclopedia of Philosophy* (New York: Macmillan, 1967) and Edward Craig, *Routledge Encyclopedia of Philosophy* (New York: Routledge, 1998) are frequently useful. Consult the following books for these specific thinkers:

ANAXIMANDER: Charles H. Kahn, *Anaximander and the Origins of Greek Cosmology* (New York: Columbia University Press, 1960).

PYTHAGORAS: Walter Burkert, *Lore and Science in Ancient Pythagoreanism,* translated by Edwin L. Minar Jr. (Cambridge, MA: Harvard University Press, 1972).

HERACLITUS: G.S. Kirk, *Heraclitus: The Cosmic Fragments* (Cambridge: Cambridge University Press, 1954); and Charles H. Kahn, *The Art and Thought of Heraclitus* (Cambridge: Cambridge University Press, 1979).

PARMENIDES: Leonardo Tarán, *Parmenides: A Text with Translation, Commentary, and Critical Essays* (Princeton, NJ: Princeton University Press, 1965); A.P.D. Mourelatos, *The Route of Parmenides* (New Haven, CT: Yale University Press, 1970); David Gallop, *Parmenides of Elea* (Toronto: University of Toronto Press, 1984); and Patricia Curd, *The Legacy of Parmenides* (Princeton, NJ: Princeton University Press, 1998).

ZENO OF ELEA: Wesley C. Salmon, ed., *Zeno's Paradoxes* (Indianapolis, IN: Bobbs-Merrill, 1970); Adolf Grünbaum, *Modern Science and Zeno's Paradoxes*

(Middletown, CT: Wesleyan University Press, 1967); and J.A. Faris, *The Paradoxes of Zeno* (Avebury, UK: Ashegate, 1996).

EMPEDOCLES: Denis O'Brien, *Empedocles' Cosmic Cycle* (Cambridge: Cambridge University Press, 1969); and M.R. Wright, *Empedocles: The Extant Fragments* (Indianapolis, IN: Hackett, 1995).

ANAXAGORAS: Malcolm Schofield, *An Essay on Anaxagoras* (Cambridge: Cambridge University Press, 1980).

DEMOCRITUS (ATOMISM): Cyril Bailey, *The Greek Atomists and Epicurus* (Oxford: Clarendon Press, 1928; reprinted New York: Russell and Russell, 1964).

SOPHISTS: G.B. Kerferd, *The Sophistic Movement* (Cambridge: Cambridge University Press, 1981).

Much of the critical work on the Pre-Socratics is found only in journal articles. *The Philosophers' Index* offers a way to locate such articles. (Please note that some of the books on specific thinkers assume some knowledge of Ancient Greek and can be very technical.)

The Milesians

THALES
fl. ca. 585 B.C.

Thales lived in Miletus in Asia Minor (on the east coast of present-day Turkey) and is said to have been so scientifically skilled that he accurately predicted the eclipse of the sun on May 23, 585 B.C. He was a contemporary of the Hebrew prophet Jeremiah, of the Persian prophet Zoroaster, of the Indian sage Gautama Siddhartha (the Buddha), and of the Chinese philosophers Confucius and Lao-Tze.

Thales has traditionally been considered the first Western philosopher (though some scholars now claim that this honor belongs to Anaximander). Thales was apparently the first to ask the question, "What is the basic 'stuff' of the universe?" According to Aristotle, Thales claimed that this basic stuff was water. This claim involves three vital assumptions: (1) that the fundamental explanation of the universe must be one in number, (2) that this one reality must be a "thing," and (3) that this one thing must have within itself the ability to move and change. Later thinkers disputed Thales' choice of the universe's basic "stuff," but his bold theory encouraged them and helped them develop their own philosophical programs.

Like many other Pre-Socratics, Thales was by no means a philosopher only. He was also a statesman, an astronomer, a geometer, and a sage. The first three fragments that follow deal with Thales' life. Number one is probably the world's oldest "absent-minded professor" story, while numbers two and three appear to be defenses designed to show how practical Thales could be. The remaining fragments are reports on Thales' ideas. There are no known writings by Thales himself.

[1]* A witty and attractive Thracian servant-girl is said to have mocked Thales for falling into a well while he was observing the stars and gazing upwards; declaring that he was eager to know the things in the sky, but that what was behind him and just by his feet escaped his notice.

[2] When they reproached him because of his poverty, as though philosophy were no use, it is said that, having observed through his study of the heavenly bodies that there would be a large olive-crop, he raised a little capital while it was still winter, and paid deposits on all the olive presses in Miletus and Chios, hiring them cheaply because no one bid against him. When the appropriate time came there was a sudden rush of requests for the presses; he then hired them out on his own terms and so made a large profit, thus demonstrating that it is easy for philosophers to be rich, if they wish, but that it is not in this that they are interested.

[3] When he came to the Halys river, Croesus then, as I say, put his army across by the existing bridges; but, according to the common account of the Greeks, Thales the Milesian transferred the army for him. For it is said that Croesus was at a loss how his army should cross the river, since these bridges did not yet exist at this period; and that Thales, who was present in the army, made the river, which flowed on the left hand of the army, flow on the right hand also. He did so in this way: beginning upstream of the army he dug a deep channel, giving it a crescent shape, so that it should flow round the back of where the army was encamped, being diverted in this way from its old course by the channel, and passing the camp should flow into its old course once more. The result was that as soon as the river was divided it became fordable in both of its parts.

*   *   *

[4] Thales . . . says the principle is water (for which reason he declared that the earth rests on water), getting the notion perhaps from seeing that the nutriment of all things is moist, and that heat itself is generated from the moist and kept alive by it . . . , and from the fact that the seeds of all things have a moist nature, and that water is the origin of the nature of moist things.

[5] Moist natural substance, since it is easily formed into each different thing, is accustomed to undergo very various changes: that part of it which is exhaled is made into air, and the finest part is kindled from air into aether, while when water is compacted and changes into slime it becomes earth. Therefore Thales declared that water, of the four elements, was the most active, as it were, as cause.

[6] He [Thales] said that the world is held up by water and rides like a ship, and when it is said to "quake" it is actually rocking because of the water's movement.

[7] Thales, too, seems, from what they relate, to have supposed that the soul was something kinetic, if he said that the [Magnesian] stone possesses soul because it moves iron.

[8] Some say that it [soul] is intermingled in the universe, for which reason, perhaps, Thales also thought that all things are full of gods.

*The numbers in brackets serve the purposes of this volume. See the "Sources of the Fragments" section on page 47 for the source of each fragment.

ANAXIMANDER
ca. 610–ca. 546 B.C.

Anaximander was born in Miletus about 610 B.C., and he died around 546 B.C. During his lifetime, Nebuchadnezzar conquered Jerusalem and the prophet Ezekiel was exiled to Babylon. Anaximander traveled extensively and was so highly regarded by his fellow Milesians that he was honored with the leadership of a new colony. He may have been the first Greek to write a book of prose.

Anaximander seems to have accepted Thales' three basic assumptions (summed up in the statement that the universe must be one changeable thing), but he differed with Thales on the nature of the "stuff" underlying the "many" that we observe. In place of Thales' water, Anaximander introduced the concept of the <apeiron>—the unlimited, boundless, infinite, or indefinite—as the fundamental principle of the world. This notion was a step up in philosophical sophistication—a metaphysical principle rather than an empirically observed material thing. This idea of a basic "stuff," with properties different from anything in the observable world, has survived to the present.

Anaximander also developed a rudimentary concept of natural law—the idea that all growing things in the natural world develop according to an identical pattern. He invented the idea of models, drawing what is considered to be the first geographical map. But what has fascinated all subsequent students of philosophy, more than anything else, is the one sentence, or half-sentence, quoted by Simplicius in fragment [3] which follows. This remark, the oldest known piece of Western philosophy, has elicited a large body of literature, including a forty-eight-page essay by Martin Heidegger.

[1] Anaximander son of Praxiades, of Miletus, philosopher, was a kinsman, pupil, and successor of Thales. He first discovered the equinox and solstices and hour-indicators, and that the earth lies in the center. He introduced the gnomon [a vertical rod whose shadow indicates the sun's direction and height] and in general made known an outline of geometry. He wrote *On Nature, Circuit of the Earth* and *On the Fixed Stars and a Celestial Globe,* and some other works.

[2] [Anaximander] was the first of the Greeks whom we know who ventured to produce a written account on nature.

*   *   *

[3] Of those who say that it is one, moving, and infinite, Anaximander, son of Praxiades, a Milesian, the successor and pupil of Thales, said that the principle and element of existing things was the <*apeiron*> [indefinite, or infinite], being the first to introduce this name of the material principle. He says that it is neither water nor any other of the so-called elements, but some other <*apeiron*> nature, from which come into being all the heavens and the worlds in them. And the source of coming-to-be for existing things is that into which destruction, too, happens "according to necessity; for they pay penalty and retribution to each other for their injustice according to the assessment of time," as he describes it in these rather poetical terms. It is clear that he, seeing the changing of the four elements into each other, thought it right to make none of these the substratum, but something else besides these; and he produces coming-to-be not through the alteration of the element, but by the separation off of the opposites through the eternal motion.

[4] He says that that which is productive from the eternal of hot and cold was separated off at the coming-to-be of this world, and that a kind of sphere of flame from this was formed round the air surrounding the earth, like bark around a tree. When this was broken off and shut off in certain circles, the sun and moon and stars were formed.

[5] He says that the earth is cylindrical in shape, and that its depth is a third of its width.

[6] Its shape is curved, round, similar to the drum of a column; of its flat surfaces we walk on one, and the other is on the opposite side.

[7] Anaximander [says the sun] is a circle twenty-eight times the size of the earth, like a chariot wheel, with its [rim] hollow and full of fire, and showing the fire at a certain point through an aperture as though through the nozzle of a bellows.

[8] Anaximander said that the first living creatures were born in moisture, enclosed in thorny barks; and that as their age increased they came forth on to the drier part and, when the bark had broken off, they lived a different kind of life for a short time.

[9] Further he says that in the beginning man was born from creatures of a different kind; because other creatures are soon self-supporting, but man alone needs prolonged nursing. For this reason he would not have survived if this had been his original form.

[10] Therefore they [the Syrians] actually revere the fish as being of similar race and nurturing. In this they philosophize more suitably than Anaximander; for he declares, not that fishes and men came into being in the same parents, but that originally men came into being inside fishes, and that, having been nurtured there—like sharks—and having become adequate to look after themselves, they then came forth and took to the land.

ANAXIMENES
fl. 546 B.C.?

Very little is known about the life of Anaximenes, except that he was a Milesian and a younger contemporary of Anaximander. Anaximenes proposed air as the basic world principle. While at first this thesis may seem a step backwards from the more comprehensive (like Anaximander's unlimited) to the less comprehensive particular (like Thales' water), Anaximenes added an important point. He explained a *process* by which the underlying one (air) becomes the observable many: By rarefaction, air becomes fire, and by condensation air becomes, successively, wind, water, and earth. Observable qualitative differences (fire, wind, water, earth) are the result of quantitative changes, that is, of how densely packed is the basic principle. This view is still held by scientists.

[1] Anaximenes, son of Eurystratus of Miletus, was a pupil of Anaximander. . . . He said that the material principle was air and the infinite; and that the stars move, not under the earth, but round it. He used simple and unsuperfluous Ionic speech. He was active, according to what Apollodorus says, around the time of the capture of Sardis [by Cyrus in 546/5 B.C.?], and died in the 63rd Olympiad.

[2] He [Anaximander] left Anaximenes as his disciple and successor, who attributed all the causes of things to infinite air, and did not deny that there were gods, or pass them over in silence; yet he believed not the air was made by them, but that they arose from air.

[3] And all things are produced by a kind of condensation, and again rarefaction, of this [air]. Motion, indeed, exists from everlasting; he says that when the air melts, there first of all comes into being the earth, quite flat—therefore it accordingly rides on the air; and sun and moon and the remaining heavenly bodies have their source of generation from earth. At last, he declares the sun to be earth, but that through the rapid motion it obtains heat in great sufficiency.

Three Solitary Figures

PYTHAGORAS
ca. 571–ca. 497 B.C.

Pythagoras was a contemporary of the Hebrew prophets Haggai and Zechariah, as well as of the Buddha, who had his enlightenment about 521 B.C. Born on the island of Samos, just off the coast of Asia Minor and very close to Miletus, Pythagoras moved to southern Italy, where the Greeks had colonies, and settled at Croton, on the Bay of Tarentum.

Pythagoras was soon associated with so many legends that few scholars dare to say much about his life, his personality, or even his teachings, without adding that we cannot be sure our information is accurate. That there was a man named Pythagoras who founded the sect called the Pythagoreans, we need not doubt: Among the witnesses to his historicity was his younger contemporary, Heraclitus, who thought ill of him (see Heraclitus, section D, following). Nevertheless, it is notoriously difficult to distinguish between the teachings of Pythagoras himself and those of his followers, the Pythagoreans.

Today he is best known for the so-called Pythagorean theorem in geometry (fragment [5] following). But his interest in mathematics went far beyond this theorem. Although the Egyptians and others had been interested in mathematics for its practical uses in building, commerce, and so on, Pythagoras was interested in mathematics for its own sake. And while the Milesians searched for the *stuff* of all things, Pythagoras (or the Pythagoreans) focused on the *form* of all things. He claimed that "things are numbers," that mathematical formulas and ratios explain the physical world. (Those who think this odd might ponder the contemporary physicist's assertion that an electron is a "probability cloud.")

Pythagoras was also interested in religious salvation and established a proto-monastic religious order with strict rules of conduct (see fragments [10–27]

11

following). His religion and his philosophy might seem disconnected to us, but for Pythagoras the two were inseparable. Like Plato after him, he believed that the study of mathematics could convert the soul from the world of the senses to the contemplation of the eternal. The religious sect Pythagoras founded still existed in Plato's time, 150 years later, and decisively influenced Plato's thought— an influence, in fact, second only to that of Plato's revered teacher, Socrates.

The following Pythagorean ideas especially influenced Plato: the dualism of body and soul and the conception of the body (*soma* in Greek) as the tomb (*sema* in Greek) of the soul; the belief in the immortality of the soul; the doctrine of the transmigration of souls; the idea that knowledge and a philosophic life are required for the salvation of the soul; the notion that one might design a society that would be an instrument of salvation for its members; the admission of women to this society; the suggestion that all members of this society should hold their property in common; and, finally, the division of humankind into three basic types—tradesmen being the lowest class; those in whom the competitive spirit and ambition are highly developed, a little higher; and those who prefer contemplation, the highest. In fact, the whole of Plato's thought, from his earliest to his latest works, can be understood as a gradual and sustained departure from the heritage of Socrates to that of Pythagoras.

[1] As I have heard from the Greeks who live on the Hellespont and the Black Sea, this Salmoxis was a man, who was a slave in Samos, the slave in fact of Pythagoras son of Mnesarchus. . . .

[2] Aristoxenus says that at the age of forty, seeing that the tyranny of Polycrates was too intense . . . he made his departure for Italy [to Croton].

[3] Three hundred of the young men [followers of Pythagoras], bound to each other by oath like a brotherhood, lived segregated from the rest of the citizens, as if to form a secret band of conspirators, and brought the city [Croton] under their control.

*   *   *

[4] Ten is the very nature of number. All Greeks and all barbarians alike count up to ten, and having reached ten revert again to the unit. And again, Pythagoras maintains, the power of the number ten lies in the number four, the tetrad. This is the reason: If one starts at the unit and adds the successive numbers up to four, one will make up the number ten; and if one exceeds the tetrad, one will exceed ten, too. If, that is, one takes the unit, adds two, then three, and then four, one will make up the number ten. . . . So the Pythagoreans used to invoke the tetrad as their most binding oath: "Nay, by him that gave to our generation the tetractys, which contains the fount and root of eternal nature."

[5] The square of the hypotenuse of a right-angled triangle is equal to the sum of the squares on the sides enclosing the right angle. [The text of the next sentence is corrupt, but the sense is:] If we pay any attention to those who like to recount ancient history, we may find some of them referring this theorem to Pythagoras, and saying that he sacrificed an ox in honor of his discovery.

[6] On the subject of reincarnation, Xenophanes bears witness in an elegy which begins: "Now I will turn to another tale and show the way." What he says about Pythagoras runs thus: "Once they say that he was passing by when a puppy was being whipped, and he took pity and said: Stop, do not beat it; for it is the soul of a friend that I recognized when I heard it giving tongue."

[7] Moreover, the Egyptians are the first to have maintained the doctrine that the soul of man is immortal and that, when the body perishes, it enters into another animal that is being born at the time, and when it has been the complete round of the creatures of the dry land and of the sea and of the air it enters again into the body of a man at birth; and its cycle is completed in three thousand years. There are some Greeks who have adopted this doctrine, some in former times and some in later, as if it were their own invention; their names I know but refrain from writing down.

[8] None the less the following became universally known: first that he maintains that the soul is immortal; next, that it changes into other kinds of living things; also that events recur in certain cycles, and that nothing is ever absolutely new; and finally, that all living things should be regarded as akin. Pythagoras seems to have been the first to bring these beliefs into Greece.

[9] If one were to believe the Pythagoreans that events recur in an arithmetical cycle, and that I shall be talking to you again sitting as you are now, with this pointer in my hand, and that everything else will be just as it is now, then it is plausible to suppose that the time, too, will be the same as now.

*   *   *

[10] Let the rules to be pondered be these:

[11] When you are going out to a temple, worship first, and on your way neither say nor do anything else connected with your daily life. (1)

[12] On a journey neither enter a temple nor worship at all, not even if you are passing the very doors. (2)

[13] Sacrifice and worship without shoes on. (3)

[14] Turn aside from highways and walk by footpaths. . . . (4)

[15] Follow the gods and restrain your tongue above all else. . . . (6)

[16] Stir not the fire with iron. . . . (8)

[17] Help a man who is loading freight, but not one who is unloading. (10)

[18] Putting on your shoes, start with the right foot; washing your feet, with the left. (11)

[19] Speak not of Pythagorean matters without light. (12)

[20] Never step over a cross-bar. (13)

[21] When you are out from home, look not back, for the furies come after you. . . . (14)

[22] Do not wear a ring. . . . (22)

[23] Do not look in a mirror beside a lamp. . . . (23)

[24] Eat not the heart. . . . (30)

[25] Spit upon the trimmings of your hair and finger-nails. . . . (32)

[26] Abstain from beans. . . . (37)

[27] Abstain from living things. (39)

[28] Pythagoras turned geometrical philosophy into a form of liberal education by seeking its first principles in a higher realm of reality.

[29] Life, he said, is like a festival; just as some come to the festival to compete, some to ply their trade, but the best people come as spectators, so in life the slavish men go hunting for fame or gain, the philosophers for the truth.

XENOPHANES
ca. 570–ca. 478 B.C.

A contemporary of Pythagoras, Xenophanes was from Colophon on the mainland of Asia Minor, a few miles inland and approximately fifty miles north of Miletus and about fifteen miles north of Ephesus. He traveled a great deal, reciting his poetry, of which only a few fragments survive. At one time he was thought to have been Parmenides' teacher and the founder of the Eleatic school, no doubt because of his conception of one unmoving god—a notion readily associated with Parmenides' idea of being. But this connection is now generally rejected, and Xenophanes is seen rather as an essentially solitary figure.

Little of his work has come down to us, but the little that has is unforgettable. Xenophanes challenges Homer's and Hesiod's anthropomorphic conception of the gods and invites skepticism about the ability of humans to know the divine.

[1] Xenophanes, son of Dexios, or, according to Apollodorus, of Orthomenes, of Colophon . . . being expelled from his native land, passed his time in Zancle in Sicily and in Catana. . . . He wrote in epic metre, also elegiacs and iambics, against Hesiod and Homer, reproving them for what they said about the gods. But he himself also recited his own original poems. He is said to have held contrary opinions to Thales and Pythagoras, and to have rebuked Epimenides, too. He had an extremely long life, as he himself somewhere says: "Already there are seven and sixty years tossing my thought up and down the land of Greece; and from my birth there were another twenty-five to add to these, if I know how to speak truly about these things."

[2] Homer and Hesiod ascribed to the gods whatever is infamy and reproach among men: theft and adultery and deceiving each other.

[3] Mortals suppose that the gods are born and have clothes and voices and shapes like their own.

[4] But if oxen, horses, and lions had hands or could paint with their hands and fashion works as men do, horses would paint horse-like images of gods and oxen ox-like ones, and each would fashion bodies like their own.

[5] The Ethiopians consider the gods flat-nosed and black; the Thracians blue-eyed and red-haired.

[6] There is one god, among gods and men the greatest, not at all like mortals in body or mind.

[7] He sees as a whole, thinks as a whole, and hears as a whole.

[8] But without toil he moves everything by the thought of his mind.

[9] He always remains in the same place, not moving at all, nor is it fitting for him to change his position at different times.

[10] Everything comes from earth and returns to earth in the end.

[11] No man knows or ever will know the truth about the gods and about everything I speak of: for even if one chanced to say the complete truth, yet oneself knows it not; but seeming is wrought over all things.

[12] Not from the beginning have the gods revealed all things to mortals, but by long seeking men find what is better.

HERACLITUS
fl. 500 B.C.

Little is known about the life of Heraclitus except that he lived in Ephesus (just north of Miletus) and flourished around 500 B.C. He may have come from an aristocratic family, since his writings indicate a clear contempt for common people. The mystery of his life, together with the obscurity of his writings, led the ancients to call him the "dark philosopher." His surviving epigrammatic fragments, though often paradoxical and elusive, are immensely suggestive, invite frequent rereading, and haunt the mind. In the sayings of Heraclitus, as in no previous philosopher, one encounters the personality of the thinker. After twenty-five centuries, he still evokes instant antipathy in some and the highest admiration in others. Influential admirers include Hegel, Nietzsche, and Bergson.

Whereas Thales considered water the basic principle, and Anaximenes believed it was air, Heraclitus saw the fundamental "world stuff" in fire. Fire seems to have been associated in his mind with change, strife, and war. He may also have been influenced by the Persians and their conception of a fiery judgment (see fragment [35], following). Fire, or the process of change itself, is the "one" truth that <Logos> teaches those few who will listen.

Plato referred to Heraclitus frequently and named one of his dialogues after Heraclitus' follower, Cratylus. One of the speakers in the dialogue *Cratylus* speaks of "the opinion of Heraclitus that all things flow," and the phrase, "all things flow" <panta rhei> has often been called the quintessence of Heracliteanism. With some slight oversimplification, one can say that Plato was convinced by Heraclitus that in this sensible world all things are in flux and, if this sensible world is all there is, no rational discourse is possible. This led Plato to the conclusion that there must be another world beyond the world of sense experience—a realm utterly free from change, motion, and time. At that point Plato was probably influenced not only by the Pythagoreans but also by Parmenides, the next great Pre-Socratic.

A. THE MAN

[1] Antisthenes, in his *Successions,* quotes as a sign of his [Heraclitus'] arrogance that he resigned the hereditary "kingship" to his brother.

[2] The book said to be his is called *On Nature,* from its chief content, and is divided into three discourses: On the Universe, Politics, Theology. He dedicated it and placed it in the temple of Artemis, as some say, having purposely written it rather obscurely so that only those of rank and influence should have access to it, and it should not be easily despised by the populace.... The work had so great a reputation that from it arose disciples, those called Heracliteans.

B. LOGOS* AND SENSES

[3] Those awake have one ordered universe in common, but in sleep every man turns away to one of his own.

[4] The thinking faculty is common to all.

[5] Of the Logos, which is as I describe it, men always prove to be uncomprehending, both before they have heard it and when once they have heard it. For although all things happen according to this Logos, men are like people of no experience, even when they experience such words and deeds as I explain, when I distinguish each thing according to its constitution and declare how it is; but the rest of men fail to notice what they do after they wake up just as they forget what they do when asleep.

[6] Therefore it is necessary to follow the common; but although the Logos is common the many live as though they had a private understanding.

[7] Listening not to me but to the Logos, it is wise to agree that all things are one.

[8] The things of which there is seeing and hearing and perception, these do I prefer.

[9] The eyes are more exact witnesses than the ears.

*The term <Logos>, left untranslated in this section, is sometimes rendered as "reason," sometimes as "word" (as in the first sentence of the Gospel of John: "In the beginning was the Word"); and it may also denote a rational principle in the world.

[10] If all existing things turned to smoke, the nose would be the discriminating organ.

[11] Evil witnesses are eyes and ears for men, if they have souls that do not understand their language.

C. COSMOS

[12] The path up and down is one and the same.

[13] The sun is new each day.

[14] In the same river we both step and do not step, we are and are not.

[15] It is not possible to step twice into the same river.

[16] Upon those that step into the same rivers different and different waters flow.

[17] Sea is the most pure and polluted water: for fishes it is drinkable and salutary, but for men undrinkable and deleterious.

[18] Disease makes health pleasant and good, hunger satiety, weariness rest.

[19] What is in opposition is in concert, and from what differs comes the most beautiful harmony.

[20] War is the father of all and king of all, and some he shows as gods, others as men; some he makes slaves, others free.

[21] It is necessary to know that war is common and right is strife, and that all things happen by strife and necessity.

[22] For souls it is death to become water; for water, death to become earth; from earth, water comes-to-be, and from water, soul.

[23] Immortals are mortal, mortals immortal, living each other's death, dying each other's life.

[24] After death things await men which they do not expect or imagine.

[25] Time is a child playing a game of draughts; the kingship is in the hands of a child.

D. RELIGION AND FIRE

[26] Being a polymath does not teach understanding: else Hesiod would have had it and Pythagoras; also Xenophanes and Hekataeus.

[27] Homer deserves to be thrown out of the contests and whipped, and Archilochus, too.

[28] The most popular teacher is Hesiod. Of him people think he knew most—he who did not even know day and night: They are one.

[29] They purify themselves by staining themselves with other blood, as if one stepped into mud to wash off mud. But a man would be thought mad if one of his fellowmen saw him do that. Also, they talk to statues as one might talk with houses, in ignorance of the nature of gods and heroes.

[30] The consecrations of the mysteries, as practiced among men, are unholy.

[31] Corpses should be thrown away more than dung.

[32] To god all things are beautiful and good and just, but men have supposed some things to be unjust, others just.

[33] Man is called childish compared with divinity, just as a boy compared with a man.

[34] Fire lives the death of earth, and air the death of fire; water lives the death of air, earth that of water.

[35] Fire, having come upon them, will judge and seize upon [condemn] all things.

[36] This world-order [the same of all] did none of gods or men make, but it always was and is and shall be: an ever-living fire, kindling in measures and going out in measures.

E. MEN AND MORALS

[37] Asses prefer chaff to gold.

[38] Dogs bark at those whom they do not recognize.

[39] If happiness lay in bodily pleasures, we should call oxen happy when they find vetch to eat.

[40] It is not good for men to obtain all they wish.

[41] Sane thinking is the greatest virtue, and wisdom is speaking the truth and acting according to nature, paying heed.

[42] All men are granted what is needed for knowing oneself and sane thinking.

[43] A dry soul is wisest and best.

[44] A man when he is drunk is led by an unfledged boy, stumbling and not knowing where he goes, having his soul moist.

[45] The best choose one above all else: everlasting fame above mortals. The majority are contented like well-fed cattle.

[46] The people must fight on behalf of the law as though for the city wall.

[47] One man to me is ten thousand if he is the best.

[48] The Ephesians would do well to hang themselves, every adult man, and leave their city to adolescents, since they expelled Hermodorus, the worthiest man among them, saying: Let us not have even one worthy man; but if we do, let him go elsewhere and live among others!

F. EPILOGUE

[49] I sought myself.

[50] If one does not expect the unexpected one will not find it, for it is not reached by search or trail.

[51] Character is man's fate.

[52] Nature loves hiding.

[53] The Sybil, uttering her unlaughing, unadorned, unincensed words with raving mouth, reaches out over a thousand years with her voice, through the god.

[54] The lord whose oracle is in Delphi neither speaks out nor conceals, but gives a sign.

The Eleatics

PARMENIDES
fl. ca. 485 B.C.?

Parmenides, a younger contemporary of Heraclitus and an older contemporary of Socrates, lived in Elea in southern Italy. According to Plato's dialogue of the same name (*Parmenides,* reprinted in part in this volume), Parmenides visited Athens when he was about sixty-five, accompanied by his chief pupil, Zeno, then nearly forty, and conversed with the still "quite young" Socrates. Whether the visit to Athens really took place, we do not know; that Socrates met Parmenides is not likely; that they did not have the conversation reported in the dialogue is absolutely clear, for that discussion presupposes Plato's earlier work.

According to Parmenides, there are two ways of inquiry. The first asserts that whatever is (i.e., being), "is and cannot not-be" (see fragment [2] following). This is the path of truth that leads us to see that being is one and cannot be created, destroyed, or changed. (If any of these alterations in being were possible, being would no longer be what "is" and would become what "is not"—but by definition there *is* no "is not" from which being could arise or into which being could change.) Being must be one seamless unchanging whole. The other path of inquiry, the path of opinion, which claims that something arises from not-being, is not only impossible, it is unthinkable.

Parmenides, the philosopher of changeless being, has often been contrasted with Heraclitus, the philosopher of change and becoming. But it should not be overlooked that both are one in repudiating the wisdom of tradition and of common sense. Both claim that things may not be what they seem to be. One is as radical as the other.

Plato was greatly impressed by Parmenides' thought and freely acknowledged his debt to the Eleatic philosopher. In the Platonic *Parmenides,* the character

Charioteer, 475 B.C. The Charioteer stands in solemn grandeur commemorating the serious nature of competition for the ancient Greeks. This statue comes from the same time and place as Parmenides' poem with its image of a chariot ride to truth. *(Photographer: Alison Frantz, Delphi Museum)*

"Parmenides" instructs the young Socrates, while in most dialogues Socrates bests or teaches others. Plato's dichotomies—of knowledge/belief and of unchanging, eternal, timeless reality/ever-changing, temporal appearance—were derived from Parmenides. However, Plato did not accept Parmenides' idea that reality is one, devoid of any plurality: Plato occupied the "real" world with a number of unchanging, eternal forms.

The following fragments are part of a poem which, after an imposing prologue, distinguishes the ways of knowledge and belief, of being and nonbeing.

[1] The mares that carry me as far as my heart ever aspires sped me on, when they had brought and set me on the far-famed road of the god, which bears the man who knows over all cities. On that road was I borne, for that way the wise horses bore me, straining at the chariot, and maidens led the way. And the axle in the naves gave out the whistle of a pipe, blazing, for it was pressed hard on either side by the two well-turned wheels as the daughters of the Sun made haste to escort me, having left the halls of Night for the light, and having thrust the veils from their heads with their hands.

There are the gates of the paths of Night and Day, and a lintel and a stone threshold enclose them. They themselves, high in the air, are blocked with great doors, and avenging Justice holds the alternate bolts. Her the maidens beguiled with gentle words and cunningly persuaded to push back swiftly from the gates the bolted bar. And the gates created a yawning gap in the door frame when they flew open, swinging in turn in their sockets the bronze-bound pivots made fast with dowels and rivets. Straight through them, on the broad way, did the maidens keep the horses and the chariot.

And the goddess greeted me kindly, and took my right hand in hers, and addressed me with these words: "Young man, you who come to my house in the company of immortal charioteers with the mares which bear you, greetings. No ill fate has sent you to travel this road—far indeed does it lie from the steps of men but right and justice. It is proper that you should learn all things, both the unshaken heart of well-rounded truth, and the opinions of mortals, in which there is no true reliance. But nonetheless you shall learn these things too, how what is believed would have to be assuredly, pervading all things throughout."

[2] Come now, and I will tell you (and you must carry my account away with you when you have heard it) the only ways of enquiry that are to be thought of. The one, that [it] is and that it is impossible for [it] not to be, is the path of Persuasion (for she attends upon Truth); the other, that [it] is not and that it is needful that [it] not be, that I declare to you is an altogether indiscernible track: for you could not know what is not—that cannot be done—nor indicate it.

[3] For the same thing is there both to be thought of and to be.

[4] But look at things which, though far off, are securely present to the mind; for you will not cut off for yourself what is from holding to what is, neither scattering everywhere in every way in order [i.e., cosmic order] nor drawing together.

[5] It is a common point from which I start; for there again and again I shall return.

[6] What is there to be said and thought needs must be; for it is there for being, but nothing is not. I bid you ponder that, for this is the first way of enquiry from which I hold you back, but then from that on which mortals wander knowing nothing, two-headed; for helplessness guides the wandering thought in their breasts, and they are carried along, deaf and blind at once, dazed, undiscriminating hordes, who believe that to be and not to be are the same and not the same, and the path taken by them is backward-turning.

[7] For never shall this be forcibly maintained, that things that are not are, but you must hold back your thought from this way of enquiry, nor let habit, born of much experience, force you down this way, by making you use an aimless eye or an ear and a tongue full of meaningless sound: judge by reason the strife-encompassed refutation spoken by me.

[8] Only one way remains; that it is. To this way there are very many sign-posts: that being has no coming-into-being and no destruction, for it is whole of limb, without

motion, and without end. And it never was, nor will be, because it is now, a whole all together, one, continuous; for what creation of it will you look? How, whence sprung? Nor shall I allow you to speak or think of it as springing from not-being; for it is nei-ther expressible nor thinkable that what-is-not is. Also, what necessity impelled it, if it did spring from nothing, to be produced later or earlier? Thus it must be absolutely, or not at all. Nor will the force of credibility ever admit that anything should come into being, beside being itself, out of not-being. So far as that is concerned, justice has never released *(being)* from its fetters and set it free either to come into being or to per-ish, but holds it fast. The decision on these matters depends on the following: it is, or it is not. It is therefore decided, as is inevitable: ignore the one way as unthinkable and inexpressible (for it is no true way) and take the other as the way of being and reality. How could being perish? How could it come into being? If it came into being, it is not, and so too if it is about-to-be at some future time. Thus coming-into-being is quenched, and destruction also into the unseen.

Nor is being divisible, since it is all alike. Nor is there anything there which could prevent it from holding together, nor any lesser thing, but all is full of being. Therefore it is altogether continuous; for being is close to being.

But it is motionless in the limits of mighty bonds, without beginning, without cease, since becoming and destruction have been driven very far away, and true con-viction has rejected them. And remaining the same in the same place, it rests by itself and thus remains there fixed; for powerful necessity holds it in the bonds of a limit, which constrains it round about, because it is decreed by divine law that being shall not be without boundary. For it is not lacking; but if it were *(spatially infinite),* it would be lacking everything.

To think is the same as the thought that it is; for you will not find thinking with-out being to which it refers. For nothing else either is or shall be except being, since fate has tied it down to be a whole and motionless; therefore all things that mortals have established, believing in their truth, are just a name: becoming and perishing, being and not-being, and change of position, and alteration of bright color.

But since there is a *(spatial)* limit, it is complete on every side, like the mass of a well-rounded sphere, equally balanced from its center in every direction; for it is not bound to be at all either greater or less in this direction or that; nor is there not-being which could check it from reaching to the same point, nor is it possible for being to be more in this direction, less in that, than being, because it is an inviolate whole. For, in all directions equal to itself, it reaches its limits uniformly.

At this point I cease my reliable theory <*Logos*> and thought, concerning Truth; from here onwards you must learn the opinions of mortals, listening to the deceptive order of my words.

They have established *(the custom of)* naming two forms, one of which ought not to be *(mentioned):* that is where they have gone astray. They have distinguished them as opposite in form, and have marked them off from another by giving them different signs: on one side the flaming fire in the heavens, mild, very light *(in weight),* the same as itself in every direction, and not the same as the other. This *(other)* also is by itself and opposite: dark night, a dense and heavy body. This world-order I describe to you throughout as it appears with all its phenomena, in order that no intellect of mortal men may outstrip you.

[9] But since all things are named light and night, and names have been given to each class of things according to the power of one or the other, everything is full equally of light and invisible night, as both are equal, because to neither of them be-longs any share (of the other).

[10] You shall know the nature of the heavens, and all the signs in the heavens, and the destructive works of the pure bright torch of the sun, and whence they came into being. And you shall learn of the wandering works of the round-faced moon, and its nature; and you shall know also the surrounding heaven, whence it sprang and how necessity brought and constrained it to hold the limits of the stars.

[11] *(I will describe)* how earth and sun and moon, and the aether common to all, and the Milky Way in the heavens, and outermost Olympus, and the hot power of the stars, hastened to come into being.

[12] For the narrower rings were filled with unmixed fire, and those next to them with night, but between (these) rushes the portion of flame. And in the center of these is the goddess who guides everything; for throughout she rules over cruel birth and mating, sending the female to mate with the male, and conversely again the male with the female.

[13] First of all the gods she devised Love.

[14] *(The moon):* Shining by night with a light not her own, wandering round the earth.

ZENO OF ELEA
fl. ca. 465 B.C.

All the ancient authorities agree that Zeno of Elea was a pupil and associate of Parmenides. Zeno is noted for his writings in defense of Parmenides' concept of the One. Zeno showed the paradoxes that result from the theses of plurality held by philosophers like Pythagoras. Zeno's paradoxes were designed to prove that plurality and change are not possible.

Zeno's puzzles have fascinated philosophers, logicians, and mathematicians ever since, and never more than in our own time: Probably more has been written on his paradoxes in the last hundred years than in the preceding two thousand. (See the suggestions for further reading in the introduction to the Pre-Socratics.) Much of this work is cheerfully unconcerned with the connection, if any, between the writers' "Zeno" and Zeno himself. Reading the critics could give one extravagant notions of the reasoning powers of this remote Greek. Hence one will probably be surprised by reading what Zeno actually said in the fragments that follow.

The fragments have been arranged into four broad arguments: against plurality, against motion, against space, and, in a slightly different vein, against the reliability of sense experience (in the paradox of the millet seed). These paradoxes are all designed to show that Parmenides is correct: Being is one seamless unchanging whole.

The four paradoxes against motion are perhaps the most famous—and the most difficult to resolve. These paradoxes clearly bring out the discrepancy between logic and experience. For example, the second of the paradoxes logically concludes that Achilles cannot catch a tortoise—but it *seems* so obvious to experience that he can. Either there is something wrong with Zeno's logic (which is, of course, what modern discussions of the paradox have tried to show), or else experience is illusory. Zeno maintained that his logic was valid and that he had demonstrated that Parmenides was right: Change is impossible.

[1] [Zeno's] book is in fact a sort of defence of Parmenides' argument against those who try to make fun of it by showing that his supposition, that there is a One, leads to many absurdities and contradictions. This book, then, is a retort against those who assert a plurality. It pays them back in the same coin with something to spare, and aims at showing that, on a thorough examination, their own supposition that there is a plurality leads to even more absurd consequences than the hypothesis of the One.

[2] [Zeno] of Elea has an art of speaking, such that he can make the same things appear to his audience like and unlike, or one and many, or again at rest and in motion. . . .

A. ARGUMENTS AGAINST PLURALITY

[3] He [Zeno] showed earlier [i.e., prior to the arguments following in fragments 6–11] that nothing has size because each of the many is self-identical and one.

[4] For if it [something having no size] were added to another, it would make it [the latter] no larger. For having no size, it could not contribute anything by way of size when added. And thus the thing added would be nothing. If indeed when [something is] subtracted from another, the latter is not reduced, nor again increased when [something is] added [to it], it is clear that what is added or subtracted is nothing.

[5] If there are many, they must be just so many as they are, neither more nor fewer. But if they are just so many as they are, they must be finite [in number]. If there are many, the existents are infinite [in number]: for there are always other [existents] between existents, and again others between these. And thus the existents are infinite [in number].

B. ARGUMENTS AGAINST MOTION

THE RACE COURSE

[6] For we have many arguments contrary to (common) beliefs, whose solution is yet difficult, like Zeno's that it is impossible to move or to traverse the race course.

[7] For this reason Zeno's argument too assumes falsely that it is impossible to traverse or to come in contact with each one of an infinite number [of things] in a finite time.

[8] The first [of Zeno's arguments against motion "which cause difficulty to those who try to solve the problems they raise"] says that there is no motion, because the moving [body] must reach the midpoint before it gets to the end.

[9] In the same way one should reply to those who pose [literally, "ask"] Zeno's argument, claiming that it is always necessary to traverse the half [i.e., to traverse any given distance we must first traverse its first half], and these [i.e., half-distances] are infinitely numerous, while it is impossible to traverse an infinity. . . .

[10] If there is motion, the moving object must traverse an infinity in a finite [time]: and this is impossible. Hence motion does not exist. He demonstrates his hypothesis thus: The moving object must move a certain stretch. And since every stretch is infinitely divisible, the moving object must first traverse half the stretch it is moving, and then the whole; but before the whole of the half, half of that and, again, the half of that. If then these halves are infinite, since, whatever may be the given [stretch] it is possible to halve it, and [if, further,] it is impossible to traverse the infinity [of these stretches] in a finite time . . . it follows that it is impossible to traverse any given length in a finite time.

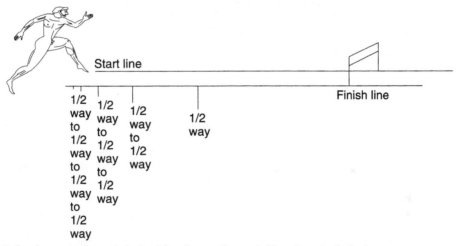

Before the runner can reach the finish line, he must first get halfway there. But before he can get halfway there, he must get halfway to the halfway point, and so on. Zeno concludes that the runner, with only a finite amount of time, could never traverse this infinite number of halfway to halfway points.

THE ACHILLES

[11] The second [of Zeno's arguments against motion] is what is known as "the Achilles," which purports to show that the slowest will never be overtaken in its course by the swiftest, inasmuch as, reckoning from any given instant, the pursuer, before he can catch the pursued, must reach the point from which the pursued started at that instant, and so the slower will always be some distance in advance of the swifter.

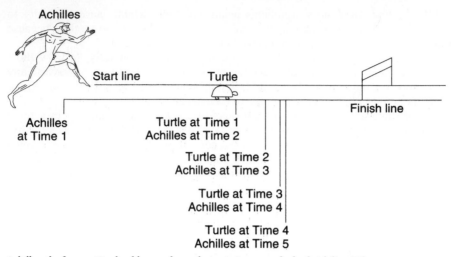

Achilles, the famous Greek athlete, and a turtle are racing towards the finish line. When they begin [at time 1], the turtle has a head start. A few seconds later [at time 2] Achilles has reached the point where the turtle *was* at the start of the race. But the turtle has moved forward slightly. Achilles continues running and a moment later [at time 3] reaches the point where the turtle *was* [at time 2]. Achilles continues to get closer and closer to the turtle, but he always arrives at a point where the turtle *was* a split-second before. Hence, Zeno concludes, Achilles can never catch the turtle.

THE ARROW

[12] The third [of Zeno's arguments against motion is] that the arrow is stationary while on its flight. . . . Since a thing is at rest when it has not shifted in any degree out of a place equal to its own dimensions, and since at any given instant during the whole of its supposed motion the supposed moving thing is in the place it occupies at that instant, the arrow is not moving at any time during its flight.

THE STADIUM

[13] The fourth [of Zeno's arguments against motion] supposes a number of objects all equal with each other in dimensions, forming two equal trains and arranged so that one train stretches from one end of a racecourse to the middle of it, and the other from the middle to the other end. Then, if you let the two trains, moving in opposite directions but at the same rate, pass each other, Zeno undertakes to show that half of the time they occupy in passing each other is equal to the whole of it. . . . This is his demonstration. Let there be a number of objects *AAAA,* equal in number and bulk to those that compose the two trains but stationary in the middle of the stadium. Then let the objects *BBBB,* in number and dimension equal to the *A*'s, form one of the trains stretching from the middle of the *A*'s in one direction; and from the inner end of the *B*'s let *CCCC* stretch in the opposite direction, being the equal in number, dimension, and rate of movement to the *B*'s.

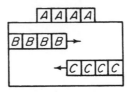

Then when they cross, the first *B* and the first *C* will simultaneously reach the extreme *A*'s in contrary directions.

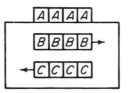

Now during this process, the first *C* has passed all the *B*'s, whereas the first *B* has only passed half the *A*'s, and therefore only taken half the time; for it takes an equal time (the minimal time) for the *C* to pass one *B* as for the *B* to pass one *A*. But during this same half-time the first *B* has also passed all the *C*'s (though the first *B* takes as long, says Zeno, to pass a *C* as an *A*) because measured by their progress through the *A*'s the *B*'s and *C*'s have had the same time in which to cross each other. Such is his argument. . . .

C. Argument Against Space

[14] If place is something that exists, where will it be? The difficulty raised by Zeno requires some answer. For if *everything* that exists has a place, it is clear that place too will have a place, and so on without limit.

D. The Paradox of the Millet Seed

[15] "Tell me, Protagoras," [Zeno] said, "does a single millet seed, or the ten-thousandth part of a seed, make a noise when they fall?" When Protagoras said they did not, he said: "Does the bushel then make a noise when it falls or not?" When Protagoras said this did, Zeno said: "Is there not then some ratio of the bushel to one seed and to a ten-thousandth of a seed?" When Protagoras said there was, Zeno said: "But then must not the respective noises stand to one another in the same ratios? For as the sounding bodies are to one another, so must be the sounds they make. This being so, if the bushel of millet makes a noise, then the single millet seed must also make a noise, and so must the ten-thousandth of a millet seed."

MELISSUS
fl. ca. 440 B.C.?

Melissus is said to have come from the island of Samos, like Pythagoras, and to have flourished during the fifth century B.C. He is reported to have been a naval commander who led the Samians to victory over the Athenians in 440 B.C. (see fragment [2] following). He wrote a book, *About Nature or Reality,* probably some time after the completion of Zeno's more celebrated work. Melissus, too, attempted to defend Parmenides, and it is therefore convenient to have a single label for the philosophy of these three men—Parmenides, Zeno, and Melissus. They are traditionally called Eleatics, after the small town in southern Italy where Parmenides made his home, Elea.

In addition to two ancient citations about his life, all of his genuine fragments are given here. These fragments show that, like Parmenides, Melissus believed that being is one seamless unchanging whole and, like Zeno, he presented *ad absurdum* arguments to show the impossibility of plurality or change. In particular, he argued against the Ionian philosophy of Anaximander that things could change into their opposites.

[1] Melissus [was the] son of Ithagenes, a Samian. He was a pupil of Parmenides. . . . He was a statesman, and was held in great honor by the citizens; and later, when he was elected admiral, he won even greater fame for his personal courage. . . .

[2] When Pericles had set sail, Melissus, son of Ithagenes, a philosopher who was then in command of Samos, was so contemptuous of the small number of the Athenian ships or of their commander's inexperience that he persuaded the Samians to attack. A battle took place which the Samians won. They took so many prisoners and

destroyed so many ships that they had command of the sea, and they devoted to the prosecution of the war certain supplies which they did not till then possess. Pericles himself, according to Aristotle, had also been defeated by Melissus in an earlier naval battle.

*   *   *

[3] That which was, always and always will be. For if it had come into being, it necessarily follows that before it came into being, nothing existed. If however nothing existed, in no way could anything come into being out of nothing.

[4] Since therefore it did not come into being, it is and always was and always will be, and has no beginning or end, but it is eternal. For if it had come into being, it would have a beginning (for it would have come into being at some time, and so begun), and an end (for since it had come into being, it would have ended). But since it has neither begun nor ended, it always was and always will be and has no beginning nor end. For it is impossible for anything to be unless it is completely.

[5] But as it is always, so also its size must always be infinite.

[6] Nothing that has a beginning and an end is either everlasting or infinite.

[7] If it were not one, it would form a boundary in relation to something else.

[8] If it were infinite, it would be one; for if it were two, *(these)* could not be *(spatially)* infinite, but each would have boundaries in relation to each other.

[9] Thus, therefore, it is everlasting and unlimited and one and like throughout *(homogeneous)*.

[10] And neither could it perish or become larger or change its *(inner)* arrangement, nor does it feel pain or grief. For if it suffered any of these things, it would no longer be one. For if being alters, it follows that it is not the same, but that that which previously was is destroyed, and that not-being has come into being. Hence if it were to become different by a single hair in ten thousand years, so it must be utterly destroyed in the whole of time.

[11] But it is not possible for it to be rearranged either, for the previous arrangement is not destroyed, nor does a nonexistent arrangement come into being. And since it is neither increased by any addition, nor destroyed, nor changed, how could it have undergone a rearrangement of what exists? For if it were different in any respect, then there would at once be a rearrangement.

[12] Nor does it feel pain; for it could not be completely if it were in pain; for a thing which is in pain could not always be. Nor has it equal power with what is healthy. Nor would it be the same if it were in pain; for it would feel pain through the subtraction or addition of something, and could no longer be the same.

[13] Nor could that which is healthy feel pain, for the healthy—that which is— would perish, and that which is not would come into being.

[14] And with regard to grief, the same reasoning applies as to pain.

[15] Nor is there any emptiness; for the empty is nothing; and so that which is nothing cannot be. Nor does it move; for it cannot withdraw in any direction, but *(all)* is full. For if there were any empty, it would have withdrawn into the empty; but as the empty does not exist, there is nowhere for it *(being)* to withdraw.

[16] And there can be no dense and rare. For the rare cannot possibly be as full as the dense, but the rare must at once become more empty than the dense.

[17] The following distinction must be made between the full and the not-full: if a thing has room for or admits something, it is not full; if it neither has room for nor admits anything, it is full.

[18] It *(being)* must necessarily be full, therefore, if there is no empty. If therefore it is full, it does not move.

[19] This argument is the greatest proof that it *(being)* is one only; but there are also the following proofs:

[20] If things were many, they would have to be of the same kind as I say the one is. For if there is earth and water and air and fire and iron and gold, and that which is living and that which is dead, and black and white and all the rest of the things which men say are real: if these things exist, and we see and hear correctly, each thing must be of such a kind as it seemed to us to be in the first place, and it cannot change or become different, but each thing must always be what it is. But now, we say we see and hear and understand correctly,

[21] and it seems to us that the hot becomes cold and the cold hot, and the hard soft and the soft hard, and that the living thing dies and comes into being from what is not living, and that all things change, and that what was and what now is are not at all the same, but iron which is hard is worn away by contact with the finger, and gold and stone and whatever seems to be entirely strong *(is worn away);* and that from water, earth and stone come into being. So that it comes about that we neither see nor know existing things.

[22] So these statements are not consistent with one another. For although we say that there are many things, ever-lasting(?), having forms and strength, it seems to us that they all alter and change from what is seen on each occasion.

[23] It is clear therefore that we have not been seeing correctly, and that those things do not correctly seem to us to be many; for they would not change if they were real, but each would be as it seemed to be. For nothing is stronger than that which is real.

[24] And if it changed, being would have been destroyed, and not-being would have come into being. Thus, therefore, if things are many, they must be such as the one is.

[25] If therefore being is, it must be one; and if it is one, it is bound not to have body. But if it had bulk, it would have parts, and would no longer be.

[26] If being is divided, it moves; and if it moved, it could not be.

The Pluralists

EMPEDOCLES
ca. 484–424 B.C.

The philosophers who came after the Eleatics, down to Plato and Aristotle, were concerned with showing how change *was* possible. The first three philosophers to attempt this are sometimes lumped together as the "Pluralists," for each of them tried to explain change by invoking several ultimate principles.

The first of these was Empedocles from Acragas on the south coast of Sicily. Born of an aristocratic family, he opposed tyranny and reputedly refused the crown of his native town. Like the more legendary Pythagoras, he fused scientific thought with religious concerns and left others with the impression he had performed miracles. Again like Pythagoras, he spoke both of the transmigration of souls and of himself as a god. He is said to have ended his life by leaping into the crater of Mount Etna.

Empedocles wrote two poems, "On Nature" and "Purifications." The former is said to have been divided into two books, totaling two thousand lines, of which fewer than four hundred have survived. According to Diogenes Laertius, the two poems together came to five thousand lines; if so, less than one-fifth of the "Purifications" has come down to us.

Empedocles was the first great synthesizer of the history of philosophy. Around 450 B.C., a full century before Aristotle's summation, Empedocles tried to find a place in his thought for all the major contributions of his predecessors. By explaining generation and destruction, if not all change, in terms of mixture and separation, Empedocles sought to reconcile Heraclitus's insistence on the reality of change with the Eleatic claim that generation and destruction are unthinkable. Going back to the Greeks' traditional belief in four elements, he found a place for Thales' water, Anaximenes' air, and Heraclitus's fire, and he added

31

earth as the fourth. In addition to these four elements, which Aristotle would later call "material causes," Empedocles postulated two "efficient causes": strife (Heraclitus's great principle) and love. He envisaged four successive ages: an age of love or perfect mixture in the beginning; then gradual separation as strife enters; then complete separation as strife rules; finally, as love enters again, a gradual remixture.

[1] Empedocles of Acragas was born not long after Anaxagoras, and was an emulator and associate of Parmenides, and even more of the Pythagoreans.

[2] Anaxagoras of Clazomenae, though older than Empedocles, was later in his philosophical activity.

*   *   *

[3] For limited are the means of grasping *(i.e., the organs of sense-perception),* which are scattered throughout their limbs, and many are the miseries that press in and blunt the thoughts. And having looked at (only) a small part of existence during their lives, doomed to perish swiftly like smoke, they are carried aloft and wafted away, believing only that upon which as individuals they chance to hit as they wander in all directions; but every man preens himself on having found the Whole: so little are these things to be seen by men or to be heard, or to be comprehended by the mind! But you, since you have come here into retirement, shall learn—not more than mortal intellect can attain.

[4] I shall tell you another thing: there is no creation of substance in any one of mortal existences, nor any end in execrable death, but only mixing and exchange of what has been mixed; and the name "substance" [*<physis>* "nature"] is applied to them by mankind. (8)

[5] But men, when these *(the Elements)* have been mixed in the form of a man and come into the light, or in the form of a species of wild animals, or plants, or birds, then say that this has "come into being"; and when they separate, this men call sad fate *(death).* The terms that right demands they do not use; but through custom I myself also apply these names. (9)

[6] From what in no wise exists, it is impossible for anything to come into being; and for being to perish completely is incapable of fulfillment and unthinkable; for it will always be there, wherever anyone may place it on any occasion. (12)

[7] Nor is there any part of the whole that is empty or overfull. (13)

[8] No part of the whole is empty; so whence could anything additional come? (14)

[9] I shall tell of a double *(process):* at one time it increased so as to be a single one out of many; at another time again it grew apart so as to be many out of one. There is a double creation of mortals and a double decline: the union of all things causes the birth and destruction of the one *(race of mortals),* the other is reared as the elements grow apart, and then flies asunder. And these *(elements)* never cease their continuous exchange, sometimes uniting under the influence of love, so that all become one, at other times again each moving apart through the hostile force of hate. Thus, in so far as they have the power to grow into one out of many, and again, when the one grows apart and many are formed, in this sense they come into being and have no stable life; but in so far as they never cease their continuous exchange, in this sense they remain always unmoved *(unaltered)* as they follow the cyclic process.

But come, listen to my discourse! For be assured, learning will increase your understanding. As I said before, revealing the aims of my discourse, I shall tell you of a double process. At one time it increased so as to be a single one out of many; at another time it grew apart so as to be many out of one—fire and water and earth and the boundless height of air, and also execrable hate apart from these, of equal weight in all directions, and love in their midst, their equal in length and breadth. Observe her with your mind, and do not sit with wondering eyes! She it is who is believed to be implanted in mortal limbs also; through her they think friendly thoughts and perform harmonious actions, calling her joy and Aphrodite. No mortal man has perceived her as she moves in and out among them. But *you* must listen to the undeceitful progress of my argument.

All these *(elements)* are equal and of the same age in their creation; but each presides over its own office, and each has its own character, and they prevail in turn in the course of time. And besides these, nothing else comes into being, nor does anything cease. For if they had been perishing continuously, they would be no more; and what could increase the whole? And whence could it have come? In what direction could it perish, since nothing is empty of these things? No, but these things alone exist, and running through one another they become different things at different times, and are ever continuously the same. (17)

[10] This process is clearly to be seen throughout the mass of mortal limbs: sometimes through love all the limbs which the body has as its lot come together into one, in the prime of flourishing life; at another time again, sundered by evil feuds, they wander severally by the breakers of the shore of life. Likewise too with shrub-plants and fish in their watery dwelling, and beasts with mountain lairs and diver-birds that travel on wings. (20)

[11] But come, observe the following witness to my previous discourse, lest in my former statements there was any substance of which the form was missing. Observe the sun, bright to see and hot everywhere, and all the immortal things *(heavenly bodies)* drenched with its heat and brilliant light; and the rain, dark and chill over everything; and from the earth issue forth things based on the soil and solid. But in *(the reign of)* wrath they are all different in form and separate, while in *(the reign of)* love they come together and long for one another. For from these *(elements)* come all things that were and are and will be; and trees spring up, and men and women, and beasts and birds and water-nurtured fish, and even the long-lived gods who are highest in honor. For these *(elements)* alone exist, but by running through one another they become different; to such a degree does mixing change them. (21)

[12] For all these things—beaming sun and earth and heaven and sea—are connected in harmony with their own parts: all those *(parts)* which have been sundered from them and exist in mortal limbs. Similarly all those things which are suitable for mixture are made like one another and united in affection by Aphrodite. But those things which differ most from one another in origin and mixture and the forms in which they are molded are completely unaccustomed to combine, and are very baneful because of the commands of hate, in that hate has wrought their origin. (22)

[13] ... Touching on summit after summit, not to follow a single path of discourse to the end. (24)

[14] For what is right can well be uttered even twice. (25)

[15] In turn they get the upper hand in the revolving cycle, and perish into one another and increase in the turn appointed by fate. For they alone exist, but running through one another they become men and the tribes of other animals, sometimes uniting under the influence of love into one ordered whole, at other times again each mov-

ing apart through the hostile force of hate, until growing together into the whole which is one, they are quelled. Thus in so far as they have the power to grow into one out of many, and again, when the one grows apart and many are formed, in this sense they come into being and have no stable life; but in so far as they never cease their continuous exchange, in this sense they remain always unmoved *(unaltered)* as they follow the cyclic process. (26)

[16] *(The sphere under the dominion of love):* Therein are articulated neither the swift limbs of the sun, nor the shaggy might of earth, nor the sea: so firmly is it *(the whole)* fixed in a close-set secrecy, a rounded Sphere enjoying a circular solitude. (27)

[17] But he *(God)* is equal in all directions to himself and altogether eternal, a rounded sphere enjoying a circular solitude. (28)

[18] For there do not start two branches from his back; *(he has)* no feet, no swift knees, no organs of reproduction; but he was a sphere, and in all directions equal to himself. (29)

[19] But I will go back to the path of song which I formerly laid down, drawing one argument from another: that *(path which shows how)* when hate has reached the bottommost abyss of the eddy, and when love reaches the middle of the whirl, then in it *(the whirl)* all these things come together so as to be one—not all at once, but voluntarily uniting, some from one quarter, others from another. And as they mixed, there poured forth countless races of mortals. But many things stand unmixed side by side with the things mixing—all those which hate *(still)* aloft checked, since it had not yet faultlessly withdrawn from the whole to the outermost limits of the circle, but was remaining in some places, and in other places departing from the limbs *(of the sphere)*. But in so far as it went on quietly streaming out, to the same extent there was entering a benevolent immortal inrush of faultless love. And swiftly those things became mortal which previously had experienced immortality, and things formerly unmixed became mixed, changing their paths. And as they mixed, there poured forth countless races of mortals, equipped with forms of every sort, a marvel to behold. (35)

[20] As they came together, hate returned to the outermost. (36)

[21] There whirls round the earth a circular borrowed light. (45)

[22] It is the earth that makes night by coming in the way of the *(sun's)* rays. (48)

[23] Sea, the sweat of earth. (55)

[24] Limbs wandered alone. (58)

[25] Creatures with rolling gait and innumerable hands. (60)

[26] The way everything breathes in and out is as follows: all have tubes of flesh, empty of blood, which extend over the surface of the body; and at the mouths of these tubes the outermost surface of the skin is perforated with frequent pores, so as to keep in the blood while a free way is cut for the passage of the air. Thus, when the thin blood flows back from here, the air, bubbling, rushes in in a mighty wave; and when the blood leaps up *(to the surface),* there is an expiration of air. As when a girl, playing with a water-catcher of shining brass—when, having placed the mouth of the pipe on her well-shaped hand, she dips the vessel into the yielding substance of silvery water, still the volume of air pressing from inside on the many holes keeps out the water, until she uncovers the condensed stream *(of air).* Then at once when the air flows out, the water flows in, in an equal quantity. Similarly, when water occupies the depths of the brazen vessel, and the opening or passage is stopped by the human flesh *(hand),* and the air outside, striving to get in, checks the water, by controlling the surface at the entrance of the noisy strainer until she lets go with her hand: then again, in exactly the opposite way from what happened before, as the air rushes in, the water flows out in equal volume. Similarly when the thin blood, rushing through the limbs, flows back

into the interior, straightway a stream of air flows in with a rush; and when the blood flows up again, again there is a breathing-out in equal volume. (100)

[27] If you press them deep into your firm mind, and contemplate them with good will and a studious care that is pure, these things will all assuredly remain with you throughout your life; and you will obtain many other things from them; for these things of themselves cause each *(element)* to increase in the character, according to the way of each man's nature. But if you intend to grasp after different things such as dwell among men in countless numbers and blunt their thoughts, miserable *(trifles)*, certainly these things will quickly desert you in the course of time, longing to return to their own original kind. For all things, be assured, have intelligence and a portion of thought. (110)

[28] You shall learn all the drugs that exist as a defence against illness and old age; for you alone will I accomplish all this. You shall check the force of the unwearying winds which rush upon the earth with their blasts and lay waste the cultivated fields. And again, if you wish, you shall conduct the breezes back again. You shall create a seasonable dryness after the dark rain for mankind, and again you shall create after summer drought the streams that nourish the trees and *(which will flow in the sky)*. And you shall bring out of Hades a dead man restored to strength. (111)

KATHARMOI (PURIFICATIONS)

[29] Friends, who dwell in the great town on the city's heights, looking down on yellow Agrigentum, you who are occupied with good deeds, who are harbors treating foreigners with respect, and who are unacquainted with wickedness: greeting! I go about among you as an immortal god, no longer a mortal, held in honor by all, as I seem *(to them to deserve)*, crowned with fillets and flowing garlands. When I come to them in their flourishing towns, to men and women, I am honored; and they follow me in thousands, to inquire where is the path of advantage, some desiring oracles, while others ask to hear a word of healing for their manifold diseases, since they have long been pierced with cruel pains. (112)

[30] But why do I lay stress on these things, as if I were achieving something as great in that I surpass mortal men who are liable to many forms of destruction? (113)

[31] Friends, I know that truth is present in the story that I shall tell; but it is actually very difficult for men, and the impact of conviction on their minds is unwelcome. (114)

[32] There is an oracle of necessity, an ancient decree of the gods, eternal, sealed fast with broad oaths, that when one of the divine spirits whose portion is long life sinfully stains his own limbs with bloodshed, and following hate has sworn a false oath— these must wander for thrice ten thousand seasons far from the company of the blessed, being born throughout the period into all kinds of mortal shapes, which exchange one hard way of life for another. For the mighty air chases them into the sea, and the sea spews them forth on to the dry land, and the earth *(drives them)* towards the rays of the blazing sun; and the sun hurls them into the eddies of the Aether. One *(Element)* receives them from the other, and all loathe them. Of this number am I too, now, a fugitive from heaven and a wanderer, because I trusted in raging Hate. (115)

[33] For by now I have been born boy, girl, plant, bird, and dumb sea-fish. (117)

[34] I wept and wailed when I saw the unfamiliar land *(at birth)*. (118)

[35] How great the honor, how deep the happiness from which *(I am exiled)!* (119)

[36] Will ye not cease from this harsh-sounding slaughter? Do you not see that you are devouring one another in the thoughtlessness of your minds? (136)

ANAXAGORAS
ca. 500–ca. 428 B.C.

Anaxagoras came from Clazomenae on the coast of Asia Minor, not far north-west of Colophon (Xenophanes' home) and Ephesus (Heraclitus' home). He was the first of the Greek philosophers to move to Athens, where he became a good friend of Pericles, the great statesman, who gave his name to the whole epoch. The dates are uncertain, but Anaxagoras may have been born about 500 B.C. and have come to Athens around 480. He lived in Athens in the time of its greatest glory, a contemporary of the classical tragedians Aeschylus, Sophocles, and Euripides. Anaxagoras was the first philosopher to be tried and condemned on a charge of heresy or impiety. He was saved by Pericles and went into exile at Lampsacus, a Milesian colony on the Hellespont, where he died about 428/7 B.C., a year after Pericles.

Anaxagoras taught that everything consists of an infinite number of particles or seeds, and that in all things there is a portion of everything. Hair could not come from what is not hair, nor could flesh come from what is not flesh. The names we apply to things are determined by the preponderance of certain seeds in them—for example, hair seeds or flesh seeds. Like Empedocles, he added to such "material causes" an "efficient cause" to account for the motion and direction of things; however, unlike Empedocles' two, Anaxagoras added only one "efficient cause," which was mind, *nous* in Greek. The introduction of mind led Aristotle to hail Anaxagoras as the only sober man among the Pre-Socratics; yet Aristotle found fault with Anaxagoras for not making more use of this new principle to explain natural events.

[1] He is said to have been twenty years old at the time of Xerxes' crossing, and to have lived to seventy-two. . . . He began to be a philosopher at Athens in the archonship of Callias [456/5 B.C.], at the age of twenty, as Demetrius Phalereus tells us in his *Register of Archons,* and is said to have spent thirty years there. . . . There are different accounts given of his trial. Sotion, in his *Succession of Philosophers,* says that he was prosecuted by Cleon for impiety, because he claimed that the sun was a red-hot mass of metal, and that after Pericles, his pupil, had made a speech in his defense, he was fined five talents and exiled. Satyrus, in his *Lives,* on the other hand, says that the charge was brought by Thucydides in his political campaign against Pericles; and he

adds that the charge was not only for impiety but for Medism [Persian leanings] as well; and he was condemned to death in absence. . . . Finally he withdrew to Lampsacus, and there died. It is said that when the rulers of the city asked him what privilege he wished to be granted, he replied that the children should be given a holiday every year in the month in which he died. The custom is preserved to the present day. When he died, the Lampsacenes buried him with full honors.

[2] Anaxagoras, the natural philosopher, was a distinguished Clazomenion, an associate of Anaximenes of Miletus; and his own pupils included Archelaus the natural philosopher and Euripides the poet.

[3] Those who wrote only one book include Melissus, Parmenides, and Anaxagoras.

* * *

[4] All Things were together, infinite in number and in smallness. For the Small also was infinite. And since all were together, nothing was distinguishable because of its smallness. For Air and Aether dominated all things, both of them being infinite. For these are the most important *(Elements)* in the total mixture, both in number and in size.

[5] Air and Aether are separated off from the surrounding multiplicity, and that which surrounds is infinite in number.

[6] For in Small there is no Least, but only a Lesser: for it is impossible that Being should Not-Be, and in Great there is always a Greater. And it is equal in number to the small, but each thing is to itself both great and small.

[7] Conditions being thus, one must believe that there are many things of all sorts in all composite products, and the seeds of all Things, which contain all kinds of shapes and colors and pleasant savors. And men too were fitted together, and all other creatures which have life. And the men possessed both inhabited cities and artificial works [cultivated fields] just like ourselves, and they had sun and moon and the rest, just as we have, and the earth produced for them many and diverse things, of which they collected the most useful, and now use them for [or, "in"] their dwellings. This I say concerning Separation, that it must have taken place not only with us, but elsewhere.

Before these things were separated off, all things were together, nor was any color distinguishable, for the mixing of all Things prevented this, *(namely)* the mixing of moist and dry, and hot and cold, and bright and dark, and there was a great quantity of earth in the mixture, and seeds infinite in number, not at all like one another. For none of the other things either is like any other. And as this was so, one must believe that all Things were present in the Whole.

[8] These things being thus separated off, one must understand that all things are in no wise less or more (for it is not possible for them to be more than All), but all things are forever equal *(in quantity)*.

[9] And since there are equal *(quantitative)* parts of Great and Small, so, too, similarly in everything there must be everything. It is not possible *(for them)* to exist apart, but all things contain a portion of everything. Since it is not possible for the Least to exist, it cannot be isolated, nor come into being by itself; but as it was in the beginning, so now, all things are together. In all things there are many things, and of the things separated off, there are equal numbers in *(the categories)* Great and Small.

[10] So that the number of the things separated off cannot be known either in thought or in fact.

[11] The things in the one Cosmos are not separated off from one another with an axe, neither the Hot from the Cold, nor the Cold from the Hot.

[12] Thus these things circulate and are separated off by force and speed. The speed makes the force. Their speed is not like the speed of any of the Things now existing among mankind, but altogether many times as fast.

[13] How can hair come from not-hair, and flesh from not-flesh?

[14] In everything there is a portion of everything except Mind; and some things contain Mind also.

[15] Other things all contain a part of everything, but Mind is infinite and self-ruling, and is mixed with no Thing, but is alone by itself. If it were not by itself, but were mixed with anything else, it would have had a share of all Things, if it were mixed with anything; for in everything there is a portion of everything, as I have said before. And the things mixed *(with Mind)* would have prevented it, so that it could not rule over any Thing in the same way as it can being alone by itself. For it is the finest of all Things, and the purest, and has complete understanding of everything, and has the greatest power. All things which have life, both the greater and the less, are ruled by Mind. Mind took command of the universal revolution, so as to make *(things)* revolve at the outset. And at first things began to revolve from some small point, but now the revolution extends over a greater area, and will spread even further. And the things which were mixed together, and separated off, and divided, were all understood by Mind. And whatever they were going to be, and whatever things were then in existence that are not now, and all things that now exist and whatever shall exist—all were arranged by Mind, as also the revolution now followed by the stars, the sun and moon, and the Air and Aether which were separated off. It was this revolution which caused the separation off. And dense separates from rare, and hot from cold, and bright from dark, and dry from wet. There are many portions of many things. And nothing is absolutely separated off or divided the one from the other except Mind. Mind is all alike, both the greater and the less. But nothing else is like anything else, but each individual thing is and was most obviously that of which it contains the most.

[16] And when Mind began the motion, there was a separating-off from all that was being moved; and all that Mind set in motion was separated *(internally);* and as things were moving and separating off *(internally),* the revolution greatly increased this *(internal)* separation.

[17] Mind, which ever Is, certainly still exists also where all other things are, *(namely)* in the multiple surrounding *(mass)* and in the things which were separated off before, and in the things already separated off [things that have been either aggregated or separated].

[18] The dense and moist and cold and dark *(Elements)* collected here, where now is Earth, and the rare and hot and dry went outwards to the furthest part of the Aether.

[19] From these, while they are separating off, Earth solidifies; for from the clouds, water is separated off, and from the water, earth, and from the earth, stones are solidified by the cold; and these rush outward rather than the water.

[20] The Greeks have an incorrect belief on Coming into Being and Passing Away. No Thing comes into being or passes away, but it is mixed together or separated from existing Things. Thus they would be correct if they called coming into being "mixing," and passing away "separation-off."

[21] It is the sun that endows the moon with its brilliance.

[22] We give the name Iris to the reflection of the sun on the clouds. It is therefore the sign of a storm, for the water which flows round the cloud produces wind or forces out rain.

[23] Through the weakness of the sense-perceptions, we cannot judge truth.

DEMOCRITUS
ca. 460–ca. 370 B.C.

LEUCIPPUS
fifth century B.C.

Democritus of Abdera, on the coast of Thrace, was probably born in 460 B.C. He wrote over sixty works, of which several hundred fragments survive. Together with Leucippus, a virtually unknown figure who was supposedly his teacher, Democritus was the prime exponent of the philosophy known as *atomism*. While Leucippus's work has perished, we have many reports about the Democritean form of atomistic philosophy.

Atomism accepted Parmenides' idea that being must be one seamless whole but posited an infinite number of such "one's." According to Democritus, the world is made up of tiny "un-cutables" *<atomos>* that move within the "void" (corresponding to Parmenides' non-being). These atoms combine in different patterns to form the material objects of the observable world. Democritus applied this understanding of reality to human beings as well. Both the soul and the body are made up of atoms. Perception occurs when atoms from objects outside the person strike the sense organs inside the person, which in turn strike the atoms of the soul further inside. Death, in turn, is simply the dissipation of the soul atoms when the body atoms no longer hold them together.

Such an understanding of the person seems to eliminate all possibility of freedom of choice and, indeed, the only known saying of Leucippus is "Nothing happens at random; everything happens out of reason and by necessity." Such a position would seem to eliminate all ethics: If you *must* act a certain way, it seems futile to talk about what you *ought* to do (since, as Kant later said, "*ought* implies *can*"). Yet Democritus wrote a great deal on ethics, including a book of ethical maxims called the *Gnomae*.

The fragments that follow are grouped into two sections: first, the ancient reports about Leucippus and Democritus; then the metaphysical and epistemological fragments.

Democritus's philosophy is important for at least two reasons. First, while atomism represents still another pluralistic answer to Parmenides, and while Leucippus was a Pre-Socratic, nevertheless Democritus was actually a slightly younger contemporary of Socrates and an older contemporary of Plato. Hence, Democritus's atomistic materialism may be viewed as an important alternative to Plato's idealism. Second, Democritus's thought continued to have an impact, being taken up first by Epicurus and then, in Roman times, by Lucretius.

A. ANCIENT REPORTS ON ATOMISM

[1] Leucippus of Elea or Miletus (both accounts are current) had associated with Parmenides in philosophy, but in his view of reality he did not follow the same path as Parmenides and Xenophanes but rather, it seems, the opposite path. For while they regarded the whole as one, motionless, uncreated, and limited, and forbade even the search for what is not, he posited innumerable elements in perpetual motion—namely the atoms—and held that the number of their shapes was infinite, on the ground that there was no reason why any atom should be of one shape rather than another; for he observed too that coming-into-being and change are incessant in the world. Further he held that not-being exists as well as being, and the two are equally the causes of things coming-into-being. The nature of atoms he supposed to be compact and full; that, he said, was being, and it moved in the void, which he called not-being and held to exist no less than being. In the same way his associate, Democritus of Abdera, posited as principles the full and the void.

[2] Apollodorus in the *Chronicles* says that Epicurus was instructed by Nausiphanes and Praxiphanes; but Epicurus himself denies this, saying in the letter to Eurylochus that he instructed himself. He and Hemarchus both maintain that there never was a philosopher Leucippus, who some (including Apollodorus the Epicurean) say was the teacher of Democritus.

[3] Leucippus postulated atoms and void, and in this Democritus resembled him, though in other respects he was more productive.

[4] Democritus ... met Leucippus and, according to some, Anaxagoras also, whose junior he was by forty years. ... As he himself says in the *Little World-system,* he was a young man in the old age of Anaxagoras, being forty years younger.

[5] Demetrius in his *Homonyms* and Antisthenes in his *Successions* say that he [Democritus] traveled to Egypt to visit the priests and learn geometry, and that he went also to Persia to visit the Chaldaeans, and to the Red Sea. Some say that he associated with the "naked philosophers" in India; also that he went to Ethiopia.

[6] Leucippus thought he had arguments which would assert what is consistent sense-perception and not do away with coming into being or perishing or motion, or the plurality of existents. He agrees with the appearances to this extent, but he concedes, to those who maintain the One [the Eleatics], that there would be no motion without void, and says that the void is non-existent, and that no part of what is is non-existent—for what is in the strict sense is wholly and fully being. But such being, he says, is not one; there is an infinite number, and they are invisible because of the small-

ness of the particles. They move in the void (for there *is* void), and when they come together they cause coming to be, and when they separate they cause perishing.

[7] They [Leucippus, Democritus, and Epicurus] said that the first principles
were infinite in number, and thought they were indivisible atoms and impassible owing
to their compactness, and without any void in them; divisibility comes about because
of the void in compound bodies.

[8] To this extent they differed, that one [Epicurus] supposed that all atoms were
very small, and on that account imperceptible; the other, Democritus, that there are
some atoms that are very large.

[9] Democritus holds the same view as Leucippus about the elements, full and
void . . . he spoke as if the things that are were in constant motion in the void; and there
are innumerable worlds which differ in size. In some worlds there is no sun and moon,
in others they are larger than in our world, and in others more numerous. The intervals
between the worlds are unequal; in some parts there are more worlds, in others fewer;
some are increasing, some at their height, some decreasing; in some parts they are arising, in others failing. They are destroyed by collision, one with another. There are
some worlds devoid of living creatures or plants or any moisture.

[10] Everything happens according to necessity; for the cause of the coming-
into-being of all things is the whirl, which he calls necessity.

[11] As they [the atoms] move, they collide and become entangled in such a way
as to cling in close contact to one another, but not so as to form one substance of them
in reality of any kind whatever; for it is very simple-minded to suppose that two or
more could ever become one. The reason he gives for atoms staying together for a
while is the intertwining and mutual hold of the primary bodies; for some of them are
angular, some hooked, some concave, some convex, and indeed with countless other
differences; so he thinks they cling to each other and stay together until such time as
some stronger necessity comes from the surrounding and shakes and scatters them
apart.

[12] Democritus says that the spherical is the most mobile of shapes; and such is
mind and fire.

[13] Democritus and the majority of natural philosophers who discuss perception
are guilty of a great absurdity; for they represent all perception as being by touch.

[14] Leucippus, Democritus, and Epicurus say that perception and thought arise
when images enter from outside; neither occurs to anybody without an image impinging.

[15] Democritus explains sight by the visual image, which he describes in a peculiar way; the visual image does not arise directly in the pupil, but the air between the
eye and the object of sight is contracted and stamped by the object seen and the seer;
for from everything there is always a sort of effluence proceeding. So this air, which is
solid and variously colored, appears in the eye, which is moist (?); the eye does not
admit the dense part, but the moist passes through.

B. Metaphysical and Epistemological Fragments

[16] We know nothing about anything really, but opinion is for all individuals an
inflowing *(? of the atoms)*.

[17] It will be obvious that it is impossible to understand how in reality each
thing is.

[18] Sweet exists by convention, bitter by convention, color by convention; atoms and void (alone) exist in reality. . . . We know nothing accurately in reality, but *(only)* as it changes according to the bodily condition, and the constitution of those things that flow upon *(the body)* and impinge upon it.

[19] It has often been demonstrated that we do not grasp how each thing is or is not.

[20] There are two sorts of knowledge, one genuine, one bastard (or *"obscure"*). To the latter belong all the following: sight, hearing, smell, taste, touch. The real is separated from this. When the bastard can do no more—neither see more minutely, nor hear, nor smell, nor taste, nor perceive by touch—and a finer investigation is needed, then the genuine comes in as having a tool for distinguishing more finely.

[21] Naught exists just as much as Aught.

Two Sophists

PROTAGORAS
ca. 490–ca. 420 B.C.

Protagoras, like Democritus, came from Abdera, on the Thracian coast. An ancient story relates that he was at first a porter and that Democritus of Abdera saw him, admired his poise, and decided to instruct him; but this story's truth is doubtful. Protagoras reflected on language and developed a system of grammar. Having settled in Athens, where he taught the youth, he won the respect of Pericles, who commissioned him to frame laws for the new colony of Thurii, in Italy. At age seventy he was accused and convicted of atheism and is said to have left for Sicily and to have drowned at sea.

Protagoras is primarily known for his claim that "of all things the measure is Man. . . ." In the dialogues *Protagoras* and *Theaetetus* (the relevant sections from the latter are reprinted in this volume), Plato takes Protagoras to mean that each person, not humanity as a whole, is the measure of all things and so attacks Protagoras's relativism.

Protagoras was the first of those traveling teachers of philosophy and rhetoric who became known as "Sophists." Sophists were not as interested in metaphysical theories as they were in the skill of <*arete*>, or "excellence," in the sense of bettering oneself. Many conservative Greeks, such as Aristophanes, considered proper speech and good manners the inherited characteristics of the upper classes. The Sophists, however, taught such skills for a fee—to the consternation of the aristocracy.

Plato considered it his task to oppose these men, and since his dialogues survived and most of their writings did not, his highly polemical pictures of the Sophists have been widely accepted as fair portraits. The very name "Sophist" has become a reproach. Yet one should not uncritically accept Plato's image of the Sophists. Although many disagree with Sophist conclusions, their question-ing of conventions, especially in ethics, and their critique of the limits of knowl-edge represent a milestone in the history of thought.

[1] Of all things the measure is Man, of the things that are, that they are, and of the things that are not, that they are not.

[2] Teaching needs endowment and practice. Learning must begin in youth.

[3] About the gods, I am not able to know whether they exist or do not exist, nor what they are like in form; for the factors preventing knowledge are many: the obscu-rity of the subject, and the shortness of human life.

[4] To make the weaker cause the stronger.

[5] When his sons, who were fine young men, died within eight days, he (Peri-cles) bore it without mourning. For he held on to his serenity, from which every day he derived great benefit in happiness, freedom from suffering, and honor in the people's eyes—for all who saw him bearing his griefs valiantly thought him great-souled and brave and superior to themselves, well knowing their own helplessness in such a calamity.

[6] Art without practice, and practice without art, are nothing.

[7] Education does not take root in the soul unless one goes deep.

GORGIAS
fl. ca. 427 B.C.

After Protagoras, Gorgias was probably the most renowned Sophist. Gorgias came from Leontini, in southern Sicily. His dates are uncertain, but he is said to have died at the age of 108, possibly as late as 375 B.C. He first came to Athens on a mission from his Sicilian countrymen, enlisting (successfully) Athenian help against Syracuse. While in Athens, he taught the art of persuasion to Isocrates, the famous rhetorician.

Like Protagoras, Gorgias is a character in Plato's dialogue bearing his name. Also like Protagoras, Gorgias held views—in this case on the impossibility of knowledge—that Plato found unacceptable. The following selections constitute the single philosophic fragment that has come down to us (a long quotation in Sextus Empiricus) and three very short pieces that may help fill out the picture of Gorgias.

[1]   I. Nothing exists.
     (a) Not-Being does not exist.
     (b) Being does not exist.

  I. Nothing exists. If anything exists, it must be either Being or Not-Being, or both Being and Not-Being.

    (a) It cannot be Not-Being, for Not-Being does not exist; if it did, it would be at the same time Being and Not-Being, which is impossible.

    (b) It cannot be Being, for Being does not exist. If Being exists, it must be either everlasting, or created, or both.

        i. It cannot be everlasting; if it were, it would have no beginning, and therefore would be boundless; if it is boundless, then it has no position, for if it had position it would be contained in something, and so it would no longer be boundless, for that which contains is greater than that which is contained, and nothing is greater than the boundless. It cannot be contained by itself, for then the thing containing and the thing contained would be the same, and Being would become two things—both position and body—which is absurd. Hence if Being is everlasting, it is boundless; if boundless, it has no position ("is nowhere"); if without position, it does not exist.

       ii. Similarly, Being cannot be created; if it were, it must come from something, either Being or Not-Being, both of which are impossible.

      iii. Similarly, Being cannot be both everlasting and created, since they are opposite. Therefore Being does not exist.

      iv. Being cannot be one, because if it exists it has size, and is therefore infinitely divisible; at least it is threefold, having length, breadth, and depth.

       v. It cannot be many, because the many is made up of an addition of ones, so that since the one does not exist, the many do not exist either.

    (c) A mixture of Being and Not-Being is impossible. Therefore since Being does not exist, nothing exists.

  II. If anything exists, it is incomprehensible. If the concepts of the mind are not realities, reality cannot be thought; if the thing thought is white, then white is thought about; if the thing thought is non-existent, then non-existence is thought about; this is equivalent to saying that "existence, reality, is not thought about, cannot be thought." Many things thought about are not realities: we can conceive of a chariot running on the sea, or a winged man. Also, since things seen are the objects of sight, and things heard are the objects of hearing, and we accept as real things seen without their being heard, and vice versa; so we would have to accept things thought without their being seen or heard; but this would mean believing in things like the chariot racing on the sea. Therefore reality is not the object of thought, and cannot be comprehended by it. Pure mind, as opposed to sense-perception, or even as an equally valid criterion, is a myth.

III. If anything is comprehensible, it is incommunicable. The things which exist are perceptibles; the objects of sight are apprehended by sight, the objects of hearing by hearing, and there is no interchange; so that these sense-perceptions cannot communicate with one another. Further, that with which we communicate is speech, and speech is not the same thing as the things that exist, the perceptibles; so that we communicate not the things which exist, but only speech; just as that which is seen cannot become that which is heard, so our speech cannot be equated with that which exists, since it is outside us. Further, speech is composed from the percepts which we receive from without, that is, from perceptibles; so that it is not speech which communicates perceptibles, but perceptibles which create speech. Further, speech can never exactly represent perceptibles, since it is different from them, and perceptibles are apprehended each by the one kind of organ, speech by another. Hence, since the objects of sight cannot be presented to any other organ but sight, and the different sense-organs cannot give their information to one another, similarly speech cannot give any information about perceptibles. Therefore, if anything exists and is comprehended, it is incommunicable.

[2] Not the looks of a woman, but her good reputation should be known to many.

[3] Tragedy, by means of legends and emotions, creates a deception in which the deceiver is more honest than the non-deceiver, and the deceived is wiser than the non-deceived.

[4] Being is unrecognizable unless it succeeds in seeming, and seeming is weak unless it succeeds in being.

Sources
of the Fragments

All of the fragments and most of the paraphrases in the preceding texts were collected by a nineteenth-century German scholar, Hermann Diels (and later modified by Walther Kranz), in *Die Fragmente der Vorsokratiker* (Berlin: Weidmann, most recent edition, 1967). Diels assembled the original Greek texts and furnished German translations for all the fragments. He also collected and printed, but did not translate, reports of ancient authors about the lives, works, and ideas of the Pre-Socratics.

Kathleen Freeman published *An Ancilla to the Pre-Socratic Philosophers: A Complete Translation of the Fragments in Diels, Fragmente der Vorsokratiker* (Cambridge, MA: Harvard University Press, 1947). Like Diels-Kranz, she translated only the fragments, not the ancient paraphrases and reports about the philosophers' lives and works. G.S. Kirk, J.E. Raven, and M. Schofield translated many of these previously untranslated items in *The Presocratic Philosophers: A Critical History with a Selection of Texts,* 2nd edition (Cambridge: Cambridge University Press, 1983). Almost all the translations I have used are either those of Freeman (marked with an *F*) or those of Kirk, Raven, and Schofield (marked with a *K*). In a few cases, the translation is Kaufmann's (marked with a *WK*) or the older first edition (1957) of Kirk and Raven (so indicated in the notes). Some of the translations have been modified by Kaufmann or myself (and are marked with an *). After direct quotations, the symbols (*K*, *F*, and *WK*) are preceded by the number that the fragment bears in the fifth edition of Diels-Kranz's standard work. (Freeman's numbering is the same as that of Diels-Kranz.) After paraphrases, the ancient works in which the paraphrases occur are cited briefly (along with the abbreviation and number from one of the above sources).

For discussions of the fragments and the paraphrases, see the Kirk, Raven, and Schofield work as well as Richard D. McKirahan Jr., *Philosophy Before Socrates* (Indianapolis, IN: Hackett, 1994).

Thales

1. Plato, *Theaetetus* 174A; K 72.
2. Aristotle, *Politics* A11, 1259a; K 73.
3. Herodotus I, 75; K 66.
4. Aristotle, *Metaphysics* A3, 983b; W.D. Ross's translation.
5. Heraclitus Homericus, *Quaest. Hom.* 22; K 87. These may not really have been Thales' reasons.
6. Seneca, *Qu. Nat.* III, 14; K 88.
7. Aristotle, *De Anima* A2, 405a; K 89.
8. Aristotle, *De Anima* A5, 411a; K 91.

Anaximander

1. Suda s.v.; K 95. Some of this has been disputed.
2. Themistius, *Or.* 26; K 96.
3. Simplicius, *Physics* 24; K 101A and 119. Some scholars believe that the quotation begins earlier and comprises the whole sentence.
4. Ps.-Plutarch, *Strom.* 2; K 121.
5. *Ibid.;* K 122A.
6. Hippolytus, *Ref.* I, 6, 3; K 122B.
7. Aetius II, 20; K 126.
8. Aetius V, 19; K 133.
9. Ps.-Plutarch, *Strom.* 2; K 134.
10. Plutarch, *Symp.* VIII, 730E; K 137.

Anaximenes

1. Diogenes Laertius II, 3; K 138.
2. Augustine, *City of God,* VIII, 2; K 146.
3. Ps.-Plutarch, *Strom.* 3; K 148.

Pythagoras

1. Herodotus IV, 95; K 257.
2. Porphyry, *V.P.* 9; K 266.
3. Iustinus *ap.* Pomp. Trog. *Hist. Phil. Epit.* XX, 4, 14; K 272.
4. Aetius I, 3, 8; 1st edition K 280.
5. Proclus, *In Eucl.,* p. 426 Friedl; 1st edition K 281.
6. Diogenes Laertius VIII, 36; Xenophanes, fragment 7; K 260.
7. Herodotus II, 123; 1st edition K 270.
8. Porphyry, *Vita Pythagorae* 19; 1st edition K 271.
9. Eudemus *ap.* Simplic. *Phys.,* 732, 30; 1st edition K 272. The doctrine of the eternal recurrence of the same events at gigantic intervals was revived in modern times by Friedrich Nietzsche; *cf.* Walter Kaufmann, *Nietzsche* (Princeton, NJ: Princeton University Press, 1950; Cleveland, OH: Meridian Books, 1956), Chapter 11, "Overman and Eternal Recurrence."

10–27. Iamblichus, *Protr.* 21; 1st edition K 275. These were some of the rules of the sect founded by Pythagoras. The numbers of the rules in K are given in parentheses after each paragraph.

28. Procl., *In Eucl.,* p. 65 Friedl.; 1st edition K 277.

29. Diogenes Laertius VIII, 8; 1st edition K 278.

Xenophanes

1. Diogenes Laertius IX, 18; K 161.
2. 11; WK.
3. 14; WK.
4. 15; WK.
5. 16; WK.
6. 23; F*.
7. 24; F.
8. 25; F*.
9. 26; F.
10. 27; F*.
11. 34; K 186.
12. 18; WK.

Heraclitus

1. Diogenes Laertius IX, 6; K 191.
2. *Ibid.,* IX, 5; K 192. Some scholars have questioned the claim about the three parts of his book; indeed, some have doubted that he wrote any book at all.
3. 89; WK.
4. 113; F.
5. 1; K 194.
6. 2; K 195.
7. 50; K 196.
8. 55; K 197.
9. 101a; F.
10. 7; F.
11. 107; K 198.
12. 60; K 200.
13. 6; F.
14. 49a; F*.
15. 91; F.
16. 12; K 214.
17. 61; K 199.
18. 111; K 201.
19. 8; F*.
20. 53; K 212.
21. 80; K 211.
22. 36; K 229.
23. 62; WK.
24. 27; F*.
25. 52; F.
26. 40; WK.
27. 42; WK.
28. 57; WK.
29. 5; F*.
30. 14; WK.
31. 96; WK. To appreciate the full measure of this heresy, one should recall Sophocles' *Antigone* and Homer's *Iliad.*
32. 102; K 206.
33. 79; F.
34. 76; F*.
35. 66; F.
36. 30; K 217.
37. 9; F*.
38. 97; F.
39. 4; F*.
40. 110; F*.
41. 112; F*.
42. 116; WK.
43. 118; K 230.
44. 117; K 231.
45. 29; WK.
46. 44; K 249.
47. 49; F*.
48. 121; F*.
49. 101; WK.
50. 18; WK.
51. 119; WK.
52. 123; WK.
53. 92; F*.
54. 93; K 244.

Parmenides

1. 1 (Lines 1–32); K 288.
2. 2; K 291.
3. 3; K 292. K construes the literal meaning as: "the same thing exists for thinking and for being"; Freeman's "For it is the same thing to think and to be" is based on Diels's *Denn (das Seiende) denken und sein ist dasselbe.* This much-discussed sentence seems to be continuous with the preceding two fragments.
4. 4; K 313.
5. 5; K 289.
6. 6; K 293. Freeman renders the final words: "in everything there is a way of opposing stress." Either way, many interpreters believe that Parmenides here alludes to Heraclitus.
7. 7; K 294.
8. 8; F*.
9. 9; Kranz takes *<epei>* with the previous line and translates: "For nothing is possible which does not come under either of the two" (i.e., everything belongs to one or other of the two categories light and night); F*.
10–14. 10–14; F.

Zeno of Elea

1. Plato, *Parmenides* 128c; F.M. Cornford's translation.
2. Plato, *Phaedrus* 261d; R. Hackforth's translation.
3. Simplicius, *Physics* 139, 18–19; WK.
4. Simplicius, *Physics* 109, 34; WK.
5. Simplicius, *Physics* 140, 30; WK.
6. Aristotle, *Topics* 160b 7; WK. Evidently the stage setting of the argument is a race course. On this ground, it is better to call the argument by this name, instead of "The Dichotomy," as is often done in the literature, keeping "The Stadium" as the generally accepted name of the fourth argument.
7. Aristotle, *Physics* 233a 21; WK.
8. Aristotle, *Physics* 239b 11; WK.
9. Aristotle, *Physics* 263a 5; WK.
10. Simplicius, *Physics* 1013, 4ff; WK.
11. Aristotle, *Physics* 239b 14; P.H. Wicksteed's translation, edited by F.M. Cornford.
12. Aristotle, *Physics* 239b 1, 30; Wicksteed's translation.
13. Aristotle, *Physics* 239b 33; Wicksteed's translation.
14. Aristotle, *Physics* 209a 23; WK.
15. Simplicius, *Physics* 1108, 18; WK.

Melissus

1. Diogenes Laertius IX, 24; 1st edition K 379.
2. Plutarch, *Pericles* 26; K 519. The great battle referred to took place in 441/40 B.C.
3–8. 1–6; F.
9–18. 7; F
19–24. 8; F
25–26. 9–10; F

Empedocles

1. Simplicius, *Physics* 25, 19; K 335.
2. Aristotle, *Metaphysics* A 3, 984a.
3–36. The fragments in this section are all from F. I have numbered them consecutively to make it easier to follow. The Diels-Freeman numbering follows each paragraph.

Anaxagoras

1. Diogenes Laertius II, 7–15; K 459.
2. Strabo 14, p. 645 Cas.; K 463.
3. Diogenes Laertius I, 16; K 466.
4–23. 1–19, 21 (Opening sentences from his book *On Natural Science*); F.

Democritus and Leucippus

1. Simplicius, *Physics* 28, 4; 1st edition of K 539.
2. Diogenes Laertius X, 13; K 540.
3. Cicero, *Academica* pr. II, 37, 118; K 541.
4. Diogenes Laertius IX, 34; K 542.
5. *Ibid.,* IX, 35; K 544.
6. Aristotle, *De Gen. et Corr.,* A 8, 325a; K 545.
7. Simplicius, *De Caelo* 242, 18; K 557.
8. Dionysius *ap.* Eusebium P.E. XIV, 23, 3; K 561.
9. Hyppolytus *Ref.* I, 13, 2; K 565.
10. Diogenes Laertius IX, 45; K 566; cf. "the only extant saying of Leucippus himself," K 569, Fr. 2, Aetius I, 25, 4: "Nothing occurs at random, but everything for a reason and by necessity."
11. Aristotle, *On Democritus ap.* Simplicium *De Caelo* 295, 11; K 583.
12. Aristotle, *De Anima,* A 2, 405a; K 585.
13. Aristotle, *De Sensu* 4, 442a; K 587.
14. Aetius IV, 8; K 588.
15. Theophrastus, *De Sensu* 50; R 589.
16. 7 (from "On the Forms"); F.
17. 8 (from "On the Forms"); F.
18. 9; F.
19. 10; F.
20. 11 (from "The Canon"); F.
21. 156; F.

Protagoras

1. 1 (from "Truth" or "Refutatory Arguments"); F.
2. 3 (from a treatise entitled "Great Logus"); F.
3. 4 (from "On the Gods"); F.
4. 6b; F.
5. 9; F.
6. 10; F.
7. 11; F.

Gorgias

1. 3, Sextus, from *On Not-being or on Nature;* F.
2. 22; F.
3. 23; F.
4. 26; F.

EPILOGUE: TWO VIEWS OF ATHENS

————◄○►————

While philosophy actually began on the Ionian coast of Asia Minor (in modern Turkey), with the fifth century B.C. the center of philosophical inquiry became the city-state of Athens. The Persian Empire overran the Ionian colonies, forcing Greek philosophers there to flee to Athens. In 499 B.C. the remaining Greeks in Ionia, supported by Athens, rebelled against their Persian overlords. The Persian king, Darius, used the unsuccessful rebellion as a pretext to attack the Greek mainland. The Persian Wars, as they are now known, lasted about fifty years, though most of the fighting took place between 490 and 479 B.C. While the specifics of the war are fascinating—and the names of major battles such as those at Marathon and Thermopylae are still famous today—we do not have space to treat them. (See the suggested readings for descriptions of the war.) The upshot of the conflict, however, was astounding: The vastly outnumbered Greeks, led by the Athenians, defeated the Persians.

In the years following the Persian Wars, Athens blossomed. Artists, sculptors, architects, playwrights, poets, and philosophers found a haven there. Democracy encouraged participation in government; the Parthenon, one of the most famous buildings in the world, was built (beginning in 447 B.C.); Aeschylus (525–456 B.C.), Sophocles (c. 496–406 B.C.), Euripides (c. 485–406 B.C.), and Aristophanes (c. 450–c. 385 B.C.), invented theater as we know it; sculptors such as Myron produced magnificent statues like the *Discus Thrower* (c. 450 B.C.); Hippocrates (c. 460–c. 377 B.C.) developed the concept of compassionate medicine (the "Hippocratic Oath" is still taken by physicians today); Thucydides (c. 460–c. 400 B.C.) introduced the concept of factual history; while the man whose name is synonymous with the age, Pericles (c. 495–429 B.C.), presided wisely over the state.

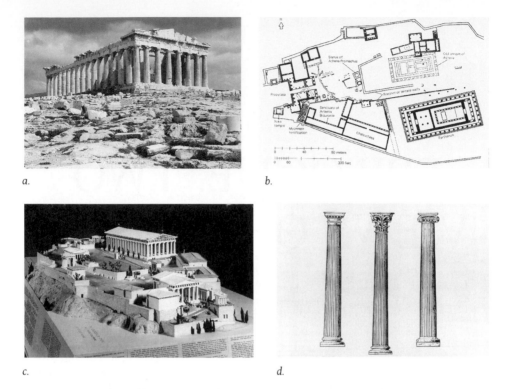

a.

b.

c.

d.

The Acropolis and the Parthenon

a. The *Parthenon*, Athens, built 477–438 B.C. The Parthenon, dedicated to Athena, patron deity of Athens, was at one period rededicated to the Christian Virgin Mary and then later became a Turkish mosque. In 1687 a gunpowder explosion created the ruin we see today. The Doric shell remains as a monument to ancient architectural engineering expertise and to a sense of classical beauty and order. (*Stergios Svaraas/D.A. Harissladis Photographic Agency*)

b. Restored plan of the Acropolis, 400 B.C. The history of the Acropolis is as varied as the style and size of the temples and buildings constructed atop the ancient site. (*Pearson Education/PH College*)

c. This model of the Acropolis of Athens recreates the complexity of fifth century B.C. public space, which included centers for worship, public forum, and entertainment. (*Royal Ontario Museum, Toronto*)

d. Doric, Ionic, and Corinthian columns with their characteristic capitals. (*Library of Congress*)

However, the Golden Age of Athens did not last long. Beginning in 431, the Athenians entered into a conflict with the Spartans, their allies in the Persian Wars. At the end of the first year of the Peloponnesian Wars (named for the Peloponnesian Peninsula, southwest of Athens, where Sparta was located), Pericles gave a famous speech at the funeral of the slain Athenians. The speech, reprinted here (as recorded by Thucydides, translated by Richard Crawley) movingly defends Athenian democracy and shows Athenians at their best.

Shortly after this speech, the tide of war turned against the Athenians. Ensconced behind safe walls, the Athenians had hoped to wait out the Spartans. But plague hit the city in 429 B.C. and among its victims was Pericles himself. Without the wise leadership of Pericles, the Athenians made a series of political and military blunders that eventually led to their defeat at the hands of the Spartans in 404 B.C. But before this, during the war, the Athenians had attempted to force all other Greek city-states to join them against the Spartans. In 416 B.C., the Athenians even sent a military delegation to neutral Melos demanding that the Melians submit or be destroyed. The Melians refused the ultimatum and the Athenians responded by killing all the men and selling the women and children as slaves. Thucydides' unwaveringly honest description of the Melian conference (given here complete) shows a side of the Athenians not visible in Pericles' oration and helps to explain why and how these democrats and lovers of ideas and arts could later execute Socrates.

* * *

General histories of this period include Russell Meiggs, *The Athenian Empire* (Oxford: Clarendon Press, 1972); Simon Hornblower, *The Greek World, 479–323 B.C.* (London: Methuen, 1983); Joint Association of Classical Teachers, *The World of Athens: An Introduction to Classical Athenian Culture* (Cambridge: Cambridge University Press, 1984); Charles W. Fornara and Loren J. Samons II, *Athens from Cleisthenes to Pericles* (Berkeley, CA: University of California Press, 1991); J.F. Lazenby, *The Defence of Greece, 490–479 B.C.* (Warminster, England: Aris & Phillips, 1993) and Paul Cartledge, *The Cambridge Illustrated History of Ancient Greece* (Cambridge: Cambridge University Press, 1998). For discussions of the Athenian city-state, see Frank J. Frost, ed., *Democracy and the Athenians; Aspects of Ancient Politics* (New York: Wiley, 1969); Jack Cargill, *The Second Athenian League: Empire or Free Alliance?* (Berkeley, CA: University of California Press, 1981); Malcolm F. McGregor, *The Athenians and Their Empire* (Vancouver, BC: University of British Columbia Press, 1987); David Stockton, *The Classical Athenian Democracy* (Oxford: Oxford University Press, 1990); Roger Just, *Women in Athenian Law and Life* (London Routledge, 1991); and Jennifer Tolbert Roberts, *Athens on Trial: The Antidemocratic Tradition in Western Thought* (Princeton, NJ: Princeton University Press, 1997). A.R. Burns, *Persia and the Greeks,* 2nd ed. (Stanford, CA: Stanford University Press, 1984) gives a description of the Persian Wars while Donald Kagan, *The Outbreak of the Peloponnesian War* (Ithaca, NY: Cornell University Press, 1969) and G.E.M. de Ste. Croix, *The Origins of the Peloponnesian War* (Ithaca, NY: Cornell University Press, 1972) discuss the Peloponnesian War. For a commentary on Thucydides' history of the Peloponnesian War, see David Cartwright, *A Historical Commentary on Thucydides* (Ann Arbor, MI: University of Michigan Press, 1997).

The classical work, *Twelve Lives,* by Plutarch is a good place to begin a study of Pericles. More recent works include Charles Alexander Robinson, *Athens in the Age of Pericles* (Norman, OK: University of Oklahoma Press, 1959); Rex Warner, *Pericles the Athenian* (Boston: Little, Brown, 1963); and Donald Kagan, *Pericles of Athens and the Birth of Democracy* (New York: Free Press, 1991). For discussions of Thucydides as an historian and as a person, see Francis Macdonald Cornford, *Thucydides Mythistoricus* (London: Routledge, 1965); Peter R. Pouncey, *The Necessities of War: A Study of Thucydides' Pessimism* (New York: Columbia University Press, 1980); Marc Cogan, *The Human Thing: The Speeches and Principles of Thucydides' History* (Chicago: University of Chicago Press, 1981); Simon Hornblower, *Thucydides* (Baltimore: Johns Hopkins University Press, 1987); and Clifford Orwin, *The Humanity of Thucydides* (Princeton, NJ: Princeton University Press, 1997).

PERICLES, FUNERAL ORATION

Book II, Chapter 6: The Funeral Oration of Pericles

After the bodies have been laid in the earth, a man chosen by the state, of approved wisdom and eminent reputation, pronounces over them an appropriate panegyric; after which all retire. Such is the manner of the burying; and throughout the whole of the war, whenever the occasion arose, the established custom was observed. Meanwhile these were the first that had fallen, and Pericles, son of Xanthippus, was chosen to pronounce their eulogium. When the proper time arrived, he advanced from the sepulchre to an elevated platform in order to be heard by as many of the crowd as possible, and spoke as follows:

Funeral Oration

Most of my predecessors in this place have commended him who made this speech part of the law, telling us that it is well that it should be delivered at the burial of those who fall in battle. For myself, I should have thought that the worth which had displayed itself in deeds would be sufficiently rewarded by honours also shown by deeds; such as you now see in this funeral prepared at the people's cost. And I could have wished that the reputations of many brave men were not to be imperilled in the mouth of a single individual, to stand or fall according as he spoke well or ill. For it is hard to speak properly upon a subject where it is even difficult to convince your hearers that you are speaking the truth. On the one hand, the friend who is familiar with every fact of the story may think that some point has not been set forth with that fullness which he wishes and knows it to deserve; on the other, he who is a stranger to the matter may be led by envy to suspect exaggeration if he hears anything above his own nature. For men can endure to hear others praised only so long as they can severally persuade themselves of their own ability to equal the actions recounted: when this point is passed, envy comes in and with it incredulity. However, since our ancestors have stamped this custom with their approval, it becomes my duty to obey the law and to try to satisfy your several wishes and opinions as best I may.

I shall begin with our ancestors: it is both just and proper that they should have the honour of the first mention on an occasion like the present. They dwelt in the country without break in the succession from generation to generation, and handed it down free to the present time by their valour. And if our more remote ancestors deserve praise, much more do our own fathers, who added to their inheritance the empire which we now possess, and spared no pains to be able to leave their acquisitions to us of the present generation. Lastly, there are few parts of our dominions that have not been augmented by those of us here, who are still more or less in the vigour of life; while the mother country has been furnished by us with everything that can enable her to depend on her own resources whether for war or for peace. That part of our history which tells of the military achievements which gave us our several possessions, or of

Thucydides, *The Peloponnesian War*, translated by Richard Crawley

the ready valour with which either we or our fathers stemmed the tide of Hellenic or foreign aggression, is a theme too familiar to my hearers for me to dilate on, and I shall therefore pass it by. But what was the road by which we reached our position, what the form of government under which our greatness grew, what the national habits out of which it sprang; these are questions which I may try to solve before I proceed to my panegyric upon these men; since I think this to be a subject upon which on the present occasion a speaker may properly dwell, and to which the whole assemblage, whether citizens or foreigners, may listen with advantage.

Our constitution does not copy the laws of neighbouring states; we are rather a pattern to others than imitators ourselves. Its administration favours the many instead of the few; this is why it is called a democracy. If we look to the laws, they afford equal justice to all in their private differences; if no social standing, advancement in public life falls to reputation for capacity, class considerations not being allowed to interfere with merit; nor again does poverty bar the way, if a man is able to serve the state, he is not hindered by the obscurity of his condition. The freedom which we enjoy in our government extends also to our ordinary life. There, far from exercising a jealous surveillance over each other, we do not feel called upon to be angry with our neighbour for doing what he likes, or even to indulge in those injurious looks which cannot fail to be offensive, although they inflict no positive penalty. But all this case in our private relations does not make us lawless as citizens. Against this fear is our chief safeguard, teaching us to obey the magistrates and the laws, particularly such as regard the protection of the injured, whether they are actually on the statute book, or belong to that code which, although unwritten, yet cannot be broken without acknowledged disgrace.

Further, we provide plenty of means for the mind to refresh itself from business. We celebrate games and sacrifices all the year round, and the elegance of our private establishments forms a daily source of pleasure and helps to banish the spleen; while the magnitude of our city draws the produce of the world into our harbour, so that to the Athenian the fruits of other countries are as familiar a luxury as those of his own.

If we turn to our military policy, there also we differ from our antagonists. We throw open our city to the world, and never by alien acts exclude foreigners from any opportunity of learning or observing, although the eyes of an enemy may occasionally profit by our liberality; trusting less in system and policy than to the native spirit of our citizens; while in education, where our rivals from their very cradles by a painful discipline seek after manliness, at Athens we live exactly as we please, and yet are just as ready to encounter every legitimate danger. In proof of this it may be noticed that the Lacedaemonians do not invade our country alone, but bring with them all their confederates; while we Athenians advance unsupported into the territory of a neighbour, and fighting upon a foreign soil usually vanquish with ease men who are defending their homes. Our united force was never yet encountered by any enemy, because we have at once to attend to our marine and to dispatch our citizens by land upon a hundred different services; so that, wherever they engage with some such fraction of our strength, a success against a detachment is magnified into a victory over the nation, and a defeat into a reverse suffered at the hands of our entire people. And yet if with habits not of labour but of ease, and courage not of art but of nature, we are still willing to encounter danger, we have the double advantage of escaping the experience of hardships in anticipation and of facing them in the hour of need as fearlessly as those who are never free from them.

Nor are these the only points in which our city is worthy of admiration. We cultivate refinement without extravagance and knowledge without effeminacy; wealth we employ more for use than for show, and place the real disgrace of poverty not in owning to the fact but in declining the struggle against it. Our public men have, besides politics, their private affairs to attend to, and our ordinary citizens, though occupied with the pursuits of industry, are still fair judges of public matters; for, unlike any other nation, regarding him who takes no part in these duties not as unambitious but as useless, we Athenians are able to judge at all events if we cannot originate, and, instead of looking on discussion as a stumbling-block in the way of action, we think it an indispensable preliminary to any wise action at all. Again, in our enterprises we present the singular spectacle of daring and deliberation, each carried to its highest point, and both united in the same persons; although usually decision is the fruit of ignorance, hesitation of reflection. But the palm of courage will surely be adjudged most justly to those, who best know the difference between hardship and pleasure and yet are never tempted to shrink from danger. In generosity we are equally singular, acquiring our friends by conferring, not by receiving, favours. Yet, of course, the doer of the favour is the firmer friend of the two, in order by continued kindness to keep the recipient in his debt; while the debtor feels less keenly from the very consciousness that the return he makes will be a payment, not a free gift. And it is only the Athenians, who, fearless of consequences, confer their benefits not from calculations of expediency, but in the confidence of liberality.

In short, I say that as a city we are the school of Hellas; while I doubt if the world can produce a man who, where he has only himself to depend upon, is equal to so many emergencies, and graced by so happy a versatility, as the Athenian. And that this is no mere boast thrown out for the occasion, but plain matter of fact, the power of the state acquired by these habits proves. For Athens alone of her contemporaries is found when tested to be greater than her reputation, and alone gives no occasion to her assailants to blush at the antagonist by whom they have been worsted, or to her subjects to question her title by merit to rule. Rather, the admiration of the present and succeeding ages will be ours, since we have not left our power without witness, but have shown it by mighty proofs; and far from needing a Homer for our panegyrist, or other of his craft whose verses might charm for the moment only for the impression which they gave to melt at the touch of fact, we have forced every sea and land to be the highway of our daring, and everywhere, whether for evil or for good, have left imperishable monuments behind us. Such is the Athens for which these men, in the assertion of their resolve not to lose her, nobly fought and died; and well may every one of their survivors be ready to suffer in her cause.

Indeed if I have dwelt at some length upon the character of our country, it has been to show that our stake in the struggle is not the same as theirs who have no such blessings to lose, and also that the panegyric of the men over whom I am now speaking might be by definite proofs established. That panegyric is now in a great measure complete; for the Athens that I have celebrated is only what the heroism of these and their like have made her, men whose fame, unlike that of most Hellenes, will be found to be only commensurate with their deserts. And if a test of worth be wanted, it is to be found in their closing scene, and this not only in the cases in which it set the final seal upon their merit, but also in those in which it gave the first intimation of their having any. For there is justice in the claim that steadfastness in his country's battles should be as a cloak to cover a man's other imperfections; since the good action has blotted out the bad, and his merit as a citizen more than outweighed his demerits as an individual. But none of these allowed either wealth with its prospect of future enjoyment to unnerve his spirit, or poverty with its hope of a day of freedom and riches to tempt him to shrink from danger. No, holding that vengeance upon their enemies was more to be desired than any personal blessings, and reckoning this to be the most glorious of hazards, they joyfully determined to accept the risk, to make sure of their vengeance, and to let their wishes wait; and while committing to hope the uncertainty of final success, in the business before them they thought fit to act boldly and trust in themselves. Thus choosing to die resisting, rather than to live submitting, they fled only from dishonour, but met danger face to face, and after one brief moment, while at the summit of their fortune, escaped, not from their fear, but from their glory.

So died these men as became Athenians. You, their survivors, must determine to have as unfaltering a resolution in the field, though you may pray that it may have a happier issue. And not contented with ideas derived only from words of the advantages which are bound up with the defence of your country, though these would furnish a valuable text to a speaker even before an audience so alive to them as the present, you must yourselves realize the power of Athens, and feed your eyes upon her from day to day, till love of her fills your hearts; and then, when all her greatness shall break upon you, you must reflect that it was by courage, sense of duty, and a keen feeling of honour in action that men were enabled to win all this, and that no personal failure in an enterprise could make them consent to deprive their country of their valour, but they laid it at her feet as the most glorious contribution that they could offer. For this offering of their lives made in common by them all they each of them individually received that renown which never grows old, and for a sepulchre, not so much that in which their bones have been deposited, but that noblest of shrines wherein their glory is laid up to be eternally remembered upon every occasion on which deed or story shall call for its commemoration. For heroes have the whole earth for their tomb; and in lands far from their own, where the column with its epitaph declares it, there is enshrined in every breast a record unwritten with no tablet to preserve it, except that of the heart. These take as your model and, judging happiness to be the fruit of freedom and freedom of valour, never decline the dangers of war. For it is not the miserable that would most justly be unsparing of their lives; these have nothing to hope for: it is rather they to whom continued life may bring reverses as yet unknown, and to whom a fall, if it came, would be most tremendous in its consequences. And surely, to a man of spirit, the degradation of cowardice must be immeasurably more grievous than the unfelt death which strikes him in the midst of his strength and patriotism!

Comfort, therefore, not condolence, is what I have to offer to the parents of the dead who may be here. Numberless are the chances to which, as they know, the life of man is subject; but fortunate indeed are they who draw for their lot a death so glorious as that which has caused your mourning, and to whom life has been so exactly measured as to terminate in the happiness in which it has been passed. Still I know that this is a hard saying, especially when those are in question of whom you will constantly be reminded by seeing in the homes of others blessings of which once you also boasted: for grief is felt not so much for the want of what we have never known, as for the loss of that to which we have been long accustomed. Yet you who are still of an age to beget children must bear up in the hope of having others in their stead; not only will they help you to forget those whom you have lost, but will be to the state at once a reinforcement and a security; for never can a fair or just policy be expected of the citizen who does not, like his fellows, bring to the decision the interests and apprehensions of a father. While those of you who have passed your prime must congratulate yourselves with the thought that the best part of your life was fortunate, and that the brief span that remains will be cheered by the fame of the departed. For it is only the love of honour that never grows old; and honour it is, not gain, as some would have it, that rejoices the heart of age and helplessness.

Turning to the sons or brothers of the dead, I see an arduous struggle before you. When a man is gone, all are wont to praise him, and should your merit be ever so transcendent, you will still find it difficult not merely to overtake, but even to approach their renown. The living have envy to contend with, while those who are no longer in our path are honoured with a goodwill into which rivalry does not enter. On the other hand, if I must say anything on the subject of female excellence to those of you who will now be in widowhood, it will be all comprised in this brief exhortation. Great will be your glory in not falling short of your natural character; and greatest will be hers who is least talked of among the men, whether for good or for bad.

My task is now finished. I have performed it to the best of my ability, and in word, at least, the requirements of the law are now satisfied. If deeds be in question, those who are here interred have received part of their honours already, and for the rest, their children will be brought up till manhood at the public expense: the state thus offers a valuable prize, as the garland of victory in this race of valour, for the reward both of those who have fallen and their survivors. And where the rewards for merit are greatest, there are found the best citizens.

And now that you have brought to a close your lamentations for your relatives, you may depart.

THUCYDIDES, THE MELIAN CONFERENCE

BOOK V, CHAPTER 17: THE ATHENIAN DESTRUCTION OF MELOS

The next summer Alcibiades sailed with twenty ships to Argos and seized the suspected persons still left of the Lacedæmonian [Spartan] faction to the number of three hundred, whom the Athenians forthwith lodged in the neighboring islands of their empire. The Athenians also made an expedition against the isle of Melos with thirty ships of their own, six Chian, and two Lesbian vessels, sixteen hundred heavy infantry, three hundred archers, and twenty mounted archers from Athens, and about fifteen hundred heavy infantry from the allies and the islanders. The Melians are a colony of Lacedæmonian that would not submit to the Athenians like the other islanders, and at first remained neutral and took no part in the struggle, but afterwards upon the Athenians using violence and plundering their territory, assumed an attitude of open hostility. Cleomedes son of Lycomedes, and Tisias, son of Tisimachus, the generals, encamping in their territory with the above armament, before doing any harm to their land, sent envoys to negotiate. These the Melians did not bring before the people, but bade them state the object of their mission to the magistrates and the few; upon which the Athenian envoys spoke as follows:

ATHENIANS: Since the negotiations are not to go on before the people, in order that we may not be able to speak straight on without interruption, and deceive the ears of the multitude by seductive arguments which would pass without refutation (for we know that this is the meaning of our being brought before the few), what if you who sit

Thucydides, *The Peloponnesian War*, translated by Richard Crawley there were to pursue a method more cautious still? Make no set speech yourselves, but take us up at whatever you do not like, and settle that before going any farther. And first tell us if this proposition of ours suits you.

The Melian commissioners answered:

MELIANS: To the fairness of quietly instructing each other as you propose there is nothing to object; but your military preparations are too far advanced to agree with what you say, as we see you are come to be judges in your own cause, and that all we can reasonably expect from this negotiation is war, if we prove to have right on our side and refuse to submit, and in the contrary case, slavery.

ATHENIANS: If you have met to reason about presentiments of the future, or for anything else than to consult for the safety of your state upon the facts that you see before you, we will give over; otherwise we will go on.

MELIANS: It is natural and excusable for men in our position to turn more ways than one both in thought and utterance. However, the question in this conference is, as you say, the safety of our country; and the discussion, if you please, can proceed in the way which you propose.

ATHENIANS: For ourselves, we shall not trouble you with specious pretences—either of how we have a right to our empire because we overthrew the Mede, or are now attacking you because of wrong that you have done us—and make a long speech which would not be believed; and in return we hope that you, instead of thinking to influence us by saying that you did not join the Lacedæmonianians, although their colonists, or that you have done us no wrong, will aim at what is feasible, holding in view the real sentiments of us both; since you know as well as we do that right, as the world goes, is only in question between equals in power, while the strong do what they can and the weak suffer what they must.

MELIANS: As we think, at any rate, it is expedient—we speak as we are obliged, since you enjoin us to let right alone and talk only of interest—that you should not destroy what is our common protection, the privilege of being allowed in danger to invoke what is fair and right, and even to profit by arguments not strictly valid if they can be got to pass current. And you are as much interested in this as any, as your fall would be a signal for the heaviest vengeance and an example for the world to meditate upon.

ATHENIANS: The end of our empire, if end it should, does not frighten us: a rival empire like Lacedæmonian, even if Lacedæmonian was our real antagonist, is not so terrible to the vanquished as subjects who by themselves attack and overpower their rulers. This, however, is a risk that we are content to take. We will now proceed to show you that we are come here in the interest of our empire, and that we shall say what we are now going to say, for the preservation of your country; as we would fain exercise that empire over you without trouble, and see you preserved for the good of us both.

MELIANS: And how, pray, could it turn out as good for us to serve as for you to rule?

ATHENIANS: Because you would have the advantage of submitting before suffering the worst, and we should gain by not destroying you.

MELIANS: So that you would not consent to our being neutral, friends instead of enemies, but allies of neither side.

ATHENIANS: No; for your hostility cannot so much hurt us as your friendship will be an argument to our subjects of our weakness, and your enmity of our power.

MELIANS: Is that your subjects' idea of equity, to put those who have nothing to do with you in the same category with peoples that are most of them your own colonists, and some conquered rebels?

ATHENIANS: As far as right goes they think one has as much of it as the other, and that if any maintain their independence it is because they are strong, and that if we do not molest them it is because we are afraid; so that besides extending our empire we should gain in security by your subjection; the fact that you are islanders and weaker than others rendering it all the more important that you should not succeed in baffling the masters of the sea.

MELIANS: But do you consider that there is no security in the policy which we indicate? For here again if you debar us from talking about justice and invite us to obey your interest, we also must explain ours, and try to persuade you, if the two happen to coincide. How can you avoid making enemies of all existing neutrals who shall look at our case and conclude from it that one day or another you will attack them? And what is this but to make greater the enemies that you have already, and to force others to become so who would otherwise have never thought of it?

ATHENIANS: Why, the fact is that continentals generally give us but little alarm; the liberty which they enjoy will long prevent their taking precautions against us; it is rather islanders like yourselves, outside our empire, and subjects smarting under the yoke, who would be the most likely to take a rash step and lead themselves and us into obvious danger.

MELIANS: Well then, if you risk so much to retain your empire, and your subjects to get rid of it, it were surely great baseness and cowardice in us who are still free not to try everything that can be tried, before submitting to your yoke.

ATHENIANS: Not if you are well advised, the contest not being an equal one, with honour as the prize and shame as the penalty, but a question of self-preservation and of not resisting those who are far stronger than you are.

MELIANS: But we know that the fortune of war is sometimes more impartial than the disproportion of numbers might lead one to suppose; to submit is to give ourselves over to despair, while action still preserves for us a hope that we may stand erect.

ATHENIANS: Hope, danger's comforter, may be indulged in by those who have abundant resources, if not without loss at all events without ruin; but its nature is to be extravagant, and those who go so far as to put their all upon the venture see it in its true colours only when they are ruined; but so long as the discovery would enable them to guard against it, it is never found wanting. Let not this be the case with you, who are weak and hang on a single turn of the scale; nor be like the vulgar, who, abandoning such security as human means may still afford, when visible hopes fail them in extremity, turn to invisible, to prophecies and oracles, and other such inventions that delude men with hopes to their destruction.

MELIANS: You may be sure that we are as well aware as you of the difficulty of contending against your power and fortune, unless the terms be equal. But we trust that the gods may grant us fortune as good as yours, since we are just men fighting against unjust, and that what we want in power will be made up by the alliance of the Lacedæmonianians, who are bound, if only for very shame, to come to the aid of their kindred. Our confidence, therefore, after all is not so utterly irrational.

ATHENIANS: When you speak of the favour of the gods, we may as fairly hope for that as yourselves; neither our pretensions nor our conduct being in any way contrary to what men believe of the gods, or practise among themselves. Of the gods we believe, and of men we know, that by a necessary law of their nature they rule wherever they can. And it is not as if we were the first to make this law, or to act upon it when made: we found it existing before us, and shall leave it to exist for ever after us; all we do is to make use of it, knowing that you and everybody else, having the same power as we have, would do the same as we do. Thus, as far as the gods are concerned, we have no fear and no reason to fear that we shall be at a disadvantage. But when we come to your notion about the Lacedæmonianians, which leads you to believe that shame will make them help you, here we bless your simplicity but do not envy your folly. The Lacedæmonian, when their own interests or their country's laws are in question, are the worthiest men alive; of their conduct towards others much might be said, but no clearer idea of it could be given than by shortly saying that of all the men we know they are most conspicuous in considering what is agreeable honourable, and what is expedient just. Such a way of thinking does not promise much for the safety which you now unreasonably count upon.

MELIANS: But it is for this very reason that we now trust to their respect for expediency to prevent them from betraying the Melians, their colonists, and thereby losing the confidence of their friends in Hellas and helping their enemies.

ATHENIANS: Then you do not adopt the view that expediency goes with security, while justice and honour cannot be followed without danger; and danger the Lacedæmonianians generally court as little as possible.

MELIANS: But we believe that they would be more likely to face even danger for our sake, and with more confidence than for others, as our nearness to Peloponnese makes it easier for them to act, and our common blood insures our fidelity.

ATHENIANS: Yes, but what an intending ally trusts to, is not the goodwill of those who ask his aid, but a decided superiority of power for action; and the Lacedæmonianians look to this even more than others. At least, such is their distrust of their home resources that it is only with numerous allies that they attack a neighbour; now is it likely that while we are masters of the sea they will cross over to an island?

MELIANS: But they would have others to send. The Cretan sea is a wide one, and it is more difficult for those who command it to intercept others, than for those who wish to elude them to do so safely. And should the Lacedæmonianians miscarry in this, they would fall upon your land, and upon those left of your allies whom Brasidas did not reach; and instead of places which are not yours, you will have to fight for your own country and your own confederacy.

ATHENIANS: Some diversion of the kind you speak of you may one day experience, only to learn as others have done, that the Athenians never once yet withdrew from a siege for fear of any. But we are struck by the fact, that after saying you would consult for the safety of your country, in all this discussion you have mentioned nothing which men might trust in and think to be saved by. Your strongest arguments depend upon hope and the future, and your actual resources are too scanty, as compared with those arrayed against you, for you to come out victorious. You will therefore show great blindness of judgment, unless, after allowing us to retire, you can find some counsel more prudent than this. You will surely not be caught by that idea of disgrace, which in dangers that are disgraceful, and at the same time too plain to be mistaken, proves so fatal to mankind; since in too many cases the very men that have their eyes perfectly open to what they are rushing into, let the thing called disgrace, by the mere influence of a seductive name, lead them on to a point at which they become so enslaved by the phrase as in fact to fall wilfully into hopeless disaster, and incur disgrace more disgraceful as the companion of error, than when it comes as the result of misfortune. This, if you are well advised, you will guard against; and you will not think it dishonourable to submit to the greatest city in Hellas, when it makes you the moderate offer of becoming its tributary ally, without ceasing to enjoy the country that belongs to you; nor when you have the choice given you between war and security, will you be so blinded as to choose the worse. And it is certain that those who do not yield to their equals, who keep terms with their superiors, and are moderate towards their inferiors, on the whole succeed best. Think over the matter, therefore, after our withdrawal, and reflect once and again that it is for your country that you are consulting, that you have not more than one, and that upon this one deliberation depends its prosperity or ruin.

The Athenians now withdrew from the conference; and the Melians, left to themselves, came to a decision corresponding with what they had maintained in the discussion, and answered, "Our resolution, Athenians, is the same as it was at first. We will not in a moment deprive of freedom a city that has been inhabited these seven hundred years; but we put our trust in the fortune by which the gods have preserved it until now, and in the help of men that is, of the Lacedæmonianians; and so we will try and save ourselves. Meanwhile we invite you to allow us to be friends to you and foes to neither party, and to retire from our country after making such a treaty as shall seem fair to us both."

Such was the answer of the Melians. The Athenians now departing from the conference said, "Well, you alone, as it seems to us, judging from these resolutions, regard what is future as more certain than what is before your eyes, and what is out of sight, in your eagerness, as already coming to pass; and as you have staked most on, and trusted most in, the Lacedæmonianians, your fortune, and your hopes, so will you be most completely deceived."

The Athenian envoys now returned to the army; and the Melians showing no signs of yielding, the generals at once betook themselves to hostilities, and drew a line of circumvallation round the Melians, dividing the work among the different states. Subsequently the Athenians returned with most of their army, leaving behind them a certain number of their own citizens and of the allies to keep guard by land and sea. The force thus left stayed on and besieged the place.

About the same time the Argives invaded the territory of Phlius and lost eighty men cut off in an ambush by the Phliasians and Argive exiles. Meanwhile the Athenians at Pylos took so much plunder from the Lacedæmonianians that the latter, although they still refrained from breaking off the treaty and going to war with Athens, yet proclaimed that any of their people that chose might plunder the Athenians. The Corinthians also commenced hostilities with the Athenians for private quarrels of their own; but the rest of the Peloponnesians stayed quiet. Meanwhile the Melians attacked by night and took the part of the Athenian lines over against the market, and killed some of the men, and brought in corn and all else that they could find useful to them, and so returned and kept quiet, while the Athenians took measures to keep better guard in future.

Summer was now over. The next winter the Lacedæmonianians intended to invade the Argive territory, but arriving at the frontier found the sacrifices for crossing unfavourable, and went back again. This intention of theirs gave the Argives suspicions of certain of their fellow-citizens, some of whom they arrested; others, however, escaped them. About the same time the Melians again took another part of the Athenian lines which were but feebly garrisoned. Reinforcements afterwards arriving from Athens in consequence, under the command of Philocrates, son of Demeas, the siege was now pressed vigorously; and some treachery taking place inside, the Melians surrendered at discretion to the Athenians, who put to death all the grown men whom they took, and sold the women and children for slaves, and subsequently sent out five hundred colonists and inhabited the place themselves.

SOCRATES
470–399 B.C.

PLATO
428/7–348/7 B.C.

Socrates has fascinated and inspired men and women for over two thousand years. All five of the major "schools" of ancient Greece (Academics, Peripatetics, Epicureans, Stoics, and Cynics) were influenced by his thought. Some of the early Christian thinkers, such as Justin Martyr, considered him a "proto-Christian," while others, such as St. Augustine (who rejected this view) still expressed deep admiration for Socrates' ethical life. More recently, existentialists have found in Socrates' admonition "know thyself" an encapsulation of their thought, and opponents of unjust laws have seen in Socrates' trial a blueprint for civil disobedience. In short, Socrates is one of the most admired men who ever lived.

The Athens into which Socrates was born in 470 B.C. was a city still living in the flush of its epic victory over the Persians, and it was bursting with new ideas. The playwrights Euripides and Sophocles were young boys, and Pericles, the great Athenian democrat, was still a young man. The Parthenon's foundation was laid when Socrates was twenty-two, and its construction was completed fifteen years later.

Socrates was the son of Sophroniscus, a sculptor, and of Phaenarete, a midwife. As a boy, Socrates received a classical Greek education in music, gymnastics, and grammar (or the study of language), and he decided early on to become a sculptor like his father. Tradition says he was a gifted artist who fashioned impressively simple statues of the Graces. He married a woman named Xanthippe, and together they had three children. He took an early interest in the developing science of the Milesians, and then he served for a time in the army.

When he was a middle-aged man, Socrates' friend, Chaerephon, asked the oracle at Delphi "if there was anyone wiser than Socrates." For once the mysterious oracle gave an unambiguous answer: "None." When Socrates heard of the incident, he was confused. He knew that he was not a wise man. So he set out to find a wiser man as "an excuse for going back and cross-examining the oracle." Socrates later described the method and results of his mission:

> So I examined this man—there's no need for me to mention his name, let's just say he was a politician—and the result of my examination . . . and of my conversations with him, was this. I decided that although the man seemed to many people, and above all to himself, to be wise, in reality he was not wise. I tried to demonstrate to him that he thought he was wise, but actually was not, and as a result I made an enemy of him, and of many of those present. To myself, as I left him, I reflected, "Here is *one* man less wise than I. In all probability neither of us knows anything worth knowing; but he *thinks* he knows when he doesn't, whereas I, given that I don't in fact know, am at least *aware* I don't know. Apparently, therefore, I am wiser than him in just this one small detail, that when I don't know something, I don't *think* I know it either." From him I went to another man, one of those who seemed wiser than the first. I came to exactly the same conclusion, and made an enemy of him and of many others besides. (*Apology* 21c)

As Socrates continued his mission by interviewing the politicians, poets, and artisans of Athens, young men followed along. They enjoyed seeing the authority figures humiliated by Socrates' intense questioning. Those in authority, however, were not amused. Athens was no longer the powerful, self-confident city of 470 B.C., the year of Socrates' birth. An exhausting succession of wars with Sparta (the Peloponnesian Wars) and an enervating series of political debacles had left the city narrow in vision and suspicious of new ideas and of dissent. In 399 B.C., Meletus and Anytus brought an indictment of "impiety and corrupting the youth" against Socrates. As recorded in the *Apology,* the Athenian assembly found him guilty by a vote of 280 to 220 and sentenced him to death. His noble death is described incomparably in the closing pages of the *Phaedo* by Plato.

Socrates wrote nothing, and our knowledge of his thought comes exclusively from the report of others. The playwright Aristophanes (455–375 B.C.) satirized Socrates in his comedy *The Clouds.* His caricature of Socrates as a cheat and charlatan was apparently so damaging that Socrates felt compelled to offer a rebuttal before the Athenian assembly (see the *Apology,* following). The military general Xenophon (ca. 430–350 B.C.) honored his friend Socrates in his *Apology of Socrates,* his *Symposium,* and, later, in his *Memorabilia* ("Recollections of Socrates"). In an effort to defend his dead friend's memory, Xenophon's writings illumine Socrates' life and character. Though born fifteen years after the death of Socrates, Aristotle (384–322 B.C.) left many fascinating allusions to Socrates in his philosophic works, as did several later Greek philosophers. But the primary source of our knowledge of Socrates comes from one of those young men who followed him: Plato.

*   *   *

Plato was probably born in 428/7 B.C. He had two older brothers, Adeimantus and Glaucon, who appear in Plato's *Republic,* and a sister, Potone. Though he may have known Socrates since childhood, Plato was probably nearer twenty when he came under the intellectual spell of Socrates. The death of Socrates made an enormous impression on Plato and contributed to his call to bear witness to posterity of "the best, . . . the wisest and most just" person that he knew (*Phaedo,* 118). Though Plato was from a distinguished family and might have followed his relatives into politics, he chose philosophy.

Following Socrates' execution, the twenty-eight-year-old Plato left Athens and traveled for a time. He is reported to have visited Egypt and Cyrene—though some scholars doubt this. During this time he wrote his early dialogues on Socrates' life and teachings. He also visited Italy and Sicily, where he became the friend of Dion, a relative of Dionysius, the tyrant of Syracuse, Sicily.

On returning to Athens from Sicily, Plato founded a school, which came to be called the Academy. One might say it was the world's first university, and it endured as a center of higher learning for nearly one thousand years, until the Roman emperor Justinian closed it in A.D. 529. Except for two later trips to Sicily, where he unsuccessfully sought to institute his political theories, Plato spent the rest of his life at the Athenian Academy. Among his students was Aristotle. Plato died at eighty in 348/7 B.C.

Plato's influence was best described by the twentieth-century philosopher Alfred North Whitehead when he said, "The safest general characterization of the European philosophical tradition is that it consists of a series of footnotes to Plato."

*   *   *

It is difficult to separate the ideas of Plato from those of his teacher, Socrates. In virtually all of Plato's dialogues, Socrates is the main character, and it is possible that in the early dialogues Plato is recording his teacher's actual words. But in the later dialogues, "Socrates" gives Plato's views—views that, in some cases, in fact, the historical Socrates denied.

The first four dialogues presented in this text describe the trial and death of Socrates and are arranged in narrative order. The first, the *Euthyphro,* takes place as Socrates has just learned of the indictment against him. He strikes up a conversation with a "theologian" so sure of his piety that he is prosecuting his own father for murder. The dialogue moves on, unsuccessfully, to define piety. Along the way, Socrates asks a question that has vexed philosophers and theologians for centuries: Is something good because the gods say it is, or do the gods say it is good because it is? This dialogue is given in the F.J. Church translation.

The next dialogue, the *Apology,* is generally regarded as one of Plato's first, and as eminently faithful to what Socrates said at his trial on charges of impiety and corruption of youth. The speech was delivered in public and heard by a large audience; Plato has Socrates mention that Plato was present; and there is no need to doubt the historical veracity of the speech, at least in essentials. There are two breaks in the narrative: one after Socrates' defense (during which the Athenians vote "guilty") and one after Socrates proposes an alternative to the death penalty (during which the Athenians decide on death). This dialogue includes Socrates' famous characterization of his mission and purpose in life.

In the *Crito,* Plato has Crito visit Socrates in prison to assure him that his escape from Athens has been well prepared and to persuade him to consent to leave. Socrates argues that one has an obligation to obey the state even when it orders one to suffer wrong. That Socrates, in fact, refused to leave is certain; that he used the arguments Plato ascribes to him is less certain. In any case, anyone who has read the *Apology* will agree that after his speech Socrates could not well escape. For this series, both the *Apology* and the *Crito* are given in translations by Tom Griffith.

The moving account of Socrates' death is given at the end of the *Phaedo,* the last of our group of dialogues. There is common agreement that this dialogue was written much later than the other three and that the earlier part of the dialogue, with its Platonic doctrine of Forms and immortality, uses "Socrates" as a vehicle for Plato's own ideas. These ideas owe much to Pythagoreanism, which exerted an ever-increasing influence on Plato's thought. (See the introduction to the Pythagorean selections, pages 11–12.) Once again, the translation is that of F.J. Church.

Like the *Phaedo,* the *Meno, Symposium,* and *Republic* were written during Plato's "middle period," when he had returned from Sicily to Athens and had established the Academy. The *Meno* gives a fine and faithful picture of Socrates practicing the art of dialogue; it also marks the point at which Plato moves beyond his master. This dialogue answers the question, "Can virtue be taught?" and treats the issues of knowledge and belief. The *Meno* is given in W.K.C. Guthrie's authoritative translation.

The *Symposium* represents the high point of Plato's literary skill. In this collection of speeches on love, Plato uses several styles of speaking, including some light-hearted banter. The *Symposium* is a work of art and surely makes no claim to historic accuracy, except for Alcibiades' speech on Socrates. As for the rest, we need not believe that Aristophanes, for example, really told the fanciful myth ascribed to him here. (Some commentators see Plato paying Aristophanes back for his earlier ridicule of Socrates.) Tom Griffith's excellent translation is given here.

Note that when reading the *Symposium,* a modern reader should keep in mind that among some—but by no means all—Greek intellectuals, homosexuality was not only accepted, it was considered a superior form of love. Since women were rarely educated, it was thought that only with males could a man move beyond "inferior" physical attraction to reach the heights of love.

There are few books in Western civilization that have had the impact of Plato's *Republic*—aside from the Bible, perhaps none. Like the Bible, there are also few books whose interpretation and evaluation have differed so widely. Apparently it is a description of Plato's ideal society: a utopian vision of the just state, possible only if philosophers were kings. But some (see the following suggested readings) claim that its purpose is not to give a model of the ideal state, but to show the impossibility of such a state and to convince aspiring philosophers to shun politics. Evaluations of the *Republic* have also varied widely: from the criticisms of Karl Popper, who denounced the *Republic* as totalitarian, to the admiration of more traditional interpreters, such as Francis MacDonald Cornford and Gregory Vlastos.

Given the importance of this work and the diversity of opinions concerning its point and value, it was extremely difficult to decide which sections of the *Republic* to include in this series. I chose to include the discussion of justice from Books I and II, the descriptions of the guardians and of the "noble lie" from Book III, the discussions of the virtues and the soul in Book IV, the presentations of the guardians' qualities and life-styles in Book V, and the key sections on knowledge (including the analogy of the line and the myth of the cave) from the end of Book VI and the beginning of Book VII. I admit that space constraints have forced me to exclude important sections. Ideally, the selections chosen will whet the student's appetite to read the rest of this classic. The translation is by Cornford.

The *Parmenides* marks a move in the development of Plato's thought—from positive philosophy to critical issues. The *Parmenides* is remarkable for the honesty with which Plato attacks the problems with his own doctrine of Forms. The second half is a lengthy and confusing series of "lessons" designed (apparently) to show that "unity is." This part is omitted because it is the most abstruse and difficult work Plato ever wrote.

The *Theaetetus* deals with the problem of knowledge and contains an interesting discussion of some of the ideas of Protagoras, the Sophist. Throughout the dialogue, Socrates assumes that knowledge leads to goodness, so a clear understanding of knowledge is vitally important. However, no conclusion about the nature of knowledge is reached—only agreement about what it is *not*. Still, this lack of knowledge about knowledge is nonetheless valuable, Socrates claims, because they have at least learned not to claim knowledge when they do not possess it.

Finally the brief section from the *Timaeus* presents Plato's account of creation. The selections from the *Parmenides, Theaetetus,* and the *Timaeus* are all given in the F.M. Cornford translation.

The marginal page numbers are those of all scholarly editions, Greek, English, German, or French.

* * *

For studies of Socrates, see the classic A.E. Taylor, *Socrates: The Man and His Thought* (London: Methuen, 1933); the second half of Volume III of W.K.C. Guthrie, *The History of Greek Philosophy* (Cambridge: Cambridge University Press, 1969); Hugh H. Benson, *Essays on the Philosophy of Socrates* (Oxford: Oxford University Press, 1992); and Thomas C. Brickhouse and Nicholas D. Smith, *Plato's Socrates* (Oxford: Oxford University Press, 1994). For collections of essays, see Gregory Vlastos, ed., *The Philosophy of Socrates* (Garden City, NY: Doubleday, 1971); Hugh H. Benson, ed., *Essays on the Philosophy of Socrates* (Oxford: Oxford University Press, 1992); Terence Irwin, ed., *Socrates and His Contemporaries* (Hamden, CT: Garland Publishing, 1995); and the multi-volume William J. Prior, ed., *Socrates* (Oxford: Routledge, 1996). For discussions of the similarities and differences between the historical Socrates and the "Socrates" of the Platonic dialogues, see Gregory Vlastos, *Socrates: Ironist and Moral Philosopher* (Ithaca, NY: Cornell University Press, 1991), especially Chapters 2 and 3, and Thomas C. Brickhouse and Nicholas D. Smith, *Plato's Socrates* (Oxford: Oxford University Press, 1994).

Books about Plato are legion. Once again the work of W.K.C. Guthrie is sensible, comprehensive, yet readable. See Volumes IV and V of his *The History of Greek Philosophy* (Cambridge: Cambridge University Press, 1975 and 1978). Paul Shorey, *What Plato Said* (Chicago: Chicago University Press, 1933), and G.M.A. Grube, *Plato's Thought* (London: Methuen, 1935) are classic treatments of Plato, while Robert Brumbaugh, *Plato for a Modern Age* (New York: Macmillan, 1964), I.M. Crombie, *An Examination of Plato's Doctrines,* two volumes (New York: Humanities Press, 1963–1969), R.M. Hare, *Plato* (Oxford: Oxford University Press, 1982), and David J. Melling, *Understanding Plato* (Oxford: Oxford University Press, 1987) are more recent studies. For collections of essays, see Gregory Vlastos, ed., *Plato: A Collection of Critical Essays,* two volumes (Garden City, NY: Doubleday, 1971); Richard Kraut, ed., *The Cambridge Companion to Plato* (Cambridge: Cambridge University Press, 1991); Nancy Tuana, ed., *Feminist Interpretations of Plato* (College Park, PA: Pennsylvania State University Press, 1994); Terence Irwin, ed., *Plato's Ethics* and *Plato's Metaphysics and Epistemology* (both Hamden, CT: Garland Publishing, 1995); and Gregory Vlastos, ed., *Studies in Greek Philosophy, Volume II: Socrates, Plato,* and Their Tradition (Princeton, NJ: Princeton University Press, 1995). Jane M. Day, ed., *Plato's Meno in Focus* (Oxford: Routledge, 1994) and Robert G. Turnbull, *The Parmenides and Plato's Late Philosophy* (Toronto: University of Toronto Press, 1998) give insights on their respective dialogues. For further reading on the *Republic,* see Nicholas P. White, *A Companion to Plato's Republic* (Indianapolis, IN: Hackett, 1979); Julia Annas, *An Introduction to Plato's Republic* (Oxford: Clarendon Press, 1981); Nickolas Pappas, *Routledge Guidebook to Plato and the Republic* (Oxford: Routledge, 1995); Daryl Rice, *A Guide to Plato's Republic* (Oxford: Oxford University Press, 1997) and Richard Kraut, ed., *Plato's Republic: Critical Essays* (Lanham, MD: Rowan & Littlefield, 1997). Terence Irwin, *Plato's Ethics* (Oxford: Oxford University Press, 1995) examines several dialogues while thoroughly exploring Plato's ethical thought. Finally, for unusual interpretations of Plato and his work, see Werner Jaeger, *Paideia,* Vols. II and III, translated by Gilbert Highet (New York: Oxford University Press, 1939–1943); Karl R. Popper, *The Open Society and Its Enemies; Volume I: The Spell of Plato* (Princeton, NJ: Princeton University Press, 1962); and Allan Bloom's interpretive essay in Plato, *Republic,* translated by Allan Bloom (New York: Basic Books, 1968).

EUTHYPHRO

Characters
Socrates
Euthyphro
Scene—The Hall of the King*

2   EUTHYPHRO: What in the world are you doing here in the king's hall, Socrates? Why have you left your haunts in the Lyceum? You surely cannot have a suit before him, as I have.

SOCRATES: The Athenians, Euthyphro, call it an indictment, not a suit.

b   EUTHYPHRO: What? Do you mean that someone is prosecuting you? I cannot believe that you are prosecuting anyone yourself.

SOCRATES: Certainly I am not.

EUTHYPHRO: Then is someone prosecuting you?

SOCRATES: Yes.

EUTHYPHRO: Who is he?

SOCRATES: I scarcely know him myself, Euthyphro; I think he must be some unknown young man. His name, however, is Meletus, and his district Pitthis, if you can call to mind any Meletus of that district—a hook-nosed man with lanky hair and rather a scanty beard.

Plato, *Euthyphro, Apology, Crito,* translated by F.J. Church (New York: Macmillan/Library of the Liberal Arts, 1963).
*The anachronistic title "king" was retained by the magistrate who had jurisdiction over crimes affecting the state religion.

EUTHYPHRO: I don't know him, Socrates. But tell me, what is he prosecuting you for?

SOCRATES: What for? Not on trivial grounds, I think. It is no small thing for so young a man to have formed an opinion on such an important matter. For he, he says, knows how the young are corrupted, and who are their corrupters. He must be a wise man who, observing my ignorance, is going to accuse me to the state, as his mother, of corrupting his friends. I think that he is the only one who begins at the right point in his political reforms; for his first care is to make the young men as good as possible, just as a good farmer will take care of his young plants first, and, after he has done that, of the others. And so Meletus, I suppose, is first clearing us away who, as he says, corrupt the young men growing up; and then, when he has done that, of course he will turn his attention to the older men, and so become a very great public benefactor. Indeed, that is only what you would expect when he goes to work in this way.

EUTHYPHRO: I hope it may be so, Socrates, but I fear the opposite. It seems to me that in trying to injure you, he is really setting to work by striking a blow at the foundation of the state. But how, tell me, does he say that you corrupt the youth?

SOCRATES: In a way which sounds absurd at first, my friend. He says that I am a maker of gods; and so he is prosecuting me, he says, for inventing new gods and for not believing in the old ones.

EUTHYPHRO: I understand, Socrates. It is because you say that you always have a divine guide. So he is prosecuting you for introducing religious reforms; and he is going into court to arouse prejudice against you, knowing that the multitude are easily prejudiced about such matters. Why, they laugh even at me, as if I were out of my mind, when I talk about divine things in the assembly and tell them what is going to happen; and yet I have never foretold anything which has not come true. But they are resentful of all people like us. We must not worry about them; we must meet them boldly.

SOCRATES: My dear Euthyphro, their ridicule is not a very serious matter. The Athenians, it seems to me, may think a man to be clever without paying him much attention, so long as they do not think that he teaches his wisdom to others. But as soon as they think that he makes other people clever, they get angry, whether it be from resentment, as you say, or for some other reason.

EUTHYPHRO: I am not very anxious to test their attitude toward me in this matter.

SOCRATES: No, perhaps they think that you are reserved, and that you are not anxious to teach your wisdom to others. But I fear that they may think that I am; for my love of men makes me talk to everyone whom I meet quite freely and unreservedly, and without payment. Indeed, if I could I would gladly pay people myself to listen to me. If then, as I said just now, they were only going to laugh at me, as you say they do at you, it would not be at all an unpleasant way of spending the day—to spend it in court, joking and laughing. But if they are going to be in earnest, then only prophets like you can tell where the matter will end.

EUTHYPHRO: Well, Socrates, I dare say that nothing will come of it. Very likely you will be successful in your trial, and I think that I shall be in mine.

SOCRATES: And what is this suit of yours, Euthyphro? Are you suing, or being sued?

EUTHYPHRO: I am suing.

SOCRATES: Whom?

EUTHYPHRO: A man whom people think I must be mad to prosecute.

SOCRATES: What? Has he wings to fly away with?

EUTHYPHRO: He is far enough from flying; he is a very old man.

SOCRATES: Who is he?

EUTHYPHRO: He is my father.

SOCRATES: Your father, my good man?

EUTHYPHRO: He is indeed.

SOCRATES: What are you prosecuting him for? What is the accusation?

EUTHYPHRO: Murder, Socrates.

b   SOCRATES: Good heavens, Euthyphro! Surely the multitude are ignorant of what is right. I take it that it is not everyone who could rightly do what you are doing; only a man who was already well advanced in wisdom.

EUTHYPHRO: That is quite true, Socrates.

SOCRATES: Was the man whom your father killed a relative of yours? But, of course, he was. You would never have prosecuted your father for the murder of a stranger?

EUTHYPHRO: You amuse me, Socrates. What difference does it make whether the murdered man were a relative or a stranger? The only question that you have to ask is, did the murderer kill justly or not? If justly, you must let him alone; if unjustly, you

c   must indict him for murder, even though he share your hearth and sit at your table. The pollution is the same if you associate with such a man, knowing what he has done, without purifying yourself, and him too, by bringing him to justice. In the present case the murdered man was a poor laborer of mine, who worked for us on our farm in Naxos. While drunk he got angry with one of our slaves and killed him. My father therefore bound the man hand and foot and threw him into a ditch, while he sent to Athens to ask the priest what he should do. While the messenger was gone, he entirely neglected the man, thinking that he was a murderer, and that it would be no great matter, even if he were to die. And that was exactly what happened; hunger and cold and

d   his bonds killed him before the messenger returned. And now my father and the rest of my family are indignant with me because I am prosecuting my father for the murder of this murderer. They assert that he did not kill the man at all; and they say that, even if he had killed him over and over again, the man himself was a murderer, and that I ought not to concern myself about such a person because it is impious for a son to prosecute his father for murder. So little, Socrates, do they know the divine law of

e   piety and impiety.

SOCRATES: And do you mean to say, Euthyphro, that you think that you understand divine things and piety and impiety so accurately that, in such a case as you have stated, you can bring your father to justice without fear that you yourself may be doing something impious?

EUTHYPHRO: If I did not understand all these matters accurately, Socrates, I

5   should not be worth much—Euthyphro would not be any better than other men.

SOCRATES: Then, my dear Euthyphro, I cannot do better than become your pupil and challenge Meletus on this very point before the trial begins. I should say that I had always thought it very important to have knowledge about divine things; and that now, when he says that I offend by speaking carelessly about them, and by introducing re-

b   forms, I have become your pupil. And I should say, "Meletus, if you acknowledge Euthyphro to be wise in these matters and to hold the correct belief, then think the same of me and do not put me on trial; but if you do not, then bring a suit, not against me, but against my master, for corrupting his elders—namely, myself whom he corrupts by his teaching, and his own father whom he corrupts by admonishing and punishing him." And if I did not succeed in persuading him to release me from the suit or to indict you in my place, then I could repeat my challenge in court.

EUTHYPHRO: Yes, by Zeus! Socrates, I think I should find out his weak points if he were to try to indict me. I should have a good deal to say about him in court long c before I spoke about myself.

SOCRATES: Yes, my dear friend, and knowing this I am anxious to become your pupil. I see that Meletus here, and others too, seem not to notice you at all, but he sees through me without difficulty and at once prosecutes me for impiety. Now, therefore, please explain to me what you were so confident just now that you knew. Tell me what d are righteousness and sacrilege with respect to murder and everything else. I suppose that piety is the same in all actions, and that impiety is always the opposite of piety, and retains its identity, and that, as impiety, it always has the same character, which will be found in whatever is impious.

EUTHYPHRO: Certainly, Socrates, I suppose so.

SOCRATES: Tell me, then, what is piety and what is impiety?

EUTHYPHRO: Well, then, I say that piety means prosecuting the unjust individual who has committed murder or sacrilege, or any other such crime, as I am doing now, whether he is your father or your mother or whoever he is; and I say that impiety e means not prosecuting him. And observe, Socrates, I will give you a clear proof, which I have already given to others, that it is so, and that doing right means not letting off unpunished the sacrilegious man, whosoever he may be. Men hold Zeus to be the best and the most just of the gods; and they admit that Zeus bound his own father, Cronos, 6 for wrongfully devouring his children; and that Cronos, in his turn, castrated his father for similar reasons. And yet these same men are incensed with me because I proceed against my father for doing wrong. So, you see, they say one thing in the case of the gods and quite another in mine.

SOCRATES: Is not that why I am being prosecuted, Euthyphro? I mean, because I find it hard to accept such stories people tell about the gods? I expect that I shall be found at fault because I doubt those stories. Now if you who understand all these matters so well agree in holding all those tales true, then I suppose that I must yield to your b authority. What could I say when I admit myself that I know nothing about them? But tell me, in the name of friendship, do you really believe that these things have actually happened?

EUTHYPHRO: Yes, and more amazing things, too, Socrates, which the multitude do not know of.

SOCRATES: Then you really believe that there is war among the gods, and bitter hatreds, and battles, such as the poets tell of, and which the great painters have de- c picted in our temples, notably in the pictures which cover the robe that is carried up to the Acropolis at the great Panathenaic festival? Are we to say that these things are true, Euthyphro?

EUTHYPHRO: Yes, Socrates, and more besides. As I was saying, I will report to you many other stories about divine matters, if you like, which I am sure will astonish you when you hear them.

SOCRATES: I dare say. You shall report them to me at your leisure another time. At present please try to give a more definite answer to the question which I asked you just now. What I asked you, my friend, was, What is piety? and you have not explained d it to me to my satisfaction. You only tell me that what you are doing now, namely, prosecuting your father for murder, is a pious act.

EUTHYPHRO: Well, that is true, Socrates.

SOCRATES: Very likely. But many other actions are pious, are they not, Euthyphro?

EUTHYPHRO: Certainly.

SOCRATES: Remember, then, I did not ask you to tell me one or two of all the many pious actions that there are; I want to know what is characteristic of piety which
e   makes all pious actions pious. You said, I think, that there is one characteristic which makes all pious actions pious, and another characteristic which makes all impious actions impious. Do you not remember?

EUTHYPHRO: I do.

SOCRATES: Well, then, explain to me what is this characteristic, that I may have it to turn to, and to use as a standard whereby to judge your actions and those of other men, and be able to say that whatever action resembles it is pious, and whatever does not, is not pious.

EUTHYPHRO: Yes, I will tell you that if you wish, Socrates.

SOCRATES: Certainly I do.

7   EUTHYPHRO: Well, then, what is pleasing to the gods is pious, and what is not pleasing to them is impious.

SOCRATES: Fine, Euthyphro. Now you have given me the answer that I wanted. Whether what you say is true, I do not know yet. But, of course, you will go on to prove that it is true.

EUTHYPHRO: Certainly.

SOCRATES: Come, then, let us examine our statement. The things and the men that are pleasing to the gods are pious, and the things and the men that are displeasing to the gods are impious. But piety and impiety are not the same; they are as opposite as possible—was not that what we said?

EUTHYPHRO: Certainly.

SOCRATES: And it seems the appropriate statement?

b   EUTHYPHRO: Yes, Socrates, certainly.

SOCRATES: Have we not also said, Euthyphro, that there are quarrels and disagreements and hatreds among the gods?

EUTHYPHRO: We have.

SOCRATES: But what kind of disagreement, my friend, causes hatred and anger? Let us look at the matter thus. If you and I were to disagree as to whether one number
c   were more than another, would that make us angry and enemies? Should we not settle such a dispute at once by counting?

EUTHYPHRO: Of course.

SOCRATES: And if we were to disagree as to the relative size of two things, we should measure them and put an end to the disagreement at once, should we not?

EUTHYPHRO: Yes.

SOCRATES: And should we not settle a question about the relative weight of two things by weighing them?

EUTHYPHRO: Of course.

SOCRATES: Then what is the question which would make us angry and enemies if
d   we disagreed about it, and could not come to a settlement? Perhaps you have not an answer ready; but listen to mine. Is it not the question of the just and unjust, of the honorable and the dishonorable, of the good and the bad? Is it not questions about these matters which make you and me and everyone else quarrel, when we do quarrel, if we differ about them and can reach no satisfactory agreement?

EUTHYPHRO: Yes, Socrates, it is disagreements about these matters.

SOCRATES: Well, Euthyphro, the gods will quarrel over these things if they quarrel at all, will they not?

EUTHYPHRO: Necessarily.

SOCRATES: Then, my good Euthyphro, you say that some of the gods think one   e
thing just, the others another; and that what some of them hold to be honorable or
good, others hold to be dishonorable or evil. For there would not have been quarrels
among them if they had not disagreed on these points, would there?

EUTHYPHRO: You are right.

SOCRATES: And each of them loves what he thinks honorable, and good, and just;
and hates the opposite, does he not?

EUTHYPHRO: Certainly.

SOCRATES: But you say that the same action is held by some of them to be just,
and by others to be unjust; and that then they dispute about it, and so quarrel and fight   8
among themselves. Is it not so?

EUTHYPHRO: Yes.

SOCRATES: Then the same thing is hated by the gods and loved by them; and the
same thing will be displeasing and pleasing to them.

EUTHYPHRO: Apparently.

SOCRATES: Then, according to your account, the same thing will be pious and
impious.

EUTHYPHRO: So it seems.

SOCRATES: Then, my good friend, you have not answered my question. I did not
ask you to tell me what action is both pious and impious; but it seems that whatever is
pleasing to the gods is also displeasing to them. And so, Euthyphro, I should not be   b
surprised if what you are doing now in punishing your father is an action well pleasing
to Zeus, but hateful to Cronos and Uranus, and acceptable to Hephaestus, but hateful to
Hera; and if any of the other gods disagree about it, pleasing to some of them and displeasing to others.

EUTHYPHRO: But on this point, Socrates, I think that there is no difference of
opinion among the gods: they all hold that if one man kills another unjustly, he must be
punished.

SOCRATES: What, Euthyphro? Among mankind, have you never heard disputes   c
whether a man ought to be punished for killing another man unjustly, or for doing
some other unjust deed?

EUTHYPHRO: Indeed, they never cease from these disputes, especially in courts of
justice. They do all manner of unjust things; and then there is nothing which they will
not do and say to avoid punishment.

SOCRATES: Do they admit that they have done something unjust, and at the same
time deny that they ought to be punished, Euthyphro?

EUTHYPHRO: No, indeed, that they do not.

SOCRATES: Then it is not the case that there is nothing which they will not do and
say. I take it, they do not dare to say or argue that they must not be punished if they
have done something unjust. What they say is that they have not done anything unjust,   d
is it not so?

EUTHYPHRO: That is true.

SOCRATES: Then they do not disagree over the question that the unjust individual
must be punished. They disagree over the question, who is unjust, and what was done
and when, do they not?

EUTHYPHRO: That is true.

SOCRATES: Well, is not exactly the same thing true of the gods if they quarrel
about justice and injustice, as you say they do? Do not some of them say that the others

are doing something unjust, while the others deny it? No one, I suppose, my dear
e   friend, whether god or man, dares to say that a person who has done something unjust
must not be punished.

EUTHYPHRO: No, Socrates, that is true, by and large.

SOCRATES: I take it, Euthyphro, that the disputants, whether men or gods, if the
gods do disagree, disagree over each separate act. When they quarrel about any act,
some of them say that it was just, and others that it was unjust. Is it not so?

EUTHYPHRO: Yes.

9   SOCRATES: Come, then, my dear Euthyphro, please enlighten me on this point.
What proof have you that all the gods think that a laborer who has been imprisoned for
murder by the master of the man whom he has murdered, and who dies from his imprisonment before the master has had time to learn from the religious authorities what
he should do, dies unjustly? How do you know that it is just for a son to indict his father and to prosecute him for the murder of such a man? Come, see if you can make it
b   clear to me that the gods necessarily agree in thinking that this action of yours is just;
and if you satisfy me, I will never cease singing your praises for wisdom.

EUTHYPHRO: I could make that clear enough to you, Socrates; but I am afraid that
it would be a long business.

SOCRATES: I see you think that I am duller than the judges. To them, of course,
you will make it clear that your father has committed an unjust action, and that all the
gods agree in hating such actions.

EUTHYPHRO: I will indeed, Socrates, if they will only listen to me.

c   SOCRATES: They will listen if they think that you are a good speaker. But while you
were talking, it occurred to me to ask myself this question: suppose that Euthyphro were
to prove to me as clearly as possible that all the gods think such a death unjust, how has
he brought me any nearer to understanding what piety and impiety are? This particular
act, perhaps, may be displeasing to the gods, but then we have just seen that piety and
impiety cannot be defined in that way; for we have seen that what is displeasing to the
d   gods is also pleasing to them. So I will let you off on this point, Euthyphro; and all the
gods shall agree in thinking your father's action wrong and in hating it, if you like. But
shall we correct our definition and say that whatever all the gods hate is impious, and
whatever they all love is pious; while whatever some of them love, and others hate, is either both or neither? Do you wish us now to define piety and impiety in this manner?

EUTHYPHRO: Why not, Socrates?

SOCRATES: There is no reason why I should not, Euthyphro. It is for you to consider whether that definition will help you to teach me what you promised.

e   EUTHYPHRO: Well, I should say that piety is what all the gods love, and that impiety is what they all hate.

SOCRATES: Are we to examine this definition, Euthyphro, and see if it is a good
one? Or are we to be content to accept the bare statements of other men or of ourselves
without asking any questions? Or must we examine the statements?

EUTHYPHRO: We must examine them. But for my part I think that the definition is
right this time.

SOCRATES: We shall know that better in a little while, my good friend. Now con-
10   sider this question. Do the gods love piety because it is pious, or is it pious because
they love it?

EUTHYPHRO: I do not understand you, Socrates.

SOCRATES: I will try to explain myself: we speak of a thing being carried and carrying, and being led and leading, and being seen and seeing; and you understand that
all such expressions mean different things, and what the difference is.

EUTHYPHRO: Yes, I think I understand.

SOCRATES: And we talk of a thing being loved, of a thing loving, and the two are different?

EUTHYPHRO: Of course.

SOCRATES: Now tell me, is a thing which is being carried in a state of being car-   b
ried because it is carried, or for some other reason?

EUTHYPHRO: No, because it is carried.

SOCRATES: And a thing is in a state of being led because it is led, and of being seen because it is seen?

EUTHYPHRO: Certainly.

SOCRATES: Then a thing is not seen because it is in a state of being seen: it is in a state of being seen because it is seen; and a thing is not led because it is in a state of being led: it is in a state of being led because it is led; and a thing is not carried because it is in a state of being carried: it is in a state of being carried because it is carried. Is my meaning clear now, Euthyphro? I mean this: if anything becomes or is affected, it does not become because it is in a state of becoming: it is in a state of becoming be-   c
cause it becomes; and it is not affected because it is in a state of being affected: it is in a state of being affected because it is affected. Do you not agree?

EUTHYPHRO: I do.

SOCRATES: Is not that which is being loved in a state either of becoming or of being affected in some way by something?

EUTHYPHRO: Certainly.

SOCRATES: Then the same is true here as in the former cases. A thing is not loved by those who love it because it is in a state of being loved; it is in a state of being loved because they love it.

EUTHYPHRO: Necessarily.

SOCRATES: Well, then, Euthyphro, what do we say about piety? Is it not loved by   d
all the gods, according to your definition?

EUTHYPHRO: Yes.

SOCRATES: Because it is pious, or for some other reason?

EUTHYPHRO: No, because it is pious.

SOCRATES: Then it is loved by the gods because it is pious; it is not pious because it is loved by them?

EUTHYPHRO: It seems so.

SOCRATES: But, then, what is pleasing to the gods is pleasing to them, and is in a state of being loved by them, because they love it?

EUTHYPHRO: Of course.

SOCRATES: Then piety is not what is pleasing to the gods, and what is pleasing to the gods is not pious, as you say, Euthyphro. They are different things.

EUTHYPHRO: And why, Socrates?   e

SOCRATES: Because we are agreed that the gods love piety because it is pious, and that it is not pious because they love it. Is not this so?

EUTHYPHRO: Yes.

SOCRATES: And that what is pleasing to the gods because they love it, is pleasing to them by reason of this same love, and that they do not love it because it is pleasing to them.

EUTHYPHRO: True.

SOCRATES: Then, my dear Euthyphro, piety and what is pleasing to the gods are different things. If the gods had loved piety because it is pious, they would also have   11
loved what is pleasing to them because it is pleasing to them; but if what is pleasing

to them had been pleasing to them because they loved it, then piety, too, would have been piety because they loved it. But now you see that they are opposite things, and wholly different from each other. For the one is of a sort to be loved because it is loved, while the other is loved because it is of a sort to be loved. My question, Euthyphro, was, What is piety? But it turns out that you have not explained to me the essential character of piety; you have been content to mention an effect which be-

b longs to it—namely, that all the gods love it. You have not yet told me what its essential character is. Do not, if you please, keep from me what piety is; begin again and tell me that. Never mind whether the gods love it, or whether it has other effects: we shall not differ on that point. Do your best to make clear to me what is piety and what is impiety.

EUTHYPHRO: But, Socrates, I really don't know how to explain to you what is in my mind. Whatever statement we put forward always somehow moves round in a circle, and will not stay where we put it.

SOCRATES: I think that your statements, Euthyphro, are worthy of my ancestor

c Daedalus.* If they had been mine and I had set them down, I dare say you would have made fun of me, and said that it was the consequence of my descent from Daedalus that the statements which I construct run away, as his statues used to, and will not stay where they are put. But, as it is, the statements are yours, and the joke would have no point. You yourself see that they will not stay still.

EUTHYPHRO: Nay, Socrates, I think that the joke is very much in point. It is not

d my fault that the statement moves round in a circle and will not stay still. But you are the Daedalus, I think; as far as I am concerned, my statements would have stayed put.

SOCRATES: Then, my friend, I must be a more skillful artist than Daedalus; he only used to make his own works move, while I, you see, can make other people's works move, too. And the beauty of it is that I am wise against my will. I would rather that our statements had remained firm and immovable than have all the wisdom of

e Daedalus and all the riches of Tantalus to boot. But enough of this. I will do my best to help you to explain to me what piety is, for I think that you are lazy. Don't give in yet. Tell me, do you not think that all piety must be just?

EUTHYPHRO: I do.

12 SOCRATES: Well, then, is all justice pious, too? Or, while all piety is just, is a part only of justice pious, and the rest of it something else?

EUTHYPHRO: I do not follow you, Socrates.

SOCRATES: Yet you have the advantage over me in your youth no less than your wisdom. But, as I say, the wealth of your wisdom makes you complacent. Exert yourself, my good friend: I am not asking you a difficult question. I mean the opposite of what the poet [Stasinus] said, when he wrote:

b   "You shall not name Zeus the creator, who made all things: for where there is fear there
    also is reverence."

Now I disagree with the poet. Shall I tell you why?

EUTHYPHRO: Yes.

SOCRATES: I do not think it true to say that where there is fear, there also is reverence. Many people who fear sickness and poverty and other such evils seem to me to have fear, but no reverence for what they fear. Do you not think so?

EUTHYPHRO: I do.

---

*Daedalus' statues were reputed to have been so lifelike that they came alive.

SOCRATES: But I think that where there is reverence there also is fear. Does any man feel reverence and a sense of shame about anything, without at the same time c dreading and fearing the reputation of wickedness?

EUTHYPHRO: No, certainly not.

SOCRATES: Then, though there is fear wherever there is reverence, it is not correct to say that where there is fear there also is reverence. Reverence does not always accompany fear; for fear, I take it, is wider than reverence. It is a part of fear, just as the odd is a part of number, so that where you have the odd you must also have number, though where you have number you do not necessarily have the odd. Now I think you follow me?

EUTHYPHRO: I do.

SOCRATES: Well, then, this is what I meant by the question which I asked you. Is there always piety where there is justice? Or, though there is always justice where there is piety, yet there is not always piety where there is justice, because piety is only d a part of justice? Shall we say this, or do you differ?

EUTHYPHRO: No, I agree. I think that you are right.

SOCRATES: Now observe the next point. If piety is a part of justice, we must find out, I suppose, what part of justice it is? Now, if you had asked me just now, for instance, what part of number is the odd, and what number is an odd number, I should have said that whatever number is not even is an odd number. Is it not so?

EUTHYPHRO: Yes.

SOCRATES: Then see if you can explain to me what part of justice is piety, that I e may tell Meletus that now that I have been adequately instructed by you as to what actions are righteous and pious, and what are not, he must give up prosecuting me unjustly for impiety.

EUTHYPHRO: Well, then, Socrates, I should say that righteousness and piety are that part of justice which has to do with the careful attention which ought to be paid to the gods; and that what has to do with the careful attention which ought to be paid to men is the remaining part of justice.

SOCRATES: And I think that your answer is a good one, Euthyphro. But there is one little point about which I still want to hear more. I do not yet understand what the 13 careful attention is to which you refer. I suppose you do not mean that the attention which we pay to the gods is like the attention which we pay to other things. We say, for instance, do we not, that not everyone knows how to take care of horses, but only the trainer of horses?

EUTHYPHRO: Certainly.

SOCRATES: For I suppose that the skill that is concerned with horses is the art of taking care of horses.

EUTHYPHRO: Yes.

SOCRATES: And not everyone understands the care of dogs, but only the huntsman.

EUTHYPHRO: True.

SOCRATES: For I suppose that the huntsman's skill is the art of taking care of dogs. b

EUTHYPHRO: Yes.

SOCRATES: And the herdsman's skill is the art of taking care of cattle.

EUTHYPHRO: Certainly.

SOCRATES: And you say that piety and righteousness are taking care of the gods, Euthyphro?

EUTHYPHRO: I do.

SOCRATES: Well, then, has not all care the same object? Is it not for the good and benefit of that on which it is bestowed? For instance, you see that horses are benefited and improved when they are cared for by the art which is concerned with them. Is it not so?

EUTHYPHRO: Yes, I think so.

c   SOCRATES: And dogs are benefited and improved by the huntsman's art, and cattle by the herdsman's, are they not? And the same is always true. Or do you think care is ever meant to harm that which is cared for?

EUTHYPHRO: No, indeed; certainly not.

SOCRATES: But to benefit it?

EUTHYPHRO: Of course.

SOCRATES: Then is piety, which is our care for the gods, intended to benefit the gods, or to improve them? Should you allow that you make any of the gods better when you do a pious action?

EUTHYPHRO: No indeed; certainly not.

SOCRATES: No, I am quite sure that that is not your meaning, Euthyphro. It was
d   for that reason that I asked you what you meant by the careful attention which ought to be paid to the gods. I thought that you did not mean that.

EUTHYPHRO: You were right, Socrates. I do not mean that.

SOCRATES: Good. Then what sort of attention to the gods will piety be?

EUTHYPHRO: The sort of attention, Socrates, slaves pay to their masters.

SOCRATES: I understand; then it is a kind of service to the gods?

EUTHYPHRO: Certainly.

SOCRATES: Can you tell me what result the art which serves a doctor serves to produce? Is it not health?

EUTHYPHRO: Yes.

e   SOCRATES: And what result does the art which serves a ship-wright serve to produce?

EUTHYPHRO: A ship, of course, Socrates.

SOCRATES: The result of the art which serves a builder is a house, is it not?

EUTHYPHRO: Yes.

SOCRATES: Then tell me, my good friend: What result will the art which serves the gods serve to produce? You must know, seeing that you say that you know more about divine things than any other man.

EUTHYPHRO: Well, that is true, Socrates.

SOCRATES: Then tell me, I beg you, what is that grand result which the gods use our services to produce?

EUTHYPHRO: There are many notable results, Socrates.

14   SOCRATES: So are those, my friend, which a general produces. Yet it is easy to see that the crowning result of them all is victory in war, is it not?

EUTHYPHRO: Of course.

SOCRATES: And, I take it, the farmer produces many notable results; yet the principal result of them all is that he makes the earth produce food.

EUTHYPHRO: Certainly.

SOCRATES: Well, then, what is the principal result of the many notable results which the gods produce?

EUTHYPHRO: I told you just now, Socrates, that accurate knowledge of all these
b   matters is not easily obtained. However, broadly I say this: if any man knows that his words and actions in prayer and sacrifice are acceptable to the gods, that is what is pious; and it preserves the state, as it does private families. But the opposite of what is acceptable to the gods is sacrilegious, and this it is that undermines and destroys everything.

SOCRATES: Certainly, Euthyphro, if you had wished, you could have answered my
c   main question in far fewer words. But you are evidently not anxious to teach me. Just

now, when you were on the very point of telling me what I want to know, you stopped short. If you had gone on then, I should have learned from you clearly enough by this time what piety is. But now I am asking you questions, and must follow wherever you lead me; so tell me, what is it that you mean by piety and impiety? Do you not mean a science of prayer and sacrifice?

EUTHYPHRO: I do.

SOCRATES: To sacrifice is to give to the gods, and to pray is to ask of them, is it not?

EUTHYPHRO: It is, Socrates.

SOCRATES: Then you say that piety is the science of asking of the gods and giving   d
to them?

EUTHYPHRO: You understand my meaning exactly, Socrates.

SOCRATES: Yes, for I am eager to share your wisdom, Euthyphro, and so I am all attention; nothing that you say will fall to the ground. But tell me, what is this service of the gods? You say it is to ask of them, and to give to them?

EUTHYPHRO: I do.

SOCRATES: Then, to ask rightly will be to ask of them what we stand in need of   e
from them, will it not?

EUTHYPHRO: Naturally.

SOCRATES: And to give rightly will be to give back to them what they stand in need of from us? It would not be very skillful to make a present to a man of something that he has no need of.

EUTHYPHRO: True, Socrates.

SOCRATES: Then piety, Euthyphro, will be the art of carrying on business between gods and men?

EUTHYPHRO: Yes, if you like to call it so.

SOCRATES: But I like nothing except what is true. But tell me, how are the gods benefited by the gifts which they receive from us? What they give is plain enough. Every good thing that we have is their gift. But how are they benefited by what we give   15
them? Have we the advantage over them in these business transactions to such an extent that we receive from them all the good things we possess, and give them nothing in return?

EUTHYPHRO: But do you suppose, Socrates, that the gods are benefited by the gifts which they receive from us?

SOCRATES: But what *are* these gifts, Euthyphro, that we give the gods?

EUTHYPHRO: What do you think but honor and praise, and, as I have said, what is acceptable to them.

SOCRATES: Then piety, Euthyphro, is acceptable to the gods, but it is not prof-   b
itable to them nor loved by them?

EUTHYPHRO: I think that nothing is more loved by them.

SOCRATES: Then I see that piety means that which is loved by the gods.

EUTHYPHRO: Most certainly.

SOCRATES: After that, shall you be surprised to find that your statements move about instead of staying where you put them? Shall you accuse me of being the Daedalus that makes them move, when you yourself are far more skillful than Daedalus was, and make them go round in a circle? Do you not see that our statement has come round to where it was before? Surely you remember that we have already   c
seen that piety and what is pleasing to the gods are quite different things. Do you not remember?

EUTHYPHRO: I do.

SOCRATES: And now do you not see that you say that what the gods love is pious? But does not what the gods love come to the same thing as what is pleasing to the gods?

EUTHYPHRO: Certainly.

SOCRATES: Then either our former conclusion was wrong or, if it was right, we are wrong now.

EUTHYPHRO: So it seems.

SOCRATES: Then we must begin again and inquire what piety is. I do not mean to

d   give in until I have found out. Do not regard me as unworthy; give your whole mind to the question, and this time tell me the truth. For if anyone knows it, it is you; and you are a Proteus whom I must not let go until you have told me. It cannot be that you would ever have undertaken to prosecute your aged father for the murder of a laboring man unless you had known exactly what piety and impiety are. You would have feared to risk the anger of the gods, in case you should be doing wrong, and you would have

e   been afraid of what men would say. But now I am sure that you think that you know exactly what is pious and what is not; so tell me, my good Euthyphro, and do not conceal from me what you think.

EUTHYPHRO: Another time, then, Socrates. I am in a hurry now, and it is time for me to be off.

SOCRATES: What are you doing, my friend! Will you go away and destroy all my hopes of learning from you what is pious and what is not, and so of escaping Meletus?

16   I meant to explain to him that now Euthyphro has made me wise about divine things, and that I no longer in my ignorance speak carelessly about them or introduce reforms. And then I was going to promise him to live a better life for the future.

APOLOGY

17   Well, I don't know what effect the prosecution has had on you, men of Athens. As far as I'm concerned, they made me all but forget the position I am in, they spoke so plausibly. And yet, to all intents and purposes, there was not a word of truth in what they said.

Of their many lies, one in particular filled me with amazement. They said you should be careful to avoid being led astray by my "skill in speaking." They were not in the least embarrassed at the prospect of being immediately proved wrong by my actual

b   performance, when it becomes clear that I am not in the least skilled in speaking. That was what I found the most shameless thing about their behaviour—unless of course they call "skilled in speaking" someone who merely speaks the truth. If *that's* what they mean, then I would agree that I am in a different class from them as an orator.

As I say, they have told you little or nothing that was true, whereas from me you will hear the whole truth—certainly not a piece of polished rhetoric like theirs, men of

c   Athens, with its words and phrases so cleverly arranged. No, the speech you are going to hear from me will use everyday language, arranged in a straightforward way—after all, I have confidence in the justice of what I have to say—so I hope no-one is expecting anything different. And I shall tell the truth, because it wouldn't be appropriate to appear before you at my age making up stories like a schoolboy.

However, there is one important request and concession I am going to ask of you, men of Athens. If you hear me making my defence in the same language I generally use in the city, among people doing business—where many of you have heard me—and elsewhere, do not be surprised on that account, or start interrupting. The reason for it is this. This is the first time I have ever appeared in court, though I am now seventy years of age. The kind of speaking practised here is, quite simply, foreign to   d
me. Imagine I really were a foreigner; you wouldn't hold it against me, presumably, if I spoke in the dialect and manner in which I had been brought up. In the same way   18
now, I make this request—justified, in my view—that you pay no attention to the manner in which I speak, be it inferior or superior. Please consider one point only, and focus your attention on that. Is there any justice in what I have to say, or not? That, after all, is the function of a member of the jury; the speaker's task is to tell the truth.

First of all, then, men of Athens, I am entitled to defend myself against the earliest false accusations made against me, and against my earliest accusers; after that against the more recent falsehoods, and my present accusers. After all, there have been many people, over the years, making accusations about me to you, and speaking not a word of truth. I fear them more than I fear Anytus and his supporters, dangerous   b
though they are as well. But the earlier ones are more dangerous, gentlemen. They took you in hand from childhood, for the most part, and tried to win you over, making accusations every bit as false as these today; they told you there was this man Socrates, an intellectual, a thinker about the heavens, an expert on everything under the earth, a man who could make the weaker argument the stronger.

These people, men of Athens, the ones who have saddled me with this reputation, are my most dangerous accusers, because those who listen to them think that stu-   c
dents of these subjects do not recognise the gods. What's more, there are a great many of these accusers, and they have been accusing me for a long time now. And thirdly, they were speaking to you at the age when you were most likely to believe them, when many of you were children and adolescents. Quite simply, they were prosecuting in an uncontested case, since there was no-one there to answer their charges.

What is particularly unfair is that I cannot even know, or tell you, their names—unless maybe one of them is a writer of comedies. But all those who tried to influence   d
you, out of spite and malice, together with those who were trying to influence others because they were genuinely convinced themselves—all these accusers are very hard to deal with. It is not possible to call any of them as a witness here, or cross-examine them; I just have to make my defence like someone shadow-boxing, and conduct my cross-examination with no-one there to answer.

So I hope you will accept my claim that I have two sets of accusers—the ones who have just now brought this case against me, and the ones from way back, the ones   e
I have been telling you about. Please believe also that I must make my defence against this second set first; after all, you heard their accusations at an earlier age, and on many more occasions, than you heard the later ones.

Very well. I must make my defence, men of Athens, and try to remove from your minds, in the very brief time available, the prejudice which you have so long held. I   19
hope that is how things will turn out, provided it really *is* the best outcome for you and for me, and that I shall achieve something by my defence. But I think it is difficult, and I am well aware of the magnitude of the task. Still, let it turn out as god wills, I must obey the law, and make my defence.

b   Let us go back to the beginning, then, and see what the accusation is which has created this prejudice against me—the prejudice which Meletus was presumably counting on when he brought this case against me. What exactly did the originators of this prejudice say? We ought really to read out a sworn statement from them, just like the prosecution's. "Socrates is guilty of being a busybody. He enquires into things under the earth and in the heavens, and makes the weaker argument the stronger, and

c he teaches these same things to other people." That's roughly how it goes. You saw it for yourselves in Aristophanes' comedy; you saw a Socrates there, swinging round and round, claiming he was walking on air, and spouting a whole lot of other drivel on subjects about which I make not the slightest claim to knowledge. Not that I have anything against knowledge of this kind, if anyone is an expert on such subjects; I hope Meletus will never bring enough cases against me to reduce me to that. No, it's just that I myself have no share in such knowledge.

   Once again, I can call most of you as witnesses. I'm sure you can make the posi-

d tion clear to one another, and explain, those of you who have ever heard me talking— and a lot of you come in that category. Tell one another then, if any of you has ever heard me breathe so much as a word on such topics. That will help you to see that the rest of what is generally said about me has as little foundation.

   No, there is no truth in these stories. And if anyone has told you that I undertake

e to educate people, or that I make money out of it, there is equally little truth in that either. Mind you, if anyone *can* educate people—as Gorgias from Leontini can, or Prodicus from Ceos, or Hippias from Elis—then that seems to me to be a fine thing. Any of these men, gentlemen, can go to any city and persuade the young men, who are at liberty to spend their time, free of charge, with whichever of their fellow-citizens they

20 choose, to abandon the company of those fellow-citizens and spend time with him instead—and pay money to do so, *and* be grateful into the bargain.

   Come to that, there is even one of them here, a wise man from Paros. I found out he was living in Athens when I ran into Callias, the son of Hipponicus, the man who has paid more money to these teachers than everyone else put together. I asked him—

b you know he has two sons—"Callias," I said, "if your sons were colts or calves, we would be able to find and employ someone to look after them, someone who would turn them into outstanding examples of their particular species; and this person would be a trainer or farmer of some kind. But they aren't colts or calves; they are men. Whom do you propose to find to look after them? Who is an expert in this kind of excellence—the excellence of a human being and a citizen? I imagine, since you have sons, you must have thought about this question. Is there someone," I asked him, "or not?"

   "There certainly is," he said.

   "Who is he?" I said. "Where is he from? What does he charge?"

   "Evenus," he said. "He is from Paros, Socrates, and he charges 500 drachmas."

   I took my hat off to Evenus, if he really did have this ability, and yet taught for

c so reasonable a fee. I wouldn't. I'd start giving myself airs, and become extremely choosy, if I had this kind of knowledge. But I don't have it, men of Athens.

   I can imagine one of you interrupting me, and saying, "That's all very well, Socrates; but what *do* you do? Where have all these prejudices against you come from? I take it all this gossip and rumour about you is not the result of your behaving just like anyone else. You must be doing *something* out of the ordinary. Tell us what it is, so we

d can avoid jumping to conclusions about you." This seems to me to be a valid point, so I'll try and explain to you what it is that has given me my reputation and created the prejudice against me. Give me a hearing. It may seem to some of you that I am not being serious, but I promise you, every word I say will be the truth.

I have gained this reputation, men of Athens, as a direct result of a kind of wisdom. What sort of wisdom? The sort we might perhaps call human wisdom. In fact, if we are talking about this kind of wisdom, I probably *am* wise. The men I mentioned just now may well be wise with some more-than-human wisdom; I don't know how else to describe it. It's not a wisdom *I* know anything about. Anyone who says I do is lying, and trying to increase the prejudice against me.

    Please do not interrupt me, men of Athens, even if you find what I say a little bit boastful. The claim I'm about to make is not *my* claim; I shall appeal to a reliable authority. I shall call the god at Delphi to give evidence to you about my wisdom; he can tell you if I really do possess any, and what it is like.

    You remember Chaerephon, I imagine. He was a friend of mine, from an early age, and a friend of most of you. He shared your recent exile, and returned from exile with you. You know what Chaerephon was like, how impetuous he was when he set about something. And sure enough, he went to Delphi one day, and went so far as to put this question to the oracle—I repeat, please do not interrupt, gentlemen—he asked if there was anyone wiser than me; and the priestess of Apollo replied that there was no-one wiser. His brother here will give evidence to you about this, since Chaerephon himself is dead.

    Let me remind you of my reason for telling you this. I am trying to show you the origin of the prejudice against me. When I heard the priestess's reply, my reaction was this: "What on earth is the god saying? What is his hidden meaning? I'm well aware that I have no wisdom, great or small. So what can he mean by saying that I am so wise? He can't be lying; he's not allowed to." I spent a long time wondering what he could mean. Finally, with great reluctance, I decided to verify his claim. What I did was this: I approached one of those who seemed to be wise, thinking that there, if anywhere, I could prove the reply wrong, and say quite clearly to the oracle, "This man is wiser than I am, whereas you said that I was the wisest."

    So I examined this man—there's no need for me to mention his name, let's just say he was a politician—and the result of my examination, men of Athens, and of my conversations with him, was this. I decided that although the man seemed to many people, and above all to himself, to be wise, in reality he was not wise. I tried to demonstrate to him that he thought he was wise, but actually was not, and as a result I made an enemy of him, and of many of those present. To myself, as I left him, I reflected: "Here is *one* man less wise than I. In all probability neither of us knows anything worth knowing; but he *thinks* he knows when he doesn't, whereas I, given that I don't in fact know, am at least *aware* I don't know. Apparently, therefore, I am wiser than him in just this one small detail, that when I don't know something, I don't *think* I know it either." From him I went to another man, one of those who seemed wiser than the first. I came to exactly the same conclusion, and made an enemy of him and of many others besides.

    After that I began approaching people in a systematic way. I could see, with regret and alarm, that I was making enemies, yet I thought it was essential to take the god seriously. So on I had to go, in my enquiry into the meaning of the oracle, to everyone who seemed to have any knowledge. And I swear to you, men of Athens— after all, I am bound to tell you the truth—what I found was this. Those with the highest reputations seemed to me to be pretty nearly the most useless, if I was trying to find out the meaning of what the god had said, whereas others, who appeared of less account, were a much better bet when it came to thinking sensibly.

    I can best give an account of my quest by likening it to a set of labours—and all, as it turned out, to satisfy myself of the accuracy of the oracle. After the politicians I went to the writers—writers of plays, and songs, and the rest of them. That would be

e

21

b

c

d

e

22

b

an open-and-shut case, I thought. I should easily show myself up as less wise than them. So I took to reading their works, the ones which struck me as showing the greatest skill in composition, and asking them what they meant; I hoped to learn from them.

c   Well, I'm embarrassed to tell you the truth, gentlemen; but I must tell you. Practically anyone present could have given a better account than they did of the works they had themselves written. As a result, I quickly came to a decision about the writers too, in their turn. I realised that their achievements are not the result of wisdom, but of natural talent and inspiration, like fortune-tellers and clairvoyants, who also say many striking things, but have no idea at all of the meaning of what they say. Writers, I felt, were clearly in the same position. Moreover, I could see that their works encouraged them to think that they were the wisest of men in other areas where they were not wise. So I left them too feeling that I had got the better of them, in the same way as I had got the better of the politicians.

d   Finally I went to the craftsmen. I was well aware that I knew virtually nothing, and confident that I would find much fine knowledge in them. Nor was I disappointed. They *did* know things which I didn't know; in this respect they were wiser than I was. However, our good friends the skilled workmen seemed also to me, men of Athens, to have the same failing as the writers. Each one, because of his skill in practising his
e   craft, thought himself extremely wise in other matters of importance as well; and this presumptuousness of theirs seemed to me to obscure the wisdom they did have. So I asked myself, on behalf of the oracle, whether I should accept being the way I was— without any of their wisdom, or any of their foolishness—or whether I ought to possess both the qualities they possessed. The answer I gave myself and the oracle was that it was best for me to remain as I was.

This survey, men of Athens, has aroused much hostility against me, of the most
23   damaging and serious kind. The result has been a great deal of prejudice, and in particular, this description of me as being "wise." That is because the people who were present on such occasions think that I am an expert myself on those subjects in which I demolish the claims of others. The truth probably is, gentlemen, that in reality god is wise, and that what he means by his reply to Chaerephon is that human wisdom is of little or no value. When he refers to the man here before you—to Socrates—and goes
b   out of his way to use my name, he is probably using me as an example, as if he were saying "That man is the wisest among you, mortals, who realises, as Socrates does, that he doesn't really amount to much when it comes to wisdom."

That's why, to this day, I go round investigating and enquiring, as the god would have me do, if I think anyone—Athenian or foreigner—is wise. And when I find he is not, then, in support of the god, I demonstrate that he is not wise. My preoccupation with this task has left me no time worth speaking of to take any part in public life or family life. Instead I live in extreme poverty as a result of my service to the god.

c   Another problem is that young people follow me—the ones with the most time at their disposal, the sons of the rich—of their own free will; they love listening to people being cross-examined. They often imitate me themselves, and have a go at cross-examining others. Nor do I imagine they have any difficulty in finding people who think they know something, when in fact they know little or nothing. The result is that the victims of their cross-examination are angry with me, rather than themselves; they
d   say Socrates is some sort of criminal, and that he has a bad influence on the young. When you ask them what I do and what I teach that makes me a criminal, they can't answer; they don't know. But since they don't want to lose face, they come out with the standard accusations made against all philosophers, the stuff about "things in

heaven and things under the earth," and "not recognising the gods" and "making the weaker argument stronger." The truth, I think, they would refuse to admit, which is that they have been shown up as pretenders to knowledge who really know nothing. Since, therefore, they are ambitious and energetic, and there are a lot of them, and since they speak forcibly and persuasively about me, they have been filling your ears for some time now, and most vigorously, with their attacks on me.

That is what Meletus relied on when he brought this charge against me, with Anytus and Lycon—Meletus feeling offended as one of the poets, Anytus as one of the craftsmen and politicians, Lycon as one of the orators. The result, as I said at the beginning, is that it would surprise me if I were able to remove from your minds, in so short a time, a prejudice which has grown so strong. This is the truth, I assure you, men of Athens. I speak with absolutely no concealment or reservation. I'm pretty sure it's this way of speaking which makes me unpopular. My unpopularity is the proof that I am speaking the truth, that this *is* the prejudice against me, and these *are* the reasons for it. You can enquire into these matters—now or later—and you will find them to be so.

So much for the accusations made by my first group of accusers. I hope you'll find what I've said a satisfactory defence against them. Now let me try and defend myself against Meletus, that excellent patriot (as he claims) and my more recent accusers. Let's treat them as a separate prosecution, and consider in its turn the charge brought by them. It runs something like this: it says that Socrates is guilty of being a bad influence on the young, and of not recognising the gods whom the state recognises, but practising a new religion of the supernatural.

That's what the charge consists of. Let's examine this charge point by point. He says I am guilty of having a bad influence on the young. But *I* claim, men of Athens, that Meletus is guilty of playing games with what is deadly serious; he is too quick to bring people to trial, pretending to be serious and care about things to which he has never given a moment's thought. That this is the truth, I will try to prove to you as well. Come now, Meletus, tell me this. I take it you regard the well-being of the young as of the utmost importance?

MELETUS: I do.

SOCRATES: In that case, please tell these people who it is who is a good influence on the young. Obviously you must know, since you're so concerned about it. You've tracked down, so you say, the man who is a bad influence—me—and are bringing me here before these people and accusing me. So come on, tell them who is a good influence; point out to them who it is.

You see, Meletus? You are silent; you have nothing to say. Don't you think that's a disgrace, and a sufficient proof of what I am saying—that you haven't given it any thought? Tell us, my friend, who is a good influence?

MELETUS: The laws.

SOCRATES: Brilliant! But that's not what I'm asking. The question is what *man*—who will of course start off with just this knowledge, the laws.

MELETUS: These men, Socrates, the members of the jury.

SOCRATES: Really, Meletus? These men are capable of educating the young and being a good influence on them?

MELETUS: They certainly are.

SOCRATES: All of them? Or are some capable, and others not?

MELETUS: All of them.

SOCRATES: How remarkably fortunate—no shortage of benefactors there, then. What about the spectators in court? Do they have a good influence, or not?

MELETUS: Yes, they do, as well.

SOCRATES: What about the members of the council?

MELETUS: Yes, the members of the council also.

SOCRATES: But surely, Meletus, the people in the assembly—the citizens meeting *as* the assembly—surely they don't have a bad influence on the young? Don't they too—all of them—have a good influence?

MELETUS: Yes, they do too.

SOCRATES: Apart from me, then, the entire population of Athens, as it appears, makes the young into upright citizens. I alone am a bad influence. Is that what you mean?

MELETUS: Yes, that's exactly what I mean.

b   SOCRATES: That's certainly a great misfortune to charge me with. Answer me this, though: do you think the situation is the same with horses as well? Do the people who are good for them make up the entire population, and is there just one person who has a harmful effect on them? Isn't it the exact opposite? Isn't there just one person, or very few people—trainers—capable of doing them any good? Don't most people, if they spend time with horses, or have anything to do with them, have a harmful effect on them? Isn't that the situation, Meletus, both with horses and with all other living creatures?

It certainly is, whether you and Anytus deny it or admit it. After all, it would be a piece of great good fortune for the young, if only one person has a bad influence on them, and everyone else has a good influence. No, Meletus. You show quite clearly
c   that you have never cared in the slightest for the young; you reveal your own lack of interest quite plainly, since you've never given a moment's thought to the things you're prosecuting me for.

Another point. Tell us honestly, Meletus, is it better to live with good fellow-citizens, or with bad? Answer, can't you? It's not a difficult question. Isn't it true that bad citizens do some harm to those who are their neighbours at any particular time, while good citizens do some good?

MELETUS: Yes, of course.

SOCRATES: That being so, does anyone choose to be harmed by those close to him
d   rather than be helped by them? Answer, there's a good fellow. Besides, the law requires you to answer. Is there anyone who chooses to be harmed?

MELETUS: No, of course not.

SOCRATES: Well, then. You bring me to court for being a bad influence on the young, and making them worse people. Are you saying I do this deliberately, or without realising it?

MELETUS: Deliberately, I'm sure of it.

SOCRATES: Really, Meletus? How odd. Are you, at your age, so much wiser than me at mine? Are *you* aware that bad people generally have a harmful effect on those
e   they come into contact with, and that good people have a good effect? And have *I* reached such a height of stupidity as not even to realise that if I make one of my neighbours a worse man, I'm likely to come to some harm at his hands? And is the result that I deliberately do such great damage as you describe? On this point I don't believe you, Meletus; and nor, I think, does anyone else. No. Either I'm not a bad influence on the
26   young, or if I do have a bad influence, I do so without realising it. Either way you are wrong. And if I have a bad influence without realising it, it's not our custom to bring people here to court for errors of this sort, but to take them on one side, and instruct them privately, pointing out their mistakes. Obviously, if I'm taught, I shall stop doing what I don't at the moment realise I *am* doing. But you avoided spending time with me

and instructing me; you refused to do it. Instead you bring me here to court, where it is our custom to bring those who need punishment, not those who need to learn.

I needn't go on, men of Athens. It must now be clear, as I've said, that Meletus has never given the slightest thought to these matters. All the same, Meletus, tell us this: *in what way* do you claim I'm a bad influence on the young? Isn't it obvious I do   b
it in the way described in the charge you've brought against me—by teaching them not to recognise the gods the city recognises, but to practise this new religion of the supernatural instead? Isn't that your claim, that it's by teaching them these things that I have a bad influence?

MELETUS: Yes, that certainly is exactly what I claim.

SOCRATES: Well then, Meletus, in the name of these gods we are now talking about, make yourself a little clearer, both to me and to these gentlemen here, since *I* at   c
least cannot understand you. Do you mean I teach them to accept that there are *some* gods—not the gods the state accepts, but other gods? In that case I myself must also accept that there are gods, so I am not a complete atheist, and am not guilty on that count. Is this what you charge me with, accepting other gods? Or are you saying that I don't myself recognise any gods at all, and that I teach the same beliefs to others?

MELETUS: Yes, that's what I am saying. You don't recognise any gods at all.

SOCRATES: Meletus, you are beyond belief. What can possess you to say that?   d
Don't I accept that the sun and moon are gods, in the same way as everyone else does?

MELETUS: Good heavens, no, men of the jury. He says the sun is a stone, and the moon is made of earth.

SOCRATES: Is it Anaxagoras you think you're accusing, my dear Meletus? Do you have such contempt for these men here? Do you think them so illiterate as to be unaware that the works of Anaxagoras of Clazomenae are stuffed full of speculations of that sort? And do the young really learn these things from me, when there are often books on sale, for a drachma at the very most, in the Orchestra, in the Agora? They can laugh at Socrates if he claims these views as his own—especially such eccentric views.   e
However, as god is your witness, is that your view of me? Do I not accept the existence of any god at all?

MELETUS: No, in god's name, no god at all.

SOCRATES: What you say is unbelievable, Meletus—even, I think to yourself. This man here, men of Athens, strikes me as an arrogant lout; his prosecution of me is prompted entirely by arrogance, loutishness, and youth. It's as if he were setting a trick question, to test me: "Will Socrates the wise realise that I'm playing with words and   27
contradicting myself, or will I deceive him and the others who hear it?" He certainly seems to me to contradict himself, in his accusation. He might as well say "Socrates is guilty of not recognising the gods, but recognising the gods instead." And that is not a serious proposition.

Please join me, gentlemen, in examining the reasons why I think this is what his accusation amounts to. You, Meletus, answer us. And you *(to the jurymen),* as I asked you at the beginning, remember not to interrupt me if I construct my argument in my   b
usual way.

Is there anyone in the world, Meletus, who accepts the existence of human activity, but not of human beings? He must answer, gentlemen. Don't allow him to keep making all these interruptions. Is there anyone who denies horses, but accepts equine activity? Or denies the existence of flute-players, but accepts flute-playing? No, my very good friend, there isn't. If you refuse to answer, then I'll say it—to you and everyone else present here. But do answer my next question: is there anyone who accepts the activity of the supernatural, but denies supernatural beings?   c

MELETUS: No, there isn't.

SOCRATES: How kind of you—forced to answer, against your will, by these people here. Very well, then. You claim that I practise and teach a religion of the supernatural—whether of a new or conventional kind—so I do at least, on your own admission, accept the existence of the supernatural. You even swore to it, on oath, in your indictment. But if I accept the supernatural, it follows, I take it, that I must necessarily admit the existence of supernatural beings, must I not? I must; I take your silence for agree-
d   ment. And don't we regard supernatural beings as either gods or the children of gods? Yes or no?

MELETUS: We certainly do.

SOCRATES: In that case, if I accept supernatural beings—as you admit—and if supernatural beings are gods of some sort, then you can see what I mean when I say that you are setting trick questions, and playing with words, claiming first that I do *not* believe in gods, and then again claiming that I *do* believe in gods, since I do believe in supernatural beings. If, on the other hand, supernatural beings are some form of illegitimate children of gods—born of nymphs or of some of the other mothers they are said to be born from—who on earth could believe that there are children of gods, but no gods? It would be as absurd as saying you believed there were such things as mules,
e   the offspring of horses and donkeys, but didn't believe there were horses and donkeys.

No, Meletus, the only possible explanation for your bringing this accusation against me is that you wanted to test us—or that you didn't have any genuine offence to charge me with. There's no conceivable way you could persuade anyone in the
28   world with a grain of intelligence that belief in the supernatural and the divine does not imply belief in supernatural beings, divine beings and heroes.

So much for that, men of Athens. I don't think it takes much of a defence to show that in the terms of Meletus' indictment I am not guilty. What I have said so far should be enough. There remains what I said in the earlier part of my speech, that there is strong and widespread hostility towards me. Be in no doubt that this is true. It is this
b   which will convict me, if it does convict me—not Meletus, not Anytus, but the prejudice and malice of the many. What has convicted many other good men before me will, I think, convict me too. There's no danger of its stopping at me.

That being so, you might ask "Well, Socrates, aren't you ashamed of living a life which has resulted in your now being on trial for your life?" I would answer you, quite justifiably, "You are wrong, sir, if you think that a man who is worth anything at all should take into account the chances of life and death. No, the only thing he should think about, when he acts, is whether he is acting rightly or wrongly, and whether this
c   is the behaviour of a good man or a bad man. After all, if we accept your argument, those of the demigods who died at Troy would have been sorry creatures—and none more so than Achilles, the son of Thetis. Compared with the threat of dishonour, he regarded danger as of no importance at all. When he was eager to kill Hector, his mother, who was a goddess, said something like this to him, I imagine: 'My son, if you avenge the death of your friend Patroclus, and kill Hector, you will yourself be killed, since death awaits you immediately after Hector.' When Achilles heard this, he gave no thought to death or danger; what he feared much more was living as a coward, and not
d   avenging his friends. 'Let me die immediately,' he said, 'after making the wrong-doer pay the penalty, rather than remain here by the curved ships, a laughing-stock, like a clod of earth.' You don't imagine *he* gave any thought to death or danger."

That's the way of things, men of Athens, it really is. Where a man takes up his position—in the belief that it is the best position—or is told to take up a position by his commanding officer, there he should stay, in my view, regardless of danger. He should

not take death into account, or anything else apart from dishonour. As for me, when the e
commanders whom you chose to command me told me to take up position at Potidaea
and Amphipolis and Delium, on those occasions I stayed where they posted me, just
like anyone else, and risked death. Would it not have been very illogical of me, when
god deployed me, as I thought and believed, to live my life as a philosopher, examining myself and others, then to be afraid of death—or anything else at all—and abandon
my post?

It would indeed be illogical, and in that case you would certainly be completely 29
justified in bringing me to court for not accepting the existence of the gods, since I disobey their oracle, and am afraid of death, and think I am wise when I am not. After all,
the fear of death is just that, gentlemen—thinking one is wise when one is not—since
it's a claim to know what one doesn't know. For all anyone knows, death may in fact
be the best thing in the world that can happen to a man; yet men fear it as if they had
certain knowledge that it is the greatest of all evils. This is without doubt the most reprehensible folly—the folly of thinking one knows what one does not know. b

As for me, gentlemen, perhaps here too I *am* different from most people, in this
one particular; and if I did claim to be in any way wiser than anyone else, it would be
in this, that lacking any certain knowledge of what happens after death, I am also
aware that I have no knowledge. But that it is evil and shameful to do wrong, and disobey one's superiors, divine or human, that I *do* know. Compared therefore with the
evils which I know to be evils, I shall never fear, or try to avoid, what for all I know
may turn out to be good.

Suppose you now acquit me, rejecting Anytus' argument that either this case c
should not have been brought in the first place, or, since it *had* been brought, that it
was out of the question not to put me to death. He told you that if I got away with it,
your sons would all start putting Socrates' teachings into practice, and be totally overwhelmed by my bad influence. And suppose your response were to say to me:
"Socrates, on this occasion we will not do what Anytus wants. We acquit you—on this
condition, however, that you give up spending your time in this enquiry, and give up
the search for wisdom. If you are caught doing it again, you will be put to death."

Even if, then, to repeat, you were to acquit me on these conditions, I would say d
to you, "Men of Athens, I have the highest regard and affection for you, but I will obey
god rather than you. While I have breath and strength, I will not give up the search for
wisdom. I will carry on nagging at you, and pointing out your errors to those of you I
meet from day to day. I shall say, in my usual way, 'My very good sir, you are a citizen
of Athens, a city which is the greatest and most renowned for wisdom and power.
Aren't you ashamed to care about money, and how to make as much of it as possible,
and about reputation and public recognition, whereas for wisdom and truth, and making your soul as good as it can possibly be, you do not care, and give no thought to e
these things at all?' And if any of you objects, and says he does care, I shall not just let
him go, or walk away and leave him. No, I shall question him, cross-examine him, try
to prove him wrong. And if I find he has not achieved a state of excellence, but still
claims he has, then I shall accuse him of undervaluing what is most important, and 30
paying too much attention to what is less important.

"That is what I shall do for anyone I meet, young or old, foreigner or citizen—
but especially for my fellow-citizens, since you are more closely related to me. That is
what god tells me to do, I promise you, and I believe that this service of mine to god is
the most valuable asset you in this city have ever yet possessed. I spend my whole time
going round trying to persuade both the young and old among you not to spend your
time or energy in caring about your bodies or about money, but rather in making your b

souls as good as possible. I tell you, 'Money cannot create a good soul, but a good soul can turn money—and everything else in private life and public life—into a good thing for men.' If saying things like this is a bad influence on the young, then things like this must be harmful. But if anyone claims I say anything different from this, he is wrong. With that in mind, Athenians," I would say, "either do what Anytus wants, or don't do it; either acquit me, or don't, knowing that I will not behave differently even if I am to be put to death a thousand times over."

c   Don't interrupt, men of Athens. Please stick to what I asked you to do, which was not to interrupt what I say, but to give me a hearing. It will be in your interest, I think, to hear me. I have some more things to say which you could object to quite violently. Please don't, however.

I have just described the kind of man I am. Take my word for it, if you put me to death, you will harm yourselves more than you will harm me. As for me, no harm can d   come to me from Meletus or Anytus, who *cannot* injure me, since I do not think god ever allows a better man to be injured by a worse. Yes, I know he might put me to death, possibly, or send me into exile, or deprive me of citizen rights. And perhaps *he* regards these as great evils—as I suppose others may too. However, *I* do not. I regard it as a much greater evil to act as he is acting now, attempting to put a man to death unjustly.

It follows, men of Athens, that in this trial I am not by any means defending myself, as you might think. No, I am defending you. I don't want you to fail to recognise e   god's gift to you, and find me guilty. If you put me to death, you will not easily find another like me. I have, almost literally, settled on the city at god's command. It's as if the city, to use a slightly absurd simile, were a horse—a large horse, high-mettled, but which because of its size is somewhat sluggish, and needs to be stung into action by some kind of horsefly. I think god has caused me to settle on the city as this horsefly, 31   the sort that never stops, all day long, coming to rest on every part of you, stinging each one of you into action, and persuading and criticising each one of you.

Another like me will not easily come your way, gentlemen, so if you take my advice you will spare me. You may very likely get annoyed with me, as people do when they are dozing and somebody wakes them up. And you might then swat me, as Anytus wants you to, and kill me, quite easily. Then you could spend the rest of your lives asleep, unless god cared enough for you to send you someone else.

b   To convince yourselves that someone like me really is a gift from god to the city, look at things this way. Behaviour like mine does not seem to be natural. I have completely neglected my own affairs, and allowed my family to be neglected, all these years, while I devoted myself to looking after your interests—approaching each one of you individually, like a father or elder brother, and trying to persuade you to consider the good of your soul.

If I made anything out of it, and charged a fee for this advice, there'd be some sense in my doing it. As it is, you can see for yourselves that although the prosecution accused me, in their unscrupulous way, of everything under the sun, there was one c   point on which they were not so unscrupulous as to produce any evidence. They didn't claim that I ever made any money, or asked for any. I can produce convincing evidence, I think, that I am telling the truth—namely my poverty.

It may perhaps seem odd that in my private life I go round giving people advice like this, and interfering, without having the courage, in public life, to come forward before you, the people, and give advice on matters of public interest. The reason for this is what you have often heard me talking about, in all sorts of places, the kind of di- d   vine or supernatural sign that comes to me. This must have been what Meletus was making fun of when he wrote out the charge against me. It started when I was a child, a kind of voice which comes to me, and when it comes, always stops me doing what I'm just about to do; it never tells me what I *should* do. It's this which opposes my taking part in politics, and rightly opposes it, in my opinion. You can be sure, men of Athens, that if I had tried, at any time in the past, to go into politics, I would have been dead long ago, and been no use at all either to you or to myself.

Please don't be annoyed with me for speaking the truth. There is no-one in the world who can get away with deliberately opposing you—or any other popular assembly—or trying to put a stop to all the unjust and unlawful things which are done in politics; it is essential that the true fighter for justice, if he is to survive even for a short time, should remain a private individual, and not go into public life.

I shall give you compelling evidence for this—not words, but what you value, actions. Listen to things which have actually happened to me, and you will realise that I would never obey anyone if it was wrong to do so, simply through fear of dying. No, I would refuse to obey, even if it meant my death. What I am going to say now is the kind of boasting you often hear in the lawcourts; but it is true, for all that.

I have never, men of Athens, held any public office in the city, apart from being a member of the Council. It turned out that our tribe, Antiochis, formed the standing committee when you decided, by a resolution of the Council, to put on trial collectively the ten generals who failed to pick up the survivors from the sea battle. This was unconstitutional, as you afterwards all decided. On that occasion I was the only member of the standing committee to argue against you. I told you not to act unconstitutionally, and voted against you. The politicians were all set to bring an immediate action against me, and have me arrested on the spot, and you were encouraging them to do so, and shouting your approval, but still I thought I ought to take my chance on the side of law and justice, rather than side with you, through fear of imprisonment or death, when you were proposing to act unjustly.

That was when the city was still a democracy. When the oligarchy came to power, the junta in its turn sent for me, with four others, and gave me the task of bringing Leon of Salamis from his home in Salamis to the Council chamber, so he could be put to death. They often gave orders of this kind, to all sorts of people; they wanted to implicate as many people as possible in their crimes. Again I demonstrated—by what I did this time, rather than what I said—that my fear of death was, if you will pardon my saying so, negligible; what I was afraid of, more than anything, was acting without regard for justice or religion. I was not intimidated by the junta's power—great though it was—into acting unjustly. When we left the Council chamber, the other four went off to Salamis and fetched Leon, but I left, and went home. I might perhaps have been put to death for that, if their power hadn't soon after been brought to an end. Of these events any number of people will give evidence to you.

Do you think I would have survived all these years if I had taken part in public life, and played the part a good man should play, supporting what was just, and attaching the highest importance to it, as is right? Don't you believe it, men of Athens. Nor would anyone else in the world have survived. As for me, it will be clear that, throughout my life, if I have done anything at all in public life, my character is as I have described—and in private life the same. I was never at any time prepared to tolerate injustice in anyone at all—certainly not in any of the people my critics say were my pupils.

I have never been anyone's teacher. Equally, I never said no to anyone, young or old, who wanted to listen to me talking and pursuing my quest. Nor do I talk if I am paid, and not talk if I am not paid. I make myself available to rich and poor alike, so b   they can question me and listen, if anyone feels like it, to what I say in reply. And if any of these people turns out well or badly, I cannot legitimately be held responsible; I neither promised any knowledge, ever, to any of them, nor did I teach them. If anyone ever claims to have learnt or heard anything from me privately, beyond what anyone else learnt or heard, I can assure you he is lying.

c   Why then do some people like spending so much of their time with me? You have heard the answer to that, men of Athens; I have told you the whole truth. They like hearing the cross-examination of those who think they are wise when they are not. After all, it is quite entertaining. For me, as I say, this is a task imposed by god, through prophecies and dreams and in every way in which divine destiny has ever imposed any task on a man.

All this is the truth, men of Athens, and easily tested. If I really am a bad influ-
d   ence on some of the young, and have been a bad influence on others in the past, and if some of them, as they have grown older, have realised that I gave them bad advice at some point when they were young, they ought to come forward now, I'd have thought, to accuse me and punish me. And if they weren't prepared to do so themselves, some of the members of their families—fathers, brothers, or other close relatives—ought
e   now to remember, if those close to them came to some harm at my hands, and want to punish me. Certainly I can see plenty of them here today—Crito there, for a start, my contemporary and fellow-demesman, the father of Critobulus, who's here too. Then there's Lysanias from the deme of Sphettos, the father of Aeschines here; or indeed Antiphon over there, from Cephisus, the father of Epigenes.

Then there are the ones whose brothers have spent their time in my company:
34   Nicostratus the son of Theozotides, the brother of Theodotus—Theodotus of course is dead, so he couldn't have put any pressure on his brother; and I can see Paralius, the son of Demodocus, whose brother was Theages. Then there's Adeimantus I can see, the son of Ariston, whose brother is Plato here; or Aiantodorus, whose brother Apollodorus is present also.

There are plenty more I could name for you. Ideally, Meletus would have called some of them himself to give evidence during his speech. However, in case he forgot at the time, let him call them now—I give up my place to him—and let him say if he has any evidence of that kind.

It's the exact opposite, gentlemen. You'll find they're all on my side—although
b   I'm a bad influence, although I harm their relatives, as Meletus and Anytus claim. I can see why the actual victims of my influence might have some reason to be on my side; but those who have not been influenced, the older generation, their relatives, what reason do they have for being on my side, other than the correct and valid reason that they know Meletus is lying, and I am telling the truth?

Well, there we are, gentlemen. That, and perhaps a bit more along the same lines,
c   is roughly what I might have to say in my defence. There may possibly be those among you who find it irritating, when you remember your own experience; you may, in a trial less important than this one, have begged and pleaded with the jury, with many tears, bringing your own children, and many others among your family and friends, up here to arouse as much sympathy as possible; whereas I refuse to do any of these things—even though I am, as it probably seems to you, in the greatest danger of all.

d   Thoughts like this could make some of you feel a little antagonistic towards me. For just this reason, you might get angry, and let anger influence your vote. If any of you does feel like this—I am sure you don't, but if you did—I think I might fairly say to you: "Of course I too have a family, my good friend. I do not come, in Homer's famous words, 'from oak or rock.' No, I was born of men, so I do have a family, and sons, men of Athens, three of them. One is not quite grown-up, the other two still boys. All the same, I am not going to bring any of them up here and beg you to acquit me."

Why will I not do any of these things? Not out of obstinacy, men of Athens, nor out of contempt for you. And whether or not I am untroubled by the thought of death is beside the point. No, it's a question of what is fitting—for me, for you, and for the whole city. I don't think it's right for me to do any of these things, at my age and with the reputation I have. It may be justified or unjustified, but there's a prevailing belief that Socrates is in some way different from other people.

If those of you who seem to be outstanding in wisdom or courage, or any other quality, were to behave like this, it would be deplorable. Yet this is just the way I *have* seen men behaving when they are brought to trial. They may seem to be men of some distinction, but still they act in the most extraordinary way; they seem to think it will be a terrible disaster for them if they are put to death—as if they'd be immortal if you didn't put them to death. I think they bring disgrace on the city. A visitor to our country might imagine that in Athens people of outstanding character, those whom the Athenians themselves single out from among themselves for positions of office and other distinctions—that these men are no better than women.

Such behaviour, men of Athens, is not right for those of you with any kind of reputation at all; and if we who are on trial behave like that, you should not let us get away with it. You should make one thing absolutely clear, which is that you are much more ready to convict a defendant who stages one of these hysterical scenes, and makes our city an object of ridicule, than a defendant who behaves with decorum.

Quite apart from what is fitting, gentlemen, I think there is no justice, either, in begging favours from the jury, or being acquitted by begging; justice requires instruction and persuasion. The juryman does not sit there for the purpose of handing out justice as a favour; he sits there to decide what justice is. He has not taken an oath to do a favour to anyone he takes a fancy to, but rather to reach a verdict in accordance with the laws. So *we* should not encourage in you the habit of breaking your oath, nor should *you* allow the habit to develop. If we did, we should neither of us be showing any respect for the gods.

Do not ask me, therefore, men of Athens, to conduct myself towards you in a way which I regard as contrary to right, justice and religion—least of all, surely, when I am being accused of impiety by Meletus here. After all, if I did persuade you and coerce you, by my begging, despite your oath, then clearly I *would* be teaching you to deny the existence of the gods; my whole defence would simply amount to accusing myself of not recognising the gods. And that is far from being the case. I do recognise them, men of Athens, as none of my accusers does, and I entrust to you and to god the task of reaching a verdict in my case in whatever way will be best both for me and for you.

*   *   *

If I am not upset, men of Athens, at what has just happened—your finding me guilty— there are a number of reasons. In particular, the result was not unexpected; in fact, I'm surprised by the final number of votes on either side. Personally, I was expecting a large margin, not a narrow one; as it is, if only thirty votes had gone the other way, apparently I would have been acquitted. Indeed, on Meletus' charge, as I see it, I *have* been acquitted, even as things are. And not just acquitted; it's clear to anyone that if Anytus had not come forward, with Lycon, to accuse me, Meletus would have incurred a fine of a thousand drachmas for not receiving twenty percent of the votes.

So the man proposes the death penalty for me. Very well. What counter-proposal am I to make to you, men of Athens? What I deserve, obviously. And what is that? What do I deserve to suffer or pay, for . . . for what? For not keeping quiet all through my life, for neglecting the things most people devote their lives to: business, family life, holding office—as general, or as leader of the assembly, or in some other capacity—or the alliances and factions which occur in political life. I thought, quite hon-

c   estly, that my sense of right and wrong would not allow me to survive in politics; so I did not pursue a course in which I should have been no use either to you or to myself, but rather one in which I could give help to each one of you privately—the greatest help possible, as I claim. That is the direction I took. I tried to persuade each of you not to give any thought at all to his own affairs until he had first given some thought to himself, and tried to make himself as good and wise as possible; not to give any thought to the affairs of the city without first giving some thought to the city itself; and to observe the same priorities in other areas as well.

d   What then do I deserve for behaving like this? Something good, men of Athens, if I am really supposed to make a proposal in accordance with what I deserve. And what's more, a good of a kind which is some use to me. What then *is* of use to a poor man, your benefactor, who needs free time in which to advise you? There can't be anything more useful to a man of this sort, men of Athens, than to be given free meals at the public expense; this is much more use to him than it is to any Olympic victor among you, if one of you wins the horse race, or the two-horse or four-horse chariot

e   race. The Olympic winner makes you *seem* to be happy; I make you really happy. He doesn't need the food; I do need it. So if I must propose a penalty based on justice, on

37   what I deserve, then that's what I propose—free meals at the public expense.

Here again, I suppose, in the same sort of way as when I was talking about appeals to pity and pleas for mercy, you may think I speak as I do out of sheer obstinacy. But it's not obstinacy, men of Athens; it's like this. I myself am convinced that I don't knowingly do wrong to anyone in the world, but I can't persuade you of that; we haven't had enough time to talk to one another. Mind you, if it were the custom here, as it is in other places, to decide cases involving the death penalty over several days rather than in one day, I believe you would have been persuaded. As it is, it was not

b   easy in a short time to overcome the strong prejudice against me.

But if I am convinced that I don't do wrong to anyone else, I am certainly not going to do wrong to myself, or speak against myself—saying I deserve something bad, and proposing some such penalty for myself. Why should I? Through fear of undergoing the penalty Meletus proposes, when I claim not to know whether it is good or bad? Should I, in preference to that, choose one of the things I know perfectly well to be bad, and propose that as a penalty?

c   Imprisonment? What is the point of living in prison, and being the slave of those in the prison service at any particular time? A fine? And be imprisoned until I pay? That's the same as the first suggestion, since I haven't any money to pay a fine. Should I propose exile? I suppose you might accept that. But I'd have to be very devoted to life, men of Athens, to lose the power of rational thought so completely, and not be able to work out what would happen. If you, my fellow-citizens, couldn't stand my talk

d   and my conversation, if you found them too boring and irritating, which is why you now want to be rid of them, will people in some other country find it any easier to put up with them? Don't you believe it, men of Athens.

A fine life I should lead in exile, a man of my age—moving and being driven from city to city. I've no doubt that wherever I go, the young will listen to me, the way they do here. If I tell them to go away, they will send me into exile of their own accord,

bringing pressure to bear on their elders; if I don't tell them to go away, their fathers   e
and relatives will exile me, out of concern for them.

I can imagine someone saying, "How about keeping your mouth shut, Socrates,
and leading a quiet life? Can't you please go into exile, and live like that?" Of all
things, this is the hardest point on which to convince some of you. If I say that it is disobeying god, and that for this reason I can't lead a quiet life, you won't believe me—   38
you'll think I'm using that as an excuse. If on the other hand I say that really the greatest good in a man's life is this, to be each day discussing human excellence and the
other subjects you hear me talking about, examining myself and other people, and that
the unexamined life isn't worth living—if I say this, you will believe me even less.

All the same, the situation is as I describe it, gentlemen—hard though it is to   b
convince you. Equally, for myself, I can't get used to the idea that I deserve anything
bad. If I had any money, I would propose as large a fine as I could afford; that would-
n't do me any harm. As it is, I have no money, unless you are willing to have me propose an amount I *could* afford. I suppose I could pay you something like a hundred
drachmas of silver, if you like. So that is the amount I propose.

Plato here, men of Athens—and Crito and Critobulus and Apollodorus—tell me
to propose a penalty of three thousand drachmas; they say they guarantee it. I propose
that amount, therefore, and they will offer full security to you for the money.

*   *   *

Despite refuting his accusers (as recorded in the *Apology*), Socrates was found guilty of
impiety toward the gods and of corrupting the youth. He was sentenced to die by drinking
the poison hemlock. (*Corbis-Bettmann*)

c   For just a small gain in time, men of Athens, you will now have the reputation and responsibility, among those who want to criticise the city, of having put to death
Socrates, that wise man—they will *say* I am wise, the people who want to blame you,
even though I am not. If you'd waited a little, you could have had what you wanted
without lifting a finger. You can see what age I am—far advanced in years, and close
to death.

    I say that not to all of you, but to those who voted for the death penalty. And I
d   have something else to say to the same people. You may think, men of Athens, that I
have lost my case through inability to make the kind of speech I *could* have used to
persuade you, had I thought it right to do and say absolutely anything to secure my acquittal. Far from it. I have lost my case, not for want of a speech, but for want of effrontery and shamelessness, for refusing to make to you the kind of speech you most
enjoy listening to. You'd like to have heard me lamenting and bewailing, and doing
e   and saying all sorts of other things which are beneath my dignity, in my opinion—the
kind of things you've grown used to hearing from other people.

    I did not think it right, when I was speaking, to demean myself through fear of
danger, nor do I now regret conducting my defence in the way I did. I had much rather
defend myself like this, and be put to death, than behave in the way I have described,
and go on living. Neither in the courts, nor in time of war, is it right—either for me or
39 for anyone else—to devote one's efforts simply to avoiding death at all costs.

    In battle it is often clear that death can be escaped, by dropping your weapons
and throwing yourself on the mercy of your pursuers—and in any kind of danger there
are all sorts of other devices for avoiding death, if you can bring yourself not to mind
what you do or say. There's no difficulty in *that,* gentlemen, in escaping death. What is
much harder is avoiding wickedness, since wickedness runs faster than death. So now,
b   not surprisingly, I, who am old and slow, have been overtaken by the slower of the
two. My accusers, being swift and keen, have been overtaken by the faster, by wickedness. Now I am departing, to pay the penalty of death inflicted by you. But they have
already incurred the penalty, inflicted by truth, for wickedness and injustice. I accept
my sentence, as they do theirs. I suppose that's probably how it was bound to turn
out—and I have no complaints.

c   Having dealt with that, I now wish to make you a prophecy, those of you who
voted for my condemnation. I am at that point where people are most inclined to make
prophecies—which is when they are just about to die. To you gentlemen who have put
me to death, I say that retribution will come to you, directly after my death—retribution far worse, god knows, than the death penalty which you have inflicted on me.

    You have acted as you have today in the belief that you will avoid having to sub-
mit your lives to examination, but you will find the outcome is just the opposite; that is
my prediction. There will be more people now to examine you—the ones I have so far
been keeping in check without your realising it. They will be harder to deal with, being
d   so much younger, and you will be more troubled by them. If you think that by putting
men to death you can stop people criticising you for not living your lives in the right
way, you are miscalculating badly. As a way of escape, this is neither effective nor
creditable; the best and simplest way lies not in weeding out other people, but in making oneself as good a person as possible.

    That is my prophecy to you who voted for my condemnation, and now I am pre-
e   pared to let you go. To those who voted for my acquittal I'd like to make a few remarks about what has just happened, while the magistrates get on with the formalities,
and it is not yet time for me to go where I must go to die. Please keep me company,
gentlemen, for this little time; there's no reason why we shouldn't talk to one another

while it is permitted. I regard you as my friends, and so to you I am prepared to explain the significance of today's outcome.

Gentlemen of the jury—since you I properly *can* call jurymen—a remarkable   40 thing has happened to me. The prophetic voice I have got so used to, my supernatural voice, has always in the past been at my elbow, opposing me even in matters of little importance, if I was about to take a false step. You can see for yourselves the situation I'm now in. You might think—and this is how it is generally regarded—it was the ultimate misfortune. Yet the sign from god did not oppose my leaving home this morning,   b nor my appearance here in court, nor was there any point in my speech when it stopped me saying what I was just about to say.

Often in the past, when I have been talking, the sign has stopped me in full flow; this time it has not opposed me at any stage in the whole proceedings—either in what I have done or in what I have said. What do I take to be the reason for this? I'll tell you. The chances are that what has happened to me here is a good thing, and that it is impossible for those of us who think death is an evil to understand it correctly. I have strong evidence for this. The sign I know so well would unquestionably have opposed me, if things had not been going to turn out all right for me.   c

There is another reason for being confident that death is a good thing. Look at it like this. Death is one of two things; either it is like the dead person being nothing at all, and having no consciousness of anything at all; or, as we are told, it is actually some sort of change, a journey of the soul from this place to somewhere different. Suppose it is a total absence of consciousness—like sleep, when the sleeper isn't even dreaming. Then death would be a marvellous bonus. At least, I certainly think that if a   d man had to choose the night on which he slept so soundly that he did not even dream, and if he had to compare all the other nights and days of his life with that night, if he had to think carefully about it, and then say how many days and nights he had spent in his life that were better and more enjoyable than that night—I think that not just a private individual, but even the great king of Persia could count these dreamless nights on   e the fingers of one hand compared with the other days and nights. If death is something like that, I call it a bonus. After all, the whole of time, seen in this way, seems no longer than a single night.

If, on the other hand, death is a kind of journey from here to somewhere different, and what we're told about all the dead being there is true, what greater good could there be than that, gentlemen of the jury? Imagine arriving in the other world, getting   41 away from the people here who claim to be judges, and finding real judges, the ones who are said to decide cases there—Minos, Rhadamanthys, Aeacus, Triptolemus, and others of the demigods who acted with justice in their own lives. Wouldn't that be a worthwhile journey?

Or again, what would any of you give to join Orpheus and Musaeus, Hesiod and Homer? Personally, I am quite prepared to die many times over, if these stories are true. For me at least, time spent there would be wonderful—I'd keep meeting people   b like Palamedes, or Aias the son of Telamon, or any other of the ancients who died as a result of an unjust verdict; I could compare my own experience with theirs. That would be entertaining, I imagine. Best of all, I could spend my time questioning and examining people there, just as I do people here, to find out which of them is wise, and which thinks he is wise but isn't.

What would you give, men of the jury, to interview the man who led the great expedition to Troy—or Odysseus, or Sisyphus, or thousands of others one could mention, men and women? It would be an unimaginable pleasure to talk to them there, to   c enjoy their company, and question them. They certainly can't put you to death there for asking questions. They are better off than us in many ways—and not least because they are now immune to death for the rest of time, if what we are told is true.

You too, men of the jury, must not be apprehensive about death. You must regard one thing at least as certain—that no harm can come to a good man either in his life or after his death; what happens to him is not a matter of indifference to the gods.

d   Nor has my present situation arisen purely by chance; it is clear to me that it was better for me to die now and be released from my task. That's why my sign didn't at any point dissuade me, and why I am not in the least angry with those who voted against me, or with my accusers. Admittedly that wasn't their reason for voting against me, and accusing me; they thought they were doing me some harm. We *can* blame them for that.

However, I do have one request to make. It concerns my sons. When they grow

e   up, gentlemen, get your own back on them, if you think they are more interested in money—or in anything else—than in goodness, by annoying them in exactly the same way as I annoyed you. If they think they amount to something when they don't, then criticise them, as I criticised you. Tell them they are not giving any thought to the things that matter, and that they think they amount to something when they are worth

42   nothing. If you do this, I shall myself have been fairly treated by you—and so will my sons.

I must stop. It is time for us to go—me to my death, you to your lives. Which of us goes to the better fate, only god knows.

CRITO

---

43   SOCRATES: What are you doing here at this time, Crito? Isn't it still early?

CRITO: Yes, it is.

SOCRATES: How early, exactly?

CRITO: It's not yet started to get light.

SOCRATES: I'm surprised the warder didn't refuse to answer your knock.

CRITO: He's become something of a friend of mine, Socrates, what with my coming here so often. Besides, I've done him a bit of a favour.

SOCRATES: Have you just arrived, or have you been here some time?

CRITO: Quite some time.

b   SOCRATES: Then why on earth didn't you wake me up? What were you doing just sitting there beside me in silence?

CRITO: I wouldn't have dreamt of it, Socrates. For my part, I wouldn't choose to be in this state of sleeplessness and misery; and for some time now it has astonished me to see how soundly you sleep. I deliberately didn't wake you because I wanted you to enjoy your rest. It has often struck me in the past, throughout my life in fact, how lucky you are in your temperament—and it strikes me much more forcibly in your present misfortune. You bear it so easily and calmly.

SOCRATES: Yes, Crito, I do. It wouldn't make much sense for a man my age to get upset at the prospect of dying.

CRITO: Other people your age, Socrates, find themselves in similar predicaments;   c
their age doesn't stop them getting upset at their misfortune.

SOCRATES: That's true. Anyway, why *have* you come so early?

CRITO: To bring news, Socrates, bad news. Not bad for you, as far as I can see, but for me and all your friends it is bad and hard to bear; and I think I shall find it as hard to bear as anybody.

SOCRATES: What sort of news? Has the boat from Delos arrived—the one my exe-   d
cution has been waiting for?

CRITO: It hasn't actually arrived, but I think it will today, judging by the reports of some people who've just come from Sunium. It was there when they left. It's clear from what they said that it will arrive today, and so tomorrow, Socrates, you will be forced to end your life.

SOCRATES: Well, Crito, if that is how the gods want it, I hope it will all turn out for the best. All the same, I don't think it will come today.

CRITO: What is that based on?   44

SOCRATES: I'll tell you. My death, I assume, is to take place on the day after the ship arrives.

CRITO: Yes. At least, that's what the prison authorities say.

SOCRATES: Then I think it will come tomorrow, not today. That's based on a dream I had last night, just before I woke up. So perhaps it was lucky you didn't wake me.

CRITO: What was the dream?

SOCRATES: I saw a woman, fair and beautiful, in a white cloak. She came up to   b
me, and called my name. "Socrates," she said, "On the third day shall you come to fer-
tile Phthia."

CRITO: A strange dream, Socrates.

SOCRATES: Clear enough, though, I think, Crito.

CRITO: Only too clear, I'm afraid. Now listen, Socrates, it's not too late, even now, to do as I say and escape. For me, if you are put to death, it is a double disaster. Quite apart from losing a friend such as I shall never find again, there will also be many who will think, those who don't know the two of us well, that I had the chance to   c
save you if I'd been prepared to spend some money, and that I wasn't interested in doing so.

Can you think of a worse reputation than being thought to value money more highly than friends? Most people will never believe that it was you yourself who re-fused to leave here, and that we strongly encouraged you to do so.

SOCRATES: Really, Crito, why should we care so much about what "most people" believe? The best people, who are the ones we should worry about more, will realise that things were done in the way they actually were done.

CRITO: Yet you can see that we have no choice, Socrates, but to care about what   d
most people think as well. The present situation is a clear example of how the many can injure us in ways which are not trivial, but just about as great as can be, if they are given the wrong impression about someone.

SOCRATES: If only the many *could* do us the greatest injuries, Crito. That would mean they were capable of doing us the greatest good as well, which would be excel-lent. As it is, they're incapable of doing either. They have no power to make a man ei-ther wise or foolish; nor do they care what effect they have.

CRITO: I dare say you are right. But tell me something, Socrates. Are you worried   e
about me and the rest of your friends? Do you think, if you leave here, that we shall get

45 into trouble with the people who make a living out of bringing private prosecutions, because we smuggled you out of here? Do you think we shall be forced to forfeit all our property, or pay a very large fine, and possibly undergo some further penalty in addition?

If something like that is what you are afraid of, don't give it another thought. We are in duty bound to run this risk to save you—that goes without saying—and even greater risks, if need be. Listen to me. Don't say "no."

SOCRATES: It *is* something I worry about, Crito. That, and many other things besides.

CRITO: Well then, do not be afraid on that score. There are people prepared, for not a very large sum of money, to save you and get you out of here. And apart from them, can't you see how easily bought they are, the men who make their living out of prosecutions? It wouldn't need a lot of money to take care of them. You have my re-

b sources at your disposal; that should be plenty, I imagine. And if you're worried about me, and feel you shouldn't spend my money, look at the people we've got here who are not Athenians, who are ready to spend theirs. One of them, Simmias the Theban, has actually brought enough money for just this purpose; Cebes too is fully prepared, and so are many others.

So as I say, you should not let these fears stop you saving yourself; and do not let it be an objection, as you claimed in court, that you would not know what to do with yourself if you went into exile. There are lots of places you can go where they'll be

c glad to see you; if you want to go to Thessaly, for example, my family has friends there who will be delighted to see you, and who will give you sanctuary. Nobody in Thessaly will give you any trouble.

Apart from that, Socrates, it is actually wrong, in my opinion, to sacrifice yourself, as you are proposing to do, when you could escape. You seem to be voluntarily choosing for yourself the kind of fate your enemies would have chosen for you—and *did* choose for you when they were trying to destroy you. Worse still, I think, is the be-

d trayal of your own sons, when there is nothing to stop you bringing them up and educating them—and yet you are going to go away and leave them, and for all you care they can turn out how they will. They will have, in all probability, the kind of life orphans generally have when they lose their parents.

No. Either you shouldn't have children, or you should play your part, and go through with the labour of raising and educating them. You seem to me to be taking the easy way out. What you should do is choose what a decent and courageous man would choose—you who claim to have been concerned with human goodness all your

e life. Personally, I am ashamed both for you and for those of us who are your friends. I think this whole business of yours will be thought to be the result of some lack of resolution on our part—first of all the fact that the case came to court when it needn't have

46 done, then the actual conduct of the case in court, and now this, as the final absurdity of the whole affair, that we shall be thought to have missed the opportunity—through our own cowardice and lack of resolution, since we didn't save you, nor did you save yourself, though it was possible, and within your power, with even a modest amount of help from us. Don't let all this be a humiliation, Socrates, both for you and for us, in addition to being an evil.

Think it over—or rather, the time for thinking it over is past, you should by now have thought it over—there is only one course of action. The whole thing must be done this coming night. If we wait any longer, it will be impossible; it will not be an option any longer. I cannot urge you too strongly, Socrates. Listen to me. Do as I say.

SOCRATES: My dear Crito, your enthusiasm is most commendable, so long as there is some justification for it. Otherwise, the greater your enthusiasm, the more out

of place it is. We'd better look into whether this is the right thing to do or not. It has   b
been my practice, not just now but always, to trust, of all the guides at my disposal,
only the principle which on reflection seems most appropriate. I cannot now throw
overboard principles which I have put forward in the past, simply because of what has
happened to me. They still seem to me very much the same as they always did; I still
give pride of place to, and value, the same principles as before. Unless we can find
some better principle than these to put forward on this occasion, you can be quite sure I
am not going to agree with you, however many bugbears the power of the many pro-   c
duces to scare us with—as if we were children—letting loose on us its imprisonments,
its death sentences, and its fines.

    What then is the best way of looking into this question? Why don't we start by
going back to the argument you put forward based on what people will think? Were we
right or wrong, all those times, when we said we should listen to some opinions, but
not to others? Or were we right before I was sentenced to death, only for it now to become clear that it was a waste of breath, spoken simply for the sake of having something to say, and that it was really juvenile fantasy? Personally, Crito, I should very   d
much like to carry out a joint enquiry with you, to see whether the principle will seem
rather different to me, now that I am in this situation, or whether it will seem the
same—and whether we are going to forget about it, or follow it.

    The principle so often put forward, I think, by those among us who thought they
knew what they were talking about, was the one I referred to just now—that of the
opinions held by men, we should regard some as important, and others not. Seriously,   e
Crito, don't you think this is a sound principle? You are, barring accidents, not in the
position of having to die tomorrow, so you shouldn't be influenced by the present situ-   47
ation. Examine the question. Don't you think it a sound principle that we should not
value all human opinions equally, but should value some highly, and others not? And
the same with the people who hold the opinions. We should not value all of them, but
should value some, and not others. What do you think? Isn't this a sound principle?

    CRITO: Yes, it is.

    SOCRATES: We should value the good opinions, but not the bad ones?

    CRITO: Yes.

    SOCRATES: Aren't good opinions the opinions of the wise, whereas bad opinions
are those of the foolish?

    CRITO: Obviously.

    SOCRATES: Well then, what was the kind of analogy we used to employ? If a man   b
is taking physical exercise, and this is what he is interested in, does he listen to the
praise and criticism and opinion of just anyone, or only of one person—the person who
is in fact a medical expert or a physical training instructor?

    CRITO: Only of one person.

    SOCRATES: So he should worry about the criticisms, and welcome the praises, of
this one person, but not those of the many?

    CRITO: Clearly he should.

    SOCRATES: In what he does, then—in the exercise he takes, in what he eats and
drinks—he should be guided by the one man, the man in charge, the expert, rather than
by everyone else.

    CRITO: That is so.

    SOCRATES: All right. If he defies the one man, and doesn't value his opinion and   c
his recommendations, but does value those of the many, those who are not experts,
won't he do himself some harm?

    CRITO: Of course he will.

SOCRATES: What is this harm? What is its extent? What part of the man who de-fies the expert does it attack?

CRITO: His body, obviously. That is what it damages.

SOCRATES: Quite right. Well then, is it the same also in other situations, Crito, to save us going through all the examples—and especially with right and wrong, foul and

d fair, good and bad, the things we are now discussing? Should we follow the opinion of the many, and fear that, or the opinion of the one man, if we can find an expert on the subject? Should we respect and fear this one man more than all the rest put together? And if we don't follow his advice, we shall injure and do violence to that part which we have often agreed improves with justice and is damaged by injustice. Or is this all wrong?

CRITO: No, I think it is right, Socrates.

SOCRATES: Very well. Take that part of us which improves with health, and is damaged by disease. If we ruin it by following advice other than that of the experts, is

e life worth living once that part is injured? This is the body, of course, isn't it?

CRITO: Yes.

SOCRATES: Is life worth living, then, if our body is in poor condition and injured?

CRITO: Certainly not.

SOCRATES: How about the part of us which is attacked by injustice, and helped by justice? Is life worth living when that is injured? Or do we regard it as less important

48 than the body, this part of us—whichever of our faculties it is—the part to which jus-tice and injustice belong?

CRITO: No, we certainly don't.

SOCRATES: More important, then?

CRITO: Much more important.

SOCRATES: In that case, my dear friend, we should not pay the slightest attention, as you suggested we should, to what most people will say about us. We should listen only to the expert on justice and injustice, to the one man, and to the truth itself. So you were wrong, for a start, in one of your recommendations—when you proposed that we should be concerned about the opinion of the many on the subject of justice, right, good, and their opposites. "Ah!" you might say, "but the many are liable to put us to death."

b CRITO: That too is obviously true. You might well say that, Socrates. You are quite right.

SOCRATES: All the same, my learned friend, I think the principle we have elabo-rated still has the same force as it did. And what about this second principle? Tell me, does our belief—that the important thing is not being alive, but living a good life—still hold good, or not?

CRITO: It does still hold good.

SOCRATES: And that when we're talking about a life, good, right, and just are one and the same thing—does that still hold good, or not?

CRITO: It does.

c SOCRATES: Well then, in the light of the points we have agreed, we must look into the question whether it is right, or not right, for me to attempt to leave here without the permission of the Athenians. If it appears to be right, let us make the attempt; other-wise let us forget about it. As for the considerations you raise—questions of expense, public opinion, the upbringing of children—I suspect that these, Crito, are really the concerns of those who readily put people to death, and would as readily bring them back to life again, if they could—for absolutely no reason. I am, of course, talking about the many.

For us, though, the thing is to follow where the argument leads us, and I rather think the only question we need ask is the one we asked just now: shall we act rightly if we give our money, and our thanks, to those who will arrange my escape from here?   d
Shall we ourselves be acting rightly in arranging the escape, and allowing it to be arranged? Or shall we in fact be acting wrongly if we do all these things? If this is clearly the wrong way for us to behave, then I'm pretty sure that compared with the danger of acting wrongly, we should not take into account the certainty either of being put to death if we stay put and accept things quietly, or of suffering anything else at all.

CRITO: I am sure you are right, Socrates. You decide what we should do.

SOCRATES: Let us look into it together, my friend. And if you want to raise an ob-   e
jection at any point while I'm talking, then raise it, and I will listen to you. Otherwise, my fine friend, stop repeating the same thing over and over again—that I should leave here in defiance of the wishes of the Athenians. I attach great importance to acting with your agreement, rather than against your wishes.

Now, think about the starting-point of our enquiry. Do you regard it as satisfac-   49
tory? And when you answer the question, mind you say what you really think.

CRITO: I will try.

SOCRATES: Do we agree that we should never deliberately do wrong, or should we sometimes do wrong, and sometimes not? Is wrong-doing absolutely contrary to what is good and fine, as has often been agreed among us in the past? Or have all those things we once agreed on become, in these last few days, so much water under the bridge? Did we, grown men and at the age we were, Crito, discuss things so enthusias-   b
tically with one another, without realising we were no better than children? Or is what we said then more true now than ever? Whether "most people" agree or not, and whether we have to undergo hardships more severe even than these—or possibly less severe—isn't wrong-doing in fact, for the person who does it, wholly evil and bad? Is this what we say, or not?

CRITO: It is.

SOCRATES: A man should never do wrong, then.

CRITO: No, he should not.

SOCRATES: So even if he is wronged, he should not do wrong in return, as most people think, since he ought not *ever* to do wrong.

CRITO: Apparently not.   c

SOCRATES: What about harming people, Crito? Should a man do that, or not?

CRITO: I suppose not, Socrates.

SOCRATES: How about harming people in retaliation, if he is injured by them first—which is what most people say he should do? Is that right or wrong?

CRITO: Completely wrong.

SOCRATES: And that, I imagine, is because injuring people is the same thing as doing them wrong.

CRITO: That is right.

SOCRATES: So he should not do wrong to anyone or injure them, in retaliation, no matter how he has been treated by them. And if you say "yes" to that, Crito, make sure you are not saying "yes" against what you really think. I realise not many people ac-   d
cept this view—or ever will accept it. As a result, there is no common ground between those who do accept it and those who do not; each side necessarily regards the opinions of the other side with contempt. So you too must think very hard about it. Are you on our side? Do you agree with us in accepting this view, and shall we base our argu-   e
ment on the premise that it is never legitimate to do wrong to people, nor do them wrong in retaliation, nor, if one is injured, defend oneself by harming them in return?

Or do you disagree? Do you reject the original premise? Personally, I have held this view a long time, and I still hold it now. If you have been holding some other view, tell me; instruct me. But if you stand by what we said earlier, then listen to what follows from it.

CRITO: I do stand by it, and I do agree with you. Tell me what follows.

SOCRATES: Very well, I will tell you. Or rather, I'll ask you. If a man makes an agreement—a fair agreement—with someone, should he fulfil his side of the agreement, or should he try to get out of it?

CRITO: He should fulfil it.

50   SOCRATES: Then see what follows from that. If we leave here without persuading the city to change its mind, are we doing harm to anyone or anything—those we have least cause to injure—or not? Are we standing by our agreement—our fair agreement—or not?

CRITO: I can't answer your question, Socrates. I don't understand it.

SOCRATES: Look at it like this. Imagine that, just as we were about to run away, or whatever we are supposed to call it, from here, the laws of Athens and the state of Athens appeared before us, and said: "Tell me, Socrates, what are you trying to do?
b   Aren't you simply trying, by this action you are embarking on, to destroy both us, the laws, and the entire city, as far as lies within your power? Do you think it possible for a city to continue to exist, and not sink without trace, if the verdicts of its courts have no force, if they are rendered invalid, and nullified, by private citizens?"

What shall we say, Crito, to these questions and others like them? There's a lot that could be said, especially by the public advocate, in defence of this law we are trying to do away with—the law which lays down that verdicts arrived at in the courts
c   should be binding. Shall we say to the laws, "The city wronged us. It did not reach its verdict fairly?" Shall we say that, or what?

CRITO: Yes, we most emphatically should say that, Socrates.

SOCRATES: Suppose then the laws say, "Was *that* what was agreed between us and you, Socrates? Or was it to abide by the verdicts the city arrives at in its courts?" And if we expressed surprise at their question, they might add: "Do not be surprised by
d   our question, Socrates. Answer it. You have had enough practice at question-and-answer. Come on, then. What principle do you appeal to, against us and the city, to allow you to try and destroy us? Did we not bring you into existence, for a start? Was it not through us that your father married your mother, and fathered you? Tell us, then, those of us who are the laws governing marriage, have you some criticism of us? Is there something wrong with us?"
e   "I have no criticism," I should have to reply.

"All right, then. How about your upbringing and education after you were born? How about the laws to do with those? Did we not give your father the right instructions—those of us whose job it is to attend to this—when we told him to educate you by means of the arts and physical training?"

"No, they were the right instructions," I would say.

"Very well. Since you were born, and brought up, and educated, under our protection, you were our offspring and our slave—both you yourself and your parents. Can you deny that, for a start? And if that is so, do you think that justice gives equivalent rights to you and to us? If we decide to do something to you, do you think you have the right to do it to us in return?

"There was no equality of rights as between you and your father or your master,
51   if you had one, entitling you to do to him in retaliation what he did to you—to answer

him back if he spoke abusively to you, or beat him in retaliation if he beat you, or anything else like that. Will it then be legitimate for you to retaliate against your country and its laws? And is the result that if we decide to destroy you, because we think it right to do so, you in your turn, to the best of your ability, will set about destroying us, the laws, and your country, in retaliation? Will you claim that in acting like this you are doing what is right, you who are truly so concerned about human excellence? Are you so clever that you fail to realise that your country is an object of greater value, an   b
object of greater respect and reverence, and altogether more important, both among gods and among men, if they have any sense, than your mother and your father and all the rest of your ancestors put together? That you should revere your country, submit to it, mollify it when it is angry with you—more than you would your father—and either persuade it to change its mind, or do what it tells you? That you should quietly accept whatever treatment it ordains you should receive—beating, perhaps, or imprison-   c
ment—or if it takes you to war, to be wounded or killed, that is what you should do, and that is what is right? That you should not give way, or retreat, or abandon your position, that in war, in the lawcourts, or anywhere else, you should do what your city and your country tells you, or else convince it where justice naturally lies? And that the use of force, against a mother or a father, is against god's law—still more so the use of force against your country?"

What are we going to say in answer to this, Crito? Shall we say the laws are right, or not?

CRITO: Well, *I* think they are right.

SOCRATES: "Consider, then, Socrates," the laws might perhaps say, "Are we right in saying that you are not justified in embarking on the actions against us which you are now embarking on? We fathered you, brought you up, educated you, gave you and   d
every other citizen a share in every good thing it was in our power to give. And even then, if there is any Athenian who reaches the age of majority, takes a look at his city's constitution, and at us, the laws, and finds we are not to his satisfaction, then by granting him permission we make a public declaration to anyone who wishes that he may take what is his, and go wherever he pleases. If a man chooses to go to one of your colonies, because we and the city are not to his liking, or to leave, emigrate to some other place, and go wherever he wants, with no loss of property, not one of us laws stands in his way, or forbids him.

"To those of you who stay, aware of our way of reaching verdicts in the courts, and of making our other political arrangements, we say that you have now entered into a formal agreement with us, to do what we tell you, and we say that the man who disobeys us is doing wrong in three ways: he is disobeying us who fathered him; he is dis-   e
obeying those who brought him up; and having made an agreement to obey us, he neither obeys, nor tries to make us change our minds, if we are doing something which is not right. When we make him a fair offer, not harshly demanding that he do whatever we order, but allowing him a straight choice, either to make us change our minds, or to   52
do as we say, he does neither. These are the charges, Socrates, to which we claim that you too will render yourself liable, if you do what you are proposing to do—you in particular, more than any of the Athenians."

If I asked them why me in particular, they might perhaps have a justifiable complaint against me in that I, as much as any of the Athenians, really have entered into this agreement with them. They could say, "Socrates, we have convincing evidence to   b
suggest that we and the city *were* to your liking. You could not possibly have spent more of your time living here in Athens than any other Athenian if the place had not

been particularly to your liking; you would not have refused ever to leave the city to see famous places—except Corinth, once—or go anywhere else, unless it was to go somewhere on military service; you never went abroad, as other people do, nor were

c   you seized with a desire to know any other city, or any other laws. No, you were satisfied with us, and with our city. In fact, so strongly did you choose us, and agree to live your life as a citizen under us, that you even produced children in the city. You would not have done that if it had not been to your liking.

"Even at your trial, it was open to you to propose a penalty of exile, if you chose, and do then, with the city's permission, what you are now proposing to do without it. On that occasion you put a brave face on it; you said you didn't mind if you had to die; you preferred, so you said, death to exile. Do not those words now make you feel ashamed? Have you no feeling for us, the laws, as you set about destroying us, and do

d   what the meanest slave might do, trying to run away in breach of the contract and agreement by which you agreed to live your life as a citizen? Answer us this question, for a start: are we right in saying that you have agreed—not just verbally, but by your behaviour—to live your life as a citizen under us? Or are we wrong?"

What are we going to say to this, Crito? Can we do anything but agree?

CRITO: We have no choice, Socrates.

SOCRATES: "Aren't you simply breaking," they might say, "contracts and agree-

e   ments which you have with us? You did not enter into them under compulsion or false pretences. You were not forced to make up your mind on the spur of the moment, but over a period of seventy years, during which you were at liberty to leave, if we were

53 not to your liking, or if you thought the agreement was unfair. You did not choose Sparta or Crete instead, places which you have always described as well-governed; nor did you choose any other city, inside or outside Greece. Even people who are lame, or blind, or crippled in other ways, spend more time away from Athens than you did. *That* is an indication, quite clearly, of how you, more than any of the Athenians, found the city, and us the laws, to your liking. After all, who could find a city to his liking, and not like its laws? And do you now not stand by what you agreed? You will if you take our advice, Socrates. That way you will avoid making yourself ridiculous by leaving the city.

b   "Think about it. If you break this agreement, and put yourself in the wrong in this way, what good will you do yourself or your friends? That your friends will probably have to go into exile as well, be cut off from their city, and forfeit their property, is reasonably clear. And you? Well for a start, if you go to one of the cities nearby, say Thebes or Megara, both of which have good laws, you will come to them, Socrates, as an enemy of their constitution; those who care for their city will look at you with suspi-

c   cion, believing you to be a subverter of the laws. You will also reinforce the opinion of the jury about you. They will decide they did reach the right verdict. After all, there is a strong presumption that a man who subverts the laws will be a corrupting influence on people who are young and foolish.

"Will you then keep away from cities with good laws, and the most civilised part of mankind? If you do, will it be worth your while remaining alive? Or will you spend your time with them? And will you have the nerve, in your conversations with them—

d   what sort of conversations, Socrates? The ones you had here, about human excellence and justice being the most valuable things for mankind, together with custom and the laws? Don't you think the whole idea of Socrates will be clearly seen to be a disgrace? You certainly should.

"Or will you leave this part of the world and go to Thessaly, to Crito's family friends? Up there you will find all sorts of anarchy and self-indulgence. I am sure they would be entertained by the amusing story of your running away from prison in some costume or other—wearing a leather jerkin, perhaps, or one of the other disguises   e favoured by people running away—and altering your appearance. That an old man, in all probability with a small span of life remaining to him, could bring himself to cling to life in this limpet-like way, by transgressing the most important of the laws—will there be no-one who will say this? Perhaps not, if you can manage not to annoy any-one. Otherwise, Socrates, you will have to listen to a lot of unflattering comments about yourself. Are you going to spend your life ingratiating yourself with everyone, being a slave to them? Oh, yes, you will have a whale of a time up there in Thessaly, as if you had emigrated out to dinner in Thessaly. But what, please tell us, will become of   54 all those conversations about justice and other forms of human excellence?

"Or do you want to remain alive for your children's sake, so that you can bring them up and educate them? How do you feel about taking them to Thessaly, and bring-ing them up and educating them there, turning them into foreigners, so you can give them that privilege as well? If not, if they are brought up here, will they be any better brought up and educated because you are alive and separated from them? Your friends will be looking after them. Will they look after them if you go to Thessaly to live, and not look after them if you go to the next world? If those who claim to be your friends   b are any use at all, of course they will not.

"No, Socrates, obey us who brought you up. Do not regard your children, or life, or anything at all, as more important than justice; you do not want, when you come to the other world, to have to defend yourself on these charges to the rulers there. Neither in this world does it seem to be better, or more just or more godfearing, for you or any of your friends, if you behave like this; nor, when you come to the next world, will it be better for you there. As it is, you go there, if you do go, as one wronged—not by us,   c the laws, but by men. If on the other hand you depart, after so shamefully returning wrong for wrong, and injury for injury, breaking your own agreement and contract with us, and injuring those whom you had least cause to injure—yourself, your friends, your country, and us—then we shall be angry with you while you are alive, and in the next world our brothers, the laws in Hades, will not receive you kindly, since they will   d know that you tried, to the best of your ability, to destroy us. So do not let Crito per-suade you to follow his advice rather than ours."

That, I assure you, Crito, my very dear friend, is what I think I hear them saying, just as those gripped by religious fervour think they hear the pipes; the sound of their words rings in my head, and stops me hearing anything else. Be in no doubt. As far as I can see at the moment, if you disagree with them, you will speak in vain. All the same, though, if you think it will do any good, then speak.

CRITO: Socrates, I have nothing to say.   e

SOCRATES: Then forget about it, Crito. Let us act in the way god points out to us.

PHAEDO

Characters

Phaedo (The Narrator)
Apollodorus
Cebes
Echecrates
Crito
Socrates
Simmias
The Servant of the Eleven
Scene—The Prison of Socrates

57   ECHECRATES: Were you with Socrates yourself, Phaedo, on that day when he drank the poison in the prison, or did you hear the story from someone else?

PHAEDO: I was there myself, Echecrates.

ECHECRATES: Then what was it that our master said before his death, and how did he die? I should be very glad if you would tell me. None of our citizens go very much

b   to Athens now; and no stranger has come from there for a long time who could give us any definite account of these things, except that he drank the poison and died. We could learn nothing beyond that.

58   PHAEDO: Then have you not heard about the trial either, how that went?

ECHECRATES: Yes, we were told of that, and we were rather surprised to find that he did not die till so long after the trial. Why was that, Phaedo?

PHAEDO: It was an accident, Echecrates. The stern of the ship, which the Athenians send to Delos, happened to have been crowned on the day before the trial.

ECHECRATES: And what is this ship?

PHAEDO: It is the ship, as the Athenians say, in which Theseus took the seven

b   youths and the seven maidens to Crete, and saved them from death, and himself was saved. The Athenians made a vow then to Apollo, the story goes, to send a sacred mission to Delos every year, if they should be saved; and from that time to this they have always sent it to the god, every year. They have a law to keep the city pure as soon as the mission begins, and not to execute any sentence of death until the ship has returned

c   from Delos; and sometimes, when it is detained by contrary winds, that is a long while. The sacred mission begins when the priest of Apollo crowns the stern of the ship; and, as I said, this happened to have been done on the day before the trial. That was why Socrates lay so long in prison between his trial and his death.

ECHECRATES: But tell me about his death, Phaedo. What was said and done, and which of his friends were with our master? Or would not the authorities let them be there? Did he die alone?

d   PHAEDO: Oh, no; some of them were there, indeed several.

ECHECRATES: It would be very good of you, if you are not busy, to tell us the whole story as exactly as you can.

Plato, *Phaedo,* translated by F.J. Church (New York: Macmillan/Library of the Liberal Arts, 1951).

PHAEDO: No, I have nothing to do, and I will try to relate it. Nothing is more pleasant to me than to recall Socrates to my mind, whether by speaking of him myself or by listening to others.

ECHECRATES: Indeed, Phaedo, you will have an audience like yourself. But try to tell us everything that happened as precisely as you can.

PHAEDO: Well, I myself was strangely moved on that day. I did not feel that I was   e
being present at the death of a dear friend; I did not pity him, for he seemed to me happy, Echecrates, both in his bearing and in his words, so fearlessly and nobly did he die. I could not help thinking that the gods would watch over him still on his journey to the other world, and that when he arrived there it would be well with him, if it was ever   59
well with any man. Therefore I had scarcely any feeling of pity, as you would expect at such a mournful time. Neither did I feel the pleasure which I usually felt at our philosophical discussions; for our talk was of philosophy. A very singular feeling came over me, a strange mixture of pleasure and of pain, when I remembered that he was presently to die. All of us who were there were in much the same state, laughing and crying by turns, particularly Apollodorus. I think you know the man and his ways.   b

ECHECRATES: Of course I do.

PHAEDO: Well, he did not restrain himself at all, and I myself and the others were greatly agitated too.

ECHECRATES: Who were there, Phaedo?

PHAEDO: Of native Athenians, there was this Apollodorus, and Critobulus, and his father Crito, and Hermogenes, and Epigenes, and Aeschines, and Antisthenes. Then there was Ctesippus the Paeanian, and Menexenus, and some other Athenians. Plato I believe was ill.

ECHECRATES: Were any strangers there?

PHAEDO: Yes, there was Simmias of Thebes, and Cebes, and Phaedondes; and   c
Eucleides and Terpsion from Megara.

ECHECRATES: But Aristippus and Cleombrotus, were they present?

PHAEDO: No, they were not. They were said to be in Aegina.

ECHECRATES: Was anyone else there?

PHAEDO: No, I think that these were all.

ECHECRATES: Then tell us about your conversation.

PHAEDO: I will try to relate the whole story to you from the beginning. On the previous days I and the others had always met in the morning at the court where the   d
trial was held, which was close to the prison; and then we had gone in to Socrates. We used to wait each morning until the prison was opened, conversing, for it was not opened early. When it was opened we used to go in to Socrates, and we generally spent the whole day with him. But on that morning we met earlier than usual; for the evening   e
before we had learned, on leaving the prison, that the ship had arrived from Delos. So we arranged to be at the usual place as early as possible. When we reached the prison, the porter, who generally let us in, came out to us and bade us wait a little, and not to go in until he summoned us himself: "For the Eleven," he said, "are releasing Socrates from his fetters and giving directions for his death today." In no great while he returned and bade us enter. So we went in and found Socrates just released, and Xan-   60
thippe—you know her—sitting by him, holding his child in her arms. When Xanthippe saw us, she wailed aloud, and cried, in her woman's way, "This is the last time, Socrates, that you will talk with your friends, or they with you." And Socrates glanced at Crito, and said, "Crito, let her be taken home." So some of Crito's servants led her   b
away weeping bitterly and beating her breast. But Socrates sat up on the bed, and bent his leg and rubbed it with his hand, and while he was rubbing it said to us, How strange

a thing is what men call pleasure! How wonderful is its relation to pain, which seems to be the opposite of it! They will not come to a man together; but if he pursues the one and gains it, he is almost forced to take the other also, as if they were two distinct things united at one end.

c

And I think, said he, that if Aesop had noticed them he would have composed a fable about them, to the effect that God had wished to reconcile them when they were quarrelling, and that, when he could not do that, he joined their ends together; and that therefore whenever the one comes to a man, the other is sure to follow. That is just the case with me. There was pain in my leg caused by the chains, and now, it seems, pleasure is come following the pain.

Cebes interrupted him and said, By the bye, Socrates, I am glad that you reminded me. Several people have been inquiring about your poems, the hymn to Apollo, and Aesop's fables which you have put into meter, and only a day or two ago Evenus asked me what was your reason for writing poetry on coming here, when you had never written a line before. So if you wish me to be able to answer him when he asks me again, as I know that he will, tell me what to say.

d

Then tell him the truth, Cebes, he said. Say that it was from no wish to pose as a rival to him, or to his poems. I knew that it would not be easy to do that. I was only testing the meaning of certain dreams and acquitting my conscience about them, in case they should be bidding me make this kind of music. The fact is this. The same dream used often to come to me in my past life, appearing in different forms at different times, but always saying the same words, "Socrates, work at music and compose it." Formerly I used to think that the dream was encouraging me and cheering me on in what was already the work of my life, just as the spectators cheer on different runners in a race. I supposed that the dream was encouraging me to create the music at which I was working already, for I thought that philosophy was the highest music, and my life was spent in philosophy. But then, after the trial, when the feast of the god delayed my death, it occurred to me that the dream might possibly be bidding me create music in the popular sense, and that in that case I ought to do so, and not to disobey. I thought that it would be safer to acquit my conscience by creating poetry in obedience to the dream before I departed. So first I composed a hymn to the god whose feast it was. And then I turned such fables of Aesop as I knew, and had ready to my hand, into verse, taking those which came first; for I reflected that a man who means to be a poet has to use fiction and not facts for his poems; and I could not invent fiction myself.

e

61

b

c

Tell Evenus this, Cebes, and bid him farewell from me; and tell him to follow me as quickly as he can, if he is wise. I, it seems, shall depart today, for that is the will of the Athenians.

And Simmias said, What strange advice to give Evenus, Socrates! I have often met him, and from what I have seen of him I think that he is certainly not at all the man to take it, if he can help it.

What, he said, is not Evenus a philosopher?

Yes, I suppose so, replied Simmias.

Then Evenus will wish to die, he said, and so will every man who is worthy of having any part in this study. But he will not lay violent hands on himself; for that, they say, is wrong. And as he spoke he put his legs off the bed on to the ground, and remained sitting thus for the rest of the conversation.

d

Then Cebes asked him, What do you mean, Socrates, by saying that it is wrong for a man to lay violent hands on himself, but that the philosopher will wish to follow the dying man?

What, Cebes? Have you and Simmias been with Philolaus, and not heard about these things?

Nothing very definite, Socrates.

Well, I myself only speak of them from hearsay, yet there is no reason why I should not tell you what I have heard. Indeed, as I am setting out on a journey to the   e
other world, what could be more fitting for me than to talk about my journey and to consider what we imagine to be its nature? How could we better employ the interval between this and sunset?

Then what is their reason for saying that it is wrong for a man to kill himself, Socrates? It is quite true that I have heard Philolaus say, when he was living at Thebes, that it is not right; and I have heard the same thing from others, too, but I never heard anything definite on the subject from any of them.

You must be of good cheer, said he, possibly you will hear something some day.   62
But perhaps you will be surprised if I say that this law, unlike every other law to which mankind is subject, is absolute and without exception; and that it is not true that death is better than life only for some persons and at some times. And perhaps you will be surprised if I tell you that these men, for whom it would be better to die, may not do themselves a service, but that they must await a benefactor from without.

Oh indeed, said Cebes, laughing quietly, and speaking in his native dialect.

Indeed, said Socrates, so stated it may seem strange, and yet perhaps a reason   b
may be given for it. The reason which the secret teaching* gives, that man is in a kind of prison, and that he may not set himself free, nor escape from it, seems to me rather profound and not easy to fathom. But I do think, Cebes, that it is true that the gods are our guardians, and that we men are a part of their property. Do you not think so?

I do, said Cebes.

Well then, said he, if one of your possessions were to kill itself, though you had   c
not signified that you wished it to die, should you not be angry with it? Should you not punish it, if punishment were possible?

Certainly, he replied.

Then in this way perhaps it is not unreasonable to hold that no man has a right to take his own life, but that he must wait until God sends some necessity upon him, as has now been sent upon me.

Yes, said Cebes, that does seem natural. But you were saying just now that the philosopher will desire to die. Is not that a paradox, Socrates, if what we have just been   d
saying, that God is our guardian and that we are his property, be true? It is not reasonable to say that the wise man will be content to depart from this service, in which the gods, who are the best of all rulers, rule him. He will hardly think that when he becomes free he will take better care of himself than the gods take of him. A fool perhaps might think so, and say that he would do well to run away from his master; he might   e
not consider that he ought not to run away from a good master, but that he ought to remain with him as long as possible, and so in his thoughtlessness he might run away. But the wise man will surely desire to remain always with one who is better than himself. But if this be true, Socrates, the reverse of what you said just now seems to follow. The wise man should grieve to die, and the fool should rejoice.

I thought Socrates was pleased with Cebes' insistence. He looked at us, and said,   63
Cebes is always examining arguments. He will not be convinced at once by anything that one says.

*[The Esoteric system of the Pythagoreans.]

Yes, Socrates, said Simmias, but I do think that now there is something in what Cebes says. Why should really wise men want to run away from masters who are better than themselves, and lightly quit their service? And I think Cebes is aiming his argument at you, because you are so ready to leave us, and the gods, who are good rulers, as you yourself admit.

b   You are right, he said. I suppose you mean that I must defend myself against your charge, as if I were in a court of justice.

That is just our meaning, said Simmias.

Well then, he replied, let me try to make a more successful defense to you than I did to the judges at my trial. I should be wrong, Cebes and Simmias, he went on, not to

c   grieve at death, if I did not think that I was going to live both with other gods who are good and wise, and with men who have died and who are better than the men of this world. But you must know that I hope that I am going to live among good men, though I am not quite sure of that. But I am as sure as I can be in such matters that I am going to live with gods who are very good masters. And therefore I am not so much grieved at death; I am confident that the dead have some kind of existence, and, as has been said of old, an existence that is far better for the good than for the wicked.

Well, Socrates, said Simmias, do you mean to go away and keep this belief to

d   yourself, or will you let us share it with you? It seems to me that we too have an interest in this good. And it will also serve as your defense, if you can convince us of what you say.

I will try, he replied. But I think Crito has been wanting to speak to me. Let us first hear what he has to say.

Only, Socrates, said Crito, that the man who is going to give you the poison has

e   been telling me to warn you not to talk much. He says that talking heats people, and that the action of the poison must not be counteracted by heat. Those who excite themselves sometimes have to drink it two or three times.

Let him be, said Socrates; let him mind his own business, and be prepared to give me the poison twice, or, if need be, thrice.

I knew that would be your answer, said Crito, but the man has been importunate.

Never mind him, he replied. But I wish now to explain to you, my judges, why it seems to me that a man who has really spent his life in philosophy has reason to be

64   of good cheer when he is about to die, and may well hope after death to gain in the other world the greatest good. I will try to show you, Simmias and Cebes, how this may be.

The world, perhaps, does not see that those who rightly engage in philosophy study only dying and death. And, if this be true, it would be surely strange for a man all through his life to desire only death, and then, when death comes to him, to be vexed at it, when it has been his study and his desire for so long.

Simmias laughed, and said: Indeed, Socrates, you make me laugh, though I am

b   scarcely in a laughing humor now. If the multitude heard that, I fancy they would think that what you say of philosophers is quite true; and my countrymen would entirely agree with you that philosophers are indeed eager to die, and they would say that they know full well that philosophers deserve to be put to death.

And they would be right, Simmias, except in saying that they know it. They do

c   not know in what sense the true philosopher is eager to die, or what kind of death he deserves, or in what sense he deserves it. Let us dismiss them from our thoughts, and converse by ourselves. Do we believe death to be anything?

We do, replied Simmias.

And do we not believe it to be the separation of the soul from the body? Does not death mean that the body comes to exist by itself, separated from the soul, and that the soul exists by herself, separated from the body? What is death but that?

It is that, he said.

Now consider, my good friend, if you and I are agreed on another point which I   d think will help us to understand the question better. Do you think that a philosopher will care very much about what are called pleasures, such as the pleasures of eating and drinking?

Certainly not, Socrates, said Simmias.

Or about the pleasures of sexual passion?

Indeed, no.

And, do you think that he holds the remaining cares of the body in high esteem? Will he think much of getting fine clothes, and sandals, and other bodily adornments,   e or will he despise them, except so far as he is absolutely forced to meddle with them?

The real philosopher, I think, will despise them, he replied.

In short, said he, you think that his studies are not concerned with the body? He stands aloof from it, as far as he can, and turns toward the soul?

I do.

Well then, in these matters, first, it is clear that the philosopher releases his soul   65 from communion with the body, so far as he can, beyond all other men?

It is.

And does not the world think, Simmias, that if a man has no pleasure in such things, and does not take his share in them, his life is not worth living? Do not they hold that he who thinks nothing of bodily pleasures is almost as good as dead?

Indeed you are right.

But what about the actual acquisition of wisdom? If the body is taken as a companion in the search for wisdom, is it a hindrance or not? For example, do sight and   b hearing convey any real truth to men? Are not the very poets forever telling us that we neither hear nor see anything accurately? But if these senses of the body are not accurate or clear, the others will hardly be so, for they are all less perfect than these, are they not?

Yes, I think so, certainly, he said.

Then when does the soul attain truth? he asked. We see that, as often as she seeks to investigate anything in company with the body, the body leads her astray.

True.   c

Is it not by reasoning, if at all, that any real truth becomes manifest to her?

Yes.

And she reasons best, I suppose, when none of the senses, whether hearing, or sight, or pain, or pleasure, harasses her; when she has dismissed the body, and released herself as far as she can from all intercourse or contact with it, and so, coming to be as much alone with herself as is possible, strives after real truth.

That is so.

And here too the soul of the philosopher very greatly despises the body, and flies   d from it, and seeks to be alone by herself, does she not?

Clearly.

And what do you say to the next point, Simmias? Do we say that there is such a thing as absolute justice, or not?

Indeed we do.

And absolute beauty, and absolute good?

Of course.

Have you ever seen any of them with your eyes?

Indeed I have not, he replied.

e   Did you ever grasp them with any bodily sense? I am speaking of all absolutes, whether size, or health, or strength; in a word, of the essence or real being of everything. Is the very truth of things contemplated by the body? Is it not rather the case that the man who prepares himself most carefully to apprehend by his intellect the essence of each thing which he examines will come nearest to the knowledge of it?

Certainly.

And will not a man attain to this pure thought most completely if he goes to each thing, as far as he can, with his mind alone, taking neither sight nor any other sense

66   along with his reason in the process of thought, to be an encumbrance? In every case he will pursue pure and absolute being, with his pure intellect alone. He will be set free as far as possible from the eye and the ear and, in short, from the whole body, because intercourse with the body troubles the soul, and hinders her from gaining truth and wisdom. Is it not he who will attain the knowledge of real being, if any man will?

Your words are admirably true, Socrates, said Simmias.

b   And, he said, must not all this cause real philosophers to reflect, and make them say to each other, It seems that there is a narrow path which will bring us safely to our journey's end, with reason as our guide. As long as we have this body, and an evil of that sort is mingled with our souls, we shall never fully gain what we desire; and that is

c   truth. For the body is forever taking up our time with the care which it needs; and, besides, whenever diseases attack it, they hinder us in our pursuit of real being. It fills us with passions, and desires, and fears, and all manner of phantoms, and much foolishness; and so, as the saying goes, in very truth we can never think at all for it. It alone

d   and its desires cause wars and factions and battles; for the origin of all wars is the pursuit of wealth, and we are forced to pursue wealth because we live in slavery to the cares of the body. And therefore, for all these reasons, we have no leisure for philosophy. And last of all, if we ever are free from the body for a time, and then turn to examine some matter, it falls in our way at every step of the inquiry, and causes confusion and trouble and panic, so that we cannot see the truth for it. Verily we have

e   learned that if we are to have any pure knowledge at all, we must be freed from the body; the soul by herself must behold things as they are. Then, it seems, after we are dead, we shall gain the wisdom which we desire, and for which we say we have a passion, but not while we are alive, as the argument shows. For if it be not possible to have pure knowledge while the body is with us, one of two things must be true: either

67   we cannot gain knowledge at all, or we can gain it only after death. For then, and not till then, will the soul exist by herself, separate from the body. And while we live, we shall come nearest to knowledge, if we have no communion or intercourse with the body beyond what is absolutely necessary, and if we are not defiled with its nature. We must live pure from it until God himself releases us. And when we are thus pure and released from its follies, we shall dwell, I suppose, with others who are pure like our-

b   selves, and we shall of ourselves know all that is pure; and that my be the truth. For I think that the impure is not allowed to attain to the pure. Such, Simmias, I fancy must needs be the language and the reflections of the true lovers of knowledge. Do you not agree with me?

Most assuredly I do, Socrates.

And, my friend, said Socrates, if this be true, I have good hope that, when I reach the place whither I am going, I shall there, if anywhere, gain fully that which we have sought so earnestly in the past. And so I shall set forth cheerfully on the journey that is

appointed me today, and so may every man who thinks that his mind is prepared and   c
purified.

That is quite true, said Simmias.

And does not the purification consist, as we have said, in separating the soul from the body, as far as is possible, and in accustoming her to collect and rally herself together from the body on every side, and to dwell alone by herself as much as she can, both now and hereafter, released from the bondage of the body?   d

Yes, certainly, he said.

Is not what we call death a release and separation of the soul from the body?

Undoubtedly, he replied.

And the true philosopher, we hold, is alone in his constant desire to set his soul free? His study is simply the release and separation of the soul from the body, is it not?

Clearly.

Would it not be absurd then, as I began by saying, for a man to complain at death   e
coming to him, when in his life he has been preparing himself to live as nearly in a state of death as he could? Would not that be absurd?

Yes, indeed.

In truth, then, Simmias, he said, the true philosopher studies to die, and to him of all men is death least terrible. Now look at the matter in this way. In everything he is at enmity with his body, and he longs to possess his soul alone. Would it not then be most unreasonable if he were to fear and complain when he has his desire, instead of rejoic-   68
ing to go to the place where he hopes to gain the wisdom that he has passionately longed for all his life, and to be released from the company of his enemy? Many a man has willingly gone to the other world, when a human love or wife or son has died, in the hope of seeing there those whom he longed for, and of being with them: and will a man who has a real passion for wisdom, and a firm hope of really finding wisdom in   b
the other world and nowhere else, grieve at death, and not depart rejoicing? Nay, my friend, you ought not to think that, if he be truly a philosopher. He will be firmly convinced that there and nowhere else will he meet with wisdom in its purity. And if this be so, would it not, I repeat, be very unreasonable for such a man to fear death?

Yes, indeed, he replied, it would.

Does not this show clearly, he said, that any man whom you see grieving at the   c
approach of death is after all no lover of wisdom, but a lover of his body? He is also, most likely, a lover either of wealth, or of honor, or, it may be, of both.

Yes, he said, it is as you say.

Well then, Simmias, he went on, does not what is called courage belong especially to the philosopher?

Certainly I think so, he replied.

And does not temperance, the quality which even the world calls temperance, and which means to despise and control and govern the passions—does not temperance belong only to such men as most despise the body, and pass their lives in philosophy?

Of necessity, he replied.   d

For if you will consider the courage and the temperance of other men, said he, you will find that they are strange things.

How so, Socrates?

You know, he replied, that all other men regard death as one of the great evils to which mankind is subject?

Indeed they do, he said.

And when the brave men of them submit to death, do not they do so from a fear of still greater evils?

Yes.

Then all men but the philosopher are brave from fear and because they are afraid. Yet it is rather a strange thing for a man to be brave out of fear and cowardice.

e   Indeed it is.

And are not the orderly men of them in exactly the same case? Are not they temperate from a kind of intemperance? We should say that this cannot be; but in them this state of foolish temperance comes to that. They desire certain pleasures, and fear to

69   lose them; and so they abstain from other pleasures because they are mastered by these. Intemperance is defined to mean being under the dominion of pleasure, yet they only master certain pleasures because they are mastered by others. But that is exactly what I said just now—that, in a way, they are made temperate from intemperance.

It seems to be so.

My dear Simmias, I fear that virtue is not really to be bought in this way, by bartering pleasure for pleasure, and pain for pain, and fear for fear, and the greater for the

b   less, like coins. There is only one sterling coin for which all these things ought to be exchanged, and that is wisdom. All that is bought and sold for this and with this, whether courage, or temperance, or justice, is real; in one word, true virtue cannot be without wisdom, and it matters nothing whether pleasure, and fear, and all other such things are present or absent. But I think that the virtue which is composed of pleasures

c   and fears bartered with one another, and severed from wisdom, is only a shadow of true virtue, and that it has no freedom, nor health, nor truth. True virtue in reality is a kind of purifying from all these things; and temperance, and justice, and courage, and wisdom itself are the purification. And I fancy that the men who established our mysteries had a very real meaning: in truth they have been telling us in parables all the time that whosoever comes to Hades uninitiated and profane will lie in the mire, while

d   he that has been purified and initiated shall dwell with the gods. For "the thyrsus-bearers are many," as they say in the mysteries, "but the inspired few." And by these last, I believe, are meant only the true philosophers. And I in my life have striven as hard as I was able, and have left nothing undone, that I might become one of them. Whether I have striven in the right way, and whether I have succeeded or not, I suppose that I shall learn in a little while, when I reach the other world, if it be the will of god.

That is my defense, Simmias and Cebes, to show that I have reason for not being

e   angry or grieved at leaving you and my masters here. I believe that in the next world, no less than in this, I shall meet with good masters and friends, though the multitude are incredulous of it. And if I have been more successful with you in my defense than I was with my Athenian judges, it is well.

When Socrates had finished, Cebes replied to him, and said, I think that for the

70   most part you are right, Socrates. But men are very incredulous of what you have said of the soul. They fear that she will no longer exist anywhere when she has left the body, but that she will be destroyed and perish on the very day of death. They think that the moment that she is released and leaves the body, she will be dissolved and vanish away like breath or smoke, and thenceforward cease to exist at all. If she were

b   to exist somewhere as a whole, released from the evils which you enumerated just now, we should have good reason to hope, Socrates, that what you say is true. But it will need no little persuasion and assurance to show that the soul exists after death, and continues to possess any power or wisdom.

True, Cebes, said Socrates; but what are we to do? Do you wish to converse about these matters and see if what I say is probable?

I for one, said Cebes, should gladly hear your opinion about them.

I think, said Socrates, that no one who heard me now, even if he were a comic poet, would say that I am an idle talker about things which do not concern me. So, if c you wish it, let us examine this question.

Let us consider whether or not the souls of men exist in the next world after death, thus. There is an ancient belief, which we remember, that on leaving this world they exist there, and that they return hither and are born again from the dead. But if it be true that the living are born from the dead, our souls must exist in the other world; otherwise they could not be born again. It will be a sufficient proof that this is so if we d can really prove that the living are born only from the dead. But if this is not so, we shall have to find some other argument.

Exactly, said Cebes.

Well, said he, the easiest way of answering the question will be to consider it not in relation to men only, but also in relation to all animals and plants, and in short to all things that are generated. Is it the case that everything which has an opposite is gener- e ated only from its opposite? By opposites I mean the honorable and the base, the just and the unjust, and so on in a thousand other instances. Let us consider then whether it is necessary for everything that has an opposite to be generated only from its own opposite. For instance, when anything becomes greater, I suppose it must first have been less and then become greater?

Yes.

And if a thing becomes less, it must have been greater, and afterward become 71 less?

That is so, said he.

And further, the weaker is generated from the stronger, and the swifter from the slower?

Certainly.

And the worse is generated from the better, and the more just from the more unjust?

Of course.

Then it is sufficiently clear to us that all things are generated in this way, opposites from opposites?

Quite so.

And in every pair of opposites, are there not two generations between the two b members of the pair, from the one to the other, and then back again from the other to the first? Between the greater and the less are growth and diminution, and we say that the one grows and the other diminishes, do we not?

Yes, he said.

And there is division and composition, and cold and hot, and so on. In fact, is it not a universal law, even though we do not always express it in so many words, that opposites are generated always from one another, and that there is a process of generation from one to the other?

It is, he replied.

Well, said he, is there an opposite to life, in the same way that sleep is the oppo- c site of being awake?

Certainly, he answered.

What is it?

Death, he replied.

Then if life and death are opposites, they are generated the one from the other: they are two, and between them there are two generations. Is it not so?

Of course.

Now, said Socrates, I will explain to you one of the two pairs of opposites of which I spoke just now, and its generations, and you shall explain to me the other.

d   Sleep is the opposite of waking. From sleep is produced the state of waking, and from the state of waking is produced sleep. Their generations are, first, to fall asleep; secondly, to awake. Is that clear? he asked.

Yes, quite.

Now then, said he, do you tell me about life and death. Death is the opposite of life, is it not?

It is.

And they are generated the one from the other?

Yes.

Then what is that which is generated from the living?

The dead, he replied.

And what is generated from the dead?

I must admit that it is the living.

Then living things and living men are generated from the dead, Cebes?

e   Clearly, said he.

Then our souls exist in the other world? he said.

Apparently.

Now of these two generations the one is certain? Death I suppose is certain enough, is it not?

Yes, quite, he replied.

What then shall we do? said he. Shall we not assign an opposite generation to correspond? Or is nature imperfect here? Must we not assign some opposite generation to dying?

I think so, certainly, he said.

And what must it be?

To come to life again.

72   And if there be such a thing as a return to life, he said, it will be a generation from the dead to the living, will it not?

It will, certainly.

Then we are agreed on this point: namely, that the living are generated from the dead no less than the dead from the living. But we agreed that, if this be so, it is a sufficient proof that the souls of the dead must exist somewhere, whence they come into being again.

I think, Socrates, that that is the necessary result of our premises.

And I think, Cebes, said he, that our conclusion has not been an unfair one. For if

b   opposites did not always correspond with opposites as they are generated, moving as it were round in a circle, and there were generation in a straight line forward from one opposite only, with no turning or return to the other, then, you know, all things would come at length to have the same form and be in the same state, and would cease to be generated at all.

What do you mean? he asked.

It is not at all hard to understand my meaning, he replied. If, for example, the one opposite, to go to sleep, existed without the corresponding opposite, to wake up, which

c   is generated from the first, then all nature would at last make the tale of Endymion meaningless, and he would no longer be conspicuous; for everything else would be in the same state of sleep that he was in. And if all things were compounded together and never separated, the Chaos of Anaxagoras would soon be realized. Just in the same way, my dear Cebes, if all things in which there is any life were to die, and when they were dead were to remain in that form and not come to life again, would not the necessary result be that everything at last would be dead, and nothing alive? For if living things were generated from other sources than death, and were to die, the result is inevitable that all things would be consumed by death. Is it not so?   d

It is indeed, I think, Socrates, said Cebes; I think that what you say is perfectly true.

Yes, Cebes, he said, I think it is certainly so. We are not misled into this conclusion. The dead do come to life again, and the living are generated from them, and the souls of the dead exist; and with the souls of the good it is well, and with the souls of the evil it is evil.   e

And besides, Socrates, rejoined Cebes, if the doctrine which you are fond of stating, that our learning is only a process of recollection, be true, then I suppose we must have learned at some former time what we recollect now. And that would be impossible unless our souls had existed somewhere before they came into this human form. So that is another reason for believing the soul immortal.   73

But, Cebes, interrupted Simmias, what are the proofs of that? Recall them to me; I am not very clear about them at present.

One argument, answered Cebes, and the strongest of all, is that if you question men about anything in the right way, they will answer you correctly of themselves. But they would not have been able to do that unless they had had within themselves knowledge and right reason. Again, show them such things as geometrical diagrams, and the proof of the doctrine is complete.*   b

And if that does not convince you, Simmias, said Socrates, look at the matter in another way and see if you agree then. You have doubts, I know, how what is called knowledge can be recollection.

Nay, replied Simmias, I do not doubt. But I want to recollect the argument about recollection. What Cebes undertook to explain has nearly brought your theory back to me and convinced me. But I am nonetheless ready to hear you undertake to explain it.

In this way, he returned. We are agreed, I suppose, that if a man remembers anything, he must have known it at some previous time.   c

Certainly, he said.

And are we agreed that when knowledge comes in the following way, it is recollection? When a man has seen or heard anything, or has perceived it by some other sense, and then knows not that thing only, but has also in his mind an impression of some other thing, of which the knowledge is quite different, are we not right in saying that he remembers the thing of which he has an impression in his mind?   d

What do you mean?

I mean this. The knowledge of a man is different from the knowledge of a lyre, is it not?

Certainly.

And you know that when lovers see a lyre, or a garment, or anything that their favorites are wont to use, they have this feeling. They know the lyre, and in their mind they receive the image of the youth whose the lyre was. That is recollection. For instance, someone seeing Simmias often is reminded of Cebes; and there are endless examples of the same thing.

Indeed there are, said Simmias.

---

*[For an example of this see Meno 82a–86b (pp. 153ff in this volume).]

e   Is not that a kind of recollection, he said; and more especially when a man has this feeling with reference to things which the lapse of time and inattention have made him forget?

Yes, certainly, he replied.

Well, he went on, is it possible to recollect a man on seeing the picture of a horse, or the picture of a lyre? Or to recall Simmias on seeing a picture of Cebes?

Certainly.

And it is possible to recollect Simmias himself on seeing a picture of Simmias?

74   No doubt, he said.

Then in all these cases there is recollection caused by similar objects, and also by dissimilar objects?

There is.

But when a man has a recollection caused by similar objects, will he not have a further feeling and consider whether the likeness to that which he recollects is defective in any way or not?

He will, he said.

Now see if this is true, he went on. Do we not believe in the existence of equality—not the equality of pieces of wood or of stones, but something beyond that—equality in the abstract? Shall we say that there is such a thing, or not?

b   Yes indeed, said Simmias, most emphatically we will.

And do we know what this abstract equality is?

Certainly, he replied.

Where did we get the knowledge of it? Was it not from seeing the equal pieces of wood, and stones, and the like, which we were speaking of just now? Did we not form from them the idea of abstract equality, which is different from them? Or do you think that it is not different? Consider the question in this way. Do not equal pieces of wood and stones appear to us sometimes equal and sometimes unequal, though in fact they remain the same all the time?

Certainly they do.

c   But did absolute equals ever seem to you to be unequal, or abstract equality to be inequality?

No, never, Socrates.

Then equal things, he said, are not the same as abstract equality?

No, certainly not, Socrates.

Yet it was from these equal things, he said, which are different from abstract equality, that you have conceived and got your knowledge of abstract equality?

That is quite true, he replied.

And that whether it is like them or unlike them?

Certainly.

d   But that makes no difference, he said. As long as the sight of one thing brings another thing to your mind, there must be recollection, whether or no the two things are like.

That is so.

Well then, said he, do the equal pieces of wood, and other similar equal things, of which we have been speaking, affect us at all this way? Do they seem to us to be equal, in the way that abstract equality is equal? Do they come short of being like abstract equality, or not?

Indeed, they come very short of it, he replied.

Are we agreed about this? A man sees something and thinks to himself, "This
e   thing that I see aims at being like some other thing, but it comes short and cannot be

like that other thing; it is inferior"; must not the man who thinks that have known at some previous time that other thing, which he says that it resembles, and to which it is inferior?

He must.

Well, have we ourselves had the same sort of feeling with reference to equal things, and to abstract equality?

Yes, certainly.

Then we must have had knowledge of equality before we first saw equal things, 75 and perceived that they all strive to be like equality, and all come short of it.

That is so.

And we are agreed also that we have not, nor could we have, obtained the idea of equality except from sight or touch or some other sense; the same is true of all the senses.

Yes, Socrates, for the purposes of the argument that is so.

At any rate, it is by the senses that we must perceive that all sensible objects b strive to resemble absolute equality, and are inferior to it. Is not that so?

Yes.

Then before we began to see, and to hear, and to use the other senses, we must have received the knowledge of the nature of abstract and real equality; otherwise we could not have compared equal sensible objects with abstract equality, and seen that the former in all cases strive to be like the latter, though they are always inferior to it?

That is the necessary consequence of what we have been saying, Socrates.

Did we not see, and hear, and possess the other senses as soon as we were born?

Yes, certainly.

And we must have received the knowledge of abstract equality before we had c these senses?

Yes.

Then, it seems, we must have received that knowledge before we were born?

It does.

Now if we received this knowledge before our birth, and were born with it, we knew, both before and at the moment of our birth, not only the equal, and the greater, and the less, but also everything of the same kind, did we not? Our present reasoning does not refer only to equality. It refers just as much to absolute good, and absolute d beauty, and absolute justice, and absolute holiness; in short, I repeat, to everything which we mark with the name of the real, in the questions and answers of our dialectic. So we must have received our knowledge of all realities before we were born.

That is so.

And we must always be born with this knowledge, and must always retain it throughout life, if we have not each time forgotten it, after having received it. For to know means to receive and retain knowledge, and not to have lost it. Do not we mean by forgetting, the loss of knowledge, Simmias?

Yes, certainly, Socrates, he said.   e

But, I suppose, if it be the case that we lost at birth the knowledge which we received before we were born, and then afterward, by using our senses on the objects of sense, recovered the knowledge which we had previously possessed, then what we call learning is the recovering of knowledge which is already ours. And are we not right in calling that recollection?

Certainly.

For we have found it possible to perceive a thing by sight, or hearing, or any 76 other sense, and thence to form a notion of some other thing, like or unlike, which had been forgotten, but with which this thing was associated. And therefore, I say, one of two things must be true. Either we are all born with this knowledge and retain it all our life; or, after birth, those whom we say are learning are only recollecting, and our knowledge is recollection.

Yes indeed, that is undoubtedly true, Socrates.

Then which do you choose, Simmias? Are we born with knowledge or do we recollect the things of which we have received knowledge before our birth?

I cannot say at present, Socrates.

Well, have you an opinion about this question? Can a man who knows give an account of what he knows, or not? What do you think about that?

Yes, of course he can, Socrates.

And do you think that everyone can give an account of the ideas of which we have been speaking?

I wish I did, indeed, said Simmias, but I am very much afraid that by this time tomorrow there will no longer be any man living able to do so as it should be done.

Then, Simmias, he said, you do not think that all men know these things?

Certainly not.

Then they recollect what they once learned?

Necessarily.

And when did our souls gain this knowledge? It cannot have been after we were born men.

No, certainly not.

Then it was before?

Yes.

Then, Simmias, our souls existed formerly, apart from our bodies, and possessed intelligence before they came into man's shape.

Unless we receive this knowledge at the moment of birth, Socrates. That time still remains.

Well, my friend, and at what other time do we lose it? We agreed just now that we are not born with it; do we lose it at the same moment that we gain it, or can you suggest any other time?

I cannot, Socrates. I did not see that I was talking nonsense.

Then, Simmias, he said, is not this the truth? If, as we are forever repeating, beauty, and good, and the other ideas really exist, and if we refer all the objects of sensible perception to these ideas which were formerly ours, and which we find to be ours still, and compare sensible objects with them, then, just as they exist, our souls must have existed before ever we were born. But if they do not exist, then our reasoning will have been thrown away. Is it so? If these ideas exist, does it not at once follow that our souls must have existed before we were born, and if they do not exist, then neither did our souls?

Admirably put, Socrates, said Simmias. I think that the necessity is the same for the one as for the other. The reasoning has reached a place of safety in the common proof of the existence of our souls before we were born and of the existence of the ideas of which you spoke. Nothing is so evident to me as that beauty, and good, and the other ideas which you spoke of just now have a very real existence indeed. Your proof is quite sufficient for me.

But what of Cebes? said Socrates. I must convince Cebes too.

I think that he is satisfied, said Simmias, though he is the most skeptical of men in argument. But I think that he is perfectly convinced that our souls existed before we were born.

But I do not think myself, Socrates, he continued, that you have proved that the soul will continue to exist when we are dead. The common fear which Cebes spoke of, b that she [the soul] may be scattered to the winds at death, and that death may be the end of her existence, still stands in the way. Assuming that the soul is generated and comes together from some other elements, and exists before she ever enters the human body, why should she not come to an end and be destroyed, after she has entered into the body, when she is released from it?

You are right, Simmias, said Cebes. I think that only half the required proof has c been given. It has been shown that our souls existed before we were born; but it must also be shown that our souls will continue to exist after we are dead, no less than that they existed before we were born, if the proof is to be complete.

That has been shown already, Simmias and Cebes, said Socrates, if you will combine this reasoning with our previous conclusion, that all life is generated from d death. For if the soul exists in a previous state and if, when she comes into life and is born, she can only be born from death, and from a state of death, must she not exist after death too, since she has to be born again? So the point which you speak of has been already proved.

Still I think that you and Simmias would be glad to discuss this question further. Like children, you are afraid that the wind will really blow the soul away and disperse her when she leaves the body, especially if a man happens to die in a storm and not in a e calm.

Cebes laughed and said, Try and convince us as if we were afraid, Socrates; or rather, do not think that we are afraid ourselves. Perhaps there is a child within us who has these fears. Let us try and persuade him not to be afraid of death, as if it were a bugbear.

You must charm him every day, until you have charmed him away, said Socrates.

And where shall we find a good charmer, Socrates, he asked, now that you are 78 leaving us?

Hellas is a large country, Cebes, he replied, and good men may doubtless be found in it; and the nations of the Barbarians are many. You must search them all through for such a charmer, sparing neither money nor labor; for there is nothing on which you could spend money more profitably. And you must search for him among yourselves too, for you will hardly find a better charmer than yourselves.

That shall be done, said Cebes. But let us return to the point where we left off, if you will. b

Yes, I will: why not?

Very good, he replied.

Well, said Socrates, must we not ask ourselves this question? What kind of thing is liable to suffer dispersion, and for what kind of thing have we to fear dispersion? And then we must see whether the soul belongs to that kind or not, and be confident or afraid about our own souls accordingly.

That is true, he answered.

Now is it not the compound and composite which is naturally liable to be dis- c solved in the same way in which it was compounded? And is not what is uncompounded alone not liable to dissolution, if anything is not?

I think that that is so, said Cebes.

And what always remains in the same state and unchanging is most likely to be uncompounded, and what is always changing and never the same is most likely to be compounded, I suppose?

Yes, I think so.

Now let us return to what we were speaking of before in the discussion, he said.
d   Does the being, which in our dialectic we define as meaning absolute existence, remain always in exactly the same state, or does it change? Do absolute equality, absolute beauty, and every other absolute existence, admit of any change at all? Or does absolute existence in each case, being essentially uniform, remain the same and unchanging, and never in any case admit of any sort or kind of change whatsoever?

It must remain the same and unchanging, Socrates, said Cebes.

And what of the many beautiful things, such as men, and horses, and garments, and the like, and of all which bears the names of the ideas, whether equal, or beautiful,
e   or anything else? Do they remain the same or is it exactly the opposite with them? In short, do they never remain the same at all, either in themselves or in their relations?

These things, said Cebes, never remain the same.
79   You can touch them, and see them, and perceive them with the other senses, while you can grasp the unchanging only by the reasoning of the intellect. These latter are invisible and not seen. Is it not so?

That is perfectly true, he said.

Let us assume then, he said, if you will, that there are two kinds of existence, the one visible, the other invisible.

Yes, he said.

And the invisible is unchanging, while the visible is always changing.

Yes, he said again.
b   Are not we men made up of body and soul?

There is nothing else, he replied.

And which of these kinds of existence should we say that the body is most like, and most akin to?

The visible, he replied; that is quite obvious.

And the soul? Is that visible or invisible?

It is invisible to man, Socrates, he said.

But we mean by visible and invisible, visible and invisible to man; do we not?

Yes; that is what we mean.

Then what do we say of the soul? Is it visible or not visible?

It is not visible.

Then is it invisible?

Yes.

Then the soul is more like the invisible than the body; and the body is like the visible.
c   That is necessarily so, Socrates.

Have we not also said that, when the soul employs the body in any inquiry, and makes use of sight, or hearing, or any other sense—for inquiry with the body means inquiry with the senses—she is dragged away by it to the things which never remain the same, and wanders about blindly, and becomes confused and dizzy, like a drunken man, from dealing with things that are ever changing?

Certainly.
d   But when she investigates any question by herself, she goes away to the pure, and eternal, and immortal, and unchangeable, to which she is akin, and so she comes to be ever with it, as soon as she is by herself, and can be so; and then she rests from her wanderings and dwells with it unchangingly, for she is dealing with what is unchanging. And is not this state of the soul called wisdom?

Indeed, Socrates, you speak well and truly, he replied.

Which kind of existence do you think from our former and our present argu-   e
ments that the soul is more like and more akin to?

I think, Socrates, he replied, that after this inquiry the very dullest man would
agree that the soul is infinitely more like the unchangeable than the changeable.

And the body?

That is like the changeable.

Consider the matter in yet another way. When the soul and the body are united,
nature ordains the one to be a slave and to be ruled, and the other to be master and to   80
rule. Tell me once again, which do you think is like the divine, and which is like the
mortal? Do you not think that the divine naturally rules and has authority, and that the
mortal naturally is ruled and is a slave?

I do.

Then which is the soul like?

That is quite plain, Socrates. The soul is like the divine, and the body is like the
mortal.

Now tell me, Cebes, is the result of all that we have said that the soul is most like
the divine, and the immortal, and the intelligible, and the uniform, and the indissoluble,   b
and the unchangeable; while the body is most like the human, and the mortal, and the
unintelligible, and the multiform, and the dissoluble, and the changeable? Have we any
other argument to show that this is not so, my dear Cebes?

We have not.

Then if this is so, is it not the nature of the body to be dissolved quickly, and of
the soul to be wholly or very nearly indissoluble?

Certainly.   c

You observe, he said, that after a man is dead, the visible part of him, his body,
which lies in the visible world and which we call the corpse, which is subject to dissolution and decomposition, is not dissolved and decomposed at once? It remains as it
was for a considerable time, and even for a long time, if a man dies with his body in
good condition and in the vigor of life. And when the body falls in and is embalmed,
like the mummies of Egypt, it remains nearly entire for an immense time. And should   d
it decay, yet some parts of it, such as the bones and muscles, may almost be said to be
immortal. Is it not so?

Yes.

And shall we believe that the soul, which is invisible, and which goes hence to a
place that is like herself, glorious, and pure, and invisible, to Hades, which is rightly
called the unseen world, to dwell with the good and wise God, whither, if it be the will
of God, my soul too must shortly go—shall we believe that the soul, whose nature is so
glorious, and pure, and invisible, is blown away by the winds and perishes as soon as   e
she leaves the body, as the world says? Nay, dear Cebes and Simmias, it is not so. I
will tell you what happens to a soul which is pure at her departure, and which in her
life has had no intercourse that she could avoid with the body, and so draws after her,
when she dies, no taint of the body, but has shunned it, and gathered herself into herself, for such has been her constant study—and that only means that she has loved wis-   81
dom rightly, and has truly practiced how to die. Is not this the practice of death?

Yes, certainly.

Does not the soul, then, which is in that state, go away to the invisible that is like
herself, and to the divine, and the immortal, and the wise, where she is released from
error, and folly, and fear, and fierce passions, and all the other evils that fall to the lot
of men, and is happy, and for the rest of time lives in very truth with the gods, as they
say that the initiated do? Shall we affirm this, Cebes?

Yes, certainly, said Cebes.

b   But if she be defiled and impure when she leaves the body, from being ever with it, and serving it and loving it, and from being besotted by it and by its desires and pleasures, so that she thinks nothing true but what is bodily and can be touched, and seen, and eaten, and drunk, and used for men's lusts; if she has learned to hate, and tremble

c   at, and fly from what is dark and invisible to the eye, and intelligible and apprehended by philosophy—do you think that a soul which is in that state will be pure and without alloy at her departure?

No, indeed, he replied.

She is penetrated, I suppose, by the corporeal, which the unceasing intercourse and company and care of the body has made a part of her nature.

Yes.

And, my dear friend, the corporeal must be burdensome, and heavy, and earthy, and visible; and it is by this that such a soul is weighed down and dragged back to the

d   visible world, because she is afraid of the invisible world of Hades, and haunts, it is said, the graves and tombs, where shadowy forms of souls have been seen, which are the phantoms of souls which were impure at their release and still cling to the visible; which is the reason why they are seen.

That is likely enough, Socrates.

That is likely, certainly, Cebes; and these are not the souls of the good, but of the evil, which are compelled to wander in such places as a punishment for the wicked lives that they have lived; and their wanderings continue until, from the desire for the

e   corporeal that clings to them, they are again imprisoned in a body.

And, he continued, they are imprisoned, probably, in the bodies of animals with habits similar to the habits which were theirs in their lifetime.

What do you mean by that, Socrates?

I mean that men who have practiced unbridled gluttony, and wantonness, and

82   drunkenness probably enter the bodies of asses and suchlike animals. Do you not think so?

Certainly that is very likely.

And those who have chosen injustice, and tyranny, and robbery enter the bodies of wolves, and hawks, and kites. Where else should we say that such souls go?

No doubt, said Cebes, they go into such animals.

In short, it is quite plain, he said, whither each soul goes; each enters an animal with habits like its own.

Certainly, he replied, that is so.

And of these, he said, the happiest, who go to the best place, are those who have

b   practiced the popular and social virtues which are called temperance and justice, and which come from habit and practice, without philosophy or reason.

And why are they the happiest?

Because it is probable that they return into a mild and social nature like their own, such as that of bees, or wasps, or ants; or, it may be, into the bodies of men, and that from them are made worthy citizens.

Very likely.

c   But none but the philosopher or the lover of knowledge, who is wholly pure when he goes hence, is permitted to go to the race of the gods; and therefore, my friends, Simmias and Cebes, the true philosopher is temperate and refrains from all the pleasures of the body, and does not give himself up to them. It is not squandering his substance and poverty that he fears, as the multitude and the lovers of wealth do; nor again does he dread the dishonor and disgrace of wickedness, like the lovers of power and honor. It is not for these reasons that he is temperate.

No, it would be unseemly in him if he were, Socrates, said Cebes.

Indeed it would, he replied, and therefore all those who have any care for their   d souls, and who do not spend their lives in forming and molding their bodies, bid farewell to such persons, and do not walk in their ways, thinking that they know not whither they are going. They themselves turn and follow whithersoever philosophy leads them, for they believe that they ought not to resist philosophy, or its deliverance and purification.

How, Socrates?

I will tell you, he replied. The lovers of knowledge know that when philosophy receives the soul, she is fast bound in the body, and fastened to it; she is unable to con-   e template what is, by herself, or except through the bars of her prison house, the body; and she is wallowing in utter ignorance. And philosophy sees that the dreadful thing about the imprisonment is that it is caused by lust, and that the captive herself is an ac-   83 complice in her own captivity. The lovers of knowledge, I repeat, know that philoso- phy takes the soul when she is in this condition, and gently encourages her, and strives to release her from her captivity, showing her that the perceptions of the eye, and the ear, and the other senses are full of deceit, and persuading her to stand aloof from the senses and to use them only when she must, and exhorting her to rally and gather her-   b self together, and to trust only to herself and to the real existence which she of her own self apprehends, and to believe that nothing which is subject to change, and which she perceives by other faculties, has any truth, for such things are visible and sensible, while what she herself sees is apprehended by reason and invisible. The soul of the true philosopher thinks that it would be wrong to resist this deliverance from captivity, and therefore she holds aloof, so far as she can, from pleasure, and desire, and pain, and   c fear; for she reckons that when a man has vehement pleasure, or fear, or pain, or desire, he suffers from them not merely the evils which might be expected, such as sickness or some loss arising from the indulgence of his desires; he suffers what is the greatest and last of evils, and does not take it into account.

What do you mean, Socrates? asked Cebes.

I mean that when the soul of any man feels vehement pleasure or pain, she is forced at the same time to think that the object, whatever it be, of these sensations is the most distinct and truest, when it is not. Such objects are chiefly visible ones, are they not?

They are.

And is it not in this state that the soul is most completely in bondage to the body?   d How so?

Because every pleasure and pain has a kind of nail, and nails and pins her to the body, and gives her a bodily nature, making her think that whatever the body says is true. And so, from having the same fancies and the same pleasures as the body, she is obliged, I suppose, to come to have the same ways, and way of life: she must always be defiled with the body when she leaves it, and cannot be pure when she reaches the   e other world; and so she soon falls back into another body and takes root in it, like seed that is sown. Therefore she loses all part in intercourse with the divine, and pure, and uniform.

That is very true, Socrates, said Cebes.

It is for these reasons then, Cebes, that the real lovers of knowledge are temper- ate and brave; and not for the world's reasons. Or do you think so?   84

No, certainly I do not.

Assuredly not. The soul of a philosopher will consider that it is the office of philosophy to set her free. She will know that she must not give herself up once more to the bondage of pleasure and pain, from which philosophy is releasing her, and, like Penelope, do a work, only to undo it continually, weaving instead of unweaving her web. She gains for herself peace from these things, and follows reason and ever abides

b   in it, contemplating what is true and divine and real, and fostered up by them. So she thinks that she should live in this life, and when she dies she believes that she will go to what is akin to and like herself, and be released from human ills. A soul, Simmias and Cebes, that has been so nurtured and so trained will never fear lest she should be torn in pieces at her departure from the body, and blown away by the winds, and vanish, and utterly cease to exist.

c   At these words there was a long silence. Socrates himself seemed to be absorbed in his argument, and so were most of us. Cebes and Simmias conversed for a little by themselves. When Socrates observed them, he said: What? Do you think that our reasoning is incomplete? It still offers many points of doubt and attack, if it is to be examined thoroughly. If you are discussing another question, I have nothing to say. But if

d   you have any difficulty about this one, do not hesitate to tell me what it is, and, if you are of the opinion that the argument should be stated in a better way, explain your views yourselves, and take me along with you if you think that you will be more successful in my company.

Simmias replied: Well, Socrates, I will tell you the truth. Each of us has a difficulty, and each has been pushing on the other and urging him to ask you about it. We were anxious to hear what you have to say; but we were reluctant to trouble you, for we were afraid that it might be unpleasant to you to be asked questions now.

Socrates smiled at this answer and said, Dear me! Simmias; I shall find it hard to

e   convince other people that I do not consider my fate a misfortune when I cannot convince even you of it, and you are afraid that I am more peevish now than I used to be. You seem to think me inferior in prophetic power to the swans, which, when they find

85   that they have to die, sing more loudly than they ever sang before, for joy that they are about to depart into the presence of God, whose servants they are. The fear which men have of death themselves makes them speak falsely of the swans, and they say that the swan is wailing at its death, and that it sings loud for grief. They forget that no bird sings when it is hungry, or cold, or in any pain; not even the nightingale, nor the swal-

b   low, nor the hoopoe, which, they assert, wail and sing for grief. But I think that neither these birds nor the swan sing for grief. I believe that they have a prophetic power and foreknowledge of the good things in the next world, for they are Apollo's birds; and so they sing and rejoice on the day of their death, more than in all their life. And I believe that I myself am a fellow slave with the swans, and consecrated to the service of the same God, and that I have prophetic power from my master no less than they, and that I am not more despondent than they are at leaving this life. So, as far as vexing me goes, you may talk to me and ask questions as you please, as long as the Eleven of the Athenians* will let you.

c   Good, said Simmias; I will tell you my difficulty, and Cebes will tell you why he is dissatisfied with your statement. I think, Socrates, and I daresay you think so too, that it is very difficult, and perhaps impossible, to obtain clear knowledge about these matters in this life. Yet I should hold him to be a very poor creature who did not test what is said about them in every way, and persevere until he had examined the ques-

*[Officials whose duty it was to superintend executions.]

tion from every side, and could do no more. It is our duty to do one of two things. We must learn, or we must discover for ourselves, the truth of these matters; or, if that be   d impossible, we must take the best and most irrefragable of human doctrines and, embarking on that, as on a raft, risk the voyage of life, unless a stronger vessel, some divine word, could be found, on which we might take our journey more safely and more securely. And now, after what you have said, I shall not be ashamed to put a question to you; and then I shall not have to blame myself hereafter for not having said now what I think. Cebes and I have been considering your argument, and we think that it is hardly sufficient.

I daresay you are right, my friend, said Socrates. But tell me, where is it insuffi-   e cient?

To me it is insufficient, he replied, because the very same argument might be used of a harmony, and a lyre, and its strings. It might be said that the harmony in a tuned lyre is something unseen, and incorporeal, and perfectly beautiful, and divine, while the lyre and its strings are corporeal, and with the nature of bodies, and compounded, and   86 earthly, and akin to the mortal. Now suppose that, when the lyre is broken and the strings are cut or snapped, a man were to press the same argument that you have used, and were to say that the harmony cannot have perished and that it must still exist, for it cannot possibly be that the lyre and the strings, with their mortal nature, continue to exist, though those strings have been broken, while the harmony, which is of the same   b nature as the divine and the immortal, and akin to them, has perished, and perished before the mortal lyre. He would say that the harmony itself must still exist somewhere, and that the wood and the strings will rot away before anything happens to it. And I think, Socrates, that you too must be aware that many of us believe the soul to be most probably a mixture and harmony of the elements by which our body is, as it were, strung and held together, such as heat and cold, and dry and wet, and the like, when they are mixed together well and in due proportion. Now if the soul is a harmony, it is clear   c that, when the body is relaxed out of proportion, or overstrung by disease or other evils, the soul, though most divine, must perish at once, like other harmonies of sound and of all works of art, while what remains of each body must remain for a long time, until it be burned or rotted away. What then shall we say to a man who asserts that the soul,   d being a mixture of the elements of the body, perishes first at what is called death?

Socrates looked keenly at us, as he often used to do, and smiled. Simmias' objection is a fair one, he said. If any of you is readier than I am, why does he not answer? For Simmias looks like a formidable assailant. But before we answer him, I think that   e we had better hear what fault Cebes has to find with my reasoning, and so gain time to consider our reply. And then, when we have heard them both, we must either give in to them, if they seem to harmonize, or, if they do not, we must proceed to argue in defense of our reasoning. Come, Cebes, what is it that troubles you and makes you doubt?

I will tell you, replied Cebes. I think that the argument is just where it was, and still open to our former objection. You have shown very cleverly and, if it is not arro-   87 gant to say so, quite conclusively that our souls existed before they entered the human form. I don't retract my admission on that point. But I am not convinced that they will continue to exist after we are dead. I do not agree with Simmias' objection, that the soul is not stronger and more lasting than the body: I think that it is very much superior in those respects. "Well, then," the argument might reply, "do you still doubt, when you see that the weaker part of a man continues to exist after his death? Do you not   b think that the more lasting part of him must necessarily be preserved for as long?" See, therefore, if there is anything in what I say; for I think that I, like Simmias, shall best express my meaning in a figure. It seems to me that a man might use an argument similar to yours to prove that a weaver, who had died in old age, had not in fact perished, but was still alive somewhere, on the ground that the garment which the weaver had

c woven for himself and used to wear had not perished or been destroyed. And if anyone were incredulous, he might ask whether a human being, or a garment constantly in use and wear, lasts the longest; and on being told that a human being lasts much the longest, he might think that he had shown beyond all doubt that the man was safe, because what lasts a shorter time than the man had not perished. But that, I suppose, is not so, Simmias; for you too must examine what I say. Everyone would understand that such an argument was simple nonsense. This weaver wove himself many such gar-

d ments and wore them out; he outlived them all but the last, but he perished before that one. Yet a man is in no wise inferior to his cloak, or weaker than it, on that account. And I think that the soul's relation to the body may be expressed in a similar figure. Why should not a man very reasonably say in just the same way that the soul lasts a long time, while the body is weaker and lasts a shorter time? But, he might go on, each soul wears out many bodies, especially if she lives for many years. For if the body is in

e a state of flux and decay in the man's lifetime, and the soul is ever repairing the worn-out part, it will surely follow that the soul, on perishing, will be clothed in her last robe, and perish before that alone. But when the soul has perished, then the body will show its weakness and quickly rot away. So as yet we have no right to be confident, on

88 the strength of this argument, that our souls continue to exist after we are dead. And a man might concede even more than this to an opponent who used your argument; he might admit not only that our souls existed in the period before we were born, but also that there is no reason why some of them should not continue to exist in the future, and often come into being, and die again, after we are dead; for the soul is strong enough by nature to endure coming into being many times. He might grant that, without conceding that she suffers no harm in all these births, or that she is not at last wholly de-

b stroyed at one of the deaths; and he might say that no man knows when this death and dissolution of the body, which brings destruction to the soul, will be, for it is impossible for any man to find out that. But if this is true, a man's confidence about death must be an irrational confidence, unless he can prove that the soul is wholly indestructible and immortal. Otherwise everyone who is dying must fear that his soul will perish utterly this time in her separation from the body.

c   It made us all very uncomfortable to listen to them, as we afterward said to each other. We had been fully convinced by the previous argument; and now they seemed to overturn our conviction, and to make us distrust all the arguments that were to come, as well as the preceding ones, and to doubt if our judgment was worth anything, or even if certainty could be attained at all.

d   ECHECRATES: By the gods, Phaedo, I can understand your feelings very well. I myself felt inclined while you were speaking to ask myself, "Then what reasoning are we to believe in future? That of Socrates was quite convincing, and now it has fallen into discredit." For the doctrine that our soul is a harmony has always taken a wonderful hold of me, and your mentioning it reminded me that I myself had held it. And now I must begin again and find some other reasoning which shall convince me that a

e man's soul does not die with him at his death. So tell me, I pray you, how did Socrates pursue the argument? Did he show any signs of uneasiness, as you say that you did, or did he come to the defense of his argument calmly? And did he defend it satisfactorily or not? Tell me the whole story as exactly as you can.

89   PHAEDO: I have often, Echecrates, wondered at Socrates; but I never admired him more than I admired him then. There was nothing very strange in his having an answer. What I chiefly wondered at was, first, the kindness and good nature and respect with

which he listened to the young men's objections; and, secondly, the quickness with which he perceived their effect upon us; and, lastly, how well he healed our wounds, and rallied us as if we were beaten and flying troops, and encouraged us to follow him, and to examine the reasoning with him.

ECHECRATES: How?

PHAEDO: I will tell you. I was sitting by the bed on a stool at his right hand, and his seat was a good deal higher than mine. He stroked my head and gathered up the b
hair on my neck in his hand—you know he used often to play with my hair—and said, Tomorrow, Phaedo, I daresay you will cut off these beautiful locks.

I suppose so, Socrates, I replied.

You will not, if you take my advice.

Why not? I asked.

You and I will cut off our hair today, he said, if our argument be dead indeed, and we cannot bring it to life again. And I, if I were you, and the argument were to es- c
cape me, would swear an oath, as the Argives did, not to wear my hair long again until I had renewed the fight and conquered the argument of Simmias and Cebes.

But Heracles himself, they say, is not a match for two, I replied.

Then summon me to aid you, as your Iolaus, while there is still light.

Then I summon you, not as Heracles summoned Iolaus, but as Iolaus might summon Heracles.

It will be the same, he replied. But first let us take care not to make a mistake.

What mistake? I asked.

The mistake of becoming misologists, or haters of reasoning, as men become d
misanthropists, he replied; for to hate reasoning is the greatest evil that can happen to us. Misology and misanthropy both come from similar causes. The latter arises out of the implicit and irrational confidence which is placed in a man who is believed by his friend to be thoroughly true and sincere and trustworthy, and who is soon afterward discovered to be a bad man and untrustworthy. This happens again and again; and when a man has had this experience many times, particularly at the hands of those e
whom he has believed to be his nearest and dearest friends, and he has quarreled with many of them, he ends by hating all men and thinking that there is no good at all in anyone. Have you not seen this happen?

Yes, certainly, said I.

Is it not discreditable? he said. Is it not clear that such a man tries to deal with men without understanding human nature? Had he understood it he would have known that, in fact, good men and bad men are very few indeed, and that the majority of men 90
are neither one nor the other.

What do you mean? I asked.

Just what is true of extremely large and extremely small things, he replied. What is rarer than to find a man, or a dog, or anything else which is either extremely large or extremely small? Or again, what is rarer than to find a man who is extremely swift or slow, or extremely base or honorable, or extremely black or white? Have you not noticed that in all these cases the extremes are rare and few, and that the average specimens are abundant and many?

Yes, certainly, I replied.

And in the same way, if there were a competition in wickedness, he said, don't b
you think that the leading sinners would be found to be very few?

That is likely enough, said I.

Yes, it is, he replied. But this is not the point in which arguments are like men; it was you who led me on to discuss this point. The analogy is this. When a man believes some reasoning to be true, though he does not understand the art of reasoning, and then soon afterward, rightly or wrongly, comes to think that it is false, and this happens to him time after time, he ends by disbelieving in reasoning altogether. You know that

c   persons who spend their time in disputation, come at last to think themselves the wisest of men, and to imagine that they alone have discovered that there is no soundness or certainty anywhere, either in reasoning or in things, and that all existence is in a state of perpetual flux, like the currents of the Euripus, and never remains still for a moment.

Yes, I replied, that is certainly true.

And, Phaedo, he said, if there be a system of reasoning which is true, and certain,

d   and which our minds can grasp, it would be very lamentable that a man who has met with some of these arguments which at one time seem true and at another false should at last, in the bitterness of his heart, gladly put all the blame on the reasoning, instead of on himself and his own unskillfulness, and spend the rest of his life in hating and reviling reasoning, and lose the truth and knowledge of reality.

Indeed, I replied, that would be very lamentable.

e   First then, he said, let us be careful not to admit into our souls the notion that all reasoning is very likely unsound; let us rather think that we ourselves are not yet sound. And we must strive earnestly like men to become sound, you, my friends, for

91   the sake of all your future life, and I, because of my death. For I am afraid that at present I can hardly look at death like a philosopher; I am in a contentious mood, like the uneducated persons who never give a thought to the truth of the question about which

b   they are disputing, but are only anxious to persuade their audience that they themselves are right. And I think that today I shall differ from them only in one thing. I shall not be anxious to persuade my audience that I am right, except by the way; but I shall be very anxious indeed to persuade myself. For see, my dear friend, how selfish my reasoning is. If what I say is true, it is well to believe it. But if there is nothing after death, at any rate I shall pain my friends less by my lamentations in the interval before I die. And this ignorance will not last forever—that would have been an evil—it will soon come to an end. So prepared, Simmias and Cebes, he said, I come to the argument.

c   And you, if you take my advice, will think not of Socrates, but of the truth; and you will agree with me if you think that what I say is true; otherwise you will oppose me with every argument that you have; and be careful that, in my anxiety to convince you, I do not deceive both you and myself, and go away, leaving my sting behind me, like a bee.

Now let us proceed, he said. And first, if you find I have forgotten your arguments, repeat them. Simmias, I think, has fears and misgivings that the soul, being of

d   the nature of a harmony, may perish before the body, though she is more divine and nobler than the body. Cebes, if I am not mistaken, conceded that the soul is more enduring than the body; but he said that no one could tell whether the soul, after wearing out many bodies many times, did not herself perish on leaving her last body, and whether death be not precisely this—the destruction of the soul; for the destruction of the body is unceasing. Is there anything else, Simmias and Cebes, which we have to examine?

e   They both agreed that these were the questions.

Do you reject all our previous conclusions, he asked, or only some of them?

Only some of them, they replied.

Well, said he, what do you say of our doctrine that knowledge is recollection,

92   and that therefore our souls must necessarily have existed somewhere else, before they were imprisoned in our bodies?

I, replied Cebes, was convinced by it at the time in a wonderful way; and now there is no doctrine to which I adhere more firmly.

And I am of that mind too, said Simmias; and I shall be very much surprised if I ever change it.

But, my Theban friend, you will have to change it, said Socrates, if this opinion of yours, that a harmony is a composite thing, and that the soul is a harmony composed of the elements of the body at the right tension, is to stand. You will hardly allow your-   b self to assert that the harmony was in existence before the things from which it was to be composed? Will you do that?

Certainly not, Socrates.

But you see that that is what your assertion comes to when you say that the soul existed before she came into the form and body of man, and yet that she is composed of elements which did not yet exist? Your harmony is not like what you compare it to: the lyre and the strings and the sounds, as yet untuned, come into existence first; and   c the harmony is composed last of all, and perishes first. How will this belief of yours accord with the other?

It will not, replied Simmias.

And yet, said he, an argument about harmony is hardly the place for a discord.

No, indeed, said Simmias.

Well, there is a discord in your argument, he said. You must choose which doctrine you will retain—that knowledge is recollection or that the soul is a harmony.

The former, Socrates, certainly, he replied. The latter has never been demonstrated to me; it rests only on probable and plausible grounds, which make it a popular   d opinion. I know that doctrines which ground their proofs on probabilities are impostors and that they are very apt to mislead, both in geometry and everything else, if one is not on one's guard against them. But the doctrine about recollection and knowledge rests upon a foundation which claims belief. We agreed that the soul exists before she ever enters the body, as surely as the essence itself which has the name of real being   e exists. And I am persuaded that I believe in this essence rightly and on sufficient evidence. It follows therefore, I suppose, that I cannot allow myself or anyone else to say that the soul is a harmony.

And, consider the question in another way, Simmias, said Socrates. Do you think that a harmony or any other composition can exist in a state other than the state of the   93 elements of which it is composed?

Certainly not.

Nor, I suppose, can it do or suffer anything beyond what they do and suffer?

He assented.

A harmony therefore cannot lead the elements of which it is composed; it must follow them?

He agreed.

And much less can it be moved, or make a sound, or do anything else in opposition to its parts.

Much less, indeed, he replied.

Well, is not every harmony by nature a harmony according as it is adjusted?

I don't understand you, he replied.

If it is tuned more, and to a greater extent, he said, supposing that to be possible, will it not be more a harmony, and to a greater extent, while if it is tuned less, and to a   b smaller extent, will it not be less a harmony, and to a smaller extent?

Certainly.

Well, is this true of the soul? Can one soul be more a soul, and to a greater extent, or less a soul, and to a smaller extent, than another, even in the smallest degree?

Certainly not, he replied.

c Well then, he replied, please tell me this; is not one soul said to have intelligence and virtue and to be good, while another is said to have folly and vice and to be bad? And is it not true?

Yes, certainly.

What then will those who assert that the soul is a harmony say that the virtue and the vice which are in our souls are? Another harmony and another discord? Will they say that the good soul is in tune, and that, herself a harmony, she has within herself another harmony, and that the bad soul is out of tune herself, and has no other harmony within her?

I, said Simmias, cannot tell. But it is clear that they would have to say something of the kind.

d But it has been conceded, he said, that one soul is never more or less a soul than another. In other words, we have agreed that one harmony is never more, or to a greater extent, or less, or to a smaller extent a harmony than another. Is it not so?

Yes, certainly.

And the harmony which is neither more nor less a harmony, is not more or less tuned. Is that so?

Yes.

And has that which is neither more nor less tuned a greater, or a less, or an equal share of harmony?

An equal share.

Then, since one soul is never more nor less a soul than another, it has not been e more or less tuned either?

True.

Therefore it can have no greater share of harmony or of discord?

Certainly not.

And, therefore, can one soul contain more vice or virtue than another, if vice be discord and virtue harmony?

By no means.

94 Or rather, Simmias, to speak quite accurately, I suppose that there will be no vice in any soul if the soul is a harmony. I take it there can never be any discord in a harmony which is a perfect harmony.

Certainly not.

Neither can a soul, if it be a perfect soul, have any vice in it?

No; that follows necessarily from what has been said.

Then the result of this reasoning is that all the souls of all living creatures will be equally good if the nature of all souls is to be equally souls.

Yes, I think so, Socrates, he said.

And do you think that this is true, he asked, and that this would have been the b fate of our argument, if the hypothesis that the soul is a harmony had been correct?

No, certainly not, he replied.

Well, said he, of all the parts of a man, should you not say that it was the soul, and particularly the wise soul, which rules?

I should.

Does she yield to the passions of the body or does she oppose them? I mean this. When the body is hot and thirsty, does not the soul drag it away and prevent it from drinking, and when it is hungry does she not prevent it from eating? And do we not see her opposing the passions of the body in a thousand other ways?

Yes, certainly.

But we have also agreed that, if she is a harmony, she can never give a sound contrary to the tensions, and relaxations, and vibrations, and other changes of the elements of which she is composed; that she must follow them, and can never lead them?

Yes, he replied, we certainly have.

Well, now, do we not find the soul acting in just the opposite way, and leading all the elements of which she is said to consist, and opposing them in almost everything all through life, and lording it over them in every way, and chastising them, sometimes severely, and with a painful discipline, such as gymnastics and medicine; and sometimes lightly, sometimes threatening and sometimes admonishing the desires and passions and fears, as though she were speaking to something other than herself, as Homer makes Odysseus do in the *Odyssey*, where he says that

> He smote upon his breast, and chid his heart:
> "Endure, my heart, e'en worse hast thou endured." [XX.17]

Do you think that when Homer wrote that, he supposed the soul to be a harmony and capable of being led by the passions of the body, and not of a nature to lead them and be their lord, being herself far too divine a thing to be like a harmony?

Certainly, Socrates, I think not.

Then, my excellent friend, it is quite wrong to say that the soul is a harmony. For then, you see, we should not be in agreement either with the divine poet Homer or with ourselves.

That is true, he replied.

Very good, said Socrates; I think that we have contrived to appease our Theban Harmonia with tolerable success. But how about Cadmus, Cebes? he said. How shall we appease him, and with what reasoning?

I daresay that you will find out how to do it, said Cebes. At all events you have argued that the soul is not a harmony in a way which surprised me very much. When Simmias was stating his objection, I wondered how anyone could possibly dispose of his argument; and so I was very much surprised to see it fall before the very first onset of yours. I should not wonder if the same fate awaited the argument of Cadmus.

My good friend, said Socrates, do not be overconfident, or some evil eye will overturn the argument that is to come. However, that we will leave to God; let us, like Homer's heroes, "advancing boldly," see if there is anything in what you say. The sum of what you seek is this. You require me to prove to you that the soul is indestructible and immortal; for if it be not so, you think that the confidence of a philosopher, who is confident in death, and who believes that when he is dead he will fare infinitely better in the other world than if he had lived a different sort of life in this world, is a foolish and idle confidence. You say that to show that the soul is strong and godlike, and that she existed before we were born men, is not enough; for that does not necessarily prove her immortality, but only that she lasts a long time, and has existed an enormous while, and has known and done many things in a previous state. Yet she is not any the more immortal for that; her very entrance into man's body was, like a disease, the beginning of her destruction. And, you say, she passes this life in misery, and at last perishes in what we call death. You think that it makes no difference at all to the fears of each one of us, whether she enters the body once or many times; for everyone but a e   fool must fear death, if he does not know and cannot prove that she is immortal. That, I think, Cebes, is the substance of your objection. I state it again and again on purpose, that nothing may escape us, and that you may add to it or take away from it anything that you wish.

Cebes replied: No, that is my meaning. I don't want to add or to take away anything at present.

Socrates paused for some time and thought. Then he said, It is not an easy question that you are raising, Cebes. We must examine fully the whole subject of the causes

96   of generation and decay. If you like, I will give you my own experiences, and if you think that you can make use of anything that I say, you may employ it to satisfy your misgivings.

Indeed, said Cebes, I should like to hear your experiences.

Listen, then, and I will tell you, Cebes, he replied. When I was a young man, I had a passionate desire for the wisdom which is called Physical Science. I thought it a splendid thing to know the causes of everything; why a thing comes into being, and

b   why it perishes, and why it exists. I was always worrying myself with such questions as, Do living creatures take a definite form, as some persons say, from the fermentation of heat and cold? Is it the blood, or the air, or fire by which we think? Or is it none of these, but the brain which gives the senses of hearing and sight and smell, and do memory and opinion come from these, and knowledge from memory and opinion

c   when in a state of quiescence? Again, I used to examine the destruction of these things, and the changes of the heaven and the earth, until at last I concluded that I was wholly and absolutely unfitted for these studies. I will prove that to you conclusively. I was so completely blinded by these studies that I forgot what I had formerly seemed to myself and to others to know quite well; I unlearned all that I had been used to think that I un-

d   derstood; even the cause of man's growth. Formerly I had thought it evident on the face of it that the cause of growth was eating and drinking, and that, when from food flesh is added to flesh, and bone to bone, and in the same way to the other parts of the body their proper elements, then by degrees the small bulk grows to be large, and so the boy becomes a man. Don't you think that my belief was reasonable?

I do, said Cebes.

Then here is another experience for you. I used to feel no doubt, when I saw a

e   tall man standing by a short one, that the tall man was, it might be, a head the taller, or, in the same way, that one horse was bigger than another. I was even clearer that ten was more than eight by the addition of two, and that a thing two cubits long was longer by half its length than a thing one cubit long.

And what do you think now? asked Cebes.

I think that I am very far from believing that I know the cause of any of these things. Why, when you add one to one, I am not sure either that the one to which one is

97   added has become two, or that the one added and the one to which it is added become, by the addition, two. I cannot understand how, when they are brought together, this union, or placing of one by the other, should be the cause of their becoming two, whereas, when they were separated, each of them was one, and they were not two. Nor,

b   again, if you divide one into two, can I convince myself that this division is the cause of one becoming two; for then a thing becomes two from exactly the opposite cause. In the former case it was because two units were brought together, and the one was added to the other; while now it is because they are separated, and the one divided from the other. Nor, again, can I persuade myself that I know how one is generated; in short, this method does not show me the cause of the generation or destruction or existence of anything. I have in my own mind a confused idea of another method, but I cannot admit this one for a moment.

But one day I listened to a man who said that he was reading from a book of Anaxagoras, which affirmed that it is Mind which orders and is the cause of all things. I was delighted with this theory; it seemed to me to be right that Mind should be the   c cause of all things, and I thought to myself, If this is so, then Mind will order and arrange each thing in the best possible way. So if we wish to discover the cause of the generation or destruction or existence of a thing, we must discover how it is best for that thing to exist, or to act, or to be acted on. Man therefore has only to consider what   d is best and fittest for himself, or for other things, and then it follows necessarily that he will know what is bad; for both are included in the same science. These reflections made me very happy: I thought that I had found in Anaxagoras a teacher of the cause of existence after my own heart, and I expected that he would tell me first whether the   e earth is flat or round, and that he would then go on to explain to me the cause and the necessity, and tell me what is best, and that it is best for the earth to be of that shape. If he said that the earth was in the center of the universe, I thought that he would explain that it was best for it to be there; and I was prepared not to require any other kind of   98 cause, if he made this clear to me. In the same way I was prepared to ask questions about the sun, and the moon, and the stars, about their relative speeds, and revolutions, and changes; and to hear why it is best for each of them to act and be acted on as they are acted on. I never thought that, when he said that things are ordered by Mind, he would introduce any reason for their being as they are, except that they are best so. I thought that he would assign a cause to each thing, and a cause to the universe, and   b then would go on to explain to me what was best for each thing, and what was the common good of all. I would not have sold my hopes for a great deal: I seized the books very eagerly, and read them as fast as I could, in order that I might know what is best and what is worse.

All my splendid hopes were dashed to the ground, my friend, for as I went on reading I found that the writer made no use of Mind at all, and that he assigned no   c causes for the order of things. His causes were air, and ether, and water, and many other strange things. I thought that he was exactly like a man who should begin by saying that Socrates does all that he does by Mind, and who, when he tried to give a reason for each of my actions, should say, first, that I am sitting here now, because my body is composed of bones and muscles, and that the bones are hard and separated by joints, while the muscles can be tightened and loosened, and, together with the flesh   d and the skin which holds them together, cover the bones; and that therefore, when the bones are raised in their sockets, the relaxation and contraction of the muscles make it possible for me now to bend my limbs, and that that is the cause of my sitting here with my legs bent. And in the same way he would go on to explain why I am talking to you: he would assign voice, and air, and hearing, and a thousand other things as causes; but he would quite forget to mention the real cause, which is that since the Athenians   e thought it right to condemn me, I have thought it right and just to sit here and to submit to whatever sentence they may think fit to impose. For, by the dog of Egypt, I think that these muscles and bones would long ago have been in Megara or Boeotia,   99 prompted by their opinion of what is best, if I had not thought it better and more honorable to submit to whatever penalty the state inflicts, rather than escape by flight. But to call these things causes is too absurd! If it were said that without bones and muscles and the other parts of my body I could not have carried my resolutions into effect, that would be true. But to say that they are the cause of what I do, and that in this way I am   b acting by Mind, and not from choice of what is best, would be a very loose and careless way of talking. It simply means that a man cannot distinguish the realcause from that without which the cause cannot be the cause, and this it is, I think, which the multitude, groping about in the dark, speaks of as the cause, giving it a name which does not belong to it. And so one man surrounds the earth with a vortex, and makes the heavens sustain it. Another represents the earth as a flat kneading trough, and supports

c   it on a basis of air. But they never think of looking for a power which is involved in these things being disposed as it is best for them to be, nor do they think that such a power has any divine strength. They expect to find an Atlas who is stronger and more immortal and abler to hold the world together, and they never for a moment imagine that it is the binding force of good which really binds and holds things together. I would most gladly learn the nature of that kind of cause from any man, but I wholly

d   failed either to discover it myself or to learn it from anyone else. However, I had a second string to my bow, and perhaps, Cebes, you would like me to describe to you how I proceeded in my search for the cause.

I should like to hear very much indeed, he replied.

When I had given up inquiring into real existence, he proceeded, I thought that I must take care that I did not suffer as people do who look at the sun during an eclipse.

e   For they are apt to lose their eyesight, unless they look at the sun's reflection in water or some such medium. That danger occurred to me. I was afraid that my soul might be completely blinded if I looked at things with my eyes, and tried to grasp them with my senses. So I thought that I must have recourse to conceptions, and examine the truth of

100   existence by means of them. Perhaps my illustration is not quite accurate. I am scarcely prepared to admit that he who examines existence through conceptions is dealing with mere reflections, any more than he who examines it as manifested in sensible objects. However, I began in this way. I assumed in each case whatever principle I judged to be strongest; and then I held as true whatever seemed to agree with it, whether in the case of the cause or of anything else, and as untrue whatever seemed not to agree with it. I should like to explain my meaning more clearly; I don't think you understand me yet.

Indeed I do not very well, said Cebes.

b   I mean nothing new, he said; only what I have repeated over and over again, both in our conversation today and at other times. I am going to try to explain to you the kind of cause at which I have worked, and I will go back to what we have so often spoken of, and begin with the assumption that there exists an absolute beauty, and an absolute good, and an absolute greatness, and so on. If you grant me this, and agree that they exist, I hope to be able to show you what my cause is, and to discover that the soul is immortal.

c   You may assume that I grant it you, said Cebes; go on with your proof.

Then do you agree with me in what follows? he asked. It appears to me that if anything besides absolute beauty is beautiful, it is so simply because it partakes of absolute beauty, and I say the same of all phenomena. Do you allow that kind of cause?

I do, he answered.

Well then, he said, I do no longer recognize nor can I understand these other

d   wise causes: if I am told that anything is beautiful because it has a rich color, or a goodly form, or the like, I pay no attention, for such language only confuses me; and in a simple and plain, and perhaps a foolish way, I hold to the doctrine that the thing is only made beautiful by the presence or communication, or whatever you please to call it, of absolute beauty—I do not wish to insist on the nature of the communication, but what I am sure of is that it is absolute beauty which makes all beautiful things beauti-

ful. This seems to me to be the safest answer that I can give myself or others; I believe
that I shall never fail if I hold to this; it is a safe answer to make to myself or anyone else,   e
that it is absolute beauty which makes beautiful things beautiful. Don't you think so?

I do.

And it is largeness that makes large things large, and larger things larger, and
smallness that makes smaller things smaller?

Yes.

And if you were told that one man was taller than another by a head, and that the
shorter man was shorter by a head, you would not accept the statement. You would   101
protest that you say only that the greater is greater by size, and that size is the cause of
its being greater; and that the less is only less by smallness, and that smallness is the
cause of its being less. You would be afraid to assert that a man is greater or smaller by
a head, lest you should be met by the retort, first, that the greater is greater, and the
smaller smaller, by the same thing, and secondly, that the greater is greater by a head,   b
which is a small thing, and that it is truly marvelous that a small thing should make a
man great. Should you not be afraid of that?

Yes, indeed, said Cebes, laughing.

And you would be afraid to say that ten is more than eight by two, and that two
is the cause of the excess; you would say that ten was more than eight by number, and
that number is the cause of the excess? And in just the same way you would be afraid
to say that a thing two cubits long was longer than a thing one cubit long by half its
length, instead of by size, would you not?

Yes, certainly.

Again, you would be careful not to affirm that, if one is added to one, the addition is the cause of two, or, if one is divided, that the division is the cause of two? You   c
would protest loudly that you know of no way in which a thing can be generated, except by participation in its own proper essence; and that you can give no cause for the
generation of two except participation in duality; and that all things which are to be
two must participate in duality, while whatever is to be one must participate in unity.
You would leave the explanation of these divisions and additions and all such sub-   d
tleties to wiser men than yourself. You would be frightened, as the saying is, at your
own shadow and ignorance, and would hold fast to the safety of our principle, and so
give your answer. But if anyone should attack the principle itself, you would not mind
him or answer him until you had considered whether the consequences of it are consistent or inconsistent, and when you had to give an account of the principle itself, you
would give it in the same way, by assuming some other principle which you think the   e
strongest of the higher ones, and so go on until you had reached a satisfactory resting
place. You would not mix up the first principle and its consequences in your argument,
as mere disputants do, if you really wish to discover anything of existence. Such persons will very likely not spend a single word or thought upon that, for they are clever
enough to be able to please themselves entirely, though their argument is a chaos. But
you, I think, if you are a philosopher, will do as I say.   102

Very true, said Simmias and Cebes together.

ECHECRATES: And they were right, Phaedo. I think the clearness of his reasoning,
even to the dullest, is quite wonderful.

PHAEDO: Indeed, Echecrates, all who were there thought so too.

ECHECRATES: So do we who were not there, but who are listening to your story.
But how did the argument proceed after that?

PHAEDO: They had admitted that each of the Ideas exists and that Phenomena take
the names of the Ideas as they participate in them. Socrates, I think, then went on to ask: b

If you say this, do you not, in saying that Simmias is taller than Socrates and shorter than Phaedo, say that Simmias possesses both the attribute of tallness and the attribute of shortness?

I do.

c   But you admit, he said, that the proposition that Simmias is taller than Socrates is not exactly true, as it is stated; Simmias is not really taller because he is Simmias, but because of his height. Nor again is he taller than Socrates because Socrates is Socrates, but because of Socrates' shortness compared with Simmias' tallness.

True.

Nor is Simmias shorter than Phaedo because Phaedo is Phaedo, but because of Phaedo's tallness compared with Simmias' shortness.

That is so.

Then in this way Simmias is called both short and tall, when he is between the two; he exceeds the shortness of one by the excess of his height, and gives the other a tallness exceeding his own shortness. I daresay you think, he said, smiling, that my language is like a legal document for precision and formality. But I think that it is as I say.

He agreed.

I say it because I want you to think as I do. It seems to me not only that absolute greatness will never be great and small at once, but also that greatness in us never admits smallness, and will not be exceeded. One of two things must happen: either the greater will give way and fly at the approach of its opposite, the less, or it will perish. It will not stand its ground, and receive smallness, and be other than it was, just as I stand my ground, and receive smallness, and remain the very same small man that I was. But greatness cannot endure to be small, being great. Just in the same way again smallness in us will never become nor be great; nor will any opposite, while it remains what it was, become or be at the same time the opposite of what it was. Either it goes away or it perishes in the change.

That is exactly what I think, said Cebes.

Thereupon someone—I am not sure who—said,

But surely is not this just the reverse of what we agreed to be true earlier in the argument, that the greater is generated from the less, and the less from the greater, and, in short, that opposites are generated from opposites? But now it seems to be denied that this can ever happen.

Socrates inclined his head to the speaker and listened. Well and bravely remarked, he said, but you have not noticed the difference between the two propositions. What we said then was that a concrete thing is generated from its opposite; what we say now is that the absolute opposite can never become opposite to itself, either when it is in us, or when it is in nature. We were speaking then of things in which the opposites are, and we named them after those opposites; but now we are speaking of the opposites themselves, whose inherence gives the things their names; and they, we say, will never be generated from each other. At the same time he turned to Cebes and asked, Did his objection trouble you at all, Cebes?

No, replied Cebes; I don't feel that difficulty. But I will not deny that many other things trouble me.

Then we are quite agreed on this point, he said. An opposite will never be opposite to itself.

No never, he replied.

Now tell me again, he said; do you agree with me in this? Are there not things which you call heat and cold?

Yes.

Are they the same as snow and fire?

No, certainly not.

Heat is different from fire, and cold from snow?   d

Yes.

But I suppose, as we have said, that you do not think that snow can ever receive heat, and yet remain what it was, snow and hot: it will either retire or perish at the approach of heat.

Certainly.

And fire, again, will either retire or perish at the approach of cold. It will never endure to receive the cold and still remain what it was, fire and cold.

True, he said.   e

Then, it is true of some of these things that not only the idea itself has a right to its name for all time, but that something else too, which is not the idea, but which has the form of the idea wherever it exists, shares the name. Perhaps my meaning will be clearer by an example. The odd ought always to have the name of odd, ought it not?

Yes, certainly.

Well, my question is this. Is the odd the only thing with this name, or is there something else which is not the same as the odd, but which must always have this   104 name, together with its own, because its nature is such that it is never separated from the odd? There are many examples of what I mean: let us take one of them, the number three, and consider it. Do you not think that we must always call it by the name of odd, as well as by its own name, although the odd is not the same as the number three? Yet the nature of the number three, and of the number five, and of half the whole series of   b numbers, is such that each of them is odd, though none of them is the same as the odd. In the same way the number two, and the number four, and the whole of the other series of numbers, are each of them always even, though they are not the same as the even. Do you agree or not?

Yes, of course, he replied.

Then see what I want to show you. It is not only opposite ideas which appear not to admit their opposites; things also which are not opposites, but which always contain opposites, seem as if they would not admit the idea which is opposite to the idea that   c they contain: they either perish or retire at its approach. Shall we not say that the number three would perish or endure anything sooner than become even while it remains three?

Yes, indeed, said Cebes.

And yet, said he, the number two is not the opposite of the number three.

No, certainly not.

Then it is not only the ideas which will not endure the approach of their opposites; there are some other things besides which will not endure such an approach.

That is quite true, he said.

Shall we determine, if we can, what is their nature? he asked.

Certainly.

Will they not be those things, Cebes, which force whatever they are in to have al-   d ways not its own idea only, but the idea of some opposite as well?

What do you mean?

Only what we were saying just now. You know, I think, that whatever the idea of three is in, is bound to be not three only, but odd as well.

Certainly.

Well, we say that the opposite idea to the form which produces this result will never come to that thing.

Indeed, no.

But the idea of the odd produces it?

Yes.

And the idea of the even is the opposite of the idea of the odd?

Yes.

e　Then the idea of the even will never come to three?

Certainly not.

So three has no part in the even?

None.

Then the number three is uneven?

Yes.

So much for the definition which I undertook to give of things which are not opposites, and yet do not admit opposites; thus we have seen that the number three does not admit the even, though it is not the opposite of the even, for it always brings with it 105　the opposite of the even, and the number two does not admit the odd, nor fire cold, and so on. Do you agree with me in saying that not only does the opposite not admit the opposite, but also that whatever brings with it an opposite of anything to which it goes never admits the opposite of that which it brings? Let me recall this to you again; there is no harm in repetition. Five will not admit the idea of the even, nor will the double of five—ten—admit the idea of the odd. It is not itself an opposite, yet it will not admit b　the idea of the odd. Again, one and a half, a half, and the other numbers of that kind will not admit the idea of the whole, nor again will such numbers as a third. Do you follow and agree?

I follow you and entirely agree with you, he said.

Now begin again, and answer me, he said. And imitate me; do not answer me in the terms of my question: I mean, do not give the old safe answer which I have already spoken of, for I see another way of safety, which is the result of what we have been c　saying. If you ask me, what is that which must be in the body to make it hot, I shall not give our old safe and stupid answer, and say that it is heat; I shall make a more refined answer, drawn from what we have been saying, and reply, fire. If you ask me, what is that which must be in the body to make it sick, I shall not say sickness, but fever; and again to the question what is that which must be in number to make it odd, I shall not reply oddness, but unity, and so on. Do you understand my meaning clearly yet?

Yes, quite, he said.

Then, he went on, tell me, what is that which must be in a body to make it alive?

A soul, he replied.

d　And is this always so?

Of course, he said.

Then the soul always brings life to whatever contains her?

No doubt, he answered.

And is there an opposite to life, or not?

Yes.

What is it?

Death.

And we have already agreed that the soul cannot ever receive the opposite of what she brings?

Yes, certainly we have, said Cebes.

Well; what name did we give to that which does not admit the idea of the even?

The uneven, he replied.

And what do we call that which does not admit justice or music?

The unjust, and the unmusical.

Good; and what do we call that which does not admit death?

The immortal, he said.

And the soul does not admit death?

No.

Then the soul is immortal?

It is.

Good, he said. Shall we say that this is proved? What do you think?

Yes, Socrates, and very sufficiently.

Well, Cebes, he said, if the odd had been necessarily imperishable, must not three have been imperishable?

Of course.

And if cold had been necessarily imperishable, snow would have retired safe and unmelted, whenever warmth was applied to it. It would not have perished, and it would not have stayed and admitted the heat.

True, he said.

In the same way, I suppose, if warmth were imperishable, whenever cold attacked fire, the fire would never have been extinguished or have perished. It would have gone away in safety.

Necessarily, he replied.

And must we not say the same of the immortal? he asked. If the immortal is imperishable, the soul cannot perish when death comes upon her. It follows from what we have said that she will not ever admit death, or be in a state of death, any more than three, or the odd itself, will ever be even, or fire, or the heat itself which is in fire, cold. But, it may be said, Granted that the odd does not become even at the approach of the even; why, when the odd has perished, may not the even come into its place? We could not contend in reply that it does not perish, for the uneven is not imperishable; if we had agreed that the uneven was imperishable, we could have easily contended that the odd and three go away at the approach of the even; and we could have urged the same contention about fire and heat and the rest, could we not?

Yes, certainly.

And now, if we are agreed that the immortal is imperishable, then the soul will be not immortal only, but also imperishable; otherwise we shall require another argument.

Nay, he [Cebes] said, there is no need of that, as far as this point goes; for if the immortal, which is eternal, will admit of destruction, what will not?

And all men would admit, said Socrates, that God, and the essential form of life, and all else that is immortal, never perishes.

All men, indeed, he said; and, what is more, I think, all gods would admit that.

Then if the immortal is indestructible, must not the soul, if it be immortal, be imperishable?

Certainly, it must.

Then, it seems, when death attacks a man, his mortal part dies, but his immortal part retreats before death, and goes away safe and indestructible.

It seems so.

Then, Cebes, said he, beyond all question the soul is immortal and imperishable, and our souls will indeed exist in the other world.

I, Socrates, he replied, have no more objections to urge; your reasoning has quite satisfied me. If Simmias, or anyone else, has anything to say, it would be well for him to say it now; for I know not to what other season he can defer the discussion if he wants to say or to hear anything touching this matter.

No, indeed, said Simmias; neither have I any further ground for doubt after what
b   you have said. Yet I cannot help feeling some doubts still in my mind; for the subject
of our conversation is a vast one, and I distrust the feebleness of man.

You are right, Simmias, said Socrates, and more than that, you must re-examine
our original assumptions, however certain they seem to you; and when you have ana-
lyzed them sufficiently, you will, I think, follow the argument, as far as man can follow it; and when that becomes clear to you, you will seek for nothing more.

That is true, he said.

c   But then, my friends, said he, we must think of this. If it be true that the soul is
immortal, we have to take care of her, not merely on account of the time which we call
life, but also on account of all time. Now we can see how terrible is the danger of neglect. For if death had been a release from all things, it would have been a godsend to
the wicked; for when they died they would have been released with their souls from
the body and from their own wickedness. But now we have found that the soul is im-
d   mortal, and so her only refuge and salvation from evil is to become as perfect and wise
as possible. For she takes nothing with her to the other world but her education and
culture; and these, it is said, are of the greatest service or of the greatest injury to the
dead man at the very beginning of his journey thither. For it is said that the genius,
who has had charge of each man in his life, proceeds to lead him, when he is dead, to a
e   certain place where the departed have to assemble and receive judgment and then go to
the world below with the guide who is appointed to conduct them thither. And when
they have received their deserts there, and remained the appointed time, another guide
brings them back again after many long revolutions of ages. So this journey is not as
108 Aeschylus describes it in the *Telephus,* where he says that "a simple way leads to
Hades." But I think that the way is neither simple nor single; there would have been no
need of guides had it been so; for no one could miss the way if there were but one path.
But this road must have many branches and many windings, as I judge from the rites of
burial on earth.* The orderly and wise soul follows her leader and is not ignorant of the
things of that world; but the soul which lusts after the body flutters about the body and
the visible world for a long time, as I have said, and struggles hard and painfully, and
b   at last is forcibly and reluctantly dragged away by her appointed genius. And when she
comes to the place where the other souls are, if she is impure and stained with evil, and
has been concerned in foul murders, or if she has committed any other crimes that are
akin to these and the deeds of kindred souls, then everyone shuns her and turns aside
from meeting her, and will neither be her companion nor her guide, and she wanders
c   about by herself in extreme distress until a certain time is completed, and then she is
borne away by force to the habitation which befits her. But the soul that has spent her
life in purity and temperance has the gods for her companions and guides, and dwells
in the place which befits her. There are many wonderful places in the earth; and neither
its nature nor its size is what those who are wont to describe it imagine, as a friend has
convinced me.

What do you mean, Socrates? said Simmias. I have heard a great deal about the
d   earth myself, but I have never heard the view of which you are convinced. I should like
to hear it very much.

Well, Simmias, I don't think that it needs the skill of Glaucus to describe it to
you, but I think that it is beyond the skill of Glaucus to prove it true. I am sure that I
could not do so; and besides, Simmias, even if I knew how, I think that my life would
come to an end before the argument was finished. But there is nothing to prevent my
e   describing to you what I believe to be the form of the earth and its regions.

*[Sacrifices were offered to the gods of the lower world in places where three roads met.]

Well, said Simmias, that will do.

In the first place then, said he, I believe that the earth is a spherical body placed in the center of the heavens, and that therefore it has no need of air or of any other force to support it; the equiformity of the heavens in all their parts, and the equipoise of the earth itself, are sufficient to hold it up. A thing in equipoise placed in the center of what is equiform cannot incline in any direction, either more or less; it will remain unmoved and in perfect balance. That, said he, is the first thing that I believe. 109

And rightly, said Simmias.

Also, he proceeded, I think that the earth is of vast extent, and that we who dwell between the Phasis and the pillars of Heracles inhabit only a small portion of it, and dwell round the sea, like ants or frogs round a marsh; and I believe that many other men dwell elsewhere in similar places. For everywhere on the earth there are many hollows of every kind of shape and size, into which the water and the mist and the air collect; but the earth itself lies pure in the purity of the heavens, wherein are the stars, and which men who speak of these things commonly call ether. The water and the mist and the air, which collect into the hollows of the earth, are the sediment of it. Now we dwell in these hollows though we think that we are dwelling on the surface of the earth. We are just like a man dwelling in the depths of the ocean who thought that he was dwelling on its surface and believed that the sea was the heaven, because he saw the sun and the stars through the water; but who was too weak and slow ever to have reached the water's surface, and to have lifted his head from the sea, and come out from his depths to our world, and seen, or heard from one who had seen, how much purer and fairer our world was than the place wherein he dwelt. We are just in that state; we dwell in a hollow of the earth, and think that we are dwelling on its surface; and we call the air heaven, and think it to be the heaven wherein the stars run their courses. But the truth is that we are too weak and slow to pass through to the surface of the air. For if any man could reach the surface, or take wings and fly upward, he would look up and see a world beyond, just as the fishes look forth from the sea, and behold our world. And he would know that that was the real heaven, and the real light, and the real earth, if his nature were able to endure the sight. For this earth, and its stones, and all its regions have been spoiled and corroded, as things in the sea are corroded by the brine: nothing of any worth grows in the sea, nor, in short, is there anything therein without blemish, but, wherever land does exist, there are only caves, and sand, and vast tracts of mud and slime, which are not worthy even to be compared with the fair things of our world. But you would think that the things of that other world still further surpass the things of our world. I can tell you a tale, Simmias, about what is on the earth that lies beneath the heavens, which is worth your hearing.

b

c

d

e

110

b

Indeed, Socrates, said Simmias, we should like to hear your tale very much.

Well, my friend, he said, this is my tale. In the first place, the earth itself, if a man could look at it from above, is like one of those balls which are covered with twelve pieces of leather, and is marked with various colors, of which the colors that our painters use here are, as it were, samples. But there the whole earth is covered with them, and with others which are far brighter and purer ones than they. For part of it is purple of marvelous beauty, and part of it is golden, and the white of it is whiter than chalk or snow. It is made up of the other colors in the same way, and also of colors which are more beautiful than any that we have ever seen. The very hollows in it, that are filled with water and air, have themselves a kind of color, and glisten amid the diversity of the others, so that its form appears as one unbroken and varied surface. And what grows in this fair earth—its trees and flowers and fruit—is more beautiful than what grows with us in the same proportion; and so likewise are the hills and the stones in their smoothness and transparency and color. The pebbles which we prize in this

c

d

e   world, our cornelians, and jaspers, and emeralds, and the like, are but fragments of
them, but there all the stones are as our precious stones, and even more beautiful still.
The reason of this is that they are pure and not corroded or spoiled, as ours are, with
the decay and brine from the sediment that collects in the hollows and brings to the
stones and the earth and all animals and plants ... deformity and disease. All these

111   things, and with them gold and silver and the like, adorn the real earth; and they are
conspicuous from their multitude and size, and the many places where they are found;
so that he who could behold it would be a happy man. Many creatures live upon it; and
there are men, some dwelling inland, and others round the air, as we dwell round the
sea, and others in islands encircled by the air, which lie near the continent. In a word,

b   they use the air as we use water and the sea, and the ether as we use the air. The temperature of their seasons is such that they are free from disease, and live much longer
than we do; and in sight, and hearing, and smell, and the other senses, they are as much
more perfect than we, as air is purer than water, and ether than air. Moreover, they
have sanctuaries and temples of the gods, in which the gods dwell in very truth; they

c   hear the voices and oracles of the gods, and see them in visions, and have intercourse
with them face to face; and they see the sun and moon and stars as they really are; and
in other matters their happiness is of a piece with this.

That is the nature of the earth as a whole, and of what is upon it; and everywhere
on its globe there are many regions in the hollows, some of them deeper and more

d   open than that in which we dwell; and others also deeper, but with narrower mouths;
and others again shallower and broader than ours. All these are connected by many
channels beneath the earth, some of them narrow and others wide; and there are passages by which much water flows from one of them to another, as into basins, and vast
and never-failing rivers of both hot and cold water beneath the earth, and much fire,
and great rivers of fire, and many rivers of liquid mud, some clearer and others more

e   turbid, like the rivers of mud which precede the lava stream in Sicily, and the lava
stream itself. These fill each hollow in turn, as each stream flows round to it. All of
them are moved up and down by a certain oscillation which is in the earth and which is
produced by a natural cause of the following kind. One of the chasms in the earth is

112   larger than all the others, and pierces right through it, from side to side. Homer describes it in the words—

Far away, where is the deepest depth beneath the earth. [*Iliad* VIII.14]

And elsewhere he and many others of the poets have called it Tartarus. All the
rivers flow into this chasm and out of it again; and each of them comes to be like the

b   soil through which it flows. The reason why they all flow into and out of the chasm is
that the liquid has no bottom or base to rest on; it oscillates and surges up and down,
and the air and wind around it do the same, for they accompany it in its passage to the
other side of the earth, and in its return; and just as in breathing the breath is always in

c   process of being exhaled and inhaled, so there the wind, oscillating with the water, produces terrible and irresistible blasts as it comes in and goes out. When the water retires
with a rush to what we call the lower parts of the earth, it flows through to the regions
of those streams and fills them, as if it were pumped into them. And again, when it
rushes back hither from those regions, it fills the streams here again, and then they flow

d   through the channels of the earth and make their way to their several places, and create
seas, and lakes, and rivers, and springs. Then they sink once more into the earth, and
after making, some a long circuit through many regions, and some a shorter one
through fewer, they fall again into Tartarus, some at a point much lower than that at

which they rose, and others only a little lower; but they all flow in below their point of issue. And some of them burst forth again on the side on which they entered; others again on the opposite side; and there are some which completely encircle the earth, twining round it, like snakes, once or perhaps oftener, and then fall again into Tartarus,   e as low down as they can. They can descend as far as the center of the earth from either side but no farther. Beyond that point on either side they would have to flow uphill.

These streams are many, and great, and various; but among them all are four, of which the greatest and outermost, which flows round the whole of the earth, is called Oceanus. Opposite Oceanus, and flowing in the reverse direction, is Acheron, which   113 runs through desert places and then under the earth until it reaches the Acherusian lake, whither the souls of the dead generally go, and after abiding there the appointed time, which for some is longer and for others shorter, are sent forth again to be born as animals. The third river rises between these two, and near its source falls into a vast and fiery region and forms a lake larger than our sea, seething with water and mud. Thence it goes forth turbid and muddy round the earth, and after many windings comes to the   b end of the Acherusian lake, but it does not mingle with the waters of the lake; and after many windings more beneath the earth, it falls into the lower part of Tartarus. This is the river that men name Pyriphlegethon; and portions of it are discharged in the lava streams, wherever they are found on the earth. The fourth river is on the opposite side; it is said to fall first into a terrible and savage region, of which the color is one dark blue. It is called the Stygian stream, and the lake which its waters create is called Styx.   c After falling into the lake and receiving strange powers in its waters, it sinks into the earth, and runs winding about in the opposite direction to Pyriphlegethon, which it meets in the Acherusian lake from the opposite side. Its waters, too, mingle with no other waters; it flows round in a circle and falls into Tartarus opposite to Pyriphlegethon. Its name, the poets say, is Cocytus.

Such is the nature of these regions; and when the dead come to the place whither   d each is brought by his genius, sentence is first passed on them according as their lives have been good and holy, or not. Those whose lives seem to have been neither very good nor very bad go to the river Acheron, and, embarking on the vessels which they find there, proceed to the lake. There they dwell, and are punished for the crimes which they have committed, and are purified and absolved; and for their good deeds they are rewarded, each according to his deserts. But all who appear to be incurable from the   e enormity of their sins—those who have committed many and great sacrileges, and foul and lawless murders, or other crimes like these—are hurled down to Tartarus by the fate which is their due, whence they never come forth again. Those who have committed sins which are great, but not too great for atonement, such, for instance, as those who have used violence toward a father or a mother in wrath and then repented of it for the rest of their lives, or who have committed homicide in some similar way, have also   114 to descend into Tartarus; but then when they have been there a year, a wave casts them forth, the homicides by Cocytus, and the parricides and matricides by Pyriphlegethon; and when they have been carried as far as the Acherusian lake they cry out and call on those whom they slew or outraged, and beseech and pray that they may be allowed to   b come out into the lake, and be received as comrades. And if they prevail, they come out, and their sufferings cease; but if they do not, they are carried back to Tartarus, and thence into the rivers again, and their punishment does not end until they have prevailed on those whom they wronged: such is the sentence pronounced on them by their judges. But such as have been pre-eminent for holiness in their lives are set free and released from this world, as from a prison; they ascend to their pure habitation and dwell   c on the earth's surface. And those of them who have sufficiently purified themselves with philosophy live thenceforth without bodies and proceed to dwellings still fairer than these, which are not easily described, and of which I have not time to speak now. But for all these reasons, Simmias, we must leave nothing undone, that we may obtain virtue and wisdom in this life. Noble is the prize, and great the hope.

d   A man of sense will not insist that these things are exactly as I have described them. But I think that he will believe that something of the kind is true of the soul and her habitations, seeing that she is shown to be immortal, and that it is worth his while to stake everything on this belief. The venture is a fair one, and he must charm his doubts with spells like these. That is why I have been prolonging the fable all this time.

e   For these reasons a man should be of good cheer about his soul if in his life he has re-nounced the pleasures and adornments of the body, because they were nothing to him, and because he thought that they would do him not good but harm; and if he has in-stead earnestly pursued the pleasures of learning, and adorned his soul with the adorn-

115 ment of temperance, and justice, and courage, and freedom, and truth, which belongs to her and is her own, and so awaits his journey to the other world, in readiness to set forth whenever fate calls him. You, Simmias and Cebes, and the rest will set forth at some future day, each at his own time. But me now, as a tragic poet would say, fate calls at once; and it is time for me to betake myself to the bath. I think that I had better bathe before I drink the poison, and not give the women the trouble of washing my dead body.

b   When he had finished speaking Crito said, Be it so, Socrates. But have you any commands for your friends or for me about your children, or about other things? How shall we serve you best?

     Simply by doing what I always tell you, Crito. Take care of your own selves, and you will serve me and mine and yourselves in all that you do, even though you make no promises now. But if you are careless of your own selves, and will not follow the path of life which we have pointed out in our discussions both today and at other times,

c all your promises now, however profuse and earnest they are, will be of no avail.

     We will do our best, said Crito. But how shall we bury you?

     As you please, he answered; only you must catch me first and not let me escape you. And then he looked at us with a smile and said, My friends, I cannot convince Crito that I am the Socrates who has been conversing with you and arranging his argu-

d ments in order. He thinks that I am the body which he will presently see a corpse, and he asks how he is to bury me. All the arguments which I have used to prove that I shall not remain with you after I have drunk the poison, but that I shall go away to the happi-ness of the blessed, with which I tried to comfort you and myself, have been thrown away on him. Do you therefore be my sureties to him, as he was my surety at the trial, but in a different way. He was surety for me then that I would remain; but you must be my sureties to him that I shall go away when I am dead, and not remain with you; then

e he will feel my death less; and when he sees my body being burned or buried, he will not be grieved because he thinks that I am suffering dreadful things; and at my funeral he will not say that it is Socrates whom he is laying out, or bearing to the grave, or burying. For, dear Crito, he continued, you must know that to use words wrongly is not only a fault in itself, it also creates evil in the soul. You must be of good cheer, and say

116 that you are burying my body; and you may bury it as you please and as you think right.

     With these words he rose and went into another room to bathe. Crito went with him and told us to wait. So we waited, talking of the argument and discussing it, and then again dwelling on the greatness of the calamity which had fallen upon us: it

The Death of Socrates, 1787, by Jacques-Louis David (1748–1825). (*Oil on canvas, 51 ×
77-1/4 inches. The Metropolitan Museum of Art, Wolfe Fund, 1931. Catharine Lorillard
Wolfe Collection. [31.45]*)

seemed as if we were going to lose a father and to be orphans for the rest of our lives.   b
When he had bathed, and his children had been brought to him—he had two sons quite
little, and one grown up—and the women of his family were come, he spoke with them
in Crito's presence, and gave them his last instructions; then he sent the women and
children away and returned to us. By that time it was near the hour of sunset, for he
had been a long while within. When he came back to us from the bath he sat down, but
not much was said after that. Presently the servant of the Eleven came and stood before   c
him and said, "I know that I shall not find you unreasonable like other men, Socrates.
They are angry with me and curse me when I bid them drink the poison because the
authorities make me do it. But I have found you all along the noblest and gentlest and
best man that has ever come here; and now I am sure that you will not be angry with
me, but with those who you know are to blame. And so farewell, and try to bear what   d
must be as lightly as you can; you know why I have come." With that he turned away
weeping, and went out.

   Socrates looked up at him and replied, Farewell, I will do as you say. Then he
turned to us and said, How courteous the man is! And the whole time that I have
been here, he has constantly come in to see me, and sometimes he has talked to me,
and has been the best of men; and now, how generously he weeps for me! Come,
Crito, let us obey him; let the poison be brought if it is ready, and if it is not ready,
let it be prepared.

   Crito replied: But, Socrates, I think that the sun is still upon the hills; it has not   e
set. Besides, I know that other men take the poison quite late, and eat and drink

heartily, and even enjoy the company of their chosen friends, after the announcement has been made. So do not hurry; there is still time.

Socrates replied: And those whom you speak of, Crito, naturally do so, for they think that they will be gainers by so doing. And I naturally shall not do so, for I think that I should gain nothing by drinking the poison a little later, but my own contempt for so greedily saving a life which is already spent. So do not refuse to do as I say.

Then Crito made a sign to his slave who was standing by; and the slave went out, and after some delay returned with the man who was to give the poison, carrying it prepared in a cup. When Socrates saw him, he asked, You understand these things, my good man, what have I to do?

You have only to drink this, he replied, and to walk about until your legs feel heavy, and then lie down; and it will act of itself.

With that he handed the cup to Socrates, who took it quite cheerfully, Echecrates, without trembling, and without any change of color or of feature, and looked up at the man with that fixed glance of his, and asked, What say you to making a libation from this draught? May I, or not?

We only prepare so much as we think sufficient, Socrates, he answered.

I understand, said Socrates. But I suppose that I may, and must, pray to the gods that my journey hence may be prosperous. That is my prayer; may it be so. With these words he put the cup to his lips and drank the poison quite calmly and cheerfully.

Till then most of us had been able to control our grief fairly well; but when we saw him drinking and then the poison finished, we could do so no longer: my tears came fast in spite of myself, and I covered my face and wept for myself; it was not for him, but at my own misfortune in losing such a friend. Even before that Crito had been unable to restrain his tears, and had gone away; and Apollodorus, who had never once ceased weeping the whole time, burst into a loud wail and made us one and all break down by his sobbing, except Socrates himself.

What are you doing, my friends? he exclaimed. I sent away the women chiefly in order that they might not behave in this way; for I have heard that a man should die in silence. So calm yourselves and bear up.

When we heard that, we were ashamed, and we ceased from weeping. But he walked about, until he said that his legs were getting heavy, and then he lay down on his back, as he was told. And the man who gave the poison began to examine his feet and legs from time to time. Then he pressed his foot hard and asked if there was any feeling in it, and Socrates said, No; and then his legs, and so higher and higher, and showed us that he was cold and stiff. And Socrates felt himself and said that when it came to his heart, he should be gone. He was already growing cold about the groin, when he uncovered his face, which had been covered, and spoke for the last time. Crito, he said, I owe a cock to Asclepius; do not forget to pay it.*

It shall be done, replied Crito. Is there anything else that you wish? He made no answer to this question; but after a short interval there was a movement, and the man uncovered him, and his eyes were fixed. Then Crito closed his mouth and his eyes.

Such was the end, Echecrates, of our friend, a man, I think, who was the wisest and justest, and the best man I have ever known.

---

*[Asclepius was the Greek god of healing. When one recovered from an illness it was customary to offer a cock as a sacrifice, so Socrates' last words imply that death is a kind of healing. See, for instance 66b ff., 67c.]

MENO

PERSONS OF THE DIALOGUE

> Meno
> A Slave of Meno
> Socrates
> Anytus

MENO: Can you tell me Socrates—is virtue something that can be taught? Or   70
does it come by practice? Or is it neither teaching nor practice that gives it to a man but
natural aptitude or something else?

SOCRATES: Well Meno, in the old days the Thessalians had a great reputation
among the Greeks for their wealth and their horsemanship. Now it seems they are   b
philosophers as well—especially the men of Larissa, where your friend Aristippus
comes from. It is Gorgias who has done it. He went to that city and captured the hearts
of the foremost of the Aleuadae for his wisdom (among them your own admirer Aristippus), not to speak of other leading Thessalians. In particular he got you into the
habit of answering any question you might be asked, with the confidence and dignity   c
appropriate to those who know the answers, just as he himself invites questions of
every kind from anyone in the Greek world who wishes to ask, and never fails to answer them. But here at Athens, my dear Meno, it is just the reverse. There is a dearth of   71
wisdom, and it looks as if it had migrated from our part of the country to yours. At any
rate, if you put your question to any of our people, they will all alike laugh and say:
"You must think I am singularly fortunate, to know whether virtue can be taught or
how it is acquired. The fact is that far from knowing whether it can be taught, I have no
idea what virtue itself is."

That is my own case. I share the poverty of my fellow-countrymen in this re-   b
spect, and confess to my shame that I have no knowledge about virtue at all. And how
can I know a property of something when I don't even know what it is? Do you suppose that somebody entirely ignorant who Meno is could say whether he is handsome
and rich and well-born or the reverse? Is that possible, do you think?

MENO: No. But is this true about yourself, Socrates, that you don't even know
what virtue is? Is this the report that we are to take home about you?   c

SOCRATES: Not only that; you may say also that, to the best of my belief, I have
never yet met anyone who did know.

MENO: What! Didn't you meet Gorgias when he was here?

SOCRATES: Yes.

MENO: And you still didn't think he knew?

SOCRATES: I'm a forgetful sort of person, and I can't say just now what I thought
at the time. Probably he did know, and I expect you know what he used to say about it.
So remind me what it was, or tell me yourself if you will. No doubt you agree with   d
him.

From *Protagoras and Meno,* translated with an introduction by W.K.C. Guthrie (Harmondsworth, Middle-
sex, England: Penguin Classics, 1956). Reprinted by permission of Penguin Books Ltd.

MENO: Yes I do.

SOCRATES: Then let's leave him out of it, since after all he isn't here. What do you yourself say virtue is? I do ask you in all earnestness not to refuse me, but to speak out. I shall be only too happy to be proved wrong if you and Gorgias turn out to know this, although I said I had never met anyone who did.

e   MENO: But there is no difficulty about it. First of all, if it is manly virtue you are after, it is easy to see that the virtue of a man consists in managing the city's affairs capably, and so that he will help his friends and injure his foes while taking care to come to no harm himself. Or if you want a woman's virtue, that is easily described. She must be a good housewife, careful with her stores and obedient to her husband. Then there is

72   another virtue for a child, male or female, and another for an old man, free or slave as you like; and a great many more kinds of virtue, so that no one need be at a loss to say what it is. For every act and every time of life, with reference to each separate function, there is a virtue for each one of us, and similarly, I should say, a vice.

SOCRATES: I seem to be in luck. I wanted one virtue and I find that you have a whole swarm of virtues to offer. But seriously, to carry on this metaphor of the swarm, suppose I asked you what a bee is, what is its essential nature, and you replied that bees were of many different kinds; what would you say if I went on to ask: "And is it

b   in being bees that they are many and various and different from one another? Or would you agree that it is not in this respect that they differ, but in something else, some other quality like size or beauty?"

MENO: I should say that in so far as they are bees, they don't differ from one another at all.

SOCRATES: Suppose I then continued: "Well, this is just what I want you to tell

c   me. What is that character in respect of which they don't differ at all, but are all the same?" I presume you would have something to say?

MENO: I should.

SOCRATES: Then do the same with the virtues. Even if they are many and various, yet at least they all have some common character which makes them virtues. That is what ought to be kept in view by anyone who answers the question: "What is virtue?"

d   Do you follow me?

MENO: I think I do, but I don't yet really grasp the question as I should wish.

SOCRATES: Well, does this apply in your mind only to virtue, that there is a different one for a man and a woman and the rest? Is it the same with health and size and

e   strength, or has health the same character everywhere, if it is health, whether it be in a man or any other creature?

MENO: I agree that health is the same in a man or in a woman.

SOCRATES: And what about size and strength? If a woman is strong, will it be the same thing, the same strength, that makes her strong? My meaning is that in its character as strength, it is no different, whether it be in a man or in a woman. Or do you think it is?

MENO: No.

73   SOCRATES: And will virtue differ, in its character as virtue, whether it be in a child or an old man, a woman or a man?

MENO: I somehow feel that this is not on the same level as the other cases.

SOCRATES: Well then, didn't you say that a man's virtue lay in directing the city well, and a woman's in directing her household well?

MENO: Yes.

SOCRATES: And is it possible to direct anything well—city or household or anything else—if not temperately and justly?

MENO: Certainly not.

SOCRATES: And that means with temperance and justice? b

MENO: Of course.

SOCRATES: Then both man and woman need the same qualities, justice and temperance, if they are going to be good.

MENO: It looks like it.

SOCRATES: And what about your child and old man? Could they be good if they were incontinent and unjust?

MENO: Of course not. c

SOCRATES: They must be temperate and just?

MENO: Yes.

SOCRATES: So everyone is good in the same way, since they become good by possessing the same qualities.

MENO: So it seems.

SOCRATES: And if they did not share the same virtue, they would not be good in the same way.

MENO: No.

SOCRATES: Seeing then that they all have the same virtue, try to remember and tell me what Gorgias, and you who share his opinion, say it is.

MENO: It must be simply the capacity to govern men, if you are looking for one d quality to cover all the instances.

SOCRATES: Indeed I am. But does this virtue apply to a child or a slave? Should a slave be capable of governing his master, and if he does, is he still a slave?

MENO: I hardly think so.

SOCRATES: It certainly doesn't sound likely. And here is another point. You speak of "capacity to govern." Shall we not add "justly but not otherwise"?

MENO: I think we should, for justice is virtue.

SOCRATES: Virtue, do you say, or *a* virtue? e

MENO: What do you mean?

SOCRATES: Something quite general. Take roundness, for instance. I should say that it is a shape, not simply that it is shape, my reason being that there are other shapes as well.

MENO: I see your point, and I agree that there are other virtues besides justice.

SOCRATES: Tell me what they are. Just as I could name other shapes if you told 74 me to, in the same way mention some other virtues.

MENO: In my opinion then courage is a virtue and temperance and wisdom and dignity and many other things.

SOCRATES: This puts us back where we were. In a different way we have discovered a number of virtues when we were looking for one only. This single virtue, which permeates each of them, we cannot find.

MENO: No, I cannot yet grasp it as you want, a single virtue covering them all, as b I do in other instances.

SOCRATES: I'm not surprised, but I shall do my best to get us a bit further if I can. You understand, I expect, that the question applies to everything. If someone took the example I mentioned just now, and asked you: "What is shape?" and you replied that roundness is shape, and he then asked you as I did, "Do you mean it is shape or *a* shape?" you would reply of course that it is *a* shape.

MENO: Certainly.

SOCRATES: Your reason being that there are other shapes as well. c

MENO: Yes.

SOCRATES: And if he went on to ask you what they were, you would tell him.

MENO: Yes.

SOCRATES: And the same with colour—if he asked you what it is, and on your replying "White," took you up with: "Is white colour or *a* colour?" you would say that it is *a* colour, because there are other colours as well.

MENO: I should.

d   SOCRATES: And if he asked you to, you would mention other colours which are just as much colours as white is.

MENO: Yes.

SOCRATES: Suppose then he pursued the question as I did, and objected: "We always arrive at a plurality, but that is not the kind of answer I want. Seeing that you call these many particulars by one and the same name, and say that every one of them is a shape, even though they are the contrary of each other, tell me what this is which em-

e   braces round as well as straight, and what you mean by shape when you say that straightness is a shape as much as roundness. You do say that?"

MENO: Yes.

SOCRATES: "And in saying it, do you mean that roundness is no more round than straight, and straightness no more straight than round?"

MENO: Of course not.

SOCRATES: "Yet you do say that roundness is no more a shape than straightness, and the other way about."

MENO: Quite true.

75   SOCRATES: "Then what is this thing which is called 'shape'? Try to tell me." If when asked this question either about shape or colour you said: "But I don't understand what you want, or what you mean," your questioner would perhaps be surprised and say: "Don't you see that I am looking for what is the same in all of them?" Would you even so be unable to reply, if the question was: "What is it that is common to roundness and straightness and the other things which you call shapes?"

Do your best to answer, as practice for the question about virtue.

b   MENO: No, you do it, Socrates.

SOCRATES: Do you want me to give in to you?

MENO: Yes.

SOCRATES: And will you in your turn give me an answer about virtue?

MENO: I will.

SOCRATES: In that case I must do my best. It's in a good cause.

MENO: Certainly.

SOCRATES: Well now, let's try to tell you what shape is. See if you accept this definition. Let us define it as the only thing which always accompanies colour. Does

c   that satisfy you, or do you want it in some other way? I should be content if your definition of virtue were on similar lines.

MENO: But that's a naïve sort of definition, Socrates.

SOCRATES: How?

MENO: Shape, if I understand what you say, is what always accompanies colour. Well and good—but if somebody says that he doesn't know what colour is, but is no better off with it than he is with shape, what sort of answer have you given him, do you think?

SOCRATES: A true one; and if my questioner were one of the clever, disputatious

d   and quarrelsome kind, I should say to him: "You have heard my answer. If it is wrong, it is for you to take up the argument and refute it." However, when friendly people, like you and me, want to converse with each other, one's reply must be milder and

e   more conducive to discussion. By that I mean that it must not only be true, but must employ terms with which the questioner admits he is familiar. So I will try to answer you like that. Tell me therefore, whether you recognize the term "end"; I mean limit or boundary—all these words I use in the same sense. Prodicus might perhaps quarrel with us, but I assume you speak of something being bounded or coming to an end. That is all I mean, nothing subtle.

MENO: I admit the notion, and believe I understand your meaning.

SOCRATES: And again, you recognize "surface" and "solid," as they are used in   76 geometry?

MENO: Yes.

SOCRATES: Then with these you should by this time understand my definition of shape. To cover all its instances, I say that shape is that in which a solid terminates, or more briefly, it is the limit of a solid.

MENO: And how do you define colour?

SOCRATES: What a shameless fellow you are, Meno. You keep bothering an old man to answer, but refuse to exercise your memory and tell me what was Gorgias's   b definition of virtue.

MENO: I will, Socrates, as soon as you tell me this.

SOCRATES: Anyone talking to you could tell blindfolded that you are a handsome man and still have your admirers.

MENO: Why so?

SOCRATES: Because you are forever laying down the law as spoilt boys do, who act the tyrant as long as their youth lasts. No doubt you have discovered that I can   c never resist good looks. Well, I will give in and let you have your answer.

MENO: Do by all means.

SOCRATES: Would you like an answer à la Gorgias, such as you would most readily follow?

MENO: Of course I should.

SOCRATES: You and he believe in Empedocles's theory of effluences, do you not?

MENO: Whole-heartedly.

SOCRATES: And passages to which and through which the effluences make their way?

MENO: Yes.

SOCRATES: Some of the effluences fit into some of the passages, whereas others   d are too coarse or too fine.

MENO: That is right.

SOCRATES: Now you recognize the term "sight"?

MENO: Yes.

SOCRATES: From these notions, then, "grasp what I would tell," as Pindar says. Colour is an effluence from shapes commensurate with sight and perceptible by it.

MENO: That seems to me an excellent answer.

SOCRATES: No doubt it is the sort you are used to. And you probably see that it provides a way to define sound and smell and many similar things.

MENO: So it does.   e

SOCRATES: Yes, it's a high-sounding answer, so you like it better than the one on shape.

MENO: I do.

SOCRATES: Nevertheless, son of Alexidemus, I am convinced that the other is better; and I believe you would agree with me if you had not, as you told me yesterday, to leave before the mysteries, but could stay and be initiated.*

---

*Evidently the Athenians are about to celebrate the famous rites of the Eleusinian Mysteries, but Meno has to return to Thessaly before they fall due. Plato frequently plays upon the analogy between religious initiation, which bestows a revelation of divine secrets, and the insight that comes from initiation into the truths of philosophy.

77   MENO: I would stay, Socrates, if you gave me more answers like this.

SOCRATES: You may be sure I shan't be lacking in keenness to do so, both for your sake and mine; but I'm afraid I may not be able to do it often. However, now it is your turn to do as you promised, and try to tell me the general nature of virtue. Stop making many out of one, as the humorists say when somebody breaks a plate. Just leave virtue

b   whole and sound and tell me what it is, as in the examples I have given you.

MENO: It seems to me then, Socrates, that virtue is, in the words of the poet, "to rejoice in the fine and have power," and I define it as desiring fine things and being able to acquire them.

SOCRATES: When you speak of a man desiring fine things, do you mean it is good things he desires?

MENO: Certainly.

c   SOCRATES: Then do you think some men desire evil and others good? Doesn't everyone, in your opinion, desire good things?

MENO: No.

SOCRATES: And would you say that the others suppose evils to be good, or do they still desire them although they recognize them as evil?

MENO: Both, I should say.

SOCRATES: What? Do you really think that anyone who recognizes evils for what they are, nevertheless desires them?

MENO: Yes.

SOCRATES: Desires in what way? To possess them?

MENO: Of course.

d   SOCRATES: In the belief that evil things bring advantage to their possessor, or harm?

MENO: Some in the first belief, but some also in the second.

SOCRATES: And do you believe that those who suppose evil things bring advantage understand that they are evil?

MENO: No, that I can't really believe.

SOCRATES: Isn't it clear then that this class, who don't recognize evils for what

e   they are, don't desire evil but what they think is good, though in fact it is evil; those who through ignorance mistake bad things for good obviously desire the good.

MENO: For them I suppose that is true.

SOCRATES: Now as for those whom you speak of as desiring evils in the belief that they do harm to their possessor, these presumably know that they will be injured by them?

MENO: They must.

78   SOCRATES: And don't they believe that whoever is injured is, in so far as he is injured, unhappy?

MENO: That too they must believe.

SOCRATES: And unfortunate?

MENO: Yes.

SOCRATES: Well, does anybody want to be unhappy and unfortunate?

MENO: I suppose not.

SOCRATES: Then if not, nobody desires what is evil; for what else is unhappiness but desiring evil things and getting them?

b   MENO: It looks as if you are right, Socrates, and nobody desires what is evil.

SOCRATES: Now you have just said that virtue consists in a wish for good things plus the power to acquire them. In this definition the wish is common to everyone, and in that respect no one is better than his neighbour.

MENO: So it appears.

SOCRATES: So if one man is better than another, it must evidently be in respect of the power, and virtue, according to your account, is the power of acquiring good things.   c

MENO: Yes, my opinion is exactly as you now express it.

SOCRATES: Let us see whether you have hit the truth this time. You may well be right. The power of acquiring good things, you say, is virtue?

MENO: Yes.

SOCRATES: And by good do you mean such things as health and wealth?

MENO: I include the gaining both of gold and silver and of high and honourable office in the State.

SOCRATES: Are these the only classes of goods that you recognize?

MENO: Yes, I mean everything of that sort.

SOCRATES: Right. In the definition of Meno, hereditary guest-friend of the Great   d
King, the acquisition of gold and silver is virtue. Do you add "just and righteous" to the word "acquisition," or doesn't it make any difference to you? Do you call it virtue all the same even if they are unjustly acquired?

MENO: Certainly not.

SOCRATES: Vice then?

MENO: Most certainly.

SOCRATES: So it seems that justice or temperance or piety, or some other part of virtue, must attach to the acquisition. Otherwise, although it is a means to good things,   e
it will not be virtue.

MENO: No, how could you have virtue without these?

SOCRATES: In fact lack of gold and silver, if it results from failure to acquire it—either for oneself or another—in circumstances which would have made its acquisition unjust, is itself virtue.

MENO: It would seem so.

SOCRATES: Then to have such goods is no more virtue than to lack them. Rather we may say that whatever is accompanied by justice is virtue, whatever is without   79
qualities of that sort is vice.

MENO: I agree that your conclusion seems inescapable.

SOCRATES: But a few minutes ago we called each of these—justice, temperance, and the rest—a part of virtue?

MENO: Yes, we did.

SOCRATES: So it seems you are making a fool of me.

MENO: How so, Socrates?

SOCRATES: I have just asked you not to break virtue up into fragments, and given you models of the type of answer I wanted, but taking no notice of this you tell me that virtue consists in the acquisition of good things with justice; and justice, you agree, is a   b
part of virtue.

MENO: True.

SOCRATES: So it follows from your own statements that to act with a part of virtue is virtue, if you call justice and all the rest parts of virtue. The point I want to make is that whereas I asked you to give me an account of virtue as a whole, far from telling me what it is itself you say that every action is virtue which exhibits a part of virtue, as if you had already told me what the whole is, so that I should recognize it even if you   c
chop it up into bits. It seems to me that we must put the same old question to you, my dear Meno—the question: "What is virtue?"—if every act becomes virtue when combined with a part of virtue. That is, after all, what it means to say that every act

performed with justice is virtue. Don't you agree that the same question needs to be put? Does anyone know what a part of virtue is, without knowing the whole?

MENO: I suppose not.

d   SOCRATES: No, and if you remember, when I replied to you about shape just now, I believe we rejected the type of answer that employs terms which are still in question and not yet agreed upon.

MENO: We did, and rightly.

SOCRATES: Then please do the same. While the nature of virtue as a whole is still under question, don't suppose that you can explain it to anyone in terms of its parts, or

e   by any similar type of explanation. Understand rather that the same question remains to be answered; you say this and that about virtue, but what *is* it? Does this seem nonsense to you?

MENO: No, to me it seems right enough.

SOCRATES: Then go back to the beginning and answer my question. What do you and your friend say that virtue is?

MENO: Socrates, even before I met you they told me that in plain truth you are a

80   perplexed man yourself and reduce others to perplexity. At this moment I feel you are exercising magic and witchcraft upon me and positively laying me under your spell until I am just a mass of helplessness. If I may be flippant, I think that not only in outward appearance but in other respects as well you are exactly like the flat stingray that one meets in the sea. Whenever anyone comes into contact with it, it numbs him, and that is the sort of thing that you seem to be doing to me now. My mind and my lips are

b   literally numb, and I have nothing to reply to you. Yet I have spoken about virtue hundreds of times, held forth often on the subject in front of large audiences, and very well too, or so I thought. Now I can't even say what it is. In my opinion you are well advised not to leave Athens and live abroad. If you behaved like this as a foreigner in another country, you would most likely be arrested as a wizard.

SOCRATES: You're a real rascal, Meno. You nearly took me in.

MENO: Just what do you mean?

c   SOCRATES: I see why you used a simile about me.

MENO: Why, do you think?

SOCRATES: To be compared to something in return. All good-looking people, I know perfectly well, enjoy a game of comparisons. They get the best of it, for naturally handsome folk provoke handsome similes. But I'm not going to oblige you. As for myself, if the stingray paralyses others only through being paralysed itself, then the comparison is just, but not otherwise. It isn't that, knowing the answers myself, I perplex other people. The truth is rather that I infect them also with the perplexity I feel myself.

d   So with virtue now. I don't know what it is. You may have known before you came into contact with me, but now you look as if you don't. Nevertheless I am ready to carry out, together with you, a joint investigation and inquiry into what it is.

MENO: But how will you look for something when you don't in the least know what it is? How on earth are you going to set up something you don't know as the object of your search? To put it another way, even if you come right up against it, how will you know that what you have found is the thing you didn't know?

e   SOCRATES: I know what you mean. Do you realize that what you are bringing up is the trick argument that a man cannot try to discover either what he knows or what he does not know? He would not seek what he knows, for since he knows it there is no need of the inquiry, nor what he does not know, for in that case he does not even know what he is to look for.

81   MENO: Well, do you think it a good argument?

SOCRATES: No.

MENO: Can you explain how it fails?

SOCRATES: I can. I have heard from men and women who understand the truths of religion—

[Here he presumably pauses to emphasize the solemn change of tone that the dialogue undergoes at this point.]

MENO: What did they say?

SOCRATES: Something true, I thought, and fine.

MENO: What was it, and who were they?

SOCRATES: Those who tell it are priests and priestesses of the sort who make it their business to be able to account for the functions which they perform. Pindar   b
speaks of it too, and many another of the poets who are divinely inspired. What they say is this—see whether you think they are speaking the truth. They say that the soul of man is immortal: At one time it comes to an end—that which is called death—and at another is born again, but is never finally exterminated. On these grounds a man must live all his days as righteously as possible. For those from whom

> Persephone receives requital for ancient doom,
> In the ninth year she restores again
> Their souls to the sun above.
> From whom rise noble kings
> And the swift in strength and greatest in wisdom;   c
> And for the rest of time
> They are called heroes and sanctified by men.*

Thus the soul, since it is immortal and has been born many times, and has seen all things both here and in the other world, has learned everything that is. So we need not be surprised if it can recall the knowledge of virtue or anything else which, as we see, it once possessed. All nature is akin, and the soul has learned everything, so that   d
when a man has recalled a single piece of knowledge—*learned* it, in ordinary language—there is no reason why he should not find out all the rest, if he keeps a stout heart and does not grow weary of the search; for seeking and learning are in fact nothing but recollection.

We ought not then to be led astray by the contentious argument you quoted. It would make us lazy, and is music in the ears of weaklings. The other doctrine produces   e
energetic seekers after knowledge; and being convinced of its truth, I am ready, with your help, to inquire into the nature of virtue.

MENO: I see, Socrates. But what do you mean when you say that we don't learn anything, but that what we call learning is recollection? Can you teach me that it is so?

SOCRATES: I have just said that you're a rascal, and now you ask me if I can teach you, when I say there is no such thing as teaching, only recollection. Evidently you   82
want to catch me contradicting myself straight away.

MENO: No, honestly, Socrates, I wasn't thinking of that. It was just habit. If you can in any way make clear to me that what you say is true, please do.

SOCRATES: It isn't an easy thing, but still I should like to do what I can since you ask me. I see you have a large number of retainers here. Call one of them, anyone you   b
like, and I will use him to demonstrate it to you.

*The quotation is from Pindar.

MENO: Certainly. *(to a slave-boy)* Come here.

SOCRATES: He is a Greek and speaks our language?

MENO: Indeed yes—born and bred in the house.

SOCRATES: Listen carefully then, and see whether it seems to you that he is learning from me or simply being reminded.

MENO: I will.

SOCRATES: Now boy, you know that a square is a figure like this?

[Socrates begins to draw figures in the sand at his feet. He points to the square ABCD.]

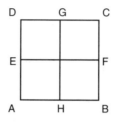

BOY: Yes.

c   SOCRATES: It has all these four sides equal?

BOY: Yes.

SOCRATES: And these lines which go through the middle of it are also equal? (The lines EF *and* GH.)

BOY: Yes.

SOCRATES: Such a figure could be either larger or smaller, could it not?

BOY: Yes.

SOCRATES: Now if this side is two feet long, and this side the same, how many feet will the whole be? Put it this way. If it were two feet in this direction and only one in that, must not the area be two feet taken once?

BOY: Yes.

d   SOCRATES: But since it is two feet this way also, does it not become twice two feet?

BOY: Yes.

SOCRATES: And how many feet is twice two? Work it out and tell me.

BOY: Four.

SOCRATES: Now could one draw another figure double the size of this, but similar, that is, with all its sides equal like this one?

BOY: Yes.

SOCRATES: It is on this line then, according to you, that we shall make the eight-foot square, by taking four of the same length?

BOY: Yes.

SOCRATES: How many feet will its area be?

BOY: Eight.

SOCRATES: Now then, try to tell me how long each of its sides will be. The pres-
e   ent figure has a side of two feet. What will be the side of the double-sized one?

BOY: It will be double, Socrates, obviously.

SOCRATES: You see, Meno, that I am not teaching him anything, only asking. Now he thinks he knows the length of the side of the eight-foot square.

MENO: Yes.

SOCRATES: But does he?

MENO: Certainly not.

SOCRATES: He thinks it is twice the length of the other.

MENO: Yes.

SOCRATES: Now watch how he recollects things in order—the proper way to recollect.

You say that the side of double length produces the double-sized figure? Like this I mean, not long this way and short that. It must be equal on all sides like the first figure, only twice its size, that is eight feet. Think a moment whether you still expect to get it from doubling the side.   83

BOY: Yes, I do.

SOCRATES: Well now, shall we have a line double the length of this (AB) if we add another the same length at this end (BJ)?

BOY: Yes.

SOCRATES: It is on this line then, according to you, that we shall make the eight-foot square, by taking four of the same length?

BOY: Yes.

SOCRATES: Let us draw in four equal lines *(that is, counting* AJ, *and adding* JK, KL, *and* LA *made complete by drawing in its second half* LD), using the first as a base.   b
Does this not give us what you call the eight-foot figure?

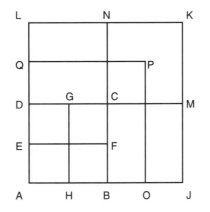

BOY: Certainly.

SOCRATES: But does it contain these four squares, each equal to the original four-foot one?

[Socrates has drawn in the lines CM, CN *to complete the squares that he wishes to point out.]*

BOY: Yes.

SOCRATES: How big is it then? Won't it be four times as big?

BOY: Of course.

SOCRATES: And is four times the same as twice?

BOY: Of course not.

SOCRATES: So doubling the side has given us not a double but a fourfold figure?   c

BOY: True.

SOCRATES: And four times four are sixteen, are they not?

BOY: Yes.

SOCRATES: Then how big is the side of the eight-foot figure? This one has given us four times the original area, hasn't it?

BOY: Yes.

SOCRATES: And a side half the length gave us a square of four feet?

BOY: Yes.

SOCRATES: Good. And isn't a square of eight feet double this one and half that?

BOY: Yes.

SOCRATES: Will it not have a side greater than this one but less than that?

d BOY: I think it will.

SOCRATES: Right. Always answer what you think. Now tell me: was not this side two feet long, and this one four?

BOY: Yes.

SOCRATES: Then the side of the eight-foot figure must be longer than two feet but shorter than four?

BOY: It must.

e SOCRATES: Try to say how long you think it is.

BOY: Three feet.

SOCRATES: If so, shall we add half of this bit (BO, *half of* BJ) and make it three feet? Here are two, and this is one, and on this side similarly we have two plus one; and here is the figure you want.

[Socrates completes the square AOPQ.*]*

BOY: Yes.

SOCRATES: If it is three feet this way and three that, will the whole area be three times three feet?

BOY: It looks like it.

SOCRATES: And that is how many?

BOY: Nine.

SOCRATES: Whereas the square double our first square had to be how many?

BOY: Eight.

SOCRATES: But we haven't yet got the square of eight feet even from a three-foot side?

BOY: No.

84 SOCRATES: Then what length will give it? Try to tell us exactly. If you don't want to count it up, just show us on the diagram.

BOY: It's no use, Socrates, I just don't know.

SOCRATES: Observe, Meno, the stage he has reached on the path of recollection. At the beginning he did not know the side of the square of eight feet. Nor indeed does he know it now, but then he thought he knew it and answered boldly, as was appropriate—he felt no perplexity. Now however he does feel perplexed. Not only does he not know the answer; he doesn't even think he knows.

b MENO: Quite true.

SOCRATES: Isn't he in a better position now in relation to what he didn't know?

MENO: I admit that too.

SOCRATES: So in perplexing him and numbing him like the sting-ray, have we done him any harm?

MENO: I think not.

SOCRATES: In fact we have helped him to some extent towards finding out the right answer, for now not only is he ignorant of it but he will be quite glad to look for it. Up to now, he thought he could speak well and fluently, on many occasions and before large audiences, on the subject of a square double the size of a given square, maintaining that it must have a side of double the length.   c

MENO: No doubt.

SOCRATES: Do you suppose then that he would have attempted to look for, or learn, what he thought he knew (though he did not), before he was thrown into perplexity, became aware of his ignorance, and felt a desire to know?

MENO: No.

SOCRATES: Then the numbing process was good for him?

MENO: I agree.

SOCRATES: Now notice what, starting from this state of perplexity, he will discover by seeking the truth in company with me, though I simply ask him questions without teaching him. Be ready to catch me if I give him any instruction or explanation instead of simply interrogating him on his own opinions.   d

[Socrates here rubs out the previous figures and starts again.]

Tell me, boy, is not this our square of four feet? *(ABCD.)* You understand?

BOY: Yes.

SOCRATES: Now we can add another equal to it like this? *(BCEF.)*

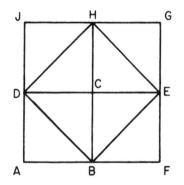

BOY: Yes.

SOCRATES: And a third here, equal to each of the others? *(CEGH.)*

BOY: Yes.

SOCRATES: And then we can fill in this one in the corner? *(DCHJ.)*

BOY: Yes.

SOCRATES: Then here we have four equal squares?

BOY: Yes.

SOCRATES: And how many times the size of the first square is the whole?   e

BOY: Four times.

SOCRATES: And we want one double the size. You remember?

BOY: Yes.

SOCRATES: Now does this line going from corner to corner cut each of these   85
squares in half?

BOY: Yes.

SOCRATES: And these are four equal lines enclosing this area? *(BEHD.)*

BOY: They are.

SOCRATES: Now think. How big is this area?

BOY: I don't understand.

SOCRATES: Here are four squares. Has not each line cut off the inner half of each of them?

BOY: Yes.

SOCRATES: And how many such halves are there in this figure? *(BEHD.)*

BOY: Four.

SOCRATES: And how many in this one? *(ABCD.)*

BOY: Two.

b   SOCRATES: And what is the relation of four to two?

BOY: Double.

SOCRATES: How big is this figure then?

BOY: Eight feet.

SOCRATES: On what base?

BOY: This one.

SOCRATES: The line which goes from corner to corner of the square of four feet?

BOY: Yes.

SOCRATES: The technical name for it is "diagonal"; so if we use that name, it is your personal opinion that the square on the diagonal of the original square is double its area.

BOY: That is so, Socrates.

c   SOCRATES: What do you think, Meno? Has he answered with any opinions that were not his own?

MENO: No, they were all his.

SOCRATES: Yet he did not know, as we agreed a few minutes ago.

MENO: True.

SOCRATES: But these opinions were somewhere in him, were they not?

MENO: Yes.

SOCRATES: So a man who does not know has in himself true opinions on a subject without having knowledge.

MENO: It would appear so.

SOCRATES: At present these opinions, being newly aroused, have a dream-like quality. But if the same questions are put to him on many occasions and in different
d   ways, you can see that in the end he will have a knowledge on the subject as accurate as anybody's.

MENO: Probably.

SOCRATES: This knowledge will not come from teaching but from questioning. He will recover it for himself.

MENO: Yes.

SOCRATES: And the spontaneous recovery of knowledge that is in him is recollection, isn't it?

MENO: Yes.

SOCRATES: Either then he has at some time acquired the knowledge which he now has, or he has always possessed it. If he always possessed it, he must always have known; if on the other hand he acquired it at some previous time, it cannot have been
e   in this life, unless somebody has taught him geometry. He will behave in the same way with all geometrical knowledge, and every other subject. Has anyone taught him all these? You ought to know, especially as he has been brought up in your household.

MENO: Yes, I know that no one ever taught him.

SOCRATES: And has he these opinions, or hasn't he?

MENO: It seems we can't deny it.

SOCRATES: Then if he did not acquire them in this life, isn't it immediately clear   86
that he possessed and had learned them during some other period?

MENO: It seems so.

SOCRATES: When he was not in human shape?

MENO: Yes.

SOCRATES: If then there are going to exist in him, both while he is and while he is
not a man, true opinions which can be aroused by questioning and turned into knowledge, may we say that his soul has been forever in a state of knowledge? Clearly he always either is or is not a man.

MENO: Clearly.

SOCRATES: And if the truth about reality is always in our soul, the soul must be   b
immortal, and one must take courage and try to discover—that is, to recollect—what
one doesn't happen to know, or (more correctly) remember, at the moment.

MENO: Somehow or other I believe you are right.

SOCRATES: I think I am. I shouldn't like to take my oath on the whole story, but
one thing I am ready to fight for as long as I can, in word and act: that is, that we shall
be better, braver, and more active men if we believe it right to look for what we don't
know than if we believe there is no point in looking because what we don't know we   c
can never discover.

MENO: There too I am sure you are right.

SOCRATES: Then, since we are agreed that it is right to inquire into something that
one does not know, are you ready to face with me the question: what is virtue?

MENO: Quite ready. All the same, I would rather consider the question as I put it
at the beginning, and hear your views on it; that is, are we to pursue virtue as something that can be taught, or do men have it as a gift of nature or how?   d

SOCRATES: If I were your master as well as my own, Meno, we should not have
inquired whether or not virtue can be taught until we had first asked the main question—what it is; but not only do you make no attempt to govern your own actions—
you prize your freedom, I suppose—but you attempt to govern mine. And you succeed
too, so I shall let you have your way. There's nothing else for it, and it seems we must
inquire into a single property of something about whose essential nature we are still in   e
the dark. Just grant me one small relaxation of your sway, and allow me, in considering whether or not it can be taught, to make use of a hypothesis—the sort of thing, I
mean, that geometers often use in their inquiries. When they are asked, for example,
about a given area, whether it is possible for this area to be inscribed as a triangle in a   87
given circle, they will probably reply: "I don't know yet whether it fulfils the conditions, but I think I have a hypothesis which will help us in the matter. It is this. If the
area is such that, when one has applied it [e.g., as a rectangle] to the given line [i.e., the
diameter] of the circle, it is deficient by another rectangle similar to the one which is
applied, then, I should say, one result follows; if not, the result is different. If you ask
me, then, about the inscription of the figure in the circle—whether it is possible or   b
not—I am ready to answer you in this hypothetical way."*

---

*[It is very difficult to understand the geometrical illustration Socrates is giving here.] Sir Thomas
Heath in his *History of Greek Mathematics* (1921), Vol. i, p. 298, says that C. Blass, writing in 1861, already
knew of thirty different interpretations, and that many more had appeared since then. Fortunately it is not
necessary to understand the example in order to grasp the hypothetical method Socrates is expounding.

Let us do the same about virtue. Since we don't know what it is or what it resembles, let us use a hypothesis in investigating whether it is teachable or not. We shall say: "What attribute of the soul must virtue be, if it is to be teachable or otherwise?" Well, in the first place, if it is anything else but knowledge, is there a possibility of anyone teaching it—or, in the language we used just now, reminding someone of it?

c   We needn't worry about which name we are to give to the process, but simply ask: will it be teachable? Isn't it plain to everyone that a man is not taught anything except knowledge?

MENO: That would be my view.

SOCRATES: If on the other hand virtue is some sort of knowledge, clearly it could be taught.

MENO: Certainly.

SOCRATES: So that question is easily settled; I mean, on what condition virtue would be teachable.

MENO: Yes.

d   SOCRATES: The next point then, I suppose, is to find out whether virtue is knowledge or something different.

MENO: That is the next question, I agree.

SOCRATES: Well then, do we assert that virtue is something good? Is that assumption a firm one for us?

MENO: Undoubtedly.

SOCRATES: That being so, if there exists any good thing different from, and not associated with, knowledge, virtue will not necessarily be any form of knowledge. If on the other hand knowledge embraces everything that is good, we shall be right to suspect that virtue is knowledge.

MENO: Agreed.

e   SOCRATES: First then, is it virtue which makes us good?

MENO: Yes.

SOCRATES: And if good, then advantageous. All good things are advantageous, are they not?

MENO: Yes.

SOCRATES: So virtue itself must be something advantageous?

MENO: That follows also.

SOCRATES: Now suppose we consider what are the sort of things that profit us. Take them in a list. Health, we may say, and strength and good looks, and wealth—these and their like we call advantageous, you agree?

MENO: Yes.

88   SOCRATES: Yet we also speak of these things as sometimes doing harm. Would you object to that statement?

MENO: No, it is so.

SOCRATES: Now look here: what is the controlling factor which determines whether each of these is advantageous or harmful? Isn't it right use which makes them advantageous, and lack of it, harmful?

MENO: Certainly.

SOCRATES: We must also take spiritual qualities into consideration. You recognize such things as temperance, justice, courage, quickness of mind, memory, nobility of character and others?

MENO: Yes, of course I do.

b   SOCRATES: Then take any such qualities which in your view are not knowledge but something different. Don't you think they may be harmful as well as advantageous? Courage for instance, if it is something thoughtless, is just a sort of confidence. Isn't it true that to be confident without reason does a man harm, whereas a reasoned confidence profits him?

MENO: Yes.

SOCRATES: Temperance and quickness of mind are no different. Learning and discipline are profitable in conjunction with wisdom, but without it harmful.

MENO: That is emphatically true.

c

SOCRATES: In short, everything that the human spirit undertakes or suffers will lead to happiness when it is guided by wisdom, but to the opposite, when guided by folly.

MENO: A reasonable conclusion.

SOCRATES: If then virtue is an attribute of the spirit, and one which cannot fail to be beneficial, it must be wisdom; for all spiritual qualities in and by themselves are neither advantageous nor harmful, but become advantageous or harmful by the presence with them of wisdom or folly. If we accept this argument, then virtue, to be something advantageous, must be a sort of wisdom.

d

MENO: I agree.

SOCRATES: To go back to the other class of things, wealth and the like, of which we said just now that they are sometimes good and sometimes harmful, isn't it the same with them? Just as wisdom when it governs our other psychological impulses turns them to advantage, and folly turns them to harm, so the mind by its right use and control of these material assets makes them profitable, and by wrong use renders them harmful.

e

MENO: Certainly.

SOCRATES: And the right user is the mind of the wise man, the wrong user the mind of the foolish.

MENO: That is so.

SOCRATES: So we may say in general that the goodness of non-spiritual assets depends on our spiritual character, and the goodness of that on wisdom. This argument shows that the advantageous element must be wisdom; and virtue, we agree, is advantageous, so that amounts to saying that virtue, either in whole or in part, is wisdom.

89

MENO: The argument seems to me fair enough.

SOCRATES: If so, good men cannot be good by nature.

MENO: I suppose not.

SOCRATES: There is another point. If they were, there would probably be experts among us who could recognize the naturally good at an early stage. They would point them out to us, and we should take them and shut them away safely in the Acropolis, sealing them up more carefully than bullion to protect them from corruption and ensure that when they came to maturity they would be of use to the State.

b

MENO: It would be likely enough.

SOCRATES: Since then goodness does not come by nature, is it got by learning?

c

MENO: I don't see how we can escape the conclusion. Indeed it is obvious on our assumption that, if virtue is knowledge, it is teachable.

SOCRATES: I suppose so. But I wonder if we were right to bind ourselves to that.

MENO: Well, it seemed all right just now.

SOCRATES: Yes, but to be sound it has got to seem all right not only "just now" but at this moment and in the future.

MENO: Of course. But what has occurred to you to make you turn against it and suspect that virtue may not be knowledge?

d

SOCRATES: I'll tell you. I don't withdraw from the position that if it is knowledge, it must be teachable; but as for its being knowledge, see whether you think my doubts on this point are well founded. If anything—not virtue only—is a possible subject of instruction, must there not be teachers and students of it?

MENO: Surely.

e   SOCRATES: And what of the converse, that if there are neither teachers nor students of a subject, we may safely infer that it cannot be taught?

MENO: That is true. But don't you think there are teachers of virtue?

SOCRATES: All I can say is that I have often looked to see if there are any, and in spite of all my efforts I cannot find them, though I have had plenty of fellow-searchers, the kind of men especially whom I believe to have most experience in such matters. But look, Meno, here's a piece of luck. Anytus has just sat down beside us. We

90   couldn't do better than make him a partner in our inquiry. In the first place, he is the son of Anthemion, a man of property and good sense, who didn't get his money out of the blue or as a gift—like Ismenias of Thebes who has just come into the fortune of a Croesus—but earned it by his own brains and hard work. Besides this, he shows himself a decent, modest citizen with no arrogance or bombast or offensiveness about him. Also he brought up his son well and had him properly educated, as the Athenian

b   people appreciate: look how they elect him into the highest offices in the State. This is certainly the right sort of man with whom to inquire whether there are any teachers of virtue, and if so who they are.

Please help us, Anytus—Meno, who is a friend of your family, and myself—to find out who may be the teachers of this subject. Look at it like this. If we wanted

c   Meno to become a good doctor, shouldn't we send him to the doctors to be taught?

ANYTUS: Of course.

SOCRATES: And if we wanted him to become a shoemaker, to the shoemakers?

ANYTUS: Yes.

SOCRATES: And so on with other trades?

ANYTUS: Yes.

SOCRATES: Now another relevant question. When we say that to make Meno a

d   doctor we should be right in sending him to the doctors, have we in mind that the sensible thing is to send him to those who profess the subject rather than to those who don't, men who charge a fee as professionals, having announced that they are prepared to teach whoever likes to come and learn?

ANYTUS: Yes.

SOCRATES: The same is surely true of flute-playing and other accomplishments. If

e   you want to make someone a performer on the flute it would be very foolish to refuse to send him to those who undertake to teach the art and are paid for it, but to go and bother other people instead and have him try to learn from them—people who don't set up to be teachers or take any pupils in the subject which we want our young man to learn. Doesn't that sound very unreasonable?

ANYTUS: Sheer stupidity I should say.

91   SOCRATES: I agree. And now we can both consult together about our visitor Meno. He has been telling me all this while that he longs to acquire the kind of wisdom and virtue which fits men to manage an estate or govern a city, to look after their parents, and to entertain and send off guests in proper style, both their own countrymen and foreigners. With this in mind, to whom would it be right to send him? What we

b   have just said seems to show that the right people are those who profess to be teachers of virtue and offer their services freely to any Greek who wishes to learn, charging a fixed fee for their instruction.

ANYTUS: Whom do you mean by that, Socrates?

SOCRATES: Surely you know yourself that they are the men called Sophists.

ANYTUS: Good heavens, what a thing to say! I hope no relative of mine or any of   c
my friends, Athenian or foreign, would be so mad as to go and let himself be ruined by
those people. That's what they are, the manifest ruin and corruption of anyone who
comes into contact with them.

SOCRATES: What, Anytus? Can they be so different from other claimants to useful
knowledge that they not only don't do good, like the rest, to the material that one puts
in their charge, but on the contrary spoil it—and have the effrontery to take money for
doing so? I for one find it difficult to believe you. I know that one of them alone, Protagoras, earned more money from being a Sophist than an outstandingly fine craftsman   d
like Phidias and ten other sculptors put together. A man who mends old shoes or re-
stores coats couldn't get away with it for a month if he gave them back in worse condition than he received them; he would soon find himself starving. Surely it is incredible
that Protagoras took in the whole of Greece, corrupting his pupils and sending them   e
away worse than when they came to him, for more than forty years. I believe he was
nearly seventy when he died, and had been practising for forty years, and all that
time—indeed to this very day—his reputation has been consistently high; and there are
plenty of others besides Protagoras, some before his time and others still alive. Are we   92
to suppose from your remark that they consciously deceive and ruin young men, or are
they unaware of it themselves? Can these remarkably clever men—as some regard
them—be mad enough for that?

ANYTUS: Far from it, Socrates. It isn't they who are mad, but rather the young
men who hand over their money; and those responsible for them, who let them get into
the Sophists' hands, are even worse. Worst of all are the cities who allow them in, or
don't expel them, whether it be a foreigner or one of themselves who tries that sort of   b
game.

SOCRATES: Has one of the Sophists done you a personal injury, or why are you so
hard on them?

ANYTUS: Heavens, no! I've never in my life had anything to do with a single one
of them, nor would I hear of any of my family doing so.

SOCRATES: So you've had no experience of them at all?

ANYTUS: And don't want any either.

SOCRATES: You surprise me. How can you know what is good or bad in some-   c
thing when you have no experience of it?

ANYTUS: Quite easily. At any rate I know *their* kind, whether I've had experience
or not.

SOCRATES: It must be second sight, I suppose; for how else you know about them,
judging from what you tell me yourself, I can't imagine. However, we are not asking
whose instruction it is that would ruin Meno's character. Let us say that those are the   d
Sophists if you like, and tell us instead about the ones we want. You can do a good turn
to a friend of your father's house if you will let him know to whom in our great city he
should apply for proficiency in the kind of virtue I have just described.

ANYTUS: Why not tell him yourself?

SOCRATES: Well, I did mention the men who in my opinion teach these things, but
apparently I was talking nonsense. So you say, and you may well be right. Now it is
your turn to direct him; mention the name of any Athenian you like.   e

ANYTUS: But why mention a particular individual? Any decent Athenian gentle-
man whom he happens to meet, if he follows his advice, will make him a better man
than the Sophists would.

SOCRATES: And did these gentlemen get their fine qualities spontaneously—self-   93
taught, as it were, and yet [they are] able to teach this untaught virtue to others?

ANYTUS: I suppose they in their turn learned it from forebears who were gentlemen like themselves. Would you deny that there have been many good men in our city?

SOCRATES: On the contrary, there are plenty of good statesmen here in Athens, and have been as good in the past. The question is, have they also been good teachers of their own virtue? That is the point we are discussing now—not whether or not there

b   are good men in Athens or whether there have been in past times, but whether virtue can be taught. It amounts to the question whether the good men of this and former times have known how to hand on to someone else the goodness that was in themselves, or whether on the contrary it is not something that can be handed over, or that one man can receive from another. That is what Meno and I have long been puzzling

c   over. Look at it from your own point of view. You would say that Themistocles was a good man?

ANYTUS: Yes, none better.

SOCRATES: And that he, if anyone, must have been a good teacher of his own virtue?

ANYTUS: I suppose so, if he wanted to be.

SOCRATES: But don't you think he must have wanted others to become worthy

d   men—above all, surely, his own son? Do you suppose he grudged him this and purposely didn't pass on his own virtue to him? You must have heard that he had his son Cleophantus so well trained in horsemanship that he could stand upright on horseback and throw a javelin from that position; and many other wonderful accomplishments the young man had, for his father had him taught and made expert in every skill that a good instructor could impart. You must have heard this from older people?

ANYTUS: Yes.

SOCRATES: No one, then, could say that there was anything wrong with the boy's natural powers?

e   ANYTUS: Perhaps not.

SOCRATES: But have you ever heard anyone, young or old, say that Cleophantus the son of Themistocles was a good and wise man in the way that his father was?

ANYTUS: Certainly not.

SOCRATES: Must we conclude then that Themistocles' aim was to educate his son in other accomplishments, but not to make him any better than his neighbours in his own type of wisdom—that is, supposing that virtue could be taught?

ANYTUS: I hardly think we can.

SOCRATES: So much then for Themistocles as a teacher of virtue, whom you yourself agree to have been one of the best men of former times. Take another example,

94   Aristides, son of Lysimachus. You accept him as a good man?

ANYTUS: Surely.

SOCRATES: He too gave his son Lysimachus the best education in Athens, in all subjects where a teacher could help; but did he make him a better man than his

b   neighbour? You know him, I think, and can say what he is like. Or again there is Pericles, that great and wise man. He brought up two sons, Paralus and Xanthippus, and had them taught riding, music, athletics, and all the other skilled pursuits till they were as good as any in Athens. Did he then not want to make them good men? Yes, he wanted that, no doubt, but I am afraid it is something that cannot be done by teaching. And in case you should think that only very few, and those the most insignificant, lacked this power, consider that Thucydides also had two sons, Melesias

c   and Stephanus, to whom he gave an excellent education. Among other things they were the best wrestlers in Athens, for he gave one to Xanthias to train and the other to Eudoxus—the two who, I understand, were considered the finest wrestlers of their time. You remember?

ANYTUS: I have heard of them.

SOCRATES: Surely then he would never have had his children taught these expen- d
sive pursuits and yet refused to teach them to be good men—which would have cost
nothing at all—if virtue could have been taught? You are not going to tell me that
Thucydides was a man of no account, or that he had not plenty of friends both at
Athens and among the allies? He came of an influential family and was a great power
both here and in the rest of Greece. If virtue could have been taught, he would have
found the man to make his sons good, either among our own citizens or abroad, supposing his political duties left him no time to do it himself. No, my dear Anytus, it e
looks as if it cannot be taught.

ANYTUS: You seem to me, Socrates, to be too ready to run people down. My ad-
vice to you, if you will listen to it, is to be careful. I dare say that in all cities it is easier
to do a man harm than good, and it is certainly so here, as I expect you know yourself. 95

SOCRATES: Anytus seems angry, Meno, and I am not surprised. He thinks I am
slandering our statesmen, and moreover he believes himself to be one of them. He
doesn't know what slander really is: if he ever finds out he will forgive me.

However, tell me this yourself: are there not similar fine characters in your country?

MENO: Yes, certainly.

SOCRATES: Do they come forward of their own accord to teach the young? Do b
they agree that they are teachers and that virtue can be taught?

MENO: No indeed, they don't agree on it at all. Sometimes you will hear them say
that it can be taught, sometimes that it cannot.

SOCRATES: Ought we then to class as teachers of it men who are not even agreed
that it can be taught?

MENO: Hardly, I think.

SOCRATES: And what about the Sophists, the only people who profess to teach it?
Do you think they do?

MENO: The thing I particularly admire about Gorgias, Socrates, is that you will c
never hear him make this claim; indeed he laughs at the others when he hears them do
so. In his view his job is to make clever speakers.

SOCRATES: So you too don't think the Sophists are teachers?

MENO: I really can't say. Like most people I waver—sometimes I think they are
and sometimes I think they are not.

SOCRATES: Has it ever occurred to you that you and our statesmen are not alone in
this? The poet Theognis likewise says in one place that virtue is teachable and in an- d
other that it is not.

MENO: Really? Where?

SOCRATES: In the elegiacs in which he writes:

Eat, drink, and sit with men of power and weight,
Nor scorn to gain the favour of the great.
For fine men's teaching to fine ways will win thee:
Low company destroys what wit is in thee.

There he speaks as if virtue can be taught, doesn't he? e

MENO: Clearly.

SOCRATES: But elsewhere he changes his ground a little:

> Were mind by art created and instilled
> Immense rewards had soon the pockets filled

of the people who could do this. Moreover

> No good man's son would ever worthless be,
> Taught by wise counsel. But no teacher's skill
> Can turn to good what is created ill.

96

Do you see how he contradicts himself?

MENO: Plainly.

SOCRATES: Can you name any other subject, in which the professed teachers are not only not recognized as teachers of others, but are thought to have no understanding of it themselves, and to be no good at the very subject they profess to teach; whereas those who are acknowledged to be the best at it are in two minds whether it can be taught or not? When people are so confused about a subject, can you say that they are in a true sense teachers?

MENO: Certainly not.

SOCRATES: Well, if neither the Sophists nor those who display fine qualities themselves are teachers of virtue, I am sure no one else can be, and if there are no teachers, there can be no students either.

MENO: I quite agree.

SOCRATES: And we have also agreed that a subject of which there were neither teachers nor students was not one which could be taught.

MENO: That is so.

SOCRATES: Now there turn out to be neither teachers nor students of virtue, so it would appear that virtue cannot be taught.

MENO: So it seems, if we have made no mistake; and it makes me wonder, Socrates, whether there are in fact no good men at all, or how they are produced when they do appear.

SOCRATES: I have a suspicion, Meno, that you and I are not much good. Our masters Gorgias and Prodicus have not trained us properly. We must certainly take ourselves in hand, and try to find someone who will improve us by hook or by crook. I say this with our recent discussion in mind, for absurdly enough we failed to perceive that it is not only under the guidance of knowledge that human action is well and rightly conducted. I believe that may be what prevents us from seeing how it is that men are made good.

MENO: What do you mean?

SOCRATES: This: We were correct, were we not, in agreeing that good men must be profitable or useful? It cannot be otherwise, can it?

MENO: No.

SOCRATES: And again that they will be of some use if they conduct our affairs aright—that also was correct?

MENO: Yes.

SOCRATES: But in insisting that knowledge was a *sine qua non* [indispensible condition] for right leadership, we look like being mistaken.

MENO: How so?

SOCRATES: Let me explain. If someone knows the way to Larissa, or anywhere else you like, then when he goes there and takes others with him he will be a good and capable guide, you would agree?

b

c

d

e

97

MENO: Of course.

SOCRATES: But if a man judges correctly which is the road, though he has never   b
been there and doesn't know it, will he not also guide others aright?

MENO: Yes, he will.

SOCRATES: And as long as he has a correct opinion on the points about which the
other has knowledge, he will be just as good a guide, believing the truth but not knowing it.

MENO: Just as good.

SOCRATES: Therefore true opinion is as good a guide as knowledge for the purpose of acting rightly. That is what we left out just now in our discussion of the nature
of virtue, when we said that knowledge is the only guide to right action. There was   c
also, it seems, true opinion.

MENO: It seems so.

SOCRATES: So right opinion is something no less useful than knowledge.

MENO: Except that the man with knowledge will always be successful, and the
man with right opinion only sometimes.

SOCRATES: What? Will he not always be successful so long as he has the right
opinion?

MENO: That must be so, I suppose. In that case, I wonder why knowledge should
be so much more prized than right opinion, and indeed how there is any difference be-   d
tween them.

SOCRATES: Shall I tell you the reason for your surprise, or do you know it?

MENO: No, tell me.

SOCRATES: It is because you have not observed the statues of Daedalus. Perhaps
you don't have them in your country.

MENO: What makes you say that?

SOCRATES: They too, if no one ties them down, run away and escape. If tied, they
stay where they are put.   e

MENO: What of it?

SOCRATES: If you have one of his works untethered, it is not worth much: it gives
you the slip like a runaway slave. But a tethered specimen is very valuable, for they are
magnificent creations. And that, I may say, has a bearing on the matter of true opinions. True opinions are a fine thing and do all sorts of good so long as they stay in their
place; but they will not stay long. They run away from a man's mind, so they are not   98
worth much until you tether them by working out the reason. That process, my dear
Meno, is recollection, as we agreed earlier. Once they are tied down, they become
knowledge, and are stable. That is why knowledge is something more valuable than
right opinion. What distinguishes one from the other is the tether.

MENO: It does seem something like that, certainly.

SOCRATES: Well of course, I have only been using an analogy myself, not knowl-   b
edge. But it is not, I am sure, a mere guess to say that right opinion and knowledge are
different. There are few things that I should claim to know, but that at least is among
them, whatever else is.

MENO: You are quite right.

SOCRATES: And is this right too, that true opinion when it governs any course of
action produces as good a result as knowledge?

MENO: Yes, that too is right, I think.

SOCRATES: So that for practical purposes right opinion is no less useful than   c
knowledge, and the man who has it is no less useful than the one who knows.

MENO: That is so.

SOCRATES: Now we have agreed that the good man is useful.

MENO: Yes.

SOCRATES: To recapitulate then: assuming that there are men good and useful to the community, it is not only knowledge that makes them so, but also right opinion, and neither of these comes by nature but both are acquired—or do you think either of them *is* natural?

MENO: No.

SOCRATES: So if both are acquired, good men themselves are not good by nature.

MENO: No.

SOCRATES: That being so, the next thing we inquired was whether their goodness was a matter of teaching, and we decided that it would be, if virtue were knowledge, and conversely, that if it could be taught, it would be knowledge.

MENO: Yes.

SOCRATES: Next, that if there were teachers of it, it could be taught, but not if there were none.

MENO: That was so.

SOCRATES: But we have agreed that there are no teachers of it, and so that it cannot be taught and is not knowledge.

MENO: We did.

SOCRATES: At the same time we agreed that it is something good, and that to be useful and good consists in giving right guidance.

MENO: Yes.

SOCRATES: And that these two, true opinion and knowledge, are the only things which direct us aright and the possession of which makes a man a true guide. We may except chance, because what turns out right by chance is not due to human direction, and say that where human control leads to right ends, these two principles are directive, true opinion and knowledge.

MENO: Yes, I agree.

SOCRATES: Now since virtue cannot be taught, we can no longer believe it to be knowledge, so that one of our two good and useful principles is excluded, and knowledge is not the guide in public life.

MENO: No.

SOCRATES: It is not then by the possession of any wisdom that such men as Themistocles, and the others whom Anytus mentioned just now, became leaders in their cities. This fact, that they do not owe their eminence to knowledge, will explain why they are unable to make others like themselves.

MENO: No doubt it is as you say.

SOCRATES: That leaves us with the other alternative, that it is well-aimed conjecture which statesmen employ in upholding their countries' welfare. Their position in relation to knowledge is no different from that of prophets and tellers of oracles, who under divine inspiration utter many truths, but have no knowledge of what they are saying.

MENO: It must be something like that.

SOCRATES: And ought we not to reckon those men divine who with no conscious thought are repeatedly and outstandingly successful in what they do or say?

MENO: Certainly.

SOCRATES: We are right therefore to give this title to the oracular priests and the prophets that I mentioned, and to poets of every description. Statesmen too, when by their speeches they get great things done yet know nothing of what they are saying, are to be considered as acting no less under divine influence, inspired and possessed by the divinity.

Meno: Certainly.

Socrates: Women, you know, Meno, do call good men "divine," and the Spartans too, when they are singing a good man's praises, say "He is divine."

Meno: And it looks as if they are right—though our friend Anytus may be annoyed with you for saying so.

Socrates: I can't help that. We will talk to him some other time. If all we have said in this discussion, and the questions we have asked, have been right, virtue will be acquired neither by nature nor by teaching. Whoever has it gets it by divine dispensation without taking thought, unless he be the kind of statesman who can create another like himself. Should there be such a man, he would be among the living practically what Homer said Tiresias was among the dead, when he described him as the only one in the underworld who kept his wits—"the others are mere flitting shades." Where virtue is concerned such a man would be just like that, a solid reality among shadows.

Meno: That is finely put, Socrates.

Socrates: On our present reasoning then, whoever has virtue gets it by divine dispensation. But we shall not understand the truth of the matter until, before asking how men get virtue, we try to discover what virtue is in and by itself. Now it is time for me to go; and my request to you is that you will allay the anger of your friend Anytus by convincing him that what you now believe is true. If you succeed, the Athenians may have cause to thank you.

SYMPOSIUM

The Speakers in the Dialogue

Agathon, a writer of tragedies
Socrates, a truth-loving eccentric
Phaedrus, an idealist
Pausanias, a realist—Agathon's lover
Aristophanes, a writer of comedies
Eryximachus, a doctor
Alcibiades, politician and playboy

Prologue—Apollodorus and a Friend

Apollodorus: You couldn't have asked anyone better. I live in Phalerum, and the day before yesterday I was going up to town when a man I know caught sight of me disappearing in the distance. He gave me a shout, calling me (a little facetiously) "You there! Citizen of Phalerum! Hey, Apollodorus! Wait a moment."

So I stopped and waited.

"Apollodorus," he said, "I've been looking for you for ages. I wanted to ask you about the time when Agathon and Socrates and Alcibiades and the others all met for dinner. I want to know what was said about love. I was told about it by a man who had talked to Phoenix, son of Philippus; he said you knew about it as well. He wasn't much help—couldn't remember anything very definite. Can you give me your version? After all, who better than you to talk about Socrates' conversations? For instance, were you at the dinner-party yourself, or not?"

"You must have been given a pretty garbled account, if you think the party you're asking about took place recently enough for me to have been at it."

"Oh! I thought you were."

"Really, Glaucon, how could I have been? It's ages since Agathon last lived in Athens, and less than three years since I became friends with Socrates, and got into the habit of keeping up with what he says and does every day. Before that my life was just a random whirl of activity. I thought I was extremely busy, but in fact I was the most pathetic creature imaginable, just as you are now, doing anything to avoid philosophical thought."

"Very funny. When *did* the party happen, then?"

"It was when we were still children, when Agathon won the prize with his first tragedy, the day after he and the members of the chorus made the usual winners' thanksgivings."

"Oh, I see. It was a long time ago, then. Who told you about it? Was it Socrates himself?"

"God, no. I got it from the man who told Phoenix, a man called Aristodemus, from Cydathenaeum. Small man, never wears shoes. He'd been at the party; in fact, I think he must have been one of Socrates' keenest admirers in those days. But I've also asked Socrates about some of the things he told me, and his version agreed with Aristodemus'."

"You must tell me all about it, and walking into town is an ideal opportunity. You can talk, and I will listen."

So we discussed the party as we went along, and that's why, as I said originally, I'm a good person to ask about it. And if I've got to tell it to you as well, I'd better get on with it. In any case, I get tremendous pleasure out of talking about philosophy myself, or listening to other people talk about it, quite apart from thinking it's good for me. Other conversation, especially your kind, about money or business, bores me stiff. You're my friends, but I feel sorry for you, because you think you're getting somewhere, when you're not. You in turn probably think me misguided, and you may well be right. However, I don't *think* you are misguided; I know for certain you are.

FRIEND: Still the old Apollodorus we know and love. Never a good word for yourself or anyone else. As far as I can see, you regard absolutely everyone, starting with yourself, as a lost cause—except for Socrates, that is. I don't know where you picked up the nickname "softy"; it certainly doesn't fit your conversation—always full of fury against yourself, and everyone else apart from Socrates.

APOLLODORUS: And if that's my opinion of myself and the rest of you, then obviously I'm crazy, or mistaken, I suppose.

FRIEND: Let's not argue about that now, Apollodorus. Just do as I ask, and tell me what was said at Agathon's party.

APOLLODORUS: The conversation went something like this . . . or better, let me try to tell it to you right from the beginning, as Aristodemus told it to me.

ARISTODEMUS' ACCOUNT

I met Socrates, all washed and brushed, and wearing shoes (a thing he hardly ever did). I asked him where he was going looking so elegant.

"I'm going to dinner with Agathon. I avoided the first celebration last night; I couldn't face the crowd. But I said I'd come this evening. I'm looking elegant, because   b
Agathon always looks elegant. What about you? How do you feel about coming to dinner uninvited?"

"I'll do anything you tell me."

"Come on then. Let's ignore the proverb, 'good men come uninvited to lesser men's feasts,' or rather let's change it, to 'good men come uninvited to Agathon's feast.' After all, Homer does worse than ignore it; he completely contradicts it. His   c
Agamemnon is an outstanding warrior, while his Menelaus is a man of straw. But when Agamemnon is sacrificing and feasting Homer lets Menelaus come to the feast without an invitation, though that's a case of a lesser man coming to dinner with a better."

"I'm afraid, in my case, that Homer is likely to be nearer the mark than you, Socrates. It'll be a question of a nonentity coming to dinner uninvited with a wise man. You'd better decide what you'll say if you do take me. I'm not coming uninvited—   d
only as your guest."

"Two heads are better than one. We'll think of something to say. Come on."

So off we went. But Socrates, absorbed in his own thoughts, got left behind on the way. I was going to wait for him, but he told me to go on ahead. So I turned up at   e
Agathon's house by myself, and found the door open. In fact, it was slightly embarrassing, because one of the house-slaves met me, and took me straight in, where I found the others had just sat down to dinner. Agathon saw me come in, and at once said, "Aristodemus, you're just in time to have dinner with us. I hope that's what you've come for. If not, it'll have to wait for another time. I tried to get hold of you yesterday, to ask you, but could not find you. How come you haven't brought Socrates with you?"

I turned round and looked behind me, and couldn't see Socrates anywhere. So I explained that I had come with Socrates. In fact, but for his invitation, I wouldn't have come at all.

"I'm glad you did. But where is he?"

"He was right behind me just now. I've no more idea than you where he could   175
have got to."

Agathon turned to a slave. "Could you go and look for Socrates, please, and ask him in? Aristodemus, why don't you sit over there by Eryximachus?"

While one slave was giving me a wash, so I could sit down to dinner, another slave came in: "That Socrates you asked me to look for has gone wandering up to the front door of the wrong house. He's just standing there. I asked him to come in, but he won't."

"How odd. Still, don't give up. Keep on asking him."   b

But I said, "No, leave him alone. He's always doing this. It doesn't matter where he is. He just wanders off and stands there. I don't think he'll be long. Don't badger him; just leave him."

"Well, if you say so, I suppose we'd better." He turned to the slaves. "The rest of us will eat now. Serve the meal just as you like. No-one's going to tell you how to do it, any more than I ever tell you. Imagine we're all your guests, and try to give us a meal we'll enjoy."

c   So we started having dinner, though still no sign of Socrates. Agathon kept wanting to send people to look for him, but I wouldn't let him. When he did turn up, he hadn't been long by his standards, but even so we were about halfway through dinner. Agathon, who'd sat down last, at a table on his own, said "Come and sit next to me,

d   Socrates. Then perhaps I shall absorb whatever it was you were thinking about outside. You must have found the answer, or you wouldn't have come in to join us."

Socrates sat down. "Wouldn't it be marvellous, Agathon," he said, "if ideas were the kind of things which could be imparted simply by contact, and those of us who had few could absorb them from those who had a lot—in the same sort of way that liquid can flow from a full container to an empty one, if you put a piece of string between

e   them? If that's the nature of ideas, then I think I'm lucky to be sitting next to you, and getting a nice, substantial transfusion. My ideas aren't much use. They have an ambiguous, dreamlike quality, whereas yours are brilliant, and with so much scope for further improvement. You're only young, and yet they were particularly brilliant the day before yesterday, as more than thirty thousand Greeks can testify."

"Don't be sarcastic, Socrates. And let's settle this question of ideas a bit later. We'll give Dionysus the casting vote. But you'd better have dinner first."

176   So Socrates sat down and ate, with the others. We poured offerings, sang hymns, and did all the usual things. Then our thoughts turned to drinking, and Pausanias made a suggestion. "Well, gentlemen, how can we make things as painless for ourselves as possible? I must admit to feeling rather frail after yesterday evening. I need a breather, and I expect most of you do, too. After all, you were there as well. So, how can we

b   make our drinking as painless as possible?"

ARISTOPHANES: I couldn't agree more, Pausanias. Whatever else we do, we don't want to let ourselves in for another evening's hard drinking. I'm one of those who sank without trace last night.

ERYXIMACHUS: I'm glad you both feel like that. But we ought also to consider how strong Agathon is feeling.

AGATHON: Not at all strong.

c   ERYXIMACHUS: It would certainly be a stroke of luck for people like Aristodemus and Phaedrus and me, if you hard drinkers are prepared to take an evening off. We're not in your league. I'm not worried about Socrates—he's equally happy either way, so he won't mind what we do. But as far as I can see, no-one here is all that keen on drinking a lot, so perhaps I can tell you the truth about getting drunk without causing

d   too much offence. My experience as a doctor leaves me in no doubt that getting drunk is bad for you. I'm not keen on drinking to excess myself, and I wouldn't advise anyone else to, especially anyone who still had a hangover from yesterday.

PHAEDRUS: Well, I generally follow your advice, especially on medical matters. So will the others, if they have any sense.

e   So we all agreed just to drink what we felt like, rather than treating it as an opportunity to get drunk.

ERYXIMACHUS: Good, that's settled then. We'll all drink as much as we feel like, and there's no compulsion on anyone. And since we've got that sorted out, I've another suggestion to make. I don't think we need this flute girl who's just started playing. She can play to herself, or to the women upstairs, if she feels like it, but for this

177   evening I suggest we stick to conversation. And I've an idea what we might talk about, if you want to hear it.

Everyone said they did want to hear it, and urged him to make his suggestion.

Eros and Psyche, a Roman copy ca. 150 B.C. after a Greek statue. Caught in a tender embrace, the two youthful figures, Eros and Psyche, symbolize both love and the human soul. While his friends describe Eros as a young, beautiful god (like this statue depicts), Socrates presents a very different picture. *(Musei Capitolini, Rome, Italy. Alinari/Art Resource, NY.)*

ERYXIMACHUS: Well, it arises out of Euripides' *Melanippe*. And it isn't really my idea. It's Phaedrus'. He gets quite worked up about it. "Don't you think it's odd, Eryximachus," he says, "that most of the other gods have had hymns and songs of praise

b   written to them by the poets, but never a word in praise of Eros, the oldest and greatest god? And it's not for want of good poets, either. Or think of the great teachers—they've recorded the exploits of Heracles and other heroes, in prose. Prodicus, for example, does that sort of thing beautifully. Now maybe that's not very surprising, but I came across a book the other day, by a well-known writer, with an extraordinary eulogy in it on the value of salt. You can find any number of things singled out for praise

c   in this way. What is surprising is that there should be so much enthusiasm for that kind of thing, and yet no-one, up to the present day, has ever found himself able to praise Eros as he deserves. He is a remarkable god, but he has been totally neglected."

I agree with Phaedrus. I'd like to do him a favour and make my contribution. What's more, the present gathering seems an ideal opportunity to praise the god. So, if

d   you agree, we can quite happily spend our time in talk. I propose that each of us in turn, going round anticlockwise, should make a speech, the best he can, in praise of Eros. Phaedrus can start, since he is in the position of honour, and since the whole thing was his idea.

SOCRATES: I don't think anyone will vote against you, Eryximachus. I'm certainly not going to refuse, since love is the only thing I ever claim to know anything about.

e   Agathon and Pausanias won't mind—still less Aristophanes, since his only interests in life are Dionysus and Aphrodite. In fact I can't see anyone here who *will* object. It's a little unfair on those of us sitting here in the last positions. Still, if you first speakers speak well enough, we shan't have to worry. Good luck, Phaedrus. You go first, and make your speech in praise of Eros.

178   They all agreed with Socrates, and told Phaedrus to start. Aristodemus couldn't remember the exact details of everybody's speech, nor in turn can I remember precisely what he said. But I can give you the gist of those speeches and speakers which were most worth remembering.

Phaedrus, as I said, began—something like this.

PHAEDRUS

Eros is a great god, a marvel to men and gods alike. This is true in many ways, and it is especially true of his birth. He is entitled to our respect, as the oldest of the gods—as I

b   can prove. Eros has no parents, either in reality or in works of prose and poetry. Take Hesiod, for example. All he says is that in the beginning there was Chaos . . . "and then came the full-breasted Earth, the eternal and immovable foundation of everything, and Eros." Acusilaus agrees with Hesiod, that after Chaos there were just these two, Earth and Eros. And then there's Parmenides' theory about his birth, that "Eros was created

c   first of the Gods." So there is widespread agreement that Eros is of great antiquity. And being very old he also brings us very great benefits. I can see nothing better in life for a young boy, as soon as he is old enough, than finding a good lover, nor for a lover than finding a boyfriend. Love, more than anything (more than family, or position, or wealth), implants in men the thing which must be their guide if they are to live a good

d   life. And what is that? It is a horror of what is degrading, and a passionate desire for what is good. These qualities are essential if a state or an individual is to accomplish anything great or good. Imagine a man in love being found out doing something humiliating, or letting someone else do something degrading to him, because he was too cowardly to stop it. It would embarrass him more to be found out by the boy he loved than by his father or his friends, or anyone. And you can see just the same thing happening with the boy. He is more worried about being caught behaving badly by his admirers than by anyone else. So if there were some way of arranging that a state, or an army, could be made up entirely of pairs of lovers, it is impossible to imagine a finer population. They would avoid all dishonour, and compete with one another for glory: in battle, this kind of army, though small, fighting side by side could conquer virtually the whole world. After all, a lover would sooner be seen by anyone deserting his post or throwing away his weapons, rather than by his boyfriend. He would normally choose to die many times over instead. And as for abandoning the boy, or not trying to save him if he is in danger—no-one is such a coward as not to be inspired with courage by Eros, making him the equal of the naturally brave man. Homer says, and rightly, that god breathes fire into some of his heroes. And it is just this quality, whose origin is to be found within himself, that Eros imparts to lovers.

What is more, lovers are the only people prepared to die for others. Not just men, either; women also sometimes. A good example is Alcestis, the daughter of Pelias. She alone was willing to die for her husband. He had a father and mother but she so far surpassed them in devotion, because of her passion for him, that she showed them to be strangers to their son, relations in name only. In so doing she was thought, by men and gods alike, to have performed a deed of supreme excellence. Indeed the gods were so pleased with her action that they brought her soul back from the underworld—a privilege they granted to only a fortunate handful of the many people who have done good deeds. That shows how highly even the gods value loyalty and courage in love. Orpheus, the son of Oeagrus, on the other hand, was sent away from the underworld empty handed; he was shown a mere phantom of the woman he came to find, and not given the woman herself. Of course Orpheus was a musician, and the gods thought he was a bit of a coward, lacking the courage to die for his love, as Alcestis did, but trying to find a way of getting into the underworld alive. They punished him further for that, giving him death at the hands of women.

In contrast, the man whom the gods honoured above all was Achilles, the son of Thetis. They sent him to the Islands of the Blessed. His mother had warned him that if he killed Hector he would himself be killed, but if he didn't, he would return home and live to a ripe old age. Nevertheless out of loyalty to his lover Patroclus he chose without hesitation to die—not to save him, but to avenge him; for Patroclus had already been killed. The gods were full of admiration, and gave him the highest possible honour, because he valued his lover so highly.

Incidentally, Aeschylus' view, that it was Achilles who was in love with Patroclus, is nonsense. Quite apart from the fact that he was more beautiful than Patroclus (and all the other Greek heroes, come to that) and had not yet grown a beard, he was also, according to Homer, much younger. And he must have been younger because it is an undoubted fact that the gods, though they always value courage which comes from love, are most impressed and pleased, and grant the greatest rewards, when the younger man is loyal to his lover, than when the lover is loyal to him. That's because the lover is a more divine creature than the younger man, since he is divinely inspired. And that's why they honoured Achilles more than Alcestis, and sent him to the Islands of the Blessed.

There you are then. I claim that Eros is the oldest of the gods, the most deserving of our respect, and the most useful, for those men, past and present, who want to attain excellence and happiness.

c   That was the gist of Phaedrus' speech. After him, several other people spoke, but Aristodemus couldn't really remember what they said. So he left them out and recounted Pausanias' speech.

PAUSANIAS

Phaedrus, I don't think we've been very accurate in defining our subject for discussion. We've simply said that we must make a speech in praise of Eros. That would be fine, if there were just one Eros. In fact, however, there isn't. And since there isn't, we would
d   do better to define first which Eros we are to praise. I am going to try to put things straight—first defining which Eros we are supposed to be praising, and then trying to praise the god as he deserves.

We are all well aware, I take it, that without Eros there is no Aphrodite. If there were only one Aphrodite, there would be one Eros. However, since there are in fact two Aphrodites, it follows that Eros likewise must be two. There's no doubt about there being two Aphrodites; the older has no mother, and is the daughter of Heaven.
e   We call her Heavenly Aphrodite. The younger is the daughter of Zeus and Dione, and we call her Common Aphrodite. It follows that the Eros who assists this Aphrodite should also, properly speaking, be called Common Eros, and the other Heavenly Eros. We certainly ought to praise all the gods, but we should also attempt to define what is the proper province of each.

181   It is in general true of any activity that, simply in itself, it is neither good nor bad. Take what we're doing now, for example—that is to say drinking, or singing, or talking. None of these is good or bad in itself, but each becomes so, depending on the way it is done. Well and rightly done, it is good; wrongly done, it is bad. And it's just the same with loving, and Eros. It's not all good, and doesn't all deserve praise. The Eros we should praise is the one which encourages people to love in the right way.

b   The Eros associated with Common Aphrodite is, in all senses of the word, common, and quite haphazard in his operation. This is the love of the man in the street. For a start, he is as likely to fall in love with women as with boys. Secondly, he falls in love with their bodies rather than their minds. Thirdly, he picks the most unintelligent people he can find, since all he's interested in is the sexual act. He doesn't care whether it's done in the right way or not. That is why the effect of this Eros is haphaz-
c   ard—sometimes good, sometimes the reverse. This love derives its existence from the much younger Aphrodite, the one composed equally of the female and male elements.

The other Eros springs from Heavenly Aphrodite, and in the first place is composed solely of the male element, with none of the female (so it is the love of boys we are talking about), and in the second place is older, and hence free from lust. In consequence, those inspired by this love turn to the male, attracted by what is naturally
d   stronger and of superior intelligence. And even among those who love boys you can tell the ones whose love is purely heavenly. They only fall in love with boys old enough to think for themselves—in other words, with boys who are nearly grown up.

Those who start a love affair with boys of that age are prepared, I think, to be friends, and live together, for life. The others are deceivers, who take advantage of

youthful folly, and then quite cheerfully abandon their victims in search of others.   e
There ought really to be a law against loving young boys, to stop so much energy
being expended on an uncertain end. After all, no-one knows how good or bad, in
mind and body, young boys will eventually turn out. Good men voluntarily observe
this rule, but the common lovers I am talking about should be compelled to do the
same, just as we stop them, so far as we can, falling in love with free women. They are
actually the people who have brought the thing into disrepute, with the result that some
people even go so far as to say that it is wrong to satisfy your lover. It is the common   182
lover they have in mind when they say this, regarding his demands as premature and
unfair to the boy. Surely nothing done with restraint and decency could reasonably
incur criticism.

What is more, while sexual conventions in other states are clearcut and easy to
understand, here and in Sparta, by contrast, they are complex. In Elis, for example, or   b
Boeotia, and places where they are not sophisticated in their use of language, it is laid
down, quite straightforwardly, that it is right to satisfy your lover. No-one, old or
young, would say it was wrong, and the reason, I take it, is that they don't want to have
all the trouble of trying to persuade them verbally, when they're such poor speakers.
On the other hand, in Ionia and many other places under Persian rule, it is regarded as   c
wrong. That is because the Persians' system of government (dictatorships) makes them
distrust it, just as they distrust philosophy and communal exercise. It doesn't suit the
rulers that their subjects should think noble thoughts, nor that they should form the
strong friendships or attachments which these activities, and in particular love, tend to   d
produce. Dictators here in Athens learnt the same lesson, by experience. The relationship between Harmodius and his lover, Aristogeiton, was strong enough to put an end
to the dictators' rule.

In short, the convention that satisfying your lover is wrong is a result of the
moral weakness of those who observe the convention—the rulers' desire for power,
and their subjects' cowardice. The belief that it is always right can be attributed to
mental-laziness. Our customs are much better but, as I said, not easy to understand.
Think about it—let's take the lover first. Open love is regarded as better than secret
love, and so is love of the noblest and best people, even if they are not the best-
looking. In fact, there is remarkable encouragement of the lover from all sides. He is   e
not regarded as doing anything wrong; it is a good thing if he gets what he wants, and a
shame if he doesn't. And when it comes to trying to get what he wants, we give the
lover permission to do the most amazing things, and be applauded for them—things
which, if he did them with any other aim or intention, would cover him in reproach.   183
Think of the way lovers behave towards the boys they love—think of the begging and
entreating involved in their demands, the oaths they swear, the nights they spend sleeping outside the boys' front doors, the slavery they are prepared to endure (which no
slave would put up with). If they behaved like this for money, or position, or influence
of any kind, they would be told to stop by friends and enemies alike. Their enemies
would call their behaviour dependent and servile, while their friends would censure
them sharply, and even be embarrassed for them. And yet a lover can do all these   b
things, and be approved of. Custom attaches no blame to his actions, since he is reckoned to be acting in a wholly honourable way. The strangest thing of all is that, in most
people's opinion, the lover has a unique dispensation from the gods to swear an oath
and then break it. Lovers' vows, apparently, are not binding.

So far, then, gods and men alike give all kinds of licence to the lover, and an ob-   c
server of Athenian life might conclude that it was an excellent thing, in this city, both
to be a lover and to be friendly to lovers. But when we come to the boy, the position is

quite different. Fathers give their sons escorts, when men fall in love with them, and don't allow them to talk to their lovers—and those are the escort's instructions as well. The boy's peers and friends jeer at him if they see anything of the kind going on, and when their elders see them jeering, they don't stop them, or tell them off, as they should if the jeers were unjustified. Looking at this side of things, you would come to the opposite conclusion—that this kind of thing is here regarded as highly reprehensible.

d

The true position, I think, is this. Going back to my original statement, there isn't one single form of love. So love is neither right nor wrong in itself. Done rightly, it is right; done wrongly, it is wrong. It is wrong if you satisfy the wrong person, for the wrong reasons, and right if you satisfy the right person, for the right reasons. The wrong person is the common lover I was talking about—the one who loves the body rather than the mind. His love is not lasting, since *what* he loves is not lasting either. As soon as the youthful bloom of the body (which is what he loves) starts to fade, he "spreads his wings and is off," as they say, making a mockery of all his speeches and promises. On the other hand, the man who loves a boy for his good character will stick to him for life, since he has attached himself to what is lasting.

e

Our customs are intended to test these lovers well and truly, and get the boys to satisfy the good ones, and avoid the bad. That's why we encourage lovers to chase after boys, but tell the boys not to be caught. In this way we set up a trial and a test, to see which category the lover comes in, and which category the boy he loves comes in. This explains a number of things—for instance, why it's thought wrong for a boy to let himself be caught too quickly. It is felt that some time should elapse, since time is a good test of most things. Also why it is wrong to be caught by means of money or political influence—whether it's a case of the boy being threatened, and yielding rather than holding out, or a case of being offered some financial or political inducement, and not turning it down. No affair of this kind is likely to be stable or secure, quite apart from the fact that it is no basis for true friendship.

184

b

There is just one way our customs leave it open for a boy to satisfy his lover, and not be blamed for it. It is permissible, as I have said, for a lover to enter upon any kind of voluntary slavery he may choose, and be the slave of the boy he loves. This is not regarded as self-seeking, or in any way demeaning. Similarly there is one other kind of voluntary slavery which is not regarded as demeaning. This is the slavery of the boy, in his desire for improvement. It can happen that a boy chooses to serve a man, because he thinks that by association with him he will improve in wisdom in some way, or in some other form of goodness. This kind of voluntary slavery, like the other, is widely held among us not to be wrong, and not to be self-seeking.

c

So it can only be regarded as right for a boy to satisfy his lover if both these conditions are satisfied—both the lover's behaviour, and the boy's desire for wisdom and goodness. Then the lover and the boy have the same aim, and each has the approval of convention—the lover because he is justified in performing any service he chooses for a boy who satisfies him, the boy because he is justified in submitting, in any way he will, to the man who can make him wise and good. So if the lover has something to offer in the way of sound judgment and moral goodness, and if the boy is eager to accept this contribution to his education and growing wisdom, then, and only then, this favourable combination makes it right for a boy to satisfy his lover. In no other situation is it right.

d

e

Nor, in this situation, is there any disgrace in making a mistake, whereas in all other situations it is equally a disgrace to be mistaken or not. For example, suppose a boy satisfies his lover for money, taking him to be rich. If he gets it wrong, and doesn't get any money, because the lover turns out to be poor, it is still regarded as immoral, because the boy who does this seems to be revealing his true character, and declaring that he would do anything for anyone in return for money. And that is not a good way

185

to behave. Equally, a boy may satisfy a man because he thinks he is a good man, and that he himself will become better through his friendship. If he gets it wrong, and his lover turns out to be a bad man, of little moral worth, still there is something creditable   b
about his mistake. He too seems to have revealed his true character—namely, that he is eager to do anything for anyone in return for goodness and self-improvement. And this is the finest of all qualities.

So it is absolutely correct for boys to satisfy their lovers, if it is done in pursuit of goodness. This is the love which comes from the heavenly goddess; it is itself heavenly, and of great value to state and individual alike, since it compels both lover and boy to devote a lot of attention to their own moral improvement. All other sorts of love   c
derive from the other goddess, the common one.

Well, Phaedrus, that's the best I can offer, without preparation, on the subject of Eros.

Pausanias paused (sorry about the pun—sophistic influence). After that it was Aristophanes' turn to speak. But he had just got hiccups. I don't know if it was from eating too much, or for some other reason; anyway he was unable to make his speech. All he could say, since Eryximachus, the doctor, happened to be sitting just below him,   d
was this: "Eryximachus, you're just the man. Either get rid of my hiccups, or speak instead of me until they stop."

"I'll do both. I'll take your turn to speak, and when you get rid of your hiccups, you can take mine. While I'm speaking, try holding your breath for a long time, to see   e
if they stop. Failing that, gargle with some water. And if they are very severe, tickle your nose and make yourself sneeze. Do that once or twice, and they'll stop, however severe."

"Will you please speak first, then?" said Aristophanes. "And I'll do as you suggest."

ERYXIMACHUS

Pausanias made an impressive start to his speech, but I do not think he brought it to a very satisfactory conclusion. So I think it is important that I should try to complete his   186
account. His analysis of the twofold nature of Eros seems to me to be a valuable distinction. But I cannot accept his implication that Eros is found only in human hearts, and is aroused only by human beauty. I am a doctor by profession, and it has been my observation, I would say, throughout my professional career, that Eros is aroused by many other things as well, and that he is found also in nature—in the physical life of all animals, in plants that grow in the ground, and in virtually all living organisms. My conclusion is that he is great and awe-inspiring, this god, and that his influence is un-   b
bounded, both in the human realm and in the divine.

I will begin by talking about my medical experience, to show my respect for my profession. The nature of the human body shows this twofold Eros, since it is generally agreed that health and sickness in the body are separate and unalike, and that unlike is attracted to unlike, and desires it. So there is one force of attraction for the healthy, and another for the sick. Pausanias was talking just now about it being right to satisfy men, if they are good men, but wrong if all they are interested in is physical pleasure. It is   c
just the same with the body. It is right to satisfy the good and healthy elements in the body, and one should do so. We call this "medicine." Conversely it is wrong to satisfy the bad, unhealthy elements, and anyone who is going to be a skilled doctor should deny these elements.

d   Medical knowledge is thus essentially knowledge of physical impulses or desires for ingestion or evacuation. In this, the man who can distinguish healthy desires from unhealthy is the best doctor. Moreover he needs the ability to change people's desires, so that they lose one and gain another. There are people who lack desires which they should have. If the doctor can produce these desires, and remove the existing ones, then he is a good doctor. He must, in fact, be able to reconcile and harmonise the most disparate elements in the body. By "the most disparate" I mean those most opposed to one another—cold and hot, bitter and sweet, dry and wet, and so forth. It was by know-

e   ing how to produce mutual desire and harmony among these that our forerunner Asclepius, as the poets say (and I believe), established this art of ours.

187   Medicine, then, as I say, is completely governed by this god—likewise physical training and farming. Music too is no exception, as must be clear to anyone who gives the matter a moment's thought. Perhaps that is what Heraclitus means, though he does not actually express it very clearly, when he says that "the One" is "in conflict and harmony with itself," . . . "like the stringing of a bow or lyre." Clearly there is a contradiction in saying that a harmony is in conflict, or is composed of conflicting elements.

b   Perhaps what he meant was that, starting from initially discordant high and low notes, the harmony is only created when these are brought into agreement by the skill of the musician. Clearly there could be no harmony between high and low, if they were still in conflict. For harmony is a consonance, and consonance is a kind of agreement. Thus it is impossible that there should be a harmony of conflicting elements, in which those elements still conflict, nor can one harmonise what is different, and incapable of agree-

c   ment. Or take rhythm as another example; it arises out of the conflict of quick and slow, but only when they cease to conflict. Here it is the art of music which imposes harmony on all the elements, by producing mutual attraction and agreement between them, whereas in the body it is the art of medicine. So music, again, is a knowledge of Eros applied to harmony and rhythm.

In the actual formation of harmony and rhythm it is a simple matter to detect the hand of Eros, which at this stage is not the twofold Eros. It is altogether more complicated when we come to apply rhythm and harmony to human activity, either to the

d   making of music, which we call composing, or to the correct use of melody and tempo in what we call education. This really does demand a high degree of skill. And the same argument again holds good, that one should satisfy the most well-ordered people, in the interests of those as yet less well-ordered; one should pay due regard to their desires, which are in fact the good, heavenly Eros, companion of the heavenly muse,

e   Ourania. Common Eros, by contrast, goes with the common muse, Polymnia. The greatest caution is called for in its employment, if one is to gain enjoyment from it without encouraging pure self-indulgence. Similarly, in my profession, there is a great art in the correct treatment of people's desire for rich food, so that they can enjoy it without ill effects.

Thus in music and medicine, and in all other spheres of activity, human and di-

188   vine, we must keep a careful eye, so far as is practicable, on both forms of Eros. For both are present. The seasons of the year likewise fully illustrate their joint operation. When all the things I was talking about just now (such as hot and cold, wet and dry) hit upon the right Eros in their relation to one another, and consequently form the right sort of mixture and harmony, then they bring what is seasonable and healthy, to men and to the rest of the world of animals and plants; and all is as it should be. But when

b   the other Eros, in violence and excess, takes over in the natural seasons of the year, it does all sorts of damage, and upsets the natural order. When that happens the result, generally, is plague and a variety of diseases—for animals and plants alike. Frost, hail, and mildew are the result of this kind of competition and disorder involving Eros.

Knowledge of Eros in connection with the movements of the stars and the seasons of the year is called astronomy.

Then again, all sacrifices, and everything which comes under the direction of the prophetic arts (that is to say, the whole relationship of gods and men to one another), have as their sole concern the observance and correct treatment of Eros. If, in their behaviour towards their parents, the living and the dead, or the gods, people stop satisfying the good, well-ordered Eros, if they stop honouring him and consulting him in every enterprise, and start to follow the other Eros, then the result is all kinds of wickedness. So the prophetic arts have to keep an eye on, and treat, the two forms of Eros. Their knowledge of Eros in human affairs, the Eros who is conducive to piety and correct observance, makes them the architects of friendship between gods and men.   d

So great and widespread—in fact, universal—is the power possessed, in general by all Eros, but in particular by the Eros which, in the moral sphere, acts with good sense and justice both among us and among the gods. And not only does it possess absolute power; it also brings us complete happiness, enabling us to be companions and friends both of each other and of our superiors, the gods.

Well, I too may have left a lot out in my praise of Eros, but I have not done so   e
deliberately. And if I have left anything out, it is up to you, Aristophanes, to fill the gap. Or if you intend to praise the god in some other way, go ahead and do that, now that you have got rid of your hiccups.

ARISTOPHANES: Yes, they've stopped, but not without resort to the sneezing treat-   189
ment. I wondered if it was the "well-ordered" part of my body which demanded all the noise and tickling involved in sneezing. Certainly the hiccups stopped the moment I tried sneezing.

ERYXIMACHUS: Careful, my dear friend. You haven't started yet, and already you're playing the fool. You'll force me to act as censor for your speech, if you start   b
fooling around as soon as you get a chance to speak in peace.

ARISTOPHANES (laughing): Fair enough, Eryximachus. Regard my remarks so far as unsaid. But don't be too censorious. I'm worried enough already about what I'm going to say—not that it may arouse laughter (after all, there would be some point in that, and it would be appropriate to my profession), but that it may be laughed out of court.

ERYXIMACHUS: Aristophanes, you're trying to eat your cake and have it. Come on, concentrate. You'll have to justify what you say, but perhaps, if I see fit, I will acquit you.   c

ARISTOPHANES

Well, Eryximachus, I do intend to make a rather different kind of speech from the kind you and Pausanias made. It's my opinion that mankind is quite unaware of the power of Eros. If they were aware of it, they would build vast temples and altars to him, and make great offerings to him. As it is, though it is of crucial importance that this observance should be paid to him, none of these things is done.

Of all the gods, Eros is the most friendly towards men. He is our helper, and   d
cures those evils whose cure brings the greatest happiness to the human race. I'll try to explain his power to you, and then you can go off and spread the word to others.

First of all you need to know about human nature and what has happened to it. Our original nature was not as it is now, but quite different. For one thing there were three sexes, rather than the two (male and female) we have now. The third sex was a combination of these two. Its name has survived, though the phenomenon itself has   e disappeared. This single combination, comprising both male and female, was, in form and name alike, hermaphrodite. Now it survives only as a term of abuse.

190   Secondly, each human being formed a complete whole, spherical, with back and ribs forming a circle. They had four hands, four legs, and two faces, identical in every way, on a circular neck. They had a single head for the two faces, which looked in opposite directions; four ears, two sets of genitals, and everything else as you'd expect from the description so far. They walked upright, as we do, in whichever direction they wanted. And when they started to run fast, they were just like people doing cartwheels. They stuck their legs straight out all round, and went bowling along, supported on their eight limbs, and rolling along at high speed.

          The reason for having three sexes, and of this kind, was this: the male was originally the offspring of the sun, the female of the earth, and the one which was half-and-

b   half was the offspring of the moon, because the moon likewise is half-sun and half-earth. They were circular, both in themselves and in their motion, because of their similarity to their parents. They were remarkable for their strength and vigour, and their ambition led them to make an assault upon the gods. The story which Homer tells

c   of the giants, Ephialtes and Otus, is told of them—that they tried to make a way up to heaven, to attack the gods. Zeus and the other gods wondered what to do about them, and couldn't decide. They couldn't kill them, as they had the giants—striking them with thunderbolts and doing away with the whole race—because the worship and sacrifices they received from men would have been done away with as well. On the other hand, they couldn't go on allowing them to behave so outrageously.

          In the end Zeus, after long and painful thought, came up with a suggestion. "I think I have an idea. Men could go on existing, but behave less disgracefully, if we

d   made them weaker. I'm going to cut each of them in two. This will have two advantages: it will make them weaker, and also more useful to us, because of the increase in their numbers. They will walk upright, on two legs. And if it's clear they still can't behave, and they refuse to lead a quiet life, I'll cut them in half again and they can go hopping along on one leg."

          That was his plan. So he started cutting them in two, like someone slicing veg-

e   etables for pickling, or slicing eggs with a wire. And each time he chopped one up, he told Apollo to turn the face and the half-neck round towards the cut side (so that the man could see where he'd been split, and be better behaved in future), and then to heal the rest of the wound. So Apollo twisted the faces round and gathered up the skin all round to what is now called the stomach, like a purse with strings. He made a single outlet, and tied it all up securely in the middle of the stomach; this we now call the

191   navel. He smoothed out most of the wrinkles, and formed the chest, using a tool such as cobblers use for smoothing out wrinkles in a hide stretched over a last. He left a few wrinkles, however, those around the stomach itself and the navel, as a reminder of what happened in those far-off days.

          When man's natural form was split in two, each half went round looking for its other half. They put their arms round one another, and embraced each other, in their

b   desire to grow together again. They started dying of hunger, and also from lethargy, because they refused to do anything separately. And whenever one half died, and the other was left, the survivor began to look for another, and twined itself about it [the other], either encountering half of a complete woman (i.e., what we now call a woman) or half a complete man. In this way they kept on dying.

          Zeus felt sorry for them, and thought of a second plan. He moved their genitals to the front—up till then they had had them on the outside, and had reproduced, not by

c   copulation, but by discharge on to the ground, like grasshoppers. So, as I say, he moved their genitals to the front, and made them use them for reproduction by insemination, the male in the female. The idea was that if, in embracing, a man chanced upon a woman, they could produce children, and the race would increase. If man chanced upon man, they could get full satisfaction from one another's company, then separate, get on with their work, and resume the business of life.

That is why we have this innate love of one another. It brings us back to our orig- d inal state, trying to reunite us and restore us to our true human form. Each of us is a mere fragment of a man (like half a tally-stick); we've been split in two, like filleted plaice. We're all looking for our "other half." Men who are a fragment of the common sex (the one called hermaphrodite), are womanisers, and most adulterers are to be found in this category. Similarly, women of this type are nymphomaniacs and adulter- esses. On the other hand, women who are part of an original woman pay very little at- tention to men. Their interest is in women; Lesbians are found in this class. And those who are part of a male pursue what is male. As boys, because they are slices of the 192 male, they are fond of men, and enjoy going to bed with men and embracing them. These are the best of the boys and young men, since they are by nature the most manly. Some people call them immoral—quite wrongly. It is not immorality, but boldness, courage and manliness, since they take pleasure in what is like themselves. This is proved by the fact that, when they grow up and take part in public life, it's only this kind who prove themselves men. When they come to manhood, they are lovers of boys, and don't naturally show any interest in marriage or producing children; they b have to be forced into it by convention. They're quite happy to live with one another, and not get married.

People like this are clearly inclined to have boyfriends or (as boys) inclined to have lovers, because they always welcome what is akin. When a lover of boys (or any sort of lover) meets the real thing (that is, his other half), he is completely over- whelmed by friendship and affection and desire, more or less refusing to be separated for any time at all. These are the people who spend their whole lives together, and yet c they cannot find words for what they want from one another. No one imagines that it's simply sexual intercourse, or that sex is the reason why one gets such enormous plea- sure out of the other's company. No, it's obvious that the soul of each has some other desire, which it cannot express. It can only give hints and clues to its wishes. d

Imagine that Hephaestus came and stood over them, with his smith's tools, as they lay in bed together. Suppose he asked them, "What is it you want from one an- other, mortals?" If they couldn't tell him, he might ask again, "Do you want to be to- gether as much as possible, and not be separated, day or night? If that's what you want, e I'm quite prepared to weld you together, and make you grow into one. You can be united, the two of you, and live your whole life together, as one. Even down in Hades, when you die, you can be a single dead person, rather than two. Decide whether that's what you want, and whether that would satisfy you." We can be sure that no-one would refuse this offer. Quite clearly, it would be just what they wanted. They'd sim- ply think they'd been offered exactly what they'd always been after, in sexual inter- course, trying to melt into their lovers, and so be united.

So that's the explanation; it's because our original nature was as I have de- 193 scribed, and because we were once complete. And the name of this desire and pursuit of completeness is Eros, or love. Formerly, as I say, we were undivided, but now we've been split up by god for our misdeeds—like the Arcadians by the Spartans. And the danger is that, if we don't treat the gods with respect, we may be divided again, and go round looking like figures in a bas-relief, sliced in half down the line of our noses. We'd be like torn-off counterfoils. That's why we should all encourage the utmost piety towards the gods. We're trying to avoid this fate, and achieve the other. So we take Eros as our guide and leader. Let no-one oppose this aim—and incurring divine b displeasure is opposing this aim—since if we are friends with god, and make our peace with him, we shall find and meet the boys who are part of ourselves, which few people these days succeed in doing.

c
I hope Eryximachus won't misunderstand me, and make fun of my speech, and say it's about Pausanias and Agathon. Perhaps they do come in this class, and are both males by nature. All I'm saying is that in general (and this applies to men and women) this is where happiness for the human race lies—in the successful pursuit of love, in finding the love who is part of our original self, and in returning to our former state. This is the ideal, but in an imperfect world we must settle for the nearest to this we can

d
get, and this is finding a boyfriend who is mentally congenial. And if we want to praise the god who brings this about, then we should praise Eros, who in this predicament is our great benefactor, attracting us to what is part of ourselves, and who gives us great hope for the future that he will reward respect for the gods by returning us to our original condition, healing us, and making us blessed and perfectly happy.

There you are then, Eryximachus. There is my speech about Eros. A bit different from yours, I'm afraid. So please, again, don't laugh at it, and let's hear what all the

e
others have to say—or rather, both the others, since only Agathon and Socrates are left.

ERYXIMACHUS: All right, I won't laugh. In any case, I thought it was a most enjoyable speech. In fact, if I did not know Socrates and Agathon to be experts on love, I would be very worried that they might have nothing to say, so abundant and varied have been the speeches so far. But knowing them as I do, I have no such anxiety.

194
SOCRATES: It's fine for you, Eryximachus. You've already made an excellent speech. If you were in my shoes—or rather, perhaps, the shoes I will be in when Agathon has made a good speech as well—then you might well be alarmed, and be in precisely the state that I am in now.

b
AGATHON: Ah! Trying a little black magic, are you, Socrates? Are you hoping it'll make me nervous if I think the audience is expecting a great speech from me?

SOCRATES: Agathon, I've seen your nerve and courage in going up on the platform with the actors, to present your plays, before the eyes of that vast audience. You were quite unperturbed by that, so it'd be pretty stupid of me to imagine that you'd be nervous in front of the few people here.

AGATHON: I may be stagestruck, Socrates, but I'm still aware that, to anyone with any sense, a small critical audience is far more daunting than a large uncritical one.

c
SOCRATES: It would be quite wrong for me, of all people, to suggest that you are lacking in taste or judgement. I'm well aware that in all your contacts with those you consider discriminating, you value their opinion more highly than that of the public. But don't put us in that category—after all, we were there, we were part of "the public." Anyway, let's pursue this: if you came across truly discriminating people (not us), you would perhaps be daunted by them, if you thought you were producing something second-rate. Is that right?

AGATHON: It is.

SOCRATES: Whereas offering the public something second-rate would not worry you, would it?

d
PHAEDRUS: Agathon, if you answer Socrates, he won't give a thought to the rest of us, so long as he has someone to talk to, particularly someone good-looking. For myself, I love hearing Socrates talk, but it's my job to supervise the progress of the speeches in praise of Eros, and get a speech out of each of you. When you've both paid your tribute to the god, then the two of you can get on with your discussion.

e
AGATHON: Quite right, Phaedrus. There's no reason why I shouldn't make my speech. I shall have plenty of other opportunities to talk to Socrates.

AGATHON

I want first to talk about *how* I should talk, and then talk. All the speakers so far have given me the impression that they were not so much praising the god as congratulating   195 mankind on the good things the god provides. No-one has told us what the giver of these benefits is really like, in himself. And yet, in any speech of praise on any subject, the only correct procedure is to work systematically through the subject under discussion, saying what its nature is, and what benefits it gives. That is how we too should by rights be praising Eros, describing first his nature, then his gifts.

I claim, then, that though all the gods are blessed, Eros, if I may say this without offending the other gods, is the most blessed, since he is the most beautiful and the best. The most beautiful? Well, for a start, Phaedrus, he is the youngest of the gods. He proves this himself, by running away at top speed from old age. Yet old age is swift   b enough, and swifter than most of us would like. It is Eros' nature to hate old age, and steer well clear of it. He lives and exists always with the young. "Birds of a feather," and all that. So, though there was much in Phaedrus' speech with which I agreed, I didn't agree with his claim that Eros was older than Cronus or Iapetus. I would say he's the youngest of the gods—eternally young, in fact. The earliest troubles among the gods,   c which Hesiod and Parmenides write about, were, if those writers are correct, the work of Necessity, not of Eros. If Eros had been there, there would have been none of this cutting, or tying, each other up, or any of the other acts of violence. There would have been friendship and peace, as there has been since Eros became king of the gods.

So, he is young. And not only young, but delicate. You need a poet like Homer   d to show how delicate. Homer describes Ate as a god and as delicate (or at any rate, with delicate feet): "delicate are her feet; she walks not upon the ground, but goes upon the heads of men." Presumably he's giving an example here to show how delicate— she goes not on what is hard, but on what is soft. We too can use a similar argument to   e show how delicate Eros is. He does not walk upon the ground, nor yet on men's heads (which aren't that soft anyway); he lives and moves among the softest of all things, making his home in the hearts and minds of gods and men. And not in all hearts equally. He avoids any hard hearts he comes across, and settles among the tender-hearted. He must therefore be extremely delicate, since he only ever touches (either with his feet or in any other way) the softest of the soft.

Very young, then, and very delicate. Another thing about him is that he's very   196 supple. He can't be rigid and unyielding, because he wouldn't be able to insinuate himself anywhere he likes, entering and leaving men's hearts undetected. Eros' outstanding beauty is universally agreed, and this again suggests that he is well-proportioned and supple. Ugliness and Eros are ever at odds with one another. Finally, the beauty of his skin is attested by his love of flowers. He will not settle in a man's body, or heart, or anywhere else, if it is past the first flower and bloom of youth. But he does settle   b down, and remain, in any flowery and fragrant place.

So much for the god's beauty, though I've left out more than I've said. Now I must say something about his goodness. The main thing about Eros is that no-one, god or man, wrongs him or is wronged by him. Nothing is done to him, when it is done, by force. Force cannot touch Eros. When he acts, he acts without force, since everyone serves Eros quite willingly, and it's agreed by "our masters, the laws" that   c where there is mutual consent and agreement, there is justice. Moreover, he is a paragon of virtue as well as justice. After all, virtue is agreed to be control of pleasures and desires, and no pleasure is stronger than love. But if they are weaker than love, then he has control over them, and if he has control over pleasures and desires, he must be highly virtuous.

d   And what about courage? "Ares himself cannot hold his ground" against Eros. Ares does not take Eros prisoner; it is Eros—the love of Aphrodite, so the story goes—who takes Ares prisoner, and the captor is stronger than the captive. He who overcomes the bravest is himself the bravest of all.

So much for the god's justice, virtue and courage. Now for his wisdom. I must try as hard as I can not to leave anything out, and so I too, in my turn, will start with a

e   tribute to my own profession, following Eryximachus' example. Eros is an accomplished poet, so accomplished that he can turn others into poets. Everyone turns to poetry, "however Philistine he may have been before," when moved by Eros. We should take this as an indication that, in general, Eros is master of all forms of literary or artistic creation. After all, no-one can impart, or teach, a skill which he does not himself possess or know. And who will deny that the creation of all living things is the work of

197   Eros' wisdom, which makes all living things come into being and grow?

It's the same with any skilled activity. It is common knowledge that those who have this god for their teacher win fame and reputation; those he passes by remain in obscurity. For example, Apollo's discoveries (archery, medicine and prophecy) were all guided by

b   desire and love, so he too can be called a disciple of Eros. Likewise with the Muses and the arts, Hephaestus and metalworking, Athene and weaving, and Zeus and "the governance of gods and men." And if we ask why the quarrels of the gods were settled as soon as Eros appeared, without doubt the reason was love of beauty (there being no love of ugliness). In earlier times, as I said originally, there were many violent quarrels among the gods—or so we are told—because they were in the grip of Necessity. But since Eros' birth, all manner of good has resulted, for gods and men, from the love of beauty.

c   Such, Phaedrus, is my view of Eros. He stands out as beautiful and excellent in himself; and secondly, he is the origin of similar qualities in others. I am tempted to speak in verse, and say he brings

> Sweet peace to men, and calm o'er all the deep,
> Rest to the winds, to those who sorrow, sleep.

d   He gives us the feeling, not of longing, but of belonging, since he is the moving spirit behind all those occasions when we meet and gather together. Festivals, dances, sacrifices—in these he is the moving spirit. Implanter of gentleness, supplanter of fierceness; generous with his kindness, ungenerous with unkindness; gracious, gentle; an example to the wise, a delight to the gods; craved by those without him, saved by those who have him; of luxury, delicacy, elegance, charm, yearning, and desire he is the father; heedful

e   of the good, heedless of the bad; in hardship and in fear, in need and in argument, he is the best possible helmsman, comrade, ally, and saviour; the glory of gods and men; the best and finest guide, whom every man should follow, singing glorious praises to him, and sharing in the song which he sings to enchant the minds of gods and men.

That is my speech, Phaedrus, in part fun, in part (as far as I could make it) fairly serious. Let it be an offering to the god.

198   When Agathon finished speaking, we all burst into applause. We thought the young man had done full justice both to himself and to the god.

SOCRATES *(to Eryximachus):* Well, son of Acumenus, do you still think my earlier fear unfounded? Wasn't I right when I predicted Agathon would make a brilliant speech, and there would be nothing left for me to say?

ERYXIMACHUS: Your prediction was half-true. Agathon did make a good speech. But I don't think you will find nothing to say.

SOCRATES: My dear fellow, what is there left for me or anyone else to say, after such a fine and varied speech? Maybe it wasn't all equally brilliant, but that bit at the end was enough to silence anyone with the beauty of its language and phraseology. When I realised I wasn't going to be able to make anything like such a good speech, I nearly ran away and disappeared, in embarrassment, only there was nowhere to go. The speech reminded me of Gorgias, and put me in exactly the position described by Homer. I was afraid, at the end of his speech there, that Agathon was going to brandish the head of Gorgias, the great speaker, at my speech, turning me to stone and silencing me. I realised then how fatuous it was to have agreed to take my turn with you in praising Eros, and to have claimed to be an expert on love. It turns out now that I know nothing at all about making speeches of praise. I was naive enough to suppose that one should speak the truth about whatever it was that was being praised, and that from this raw material one should select the most telling points, and arrange them as pleasingly as possible. I was pretty confident I would make a good speech, because I thought I knew about speeches of praise. However, it now seems that praising things well isn't like that; it seems to be a question of hyperbole and rhetoric, regardless of truth or falsehood. And if it's false, that's immaterial. So our original agreement, as it now seems, was that each of us should pretend to praise Eros, rather than really praise him.

That, I imagine, is why you credit Eros with all the good points you have dug out in his favour. You say his nature is this, and the blessings he produces are these; your object is to make him appear as noble and fine as possible (in the eyes of the ignorant, presumably, since those who know about Eros clearly aren't going to believe you). Certainly your praise of him looks very fine and impressive, but I didn't realise this was what was called for; if I had known I wouldn't have agreed to take my turn in praising him. "My tongue promised, not my heart." Anyway, it can't be helped, but I don't propose to go on praising him like that—I wouldn't know how to. What I am prepared to do, if you like, is tell the truth, in my own way, and not in competition with your speeches. I don't want to make a complete fool of myself. What do you think, Phaedrus? Do you want a speech of that sort? Do you want to hear the truth told about Eros? And may I use whatever language and forms of speech come naturally?

Phaedrus and the others told him to make his speech, in whatever way he thought best.

SOCRATES: One other point before I start, Phaedrus. Will you let me ask Agathon a few brief questions? I'd like to get his agreement before I begin.

PHAEDRUS: Yes, I'll let you. Ask away.

So Socrates began his speech, something like this.

SOCRATES

Well, my dear Agathon, I liked the beginning of your speech. You said the first thing to do was to reveal the nature of Eros; after that his achievements. I think that was an excellent starting point. And since you've explained everything else about the nature of Eros so impressively and so well, can you tell me one more thing? Is Eros' nature such that he is love produced by something, or by nothing? I don't mean, is he *the son of* a father or a mother—it would be an absurd question, to ask whether Eros is the son of a father or mother. But suppose I asked you about this thing "father," whether a father is father of something or not? If you wanted to give an accurate answer, you would say, presumably, that a father is father of a son or a daughter, wouldn't you?

AGATHON: Yes, I would.

SOCRATES: And the same with a mother?

AGATHON: Yes, the same.

e SOCRATES: Let's take a few more questions, so you can be quite clear what I mean. Suppose I ask, "What about a brother, simply as a brother? Is he someone's brother, or not?"

AGATHON: Yes, he is.

SOCRATES: His brother's or sister's, I take it?

AGATHON: Yes.

SOCRATES: Try, then, to answer my question about Eros. Is Eros love of nothing, or of something?

AGATHON: Of something, certainly.

200 SOCRATES: Good. Hold on to that answer. Keep it in mind, and make a mental note what it is that Eros is love of. But first tell me this: this thing which Eros is love of, does he desire it, or not?

AGATHON: Certainly.

SOCRATES: And does he possess that which he desires and loves, or not?

AGATHON: Probably not.

SOCRATES: I'm not interested in probability, but in certainty. Consider this proposition: anything which desires something desires what it does not have, and it only desires when it is lacking something. This proposition, Agathon, seems to me to be absolutely certain. How does it strike you?

AGATHON: Yes, it seems certain to me too.

SOCRATES: Quite right. So would a big man want to be big, or a strong man want to be strong?

AGATHON: No, that's impossible, given what we have agreed so far.

SOCRATES: Because if he possesses these qualities, he cannot also lack them.

AGATHON: True.

SOCRATES: So if a strong man wanted to be strong, or a fast runner to be fast, or a healthy man to be healthy—but perhaps I'd better explain what I'm on about. I'm a bit worried that you may think that people like this, people having these qualities, can also

c want the qualities which they possess. So I'm trying to remove this misapprehension. If you think about it, Agathon, people cannot avoid possession of whichever of these qualities they do possess, whether they like it or not. So obviously there's no point in desiring to do so. When anyone says, "I'm in good health, and I also desire to be in good health," or "I am rich and also desire to be rich," [that is] "I desire those things

d which I already have," then we should answer him: "What you want is to go on possessing, in the future, the wealth, health, or strength you possess now, since you have them now, like it or not. So when you say you desire what you've already got, are you sure you don't just mean you want to continue to possess in the future what you possess now?" Would he deny this?

AGATHON: No, he would agree.

SOCRATES: But isn't this a question of desiring what he doesn't already have in his possession—that is, the desire that what he does have should be safely and perma-

e nently available to him in the future?

AGATHON: Yes, it is.

SOCRATES: So in this, or any other, situation, the man who desires something desires what is not available to him, and what he doesn't already have in his possession. And what he neither has nor himself is—that which he lacks—this is what he wants and desires.

AGATHON: Absolutely.

SOCRATES: Right then, let's agree on the argument so far. Eros has an existence of his own; he is in the first place love of something, and secondly, he is love of that which he is without.

AGATHON: Yes.

SOCRATES: Keeping that in mind, just recall what you said were the objects of Eros, in your speech. I'll remind you, if you like. I think what you said amounted to this: trouble among the gods was ended by their love of beauty, since there could be no love of what is ugly. Isn't that roughly what you said?

AGATHON: Yes, it is.

SOCRATES: And a very reasonable statement, too, my friend. And this being so, Eros must have an existence as love of beauty, and not love of ugliness, mustn't he?

AGATHON: Yes.

SOCRATES: But wasn't it agreed that he loves what he lacks, and does not possess?

AGATHON: Yes, it was.

SOCRATES: So Eros lacks, and does not possess, beauty.

AGATHON: That is the inevitable conclusion.

SOCRATES: Well then, do you describe as beautiful that which lacks beauty and has never acquired beauty?

AGATHON: No.

SOCRATES: If that is so, do you still maintain that Eros is beautiful?

AGATHON: I rather suspect, Socrates, that I didn't know what I was talking about.

SOCRATES: It sounded marvellous, for all that, Agathon. Just one other small point. Would you agree that what is good is also beautiful?

AGATHON: Yes, I would.

SOCRATES: So if Eros lacks beauty, and if what is good is beautiful, then Eros would lack what is good also.

AGATHON: I can't argue with you, Socrates. Let's take it that it is as you say.

SOCRATES: What you mean, Agathon, my very good friend, is that you can't argue with the truth. Any fool can argue with Socrates. Anyway, I'll let you off for now, because I want to pass on to you the account of Eros which I once heard given by a woman called Diotima, from Mantinea. She was an expert on this subject, as on many others. In the days before the plague she came to the help of the Athenians in their sacrifices, and managed to gain them a ten-years' reprieve from the disease. She also taught me about love.

I'll start from the position on which Agathon and I reached agreement, and I'll give her account, as best I can, in my own words. So first I must explain, as you rightly laid down, Agathon, what Eros is and what he is like; then I must describe what he does. I think it'll be easiest for me to explain things as she explained them when she was questioning me, since I gave her pretty much the same answers Agathon has just been giving me. I said Eros was a great god, and a lover of beauty. Diotima proved to me, using the same argument by which I have just proved it to Agathon, that, according to my own argument, Eros was neither beautiful nor good.

"What do you mean, Diotima," I said, "Is Eros then ugly or bad?"

"Careful what you say. Do you think what is not beautiful must necessarily be ugly?"

"Obviously."

202   "And that what is not wise is ignorant? Don't you realise there is an intermediate state, between wisdom and ignorance?"

"And what is that?"

"Think of someone who has a correct opinion, but can give no rational explanation of it. You wouldn't call this knowledge (how can something irrational be knowledge?), yet it isn't ignorance either, since an opinion which accords with reality cannot be ignorance. So correct opinion is the kind of thing we are looking for, between understanding and ignorance."

b   "That's true."

"So don't insist that what is not beautiful must necessarily be ugly, nor that what is not good must be bad. The same thing is equally true of Eros; just because, as you yourself admit, he is not good or beautiful, you need not regard him as ugly and bad, but as something between these extremes."

"Yet he is universally agreed to be a great god."

"By those who don't know what they are talking about, do you mean? Or those who do?"

"I mean by absolutely everyone."

c   Diotima laughed. "How can Eros be agreed to be a great god by people who don't even admit that he's a god at all?"

"What people?"

"Well, you, for one. And me, for another."

"What do you mean?"

"Quite simple. The gods are all happy and beautiful, aren't they? You wouldn't go so far as to claim that any of the gods is not happy and beautiful?"

"Good Lord, no!"

"And you agree that 'happy' means 'possessing what is good and beautiful'?"

"Certainly."

d   "But you have already admitted that Eros lacks what is good and beautiful, and that he desires them because he lacks them."

"Yes, I have."

"How can he be a god, then, if he is without beauty and goodness?"

"He can't, apparently."

"You see, even you don't regard Eros as a god."

"What can Eros be, then? A mortal?"

"Far from it."

"What, then?"

"As in the other examples, something between a mortal and an immortal."

"And what is that, Diotima?"

e   "A great spirit, Socrates. Spirits are midway between what is divine and what is human."

"What power does such a spirit possess?"

"He acts as an interpreter and means of communication between gods and men. He takes requests and offerings to the gods, and brings back instructions and benefits in return. Occupying this middle position he plays a vital role in holding the world together. He is the medium of all prophecy and religion, whether it concerns sacrifice,

203   forms of worship, incantations, or any kind of divination or sorcery. There is no direct contact between god and man. All association and communication between them, wak-

ing or sleeping, takes place through Eros. This kind of knowledge is knowledge of the spirit; any other knowledge (occupational or artistic, for example) is purely utilitarian. Such spirits are many and varied, and Eros is one of them."

"Who are his parents?"

"That is not quite so simple, but I'll tell you, all the same. When Aphrodite was b born, the gods held a banquet, at which one of the guests was Resource, the son of Ingenuity. When they finished eating, Poverty came begging, as you would expect (there being plenty of food), and hung around the doorway. Resource was drunk (on nectar, since wine hadn't been invented), so he went into Zeus' garden, and was overcome by sleep. Poverty, seeing here the solution to her own lack of resources, decided to have a child by him. So she lay with him, and conceived Eros. That's why Eros is a follower and servant of Aphrodite, because he was conceived at her birthday party—and also c because he is naturally attracted to what is beautiful, and Aphrodite is beautiful.

So Eros' attributes are what you would expect of a child of Resource and Poverty. For a start, he's always poor, and so far from being soft and beautiful (which is most people's view of him), he is hard, unkempt, barefoot, homeless. He sleeps on the ground, without a bed, lying in doorways or in the open street. He has his mother's d nature, and need is his constant companion. On the other hand, from his father he has inherited an eye for beauty and the good. He is brave, enterprising and determined—a marvelous huntsman, always intriguing. He is intellectual, resourceful, a lover of wisdom his whole life through, a subtle magician, sorcerer and thinker.

His nature is neither that of an immortal nor that of a mortal. In one and the same e day he can be alive and flourishing (when things go well), then at death's door, later still reviving as his father's character asserts itself again. But his resources are always running out, so that Eros is never either totally destitute or affluent. Similarly he is midway between wisdom and folly, as I will show you. None of the gods searches for wisdom, or tries to become wise—they are wise already. Nor does anyone else wise search for wisdom. On the other hand, the foolish do not search for wisdom or try to become wise either, since folly is precisely the failing which consists in not being fine 204 and good, or intelligent—and yet being quite satisfied with the way one is. You cannot desire what you do not realise you lack."

"Who then are the lovers of wisdom, Diotima, if they are neither the wise nor the foolish?"

"That should by now be obvious, even to a child. They must be the intermediate b class, among them Eros. We would classify wisdom as very beautiful, and Eros is love of what is beautiful, so it necessarily follows that Eros is a lover of wisdom (lovers of wisdom being the intermediate class between the wise and the foolish). The reason for this, too, is to be found in his parentage. His father is wise and resourceful, while his mother is foolish and resourceless.

"Such is the nature of this spirit, Socrates. Your views on Eros revealed a quite c common mistake. You thought (or so I infer from your comments) that Eros was what was loved, rather than the lover. That is why you thought Eros was beautiful. After all, what we love really *is* beautiful and delicate, perfect and delightful, whereas the lover has the quite different character I have outlined."

"Fair enough, my foreign friend, I think you're right. But if that's what Eros is like, what use is he to men?"

"That's the next point I want to explain to you, Socrates. I've told you what Eros d is like, and what his parentage is; he is also love of what is beautiful, as you say. Now let's imagine someone asking us, 'Why is Eros love of the beautiful, Socrates and Diotima?' Let me put it more clearly: what is it that the lover of beauty desires?" e

"To possess it."

"That prompts the further question, 'What good does it do someone to possess beauty?'"

"I don't quite know how to give a quick answer to that question."

"Well, try a different question, about goodness rather than beauty: Socrates, what does the lover of goodness want?"

"To possess it."

"What good will it do him to possess it?"

"That's easier. It will make him happy."

205   "Yes, because those who are happy are happy because they possess what is good. The enquiry seems to have reached a conclusion, and there is no need to ask the further question, 'If someone wants to be happy, why does he want to be happy?'"

"True."

"Do you think this wish and this desire are common to all mankind, and that everyone wants always to possess what is good? Or what do you think?"

"I think it is common to all men."

"In that case, Socrates, why do we not describe all men as lovers, if everyone al-
b   ways loves the same thing? Why do we describe some people as lovers, but not others?"

"I don't know. I agree with you, it *is* surprising."

"Not really. We abstract a part of love, and call it by the name of the whole—
love—and then for the other parts we use different names."

"What names? Give me an example."

"What about this? Take a concept like creation, or composition. Composition means putting things together, and covers a wide range of activities. Any activity which brings anything at all into existence is an example of creation. Hence the exer-
c   cise of any skill is composition, and those who practise it are composers."

"True."

"All the same, they aren't all called composers. They all have different names, and it's only one subdivision of the whole class (that which deals with music and rhythm) which is called by the general name. Only this kind of creation is called composing, and its practitioners composers."

"True."

d   "Well, it's the same with love. In general, for anyone, any desire for goodness and happiness is love—and it is a powerful and unpredictable force. But there are vari-
ous ways of pursuing this desire—through money-making, through physical fitness, through philosophy—which do not entitle their devotees to call themselves lovers, or describe their activity as loving. Those who pursue one particular mode of loving, and make that their concern, have taken over the name of the whole (love, loving, and lovers)."

"You may well be right."

e   "There is a theory that lovers are people in search of their other half. But accord-
ing to my theory, love is not love of a half, nor of a whole, unless it is good. After all, men are prepared to have their own feet and hands cut off, if they think there's something wrong with them. They're not particularly attached to what is their own, except
206   in so far as they regard the good as their own property, and evil as alien to them. And that's because the good is the only object of human love, as I think you will agree."

"Yes, I certainly do agree."

"Can we say, then, quite simply, that men love the good?"

"Yes."

"And presumably we should add that they want to possess the good?"

"Yes, we should."

"And not merely to possess it, but to possess it forever."

"That also."

"In short, then, love is the desire for permanent possession of the good."

"Precisely."

"If this is always the object of our desire, what is the particular manner of pur-   b
suit, and the particular sphere of activity, in which enthusiasm and effort qualify for
the title 'love'? What is this activity? Do you know?"

"No, I don't. That's why I find your knowledge so impressive. In fact, I've kept
coming to see you, because I want an answer to just that question."

"Very well, I'll tell you. The activity we're talking about is the use of what is
beautiful for the purpose of reproduction, whether physical or mental."

"I'm no good at riddles. I don't understand what you mean."   c

"I'll try to make myself clearer. Reproduction, Socrates, both physical and mental, is a universal human activity. At a certain age our nature desires to give birth. To
do so, it cannot employ an ugly medium, but insists on what is beautiful. Sexual intercourse between man and woman is this reproduction. So there is the divine element,
this germ of immortality, in mortal creatures—[that is] conception and begetting.
These cannot take place in an uncongenial medium, and ugliness is uncongenial to
everything divine, while beauty is congenial. Therefore procreation has Beauty as its   d
midwife and its destiny, which is why the urge to reproduce becomes gentle and happy
when it comes near beauty: then conception and begetting become possible. By contrast, when it comes near ugliness it becomes sullen and offended, it contracts, withdraws, and shrinks away and does not beget. It stifles the reproductive urge, and is
frustrated. So in anyone who is keen (one might almost say bursting) to reproduce,
beauty arouses violent emotion, because beauty can release its possessor from the
agony of reproduction. Your opinion, Socrates, that love is desire for beauty, is mis-   e
taken."

"What is the correct view, then?"

"It is the desire to use beauty to beget and bear offspring."

"Perhaps."

"Certainly! And why to beget? Because begetting is, by human standards, something eternal and undying. So if we were right in describing love as the desire always
to possess the good, then the inevitable conclusion is that we desire immortality as well
as goodness. On this argument, love must be desire for immortality as much as for   207
beauty."

Those were her teachings, when she talked to me about love. And one day she
asked me, "What do you think is the reason for this love and this desire? You know
how strangely animals behave when they want to mate. Animals and birds, they're just   b
the same. Their health suffers, and they get all worked up, first over sexual intercourse,
and then over raising the young. For these ends they will fight, to the death, against far
stronger opponents. They will go to any lengths, even starve themselves, to bring up
their offspring. We can easily imagine human beings behaving like this from rational
motives, but what can be the cause of such altruistic behaviour in animals? Do you   c
know?"

"No, I don't."

"Do you think you can become an expert on love without knowing?"

"Look, Diotima, I know I have a lot to learn. I've just admitted that. That's why
I've come to you. So please tell me the cause of these phenomena, and anything else I
should know about love."

"Well, if you believe that the natural object of love is what we have often agreed it to be, then the answer is not surprising, since the same reasoning still holds good. What is mortal tries, to the best of its ability, to be everlasting and immortal. It does this in the only way it can, by always leaving a successor to replace what decays. Think of what we call the life-span and identity of an individual creature. For example, a man is said to be the same individual from childhood until old age. The cells in his body are always changing, yet he is still called the same person, despite being perpetually reconstituted as parts of him decay—hair, flesh, bones, blood, his whole body, in fact. And not just his body, either. Precisely the same happens with mental attributes. Habits, dispositions, beliefs, opinions, desires, pleasures, pains and fears are all varying all the time for everyone. Some disappear, others take their place. And when we come to knowledge, the situation is even odder. It is not just a question of one piece of knowledge disappearing and being replaced by another, so that we are never the same people, as far as knowledge goes: the same thing happens with each individual piece of knowledge. What we call studying presupposes that knowledge is transient. Forgetting is loss of knowledge, and studying preserves knowledge by creating memory afresh in us, to replace what is lost. Hence we have the illusion of continuing knowledge.

"All continuous mortal existence is of this kind. It is not the case that creatures remain always, in every detail, precisely the same—only the divine does that. It is rather that what is lost, and what decays, always leaves behind a fresh copy of itself. This, Socrates, is the mechanism by which mortal creatures can taste immortality—both physical immortality, and other sorts. (For immortals, of course, it's different.) So it's not surprising that everything naturally values its own offspring. They all feel this concern, and this love, because of their desire for immortality."

I found these ideas totally novel, and I said, "Well, Diotima, that's a very clever explanation. Is it really all true?"

And she, in her best lecturer's manner, replied, "There can be no question of it. Take another human characteristic, ambition. It seems absurdly irrational until you remember my explanation. Think of the extraordinary behaviour of those who, prompted by Eros, are eager to become famous, and 'amass undying fame for the whole of time to come.' For this they will expose themselves to danger even more than they will for their children. They will spend money, endure any hardship, even die for it. Think of Alcestis' willingness to die for Admetus, or Achilles' determination to follow Patroclus in death, or your Athenian king Codrus and his readiness to give up his life for his children's right to rule. Would they have done these things if they hadn't thought they were leaving behind them an undying memory—which we still possess—of their courage? Of course not. The desire for undying nobility, and the good reputation which goes with it, is a universal human motive. The nobler people are, the more strongly they feel it. They desire immortality.

"Those whose creative urge is physical tend to turn to women, and pursue Eros by this route. The production of children gains them, as they imagine, immortality and a name and happiness for themselves, for all time. In others the impulse is mental or spiritual—people who are creative mentally, much more than physically. They produce what you would expect the mind to conceive and produce. And what is that? Thought, and all other human excellence. All poets are creators of this kind, and so are those artists who are generally regarded as inventive. However, under the general heading 'thought,' by far the finest and most important item is the art of political and domestic economy, what we call good judgment, and justice.

"Someone who, right from his youth, is mentally creative in these areas, when he is ready, and the time comes, feels a strong urge to give birth, or beget. So he goes around, like everyone else, searching, as I see it, for a medium of beauty in which he can create. He will never create in an ugly medium. So in his desire to create he is attracted to what is physically beautiful rather than ugly. But if he comes across a beautiful, noble, well-formed mind, then he finds the combination particularly attractive. He'll drop everything and embark on long conversations about goodness, with such a companion, trying to teach him about the nature and behaviour of the good man. Now that he's made contact with someone beautiful, and made friends with him, he can produce and bring to birth what he long ago conceived. Present or absent, he keeps it in mind, and joins with his friends in bringing his conception to maturity. In consequence such people have a far stronger bond between them than there is between the parents of children; and they form much firmer friendships, because they are jointly responsible for finer, and more lasting, offspring.

"We would all choose children of this kind for ourselves, rather than human children. We look with envy at Homer and Hesiod, and the other great poets, and the marvellous progeny they left behind, which have brought them undying fame and memory; or, if you like, at children of the kind which Lycurgus left in Sparta, the salvation of Sparta and practically all Greece. In your city, Solon is highly thought of, as the father of your laws, as are many other men in other states, both Greek and foreign. They have published to the world a variety of noble achievements, and created goodness of every kind. There are shrines to such people in honour of their offspring, but none to the producers of ordinary children.

"You, too, Socrates, could probably be initiated this far into knowledge of Eros. But all this, rightly pursued, is a mere preliminary to the full rites, and final revelation, which might well be beyond you. Still, I'll tell you about it, so that if I fail, it won't be for want of trying. Try to follow, if you can.

"The true follower of this subject must begin, as a young man, with the pursuit of physical beauty. In the first place, if his mentor advises him properly, he should be attracted, physically, to one individual; at this stage his offspring are beautiful discussions and conversations. Next he should realise that the physical beauty of one body is akin to that of any other body, and that if he's going to pursue beauty of appearance, it's the height of folly not to regard the beauty which is in all bodies as one and the same. This insight will convert him into a lover of all physical beauty, and he will become less obsessive in his pursuit of his one former passion, as he realises its unimportance.

"The next stage is to put a higher value on mental than on physical beauty. The right qualities of mind, even in the absence of any great physical beauty, will be enough to awaken his love and affection. He will generate the kind of discussions which are improving to the young. The aim is that, as the next step, he should be compelled to contemplate the beauty of customs and institutions, to see that all beauty of this sort is related, and consequently to regard physical beauty as trivial.

"From human institutions his teacher should direct him to knowledge, so that he may, in turn, see the beauty of different types of knowledge. Whereas before, in servile and contemptible fashion, he was dominated by the individual case, loving the beauty of a boy, or a man, or a single human activity, now he directs his eyes to what is beautiful in general, as he turns to gaze upon the limitless ocean of beauty. Now he produces many fine and inspiring thoughts and arguments, as he gives his undivided attention to philosophy. Here he gains in strength and stature until his attention is caught by that one special knowledge—the knowledge of a beauty which I will now try to describe to you. So pay the closest possible attention.

"When a man has reached this point in his education in love, studying the different types of beauty in correct order, he will come to the final end and goal of this education. Then suddenly he will see a beauty of a breathtaking nature, Socrates, the

211   beauty which is the justification of all his efforts so far. It is eternal, neither coming to be nor passing away, neither increasing nor decreasing. Moreover it is not beautiful in part, and ugly in part, nor is it beautiful at one time, and not at another; nor beautiful

b   in some respects, but not in others; nor beautiful here and ugly there, as if beautiful in some people's eyes, but not in others. It will not appear to him as the beauty of a face, or hands, or anything physical—nor as an idea or branch of knowledge, nor as existing in any determinate place, such as a living creature, or the earth, or heaven, or anywhere like that. It exists for all time, by itself and with itself, unique. All other forms of beauty derive from it, but in such a way that their creation or destruction does not strengthen or weaken it, or affect it in any way at all. If a man progresses (as he will do, if he goes about his love affairs in the right way) from the lesser beauties, and begins to catch sight of this beauty, then he is within reach of the final revelation. Such is

c   the experience of the man who approaches, or is guided towards, love in the right way, beginning with the particular examples of beauty, but always returning from them to the search for that one beauty. He uses them like a ladder, climbing from the love of one person to love of two; from two to love of all physical beauty; from physical beauty to beauty in human behaviour; thence to beauty in subjects of study; from them he arrives finally at that branch of knowledge which studies nothing but ultimate beauty. Then at last he understands what true beauty is.

d   "That, if ever, is the moment, my dear Socrates, when a man's life is worth living, as he contemplates beauty itself. Once seen, it will not seem to you to be a good such as gold, or fashionable clothes, or the boys and young men who have such an effect on you now when you see them. You, and any number of people like you, when you see your boyfriends and spend all your time with them, are quite prepared (or would be, if it were possible) to go without food and drink, just looking at them and

e   being with them. But suppose it were granted to someone to see beauty itself quite clearly, in its pure, undiluted form—not clogged up with human flesh and colouring, and a whole lot of other worthless and corruptible matter. No, imagine he were able to

212   see the divine beauty itself in its unique essence. Don't you think he would find it a wonderful way to live, looking at it, contemplating it as it should be contemplated, and spending his time in its company? It cannot fail to strike you that only then will it be possible for him, seeing beauty as it should be seen, to produce, not likenesses of goodness (since it is no likeness he has before him), but the real thing (since he has the real thing before him); and that this producing, and caring for, real goodness earns him the friendship of the gods and makes him, if anyone, immortal."

b   There you are, then, Phaedrus and the rest of you. That's what Diotima said to me, and I, for one, find it convincing. And it's because I'm convinced that I now try to persuade other people as well that man, in his search for this goal, could hardly hope to find a better ally than Eros. That's why I say that everyone should honour Eros, and why I myself honour him, and make the pursuit of Eros my chief concern, and encourage others to do the same. Now, and for all time, I praise the power and vigour of Eros, to the limits of my ability.

That's my speech, Phaedrus. You can take it, if you like, as a formal eulogy of

c   Eros. Or you can call it by any other name you please.

This speech was greeted with applause, and Aristophanes started saying something about Socrates' reference to his speech, when suddenly there was a tremendous sound of hammering at the front door—people going home from a party, by the sound of it. You could hear the voice of a flute-girl.

AGATHON *(to his slaves):* Could you see who that is? If it's one of my friends, ask   d
him in. Otherwise, say we've stopped drinking and are just going to bed.

Almost at once we heard Alcibiades' voice from the courtyard. He was very drunk, and shouting at the top of his voice, asking "where Agathon was," and demanding "to be taken to Agathon." So in he came, supported by the girl, and some of his followers. He stood there in the doorway, wearing a luxuriant garland of ivy and violets,   e
with his head covered in ribbons.

ALCIBIADES: Greetings, gentlemen. Will you allow me to join your gathering completely drunk? Or shall we just crown Agathon (which is what we've come for) and go away? I couldn't come yesterday, but now here I am, with ribbons in my hair, so that I can take a garland from my own head, and crown the man whom I hereby proclaim the cleverest and handsomest man in Athens. Are you going to laugh at me for being drunk? Well, you may laugh, but I'm sure I'm right, all the same. Anyway,   213
those are my terms. So tell me right away: should I come in? Will you drink with me, or not?

Then everyone started talking at once, telling him to come in and sit down. And Agathon called him over. So over he came, assisted by his companions. He was taking off his ribbons, getting ready to put the garland on Agathon, and with the ribbons in front of his eyes he didn't see Socrates. So he sat down next to Agathon, between him and Socrates, Socrates moving aside, when he saw him, to make room. As he sat down he greeted Agathon, and put the garland on his head.   b

AGATHON *(to his slaves):* Take Alcibiades' shoes off. He can make a third at this table.

ALCIBIADES: Excellent, but who is the other person drinking at our table? (Turning and seeing Socrates, and leaping to his feet.) My God, what's this? Socrates here? You've been lying in wait here for me, just as you used to do. You were always turn-   c
ing up unexpectedly, wherever I least expected you. What are you doing here this time? And come to that, how've you managed to get yourself a place next to the most attractive person in the room? You ought to be next to someone like Aristophanes; he sets out to make himself ridiculous, and succeeds. Shouldn't you be with him?

SOCRATES: I'm going to need your protection, Agathon. I've found the love of this man a bit of a nightmare. From the day I took a fancy to him, I haven't been al-   d
lowed to look at, or talk to, anyone attractive at all. If I do he gets envious and jealous, and starts behaving outrageously. He insults me, and can barely keep his hands off me. So you make sure he doesn't do anything now. You reconcile us, or defend me if he resorts to violence. His insane sexuality scares me stiff.

ALCIBIADES: There can be no reconciliation between you and me. However, I'll get my revenge another time. For the moment, give me some of those ribbons,   e
Agathon, so I can make a garland for this remarkable head of his as well. I don't want him complaining that I crowned you, and not him, though he is the international grandmaster of words—and not just the day before yesterday, like you, but all the time. *(As he said this he took some of the ribbons, made a garland for Socrates, and sat down.)* Well, gentlemen, you seem to me to be pretty sober. We can't have that. You'll have to drink. After all, that's what we agreed. So I'm going to choose a Master of Ceremonies, to see you all get enough to drink. I choose myself. Agathon, let them bring a large cup, if you've got one. No, wait! *(Suddenly catching sight of an ice-bucket holding upwards of half a gallon.)* No need for that. Boy, bring me that ice-bucket. *(He*   214
filled it, and started off by draining it himself. Then he told the slave to fill it up again for Socrates.) A useless ploy against Socrates, gentlemen. It doesn't matter how much

you give him to drink, he'll drink it and be none the worse for wear. *(So the slave filled the bucket for Socrates, who drank it.)*

b   ERYXIMACHUS: What's the plan, Alcibiades? Are we just going to sit here and drink as if we were dying of thirst? Aren't we going to talk, or sing, at all while we drink?

ALCIBIADES: Ah, Eryximachus. Most excellent scion of a most excellent and sensible father. Good evening.

ERYXIMACHUS: Good evening to you too. But what *do* you want us to do?

ALCIBIADES: Whatever you recommend. We must do as you say. After all, "a doctor is worth a dozen ordinary men." So you tell us your prescription.

c   ERYXIMACHUS: Very well, listen. We had decided, before you came, that going round anticlockwise, each of us in turn should make the best speech he could about Eros, in praise of him. We've all made our speeches. You've drunk but you haven't spoken. So it's only fair that you should speak now; after that you can give any instructions you like to Socrates, and he can do the same to the man on his right, and so on all the way round.

ALCIBIADES: That's a good idea, Eryximachus. But it's grossly unfair to ask me, drunk, to compete with you sober. Also, my dear friend, I hope you didn't pay any attention to Socrates' remarks just now. Presumably you realise the situation is the exact
d   opposite of what he said. He's the one who will resort to violence, if I praise anyone else, god or man, in his presence.

SOCRATES: Can't you hold your tongue?

ALCIBIADES: Don't worry, I wouldn't dream of praising anyone else if you're here.

ERYXIMACHUS: Well, that'll do, if you like. Praise Socrates.

e   ALCIBIADES: Really? You think I should, Eryximachus? Shall I set about him, and get my own back on him, here in front of you all?

SOCRATES: Hey! What are you up to? Are you trying to make a fool of me by praising me. Or what?

ALCIBIADES: I'm going to tell the truth. Do you mind that?

SOCRATES: Of course not. In fact, I'm all in favour of it.

ALCIBIADES: I can't wait to start. And here's what you can do. If I say anything that's not true, you can interrupt me, if you like, and tell me I'm wrong. I shan't get anything wrong on purpose, but don't be surprised if my recollection of things is a bit higgledy-piggledy. It's not easy, when you're as drunk as I am, to give a clear and orderly account of someone as strange as you.

ALCIBIADES

215   Gentlemen, I'm going to try and praise Socrates using similes. He may think I'm trying to make a fool of him, but the point of the simile is its accuracy, not its absurdity. I think he's very like one of those Silenus-figures sculptors have on their shelves. They're made with flutes or pipes. You can open them up, and when you do you find little figures of the gods inside. I also think Socrates is like the satyr Marsyas. As far as
b   your appearance goes, Socrates, even you can't claim these are poor comparisons; but I'll tell you how the likeness holds good in other ways: just listen. You're a trouble-maker, aren't you? Don't deny it, I can bring witnesses. You may not play the pipes,

like Marsyas, but what you do is much more amazing. He had only to open his mouth to delight men, but he needed a musical instrument to do it. The same goes for anyone   c nowadays who plays his music—I count what Olympus played as really Marsyas', since he learnt from him. His is the only music which carries people away, and reveals those who have a desire for the gods and their rites. Such is its divine power, and it makes no difference whether it's played by an expert, or by a mere flute-girl.

You have the same effect on people. The only difference is that you do it with words alone, without the aid of any instrument. We can all listen to anyone else talking, and it has virtually no effect on us, no matter what he's talking about, or how good   d a speaker he is. But when we listen to you, or to someone else using your arguments, even if he's a hopeless speaker, we're overwhelmed and carried away. This is true of men, women, and children alike.

For my own part, gentlemen, I would like to tell you on my honour (only you would certainly think I was drunk) the effect what he says has had on me in the past— and still does have, to this day. When I hear him, it's like the worst kind of religious hysteria. My heart pounds, and I find myself in floods of tears, such is the effect of his words. And I can tell lots of other people feel the same. I used to listen to Pericles and other powerful speakers, and I thought they spoke well. But they never had the effect   e on me of turning all my beliefs upside down, with the disturbing realisation that my whole life is that of a slave. Whereas this Marsyas here has often made me feel that, and decide that the kind of life I lead is just not worth living. You can't deny it, Socrates.   216

Even now I know in my heart of hearts that if I were to listen to him, I couldn't resist him. The same thing would happen again. He forces me to admit that with all my faults I do nothing to improve myself, but continue in public life just the same. So I tear myself away, as if stopping my ears against the Sirens; otherwise I would spend my whole life there sitting at his feet. He's the only man who can appeal to my better   b nature (not that most people would reckon I *had* a better nature), because I'm only too aware I have no answer to his arguments. I know I should do as he tells me, but when I leave him I have no defence against my own ambition and desire for recognition. So I run for my life, and avoid him, and when I see him, I'm embarrassed, when I remember conclusions we've reached in the past. I would often cheerfully have seen him   c dead, and yet I know that if that did happen, I should be even more upset. So I just can't cope with the man.

I'm by no means the only person to be affected like this by his satyr's music, but that isn't all I have to say about his similarity to those figures I likened him to, and about his remarkable powers. Believe me, none of you really knows the man. So I'll enlighten you, now that I've begun.

Your view of Socrates is of someone who fancies attractive men, spends all his   d time with them, finds them irresistible—and you know how hopelessly ignorant and uncertain he is. And yet this pose is extremely Silenus-like. It's the outward mask he wears, like the carved Silenus. Open him up, and he's a model of restraint—you wouldn't believe it, my dear fellow-drinkers. Take my word for it, it makes no differ-   e ence at all how attractive you are, he has an astonishing contempt for that kind of thing. Similarly with riches, or any of the other so-called advantages we possess. He regards all possessions as worthless, and us humans as insignificant. No, I mean it—he treats his whole life in human society as a game or puzzle.

But when he's serious, when he opens up and you see the real Socrates—I don't know if any of you has ever seen the figure inside. I saw it once, and it struck me as utterly godlike and golden and beautiful and wonderful. In fact, I thought I must simply   217 do anything he told me. And since I thought he was serious about my good looks, I congratulated myself on a fantastic stroke of luck, which had given me the chance to satisfy Socrates, and be the recipient, in return, of all his knowledge. I had, I may say, an extremely high opinion of my own looks.

b   That was my plan, so I did what I had never done up to then—I sent away my attendant, and took to seeing him on my own. You see, I'm going to tell you the whole truth, so listen carefully, and you tell them, Socrates, if I get anything wrong. Well, gentlemen, I started seeing him—just the two of us—and I thought he would start talking to me as lovers do to their boyfriends when they're alone together. I was very ex-

c   cited. But nothing like that happened at all. He spent the day talking to me as usual, and then left. I invited him to the gymnasium with me, and exercised with him there, thinking I might make some progress that way. So he exercised and wrestled with me, often completely on our own, and (needless to say) it got me nowhere at all. When that turned out to be no good, I thought I'd better make a pretty determined assault on the man, and not give up, now that I'd started. I wanted to find out what the trouble was. So I asked him to dinner, just like a lover with designs on his boyfriend.

d   He took some time to agree even to this, but finally I did get him to come. The first time he came, he had dinner, and then got up to go. I lost my nerve, that time, and let him go. But I decided to try again. He came to dinner, and I kept him talking late into the night. When he tried to go home, I made him stay, saying it was too late to go. So he stayed the night on the couch next to mine. There was no-one else sleeping in the room.

e   What I've told you so far I'd be quite happy to repeat to anyone. The next part I'm only telling you because (a) I'm drunk—*"in vino veritas,"* and all that—and (b) since I've started praising Socrates, it seems wrong to leave out an example of his superior behaviour. Besides, I'm like someone who's been bitten by an adder. They say that a man who's had this happen to him will only say what it was like to others

218   who've been bitten; they're the only people who will understand, and make allowances for, his willingness to say or do anything, such is the pain. Well, I've been bitten by something worse than an adder, and in the worst possible place. I've been stung, or bitten, in my heart or soul (whatever you care to call it) by a method of philosophical argument, whose bite, when it gets a grip on a young and intelligent mind, is sharper than

b   any adder's. It makes one willing to say or do anything. I can see all these Phaedruses and Agathons, Eryximachuses, Pausaniases, Aristodemuses and Aristophaneses here, not to mention Socrates himself and the rest of you. You've all had a taste of this wild passion for philosophy, so you'll understand me, and forgive what I did then, and what I'm telling you now. As for the servants, and anyone else who's easily shocked, or doesn't know what I'm talking about, they'll just have to put something over their ears.

c   There we were, then, gentlemen. The lamp had gone out, the slaves had gone to bed. I decided it was time to abandon subtlety, and say plainly what I was after. So I nudged him. "Socrates, are you asleep?"

"No."

"Do you know what I've decided?"

"What?"

"I think you're the ideal person to be my lover, but you seem to be a bit shy about suggesting it. So I'll tell you how I feel about it. I think I'd be crazy not to satisfy

d   you in this way, just as I'd do anything else for you if it was in my power—or in my friends' power. Nothing matters more to me than my own improvement, and I can't imagine a better helper than you. Anyone with any sense would think worse of me for not giving a man like you what he wants than most ignorant people would if I did give you what you want."

Socrates listened to this. Then, with characteristic irony, he replied. "My dear Alcibiades, you're certainly nobody's fool, if you're right in what you say about me, and I do have some power to improve you. It must be remarkable beauty you see in me, far superior to your own physical beauty. If that's the aim of your deal with me, to exchange beauty for beauty, then you're trying to get much the better of the bargain. You want to get real beauty in exchange for what is commonly mistaken for it, like Diomedes getting gold armour in return for his bronze. Better think again, however. You might be wrong about me. Judgment begins when eyesight starts to fail, and you're still a long way from that."

I listened, then said: "Well, as far as I am concerned, that's how things stand. I've told you my real feelings. You must decide what you think best for yourself and for me."

"That's good advice. We must think about it some time, and act as seems best to us, in this matter as in others."

After this exchange, thinking my direct assault had made some impact, I got up, before he could say anything more, wrapped my cloak around him (it was winter), and lay down with him under his rough cloak. I put my arms round him. I spent the whole night with him, remarkable, superhuman being that he is—still telling the truth, Socrates, you can't deny it—but he was more than equal to my advances. He rejected them, laughed at my good looks, and treated them with contempt; and I must admit that, as far as looks went, I thought I was quite something, members of the jury. (I call you that, since I'm accusing Socrates of contempt.) In short, I promise you faithfully, I fell asleep, and when I woke up in the morning I'd slept with Socrates all night, but absolutely nothing had happened. It was just like sleeping with one's father or elder brother.

Imagine how I felt after that. I was humiliated and yet full of admiration for Socrates' character—his restraint and strength of mind. I'd met a man whose equal, in intelligence and control, I didn't think I should ever meet again. I couldn't have a row with him; that would just lose me his friendship. Nor could I see any way of attracting him. I knew money would make as little impression on him as Trojan weapons on Ajax, and he'd already escaped my one sure means of ensnaring him. I didn't know what to do, and I went around infatuated with the man. No-one's ever been so infatuated.

That was the background to our military service together in Potidaea, where we were messmates. In the first place there was his toughness—not only greater than mine, but greater than anyone else's. Sometimes we were cut off and had to go without food, as happens on campaign. No one could match him for endurance. On the other hand, he was the one who really made the most of it when there was plenty. He wouldn't drink for choice, but if he had to, he drank us all under the table. Surprising as it may seem, no man has ever seen Socrates drunk. I've no doubt you'll see confirmation of that this evening. As for the weather (they have pretty savage winters up there), his indifference to it was always astonishing, but one occasion stands out in particular. There was an incredibly severe frost. No one went outside, or if they did, they went muffled up to the eyeballs, with their feet wrapped up in wool or sheepskin. In these conditions Socrates went out in the same cloak he always wore, and walked barefoot over the ice with less fuss than the rest of us who had our feet wrapped up. The men didn't like it at all; they thought he was getting at them.

So much for that. But there's another exploit of this "conquering hero" during that campaign, which I ought to tell you about. He was studying a problem one morning, and he stood there thinking about it, not making any progress, but not giving up either—just standing there, trying to find the answer. By midday people were beginning to take notice, and remark to one another in some surprise that Socrates had been standing there thinking since dawn. Finally, in the evening after supper, some of the Ionians brought out their mattresses (this was in summer), and slept in the open, keeping an eye on him to see if he'd stand there all night. And sure enough he did stand there, until dawn broke and the sun rose. Then he said a prayer to the sun and left.

Should I say something about his conduct in action? Yes, I think he's earned it. In the battle in which the generals gave me a decoration, my own life was saved by none other than Socrates. He refused to leave me when I was wounded, and saved both me and my weapons. So I recommended that the generals should give you the decoration. Isn't that true, Socrates? You can't object to that, or say I'm lying, can you? In fact the generals were inclined to favour me, because of my social position, and wanted to give it to me, but you were keener than they were that I should get it, rather than you.

And you should have seen him, gentlemen, on the retreat from Delium. I was with him, but I was on horseback, and he was on foot. He was retreating, amid the general rout, with Laches. I came upon them, and when I saw them I told them not to panic, and said I'd stick by them. This time I got a better view of Socrates than I had at Potidaea, since I was on horseback, and less worried about my own safety. For a start, he was much more composed than Laches. And then I thought your description of him, Aristophanes, was as accurate there as it is here in Athens, "marching along with his head in the air, staring at all around him," calmly contemplating friend and foe alike. It was perfectly clear, even from a distance, that any attempt to lay a finger on him would arouse vigorous resistance. So he and his companion escaped unhurt. On the whole, in battle, you don't meddle with people like that. You go after the ones in headlong flight.

I could go on praising Socrates all night, and tell you some surprising things. Many of his qualities can be found in other people, and yet it's remarkable how unlike he is to anyone in the past or present. You can compare Brasidas, or someone like that, with Achilles; Pericles with Nestor or Antenor (for example); and make other similar comparisons. But you could go a long way and not find a match, dead or living, for Socrates. So unusual are the man himself and his arguments. You have to go back to my original comparison of the man and his arguments, to Silenuses and satyrs. I didn't say this at the beginning, but his arguments, when you really look at them, are also just like Silenus-figures. If you decided to listen to one, it would strike you at first as ludicrous. On the face of it, it's just a collection of irrelevant words and phrases; but those are just the outer skin of this trouble-making satyr. It's all donkeys and bronzesmiths, shoemakers and tanners. He always seems to be repeating himself, and people who haven't heard him before, and aren't too quick on the uptake, laugh at what he says. But look beneath the surface, and get inside them, and you'll find two things. In the first place, they're the only arguments which really make any sense; on top of that they are supremely inspiring, because they contain countless models of excellence and pointers towards it. In fact, they deal with everything you should be concerned about, if you want to lead a good and noble life.

That's my speech, gentlemen, in praise of Socrates—though I've included a bit of blame as well for his outrageous treatment of me. And I'm not the only sufferer. There's Charmides, the son of Glaucon, and Euthydemus, the son of Diocles, and lots of others. He seduces them, like a lover seducing his boyfriend, and then it turns out he's not their lover at all; in fact, they're his lovers. So take my advice, Agathon, and don't be seduced. Learn from our experience, rather than at first hand, like Homer's "fool who learnt too late." Don't trust him an inch.

Alcibiades' candour aroused some amusement. He seemed to be still in love with   c
Socrates.

SOCRATES: Not so drunk after all, Alcibiades; or you wouldn't have avoided, so
elegantly and so deviously, revealing the real object of your speech, just slipping it in
at the end, as if it were an afterthought. What you're really trying to do is turn Agathon
and me against one another. You think that I should be your lover, and no-one else's;
and that you, and no-one else, should be Agathon's. Well, it hasn't worked. All that   d
stuff about satyrs and Silenuses is quite transparent. You mustn't let him get away with
it, my dear Agathon; you must make sure no-one turns us against each other.

AGATHON: You may be right, Socrates. His sitting between us, to keep us apart,
bears that out. But it won't work. I'll come round and sit next to you.   e

SOCRATES: Good idea. Sit here, round this side.

ALCIBIADES: Ye gods. What I have to put up with from the man. He has to keep
scoring off me. Look, at least let Agathon sit in the middle.

SOCRATES: Out of the question. You've just praised me, and now I must praise the
person on my right. If Agathon sits next to you, he can't be expected to make *another*
speech in praise of me. I'd better make one in praise of him instead. No, you'll have to
admit defeat, my good friend, and put up with me praising the boy. I look forward to it.   223

*A Seated Man at a Greek
Symposium,* Red-figure vase,
460–450 B.C. Today the term
"symposium" usually means a
scholarly meeting; in ancient Greece
it meant a drinking party (as depicted
on this vase—and in the dialogue).
(*Smithsonian Institution*)

AGATHON: What a bit of luck. I'm certainly not staying here, Alcibiades. I'd much rather move, and get myself praised by Socrates.

ALCIBIADES: That's it, the same old story. Whenever Socrates is around, no-one else can get near anyone good looking. Like now, for example. Look how easily he finds plausible reasons why Agathon should sit next to him.

b   Agathon got up to come and sit by Socrates. Suddenly a whole crowd of people on their way home from a party turned up at the door, and finding it open (someone was just leaving), they came straight in, and sat down to join us. Things became incredibly noisy and disorderly, and we couldn't avoid having far too much to drink.

c   Eryximachus and Phaedrus and some others went home. I fell asleep, and slept for some time, the nights being long at that time of year. When I woke up it was almost light, and the cocks were crowing. I could see that everyone had gone home or to sleep, apart from Agathon, Aristophanes, and Socrates. They were still awake and drinking (passing a large bowl round anticlockwise). Socrates was holding the floor.

d   I've forgotten most of what he was saying, since I missed the beginning of it, and was still half-asleep anyway. The gist of it was that he was forcing them to admit that the same man could be capable of writing comedy and tragedy, and hence that a successful tragedian must also be able to write comedy. As they were being driven to this conclusion, though not really following the argument, they dropped off. Aristophanes went to sleep first, and then, as it was getting light, Agathon. Socrates made them both comfortable, and got up to leave himself. I followed him, as usual. He went to the Lyceum, had a bath, spent the rest of the day as he normally would, and then, towards evening, went home to bed.

REPUBLIC (in part)

BOOK I

*   *   *

336^b   All this time Thrasymachus had been trying more than once to break in upon our conversation; but his neighbours had restrained him, wishing to hear the argument to the end. In the pause after my last words he could keep quiet no longer; but gathering himself up like a wild beast he sprang at us as if he would tear us in pieces. Polemarchus and I were frightened out of our wits, when he burst out to the whole company:

c   What is the matter with you two, Socrates? Why do you go on in this imbecile way, politely deferring to each other's nonsense? If you really want to know what justice means, stop asking questions and scoring off the answers you get. You know very well it is easier to ask questions than to answer them. Answer yourself, and tell us what you think justice means. I won't have you telling us it is the same as what is obligatory

The Republic of Plato (Book I, 336b–49b, 350d–54b; Book II, 367e–382a; Book III, 412b–417b; Book IV, 427d–448e; Book V, complete: 448e–480a; Books VI–VII, 502c–521b), translated by Francis MacDonald Cornford (Oxford: Oxford University Press, 1945). Reprinted by permission of Oxford University Press.

or useful or advantageous or profitable or expedient; I want a clear and precise state-   d
ment; I won't put up with that sort of verbiage.

I was amazed by this onslaught and looked at him in terror. If I had not seen this
wolf before he saw me, I really believe I should have been struck dumb;* but fortunately I had looked at him earlier, when he was beginning to get exasperated with our
argument; so I was able to reply, though rather tremulously:

Don't be hard on us, Thrasymachus. If Polemarchus and I have gone astray in   e
our search, you may be quite sure the mistake was not intentional. If we had been looking for a piece of gold, we should never have deliberately allowed politeness to spoil
our chance of finding it; and now when we are looking for justice, a thing much more
precious than gold, you cannot imagine we should defer to each other in that foolish
way and not do our best to bring it to light. You must believe we are in earnest, my
friend; but I am afraid the task is beyond our powers, and we might expect a man of   337
your ability to pity us instead of being so severe.

Thrasymachus replied with a burst of sardonic laughter.

Good Lord, he said; Socrates at his old trick of shamming ignorance! I knew it; I
told the others you would refuse to commit yourself and do anything sooner than answer a question.

Yes, Thrasymachus, I replied; because you are clever enough to know that if you
asked someone what are the factors of the number twelve, and at the same time warned   b
him: "Look here, you are not to tell me that twelve is twice six, or three times four, or six
times two, or four times three; I won't put up with any such nonsense"—you must surely
see that no one would answer a question put like that. He would say: "What do you
mean, Thrasymachus? Am I forbidden to give any of these answers, even if one happens
to be right? Do you want me to give a wrong one?" What would you say to that?   c

Humph! said he. As if that were a fair analogy!

I don't see why it is not, said I; but in any case, do you suppose our barring a certain answer would prevent the man from giving it, if he thought it was the truth?

Do you mean that you are going to give me one of those answers I barred?

I should not be surprised, if it seemed to me true, on reflection.

And what if I give you another definition of justice, better than any of those?   d
What penalty are you prepared to pay?**

The penalty deserved by ignorance, which must surely be to receive instruction
from the wise. So I would suggest that as a suitable punishment.

I like your notion of a penalty! he said; but you must pay the costs as well.

I will, when I have any money.

That will be all right, said Glaucon; we will all subscribe for Socrates. So let us
have your definition, Thrasymachus.

Oh yes, he said; so that Socrates may play the old game of questioning and refut-   e
ing someone else, instead of giving an answer himself!

But really, I protested, what can you expect from a man who does not know the
answer or profess to know it, and, besides that, has been forbidden by no mean authority to put forward any notions he may have? Surely the definition should naturally
come from you, who say you do know the answer and can tell it us. Please do not dis-
appoint us. I should take it as a kindness, and I hope you will not be chary of giving   338
Glaucon and the rest of us the advantage of your instruction.

*A popular superstition, that if a wolf sees you first, you become dumb.
**In certain lawsuits the defendant, if found guilty, was allowed to propose a penalty alternative to
that demanded by the prosecution. The judges then decided which should be inflicted. The "costs" here
means the fee which the sophist, unlike Socrates, expected from his pupils.

Glaucon and the others added their entreaties to mine. Thrasymachus was evidently longing to win credit, for he was sure he had an admirable answer ready, though he made a show of insisting that I should be the one to reply. In the end he gave way and exclaimed:

b   So this is what Socrates' wisdom comes to! He refuses to teach, and goes about learning from others without offering so much as thanks in return.

I do learn from others, Thrasymachus; that is quite true; but you are wrong to call me ungrateful. I give in return all I can—praise; for I have no money. And how ready I am to applaud any idea that seems to me sound, you will see in a moment, when you have stated your own; for I am sure that will be sound.

c   Listen then, Thrasymachus began. What I say is that "just" or "right" means nothing but what is to the interest of the stronger party. Well, where is your applause? You don't mean to give it me.

I will, as soon as I understand, I said. I don't see yet what you mean by right being the interest of the stronger party. For instance, Polydamas, the athlete, is stronger than we are, and it is to his interest to eat beef for the sake of his muscles; but surely you don't mean that the same diet would be good for weaker men and therefore be
d   right for us?

You are trying to be funny, Socrates. It's a low trick to take my words in the sense you think will be most damaging.

No, no, I protested; but you must explain.

Don't you know, then, that a state may be ruled by a despot, or a democracy, or an aristocracy?

Of course.

And that the ruling element is always the strongest?

Yes.

e   Well then, in every case the laws are made by the ruling party in its own interest; a democracy makes democratic laws, a despot autocratic ones, and so on. By making these laws they define as "right" for their subjects whatever is for their own interest, and they call anyone who breaks them a "wrongdoer" and punish him accordingly. That is
339   what I mean: in all states alike "right" has the same meaning, namely what is for the interest of the party established in power, and that is the strongest. So the sound conclusion is that what is "right" is the same everywhere: the interest of the stronger party.

Now I see what you mean, said I; whether it is true or not, I must try to make out. When you define right in terms of interest, you are yourself giving one of those answers you forbade to me; though, to be sure, you add "to the stronger party."

An insignificant addition, perhaps!

b   Its importance is not clear yet; what is clear is that we must find out whether your definition is true. I agree myself that right is in a sense a matter of interest; but when you add "to the stronger party," I don't know about that. I must consider.

Go ahead, then.

I will. Tell me this. No doubt you also think it is right to obey the men in power?

I do.

c   Are they infallible in every type of state, or can they sometimes make a mistake?

Of course they can make a mistake.

In framing laws, then, they may do their work well or badly?

No doubt.

Well, that is to say, when the laws they make are to their own interest; badly, when they are not?

Yes.

But the subjects are to obey any law they lay down, and they will then be doing right?

Of course.

If so, by your account, it will be right to do what is not to the interest of the stronger party, as well as what is so.   d

What's that you are saying?

Just what you said, I believe; but let us look again. Haven't you admitted that the rulers, when they enjoin certain acts on their subjects, sometimes mistake their own best interests, and at the same time that it is right for the subjects to obey, whatever they may enjoin?

Yes, I suppose so.

Well, that amounts to admitting that it is right to do what is not to the interest of   e
the rulers or the stronger party. They may unwittingly enjoin what is to their own disadvantage; and you say it is right for the others to do as they are told. In that case, their
duty must be the opposite of what you said, because the weaker will have been ordered
to do what is against the interest of the stronger. You with your intelligence must see
how that follows.

Yes, Socrates, said Polemarchus, that is undeniable.

No doubt, Cleitophon broke in, if you are to be a witness on Socrates' side.   340

No witness is needed, replied Polemarchus; Thrasymachus himself admits that
rulers sometimes ordain acts that are to their own disadvantage, and that it is the subjects' duty to do them.

That is because Thrasymachus said it was right to do what you are told by the
men in power.

Yes, but he also said that what is to the interest of the stronger party is right; and,
after making both these assertions, he admitted that the stronger sometimes command   b
the weaker subjects to act against their interests. From all which it follows that what is
in the stronger's interest is no more right than what is not.

No, said Cleitophon; he meant whatever the stronger believes to be in his own
interest. That is what the subject must do, and what Thrasymachus meant to define as
right.

That was not what he said, rejoined Polemarchus.

No matter, Polemarchus, said I; if Thrasymachus says so now, let us take him in   c
that sense. Now, Thrasymachus, tell me, was that what you intended to say—that right
means what the stronger thinks is to his interest, whether it really is so or not?

Most certainly not, he replied. Do you suppose I should speak of a man as
"stronger" or "superior" at the very moment when he is making a mistake?

I did think you said as much when you admitted that rulers are not always infallible.

That is because you are a quibbler, Socrates. Would you say a man deserves to   d
be called a physician at the moment when he makes a mistake in treating his patient
and just in respect of that mistake; or a mathematician, when he does a sum wrong and
just in so far as he gets a wrong result? Of course we do commonly speak of a physician or a mathematician or a scholar having made a mistake; but really none of these, I
should say, is ever mistaken, in so far as he is worthy of the name we give him. So   e
strictly speaking—and you are all for being precise—no one who practises a craft
makes mistakes. A man is mistaken when his knowledge fails him; and at that moment
he is no craftsman. And what is true of craftsmanship or any sort of skill is true of the
ruler: he is never mistaken so long as he is acting as a ruler; though anyone might

speak of a ruler making a mistake, just as he might of a physician. You must understand that I was talking in that loose way when I answered your question just now; but the precise statement is this. The ruler, in so far as he is acting as a ruler, makes no mistakes and consequently enjoins what is best for himself; and that is what the subject is to do. So, as I said at first, "right" means doing what is to the interest of the stronger.

Very well, Thrasymachus, said I. So you think I am quibbling?

I am sure you are.

You believe my questions were maliciously designed to damage your position?

I know it. But you will gain nothing by that. You cannot outwit me by cunning, and you are not the man to crush me in the open.

Bless your soul, I answered, I should not think of trying. But, to prevent any more misunderstanding, when you speak of that ruler or stronger party whose interest the weaker ought to serve, please make it clear whether you are using the words in the ordinary way or in that strict sense you have just defined.

I mean a ruler in the strictest possible sense. Now quibble away and be as malicious as you can. I want no mercy. But you are no match for me.

Do you think me mad enough to beard a lion or try to outwit a Thrasymachus?

You did try just now, he retorted, but it wasn't a success.

Enough of this, said I. Now tell me about the physician in that strict sense you spoke of: is it his business to earn money or to treat his patients? Remember, I mean your physician who is worthy of the name.

To treat his patients.

And what of the ship's captain in the true sense? Is he a mere seaman or the commander of the crew?

The commander.

Yes, we shall not speak of him as a seaman just because he is on board a ship. That is not the point. He is called captain because of his skill and authority over the crew.

Quite true.

And each of these people has some special interest?*

No doubt.

And the craft in question exists for the very purpose of discovering that interest and providing for it?

Yes.

Can it equally be said of any craft that it has an interest, other than its own greatest possible perfection?

What do you mean by that?

Here is an illustration. If you ask me whether it is sufficient for the human body just to be itself, with no need of help from without, I should say, Certainly not; it has weaknesses and defects, and its condition is not all that it might be. That is precisely why the art of medicine was invented: it was designed to help the body and provide for its interests. Would not that be true?

It would.

But now take the art of medicine itself. Has that any defects or weaknesses? Does any art stand in need of some further perfection, as the eye would be imperfect without the power of vision or the ear without hearing, so that in their case an art is re-

---

*All the persons mentioned have some interest. The craftsman *qua* craftsman has an interest in doing his work as well as possible, which is the same thing as serving the interest of the subjects on whom his craft is exercised; and the subjects have their interest, which the craftsman is there to promote.

quired that will study their interests and provide for their carrying out those functions? Has the art itself any corresponding need of some further art to remedy its defects and look after its interests; and will that further art require yet another, and so on for ever? Or will every art look after its own interests? Or, finally, is it not true that no art needs to have its weaknesses remedied or its interests studied either by another art or by it-   b self, because no art has in itself any weakness or fault, and the only interest it is required to serve is that of its subject-matter? In itself, an art is sound and flawless, so long as it is entirely true to its own nature as an art in the strictest sense—and it is the strict sense that I want you to keep in view. Is not that true?

So it appears.

Then, said I, the art of medicine does not study its own interest, but the needs of   c the body, just as a groom shows his skill by caring for horses, not for the art of grooming. And so every art seeks, not its own advantage—for it has no deficiencies—but the interest of the subject on which it is exercised.

It appears so.

But surely, Thrasymachus, every art has authority and superior power over its subject.

To this he agreed, though very reluctantly.

So far as arts are concerned, then, no art ever studies or enjoins the interest of the superior or stronger party, but always that of the weaker over which it has authority.   d

Thrasymachus assented to this at last, though he tried to put up a fight. I then went on:

So the physician, as such, studies only the patient's interest, not his own. For as we agreed, the business of the physician, in the strict sense, is not to make money for himself, but to exercise his power over the patient's body; and the ship's captain, again, considered strictly as no mere sailor, but in command of the crew, will study and enjoin the interest of his subordinates, not his own.

He agreed reluctantly.   e

And so with government of any kind: no ruler, in so far as he is acting as ruler, will study or enjoin what is for his own interest. All that he says and does will be said and done with a view to what is good and proper for the subject for whom he practises his art.

At this point, when everyone could see that Thrasymachus' definition of justice   343 had been turned inside out, instead of making any reply, he said:

Socrates, have you a nurse?

Why do you ask such a question as that? I said. Wouldn't it be better to answer mine?

Because she lets you go about sniffling like a child whose nose wants wiping. She hasn't even taught you to know a shepherd when you see one, or his sheep either.

What makes you say that?

Why, you imagine that a herdsman studies the interests of his flocks or cattle,   b tending and fattening them up with some other end in view than his master's profit or his own; and so you don't see that, in politics, the genuine ruler regards his subjects exactly like sheep, and thinks of nothing else, night and day, but the good he can get out of them for himself. You are so far out in your notions of right and wrong, justice and injustice, as not to know that "right" actually means what is good for someone else,   c and to be "just" means serving the interest of the stronger who rules, at the cost of the subject who obeys; whereas injustice is just the reverse, asserting its authority over those innocents who are called just, so that they minister solely to their master's advantage and happiness, and not in the least degree to their own. Innocent as you are your-

d   self, Socrates, you must see that a just man always has the worst of it. Take a private business: when a partnership is wound up, you will never find that the more honest of two partners comes off with the larger share; and in their relations to the state, when there are taxes to be paid, the honest man will pay more than the other on the same amount of property; or if there is money to be distributed, the dishonest will get it all.

e   When either of them hold some public office, even if the just man loses in no other way, his private affairs at any rate will suffer from neglect, while his principles will not allow him to help himself from the public funds; not to mention the offence he will give to his friends and relations by refusing to sacrifice those principles to do them a good turn. Injustice has all the opposite advantages. I am speaking of the type I de-

344   scribed just now, the man who can get the better of other people on a large scale: you must fix your eye on him, if you want to judge how much it is to one's own interest not to be just. You can see that best in the most consummate form of injustice, which rewards wrongdoing with supreme welfare and happiness and reduces its victims, if they won't retaliate in kind, to misery. That form is despotism, which uses force or fraud to plunder the goods of others, public or private, sacred or profane, and to do it in a wholesale way. If you are caught committing any one of these crimes on a small scale,

b   you are punished and disgraced; they call it sacrilege, kidnapping, burglary, theft and brigandage. But if, besides taking their property, you turn all your countrymen into slaves, you will hear no more of those ugly names; your countrymen themselves will

c   call you the happiest of men and bless your name, and so will everyone who hears of such a complete triumph of injustice; for when people denounce injustice, it is because they are afraid of suffering wrong, not of doing it. So true is it, Socrates, that injustice, on a grand enough scale, is superior to justice in strength and freedom and autocratic power; and "right," as I said at first, means simply what serves the interest of the stronger party; "wrong" means what is for the interest and profit of oneself.

d   Having deluged our ears with this torrent of words, as the man at the baths might empty a bucket over one's head, Thrasymachus meant to take himself off; but the company obliged him to stay and defend his position. I was specially urgent in my entreaties.

      My good Thrasymachus, said I, do you propose to fling a doctrine like that at our heads and then go away without explaining it properly or letting us point out to you

e   whether it is true or not? Is it so small a matter in your eyes to determine the whole course of conduct which every one of us must follow to get the best out of life?

      Don't I realize it is a serious matter? he retorted.

      Apparently not, said I; or else you have no consideration for us, and do not care whether we shall lead better or worse lives for being ignorant of this truth you profess to know. Do take the trouble to let us into your secret; if you treat us handsomely, you

345   may be sure it will be a good investment; there are so many of us to show our gratitude. I will make no secret of my own conviction, which is that injustice is not more profitable than justice, even when left free to work its will unchecked. No; let your unjust man have full power to do wrong, whether by successful violence or by escaping detection; all the same he will not convince me that he will gain more than he would by being just. There may be others here who feel as I do, and set justice above injus-

b   tice. It is for you to convince us that we are not well advised.

      How can I? he replied. If you are not convinced by what I have just said, what more can I do for you? Do you want to be fed with my ideas out of a spoon?

      God forbid! I exclaimed; not that. But I do want you to stand by your own words; or, if you shift your ground, shift it openly and stop trying to hoodwink us as

you are doing now. You see, Thrasymachus, to go back to your earlier argument, in   c
speaking of the shepherd you did not think it necessary to keep to that strict sense you
laid down when you defined the genuine physician. You represent him, in his character
of shepherd, as feeding up his flock, not for their own sake but for the table or the market, as if he were out to make money as a caterer or a cattle-dealer, rather than a shepherd. Surely the sole concern of the shepherd's art is to do the best for the charges put   d
under its care; its own best interest is sufficiently provided for, so long as it does not
fall short of all that shepherding should imply. On that principle it followed, I thought,
that any kind of authority, in the state or in private life, must, in its character of authority, consider solely what is best for those under its care. Now what is your opinion? Do
you think that the men who govern states—I mean rulers in the strict sense—have no   e
reluctance to hold office?

I don't think so, he replied; I know it.

Well, but haven't you noticed, Thrasymachus, that in other positions of authority
no one is willing to act unless he is paid wages, which he demands on the assumption
that all the benefit of his action will go to his charges? Tell me: Don't we always distinguish one form of skill from another by its power to effect some particular result?   346
Do say what you really think, so that we may get on.

Yes, that is the distinction.

And also each brings us some benefit that is peculiar to it: medicine gives health,
for example; the art of navigation, safety at sea; and so on.

Yes.   b

And wage-earning brings us wages; that is its distinctive product. Now, speaking
with that precision which you proposed, you would not say that the art of navigation is
the same as the art of medicine, merely on the ground that a ship's captain regained his
health on a voyage, because the sea air was good for him. No more would you identify
the practice of medicine with wage-earning because a man may keep his health while
earning wages, or a physician attending a case may receive a fee.   c

No.

And, since we agreed that the benefit obtained by each form of skill is peculiar to
it, any common benefit enjoyed alike by all these practitioners must come from some
further practice common to them all?

It would seem so.

Yes, we must say that if they all earn wages, they get that benefit in so far as they
are engaged in wage-earning as well as in practising their several arts.

He agreed reluctantly.   d

This benefit, then—the receipt of wages—does not come to a man from his special art. If we are to speak strictly, the physician, as such, produces health; the builder,
a house; and then each, in his further capacity of wage-earner, gets his pay. Thus every
art has its own function and benefits its proper subject. But suppose the practitioner is
not paid; does he then get any benefit from his art?

Clearly not.

And is he doing no good to anyone either, when he works for nothing?   e

No, I suppose he does some good.

Well then, Thrasymachus, it is now clear that no form of skill or authority provides for its own benefit. As we were saying some time ago, it always studies and prescribes what is good for its subject—the interest of the weaker party, not of the
stronger. And that, my friend, is why I said that no one is willing to be in a position of
authority and undertake to set straight other men's troubles, without demanding to be
paid; because, if he is to do his work well, he will never, in his capacity of ruler, do, or   347

command others to do, what is best for himself, but only what is best for the subject. For that reason, if he is to consent, he must have his recompense, in the shape of money or honour, or of punishment in case of refusal.

What do you mean, Socrates? asked Glaucon. I recognize two of your three kinds of reward; but I don't understand what you mean by speaking of punishment as a recompense.

b   Then you don't understand the recompense required by the best type of men, or their motive for accepting authority when they do consent. You surely know that a passion for honours or for money is rightly regarded as something to be ashamed of.

Yes, I do.

For that reason, I said, good men are unwilling to rule, either for money's sake or for honour. They have no wish to be called mercenary for demanding to be paid, or thieves for making a secret profit out of their office; nor yet will honours tempt them,

c   for they are not ambitious. So they must be forced to consent under threat of penalty; that may be why a readiness to accept power under no such constraint is thought discreditable. And the heaviest penalty for declining to rule is to be ruled by someone inferior to yourself. That is the fear, I believe, that makes decent people accept power; and when they do so, they face the prospect of authority with no idea that they are coming into the enjoyment of a comfortable berth; it is forced upon them because they

d   can find no one better than themselves, or even as good, to be entrusted with power. If there could ever be a society of perfect men, there might well be as much competition to evade office as there now is to gain it; and it would then be clearly seen that the genuine ruler's nature is to seek only the advantage of the subject, with the consequence that any man of understanding would sooner have another to do the best for him than be at the pains to do the best for that other himself. On this point, then, I entirely dis-

e   agree with Thrasymachus' doctrine that right means what is to the interest of the stronger.

However, I continued, we may return to that question later. Much more important is the position Thrasymachus is asserting now: that a life of injustice is to be preferred to a life of justice. Which side do you take, Glaucon? Where do you think the truth lies?

I should say that the just life is the better worth having.

348   You heard Thrasymachus' catalogue of all the good things in store for injustice?

I did, but I am not convinced.

Shall we try to convert him, then, supposing we can find some way to prove him wrong?

By all means.

We might answer Thrasymachus' case in a set speech of our own, drawing up a corresponding list of the advantages of justice; he would then have the right to reply,

b   and we should make our final rejoinder; but after that we should have to count up and measure the advantages on each list, and we should need a jury to decide between us. Whereas, if we go on as before, each securing the agreement of the other side, we can combine the functions of advocate and judge. We will take whichever course you prefer.

I prefer the second, said Glaucon.

Come then, Thrasymachus, said I, let us start afresh with our questions. You say that injustice pays better than justice, when both are carried to the furthest point?

c   I do, he replied; and I have told you why.

And how would you describe them? I suppose you would call one of them an excellence and the other a defect?

Of course.

Justice an excellence, and injustice a defect?

Now is that likely, when I am telling you that injustice pays, and justice does not?

Then what do you say?

The opposite.

That justice is a defect?

No; rather the mark of a good-natured simpleton.

Injustice, then, implies being ill-natured?   d

No; I should call it good policy.

Do you think the unjust are positively superior in character and intelligence, Thrasymachus?

Yes, if they are the sort that can carry injustice to perfection and make themselves masters of whole cities and nations. Perhaps you think I was talking of pickpockets. There is profit even in that trade, if you can escape detection; but it doesn't come to much as compared with the gains I was describing.

I understand you now on that point, I replied. What astonished me was that you   e
should class injustice with superior character and intelligence and justice with the reverse.

Well, I do, he rejoined.

That is a much more stubborn position, my friend; and it is not so easy to see how to assail it. If you would admit that injustice, however well it pays, is nevertheless, as some people think, a defect and a discreditable thing, then we could argue on generally accepted principles. But now that you have gone so far as to rank it with superior character and intelligence, obviously you will say it is an admirable thing as   349
well as a source of strength, and has all the other qualities we have attributed to justice.

You read my thoughts like a book, he replied.

However, I went on, it is no good shirking; I must go through with the argument, so long as I can be sure you are really speaking your mind. I do believe you are not playing with us now, Thrasymachus, but stating the truth as you conceive it.

Why not refute the doctrine? he said. What does it matter to you whether I believe it or not?

It does not matter, I replied.   b

*   *   *

Thrasymachus' assent was dragged out of him with a reluctance of which my account gives no idea. He was sweating at every pore, for the weather was hot; and I saw   350^d
then what I had never seen before—Thrasymachus blushing. However, now that we had agreed that justice implies superior character and intelligence, injustice a deficiency in both respects, I went on:

Good; let us take that as settled. But we were also saying that injustice was a source of strength. Do you remember, Thrasymachus ?

I do remember; only your last argument does not satisfy me, and I could say a good deal about that. But if I did, you would tell me I was haranguing you like a public meeting. So either let me speak my mind at length, or else, if you want to ask ques-   e
tions, ask them, and I will nod or shake my head, and say "Hm?" as we do to encourage an old woman telling us a story.

No, please, said I; don't give your assent against your real opinion.

Anything to please you, he rejoined, since you won't let me have my say. What more do you want?

Nothing. I replied. If that is what you mean to do, I will go on with my questions.

Go on, then.

351   Well, to continue where we left off. I will repeat my question What is the nature and quality of justice as compared with injustice? It was suggested, I believe, that injustice is the stronger and more effective of the two; but now we have seen that justice implies superior character and intelligence, it will not be hard to show that it will also be superior in power to injustice, which implies ignorance and stupidity; that must be obvious to anyone. However, I would rather look deeper into this matter than take it as settled off-hand. Would you agree that a state may be unjust and may try to enslave
b   other states or to hold a number of others in subjection unjustly?

Of course it may, he said; above all if it is the best sort of state, which carries injustice to perfection.

I understand, said I; that was your view. But I am wondering whether a state can do without justice when it is asserting its superior power over another in that way.

c   Not if you are right, that justice implies intelligence; but if I am right, injustice will be needed.

I am delighted with your answer, Thrasymachus; this is much better than just nodding and shaking your head.

It is all to oblige you.

Thank you. Please add to your kindness by telling me whether any set of men—a state or an army or a band of robbers or thieves —who were acting together for some
d   unjust purpose would be likely to succeed, if they were always trying to injure one another. Wouldn't they do better, if they did not?

Yes, they would.

Because, of course, such injuries must set them quarrelling and hating each other. Only fair treatment can make men friendly and of one mind.

Be it so, he said; I don't want to differ from you.

Thank you once more, I replied. But don't you agree that, if injustice has this effect of implanting hatred wherever it exists, it must make any set of people, whether
e   freemen or slaves, split into factions, at feud with one another and incapable of any joint action?

Yes.

And so with any two individuals: injustice will set them at variance and make them enemies to each other as well as to everyone who is just.

It will.

And will it not keep its character and have the same effect, if it exists in a single person?

Let us suppose so.

The effect being, apparently, wherever it occurs—in a state or a family or an
352   army or anywhere else—to make united action impossible because of factions and quarrels, and moreover to set whatever it resides in at enmity with itself as well as with any opponent and with all who are just.

Yes, certainly.

Then I suppose it will produce the same natural results in an individual. He will have a divided mind and be incapable of action, for lack of singleness of purpose; and he will be at enmity with all who are just as well as with himself?

Yes.

And "all who are just" surely includes the gods?

Let us suppose so.

b   The unjust man, then, will be a god-forsaken creature; the goodwill of heaven will be for the just.

Enjoy your triumph, said Thrasymachus. You need not fear my contradicting you. I have no wish to give offence to the company.

You will make my enjoyment complete, I replied, if you will answer my further questions in the same way. We have made out so far that just men are superior in character and intelligence and more effective in action. Indeed without justice men cannot act together at all; it is not strictly true to speak of such people as ever having effected any c strong action in common. Had they been thoroughly unjust, they could not have kept their hands off one another; they must have had some justice in them, enough to keep them from injuring one another at the same time with their victims. This it was that enabled them to achieve what they did achieve: their injustice only partially incapacitated them for their career of wrongdoing; if perfect, it would have disabled them for any action whatsoever. I can see that all this is true, as against your original position. But there is a further question which we postponed: Is the life of justice the better and happier life?   d What we have said already leaves no doubt in my mind; but we ought to consider more carefully, for this is no light matter: it is the question, what is the right way to live?

Go on, then.

I will, said I. Some things have a function*; a horse, for instance, is useful for certain kinds of work. Would you agree to define a thing's function in general as the   e work for which that thing is the only instrument or the best one?

I don't understand.

Take an example. We can see only with the eyes, hear only with the ears; and seeing and hearing might be called the functions of those organs.

Yes.

Or again, you might cut vine-shoots with a carving-knife or a chisel or many   353 other tools, but with none so well as with a pruning knife made for the purpose; and we may call that its function.

True.

Now, I expect, you see better what I meant by suggesting that a thing's function is the work that it alone can do, or can do better than anything else.

Yes, I will accept that definition.   b

Good, said I; and to take the same examples, the eye and the ear, which we said have each its particular function: have they not also a specific excellence or virtue? Is not that always the case with things that have some appointed work to do?

Yes.

Now consider: is the eye likely to do its work well, if you take away its peculiar   c virtue and substitute the corresponding defect?

Of course not, if you mean substituting blindness for the power of sight.

I mean whatever its virtue may be; I have not come to that yet. I am only asking, whether it is true of things with a function—eyes or ears or anything else—that there is always some specific virtue which enables them to work well; and if they are deprived of that virtue, they work badly.

I think that is true.   d

Then the next point is this. Has the soul a function that can be performed by nothing else? Take for example such actions as deliberating or taking charge and exercising control: is not the soul the only thing of which you can say that these are its proper and peculiar work?

*The word translated "function" is the common word for "work." Hence the need for illustrations to confine it to the narrower sense of "function" here defined for the first time.

That is so.

And again, living—is not that above all the function of the soul?

No doubt.

And we also speak of the soul as having a certain specific excellence or virtue?

Yes.

e   Then, Thrasymachus, if the soul is robbed of its peculiar virtue, it cannot possibly do its work well. It must exercise its power of controlling and taking charge well or ill according as it is itself in a good or a bad state.

That follows.

And did we not agree that the virtue of the soul is justice, and injustice its defect?

We did.

So it follows that a just soul, or in other words a just man, will live well; the unjust will not.

Apparently, according to your argument.

354   But living well involves well-being and happiness.

Naturally.

Then only the just man is happy; injustice will involve unhappiness.

Be it so.

But you cannot say it pays better to be unhappy.

Of course not.

Injustice then, my dear Thrasymachus, can never pay better than justice.

Well, he replied, this is a feast-day, and you may take all this as your share of the entertainment.

For which I have to thank you, Thrasymachus; you have been so gentle with me

b   since you recovered your temper. It is my own fault if the entertainment has not been satisfactory. I have been behaving like a greedy guest, snatching a taste of every new dish that comes round before he has properly enjoyed the last. We began by looking for a definition of justice; but before we had found one, I dropped that question and hurried on to ask whether or not it involved superior character and intelligence; and then, as soon as another idea cropped up, that injustice pays better, I could not refrain from pursuing that.

So now the whole conversation has left me completely in the dark; for so long as I do not know what justice is, I am hardly likely to know whether or not it is a virtue, or whether it makes a man happy or unhappy.

BOOK II

*   *   *

[Socrates responds to speeches by Glaucon and Adeimantus]: There must indeed be some divine quality in your nature, if you can plead the cause of injustice so eloquently

368ᵃ   and still not be convinced yourselves that it is better than justice. That you are not really convinced I am sure from all I know of your dispositions, though your words might well have left me in doubt. But the more I trust you, the harder I find it to reply. How can I come to the rescue? I have no faith in my own powers, when I remember that you were not satisfied with the proof I thought I had given to Thrasymachus that it is better to be just. And yet I cannot stand by and hear justice reviled without lifting a

finger. I am afraid to commit a sin by holding aloof while I have breath and strength to   c
say a word in its defence. So there is nothing for it but to do the best I can.

Glaucon and the others begged me to step into the breach and carry through our
inquiry into the real nature of justice and injustice, and the truth about their respective
advantages. So I told them what I thought. This is a very obscure question, I said, and
we shall need keen sight to see our way. Now, as we are not remarkably clever, I will   d
make a suggestion as to how we should proceed. Imagine a rather short-sighted person
told to read an inscription in small letters from some way off. He would think it a godsend if someone pointed out that the same inscription was written up elsewhere on a
bigger scale, so that he could first read the larger characters and then make out whether
the smaller ones were the same.

No doubt, said Adeimantus; but what analogy do you see in that to our inquiry?   e

I will tell you. We think of justice as a quality that may exist in a whole community as well as in an individual, and the community is the bigger of the two. Possibly,
then, we may find justice there in larger proportions, easier to make out. So I suggest
that we should begin by inquiring what justice means in a state. Then we can go on to   369
look for its counterpart on a smaller scale in the individual.

That seems a good plan, he agreed.

Well then, I continued, suppose we imagine a state coming into being before our
eyes. We might then be able to watch the growth of justice or of injustice within it.
When that is done, we may hope it will be easier to find what we are looking for.

Much easier.   b

Shall we try, then, to carry out this scheme? I fancy it will be no light undertaking; so you had better think twice.

No need for that, said Adeimantus. Don't waste any more time.

My notion is, said I, that a state comes into existence because no individual is
self-sufficing; we all have many needs. But perhaps you can suggest some different
origin for the foundation of a community?

No, I agree with you.

So, having all these needs, we call in one another's help to satisfy our various re-   c
quirements; and when we have collected a number of helpers and associates to live together in one place, we call that settlement a state.

Yes.

So if one man gives another what he has to give in exchange for what he can get,
it is because each finds that to do so is for his own advantage.

Certainly.

Very well, said I. Now let us build up our imaginary state from the beginning.
Apparently, it will owe its existence to our needs, the first and greatest need being the   d
provision of food to keep us alive. Next we shall want a house; and thirdly, such things
as clothing.

True.

How will our state be able to supply all these demands? We shall need at least
one man to be a farmer, another a builder, and a third a weaver. Will that do, or shall
we add a shoemaker and one or two more to provide for our personal wants?

By all means.

The minimum state, then, will consist of four or five men.

Apparently.   e

Now here is a further point. Is each one of them to bring the product of his work
into a common stock? Should our one farmer, for example, provide food enough for

370   four people and spend the whole of his working time in producing corn, so as to share with the rest; or should he take no notice of them and spend only a quarter of his time on growing just enough corn for himself, and divide the other three-quarters between building his house, weaving his clothes, and making his shoes, so as to save the trouble of sharing with others and attend himself to all his own concerns?

The first plan might be the easier, replied Adeimantus.

That may very well be so, said I; for, as you spoke, it occurred to me, for one

b   thing, that no two people are born exactly alike. There are innate differences which fit them for different occupations.

I agree.

And will a man do better working at many trades, or keeping to one only?

Keeping to one.

And there is another point: obviously work may be ruined, if you let the right time go by. The workman must wait upon the work; it will not wait upon his leisure and allow itself to be done in a spare moment. So the conclusion is that more things will be produced and the work be more easily and better done, when every man is set

c   free from all other occupations to do, at the right time, the one thing for which he is naturally fitted.

That is certainly true.

We shall need more than four citizens, then, to supply all those necessaries we mentioned. You see, Adeimantus, if the farmer is to have a good plough and spade and other tools, he will not make them himself. No more will the builder and weaver and

d   shoemaker make all the many implements they need. So quite a number of carpenters and smiths and other craftsmen must be enlisted. Our miniature state is beginning to grow.

It is.

Still, it will not be very large, even when we have added cowherds and shepherds

e   to provide the farmers with oxen for the plough, and the builders as well as the farmers with draught-animals, and the weavers and shoemakers with wool and leather.

No; but it will not be so very small either.

And yet, again, it will be next to impossible to plant our city in a territory where it will need no imports. So there will have to be still another set of people, to fetch what it needs from other countries.

There will.

371   Moreover, if these agents take with them nothing that those other countries require in exchange, they will return as empty handed as they went. So, besides everything wanted for consumption at home, we must produce enough goods of the right kind for the foreigners whom we depend on to supply us. That will mean increasing the number of farmers and craftsmen.

Yes.

b   And then, there are these agents who are to import and export all kinds of goods—merchants, as we call them. We must have them; and if they are to do business overseas, we shall need quite a number of ship-owners and others who know about that branch of trading.

We shall.

Again, in the city itself how are the various sets of producers to exchange their products? That was our object, you will remember, in forming a community and so laying the foundation of our state.

Obviously, they must buy and sell.

That will mean having a market-place, and a currency to serve as a token for pur-   c
poses of exchange.

Certainly.

Now suppose a farmer, or an artisan, brings some of his produce to market at a
time when no one is there who wants to exchange with him. Is he to sit there idle,
when he might be at work?

No, he replied; there are people who have seen an opening here for their services. In well-ordered communities they are generally men not strong enough to be of
use in any other occupation. They have to stay where they are in the market-place and   d
take goods for money from those who want to sell, and money for goods from those
who want to buy.

That, then, is the reason why our city must include a class of shopkeepers—so
we call these people who sit still in the marketplace to buy and sell, in contrast with
merchants who travel to other countries.

Quite so.

There are also the services of yet another class, who have the physical strength   e
for heavy work, though on intellectual grounds they are hardly worth including in our
society—hired labourers, as we call them, because they sell the use of their strength for
wages. They will go to make up our population.

Yes.

Well, Adeimantus, has our state now grown to its full size?

Perhaps.

Then, where in it shall we find justice or injustice? If they have come in with one
of the elements we have been considering, can you say with which one?

I have no idea, Socrates; unless it be somewhere in their dealings with one an-   372
other.

You may be right, I answered. Anyhow, it is a question which we shall have to
face.

Let us begin, then, with a picture of our citizens' manner of life, with the provision we have made for them. They will be producing corn and wine, and making
clothes and shoes. When they have built their houses, they will mostly work without
their coats or shoes in summer, and in winter be well shod and clothed. For their food,   b
they will prepare flour and barley-meal for kneading and baking, and set out a grand
spread of loaves and cakes on rushes or fresh leaves. Then they will lie on beds of
myrtle-boughs and bryony [a type of gourd vine] and make merry with their children,
drinking their wine after the feast with garlands on their heads and singing the praises
of the gods. So they will live pleasantly together; and a prudent fear of poverty or war   c
will keep them from begetting children beyond their means.

Here Glaucon interrupted me: You seem to expect your citizens to feast on dry
bread.

True, I said; I forgot that they will have something to give it a relish, salt, no
doubt, and olives, and cheese, and country stews of roots and vegetables. And for
dessert we will give them figs and peas and beans; and they shall roast myrtle-berries
and acorns at the fire, while they sip their wine. Leading such a healthy life in peace,
they will naturally come to a good old age, and leave their children to live after them in
the same manner.   d

That is just the sort of provender you would supply, Socrates, if you were founding a community of pigs.

Well, how are they to live, then, Glaucon?

With the ordinary comforts. Let them lie on couches and dine off tables on such

e   dishes and sweets as we have nowadays.

Ah, I see, said I; we are to study the growth, not just of a state, but of a luxurious one. Well, there may be no harm in that; the consideration of luxury may help us to discover how justice and injustice take root in society. The community I have described seems to me the ideal one, in sound health as it were: but if you want to see one suffering from inflammation, there is nothing to hinder us. So some people, it seems,

373   will not be satisfied to live in this simple way; they must have couches and tables and furniture of all sorts; and delicacies too, perfumes, unguents, courtesans, sweetmeats, all in plentiful variety. And besides, we must not limit ourselves now to those bare necessaries of house and clothes and shoes; we shall have to set going the arts of embroidery and painting, and collect rich materials, like gold and ivory.

b   Yes.

Then we must once more enlarge our community. The healthy one will not be big enough now; it must be swollen up with a whole multitude of callings not ministering to any bare necessity: hunters and fishermen, for instance; artists in sculpture, painting, and music; poets with their attendant train of professional reciters, actors, dancers, producers; and makers of all sorts of household gear, including everything for

c   women's adornment. And we shall want more servants: children's nurses and attendants, lady's maids, barbers, cooks and confectioners. And then swineherds—there was no need for them in our original state, but we shall want them now; and a great quantity of sheep and cattle too, if people are going to live on meat.

Of course.

d   And with this manner of life physicians will be in much greater request.

No doubt.

The country, too, which was large enough to support the original inhabitants, will now be too small. If we are to have enough pasture and plough land, we shall have to cut off a slice of our neighbours' territory; and if they too are not content with necessaries, but give themselves up to getting unlimited wealth, they will want a slice of ours.

e   That is inevitable, Socrates.

So the next thing will be, Glaucon, that we shall be at war.

No doubt.

We need not say yet whether war does good or harm, but only that we have discovered its origin in desires which are the most fruitful source of evils both to individuals and to states.

Quite true.

374   This will mean a considerable addition to our community—a whole army, to go out to battle with any invader, in defence of all this property and of the citizens we have been describing.

Why so? Can't they defend themselves?

Not if the principle was right, which we all accepted in framing our society. You remember we agreed that no one man can practise many trades or arts satisfactorily.

True.

b   Well, is not the conduct of war an art, quite as important as shoemaking?

Yes.

But we would not allow our shoemaker to try to be also a farmer or weaver or builder, because we wanted our shoes well made. We gave each man one trade, for

c   which he was naturally fitted; he would do good work, if he confined himself to that all his life, never letting the right moment slip by. Now in no form of work is efficiency so important as in war; and fighting is not so easy a business that a man can follow another trade, such as farming or shoemaking, and also be an efficient soldier. Why, even d a game like draughts or dice must be studied from childhood; no one can become a fine player in his spare moments. Just taking up a shield or other weapon will not make a man capable of fighting that very day in any sort of warfare, any more than taking up a tool or implement of some kind will make a man a craftsman or an athlete, if he does not understand its use and has never been properly trained to handle it.

No; if that were so, tools would indeed be worth having.

These guardians of our state, then, inasmuch as their work is the most important of all, will need the most complete freedom from other occupations and the greatest e amount of skill and practice.

I quite agree.

And also a native aptitude for their calling.

Certainly.

So it is our business to define, if we can, the natural gifts that fit men to be guardians of a commonwealth, and to select them accordingly. It will certainly be a formidable task; but we must grapple with it to the best of our power. Yes.

Don't you think then, said I, that, for the purpose of keeping guard, a young man 375 should have much the same temperament and qualities as a well-bred watch-dog? I mean, for instance, that both must have quick senses to detect an enemy, swiftness in pursuing him, and strength, if they have to fight when they have caught him.

Yes, they will need all those qualities.

And also courage, if they are to fight well.

Of course.

And courage, in dog or horse or any other creature, implies a spirited disposition. You must have noticed that a high spirit is unconquerable. Every soul possessed of it is b fearless and indomitable in the face of any danger.

Yes, I have noticed that.

So now we know what physical qualities our Guardian must have, and also that he must be of a spirited temper.

Yes.

Then, Glaucon, how are men of that natural disposition to be kept from behaving pugnaciously to one another and to the rest of their countrymen?

It is not at all easy to see.

And yet they must be gentle to their own people and dangerous only to enemies; c otherwise they will destroy themselves without waiting till others destroy them.

True.

What are we to do, then? If gentleness and a high temper are contraries, where d shall we find a character to combine them? Both are necessary to make a good Guardian, but it seems they are incompatible. So we shall never have a good Guardian.

It looks like it.

Here I was perplexed, but on thinking over what we had been saying, I remarked that we deserved to be puzzled, because we had not followed up the comparison we had just drawn.

What do you mean? he asked.

We never noticed that, after all, there are natures in which these contraries are combined. They are to be found in animals, and not least in the kind we compared to e our Guardian. Well-bred dogs, as you know, are by instinct perfectly gentle to people whom they know and are accustomed to, and fierce to strangers. So the combination of qualities we require for our Guardian is, after all, possible and not against nature.

Evidently.

Do you further agree that, besides this spirited temper, he must have a philosophical element in his nature?

I don't see what you mean.

376   This is another trait you will see in the dog. It is really remarkable how the creature gets angry at the mere sight of a stranger and welcomes anyone he knows, though he may never have been treated unkindly by the one or kindly by the other. Did that never strike you as curious?

I had not thought of it before; but that certainly is how a dog behaves.

b   Well, but that shows a fine instinct, which is philosophic in the true sense.

How so?

Because the only mark by which he distinguishes a friendly and an unfriendly face is that he knows the one and does not know the other; and if a creature makes that the test of what it finds congenial or otherwise, how can you deny that it has a passion for knowledge and understanding?

Of course, I cannot.

And that passion is the same thing as philosophy—the love of wisdom.

Yes.

Shall we boldly say, then, that the same is true of human beings? If a man is to
c   be gentle towards his own people whom he knows, he must have an instinctive love of wisdom and understanding.

Agreed.

So the nature required to make a really noble Guardian of our commonwealth will be swift and strong, spirited, and philosophic.

Quite so.

Given those natural qualities, then, how are these Guardians to be brought up and educated? First, will the answer to that question help the purpose of our whole in-
d   quiry, which is to make out how justice and injustice grow up in a state? We want to be thorough, but not to draw out this discussion to a needless length.

Glaucon's brother answered: I certainly think it will help.

If so, I said, we must not think of dropping it, though it may be rather a long business.

I agree.

Come on then. We will take our time and educate our imaginary citizens.

e   Yes, let us do so.

*   *   *

BOOK III

*   *   *

Good, said I; and what is the next point to be settled? Is it not the question, which of these Guardians are to be rulers and which are to obey?

412ᵇ   No doubt.

Well, it is obvious that the elder must have authority over the young, and that the rulers must be the best.

Yes.

And as among farmers the best are those with a natural turn for farming, so, if we want the best among our Guardians, we must take those naturally fitted to watch over a commonwealth. They must have the right sort of intelligence and ability; and also they must look upon the commonwealth as their special concern—the sort of concern that is felt for something so closely bound up with oneself that its interests and fortunes, for good or ill, are held to be identical with one's own.   d

Exactly.

So the kind of men we must choose from among the Guardians will be those who, when we look at the whole course of their lives, are found to be full of zeal to do whatever they believe is for the good of the commonwealth and never willing to act against its interest.   e

Yes, they will be the men we want.

We must watch them, I think, at every age and see whether they are capable of preserving this conviction that they must do what is best for the community, never forgetting it or allowing themselves to be either forced or bewitched into throwing it over.

How does this throwing over come about?

I will explain. When a belief passes out of the mind, a man may be willing to part with it, if it is false and he has learnt better, or unwilling, if it is true.   413

I see how he might be willing to let it go; but you must explain how he can be unwilling.

Where is your difficulty? Don't you agree that men are unwilling to be deprived of good, though ready enough to part with evil? Or that to be deceived about the truth is evil, to possess it good? Or don't you think that possessing truth means thinking of things as they really are?

You are right. I do agree that men are unwilling to be robbed of a true belief.

When that happens to them, then, it must be by theft, or violence, or bewitch-   b
ment.

Again I do not understand.

Perhaps my metaphors are too high-flown. I call it theft when one is persuaded out of one's belief or forgets it. Argument in the one case, and time in the other, steal it away without one's knowing what is happening. You understand now?

Yes.

And by violence I mean being driven to change one's mind by pain or suffering.

That too I understand, and you are right.

And bewitchment, as I think you would agree, occurs when a man is beguiled   c
out of his opinion by the allurements of pleasure or scared out of it under the spell of panic.

Yes, all delusions are like a sort of bewitchment.

As I said just now, then, we must find out who are the best guardians of this inward conviction that they must always do what they believe to be best for the commonwealth. We shall have to watch them from earliest childhood and set them tasks in which they would be most likely to forget or to be beguiled out of this duty. We shall then choose only those whose memory holds firm and who are proof against delusion.   d

Yes.

We must also subject them to ordeals of toil and pain and watch for the same qualities there. And we must observe them when exposed to the test of yet a third kind of bewitchment. As people lead colts up to alarming noises to see whether they are

timid, so these young men must be brought into terrifying situations and then into
e   scenes of pleasure, which will put them to severer proof than gold tried in the furnace. If we find one bearing himself well in all these trials and resisting every enchantment, a true guardian of himself, preserving always that perfect rhythm and harmony of being which he has acquired from his training in music and poetry, such a one will be of the greatest service to the commonwealth as well as to himself. Whenever we find one
414 who has come unscathed through every test in childhood, youth, and manhood, we shall set him as a Ruler to watch over the commonwealth; he will be honoured in life, and after death receive the highest tribute of funeral rites and other memorials. All who do not reach this standard we must reject. And that, I think, my dear Glaucon, may be taken as an outline of the way in which we shall select Guardians to be set in authority as Rulers.

I am very much of your mind.

b   These, then, may properly be called Guardians in the fullest sense, who will ensure that neither foes without shall have the power, nor friends within the wish, to do harm. Those young men whom up to now we have been speaking of as Guardians, will be better described as Auxiliaries, who will enforce the decisions of the Rulers.

I agree.

Now, said I, can we devise something in the way of those convenient fictions we
c   spoke of earlier, a single bold flight of invention,* which we may induce the community in general, and if possible the Rulers themselves, to accept?

What kind of fiction?

Nothing new; something like an Eastern tale of what, according to the poets, has happened before now in more than one part of the world. The poets have been believed; but the thing has not happened in our day, and it would be hard to persuade anyone that it could ever happen again.

You seem rather shy of telling this story of yours.

With good reason, as you will see when I have told it.

Out with it; don't be afraid.

d   Well, here it is; though I hardly know how to find the courage or the words to express it. I shall try to convince, first the Rulers and the soldiers, and then the whole community, that all that nurture and education which we gave them was only something they seemed to experience as it were in a dream. In reality they were the whole time down inside the earth, being moulded and fostered while their arms and all their equipment were being fashioned also; and at last, when they were complete, the earth sent them up from her womb into the light of day. So now they must think of the land
e   they dwell in as a mother and nurse, whom they must take thought for and defend against any attack, and of their fellow citizens as brothers born of the same soil.

You might well be bashful about coming out with your fiction.

415 No doubt; but still you must hear the rest of the story. It is true, we shall tell our people in this fable, that all of you in this land are brothers; but the god who fashioned you mixed gold in the composition of those among you who are fit to rule, so that they are of the most precious quality; and he put silver in the Auxiliaries, and iron and brass in the farmers and craftsmen. Now, since you are all of one stock, although your chil-
b   dren will generally be like their parents, sometimes a golden parent may have a silver child or a silver parent a golden one, and so on with all the other combinations. So the

---

*[What Cornford translates as "bold flight of invention" is usually rendered "noble lie." Cornford claims this common translation is unfair to "Plato's harmless allegory." Other scholars are not so generous. For a discussion of the issues, see the bibliography for books on the *Republic*.]

first and chief injunction laid by heaven upon the Rulers is that, among all the things of
which they must show themselves good guardians, there is none that needs to be so
carefully watched as the mixture of metals in the souls of the children. If a child of
their own is born with an alloy of iron or brass, they must, without the smallest pity,   c
assign him the station proper to his nature and thrust him out among the craftsmen or
the farmers. If, on the contrary, these classes produce a child with gold or silver in his
composition, they will promote him, according to his value, to be a Guardian or an
Auxiliary. They will appeal to a prophecy that ruin will come upon the state when it
passes into the keeping of a man of iron or brass. Such is the story; can you think of
any device to make them believe it?

Not in the first generation; but their sons and descendants might believe it, and fi-   d
nally the rest of mankind.

Well, said I, even so it might have a good effect in making them care more for
the commonwealth and for one another; for I think I see what you mean.

So, I continued, we will leave the success of our story to the care of popular tradition; and now let us arm these sons of Earth and lead them, under the command of
their Rulers, to the site of our city. There let them look round for the best place to fix
their camp, from which they will be able to control any rebellion against the laws from   e
within and to beat off enemies who may come from without like wolves to attack the
fold. When they have pitched their camp and offered sacrifice to the proper divinities,
they must arrange their sleeping quarters; and these must be sufficient to shelter them
from winter cold and summer heat.

Naturally. You mean they are going to live there?

Yes, said I; but live like soldiers, not like men of business.

What is the difference?   416

I will try to explain. It would be very strange if a shepherd were to disgrace himself by keeping, for the protection of his flock, dogs who were so ill-bred and badly
trained that hunger or unruliness or some bad habit or other would set them worrying
the sheep and behaving no better than wolves. We must take every precaution against   b
our Auxiliaries treating the citizens in any such way and, because they are stronger,
turning into savage tyrants instead of friendly allies; and they will have been furnished
with the best of safeguards, if they have really been educated in the right way.

But surely there is nothing wrong with their education.

We must not be too positive about that, my dear Glaucon; but we can be sure of
what we said not long ago, that if they are to have the best chance of being gentle and   c
humane to one another and to their charges, they must have the right education, whatever that may be.

We were certainly right there.

Then besides that education, it is only common sense to say that the dwellings
and other belongings provided for them must be such as will neither make them less
perfect Guardians nor encourage them to maltreat their fellow citizens.   d

True.

With that end in view, let us consider how they should live and be housed. First,
none of them must possess any private property beyond the barest necessaries. Next,
no one is to have any dwelling or store-house that is not open for all to enter at will.
Their food, in the quantities required by men of temperance and courage who are in   e
training for war, they will receive from the other citizens as the wages of their
guardianship, fixed so that there shall be just enough for the year with nothing over;
and they will have meals in common and all live together like soldiers in a camp. Gold

and silver, we shall tell them, they will not need, having the divine counterparts of those metals always in their souls as a god-given possession, whose purity it is not

417   lawful to sully by the acquisition of that mortal dross, current among mankind, which has been the occasion of so many unholy deeds. They alone of all the citizens are forbidden to touch and handle silver or gold, or to come under the same roof with them, or wear them as ornaments, or drink from vessels made of them. This manner of life will be their salvation and make them the saviours of the commonwealth. If ever they should come to possess land of their own and houses and money, they will give up

b   their guardianship for the management of their farms and households and become tyrants at enmity with their fellow citizens instead of allies. And so they will pass all their lives in hating and being hated, plotting and being plotted against, in much greater fear of their enemies at home than of any foreign foe, and fast heading for the destruction that will soon overwhelm their country with themselves. For all these reasons let us say that this is how our Guardians are to be housed and otherwise provided for, and let us make laws accordingly.

By all means, said Glaucon.

BOOK IV

*   *   *

So now at last, son of Ariston, said I, your commonwealth is established. The

427^d next thing is to bring to bear upon it all the light you can get from any quarter, with the help of your brother and Polemarchus and all the rest, in the hope that we may see where justice is to be found in it and where injustice, how they differ, and which of the two will bring happiness to its possessor, no matter whether gods and men see that he has it or not.

e   Nonsense, said Glaucon; you promised to conduct the search yourself, because it would be a sin not to uphold justice by every means in your power.

That is true; I must do as you say, but you must all help.

We will.

I suspect, then, we may find what we are looking for in this way. I take it that our state, having been founded and built up on the right lines, is good in the complete sense of the word.

It must be.

Obviously, then, it is wise, brave, temperate, and just.

Obviously.

Then if we find some of these qualities in it, the remainder will be the one we

428   have not found. It is as if we were looking somewhere for one of any four things: if we detected that one immediately, we should be satisfied; whereas if we recognized the other three first, that would be enough to indicate the thing we wanted; it could only be the remaining one. So here we have four qualities. Had we not better follow that method in looking for the one we want?

Surely.

To begin then: the first quality to come into view in our state seems to be its wis-

b   dom; and there appears to be something odd about this quality.

What is there odd about it?

I think the state we have described really has wisdom; for it will be prudent in counsel, won't it?

Yes.

And prudence in counsel is clearly a form of knowledge; good counsel cannot be due to ignorance and stupidity.

Clearly.

But there are many and various kinds of knowledge in our commonwealth. There   c
is the knowledge possessed by the carpenters or the smiths, and the knowledge how to raise crops. Are we to call the state wise and prudent on the strength of these forms of skill?

No; they would only make it good at furniture-making or working in copper or agriculture.

Well then, is there any form of knowledge, possessed by some among the citizens of our new-founded commonwealth, which will enable it to take thought, not for   d
some particular interest, but for the best possible conduct of the state as a whole in its internal and external relations?

Yes, there is.

What is it, and where does it reside?

It is precisely that art of guardianship which resides in those Rulers whom we just now called Guardians in the full sense.

And what would you call the state on the strength of that knowledge?

Prudent and truly wise.   e

And do you think there will be more or fewer of these genuine Guardians in our state than there will be smiths?

Far fewer.

Fewer, in fact, than any of those other groups who are called after the kind of skill they possess?

Much fewer.

So, if a state is constituted on natural principles, the wisdom it possesses as a whole will be due to the knowledge residing in the smallest part, the one which takes the lead and governs the rest. Such knowledge is the only kind that deserves the name   429
of wisdom, and it appears to be ordained by nature that the class privileged to possess it should be the smallest of all.

Quite true.

Here then we have more or less made out one of our four qualities and its seat in the structure of the commonwealth.

To my satisfaction, at any rate.

Next there is courage. It is not hard to discern that quality or the part of the community in which it resides so as to entitle the whole to be called brave.

Why do you say so?

Because anyone who speaks of a state as either brave or cowardly can only be   b
thinking of that part of it which takes the field and fights in its defence; the reason being, I imagine, that the character of the state is not determined by the bravery or cowardice of the other parts.

No.

Courage, then, is another quality which a community owes to a certain part of itself. And its being brave will mean that, in this part, it possesses the power of preserving, in all circumstances, a conviction about the sort of things that it is right to be   c
afraid of—the conviction implanted by the education which the law-giver has established. Is not that what you mean by courage?

I do not quite understand. Will you say it again?

I am saying that courage means preserving something.

Yes, but what?

The conviction, inculcated by lawfully established education, about the sort of things which may rightly be feared. When I added "in all circumstances," I meant preserving it always and never abandoning it, whether under the influence of pain or of pleasure, of desire or of fear. If you like, I will give an illustration.

Please do.

You know how dyers who want wool to take a purple dye, first select the white wool from among all the other colours, next treat it very carefully to make it take the dye in its full brilliance, and only then dip it in the vat. Dyed in that way, wool gets a fast colour, which no washing, even with soap, will rob of its brilliance; whereas if they choose wool of any colour but white, or if they neglect to prepare it, you know what happens.

Yes, it looks washed-out and ridiculous.

That illustrates the result we were doing our best to achieve when we were choosing our fighting men and training their minds and bodies. Our only purpose was to contrive influences whereby they might take the colour of our institutions like a dye, so that, in virtue of having both the right temperament and the right education, their convictions about what ought to be feared and on all other subjects might be indelibly fixed, never to be washed out by pleasure and pain, desire and fear, solvents more terribly effective than all the soap and fuller's earth in the world. Such a power of constantly preserving, in accordance with our institutions, the right conviction about the things which ought, or ought not, to be feared, is what I call courage. That is my position, unless you have some objection to make.

None at all, he replied; if the belief were such as might be found in a slave or an animal—correct, but not produced by education—you would hardly describe it as in accordance with our institutions, and you would give it some other name than courage.

Quite true.

Then I accept your account of courage.

You will do well to accept it, at any rate as applying to the courage of the ordinary citizen; if you like we will go into it more fully some other time. At present we are in search of justice, rather than of courage; and for that purpose we have said enough.

I quite agree.

Two qualities, I went on, still remain to be made out in our state, temperance and the object of our whole inquiry, justice. Can we discover justice without troubling ourselves further about temperance?

I do not know, and I would rather not have justice come to light first, if that means that we should not go on to consider temperance. So if you want to please me, take temperance first.

Of course I have every wish to please you.

Do go on then.

I will. At first sight, temperance seems more like some sort of concord or harmony than the other qualities did.

How so?

Temperance surely means a kind of orderliness, a control of certain pleasures and appetites. People use the expression, "master of oneself," whatever that means, and various other phrases that point the same way.

Quite true.

Is not "master of oneself" an absurd expression? A man who was master of him-   431
self would presumably be also subject to himself, and the subject would be master; for
all these terms apply to the same person.

No doubt.

I think, however, the phrase means that within the man himself, in his soul, there
is a better part and a worse; and that he is his own master when the part which is better
by nature has the worse under its control. It is certainly a term of praise; whereas it is
considered a disgrace, when, through bad breeding or bad company, the better part is
overwhelmed by the worse, like a small force outnumbered by a multitude. A man in   b
that condition is called a slave to himself and intemperate.

Probably that is what is meant.

Then now look at our newly founded state and you will find one of these two
conditions realized there. You will agree that it deserves to be called master of itself, if
temperance and self-mastery exist where the better part rules the worse.

Yes, I can see that is true.

It is also true that the great mass of multifarious appetites and pleasures and
pains will be found to occur chiefly in children and women and slaves, and, among free
men so called, in the inferior multitude; whereas the simple and moderate desires   c
which, with the aid of reason and right belief, are guided by reflection, you will find
only in a few, and those with the best inborn dispositions and the best educated.

Yes, certainly.

Do you see that this state of things will exist in your commonwealth, where the
desires of the inferior multitude will be controlled by the desires and wisdom of the su-   d
perior few? Hence, if any society can be called master of itself and in control of pleasures and desires, it will be ours.

Quite so.

On all these grounds, then, we may describe it as temperate. Furthermore, in our
state, if anywhere, the governors and the governed will share the same conviction on
the question of who ought to rule. Don't you think so?   e

I am quite sure of it.

Then, if that is their state of mind, in which of the two classes of citizens will
temperance reside—in the governors or in the governed?

In both, I suppose.

So we were not wrong in divining a resemblance between temperance and some
kind of harmony. Temperance is not like courage and wisdom, which made the state
wise and brave by residing each in one particular part. Temperance works in a different   432
way; it extends throughout the whole gamut of the state, producing a consonance of all
its elements from the weakest to the strongest as measured by any standard you like to
take—wisdom, bodily strength, numbers, or wealth. So we are entirely justified in
identifying with temperance this unanimity or harmonious agreement between the naturally superior and inferior elements on the question which of the two should govern,
whether in the state or in the individual.

I fully agree.   b

Good, said I. We have discovered in our commonwealth three out of our four
qualities, to the best of our present judgment. What is the remaining one, required to
make up its full complement of goodness? For clearly this will be justice.

Clearly.

Now is the moment, then, Glaucon, for us to keep the closest watch, like hunts-
men standing round a covert, to make sure that justice does not slip through and vanish

c   undetected. It must certainly be somewhere hereabouts; so keep your eyes open for a view of the quarry, and if you see it first, give me the alert.

I wish I could, he answered; but you will do better to give me a lead and not count on me for more than eyes to see what you show me.

Pray for luck, then, and follow me.

I will, if you will lead on.

The thicket looks rather impenetrable, said I; too dark for it to be easy to start up

d   the game. However, we must push on.

Of course we must.

Here I gave the view halloo. Glaucon, I exclaimed, I believe we are on the track and the quarry is not going to escape us altogether.

That is good news.

Really, I said, we have been extremely stupid. All this time the thing has been

e   under our very noses from the start, and we never saw it. We have been as absurd as a person who hunts for something he has all the time got in his hand. Instead of looking at the thing, we have been staring into the distance. No doubt that is why it escaped us.

What do you mean?

I believe we have been talking about the thing all this while without ever understanding that we were giving some sort of account of it.

Do come to the point. I am all ears.

433   Listen, then, and judge whether I am right. You remember how, when we first began to establish our commonwealth and several times since, we have laid down, as a universal principle, that everyone ought to perform the one function in the community for which his nature best suited him. Well, I believe that that principle, or some form of it, is justice.

We certainly laid that down.

Yes, and surely we have often heard people say that justice means minding one's

b   own business and not meddling with other men's concerns; and we have often said so ourselves.

We have.

Well, my friend, it may be that this minding of one's own business, when it takes a certain form, is actually the same thing as justice. Do you know what makes me think so?

No, tell me.

I think that this quality which makes it possible for the three we have already considered, wisdom, courage, and temperance, to take their place in the commonwealth, and so long as it remains present secures their continuance, must be the re-

c   maining one. And we said that, when three of the four were found, the one left over would be justice.

It must be so.

Well now, if we had to decide which of these qualities will contribute most to the excellence of our commonwealth, it would be hard to say whether it was the unanimity of rulers and subjects, or the soldier's fidelity to the established conviction about what is, or is not, to be feared, or the watchful intelligence of the Rulers; or whether its ex-

d   cellence were not above all due to the observance by everyone, child or woman, slave or freeman or artisan, ruler or ruled, of this principle that each one should do his own proper work without interfering with others.

It would be hard to decide, no doubt.

It seems, then, that this principle can at any rate claim to rival wisdom, temperance, and courage as conducive to the excellence of a state. And would you not say that the only possible competitor of these qualities must be justice?

Yes, undoubtedly.

Here is another thing which points to the same conclusion. The judging of law-suits is a duty that you will lay upon your Rulers, isn't it?

Of course.

And the chief aim of their decisions will be that neither party shall have what belongs to another or be deprived of what is his own.

Yes.

Because that is just?

Yes.

So here again justice admittedly means that a man should possess and concern himself with what properly belongs to him.

True.

Again, do you agree with me that no great harm would be done to the community by a general interchange of most forms of work, the carpenter and the cobbler exchanging their positions and their tools and taking on each other's jobs, or even the same man undertaking both?

Yes, there would not be much harm in that.

But I think you will also agree that another kind of interchange would be disastrous. Suppose, for instance, someone whom nature designed to be an artisan or tradesman should be emboldened by some advantage, such as wealth or command of votes or bodily strength, to try to enter the order of fighting men; or some member of that order should aspire, beyond his merits, to a seat in the council-chamber of the Guardians. Such interference and exchange of social positions and tools, or the attempt to combine all these forms of work in the same person, would be fatal to the commonwealth.

Most certainly.

Where there are three orders, then, any plurality of functions or shifting from one order to another is not merely utterly harmful to the community, but one might fairly call it the extreme of wrongdoing. And you will agree that to do the greatest of wrongs to one's own community is injustice.

Surely.

This, then, is injustice. And, conversely, let us repeat that when each order—tradesman, Auxiliary, Guardian—keeps to its own proper business in the commonwealth and does its own work, that is justice and what makes a just society.

I entirely agree.

We must not be too positive yet, said I. If we find that this same quality when it exists in the individual can equally be identified with justice, then we can at once give our assent; there will be no more to be said; otherwise, we shall have to look further. For the moment, we had better finish the inquiry which we began with the idea that it would be easier to make out the nature of justice in the individual if we first tried to study it in something on a larger scale. That larger thing we took to be a state, and so we set about constructing the best one we could, being sure of finding justice in a state that was good. The discovery we made there must now be applied to the individual. If it is confirmed, all will be well; but if we find that justice in the individual is something different, we must go back to the state and test our new result. Perhaps if we brought the two cases into contact like flint and steel, we might strike out between them the spark of justice, and in its light confirm the conception in our own minds.

A good method. Let us follow it.

Now, I continued, if two things, one large, the other small, are called by the same name, they will be alike in that respect to which the common name applies. Accordingly, in so far as the quality of justice is concerned, there will be no difference between a just man and a just society.

No.

Well, but we decided that a society was just when each of the three types of human character it contained performed its own function; and again, it was temperate and brave and wise by virtue of certain other affections and states of mind of those same types.

True.

c   Accordingly, my friend, if we are to be justified in attributing those same virtues to the individual, we shall expect to find that the individual soul contains the same three elements and that they are affected in the same way as are the corresponding types in society.

That follows.

Here, then, we have stumbled upon another little problem: Does the soul contain these three elements or not?

Not such a very little one, I think. It may be a true saying, Socrates, that what is worthwhile is seldom easy.

Apparently; and let me tell you, Glaucon, it is my belief that we shall never reach
d   the exact truth in this matter by following our present methods of discussion; the road leading to that goal is longer and more laborious. However, perhaps we can find an answer that will be up to the standard we have so far maintained in our speculations.

Is not that enough? I should be satisfied for the moment.

Well, it will more than satisfy me, I replied.

Don't be disheartened, then, but go on.

e   Surely, I began, we must admit that the same elements and characters that appear in the state must exist in every one of us; where else could they have come from? It would be absurd to imagine that among peoples with a reputation for a high-spirited character, like the Thracians and Scythians and northerners generally, the states have not derived that character from their individual members; or that it is otherwise with the love of knowledge, which would be ascribed chiefly to our own part of the world,
436   or with the love of money, which one would specially connect with Phoenicia and Egypt.

Certainly.

So far, then, we have a fact which is easily recognized. But here the difficulty begins. Are we using the same part of ourselves in all these three experiences, or a different part in each? Do we gain knowledge with one part, feel anger with another, and with yet a third desire the pleasures of food, sex, and so on? Or is the whole soul at
b   work in every impulse and in all these forms of behaviour? The difficulty is to answer that question satisfactorily.

I quite agree.

Let us approach the problem whether these elements are distinct or identical in this way. It is clear that the same thing cannot act in two opposite ways or be in two opposite states at the same time, with respect to the same part of itself, and in relation
c   to the same object. So if we find such contradictory actions or states among the elements concerned, we shall know that more than one must have been involved.

Very well.

Consider this proposition of mine, then. Can the same thing, at the same time and with respect to the same part of itself, be at rest and in motion?

Certainly not.

We had better state this principle in still more precise terms, to guard against misunderstanding later on. Suppose a man is standing still, but moving his head and arms. We should not allow anyone to say that the same man was both at rest and in   d motion at the same time, but only that part of him was at rest, part in motion. Isn't that so?

Yes.

An ingenious objector might refine still further and argue that a peg-top, spinning with its peg fixed at the same spot, or indeed any body that revolves in the same place, is both at rest and in motion as a whole. But we should not agree, because the parts in respect of which such a body is moving and at rest are not the same. It contains an axis and a circumference; and in respect of the axis it is at rest inasmuch as the axis   e is not inclined in any direction, while in respect of the circumference it revolves; and if, while it is spinning, the axis does lean out of the perpendicular in all directions, then it is in no way at rest.

That is true.

No objection of that sort, then, will disconcert us or make us believe that the same thing can ever act or be acted upon in two opposite ways, or be two opposite   437 things, at the same time, in respect of the same part of itself, and in relation to the same object.

I can answer for myself at any rate.

Well, anyhow, as we do not want to spend time in reviewing all such objections to make sure that they are unsound, let us proceed on this assumption, with the understanding that, if we ever come to think otherwise, all the consequences based upon it will fall to the ground.

Yes, that is a good plan.

Now, would you class such things as assent and dissent, striving after something   b and refusing it, attraction and repulsion, as pairs of opposite actions or states of mind—no matter which?

Yes, they are opposites.

And would you not class all appetites such as hunger and thirst, and again willing and wishing, with the affirmative members of those pairs I have just mentioned? For instance, you would say that the soul of a man who desires something is striving   c after it, or trying to draw to itself the thing it wishes to possess, or again, in so far as it is willing to have its want satisfied, it is giving its assent to its own longing, as if to an inward question.

Yes.

And, on the other hand, disinclination, unwillingness, and dislike, we should class on the negative side with acts of rejection or repulsion.

Of course.   d

That being so, shall we say that appetites form one class, the most conspicuous being those we call thirst and hunger?

Yes.

Thirst being desire for drink, hunger for food?

Yes.

Now, is thirst, just in so far as it is thirst, a desire in the soul for anything more than simply drink? Is it, for instance, thirst for hot drink or for cold, for much drink or for little, or in a word for drink of any particular kind? Is it not rather true that you will   e have a desire for cold drink only if you are feeling hot as well as thirsty, and for hot drink only if you are feeling cold; and if you want much drink or little, that will be because your thirst is a great thirst or a little one? But, just in itself, thirst or hunger is a desire for nothing more than its natural object, drink or food, pure and simple.

Yes, he agreed, each desire, just in itself, is simply for its own natural object. When the object is of such and such a particular kind, the desire will be correspondingly qualified.

438   We must be careful here, or we might be troubled by the objection that no one desires mere food and drink, but always wholesome food and drink. We shall be told that what we desire is always something that is good; so if thirst is a desire, its object must be, like that of any other desire, something—drink or whatever it may be—that will be good for one.

Yes, there might seem to be something in that objection.

But surely, wherever you have two correlative terms, if one is qualified, the other

b   must always be qualified too; whereas if one is unqualified, so is the other.

I don't understand.

Well, "greater" is a relative term; and the greater is greater than the less; if it is much greater, then the less is much less; if it is greater at some moment, past or future, then the less is less at that same moment. The same principle applies to all such correl-

c   atives, like "more" and "fewer," "double" and "half"; and again to terms like "heavier" and "lighter," "quicker" and "slower," and to things like hot and cold.

Yes.

Or take the various branches of knowledge: is it not the same there? The object of knowledge pure and simple is the knowable—if that is the right word—without any qualification; whereas a particular kind of knowledge has an object of a particular kind.

d   For example, as soon as men learnt how to build houses, their craft was distinguished from others under the name of architecture, because it had a unique character, which was itself due to the character of its object; and all other branches of craft and knowledge were distinguished in the same way.

True.

This, then, if you understand me now, is what I meant by saying that, where

e   there are two correlatives, the one is qualified if, and only if, the other is so. I am not saying that the one must have the same quality as the other—that the science of health and disease is itself healthy and diseased, or the knowledge of good and evil is itself good and evil—but only that, as soon as you have a knowledge that is restricted to a particular kind of object, namely health and disease, the knowledge itself becomes a particular kind of knowledge. Hence we no longer call it merely knowledge, which would have for its object whatever can be known, but we add the qualification and call it medical science.

I understand now and I agree.

439   Now, to go back to thirst: is not that one of these relative terms? It is essentially thirst for something.

Yes, for drink.

And if the drink desired is of a certain kind, the thirst will be correspondingly qualified. But thirst which is just simply thirst is not for drink of any particular sort—much or little, good or bad—but for drink pure and simple.

Quite so.

We conclude, then, that the soul of a thirsty man, just in so far as he is thirsty,

b   has no other wish than to drink. That is the object of its craving, and towards that it is impelled.

That is clear.

Now if there is ever something which at the same time pulls it the opposite way, that something must be an element in the soul other than the one which is thirsting and driving it like a beast to drink; in accordance with our principle that the same thing cannot behave in two opposite ways at the same time and towards the same object with the same part of itself. It is like an archer drawing the bow: it is not accurate to say that his hands are at the same time both pushing and pulling it. One hand does the pushing, the other the pulling.

Exactly.   c

Now, is it sometimes true that people are thirsty and yet unwilling to drink?

Yes, often.

What, then, can one say of them, if not that their soul contains something which urges them to drink and something which holds them back, and that this latter is a distinct thing and overpowers the other?

I agree.

And is it not true that the intervention of this inhibiting principle in such cases al-   d
ways has its origin in reflection; whereas the impulses driving and dragging the soul are engendered by external influences and abnormal conditions?

Evidently.

We shall have good reason, then, to assert that they are two distinct principles. We may call that part of the soul whereby it reflects, rational; and the other, with which it feels hunger and thirst and is distracted by sexual passion and all the other desires, we will call irrational appetite, associated with pleasure in the replenishment of certain wants.

Yes, there is good ground for that view.   e

Let us take it, then, that we have now distinguished two elements in the soul. What of that passionate element which makes us feel angry and indignant? Is that a third, or identical in nature with one of those two?

It might perhaps be identified with appetite.

I am more inclined to put my faith in a story I once heard about Leontius, son of Aglaion. On his way up from the Piraeus outside the north wall, he noticed the bodies of some criminals lying on the ground, with the executioner standing by them. He wanted to go and look at them, but at the same time he was disgusted and tried to turn away. He struggled for some time and covered his eyes, but at last the desire was too much for him. Opening his eyes wide, he ran up to the bodies and cried, "There you   440
are, curse you; feast yourselves on this lovely sight!"

Yes, I have heard that story too.

The point of it surely is that anger is sometimes in conflict with appetite, as if they were two distinct principles. Do we not often find a man whose desires would   b
force him to go against his reason, reviling himself and indignant with this part of his nature which is trying to put constraint on him? It is like a struggle between two factions, in which indignation takes the side of reason. But I believe you have never observed, in yourself or anyone else, indignation make common cause with appetite in behaviour which reason decides to be wrong.

No, I am sure I have not.

Again, take a man who feels he is in the wrong. The more generous his nature,   c
the less can he be indignant at any suffering, such as hunger and cold, inflicted by the man he has injured. He recognizes such treatment as just, and, as I say, his spirit refuses to be roused against it.

That is true.

But now contrast one who thinks it is he that is being wronged. His spirit boils
d   with resentment and sides with the right as he conceives it. Persevering all the more for
the hunger and cold and other pains he suffers, it triumphs and will not give in until its
gallant struggle has ended in success or death; or until the restraining voice of reason,
like a shepherd calling off his dog, makes it relent.

An apt comparison, he said; and in fact it fits the relation of our Auxiliaries to the
Rulers: they were to be like watch-dogs obeying the shepherds of the commonwealth.

e   Yes, you understand very well what I have in mind. But do you see how we have
changed our view? A moment ago we were supposing this spirited element to be something of the nature of appetite; but now it appears that, when the soul is divided into
factions, it is far more ready to be up in arms on the side of reason.

Quite true.

Is it, then, distinct from the rational element or only a particular form of it, so
that the soul will contain no more than two elements, reason and appetite? Or is the
441   soul like the state, which had three orders to hold it together, traders, Auxiliaries, and
counsellors? Does the spirited element make a third, the natural auxiliary of reason,
when not corrupted by bad upbringing?

It must be a third.

Yes, I said, provided it can be shown to be distinct from reason, as we saw it was
from appetite.

That is easily proved. You can see that much in children: they are full of passion-
b   ate feelings from their very birth; but some, I should say, never become rational, and
most of them only late in life.

A very sound observation, said I, the truth of which may also be seen in animals.
And besides, there is the witness of Homer in that line I quoted before: "He smote his
breast and spoke, chiding his heart." The poet is plainly thinking of the two elements
c   as distinct, when he makes the one which has chosen the better course after reflection
rebuke the other for its unreasoning passion.

I entirely agree.

And so, after a stormy passage, we have reached the land. We are fairly agreed
that the same three elements exist alike in the state and in the individual soul.

That is so.

d   Does it not follow at once that state and individual will be wise or brave by
virtue of the same element in each and in the same way? Both will possess in the same
manner any quality that makes for excellence.

That must be true.

Then it applies to justice: we shall conclude that a man is just in the same way
that a state was just. And we have surely not forgotten that justice in the state meant
that each of the three orders in it was doing its own proper work. So we may hence-
e   forth bear in mind that each one of us likewise will be a just person, fulfilling his
proper function, only if the several parts of our nature fulfil theirs.

Certainly.

And it will be the business of reason to rule with wisdom and forethought on behalf of the entire soul; while the spirited element ought to act as its subordinate and
ally. The two will be brought into accord, as we said earlier, by that combination of
442   mental and bodily training which will tune up one string of the instrument and relax
the other, nourishing the reasoning part on the study of noble literature and allaying the
other's wildness by harmony and rhythm. When both have been thus nurtured and
trained to know their own true functions, they must be set in command over the appetites, which form the greater part of each man's soul and are by nature insatiably

covetous. They must keep watch lest this part, by battening on the pleasures that are called bodily, should grow so great and powerful that it will no longer keep to its own work, but will try to enslave the others and usurp a dominion to which it has no right,   b thus turning the whole of life upside down. At the same time, those two together will be the best of guardians for the entire soul and for the body against all enemies from without: the one will take counsel, while the other will do battle, following its ruler's commands and by its own bravery giving effect to the ruler's designs.

Yes, that is all true.

And so we call an individual brave in virtue of this spirited part of his nature,   c when, in spite of pain or pleasure, it holds fast to the injunctions of reason about what he ought or ought not to be afraid of.

True.

And wise in virtue of that small part which rules and issues these injunctions, possessing as it does the knowledge of what is good for each of the three elements and for all of them in common.

Certainly.

And, again, temperate by reason of the unanimity and concord of all three, when   d there is no internal conflict between the ruling element and its two subjects, but all are agreed that reason should be ruler.

Yes, that is an exact account of temperance, whether in the state or in the individual.

Finally, a man will be just by observing the principle we have so often stated.

Necessarily.

Now is there any indistinctness in our vision of justice, that might make it seem somehow different from what we found it to be in the state?   e

I don't think so.

Because, if we have any lingering doubt, we might make sure by comparing it with some commonplace notions. Suppose, for instance, that a sum of money were entrusted to our state or to an individual of corresponding character and training, would   443 anyone imagine that such a person would be specially likely to embezzle it?

No.

And would he not be incapable of sacrilege and theft, or of treachery to friend or country; never false to an oath or any other compact; the last to be guilty of adultery or of neglecting parents or the due service of the gods?

Yes.

And the reason for all this is that each part of his nature is exercising its proper   b function, of ruling or of being ruled.

Yes, exactly.

Are you satisfied, then, that justice is the power which produces states or individuals of whom that is true, or must we look further?

There is no need; I am quite satisfied.

And so our dream has come true—I mean the inkling we had that, by some happy chance, we had lighted upon a rudimentary form of justice from the very mo-   c ment when we set about founding our commonwealth. Our principle that the born shoemaker or carpenter had better stick to his trade turns out to have been an adumbration of justice; and that is why it has helped us. But in reality justice, though evidently analogous to this principle, is not a matter of external behaviour, but of the inward self and of attending to all that is, in the fullest sense, a man's proper concern. The just man   d does not allow the several elements in his soul to usurp one another's functions; he is indeed one who sets his house in order, by self-mastery and discipline coming to be at

peace with himself, and bringing into tune those three parts, like the terms in the proportion of a musical scale, the highest and lowest notes and the mean between them,
with all the intermediate intervals. Only when he has linked these parts together in
e   well-tempered harmony and has made himself one man instead of many, will he be
ready to go about whatever he may have to do, whether it be making money and satisfying bodily wants, or business transactions, or the affairs of state. In all these fields
when he speaks of just and honourable conduct, he will mean the behaviour that helps
to produce and to preserve this habit of mind; and by wisdom he will mean the knowledge which presides over such conduct. Any action which tends to break down this
444   habit will be for him unjust; and the notions governing it he will call ignorance and
folly.

That is perfectly true, Socrates.

Good, said I. I believe we should not be thought altogether mistaken, if we
claimed to have discovered the just man and the just state, and wherein their justice
consists.

Indeed we should not.

Shall we make that claim, then?

Yes, we will.

So be it, said I. Next, I suppose, we have to consider injustice.

Evidently.

b   This must surely be a sort of civil strife among the three elements, whereby they
usurp and encroach upon one another's functions and some one part of the soul rises
up in rebellion against the whole, claiming a supremacy to which it has no right because its nature fits it only to be the servant of the ruling principle. Such turmoil and
aberration we shall, I think, identify with injustice, intemperance, cowardice, ignorance, and in a word with all wickedness.

Exactly.

c   And now that we know the nature of justice and injustice, we can be equally
clear about what is meant by acting justly and again by unjust action and wrongdoing.

How do you mean?

Plainly, they are exactly analogous to those wholesome and unwholesome activities which respectively produce a healthy or unhealthy condition in the body; in the
d   same way just and unjust conduct produce a just or unjust character. Justice is produced in the soul, like health in the body, by establishing the elements concerned in
their natural relations of control and subordination, whereas injustice is like disease
and means that this natural order is inverted.

Quite so.

e   It appears, then, that virtue is as it were the health and comeliness and well-being
of the soul, as wickedness is disease, deformity, and weakness.

True.

And also that virtue and wickedness are brought about by one's way of life, honourable or disgraceful.

That follows.

445   So now it only remains to consider which is the more profitable course: to do
right and live honourably and be just, whether or not anyone knows what manner of
man you are, or to do wrong and be unjust, provided that you can escape the chastise-
ment which might make you a better man.

But really, Socrates, it seems to me ridiculous to ask that question now that the
nature of justice and injustice has been brought to light. People think that all the luxury

and wealth and power in the world cannot make life worth living when the bodily con-   b
stitution is going to rack and ruin; and are we to believe that, when the very principle
whereby we live is deranged and corrupted, life will be worth living so long as a man
can do as he will, and wills to do anything rather than to free himself from vice and
wrong doing and to win justice and virtue?

Yes, I replied, it is a ridiculous question.

Nevertheless, I continued, we are now within sight of the clearest possible proof
of our conclusions, and we ought not to slacken our efforts.

No, anything rather than that.

If you will take your stand with me, then, on this point of vantage to which we   c
have climbed, you shall see all the forms that evil takes, or at least all that it seems
worthwhile to look at.

Lead the way and tell me what you see.

What I see is that, whereas there is only one form of excellence, imperfection exists in innumerable shapes, of which there are four that specially deserve notice.

What do you mean?

It looks as if there were as many types of character as there are distinct varieties
of political constitution.

How many?

Five of each.   d

Will you define them?

Yes, I said. One form of constitution will be the form we have been describing,
though it may be called by two names: monarchy, when there is one man who stands
out above the rest of the Rulers; aristocracy, when there are more than one.

True.

That, then, I regard as a single form; for, so long as they observe our principles
of upbringing and education, whether the Rulers be one or more, they will not subvert   e
the important institutions in our commonwealth.

Naturally not.

Book V

Such, then, is the type of state or constitution that I call good and right, and the corre-   449
sponding type of man. By this standard, the other forms in which a state or an individual character may be organized are depraved and wrong. There are four of these vicious forms.

What are they?

Here I was going on to describe these forms in the order in which, as I thought,
they develop one from another, when Polemarchus, who was sitting a little way from   b
Adeimantus, reached out his hand and took hold of his garment by the shoulder. Lean-
ing forward and drawing Adeimantus towards him, he whispered something in his ear,
of which I only caught the words: What shall we do? Shall we leave it alone?

Certainly not, said Adeimantus, raising his voice.

What is this, I asked, that you are not going to leave alone?

You, he replied.

Why, in particular? I inquired.   c

Because we think you are shirking the discussion of a very important part of the subject and trying to cheat us out of an explanation. Everyone, you said, must of course see that the maxim "friends have all things in common" applies to women and children. You thought we should pass over such a casual remark!

But wasn't that right, Adeimantus? said I.

Yes, he said, but "right" in this case, as in others, needs to be defined. There may d be many ways of having things in common, and you must tell us which you mean. We have been waiting a long time for you to say something about the conditions in which children are to be born and brought up and your whole plan of having wives and children held in common. This seems to us a matter in which right or wrong management will make all the difference to society; and now, instead of going into it thoroughly, you are passing on to some other form of constitution. So we came to the resolution 450 which you overheard, not to let you off discussing it as fully as all the other institutions.

I will vote for your resolution too, said Glaucon.

In fact, Socrates, Thrasymachus added, you may take it as carried unanimously.

You don't know what you are doing, I said, in holding me up like this. You want to start, all over again, on an enormous subject, just as I was rejoicing at the idea that b we had done with this form of constitution. I was only too glad that my casual remark should be allowed to pass. And now, when you demand an explanation, you little know what a swarm of questions you are stirring up. I let it alone, because I foresaw no end of trouble.

Well, said Thrasymachus, what do you think we came here for—to play pitch-and-toss or to listen to a discussion?

A discussion, no doubt, I replied; but within limits.

No man of sense, said Glaucon, would think the whole of life too long to spend on questions of this importance. But never mind about us; don't be faint-hearted your- c self. Tell us what you think about this question: how our Guardians are to have wives and children in common, and how they will bring up the young in the interval between their birth and education, which is thought to be the most difficult time of all. Do try to explain how all this is to be arranged.

I wish it were as easy as you seem to think, I replied. These arrangements are even more open to doubt than any we have so far discussed. It may be questioned d whether the plan is feasible, and even if entirely feasible, whether it would be for the best. So I have some hesitation in touching on what may seem to be an idle dream.

You need not hesitate, he replied. This is not an unsympathetic audience; we are neither incredulous nor hostile.

Thank you, I said; I suppose that remark is meant to be encouraging.

Certainly it is.

Well, I said, it has just the opposite effect. You would do well to encourage me, if I had any faith in my own understanding of these matters. If one knows the truth, e there is no risk to be feared in speaking about the things one has most at heart among intelligent friends; but if one is still in the position of a doubting inquirer, as I am now, talking becomes a slippery venture. Not that I am afraid of being laughed at—that would be childish—but I am afraid I may miss my footing just where a false step is 451 most to be dreaded and drag my friends down with me in my fall. I devoutly hope, Glaucon, that no nemesis will overtake me for what I am going to say; for I really believe that to kill a man unintentionally is a lighter offence than to mislead him concerning the goodness and justice of social institutions. Better to run that risk among ene- b mies than among friends; so your encouragement is out of place.

Glaucon laughed at this. No, Socrates, he said, if your theory has any untoward effect on us, our blood shall not be on your head; we absolve you of any intention to mislead us. So have no fear.

Well, said I, when a homicide is absolved of all intention, the law holds him clear of guilt; and the same principle may apply to my case.

Yes, so far as that goes, you may speak freely.

We must go back, then, to a subject which ought, perhaps, to have been treated earlier in its proper place; though, after all, it may be suitable that the women should c
have their turn on the stage when the men have quite finished their performance, especially since you are so insistent. In my judgement, then, the question under what conditions people born and educated as we have described should possess wives and children, and how they should treat them, can be rightly settled only by keeping to the course on which we started them at the outset. We undertook to put these men in the position of watch-dogs guarding a flock. Suppose we follow up the analogy and imagine them bred and reared in the same sort of way. We can then see if that plan will suit d
our purpose.

How will that be?

In this way. Which do we think right for watch-dogs: should the females guard the flock and hunt with the males and take a share in all they do, or should they be kept within doors as fit for no more than bearing and feeding their puppies, while all the hard work of looking after the flock is left to the males?

They are expected to take their full share, except that we treat them as not quite e
so strong.

Can you employ any creature for the same work as another, if you do not give them both the same upbringing and education?

No.

Then, if we are to set women to the same tasks as men, we must teach them the 452
same things. They must have the same two branches of training for mind and body and also be taught the art of war, and they must receive the same treatment.

That seems to follow.

Possibly, if these proposals were carried out, they might be ridiculed as involving a good many breaches of custom.

They might indeed.

The most ridiculous—don't you think?—being the notion of women exercising naked along with the men in the wrestling-schools; some of them elderly women too, b
like the old men who still have a passion for exercise when they are wrinkled and not very agreeable to look at.

Yes, that would be thought laughable, according to our present notions.

Now we have started on this subject, we must not be frightened of the many witticisms that might be aimed at such a revolution, not only in the matter of bodily exercise but in the training of women's minds, and not least when it comes to their bearing c
arms and riding on horseback. Having begun upon these rules, we must not draw back from the harsher provisions. The wits may be asked to stop being witty and try to be serious; and we may remind them that it is not so long since the Greeks, like most foreign nations of the present day, thought it ridiculous and shameful for men to be seen naked. When gymnastic exercises were first introduced in Crete and later at Sparta, the humorists had their chance to make fun of them; but when experience had shown that d
nakedness is better uncovered than muffled up, the laughter died down and a practice which the reason approved ceased to look ridiculous to the eye. This shows how idle it is to think anything ludicrous but what is base. One who tries to raise a laugh at any

e   spectacle save that of baseness and folly will also, in his serious moments, set before himself some other standard than goodness of what deserves to be held in honour.

Most assuredly.

453   The first thing to be settled, then, is whether these proposals are feasible; and it must be open to anyone, whether a humorist or serious-minded, to raise the question whether, in the case of mankind, the feminine nature is capable of taking part with the other sex in all occupations, or in none at all, or in some only; and in particular under which of these heads this business of military service falls. Well begun is half done, and would not this be the best way to begin?

Yes.

Shall we take the other side in this debate and argue against ourselves? We do not want the adversary's position to be taken by storm for lack of defenders.

b   I have no objection.

Let us state his case for him. "Socrates and Glaucon," he will say, "there is no need for others to dispute your position; you yourselves, at the very outset of founding your commonwealth, agreed that everyone should do the one work for which nature fits him." Yes, of course; I suppose we did. "And isn't there a very great difference in

c   nature between man and woman?" Yes, surely. "Does not that natural difference imply a corresponding difference in the work to be given to each?" Yes. "But if so, surely you must be mistaken now and contradicting yourselves when you say that men and women, having such widely divergent natures, should do the same things? What is your answer to that, my ingenious friend?"

It is not easy to find one at the moment. I can only appeal to you to state the case on our own side, whatever it may be.

d   This, Glaucon, is one of many alarming objections which I foresaw some time ago. That is why I shrank from touching upon these laws concerning the possession of wives and the rearing of children.

It looks like anything but an easy problem.

True, I said; but whether a man tumbles into a swimming-pool or into mid-ocean, he has to swim all the same. So must we, and try if we can reach the shore, hoping for some Arion's dolphin or other miraculous deliverance to bring us safe to land.

e   I suppose so.

Come then, let us see if we can find the way out. We did agree that different natures should have different occupations, and that the natures of man and woman are different; and yet we are now saying that these different natures are to have the same occupations. Is that the charge against us?

Exactly.

454   It is extraordinary, Glaucon, what an effect the practice of debating has upon people.

Why do you say that?

Because they often seem to fall unconsciously into mere disputes which they mistake for reasonable argument, through being unable to draw the distinctions proper to their subject; and so, instead of a philosophical exchange of ideas, they go off in chase of contradictions which are purely verbal.

I know that happens to many people; but does it apply to us at this moment?

b   Absolutely. At least I am afraid we are slipping unconsciously into a dispute about words. We have been strenuously insisting on the letter of our principle that different natures should not have the same occupations, as if we were scoring a point in a debate; but we have altogether neglected to consider what sort of sameness or difference we meant and in what respect these natures and occupations were to be defined as different or the same. Consequently, we might very well be asking one another whether there is not an opposition in nature between bald and long-haired men, and, when that was admitted, forbid one set to be shoemakers, if the other were following that trade.

That would be absurd.

Yes, but only because we never meant any and every sort of sameness or difference in nature, but the sort that was relevant to the occupations in question. We meant, for instance, that a man and a woman have the same nature if both have a talent for medicine; whereas two men have different natures if one is a born physician, the other a born carpenter.

Yes, of course.

If, then, we find that either the male sex or the female is specially qualified for any particular form of occupation, then that occupation, we shall say, ought to be assigned to one sex or the other. But if the only difference appears to be that the male begets and the female brings forth, we shall conclude that no difference between man and woman has yet been produced that is relevant to our purpose. We shall continue to think it proper for our Guardians and their wives to share in the same pursuits.

And quite rightly.

The next thing will be to ask our opponent to name any profession or occupation in civic life for the purposes of which woman's nature is different from man's.

That is a fair question.

He might reply, as you did just now, that it is not easy to find a satisfactory answer on the spur of the moment, but that there would be no difficulty after a little reflection.

Perhaps.

Suppose, then, we invite him to follow us and see if we can convince him that there is no occupation concerned with the management of social affairs that is peculiar to women. We will confront him with a question: When you speak of a man having a natural talent for something, do you mean that he finds it easy to learn, and after a little instruction can find out much more for himself; whereas a man who is not so gifted learns with difficulty and no amount of instruction and practice will make him even remember what he has been taught? Is the talented man one whose bodily powers are readily at the service of his mind, instead of being a hindrance? Are not these the marks by which you distinguish the presence of a natural gift for any pursuit?

Yes, precisely.

Now do you know of any human occupation in which the male sex is not superior to the female in all these respects? Need I waste time over exceptions like weaving and watching over saucepans and batches of cakes, though women are supposed to be good at such things and get laughed at when a man does them better?

It is true, he replied, in almost everything one sex is easily beaten by the other. No doubt many women are better at many things than many men; but taking the sexes as a whole, it is as you say.

To conclude, then, there is no occupation concerned with the management of social affairs which belongs either to woman or to man, as such. Natural gifts are to be found here and there in both creatures alike; and every occupation is open to both, so far as their natures are concerned, though woman is for all purposes the weaker.

Certainly.

Is that a reason for making over all occupations to men only?

Of course not.

Steps in Cloth-Making. Black-figure lekythos (oil jug) attributed to the potter Amasis (sixth century B.C.). The women on the left are hand spinning thread; those in the center are weaving wool. Given that Greek women generally remained at home fulfilling such domestic occupations, Plato's suggestions in the *Republic* were quite revolutionary. Though he claims that women are "for all purposes the weaker [sex]," Plato's character, Socrates, concludes, "There is no occupation concerned with the management of social affairs which belongs to woman or to man, as such. Natural gifts are to be found here and there in both . . . alike; and every occupation is open to both. . . ." (*The Metropolitan Museum of Art, Fletcher Fund, 1931*)

No, because one woman may have a natural gift for medicine or for music, another may not.

Surely.

456   Is it not also true that a woman may, or may not, be warlike or athletic?

I think so.

And again, one may love knowledge, another hate it; one may be high-spirited, another spiritless?

True again.

It follows that one woman will be fitted by nature to be a Guardian, another will not; because these were the qualities for which we selected our men Guardians. So for the purpose of keeping watch over the commonwealth, woman has the same nature as man, save in so far as she is weaker.

So it appears.

b   It follows that women of this type must be selected to share the life and duties of Guardians with men of the same type, since they are competent and of a like nature, and the same natures must be allowed the same pursuits.

Yes.

We come round, then, to our former position, that there is nothing contrary to

c   nature in giving our Guardians' wives the same training for mind and body. The practice we proposed to establish was not impossible or visionary, since it was in accordance with nature. Rather, the contrary practice which now prevails turns out to be unnatural.

So it appears.

Well, we set out to inquire whether the plan we proposed was feasible and also the best. That it is feasible is now agreed; we must next settle whether it is the best.

Obviously.

Now, for the purpose of producing a woman fit to be a Guardian, we shall not have one education for men and another for women, precisely because the nature to be taken in hand is the same.   d

True.

What is your opinion on the question of one man being better than another? Do you think there is no such difference?

Certainly I do not.

And in this commonwealth of ours which will prove the better men—the Guardians who have received the education we described, or the shoemakers who have been trained to make shoes?

It is absurd to ask such a question.

Very well. So these Guardians will be the best of all the citizens?   e

By far.

And these women the best of all the women?

Yes.

Can anything be better for a commonwealth than to produce in it men and women of the best possible type?

No.

And that result will be brought about by such a system of mental and bodily   457 training as we have described?

Surely.

We may conclude that the institution we proposed was not only practicable, but also the best for the commonwealth.

Yes.

The wives of our Guardians, then, must strip for exercise, since they will be clothed with virtue, and they must take their share in war and in the other social duties of guardianship. They are to have no other occupation; and in these duties the lighter part must fall to the women, because of the weakness of their sex. The man who laughs   b at naked women, exercising their bodies for the best of reasons, is like one that "gathers fruit unripe," for he does not know what it is that he is laughing at or what he is doing. There will never be a finer saying than the one which declares that whatever does good should be held in honour, and the only shame is in doing harm.

That is perfectly true.

So far, then, in regulating the position of women, we may claim to have come safely through with one hazardous proposal, that male and female Guardians shall   c have all occupations in common. The consistency of the argument is an assurance that the plan is a good one and also feasible. We are like swimmers who have breasted the first wave without being swallowed up.

Not such a small wave either.

You will not call it large when you see the next.

Let me have a look at the next one, then.

Here it is: a law which follows from that principle and all that has gone before,   d namely that, of these Guardians, no one man and one woman are to set up house together privately: wives are to be held in common by all; so too are the children, and no parent is to know his own child, nor any child his parent.

It will be much harder to convince people that that is either a feasible plan or a good one.

As to its being a good plan, I imagine no one would deny the immense advantage of wives and children being held in common, provided it can be done. I should expect dispute to arise chiefly over the question of whether it is possible.

e   There may well be a good deal of dispute over both points.

You mean, I must meet attacks on two fronts. I was hoping to escape one by running away: if you agreed it was a good plan, then I should only have had to inquire whether it was feasible.

No, we have seen through that manoeuvre. You will have to defend both positions.

Well, I must pay the penalty for my cowardice. But grant me one favour. Let me
458   indulge my fancy, like one who entertains himself with idle day-dreams on a solitary walk. Before he has any notion how his desires can be realized, he will set aside that question, to save himself the trouble of reckoning what may or may not be possible. He will assume that his wish has come true, and amuse himself with settling all the details of what he means to do then. So a lazy mind encourages itself to be lazier than ever;
b   and I am giving way to the same weakness myself. I want to put off till later that question, how the thing can be done. For the moment, with your leave, I shall assume it to be possible, and ask how the Rulers will work out the details in practice; and I shall argue that the plan, once carried into effect, would be the best thing in the world for our commonwealth and for its Guardians. That is what I shall now try to make out with your help, if you will allow me to postpone the other question.

Very good; I have no objection.

Well, if our Rulers are worthy of the name, and their Auxiliaries likewise, these
c   latter will be ready to do what they are told, and the Rulers, in giving their commands, will themselves obey our laws and will be faithful to their spirit in any details we leave to their discretion.

No doubt.

It is for you, then, as their lawgiver, who has already selected the men, to select for association with them women who are so far as possible of the same natural capac-
d   ity. Now since none of them will have any private home of his own, but they will share the same dwelling and eat at common tables, the two sexes will be together; and meeting without restriction for exercise and all through their upbringing, they will surely be drawn towards union with one another by a necessity of their nature—necessity is not too strong a word, I think?

Not too strong for the constraint of love, which for the mass of mankind is more persuasive and compelling than even the necessity of mathematical proof.

Exactly. But in the next place, Glaucon, anything like unregulated unions would
e   be a profanation in a state whose citizens lead the good life. The Rulers will not allow such a thing.

No, it would not be right.

Clearly, then, we must have marriages, as sacred as we can make them; and this sanctity will attach to those which yield the best results.

Certainly.
459   How are we to get the best results? You must tell me, Glaucon, because I see you keep sporting dogs and a great many game birds at your house; and there is something about their mating and breeding that you must have noticed.

What is that?

In the first place, though they may all be of good stock, are there not some that turn out to be better than the rest?

There are.

And do you breed from all indiscriminately? Are you not careful to breed from the best so far as you can?

Yes.

And from those in their prime, rather than the very young or the very old?   b

Yes.

Otherwise, the stock of your birds or dogs would deteriorate very much, wouldn't it?

It would.

And the same is true of horses or of any animal?

It would be very strange if it were not.

Dear me, said I; we shall need consummate skill in our Rulers, if it is also true of the human race.

Well, it is true. But why must they be so skilful?   c

Because they will have to administer a large dose of that medicine we spoke of earlier. An ordinary doctor is thought good enough for a patient who will submit to be dieted and can do without medicine; but he must be much more of a man if drugs are required.

True, but how does that apply?

It applies to our Rulers: it seems they will have to give their subjects a considerable dose of imposition and deception for their good. We said, if you remember, that   d such expedients would be useful as a sort of medicine.

Yes, a very sound principle.

Well, it looks as if this sound principle will play no small part in this matter of marriage and child-bearing.

How so?

It follows from what we have just said that, if we are to keep our flock at the highest pitch of excellence, there should be as many unions of the best of both sexes, and as few of the inferior, as possible, and that only the offspring of the better unions   e should be kept. And again, no one but the Rulers must know how all this is being effected; otherwise our herd of Guardians may become rebellious.

Quite true.

We must, then, institute certain festivals at which we shall bring together the brides and the bridegrooms. There will be sacrifices, and our poets will write songs be-   460 fitting the occasion. The number of marriages we shall leave to the Rulers' discretion. They will aim at keeping the number of the citizens as constant as possible, having regard to losses caused by war, epidemics, and so on; and they must do their best to see that our state does not become either great or small.

Very good.

I think they will have to invent some ingenious system of drawing lots, so that, at each pairing off, the inferior candidate may blame his luck rather than the Rulers.

Yes, certainly.

Moreover, young men who acquit themselves well in war and other duties,   b should be given, among other rewards and privileges, more liberal opportunities to sleep with a wife, for the further purpose that, with good excuse, as many as possible of the children may be begotten of such fathers.

Yes.

As soon as children are born, they will be taken in charge by officers appointed for the purpose, who may be men or women or both, since offices are to be shared by both sexes. The children of the better parents they will carry to the creche to be reared in the care of nurses living apart in a certain quarter of the city. Those of the inferior parents and any children of the rest that are born defective will be hidden away, in some appropriate manner that must be kept secret.

They must be, if the breed of our Guardians is to be kept pure.

These officers will also superintend the nursing of the children. They will bring the mothers to the creche when their breasts are full, while taking every precaution that no mother shall know her own child; and if the mothers have not enough milk, they will provide wet-nurses. They will limit the time during which the mothers will suckle their children, and hand over all the hard work and sitting up at night to nurses and attendants.

That will make child-bearing an easy business for the Guardians' wives.

So it should be. To go on with our scheme: we said that children should be born from parents in the prime of life. Do you agree that this lasts about twenty years for a woman, and thirty for a man? A woman should bear children for the commonwealth from her twentieth to her fortieth year; a man should begin to beget them when he has passed "the racer's prime in swiftness," and continue till he is fifty-five.

Those are certainly the years in which both the bodily and the mental powers of man and woman are at their best.

If a man either above or below this age meddles with the begetting of children for the commonwealth, we shall hold it an offence against divine and human law. He will be begetting for his country a child conceived in darkness and dire incontinence, whose birth, if it escape detection, will not have been sanctioned by the sacrifices and prayers offered at each marriage festival, when priests and priestesses join with the whole community in praying that the children to be born may be even better and more useful citizens than their parents.

You are right.

The same law will apply to any man within the prescribed limits who touches a woman also of marriageable age when the Ruler has not paired them. We shall say that he is foisting on the commonwealth a bastard, unsanctioned by law or by religion.

Perfectly right.

As soon, however, as the men and the women have passed the age prescribed for producing children, we shall leave them free to form a connexion with whom they will, except that a man shall not take his daughter or daughter's daughter or mother or mother's mother, nor a woman her son or father or her son's son or father's father; and all this only after we have exhorted them to see that no child, if any be conceived, shall be brought to light, or, if they cannot prevent its birth, to dispose of it on the understanding that no such child can be reared.

That too is reasonable. But how are they to distinguish fathers and daughters and those other relations you mentioned?

They will not, said I. But, reckoning from the day when he becomes a bridegroom, a man will call all children born in the tenth or the seventh month sons and daughters, and they will call him father. Their children again he will call grandchildren, and they will call his group grandfathers and grandmothers; and all who are born within the period during which their mothers and fathers were having children will be called brothers and sisters. This will provide for those restrictions on unions that we mentioned; but the law will allow brothers and sisters to live together, if the lot so falls out and the Delphic oracle also approves.

Very good.

This, then, Glaucon, is the manner in which the Guardians of your commonwealth are to hold their wives and children in common. Must we not next find arguments to establish that it is consistent with our other institutions and also by far the best plan?

Yes, surely.   462

We had better begin by asking what is the greatest good at which the lawgiver should aim in laying down the constitution of a state, and what is the worst evil. We can then consider whether our proposals are in keeping with that good and irreconcilable with the evil.

By all means.

Does not the worst evil for a state arise from anything that tends to rend it asunder and destroy its unity, while nothing does it more good than whatever tends to bind   b
it together and make it one?

That is true.

And are not citizens bound together by sharing in the same pleasures and pains, all feeling glad or grieved on the same occasions of gain or loss; whereas the bond is broken when such feelings are no longer universal, but any event of public or personal   c
concern fills some with joy and others with distress?

Certainly.

And this disunion comes about when the words "mine" and "not mine," "another's" and "not another's" are not applied to the same things throughout the community. The best ordered state will be the one in which the largest number of persons use these terms in the same sense, and which accordingly most nearly resembles a single person. When one of us hurts his finger, the whole extent of those bodily connexions which are gathered up in the soul and unified by its ruling element is made aware and it   d
all shares as a whole in the pain of the suffering part; hence we say that the man has a pain in his finger. The same thing is true of the pain or pleasure felt when any other part of the person suffers or is relieved.

Yes; I agree that the best organized community comes nearest to that condition.

And so it will recognize as a part of itself the individual citizen to whom good or   e
evil happens, and will share as a whole in his joy or sorrow.

It must, if the constitution is sound.

It is time now to go back to our own commonwealth and see whether these conclusions apply to it more than to any other type of state. In all alike there are rulers and   463
common people, all of whom will call one another fellow citizens.

Yes.

But in other states the people have another name as well for their rulers, haven't they?

Yes; in most they call them masters; in democracies, simply the government.

And in ours?

The people will look upon their rulers as preservers and protectors.   b

And how will our rulers regard the people?

As those who maintain them and pay them wages.

And elsewhere?

As slaves.

And what do rulers elsewhere call one another?

Colleagues.

And ours?

Fellow Guardians.

And in other states may not a ruler regard one colleague as a friend in whom he
c   has an interest, and another as a stranger with whom he has nothing in common?

Yes, that often happens.

But that could not be so with your Guardians? None of them could ever treat a
fellow Guardian as a stranger.

Certainly not. He must regard everyone whom he meets as brother or sister, father or mother, son or daughter, grandchild or grandparent.

Very good; but here is a further point. Will you not require them, not merely to
d   use these family terms, but to behave as a real family? Must they not show towards all
whom they call "father" the customary reverence, care, and obedience due to a parent,
if they look for any favour from gods or men, since to act otherwise is contrary to divine and human law? Should not all the citizens constantly reiterate in the hearing of
the children from their earliest years such traditional maxims of conduct towards those
whom they are taught to call father and their other kindred?

e   They should. It would be absurd that terms of kinship should be on their lips
without any action to correspond.

In our community, then, above all others, when things go well or ill with any individual everyone will use that word "mine" in the same sense and say that all is going
well or ill with him and his.

Quite true.

464   And, as we said, this way of speaking and thinking goes with fellow-feeling; so
that our citizens, sharing as they do in a common interest which each will call his own,
will have all their feelings of pleasure or pain in common.

Assuredly.

A result that will be due to our institutions, and in particular to our Guardians'
holding their wives and children in common.

Very much so.

b   But you will remember how, when we compared a well-ordered community to
the body which shares in the pleasures and pains of any member, we saw in this unity
the greatest good that a state can enjoy. So the conclusion is that our commonwealth
owes to this sharing of wives and children by its protectors its enjoyment of the greatest of all goods.

Yes, that follows.

Moreover, this agrees with our principle that they were not to have houses or
c   lands or any property of their own, but to receive sustenance from the other citizens, as
wages for their guardianship, and to consume it in common. Only so will they keep to
their true character; and our present proposals will do still more to make them genuine
Guardians. They will not rend the community asunder by each applying that word
d   "mine" to different things and dragging off whatever he can get for himself into a private home, where he will have his separate family, forming a centre of exclusive joys
and sorrows. Rather they will all, so far as may be, feel together and aim at the same
ends, because they are convinced that all their interests are identical.

Quite so.

Again, if a man's person is his only private possession, lawsuits and prosecutions
will all but vanish, and they will be free of those quarrels that arise from ownership of
property and from having family ties. Nor would they be justified even in bringing ac-
e   tions for assault and outrage; for we shall pronounce it right and honourable for a man
to defend himself against an assailant of his own age, and in that way they will be compelled to keep themselves fit.

That would be a sound law.

And it would also have the advantage that, if a man's anger can be satisfied in   465
this way, a fit of passion is less likely to grow into a serious quarrel.

True.

But an older man will be given authority over all younger persons and power to
correct them; whereas the younger will, naturally, not dare to strike the elder or do him
any violence, except by command of a Ruler. He will not show him any sort of disre-
spect. Two guardian spirits, fear and reverence, will be enough to restrain him—reverence forbidding him to lay hands on a parent, and fear of all those others who as sons   b
or brothers or fathers would come to the rescue.

Yes, that will be the result.

So our laws will secure that these men will live in complete peace with one another; and if they never quarrel among themselves, there is no fear of the rest of the
community being divided either against them or against itself.

No.

There are other evils they will escape, so mean and petty that I hardly like to
mention them: the poor man's flattery of the rich, and all the embarrassments and vex-   c
ations of rearing a family and earning just enough to maintain a household; now borrowing and now refusing to repay, and by any and every means scraping together
money to be handed over to wife and servants to spend. These sordid troubles are familiar and not worth describing.

Only too familiar.   d

Rid of all these cares, they will live a more enviable life than the Olympic victor,
who is counted happy on the strength of far fewer blessings than our Guardians will
enjoy. Their victory is the nobler, since by their success the whole commonwealth is
preserved; and their reward of maintenance at the public cost is more complete, since
their prize is to have every need of life supplied for themselves and for their children;
their country honours them while they live, and when they die they receive a worthy   e
burial.

Yes, they will be nobly rewarded.

Do you remember, then, how someone who shall be nameless reproached us for
not making our Guardians happy: they were to possess nothing, though all the wealth   466
of their fellow citizens was within their grasp? We replied, I believe, that we would
consider that objection later, if it came in our way: for the moment we were bent on
making our Guardians real guardians, and moulding our commonwealth with a view to
the greatest happiness, not of one section of it, but of the whole.

Yes, I remember.

Well, it appears now that these protectors of our state will have a life better and
more honourable than that of any Olympic victor; and we can hardly rank it on a level   b
with the life of a shoemaker or other artisan or of a farmer.

I should think not.

However, it is right to repeat what I said at the time: if ever a Guardian tries to
make himself happy in such a way that he will be a guardian no longer; if, not content
with the moderation and security of this way of living which we think the best, he becomes possessed with some silly and childish notion of happiness, impelling him to
make his power a means to appropriate all the citizens' wealth, then he will learn the   c
wisdom of Hesiod's saying that the half is more than the whole.

My advice would certainly be that he should keep to his own way of living.

You do agree, then, that women are to take their full share with men in education, in the care of children, and in the guardianship of the other citizens; whether they
stay at home or go out to war, they will be like watch-dogs which take their part either

in guarding the fold or in hunting and share in every task so far as their strength allows.

d   Such conduct will not be unwomanly, but all for the best and in accordance with the natural partnership of the sexes.

Yes, I agree.

It remains to ask whether such a partnership can be established among human beings, as it can among animals, and if so, how.

I was just going to put that question.

e   So far as fighting is concerned, it is easy to see how they will go out to war.

How?

Men and women will take the field together and moreover bring with them the children who are sturdy enough, to learn this trade, like any other, by watching what they will have to do themselves when they are grown up; and besides looking on, they will fetch and carry for their fathers and mothers and see to all their needs in time of

467   war. You must have noticed how, in the potter's trade for example, the children watch their fathers and wait on them long before they may touch the wheel. Ought our Guardians to be less careful to train theirs by letting them look on and become familiar with their duties?

No, that would be absurd.

b   Moreover, any creature will fight better in the presence of its young.

That is so. But in case of defeat, which may always happen in war, there will be serious danger of their children's lives being lost with their own, so that the country could never recover.

True; but, in the first place, do you think we must make sure that they never run any risk?

No, far from it.

c   Well, if they are ever to take their chance, should it not be on some occasion when, if all goes well, they will be the better for it?

No doubt.

And is it of no importance that men who are to be warriors should see something of war in childhood? Is that not worth some danger?

Yes; it is important.

Granted, then, that the children are to go to war as spectators, all will be well if

d   we can contrive that they shall do so in safety. To begin with, their fathers will not be slow to judge, so far as human foresight can, which expeditions are hazardous and which are safe; and they will be careful not to take the children into danger. Also they will put them in charge of officers qualified by age and experience to lead and take care of them.

Yes, that would be the proper way.

All the same, the unexpected often happens; and to guard against such chances we must see that they have, from their earliest years, wings to fly away with if need be.

e   What do you mean by wings?

Horses, which they must be taught to ride at the earliest possible age; then, when they are taken to see the fighting, their mounts must not be spirited chargers but the swiftest we can find and the easiest to manage. In that way they will get a good view of their future business, and in case of need they will be able to keep up with their older leaders and escape in safety.

That seems an excellent plan.

468   Now, as to the conduct of war and your soldiers' relations to one another and to the enemy: am I right in thinking that anyone guilty of an act of cowardice, such as deserting his post or throwing away his arms, should be reduced to the artisan or farmer

class; while if any fall alive into the enemy's hands, we shall make them a present of him, and they may do what they like with their prey?

Certainly.   b

And what shall be done to the hero who has distinguished himself by his valour? First, should he not be crowned on the field by the youths and children each in turn?

Surely.

And they might shake his hand?

Yes.

But you would stop there, no doubt. I am sure you would not approve of his ex-   c changing kisses with them all?

I am all for that; indeed I would add to the law the provision that, so long as they are on the campaign, no one whom he wishes to kiss may refuse. That would make any soldier who chanced to be in love with a youth or a girl all the more eager to win the prize of valour.

Very well. We have already said that the brave man is to be selected for marriage more frequently than the rest, so that as many children as possible may have such a man for their father. But besides that, these valiant youths may well be rewarded in the   d Homeric manner. When Ajax distinguished himself in the war, he was "honoured with slices of the chine's full length," a suitable compliment to a lusty young hero, and one that would at the same time strengthen his muscles.

An excellent idea.

Then here at any rate we will follow Homer. At sacrificial feasts and all such occasions, we shall reward the brave, in proportion to their merit, not only with songs and those privileges we mentioned but "with seats of honour, meat, and cups brimful"; and so   e at once pay tribute to the bravery of these men and women and improve their physique.

Nothing could be better.

Good. And of those who are slain in the field, we shall say that all who fell with honour are of that Golden Race, who, when they die,

> Dwell here on earth, pure spirits, beneficent.   469
> Guardians to shield us mortal men from harm.

Shall we not believe those words of Hesiod?

We shall.

Then we shall ask the Oracle with what special rites these men of more than human mould should be buried, and we shall do as it prescribes. And for all time to   b come we shall reverence their tombs and worship them as demigods. Others, too, who die in the natural course of old age or otherwise shall be honoured in the same way, if they are judged to have led an exceptionally noble life.

That is but fair.

And next, how will our soldiers deal with enemies?

In what respect?

First take slavery. Is it right that Greek states should sell Greeks into slavery? Ought they not rather to do all they can to stop this practice and substitute the custom   c of sparing their own race, for fear of falling into bondage to foreign nations?

That would be better, beyond all comparison.

They must not, then, hold any Greek in slavery themselves, and they should advise the rest of Greece not to do so.

Certainly. Then they would be more likely to keep their hands off one another and turn their energies against foreigners.

Next, is it well to strip the dead, after a victory, of anything but their arms? It
d   only gives cowards an excuse for not facing the living enemy, as if they were usefully
employed in poking about over a dead body. Many an army has been lost through this
pillaging. There is something mean and greedy in plundering a corpse; and a sort of
womanish pettiness in treating the body as an enemy, when the spirit, the real enemy,
has flown, leaving behind only the instrument with which he fought. It is to behave no
e   better than a dog who growls at the stone that has hit him and leaves alone the man
who threw it.

True.

So we will have no stripping of the slain and we shall not prevent their comrades
from burying them. Nor shall we dedicate in the temples trophies of their weapons,
least of all those of Greeks, if we are concerned to show loyalty towards the rest of
470   Hellas. We shall rather be afraid of desecrating a sanctuary by bringing to it such spoils
of our own people, unless indeed the Oracle should pronounce otherwise.

That is very right.

And what of ravaging Greek lands and burning houses? How will your soldiers
deal with their enemies in this matter?

I should like to hear your own opinion.

b   I think they should do neither, but only carry off the year's harvest. Shall I tell
you why?

Please do.

It seems to me that war and civil strife differ in nature as they do in name, according to the two spheres in which disputes may arise: at home or abroad, among men
of the same race or with foreigners. War means fighting with a foreign enemy; when
the enemy is of the same kindred, we call it civil strife.

That is a reasonable distinction.

c   Is it not also reasonable to assert that Greeks are a single people, all of the same
kindred and alien to the outer world of foreigners?

Yes.

Then we shall speak of war when Greeks fight with foreigners, whom we may
call their natural enemies. But Greeks are by nature friends of Greeks, and when they
d   fight, it means that Hellas is afflicted by dissension which ought to be called civil
strife.

I agree with that view.

Observe, then, that in what is commonly known as civil strife, that is to say,
when one of our Greek states is divided against itself, it is thought an abominable outrage for either party to ravage the lands or burn the houses of the other. No lover of his
country would dare to mangle the land which gave him birth and nursed him. It is
thought fair that the victors should carry off the others' crops, but do no more. They
e   should remember that the war will not last forever; some day they must make friends
again.

That is a much more civilized state of mind.

Well then, is not this commonwealth you are founding a Greek state, and its citizens good and civilized people?

Very much so.

And lovers of Greece, who will think of all Hellas as their home, where they
share in one common religion with the rest?

Most certainly.

Accordingly, the Greeks being their own people, a quarrel with them will not be
471   called a war. It will only be civil strife, which they will carry on as men who will some

day be reconciled. So they will not behave like a foreign enemy seeking to enslave or destroy, but will try to bring their adversaries to reason by well-meant correction. As Greeks they will not devastate the soil of Greece or burn the homesteads; nor will they allow that all the inhabitants of any state, men, women, and children, are their enemies, but only the few who are responsible for the quarrel. The greater number are friends, whose land and houses, on all these accounts, they will not consent to lay waste and   b destroy. They will pursue the quarrel only until the guilty are compelled by the innocent sufferers to give satisfaction.

For my part, I agree that our citizens should treat their adversaries in that way, and deal with foreigners as Greeks now deal with one another.

We will make this a law, then, for our Guardians: they are not to ravage lands or   c burn houses.

Yes, we will; it is as satisfactory as all our other laws.

But really, Socrates, Glaucon continued, if you are allowed to go on like this, I am afraid you will forget all about the question you thrust aside some time ago: whether a society so constituted can ever come into existence, and if so, how. No doubt, if it did exist, all manner of good things would come about. I can even add some that you have passed over. Men who acknowledged one another as fathers, sons, or   d brothers and always used those names among themselves would never desert one another; so they would fight with unequaled bravery. And if their womenfolk went out with them to war, either in the ranks or drawn up in the rear to intimidate the enemy and act as a reserve in case of need, I am sure all this would make them invincible. At home, too, I can see many advantages you have not mentioned. But, since I admit that our commonwealth would have all these merits and any number more, if once it came   e into existence, you need not describe it in further detail. All we have now to do is to convince ourselves that it can be brought into being and how.

This is a very sudden onslaught, said I; you have no mercy on my shilly-shally-   472 ing. Perhaps you do not realize that, after I have barely escaped the first two waves, the third, which you are now bringing down upon me, is the most formidable of all. When you have seen what it is like and heard my reply, you will be ready to excuse the very natural fears which made me shrink from putting forward such a paradox for discussion.

The more you talk like that, he said, the less we shall be willing to let you off from telling us how this constitution can come into existence; so you had better waste   b no more time.

Well, said I, let me begin by reminding you that what brought us to this point was our inquiry into the nature of justice and injustice.

True; but what of that?

Merely this: suppose we do find out what justice is, are we going to demand that a man who is just shall have a character which exactly corresponds in every respect to the ideal of justice? Or shall we be satisfied if he comes as near to the ideal as possible and has in him a larger measure of that quality than the rest of the world?   c

That will satisfy me.

If so, when we set out to discover the essential nature of justice and injustice and what a perfectly just and a perfectly unjust man would be like, supposing them to exist, our purpose was to use them as ideal patterns: we were to observe the degree of happiness or unhappiness that each exhibited, and to draw the necessary inference that our own destiny would be like that of the one we most resembled. We did not set out to show that these ideals could exist in fact.   d

That is true.

Then suppose a painter had drawn an ideally beautiful figure complete to the last touch, would you think any the worse of him, if he could not show that a person as beautiful as that could exist?

No, I should not.

e   Well, we have been constructing in discourse the pattern of an ideal state. Is our theory any the worse, if we cannot prove it possible that a state so organized should be actually founded?

Surely not.

That, then, is the truth of the matter. But if, for your satisfaction, I am to do my best to show under what conditions our ideal would have the best chance of being real-

473   ized, I must ask you once more to admit that the same principle applies here. Can theory ever be fully realized in practice? Is it not in the nature of things that action should come less close to truth than thought? People may not think so; but do you agree or not?

I do.

Then you must not insist upon my showing that this construction we have traced in thought could be reproduced in fact down to the last detail. You must admit that we shall have found a way to meet your demand for realization, if we can discover how a

b   state might be constituted in the closest accordance with our description. Will not that content you? It would be enough for me.

And for me too.

Then our next attempt, it seems, must be to point out what defect in the working of existing states prevents them from being so organized, and what is the least change that would effect a transformation into this type of government—a single change if possible, or perhaps two; at any rate let us make the changes as few and insignificant as may be.

c   By all means.

Well, there is one change which, as I believe we can show, would bring about this revolution—not a small change, certainly, nor an easy one, but possible.

What is it?

I have now to confront what we called the third and greatest wave. But I must state my paradox, even though the wave should break in laughter over my head and drown me in ignominy. Now mark what I am going to say.

Go on.

Unless either philosophers become kings in their countries or those who are now called kings and rulers come to be sufficiently inspired with a genuine desire for wis-

d   dom; unless, that is to say, political power and philosophy meet together, while the many natures who now go their several ways in the one or the other direction are

e   forcibly debarred from doing so, there can be no rest from troubles, my dear Glaucon, for states, nor yet, as I believe, for all mankind; nor can this commonwealth which we have imagined ever till then see the light of day and grow to its full stature. This it was that I have so long hung back from saying; I knew what a paradox it would be, because it is hard to see that there is no other way of happiness either for the state or for the individual.

Socrates, exclaimed Glaucon, after delivering yourself of such a pronouncement as that, you must expect a whole multitude of by no means contemptible assailants to fling off their coats, snatch up the handiest weapon, and make a rush at you, breathing

474   fire and slaughter. If you cannot find arguments to beat them off and make your escape, you will learn what it means to be the target of scorn and derision.

Well, it was you who got me into this trouble.

Yes, and a good thing too. However, I will not leave you in the lurch. You shall have my friendly encouragement for what it is worth; and perhaps you may find me more complaisant than some would be in answering your questions. With such backing b
you must try to convince the unbelievers.

I will, now that I have such a powerful ally.

Now, I continued, if we are to elude those assailants you have described, we must, I think, define for them whom we mean by these lovers of wisdom who, we have dared to assert, ought to be our rulers. Once we have a clear view of their character, we shall be able to defend our position by pointing to some who are naturally fitted to c
combine philosophic study with political leadership, while the rest of the world should accept their guidance and let philosophy alone.

Yes, this is the moment for a definition.

Here, then, is a line of thought which may lead to a satisfactory explanation. Need I remind you that a man will deserve to be called a lover of this or that, only if it is clear that he loves that thing as a whole, not merely in parts?

You must remind me, it seems; for I do not see what you mean. d

That answer would have come better from someone less susceptible to love than yourself, Glaucon. You ought not to have forgotten that any boy in the bloom of youth will arouse some sting of passion in a man of your amorous temperament and seem worthy of his attentions. Is not this your way with your favourites? You will praise a snub nose as piquant and a hooked one as giving a regal air, while you call a straight e
nose perfectly proportioned; the swarthy, you say, have a manly look, the fair are children of the gods; and what do you think is that word "honey-pale," if not the euphemism of some lover who had no fault to find with sallowness on the cheek of youth? In a word, you will carry pretence and extravagance to any length sooner than 475
reject a single one that is in the flower of his prime.

If you insist on taking me as an example of how lovers behave, I will agree for the sake of argument.

Again, do you not see the same behaviour in people with a passion for wine? They are glad of any excuse to drink wine of any sort. And there are the men who covet honour, who, if they cannot lead an army, will command a company, and if they b
cannot win the respect of important people, are glad to be looked up to by nobodies, because they must have someone to esteem them.

Quite true.

Do you agree, then, that when we speak of a man as having a passion for a certain kind of thing, we mean that he has an appetite for everything of that kind without discrimination?

Yes.

So the philosopher, with his passion for wisdom, will be one who desires all wisdom, not only some part of it. If a student is particular about his studies, especially while he is too young to know which are useful and which are not, we shall say he is c
no lover of learning or of wisdom; just as, if he were dainty about his food, we should say he was not hungry or fond of eating, but had a poor appetite. Only the man who has a taste for every sort of knowledge and throws himself into acquiring it with an insatiable curiosity will deserve to be called a philosopher. Am I not right?

That description, Glaucon replied, would include a large and ill assorted com- d
pany. It is curiosity, I suppose, and a delight in fresh experience that gives some people a passion for all that is to be seen and heard at theatrical and musical performances. But they are a queer set to reckon among philosophers, considering that they would never go near anything like a philosophical discussion, though they run round at all the

Dionysiac festivals in town or country as if they were under contract to listen to every company of performers without fail. Will curiosity entitle all these enthusiasts, not to

e   mention amateurs of the minor arts, to be called philosophers?

Certainly not; though they have a certain counterfeit resemblance.

And whom do you mean by the genuine philosophers?

Those whose passion it is to see the truth.

That must be so; but will you explain?

It would not be easy to explain to everyone; but you, I believe, will grant my premise.

Which is—?

That since beauty and ugliness are opposite, they are two things; and conse-

476   quently each of them is one. The same holds of justice and injustice, good and bad, and all the essential Forms: each in itself is one; but they manifest themselves in a great variety of combinations, with actions, with material things, and with one another, and so each seems to be many.

That is true.

On the strength of this premise, then, I can distinguish your amateurs of the arts

b   and men of action from the philosophers we are concerned with, who are alone worthy of the name.

What is your distinction?

Your lovers of sights and sounds delight in beautiful tones and colours and shapes and in all the works of art into which these enter; but they have not the power of thought to behold and to take delight in the nature of Beauty itself. That power to approach Beauty and behold it as it is in itself, is rare indeed.

c   Quite true.

Now if a man believes in the existence of beautiful things, but not of Beauty itself, and cannot follow a guide who would lead him to a knowledge of it, is he not living in a dream? Consider: does not dreaming, whether one is awake or asleep, consist in mistaking a semblance for the reality it resembles?

I should certainly call that dreaming.

Contrast with him the man who holds that there is such a thing as Beauty itself

d   and can discern that essence as well as the things that partake of its character, without ever confusing the one with the other—is he a dreamer or living in a waking state?

He is very much awake.

So may we say that he knows, while the other has only a belief in appearances; and might we call their states of mind knowledge and belief?

Certainly.

But this person who, we say, has only belief without knowledge may be ag-

e   grieved and challenge our statement. Is there any means of soothing his resentment and converting him gently, without telling him plainly that he is not in his right mind?

We surely ought to try.

Come then, consider what we are to say to him. Or shall we ask him a question, assuring him that, far from grudging him any knowledge he may have, we shall be only too glad to find that there is something he knows? But, we shall say, tell us this: When a man knows, must there not be something that he knows? Will you answer for him, Glaucon?

My answer will be, that there must.

Something real or unreal?

477   Something real; how could a thing that is unreal ever be known?

Are we satisfied, then, on this point, from however many points of view we might examine it: that the perfectly real is perfectly knowable, and the utterly unreal is entirely unknowable?

Quite satisfied.

Good. Now if there is something so constituted that it both *is* and *is not,* will it not lie between the purely real and the utterly unreal?

It will.

Well then, as knowledge corresponds to the real, and absence of knowledge necessarily to the unreal, so, to correspond to this intermediate thing, we must look for   b something between ignorance and knowledge, if such a thing there be.

Certainly.

Is there not a thing we call belief?

Surely.

A different power from knowledge, or the same?

Different.

Knowledge and belief, then, must have different objects, answering to their respective powers.

Yes.

And knowledge has for its natural object the real—to know the truth about reality. However, before going further, I think we need a definition. Shall we distinguish   c under the general name of "faculties" those powers which enable us—or anything else—to do what we can do? Sight and hearing, for instance, are what I call faculties, if that will help you to see the class of things I have in mind.

Yes, I understand.

Then let me tell you what view I take of them. In a faculty I cannot find any of those qualities, such as colour or shape, which, in the case of many other things, enable me to distinguish one thing from another. I can only look to its field of objects and the state of mind it produces, and regard these as sufficient to identify it and to distinguish   d it from faculties which have different fields and produce different states. Is that how you would go to work?

Yes.

Let us go back, then, to knowledge. Would you class that as a faculty?

Yes; and I should call it the most powerful of all.

And is belief also a faculty?   e

It can be nothing else, since it is what gives us the power of believing.

But a little while ago you agreed that knowledge and belief are not the same thing.

Yes; there could be no sense in identifying the infallible with the fallible.

Good. So we are quite clear that knowledge and belief are different things?   478

They are.

If so, each of them, having a different power, must have a different field of objects.

Necessarily.

The field of knowledge being the real; and its power, the power of knowing the real as it is.

Yes.

Whereas belief, we say, is the power of believing. Is its object the same as that which knowledge knows? Can the same things be possible objects both of knowledge and of belief?

Not if we hold to the principles we agreed upon. If it is of the nature of a different
b   faculty to have a different field, and if both knowledge and belief are faculties and, as we
assert, different ones, it follows that the same things cannot be possible objects of both.

So if the real is the object of knowledge, the object of belief must be something
other than the real.

Yes.

c   Can it be the unreal? Or is that an impossible object even for belief? Consider: if
a man has a belief, there must be something before his mind; he cannot be believing
nothing, can he?

No.

He is believing something, then; whereas the unreal could only be called nothing
at all.

Certainly.

Now we said that ignorance must correspond to the unreal, knowledge to the
real. So what he is believing cannot be real nor yet unreal.

True.

Belief, then, cannot be either ignorance or knowledge.

It appears not.

d   Then does it lie outside and beyond these two? Is it either more clear and certain
than knowledge or less clear and certain than ignorance?

No, it is neither.

It rather seems to you to be something more obscure than knowledge, but not so
dark as ignorance, and so to lie between the two extremes?

Quite so.

Well, we said earlier that if some object could be found such that it both *is* and at
the same time *is not,* that object would lie between the perfectly real and the utterly unreal; and that the corresponding faculty would be neither knowledge nor ignorance, but
a faculty to be found situated between the two.

Yes.

And now what we have found between the two is the faculty we call belief.

True.

e   It seems, then, that what remains to be discovered is that object which can be
said both to be and not to be and cannot properly be called either purely real or purely
unreal. If that can be found, we may justly call it the object of belief, and so give the
intermediate faculty the intermediate object, while the two extreme objects will fall to
the extreme faculties.

Yes.

479   On these assumptions, then, I shall call for an answer from our friend who denies
the existence of Beauty itself or of anything that can be called an essential Form of
Beauty remaining unchangeably in the same state forever, though he does recognize
the existence of beautiful things as a plurality—that lover of things seen who will not
listen to anyone who says that Beauty is one, Justice is one, and so on. I shall say to
him, Be so good as to tell us: of all these many beautiful things is there one which will
not appear ugly? Or of these many just or righteous actions, is there one that will not
appear unjust or unrighteous?

b   No, replied Glaucon, they must inevitably appear to be in some way both beautiful and ugly; and so with all the other terms your question refers to.

And again the many things which are doubles are just as much halves as they are
doubles. And the things we call large or heavy have just as much right to be called
small or light.

Yes; any such thing will always have a claim to both opposite designations.

Then, whatever any one of these many things may be said to be, can you say that it absolutely *is* that, any more than that it *is not* that?

They remind me of those punning riddles people ask at dinner parties, or the child's puzzle about what the eunuch threw at the bat and what the bat was perched on. These things have the same ambiguous character, and one cannot form any stable conception of them either as being or as not being, or as both being and not being, or as neither. c

Can you think of any better way of disposing of them than by placing them between reality and unreality? For I suppose they will not appear more obscure and so less real than unreality, or clearer and so more real than reality. d

Quite true.

It seems, then, we have discovered that the many conventional notions of the mass of mankind about what is beautiful or honourable or just and so on are adrift in a sort of twilight between pure reality and pure unreality.

We have.

And we agreed earlier that, if any such object were discovered, it should be called the object of belief and not of knowledge. Fluctuating in that half-way region, it would be seized upon by the intermediate faculty.

Yes.

So when people have an eye for the multitude of beautiful things or of just actions or whatever it may be, but can neither behold Beauty or Justice itself nor follow a guide who would lead them to it, we shall say that all they have is beliefs, without any real knowledge of the objects of their belief. e

That follows.

But what of those who contemplate the realities themselves as they are forever in the same unchanging state? Shall we not say that they have, not mere belief, but knowledge?

That too follows.

And, further, that their affection goes out to the objects of knowledge, whereas the others set their affections on the objects of belief; for it was they, you remember, who had a passion for the spectacle of beautiful colours and sounds, but would not hear of Beauty itself being a real thing. 480

I remember.

So we may fairly call them lovers of belief rather than of wisdom—not philosophical, in fact, but philodoxical. Will they be seriously annoyed by that description?

Not if they will listen to my advice. No one ought to take offence at the truth.

The name of philosopher, then, will be reserved for those whose affections are set, in every case, on the reality.

By all means.

BOOK VI

*   *   *

One difficulty, then, has been surmounted. It remains to ask how we can make sure of having men who will preserve our constitution. What must they learn, and at what age should they take up each branch of study? 502^d

Yes, that is the next point.

I gained nothing by my cunning in putting off those thorny questions of the posses-sion of wives and children and the appointment of Rulers. I knew that the ideal plan would give offence and be hard to carry out; none the less I have had to discuss these matters. We have now disposed of the women and children, but we must start all over again upon the training of the Rulers. You remember how their love for their country was to be proved, by the tests of pain and pleasure, to be a faith that no toil or danger, no turn of fortune could make them abandon. All who failed were to be rejected; only the man who came out flawless, like gold tried in the fire, was to be made a Ruler with privileges and rewards in life and after death. So much was said, when our argument turned aside, as if hoping, with veiled face, to slip past the danger that now lies in our path.

Quite true, I remember.

Yes, I shrank from the bold words which have now been spoken; but now we have ventured to declare that our Guardians in the fullest sense must be philosophers. So much being granted, you must reflect how few are likely to be available. The nat-ural gifts we required will rarely grow together into one whole; they tend to split apart.

How do you mean?

Qualities like ready understanding, a good memory, sagacity, quickness, to-gether with a high-spirited, generous temper, are seldom combined with willingness to live a quiet life of sober constancy. Keen wits are apt to lose all steadiness and to veer about in every direction. On the other hand, the steady reliable characters, whose im-passivity is proof against the perils of war, are equally proof against instruction. Con-fronted with intellectual work, they become comatose and do nothing but yawn.

That is true.

But we insist that no one must be given the highest education or hold office as Ruler, who has not both sets of qualities in due measure. This combination will be rare. So, besides testing it by hardship and danger and by the temptations of pleasure, we may now add that its strength must be tried in many forms of study, to see whether it has the courage and endurance to pursue the highest kind of knowledge, without flinching as others flinch under physical trials.

By all means; but what kinds of study do you call the highest?

You remember how we deduced the definitions of justice, temperance, courage, and wisdom by distinguishing three parts of the soul?

If I had forgotten that, I should not deserve to hear any more.

Do you also remember my warning you beforehand that in order to gain the clearest possible view of these qualities we should have to go round a longer way, al-though we could give a more superficial account in keeping with our earlier argument. You said that would do; and so we went on in a way which seemed to me not suffi-ciently exact; whether you were satisfied, it is for you to say.

We all thought you gave us a fair measure of truth.

No measure that falls in the least degree short of the whole truth can be quite fair in so important a matter. What is imperfect can never serve as a measure; though peo-ple sometimes think enough has been done and there is no need to look further.

Yes, indolence is common enough.

But the last quality to be desired in the Guardian of a commonwealth and its laws. So he will have to take the longer way and work as hard at learning as at training his body; otherwise he will never reach the goal of the highest knowledge, which most of all concerns him.

Why, are not justice and the other virtues we have discussed the highest? Is there something still higher to be known?

There is; and of those virtues themselves we have as yet only a rough outline, where nothing short of the finished picture should content us. If we strain every nerve   e
to reach precision and clearness in things of little moment, how absurd not to demand the highest degree of exactness in the things that matter most.

Certainly. But what do you mean by the highest kind of knowledge and with what is it concerned? You cannot hope to escape that question.

I do not; you may ask me yourself. All the same, you have been told many a time; but now either you are not thinking or, as I rather suspect, you mean to put me to   505
some trouble with your insistence. For you have often been told that the highest object of knowledge is the essential nature of the Good, from which everything that is good and right derives its value for us. You must have been expecting me to speak of this now, and to add that we have no sufficient knowledge of it. I need not tell you that, without that knowledge, to know everything else, however well, would be of no value to us, just as it is of no use to possess anything without getting the good of it. What advantage can there be in possessing everything except what is good, or in understanding   b
everything else while of the good and desirable we know nothing?

None whatever.

Well then, you know too that most people identify the Good with pleasure, whereas the more enlightened think it is knowledge.

Yes, of course.

And further that these latter cannot tell us what knowledge they mean, but are reduced at last to saying, "knowledge of the Good."

That is absurd.   c

It is; first they reproach us with not knowing the Good, and then tell us that it is knowledge of the Good, as if we did after all understand the meaning of that word "Good" when they pronounce it.

Quite true.

What of those who define the Good as pleasure? Are they any less confused in their thoughts? They are obliged to admit that there are bad pleasures; from which it follows that the same things are both good and bad.

Quite so.

Evidently, then, this is a matter of much dispute. It is also evident that, although   d
many are content to do what seems just or honourable without really being so, and to possess a mere semblance of these qualities, when it comes to good things, no one is   e
satisfied with possessing what only seems good: here all reject the appearance and demand the reality.

Certainly.

A thing, then, that every soul pursues as the end of all her actions, dimly divining its existence, but perplexed and unable to grasp its nature with the same clearness and assurance as in dealing with other things, and so missing whatever value those other things might have—a thing of such supreme importance is not a matter about which those cho-   506
sen Guardians of the whole fortunes of our commonwealth can be left in the dark.

Most certainly not.

At any rate, institutions or customs which are desirable and right will not, I imagine, find a very efficient guardian in one who does not know in what way they are good. I should rather guess that he will not be able to recognize fully that they are right and desirable.

No doubt.

So the order of our commonwealth will be perfectly regulated only when it is   b
watched over by a Guardian who does possess this knowledge.

That follows. But, Socrates, what is your own account of the Good? Is it knowledge, or pleasure, or something else?

There you are! I exclaimed; I could see all along that you were not going to be content with what other people think.

Well, Socrates, it does not seem fair that you should be ready to repeat other people's opinions but not to state your own, when you have given so much thought to this subject.

c   And do you think it fair of anyone to speak as if he knew what he does not know?

No, not as if he knew, but he might give his opinion for what it is worth.

Why, have you never noticed that opinion without knowledge is always a shabby sort of thing? At the best it is blind. One who holds a true belief without intelligence is just like a blind man who happens to take the right road, isn't he?

No doubt.

d   Well, then, do you want me to produce one of these poor blind cripples, when others could discourse to you with illuminating eloquence?

No, really, Socrates, said Glaucon, you must not give up within sight of the goal. We should be quite content with an account of the Good like the one you gave us of justice and temperance and the other virtues.

So should I be, my dear Glaucon, much more than content! But I am afraid it is beyond my powers; with the best will in the world I should only disgrace myself and

e   be laughed at. No, for the moment let us leave the question of the real meaning of good; to arrive at what I at any rate believe it to be would call for an effort too ambitious for an inquiry like ours. However, I will tell you, though only if you wish it, what I picture to myself as the offspring of the Good and the thing most nearly resembling it.

Well, tell us about the offspring, and you shall remain in our debt for an account of the parent.

507   I only wish it were within my power to offer, and within yours to receive, a settlement of the whole account. But you must be content now with the interest only; and you must see to it that, in describing this offspring of the Good, I do not inadvertently cheat you with false coin.

We will keep a good eye on you. Go on.

First we must come to an understanding. Let me remind you of the distinction we

b   drew earlier and have often drawn on other occasions, between the multiplicity of things that we call good or beautiful or whatever it may be and, on the other hand, Goodness itself or Beauty itself and so on. Corresponding to each of these sets of many things, we postulate a single Form or real essence, as we call it.

Yes, that is so.

Further, the many things, we say, can be seen, but are not objects of rational thought; whereas the Forms are objects of thought, but invisible.

c   Yes, certainly.

And we see things with our eyesight, just as we hear sounds with our ears and, to speak generally, perceive any sensible thing with our sense-faculties.

Of course.

Have you noticed, then, that the artificer who designed the senses has been exceptionally lavish of his materials in making the eyes able to see and their objects visible?

That never occurred to me.

Well, look at it in this way. Hearing and sound do not stand in need of any third

d   thing, without which the ear will not hear nor sound be heard; and I think the same is true of most, not to say all, of the other senses. Can you think of one that does require anything of the sort?

No, I cannot.

But there is this need in the case of sight and its objects. You may have the power of vision in your eyes and try to use it, and colour may be there in the objects; but sight will see nothing and the colours will remain invisible in the absence of a third e
thing peculiarly constituted to serve this very purpose.

By which you mean—?

Naturally I mean what you call light; and if light is a thing of value, the sense of sight and the power of being visible are linked together by a very precious bond, such 508
as unites no other sense with its object.

No one could say that light is not a precious thing.

And of all the divinities in the skies is there one whose light, above all the rest, is responsible for making our eyes see perfectly and making objects perfectly visible?

There can be no two opinions: of course you mean the Sun.

And how is sight related to this deity? Neither sight nor the eye which contains it is the Sun, but of all the sense-organs it is the most sun-like; and further, the power it b
possesses is dispensed by the Sun, like a stream flooding the eye. And again, the Sun is not vision, but it is the cause of vision and also is seen by the vision it causes.

Yes.

It was the Sun, then, that I meant when I spoke of that offspring which the Good has created in the visible world, to stand there in the same relation to vision and visible things as that which the Good itself bears in the intelligible world to intelligence and to c
intelligible objects.

How is that? You must explain further.

You know what happens when the colours of things are no longer irradiated by the daylight, but only by the fainter luminaries of the night: when you look at them, the eyes are dim and seem almost blind, as if there were no unclouded vision in them. But d
when you look at things on which the Sun is shining, the same eyes see distinctly and it becomes evident that they do contain the power of vision.

Certainly.

Apply this comparison, then, to the soul. When its gaze is fixed upon an object irradiated by truth and reality, the soul gains understanding and knowledge and is manifestly in possession of intelligence. But when it looks towards that twilight world of things that come into existence and pass away, its sight is dim and it has only opinions and beliefs which shift to and fro, and now it seems like a thing that has no intelligence.

That is true.

This, then, which gives to the objects of knowledge their truth and to him who knows them his power of knowing, is the Form or essential nature of Goodness. It is e
the cause of knowledge and truth; and so, while you may think of it as an object of knowledge, you will do well to regard it as something beyond truth and knowledge and, precious as these both are, of still higher worth. And, just as in our analogy light and vision were to be thought of as like the Sun, but not identical with it, so here both 509
knowledge and truth are to be regarded as like the Good, but to identify either with the Good is wrong. The Good must hold a yet higher place of honour.

You are giving it a position of extraordinary splendour, if it is the source of knowledge and truth and itself surpasses them in worth. You surely cannot mean that it is pleasure.

Heaven forbid, I exclaimed. But I want to follow up our analogy still further. b
You will agree that the Sun not only makes the things we see visible, but also brings

them into existence and gives them growth and nourishment; yet he is not the same thing as existence. And so with the objects of knowledge: these derive from the Good not only their power of being known, but their very being and reality; and Goodness is not the same thing as being, but even beyond being, surpassing it in dignity and power.

c   Glaucon exclaimed with some amusement at my exalting Goodness in such extravagant terms.

It is your fault, I replied; you forced me to say what I think.

Yes, and you must not stop there. At any rate, complete your comparison with the Sun, if there is any more to be said.

There is a great deal more, I answered.

Let us hear it, then; don't leave anything out.

I am afraid much must be left unspoken. However, I will not, if I can help it, leave out anything that can be said on this occasion.

Please do not.

d   Conceive, then, that there are these two powers I speak of, the Good reigning over the domain of all that is intelligible, the Sun over the visible world—or the heaven as I might call it; only you would think I was showing off my skill in etymology. At any rate you have these two orders of things clearly before your mind: the visible and the intelligible?

I have.

Now take a line divided into two unequal parts, one to represent the visible order, the other the intelligible; and divide each part again in the same proportion,
e   symbolizing degrees of comparative clearness or obscurity. Then (A) one of the two
510 sections in the visible world will stand for images. By images I mean first shadows, and then reflections in water or in close-grained, polished surfaces, and everything of that kind, if you understand.

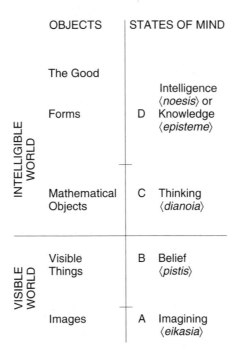

	OBJECTS		STATES OF MIND
INTELLIGIBLE WORLD	The Good		
	Forms	D	Intelligence ⟨*noesis*⟩ or Knowledge ⟨*episteme*⟩
	Mathematical Objects	C	Thinking ⟨*dianoia*⟩
VISIBLE WORLD	Visible Things	B	Belief ⟨*pistis*⟩
	Images	A	Imagining ⟨*eikasia*⟩

Yes, I understand.

Let the second section (B) stand for the actual things of which the first are likenesses, the living creatures about us and all the works of nature or of human hands.

So be it.

Will you also take the proportion in which the visible world has been divided as corresponding to degrees of reality and truth, so that the likeness shall stand to the original in the same ratio as the sphere of appearances and belief to the sphere of knowledge?

Certainly.   b

Now consider how we are to divide the part which stands for the intelligible world. There are two sections. In the first (C) the mind uses as images those actual things which themselves had images in the visible world; and it is compelled to pursue its inquiry by starting from assumptions and travelling, not up to a principle, but down to a conclusion. In the second (D) the mind moves in the other direction, from an assumption up towards a principle which is not hypothetical; and it makes no use of the images employed in the other section, but only of Forms, and conducts its inquiry solely by their means.

I don't quite understand what you mean.

Then we will try again; what I have just said will help you to understand. (C)   c
You know, of course, how students of subjects like geometry and arithmetic begin by postulating odd and even numbers, or the various figures and the three kinds of angle, and other such data in each subject. These data they take as known; and, having adopted them as assumptions, they do not feel called upon to give any account of them to themselves or to anyone else, but treat them as self-evident. Then, starting from these assumptions, they go on until they arrive, by a series of consistent steps, at all the   d
conclusions they set out to investigate.

Yes, I know that.

You also know how they make use of visible figures and discourse about them, though what they really have in mind is the originals of which these figures are images: they are not reasoning, for instance, about this particular square and diagonal which they have drawn, but about *the* Square and *the* Diagonal; and so in all cases. The diagrams they draw and the models they make are actual things, which may have their   e
shadows or images in water; but now they serve in their turn as images, while the student is seeking to behold those realities which only thought can apprehend.

True.   511

This, then, is the class of things that I spoke of as intelligible, but with two qualifications: first, that the mind, in studying them, is compelled to employ assumptions, and, because it cannot rise above these, does not travel upwards to a first principle; and second, that it uses as images those actual things which have images of their own in the section below them and which, in comparison with those shadows and reflections, are reputed to be more palpable and valued accordingly.

I understand: you mean the subject-matter of geometry and of the kindred arts.   b

(D) Then by the second section of the intelligible world you may understand me to mean all that unaided reasoning apprehends by the power of dialectic, when it treats its assumptions, not as first principles, but as *hypotheses* in the literal sense, things "laid down" like a flight of steps up which it may mount all the way to something that is not hypothetical, the first principle of all; and having grasped this, may turn back and, holding on to the consequences which depend upon it, descend at last to a conclusion, never making use of any sensible object, but only of Forms, moving through   c
Forms from one to another, and ending with Forms.

I understand, he said, though not perfectly; for the procedure you describe sounds like an enormous undertaking. But I see that you mean to distinguish the field of intelligible reality studied by dialectic as having a greater certainty and truth than the subject-matter of the "arts," as they are called, which treat their assumptions as first principles. The students of these arts are, it is true, compelled to exercise thought in

d   contemplating objects which the senses cannot perceive; but because they start from assumptions without going back to a first principle, you do not regard them as gaining true understanding about those objects, although the objects themselves, when connected with a first principle, are intelligible. And I think you would call the state of mind of the students of geometry and other such arts, not intelligence, but thinking, as being something between intelligence and mere acceptance of appearances.

You have understood me quite well enough, I replied. And now you may take, as

e   corresponding to the four sections, these four states of mind: *intelligence* for the highest, *thinking* for the second, *belief* for the third, and for the last *imagining*. These you may arrange as the terms in a proportion, assigning to each a degree of clearness and certainty corresponding to the measure in which their objects possess truth and reality.

I understand and agree with you. I will arrange them as you say.

Book VII

514   Next, said I, here is a parable to illustrate the degrees in which our nature may be enlightened or unenlightened. Imagine the condition of men living in a sort of cavernous chamber underground, with an entrance open to the light and a long passage all down the cave. Here they have been from childhood, chained by the leg and also by the neck, so that they cannot move and can see only what is in front of them, because the chains

b   will not let them turn their heads. At some distance higher up is the light of a fire burning behind them; and between the prisoners and the fire is a track with a parapet built along it, like the screen at a puppet-show, which hides the performers while they show their puppets over the top.

I see, said he.

Now behind this parapet imagine persons carrying along various artificial ob-

c   jects, including figures of men and animals in wood or stone or other materials, which
515   project above the parapet. Naturally, some of these persons will be talking, others silent.

It is a strange picture, he said, and a strange sort of prisoners.

Like ourselves, I replied; for in the first place prisoners so confined would have seen nothing of themselves or of one another, except the shadows thrown by the fire-light on the wall of the Cave facing them, would they?

b   Not if all their lives they had been prevented from moving their heads.

And they would have seen as little of the objects carried past.

Of course.

Now, if they could talk to one another, would they not suppose that their words referred only to those passing shadows which they saw?

Necessarily.

And suppose their prison had an echo from the wall facing them? When one of the people crossing behind them spoke, they could only suppose that the sound came from the shadow passing before their eyes.

No doubt.

In every way, then, such prisoners would recognize as reality nothing but the   c
shadows of those artificial objects.

Inevitably.

Now consider what would happen if their release from the chains and the healing
of their unwisdom should come about in this way. Suppose one of them were set free
and forced suddenly to stand up, turn his head, and walk with eyes lifted to the light; all
these movements would be painful, and he would be too dazzled to make out the objects
whose shadows he had been used to seeing. What do you think he would say, if someone told him that what he had formerly seen was meaningless illusion, but now, being
somewhat nearer to reality and turned towards more real objects, he was getting a truer   d
view? Suppose further that he were shown the various objects being carried by and were
made to say, in reply to questions, what each of them was. Would he not be perplexed
and believe the objects now shown him to be not so real as what he formerly saw?

Yes, not nearly so real.

And if he were forced to look at the firelight itself, would not his eyes ache, so   e
that he would try to escape and turn back to the things which he could see distinctly,
convinced that they really were clearer than these other objects now being shown to
him?

Yes.

And suppose someone were to drag him away forcibly up the steep and rugged
ascent and not let him go until he had hauled him out into the sunlight, would he not
suffer pain and vexation at such treatment, and, when he had come out into the light,
find his eyes so full of its radiance that he could not see a single one of the things that   516
he was now told were real?

Certainly he would not see them all at once.

He would need, then, to grow accustomed before he could see things in that
upper world. At first it would be easiest to make out shadows, and then the images of
men and things reflected in water, and later on the things themselves. After that, it
would be easier to watch the heavenly bodies and the sky itself by night, looking at the   b
light of the moon and stars rather than the Sun and the Sun's light in the day-time.

Yes, surely.

Last of all, he would be able to look at the Sun and contemplate its nature, not as
it appears when reflected in water or any alien medium, but as it is in itself in its own
domain.

No doubt.

And now he would begin to draw the conclusion that it is the Sun that produces
the seasons and the course of the year and controls everything in the visible world, and
moreover is in a way the cause of all that he and his companions used to see.   c

Clearly he would come at last to that conclusion.

Then if he called to mind his fellow prisoners and what passed for wisdom in his
former dwelling-place, he would surely think himself happy in the change and be sorry
for them. They may have had a practice of honouring and commending one another,
with prizes for the man who had the keenest eye for the passing shadows and the best
memory for the order in which they followed or accompanied one another, so that he   d
could make a good guess as to which was going to come next. Would our released
prisoner be likely to covet those prizes or to envy the men exalted to honour and power
in the Cave? Would he not feel like Homer's Achilles, that he would far sooner "be on
earth as a hired servant in the house of a landless man" or endure anything rather than
go back to his old beliefs and live in the old way?

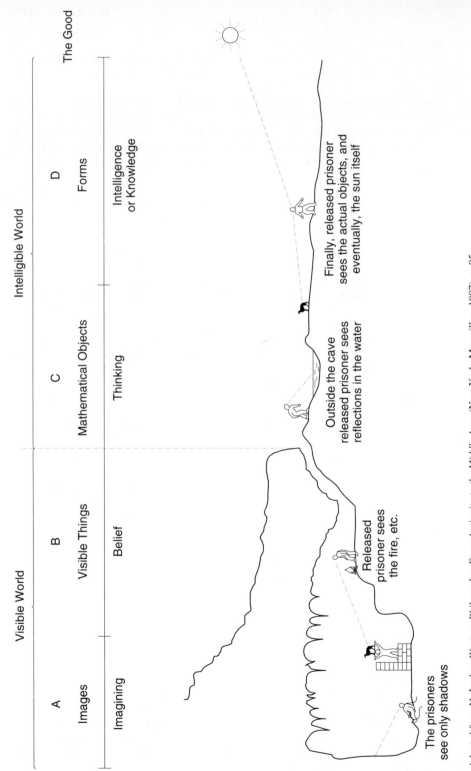

	Visible World		Intelligible World	
A	B	C	D	The Good
Images	Visible Things	Mathematical Objects	Forms	
Imagining	Belief	Thinking	Intelligence or Knowledge	

Finally, released prisoner sees the actual objects, and eventually, the sun itself

Outside the cave released prisoner sees reflections in the water

Released prisoner sees the fire, etc.

The prisoners see only shadows

Adapted from N. Jordan, *Western Philosophy: From Antiquity to the Middle Ages* (New York: Macmillan, 1987), p. 95.

Yes, he would prefer any fate to such a life.   e

Now imagine what would happen if he went down again to take his former seat
in the Cave. Coming suddenly out of the sunlight, his eyes would be filled with dark-   517
ness. He might be required once more to deliver his opinion on those shadows, in competition with the prisoners who had never been released, while his eyesight was still
dim and unsteady; and it might take some time to become used to the darkness. They
would laugh at him and say that he had gone up only to come back with his sight ruined; it was worth no one's while even to attempt the ascent. If they could lay hands on
the man who was trying to set them free and lead them up, they would kill him.

Yes, they would.

Every feature in this parable, my dear Glaucon, is meant to fit our earlier analysis. The prison dwelling corresponds to the region revealed to us through the sense of   b
sight, and the firelight within it to the power of the Sun. The ascent to see the things in
the upper world you may take as standing for the upward journey of the soul into the
region of the intelligible; then you will be in possession of what I surmise, since that is
what you wish to be told. Heaven knows whether it is true; but this, at any rate, is how
it appears to me. In the world of knowledge, the last thing to be perceived and only
with great difficulty is the essential Form of Goodness. Once it is perceived, the conclusion must follow that, for all things, this is the cause of whatever is right and good;   c
in the visible world it gives birth to light and to the lord of light, while it is itself sovereign in the intelligible world and the parent of intelligence and truth. Without having
had a vision of this Form no one can act with wisdom, either in his own life or in matters of state.

So far as I can understand, I share your belief.

Then you may also agree that it is no wonder if those who have reached this
height are reluctant to manage the affairs of men. Their souls long to spend all their   d
time in that upper world—naturally enough, if here once more our parable holds true.
Nor, again, is it at all strange that one who comes from the contemplation of divine
things to the miseries of human life should appear awkward and ridiculous when, with
eyes still dazed and not yet accustomed to the darkness, he is compelled, in a law-court
or elsewhere, to dispute about the shadows of justice or the images that cast those
shadows, and to wrangle over the notions of what is right in the minds of men who   e
have never beheld Justice itself.

It is not at all strange.

No; a sensible man will remember that the eyes may be confused in two   518
ways—by a change from light to darkness or from darkness to light; and he will recognize that the same thing happens to the soul. When he sees it troubled and unable to
discern anything clearly, instead of laughing thoughtlessly, he will ask whether, coming from a brighter existence, its unaccustomed vision is obscured by the darkness, in
which case he will think its condition enviable and its life a happy one; or whether,
emerging from the depths of ignorance, it is dazzled by excess of light. If so, he will   b
rather feel sorry for it; or, if he were inclined to laugh, that would be less ridiculous
than to laugh at the soul which has come down from the light.

That is a fair statement.

If this is true, then, we must conclude that education is not what it is said to be by
some, who profess to put knowledge into a soul which does not possess it, as if they   c
could put sight into blind eyes. On the contrary, our own account signifies that the soul
of every man does possess the power of learning the truth and the organ to see it with;
and that, just as one might have to turn the whole body round in order that the eye
should see light instead of darkness, so the entire soul must be turned away from this

changing world, until its eye can bear to contemplate reality and that supreme splen-
d   dour which we have called the Good. Hence there may well be an art whose aim would
be to effect this very thing, the conversion of the soul, in the readiest way; not to put
the power of sight into the soul's eye, which already has it, but to ensure that, instead
of looking in the wrong direction, it is turned the way it ought to be.

Yes, it may well be so.

It looks, then, as though wisdom were different from those ordinary virtues, as
they are called, which are not far removed from bodily qualities, in that they can be
produced by habituation and exercise in a soul which has not possessed them from the
e   first. Wisdom, it seems, is certainly the virtue of some diviner faculty, which never
loses its power, though its use for good or harm depends on the direction towards
519   which it is turned. You must have noticed in dishonest men with a reputation for
sagacity the shrewd glance of a narrow intelligence piercing the objects to which it is
directed. There is nothing wrong with their power of vision, but it has been forced into
the service of evil, so that the keener its sight, the more harm it works.

Quite true.

And yet if the growth of a nature like this had been pruned from earliest child-
b   hood, cleared of those clinging overgrowths which come of gluttony and all luxurious
pleasure and, like leaden weights charged with affinity to this mortal world, hang upon
the soul, bending its vision downwards; if, freed from these, the soul were turned
round towards true reality, then this same power in these very men would see the truth
as keenly as the objects it is turned to now.

Yes, very likely.

Is it not also likely, or indeed certain after what has been said, that a state can
never be properly governed either by the uneducated who know nothing of truth or by
c   men who are allowed to spend all their days in the pursuit of culture? The ignorant
have no single mark before their eyes at which they must aim in all the conduct of their
own lives and of affairs of state; and the others will not engage in action if they can
help it, dreaming that, while still alive, they have been translated to the Islands of the
Blest.

Quite true.

It is for us, then, as founders of a commonwealth, to bring compulsion to bear on
the noblest natures. They must be made to climb the ascent to the vision of Goodness,
d   which we called the highest object of knowledge; and, when they have looked upon it
long enough, they must not be allowed, as they now are, to remain on the heights, refusing to come down again to the prisoners or to take any part in their labours and rewards, however much or little these may be worth.

Shall we not be doing them an injustice, if we force on them a worse life than
they might have?

e   You have forgotten again, my friend, that the law is not concerned to make any
one class specially happy, but to ensure the welfare of the commonwealth as a whole.
520   By persuasion or constraint it will unite the citizens in harmony, making them share
whatever benefits each class can contribute to the common good; and its purpose in
forming men of that spirit was not that each should be left to go his own way, but that
they should be instrumental in binding the community into one.

True, I had forgotten.

You will see, then, Glaucon, that there will be no real injustice in compelling our
philosophers to watch over and care for the other citizens. We can fairly tell them that
b   their compeers in other states may quite reasonably refuse to collaborate: there they
have sprung up, like a self-sown plant, in despite of their country's institutions; no one

has fostered their growth, and they cannot be expected to show gratitude for a care they have never received. "But," we shall say, "it is not so with you. We have brought you into existence for your country's sake as well as for your own, to be like leaders and king-bees in a hive; you have been better and more thoroughly educated than those others and hence you are more capable of playing your part both as men of thought and as men of action. You must go down, then, each in his turn, to live with the rest and let   c
your eyes grow accustomed to the darkness. You will then see a thousand times better than those who live there always; you will recognize every image for what it is and know what it represents, because you have seen justice, beauty, and goodness in their reality; and so you and we shall find life in our commonwealth no mere dream, as it is in most existing states, where men live fighting one another about shadows and quar-   d
relling for power, as if that were a great prize; whereas in truth government can be at its best and free from dissension only where the destined rulers are least desirous of holding office."

Quite true.

Then will our pupils refuse to listen and to take their turns at sharing in the work of the community, though they may live together for most of their time in a purer air?

No; it is a fair demand, and they are fair-minded men. No doubt, unlike any ruler   e
of the present day, they will think of holding power as an unavoidable necessity.

Yes, my friend; for the truth is that you can have a well-governed society only if you can discover for your future rulers a better way of life than being in office; then   521
only will power be in the hands of men who are rich, not in gold, but in the wealth that brings happiness, a good and wise life. All goes wrong when, starved for lack of any-thing good in their own lives, men turn to public affairs hoping to snatch from thence the happiness they hunger for. They set about fighting for power, and this internecine conflict ruins them and their country. The life of true philosophy is the only one that looks down upon offices of state; and access to power must be confined to men who are not in love with it; otherwise rivals will start fighting. So whom else can you com-pel to undertake the guardianship of the commonwealth, if not those who, besides un-   b
derstanding best the principles of government, enjoy a nobler life than the politician's and look for rewards of a different kind?

There is indeed no other choice.

PARMENIDES (in part)

According to Antiphon, then, this was Pythodorus' account. Zeno and Parmenides   127[a]
once came to Athens for the Great Panathenaea. Parmenides was a man of distin-   b
guished appearance. By that time he was well advanced in years, with hair almost white; he may have been sixty-five. Zeno was nearing forty, a tall and attractive figure. It was said that he had been Parmenides' favourite. They were staying with Pythodorus outside the walls in the Ceramicus. Socrates and a few others came there, anxious to   c

Plato, *Parmenides* (127–135), translated by F.M. Cornford from *The Collected Dialogues of Plato,* edited by Edith Hamilton and Huntington Cairns. Copyright © 1961 by the Princeton University Press. Reprinted by permission of the Princeton University Press.

hear a reading of Zeno's treatise, which the two visitors had brought for the first time to Athens. Socrates was then quite young. Zeno himself read it to them; Parmenides at the moment had gone out. The reading of the arguments was very nearly over when

d   Pythodorus himself came in, accompanied by Parmenides and Aristoteles, the man who was afterwards one of the Thirty; so they heard only a small part of the treatise. Pythodorus himself, however, had heard it read by Zeno before.

When Zeno had finished, Socrates asked him to read once more the first hypothesis of the first argument. He did so, and Socrates asked: "What does this statement

e   mean, Zeno? 'If things are many,' you say, 'they must be both like and unlike. But that is impossible: unlike things cannot be like, nor like things unlike.' That is what you say, isn't it?"

Yes, replied Zeno.

And so, if unlike things cannot be like or like things unlike, it is also impossible that things should be a plurality; if many things did exist, they would have impossible attributes. Is this the precise purpose of your arguments—to maintain, against everything that is commonly said, that things are not a plurality? Do you regard every one of your arguments as evidence of exactly that conclusion, and so hold that, in each argu-

128   ment in your treatise, you are giving just one more proof that a plurality does not exist? Is that what you mean, or am I understanding you wrongly?

No, said Zeno, you have quite rightly understood the purpose of the whole treatise.

I see, Parmenides, said Socrates, that Zeno's intention is to associate himself with you by means of his treatise no less intimately than by his personal attachment. In a way, his book states the same position as your own; only by varying the form he tries

b   to delude us into thinking that his thesis is a different one. You assert, in your poem, that the All is one; and for this you advance admirable proofs. Zeno, for his part, asserts that it is not a plurality; and he too has many weighty proofs to bring forward. You assert unity, he asserts no plurality; each expresses himself in such a way that your arguments seem to have nothing in common, though really they come to very much the same thing. That is why your exposition and his seem to be rather over the heads of outsiders like ourselves.

c   Yes, Socrates, Zeno replied, but you have not quite seen the real character of my book. True, you are as quick as a Spartan hound to pick up the scent and follow the trail of the argument; but there is a point you have missed at the outset. The book makes no pretence of disguising from the public the fact that it was written with the purpose you describe, as if such deception were something to be proud of. What you have pointed out is only incidental; the book is in fact a sort of defence of Parmenides'

d   argument against those who try to make fun of it by showing that his supposition, that there is a One, leads to many absurdities and contradictions. This book, then, is a retort against those who assert a plurality. It pays them back in the same coin with something to spare, and aims at showing that, on a thorough examination, their own supposition that there is a plurality leads to even more absurd consequences than the hypothesis of the One. It was written in that controversial spirit in my young days; and someone copied it surreptitiously, so that I had not even the chance to consider whether it should

e   see the light or not. That is where you are mistaken Socrates; you imagine it was inspired, not by a youthful eagerness for controversy, but by the more dispassionate aims of an older man; though, as I said, your description of it was not far wrong.

I accept that, said Socrates, and I have no doubt it is as you say. But tell me this. Do you not recognise that there exists, just by itself, a Form of Likeness and again an-

129   other contrary Form, Unlikeness itself, and that of these two Forms you and I and all

the things we speak of as "many" come to partake? Also, that things which come to partake of Likeness come to be alike in that respect and just in so far as they do come to partake of it, and those that come to partake of Unlikeness come to be unlike, while those which come to partake of both come to be both? Even if all things come to partake of both, contrary as they are, and by having a share in both are at once like and unlike one another, what is there surprising in that? If one could point to things which are simply "alike" or "unlike" proving to be unlike or alike, that no doubt would be a portent; but when things which have a share in both are shown to have both characters, I see nothing strange in that, Zeno; nor yet in a proof that all things are one by having a share in Unity and at the same time many by sharing in Plurality. But if anyone can prove that what is simply Unity itself is many or that Plurality itself is one, then I shall begin to be surprised.

And so in all other cases; if the kinds or Forms themselves were shown to have these contrary characters among themselves, there would be good ground for astonishment; but what is there surprising in someone pointing out that I am one thing and also many? When he wants to show that I am many things, he can say that my right side is a different thing from my left, my front from my back, my upper parts from my lower, since no doubt I do partake of Plurality. When he wants to prove that I am one thing, he will say that I am one person among the seven of us, since I partake also of Unity. So both statements are true. Accordingly, if anyone sets out to show about things of this kind—sticks and stones, and so on—that the same thing is many and one, we shall say that what he is proving is that *something* is many and one, not that Unity is many or that Plurality is one; he is not telling us anything wonderful, but only what we should all admit. But, as I said just now, if he begins by distinguishing the Forms apart just by themselves—Likeness, for instance, and Unlikeness, Plurality and Unity, Rest and Motion, and all the rest—and then shows that these Forms among themselves can be combined with, or separate from, one another, then, Zeno, I should be filled with admiration. I am sure you have dealt with this subject very forcibly; but, as I say, my admiration would be much greater if anyone could show that these same perplexities are everywhere involved in the Forms themselves—among the objects we apprehend in reflection, just as you and Parmenides have shown them to be involved in the things we see.

While Socrates was speaking, Pythodorus said he was expecting every moment that Parmenides and Zeno would be annoyed; but they listened very attentively and kept on exchanging glances and smiles in admiration of Socrates. When he ended, Parmenides expressed this feeling.

Socrates, he said, your eagerness for discussion is admirable. And now tell me: have you yourself drawn this distinction you speak of and separated apart on the one side Forms themselves and on the other the things that share in them? Do you believe that there is such a thing as Likeness itself apart from the likeness that we possess, and so on with Unity and Plurality and all the terms in Zeno's argument that you have just been listening to?

Certainly I do, said Socrates.

And also in cases like these, asked Parmenides: is there, for example, a Form of Rightness or of Beauty or of Goodness, and of all such things?

Yes.

And again, a Form of Man, apart from ourselves and all other men like us—a Form of Man as something by itself? Or a Form of Fire or of Water?

I have often been puzzled about those things, Parmenides, whether one should say that the same thing is true in their case or not.

d   Are you also puzzled, Socrates, about cases that might be thought absurd, such as hair or mud or dirt or any other trivial and undignified objects? Are you doubtful whether or not to assert that each of these has a separate Form distinct from things like those we handle?

Not at all, said Socrates; in these cases, the things are just the things we see; it would surely be too absurd to suppose that they have a Form. All the same, I have sometimes been troubled by a doubt whether what is true in one case may not be true in all. Then, when I have reached that point, I am driven to retreat, for fear of tumbling into a bottomless pit of nonsense. Anyhow, I get back to the things which we were just now speaking of as having Forms, and occupy my time with thinking about them.

e   That, replied Parmenides, is because you are still young, Socrates, and philosophy has not yet taken hold of you so firmly as I believe it will some day. You will not despise any of these objects then; but at present your youth makes you still pay attention to what the world will think. However that may be, tell me this. You say you hold that there exist certain Forms, of which these other things come to partake and so to be called after their names: by coming to partake of Likeness or Largeness or Beauty or

131   Justice, they become like or large or beautiful or just?

Certainly, said Socrates.

Then each thing that partakes receives as its share either the Form as a whole or a part of it? Or can there be any other way of partaking besides this?

No, how could there be?

Do you hold, then, that the Form as a whole, a single thing, is in each of the many, or how?

Why should it not be in each, Parmenides?

b   If so, a Form which is one and the same will be at the same time, as a whole, in a number of things which are separate, and consequently will be separate from itself.

No, it would not, replied Socrates, if it were like one and the same day, which is in many places at the same time and nevertheless is not separate from itself. Suppose any given Form is in them all at the same time as one and the same thing in that way.

I like the way you make out that one and the same thing is in many places at once, Socrates. You might as well spread a sail over a number of people and then say that the one sail as a whole was over them all. Don't you think that is a fair analogy?

Perhaps it is.

c   Then would the sail as a whole be over each man, or only a part over one, another part over another?

Only a part.

In that case, Socrates, the Forms themselves must be divisible into parts, and the things which have a share in them will have a part for their share. Only a part of any given Form, and no longer the whole of it, will be in each thing.

Evidently, on that showing.

Are you, then, prepared to assert that we shall find the single Form actually being divided? Will it still be one?

Certainly not.

No, for consider this. Suppose it is Largeness itself that you are going to divide into parts, and that each of the many large things is to be large by virtue of a part of

d   Largeness which is smaller than Largeness itself. Will not that seem unreasonable?

It will indeed.

And again, if it is Equality that a thing receives some small part of, will that part, which is less than Equality itself, make its possessor equal to something else?

No, that is impossible.

Well, take Smallness. Is one of us to have a portion of Smallness, and is Smallness to be larger than that portion, which is a part of it? On this supposition again
Smallness itself will be larger, and anything to which the portion taken is added will be   e
smaller, and larger, than it was before.

That cannot be so.

Well then, Socrates, how are the other things going to partake of your Forms, if
they can partake of them neither in part nor as wholes?

Really, said Socrates, it seems no easy matter to determine in any way.

Again, there is another question.

What is that?

How do you feel about this? I imagine your ground for believing in a single
Form in each case is this. When it seems to you that a number of things are large, there   132
seems, I suppose, to be a certain single character which is the same when you look at
them all; hence you think that Largeness is a single thing.

True, he replied.

But now take Largeness itself and the other things which are large. Suppose you
look at all these in the same way in your mind's eye, will not yet another unity make its
appearance—a Largeness by virtue of which they all appear large?

So it would seem.

If so, a second Form of Largeness will present itself, over and above Largeness
itself and the things that share in it; and again, covering all these, yet another, which   b
will make all of them large. So each of your Forms will no longer be one, but an indefinite number.

But, Parmenides, said Socrates, may it not be that each of these Forms is a
thought, which cannot properly exist anywhere but in a mind. In that way each of them
can be one and the statements that have just been made would no longer be true of it.

Then, is each Form one of these thoughts and yet a thought of nothing?

No, that is impossible.

So it is a thought of something?

Yes.

Of something that is, or of something that is not?   c

Of something that is.

In fact, of some one thing which that thought observes to cover all the cases, as
being a certain single character?

Yes.

Then will not this thing that is thought of as being one and always the same in all
cases be a Form?

That again seems to follow.

And besides, said Parmenides, according to the way in which you assert that the
other things have a share in the Forms, must you not hold either that each of those
things consists of thoughts, so that all things think, or else that they are thoughts which
nevertheless do not think?

That too is unreasonable, replied Socrates. But, Parmenides, the best I can make
of the matter is this: that these Forms are as it were patterns fixed in the nature of   d
things; the other things are made in their image and are likenesses; and this participation they come to have in the Forms is nothing but their being made in their image.

Well, if a thing is made in the image of the Form, can that Form fail to be like the
image of it, in so far as the image was made in its likeness? If a thing is like, must it
not be like something that is like it?

It must.

e   And must not the thing which is like share with the thing that is like it in one and the same thing [character]?

Yes.

And will not that in which the like things share, so as to be alike, be just the Form itself that you spoke of?

Certainly.

If so, nothing can be like the Form, nor can the Form be like anything. Otherwise a second Form will always make its appearance over and above the first Form; and if

133   that second Form is like anything, yet a third; and there will be no end to this emergence of fresh Forms, if the Form is to be like the thing that partakes of it.

Quite true.

It follows that the other things do not partake of Forms by being like them; we must look for some other means by which they partake.

So it seems.

You see then, Socrates, said Parmenides, what great difficulties there are in asserting their existence as Forms just by themselves?

I do indeed.

I assure you, then, you have as yet hardly a notion of how great they will be, if

b   you are going to set up a single Form for every distinction you make among things.

How so?

The worst difficulty will be this, though there are plenty more: Suppose someone should say that the Forms, if they are such as we are saying they must be, cannot even be known. One could not convince him that he was mistaken in that objection, unless he chanced to be a man of wide experience and natural ability, and were willing to follow one through a long and remote train of argument. Otherwise there

c   would be no way of convincing a man who maintained that the Forms were unknowable.

Why so, Parmenides?

Because, Socrates, I imagine that you or anyone else who asserts that each of them has a real being "just by itself," would admit, to begin with, that no such real being exists in our world.

True; for how could it then be just by itself?

Very good, said Parmenides. And further, those Forms which are what they are with reference to one another, have their being in such references among themselves,

d   not with reference to those likenesses, or whatever we are to call them, in our world, which we possess and so come to be called by their several names. And, on the other hand, these things in our world which bear the same names as the Forms are related among themselves, not to the Forms; and all the names of that sort that they bear have reference to one another, not to the Forms.

How do you mean? asked Socrates.

Suppose, for instance, one of us is master or slave of another; he is not, of

e   course, the slave of Master itself, the essential Master, nor, if he is a master, is he master of Slave itself, the essential Slave, but, being a man, is master or slave of another man; whereas Mastership itself is what it is [mastership] of Slavery itself, and Slavery itself is slavery to Mastership itself. The significance of things in our world is not with reference to things in that other world, nor have these their significance with reference

134   to us; but as I say, the things in that world are what they are with reference to one another and towards one another; and so likewise are the things in our world. You see what I mean?

Certainly I do.

And similarly Knowledge itself, the essence of Knowledge, will be knowledge of that Reality itself, the essentially real.

Certainly.

And again any given branch of Knowledge in itself will be knowledge of some department of real things as it is in itself, will it not?

Yes.

Whereas the knowledge in our world will be knowledge of the reality in our   b
world; and it will follow again that each branch of knowledge in our world must be knowledge of some department of things that exist in our world.

Necessarily.

But, as you admit, we do not possess the Forms themselves, nor can they exist in our world.

No.

And presumably the Forms, just as they are in themselves, are known by the Form of Knowledge itself?

Yes.

The Form which we do not possess.

True.

Then, none of the Forms is known by us, since we have no part in Knowledge itself.

Apparently not.

So Beauty itself or Goodness itself and all the things we take as Forms in them-   c
selves, are unknowable to us.

I am afraid that is so.

Then here is a still more formidable consequence for you to consider.

What is that?

You will grant, I suppose, that if there is such a thing as a Form, Knowledge itself, it is much more perfect than the knowledge in our world; and so with Beauty and all the rest.

Yes.

And if anything has part in this Knowledge itself, you would agree that a god has a better title than anyone else to possess the most perfect knowledge?

Undoubtedly.

Then will the god, who possesses Knowledge itself, be able to know the things in   d
our world?

Why not?

Because we have agreed that those Forms have no significance with reference to things in our world, nor have things in our world any significance with reference to them. Each set has it only among themselves.

Yes, we did.

Then if this most perfect Mastership and most perfect Knowledge are in the gods' world, the gods' Mastership can never be exercised over us, nor their Knowledge know us or anything in our world. Just as we do not rule over them by virtue of rule as   e
it exists in our world and we know nothing that is divine by our knowledge, so they, on the same principle, being gods, are not our masters nor do they know anything of human concerns.

But surely, said Socrates, an argument which would deprive the gods of knowledge, would be too strange.

And yet, Socrates, Parmenides went on, these difficulties and many more besides   135
are inevitably involved in the Forms, if these characters of things really exist and one is

going to distinguish each Form as a thing just by itself. The result is that the hearer is perplexed and inclined either to question their existence, or to contend that, if they do exist, they must certainly be unknowable by our human nature. Moreover, there seems to be some weight in these objections, and, as we were saying, it is extraordinarily difficult to convert the objector. Only a man of exceptional gifts will be able to see that a

b   Form, or essence just by itself, does exist in each case; and it will require someone still more remarkable to discover it and to instruct another who has thoroughly examined all these difficulties.

I admit that, Parmenides; I quite agree with what you are saying.

But on the other hand, Parmenides continued, if, in view of all these difficulties

c   and others like them, a man refuses to admit that Forms of things exist or to distinguish a definite Form in every case, he will have nothing on which to fix his thought, so long as he will not allow that each thing has a character which is always the same; and in so doing he will completely destroy the significance of all discourse. But of that consequence I think you are only too well aware.

True.

What are you going to do about philosophy, then? Where will you turn while the answers to these questions remain unknown?

I can see no way out at the present moment.

That is because you are undertaking to define "Beautiful," "Just," "Good," and

d   other particular Forms, too soon, before you have had a preliminary training. I noticed that the other day when I heard you talking here with Aristoteles. Believe me, there is something noble and inspired in your passion for argument; but you must make an effort and submit yourself, while you are still young, to a severer training in what the world calls idle talk and condemns as useless. Otherwise, the truth will escape you.

THEAETETUS (in part)

148ᶜ   SOCRATES: . . . Do you fancy it is a small matter to discover the nature of knowledge? Is it not one of the hardest questions?

THEAETETUS: One of the very hardest, I should say.

SOCRATES: You may be reassured, then, about Theodorus' account of you, and set

d   your mind on finding a definition of knowledge, as of anything else, with all the zeal at your command.

THEAETETUS: If it depends on my zeal, Socrates, the truth will come to light.

SOCRATES: Forward, then, on the way you have just shown so well. Take as a model your answer about the roots: just as you found a single character to embrace all that multitude, so now try to find a single formula that applies to the many kinds of knowledge.

e   THEAETETUS: But I assure you, Socrates, I have often set myself to study that problem, when I heard reports of the questions you ask. But I cannot persuade myself

Plato, *Plato's Theory of Knowledge: The Theaetetus and the Sophist of Plato* (148c–210d), translated by F.M. Cornford (New York: Macmillan/Library of the Liberal Arts, 1957).

that I can give any satisfactory solution or that anyone has ever stated in my hearing the sort of answer you require. And yet I cannot get the question out of my mind.

SOCRATES: My dear Theaetetus, that is because your mind is not empty or barren. You are suffering the pains of travail.

THEAETETUS: I don't know about that, Socrates. I am only telling you how I feel.

SOCRATES: How absurd of you, never to have heard that I am the son of a mid-   149
wife, a fine buxom woman called Phaenarete!

THEAETETUS: I have heard that.

SOCRATES: Have you also been told that I practise the same art?

THEAETETUS: No, never.

SOCRATES: It is true, though; only don't give away my secret. It is not known that I possess this skill; so the ignorant world describes me in other terms as an eccentric person who reduces people to hopeless perplexity. Have you been told that too?   b

THEAETETUS: I have.

SOCRATES: Shall I tell you the reason?

THEAETETUS: Please do.

SOCRATES: Consider, then, how it is with all midwives; that will help you to understand what I mean. I dare say you know that they never attend other women in childbirth so long as they themselves can conceive and bear children, but only when they are too old for that.

THEAETETUS: Of course.

SOCRATES: They said that is because Artemis, the patroness of childbirth, is herself childless; and so, while she did not allow barren women to be midwives, because it is beyond the power of human nature to achieve skill without any experience, she as-   c
signed the privilege to women who were past childbearing, out of respect to their likeness to herself.

THEAETETUS: That sounds likely.

SOCRATES: And it is more than likely, is it not, that no one can tell so well as a midwife whether women are pregnant or not?

THEAETETUS: Assuredly.

SOCRATES: Moreover, with the drugs and incantations they administer, midwives can either bring on the pains of travail or allay them at their will, make a difficult   d
labour easy, and at an early stage cause a miscarriage if they so decide.

THEAETETUS: True.

SOCRATES: Have you also observed that they are the cleverest matchmakers, having an unerring skill in selecting a pair whose marriage will produce the best children?

THEAETETUS: I was not aware of that.

SOCRATES: Well, you may be sure they pride themselves on that more than on cutting the umbilical cord. Consider the knowledge of the sort of plant or seed that   e
should be sown in any given soil; does not that go together with skill in tending and harvesting the fruits of the earth? They are not two different arts?

THEAETETUS: No, the same.

SOCRATES: And so with a woman; skill in the sowing is not to be separated from skill in the harvesting?

THEAETETUS: Probably not.   150

SOCRATES: No; only, because there is that wrong and ignorant way of bringing together man and woman which they call pandering, midwives, out of self-respect, are shy even of matchmaking, for fear of falling under the accusation of pandering. Yet the genuine midwife is the only successful matchmaker.

THEAETETUS: That is clear.

SOCRATES: All this, then, lies within the midwife's province; but her performance falls short of mine. It is not the way of women sometimes to bring forth real children, sometimes mere phantoms, such that it is hard to tell the one from the other. If it were so, the highest and noblest task of the midwife would be to discern the real from the unreal, would it not?

THEAETETUS: I agree.

SOCRATES: My art of midwifery is in general like theirs; the only difference is that my patients are men, not women, and my concern is not with the body but with the soul that is in travail of birth. And the highest point of my art is the power to prove by every test whether the offspring of a young man's thought is a false phantom or instinct with life and truth. I am so far like the midwife, that I cannot myself give birth to wisdom; and the common reproach is true, that, though I question others, I can myself bring nothing to light because there is no wisdom in me. The reason is this: heaven constrains me to serve as a midwife, but has debarred me from giving birth. So of myself I have no sort of wisdom, nor has any discovery ever been born to me as the child of my soul. Those who frequent my company at first appear, some of them, quite unintelligent; but, as we go further with our discussions, all who are favoured by heaven make progress at a rate that seems surprising to others as well as to themselves, although it is clear that they have never learnt anything from me; the many admirable truths they bring to birth have been discovered by themselves from within. But the delivery is heaven's work and mine.

The proof of this is that many who have not been conscious of my assistance but have made light of me, thinking it was all their own doing, have left me sooner than they should, whether under others' influence or of their own motion, and thenceforward suffered miscarriage of their thoughts through falling into bad company; and they have lost the children of whom I had delivered them by bringing them up badly, caring more for false phantoms than for the true; and so at last their lack of understanding has become apparent to themselves and to everyone else. Such a one was Aristides, son of Lysimachus, and there have been many more. When they come back and beg for a renewal of our intercourse with extravagant protestations, sometimes the divine warning that comes to me forbids it; with others it is permitted, and these begin again to make progress. In yet another way, those who seek my company have the same experience as a woman with child: they suffer the pains of labour and, by night and day, are full of distress far greater than a woman's; and my art has power to bring on these pangs or to allay them. So it fares with these; but there are some, Theaetetus, whose minds, as I judge, have never conceived at all. I see that they have no need of me and with all goodwill I seek a match for them. Without boasting unduly, I can guess pretty well whose society will profit them. I have arranged many of these matches with Prodicus, and with other men of inspired sagacity.

And now for the upshot of this long discourse of mine. I suspect that, as you yourself believe, your mind is in labour with some thought it has conceived. Accept, then, the ministration of a midwife's son who himself practises his mother's art, and do the best you can to answer the questions I ask. Perhaps when I examine your statements I may judge one or another of them to be an unreal phantom. If I then take the abortion from you and cast it away, do not be savage with me like a woman robbed of her first child. People have often felt like that towards me and been positively ready to bite me for taking away some foolish notion they have conceived. They do not see that I am doing them a kindness. They have not learnt that no divinity is ever ill-disposed towards man, nor is such action on my part due to unkindness; it is only that I am not permitted to acquiesce in falsehood and suppress the truth.

So, Theaetetus, start again and try to explain what knowledge is. Never say it is beyond your power; it will not be so, if heaven wills and you take courage.

THEAETETUS: Well, Socrates, with such encouragement from a person like you, it would be a shame not to do one's best to say what one can. It seems to me that one e who knows something is perceiving the thing he knows, and, so far as I can see at present, knowledge is nothing but perception.

SOCRATES: Good; that is the right spirit in which to express one's opinion. But now suppose we examine your offspring together, and see whether it is a mere wind-egg or has some life in it. Perception, you say, is knowledge?

THEAETETUS: Yes.

SOCRATES: The account you give of the nature of knowledge is not, by any means, to be despised. It is the same that was given by Protagoras, though he stated it 152 in a somewhat different way. He says, you will remember, that "man is the measure of all things—alike of the being of things that are and of the not-being of things that are not." No doubt you have read that.

THEAETETUS: Yes, often.

SOCRATES: He puts it in this sort of way, doesn't he?—that any given thing "is to me such as it appears to me, and is to you such as it appears to you," you and I being men.

THEAETETUS: Yes, that is how he puts it.

SOCRATES: Well, what a wise man says is not likely to be nonsense. So let us fol- b low up his meaning. Sometimes, when the same wind is blowing, one of us feels chilly, the other does not; or one may feel slightly chilly, the other quite cold.

THEAETETUS: Certainly.

SOCRATES: Well, in that case are we to say that the wind in itself is cold or not cold? Or shall we agree with Protagoras that it is cold to the one who feels chilly, and not to the other?

THEAETETUS: That seems reasonable.

SOCRATES: And further that it so "appears" to each of us?

THEAETETUS: Yes.

SOCRATES: And "appears" means that he "perceives" it so?

THEAETETUS: True.

SOCRATES: "Appearing," then, is the same thing as "perceiving," in the case of c what is hot or anything of that kind. They are to each man such as he *perceives* them.

THEAETETUS: So it seems.

SOCRATES: Perception, then, is always of something that is, and, as being knowledge, it is infallible.

THEAETETUS: That is clear.

*   *   *

SOCRATES: . . . When we say that I, being of the height you see, without gaining 155^{b} or losing in size, may within a year be taller (as I am now) than a youth like you, and later on be shorter, not because I have lost anything in bulk, but because you have grown. For apparently I am later what I was not before, and yet have not become so; for without the process of becoming the result is impossible, and I could not be in process of becoming shorter without losing some of my bulk. I could give you count- c less other examples, if we are to accept these. For I think you follow me, Theaetetus; I fancy, at any rate, such puzzles are not altogether strange to you.

THEAETETUS: No; indeed it is extraordinary how they set me wondering whatever they can mean. Sometimes I get quite dizzy with thinking of them.

d   SOCRATES: That shows that Theodorus was not wrong in his estimate of your nature. This sense of wonder is the mark of the philosopher. Philosophy indeed has no other origin, and he was a good genealogist who made Iris [philosophy] the daughter of Thaumas [wonder]. Do you now begin to see the explanation of all this which follows from the theory we are attributing to Protagoras? Or is it not yet clear?

THEAETETUS: I can't say it is yet.

SOCRATES: Then perhaps you will be grateful if I help you to penetrate to the truth concealed in the thoughts of a man—or, I should say, of men—of such distinction.

e   THEAETETUS: Of course I shall be very grateful.

SOCRATES: Then just take a look round and make sure that none of the uninitiate overhears us. I mean by the uninitiate the people who believe that nothing is real save what they can grasp with their hands and do not admit that actions or processes or anything invisible can count as real.

THEAETETUS: They sound like a very hard and repellent sort of people.

*   *   *

161   SOCRATES: You have an absolute passion for discussion, Theodorus. I like the way you take me for a sort of bag full of arguments, and imagine I can easily pull out a proof to show that our conclusion is wrong. You don't see what is happening: The arguments never come out of me, they always come from the person I am talking with. I
b   am only at a slight advantage in having the skill to get some account of the matter from another's wisdom and entertain it with fair treatment. So now, I shall not give any explanation myself, but try to get it out of our friend.

THEODORUS: That is better, Socrates; do as you say.

*   *   *

163   SOCRATES: Let us look at it in this way, then—this question whether knowledge and perception are, after all, the same thing or not. For that, you remember, was the point to which our whole discussion was directed, and it was for its sake that we stirred up all this swarm of queer doctrines, wasn't it?

b   THEAETETUS: Quite true.

SOCRATES: Well, are we going to agree that, whenever we perceive something by sight or hearing, we also at the same time know it? Take the case of a foreign language we have not learnt. Are we to say that we do not hear the sounds that foreigners utter, or that we both hear and know what they are saying? Or again, when we don't know our letters, are we to maintain that we don't see them when we look at them, or that, since we see them, we do know them?

THEAETETUS: We shall say, Socrates, that we know just so much of them as we do
c   see or hear. The shape and colour of the letters we both see and know; we hear and at the same time know the rising and falling accents of the voice; but we neither perceive by sight and hearing nor yet know what a schoolmaster or an interpreter could tell us about them.

SOCRATES: Well done, Theaetetus. I had better not raise objections to that, for fear of checking your growth. But look, here is another objection threatening. How are we going to parry it?

THEAETETUS: What is that?

SOCRATES: It is this. Suppose someone were to ask: "Is it possible for a man who   d
has once come to know something and still preserves a memory of it, not to know just
that thing that he remembers at the moment when he remembers it?" This is, perhaps,
rather a long-winded way of putting the question. I mean: Can a man who has become
acquainted with something and remembers it, not know it?

THEAETETUS: Of course not, Socrates; the supposition is monstrous.

SOCRATES: Perhaps I am talking nonsense, then. But consider: you call seeing
"perceiving," and sight "perception," don't you?

THEAETETUS: I do.

SOCRATES: Then, according to our earlier statement, a man who sees something
acquires from that moment knowledge of the thing he sees?   e

THEAETETUS: Yes.

SOCRATES: Again, you recognise such a thing as memory?

THEAETETUS: Yes.

SOCRATES: Memory of nothing, or of something?

THEAETETUS: Of something, surely.

SOCRATES: Of what one has become acquainted with and perceived—that sort of
thing?

THEAETETUS: Of course.

SOCRATES: So a man sometimes remembers what he has seen?

THEAETETUS: He does.

SOCRATES: Even when he shuts his eyes? Or does he forget when he shuts them?

THEAETETUS: No, Socrates; that would be a monstrous thing to say.   164

SOCRATES: All the same, we shall have to say it, if we are to save our former
statement. Otherwise, it goes by the board.

THEAETETUS: I certainly have a suspicion that you are right, but I don't quite see
how. You must tell me.

SOCRATES: In this way. One who sees, we say, acquires knowledge of what he
sees, because it is agreed that sight or perception and knowledge are the same thing.

THEAETETUS: Certainly.

SOCRATES: But suppose this man who sees and acquires knowledge of what he
has seen, shuts his eyes; then he remembers the thing, but does not see it. Isn't that so?

THEAETETUS: Yes.

SOCRATES: But "does not see it" means "does not know it," since "sees" and   b
"knows" mean the same.

THEAETETUS: True.

SOCRATES: Then the conclusion is that a man who has come to know a thing and
still remembers it does not know it, since he does not see it; and we said that would be
a monstrous conclusion.

THEAETETUS: Quite true.

SOCRATES: Apparently, then, if you say that knowledge and perception are the
same thing, it leads to an impossibility.

THEAETETUS: So it seems.

SOCRATES: Then we shall have to say they are different.

THEAETETUS: I suppose so.

*   *   *

SOCRATES: . . . And now, perhaps, you may wonder what argument Protagoras   165ᵉ
will find to defend his position. Shall we try to put it into words?

THEAETETUS: By all means.

SOCRATES: No doubt, then, Protagoras will make all the points we have put for-
166   ward in our attempt to defend him, and at the same time will come to close quarters
with the assailant, dismissing us with contempt. Your admirable Socrates, he will say,
finds a little boy who is scared at being asked whether one and the same person can remember and at the same time not know one and the same thing. When the child is
frightened into saying No, because he cannot foresee the consequence, Socrates turns
the conversation so as to make a figure of fun of my unfortunate self. You take things
b   much too easily, Socrates. The truth of the matter is this: when you ask someone questions in order to canvass some opinion of mine and he is found tripping, then I am refuted only if his answers are such as I should have given; if they are different, it is he
who is refuted, not I. For instance, do you think you will find anyone to admit that
one's present memory of a past impression is an impression of the same character as
one had during the original experience, which is now over? It is nothing of the sort. Or
again, will anyone shrink from admitting that it is possible for the same person to
know and not to know the same thing? Or, if he is frightened of saying that, will he
ever allow that a person who is changed is the *same* as he was before the change occurred; or rather, that he is *one* person at all, and not several, indeed an infinite succes-
c   sion of persons, provided change goes on happening—if we are really to be on the
watch against one another's attempts to catch at words?

No, he will say; show a more generous spirit by attacking what I actually say;
and prove, if you can, that we have not, each one of us, his peculiar perceptions, or
that, granting them to be peculiar, it would not follow that what appears to each becomes—or is, if we may use the word "is"—for him alone to whom it appears. With
this talk of pigs and baboons, you are behaving like a pig yourself, and, what is more,
you tempt your hearers to treat my writings in the same way, which is not fair. For I do
d   indeed assert that the truth is as I have written: each one of us is a measure of what is
and of what is not; but there is all the difference in the world between one man and another just in the very fact that what is and appears to one is different from what is and
appears to the other. And as for wisdom and the wise man, I am very far from saying
they do not exist. By a wise man I mean precisely a man who can change any one of
us, when what is bad appears and is to him, and make what is good appear and be to
e   him. In this statement, again, don't set off in chase of words, but let me explain still
more clearly what I mean. Remember how it was put earlier in the conversation: to the
sick man his food appears sour and is so; to the healthy man it is and appears the opposite. Now there is no call to represent either of the two as wiser—that cannot be—nor
167   is the sick man to be pronounced unwise because he thinks as he does, or the healthy
man wise because he thinks differently. What is wanted is a change to the opposite
condition, because the other state is better.

And so too in education a change has to be effected from the worse condition to
the better; only, whereas the physician produces a change by means of drugs, the
sophist does it by discourse. It is not that a man makes someone who previously
thought what is false think what is true (for it is not possible either to think the thing
that is not or to think anything but what one experiences, and all experiences are true);
b   rather, I should say, when someone by reason of a depraved condition of mind has
thoughts of a like character, one makes him, by reason of a sound condition, think
other and sound thoughts, which some people ignorantly call true, whereas I should
say that one set of thoughts is better than the other, but not in any way truer. And as for
the wise, my dear Socrates, so far from calling them frogs, I call them, when they have
to do with the body, physicians, and when they have to do with plants, husbandmen.

For I assert that husbandmen too, when plants are sickly and have depraved sensations, substitute for these sensations that are sound and healthy; and moreover that wise and honest public speakers substitute in the community sound for unsound views of what is right. For I hold that whatever practices seem right and laudable to any particular State are so, for that State, so long as it holds by them. Only, when the practices are, in any particular case, unsound for them, the wise man substitutes others that are and appear sound. On the same principle the sophist, since he can in the same manner guide his pupils in the way they should go, is wise and worth a considerable fee to them when their education is completed. In this way it is true both that some men are wiser than others and that no one thinks falsely; and you, whether you like it or not, must put up with being a measure, since by these considerations my doctrine is saved from shipwreck.

Now if you can dispute this doctrine in principle, do so by argument stating the case on the other side, or by asking questions, if you prefer that method, which has no terrors for a man of sense; on the contrary it ought to be specially agreeable to him. Only there is this rule to be observed: do not conduct your questioning unfairly. It is very unreasonable that one who professes a concern for virtue should be constantly guilty of unfairness in argument. Unfairness here consists in not observing the distinction between a debate and a conversation. A debate need not be taken seriously and one may trip up an opponent to the best of one's power; but a conversation should be taken in earnest; one should help out the other party and bring home to him only those slips and fallacies that are due to himself or to his earlier instructors. If you follow this rule, your associates will lay the blame for their confusions and perplexities on themselves and not on you; they will like you and court your society, and disgusted with themselves, will turn to philosophy, hoping to escape from their former selves and become different men. But if, like so many, you take the opposite course, you will reach the opposite result: instead of turning your companions to philosophy, you will make them hate the whole business when they get older. So, if you will take my advice, you will meet us in the candid spirit I spoke of, without hostility or contentiousness, and honestly consider what we mean when we say that all things are in motion and that what seems also is, to any individual or community. The further question whether knowledge is, or is not, the same thing as perception, you will consider as a consequence of these principles, not (as you did just now) basing your argument on the common use of words and phrases, which the vulgar twist into any sense they please and so perplex one another in all sorts of ways.

* * *

SOCRATES: Let us begin, then, by coming to grips with the doctrine at the same point as before. Let us see whether or not our discontent was justified, when we criticised it as making every individual self-sufficient in wisdom. Protagoras then conceded that some people were superior in the matter of what is better or worse, and these, he said, were wise. Didn't he?

THEODORUS: Yes.

SOCRATES: If he were here himself to make that admission, instead of our conceding it for him in our defence, there would be no need to reopen the question and make sure of our ground; but, as things are, we might be said to have no authority to make the admission on his behalf. So it will be more satisfactory to come to a more complete and clear agreement on this particular point; for it makes a considerable difference, whether this is so or not.

THEODORUS: That is true.

170   SOCRATES: Let us, then, as briefly as possible, obtain his agreement, not through any third person, but from his own statement.

THEODORUS: How?

SOCRATES: In this way. He says—doesn't he?—that what seems true to anyone is true for him to whom it seems so?

THEODORUS: He does.

SOCRATES: Well now, Protagoras, we are expressing what seems true to a man, or rather to all men, when we say that everyone without exception holds that in some respects he is wiser than his neighbours and in others they are wiser than
b   he. For instance, in moments of great danger and distress, whether in war or in sickness or at sea, men regard as a god anyone who can take control of the situation and look to him as a saviour, when his only point of superiority is his knowledge. Indeed, the world is full of people looking for those who can instruct and govern men and animals and direct their doings, and on the other hand of people who think themselves quite competent to undertake the teaching and governing. In all these cases what can we say, if not that men do hold that wisdom and ignorance exist among them?

THEODORUS: We must say that.

SOCRATES: And they hold that wisdom lies in thinking truly, and ignorance in false belief?
c   THEODORUS: Of course.

SOCRATES: In that case, Protagoras, what are we to make of your doctrine? Are we to say that what men think is always true, or that it is sometimes true and sometimes false? From either supposition it results that their thoughts are not always true, but both true and false. For consider, Theodorus. Are you, or is any Protagorean, prepared to maintain that no one regards anyone else as ignorant or as making false judgments?

THEODORUS: That is incredible, Socrates.
d   SOCRATES: That, however, is the inevitable consequence of the doctrine which makes man the measure of all things.

THEODORUS: How so?

SOCRATES: When you have formed a judgment on some matter in your own mind and express an opinion about it to me, let us grant that, as Protagoras' theory says, it is true for you; but are we to understand that it is impossible for us, the rest of the company, to pronounce any judgment upon your judgment; or, if we can, that we always pronounce your opinion to be true? Do you not rather find thousands of opponents who set their opinion against yours on every occasion and hold that your judgment and belief are false?
e   THEODORUS: I should just think so, Socrates; thousands and tens of thousands, as Homer says; and they give me all the trouble in the world.

SOCRATES: And what then? Would you have us say that in such a case the opinion you hold is true for yourself and false for these tens of thousands?

THEODORUS: The doctrine certainly seems to imply that.

SOCRATES: And what is the consequence for Protagoras himself? Is it not this: supposing that not even he believed in man being the measure and the world in general
171   did not believe it either—as in fact it doesn't—then this *Truth* which he wrote would not be true for anyone? If, on the other hand, he did believe it, but the mass of mankind does not agree with him, then, you see, it is more false than true by just so much as the unbelievers outnumber the believers.

THEODORUS: That follows, if its truth or falsity varies with each individual opinion.

SOCRATES: Yes, and besides that it involves a really exquisite conclusion. Protagoras, for his part, admitting as he does that everybody's opinion is true, must acknowledge the truth of his opponents' belief about his own belief, where they think he is wrong.

THEODORUS: Certainly.

SOCRATES: That is to say, he would acknowledge his own belief to be false, if he   b
admits that the belief of those who think him wrong is true?

THEODORUS: Necessarily.

SOCRATES: But the others, on their side, do not admit to themselves that they are wrong.

THEODORUS: No.

SOCRATES: Whereas Protagoras, once more, according to what he has written, admits that this opinion of theirs is as true as any other.

THEODORUS: Evidently.

SOCRATES: On all hands, then, Protagoras included, his opinion will be disputed, or rather Protagoras will join in the general consent—when he admits to an opponent the truth of his contrary opinion, from that moment Protagoras himself will be admit-   c
ting that a dog or the man in the street is not a measure of anything whatever that he does not understand. Isn't that so?

THEODORUS: Yes.

SOCRATES: Then, since it is disputed by everyone, the *Truth* of Protagoras is true to nobody—to himself no more than to anyone else.

THEODORUS: We are running my old friend too hard, Socrates.

SOCRATES: But it is not clear that we are outrunning the truth, my friend. Of course it is likely that, as an older man, he was wiser than we are; and if at this moment   d
he could pop his head up through the ground there as far as to the neck, very probably he would expose me thoroughly for talking such nonsense and you for agreeing to it, before he sank out of sight and took to his heels. However, we must do our best with such lights as we have and continue to say what we think.

*   *   *

THEODORUS: What do you mean, Socrates?   174

SOCRATES: The same thing as the story about the Thracian maidservant who exercised her wit at the expense of Thales, when he was looking up to study the stars and tumbled down a well. She scoffed at him for being so eager to know what was happening in the sky that he could not see what lay at his feet. Anyone who gives his life to philosophy is open to such mockery. It is true that he is unaware what his next-door   b
neighbour is doing, hardly knows, indeed, whether the creature is a man at all; he spends all his pains on the question, what man is, and what powers and properties distinguish such a nature from any other. You see what I mean, Theodorus?

THEODORUS: Yes; and it is true.

SOCRATES: And so, my friend, as I said at first, on a public occasion or in private company, in a law court or anywhere else, when he is forced to talk about what lies at   c
his feet or is before his eyes, the whole rabble will join the maidservants in laughing at him, as from inexperience he walks blindly and stumbles into every pitfall. His terrible clumsiness makes him seem so stupid. He cannot engage in an exchange of abuse, for, never having made a study of anyone's peculiar weaknesses, he has no personal scan-

d   dals to bring up; so in his helplessness he looks a fool. When people vaunt their own or other men's merits, his unaffected laughter makes him conspicuous and they think he is frivolous. When a despot or king is eulogised, he fancies he is hearing some keeper of swine or sheep or cows being congratulated on the quantity of milk he has squeezed out of his flock; only he reflects that the animal that princes tend and milk is more given than sheep or cows to nurse a sullen grievance, and that a herdsman of this sort,

e   penned up in his castle, is doomed by sheer press of work to be as rude and unculti-vated as the shepherd in his mountain fold. He hears of the marvellous wealth of some landlord who owns ten thousand acres or more; but that seems a small matter to one accustomed to think of the earth as a whole. When they harp upon birth—some gentle-man who can point to seven generations of wealthy ancestors—he thinks that such

175   commendation must come from men of purblind vision, too uneducated to keep their eyes fixed on the whole or to reflect that any man has had countless myriads of ances-tors and among them any number of rich men and beggars, kings and slaves, Greeks and barbarians. To pride oneself on a catalogue of twenty-five progenitors going back to Heracles, son of Amphitryon, strikes him as showing a strange pettiness of outlook.

b   He laughs at a man who cannot rid his mind of foolish vanity by reckoning that before Amphitryon there was a twenty-fifth ancestor, and before him a fiftieth, whose fortunes were as luck would have it. But in all these matters the world has the laugh of the philosopher, partly because he seems arrogant, partly because of his helpless ignorance in matters of daily life.

    THEODORUS: Yes, Socrates, that is exactly what happens.

    SOCRATES: On the other hand, my friend, when the philosopher drags the other

c   upwards to a height at which he may consent to drop the question "What injustice have I done to you or you to me?" and to think about justice and injustice in themselves, what each is, and how they differ from one another and from anything else; or to stop quoting poetry about the happiness of kings or of men with gold in store and think about the meaning of kingship and the whole question of human happiness and misery,

d   what their nature is, and how humanity can gain the one and escape the other—in all this field, when that small, shrewd, legal mind has to render an account, then the situa-tion is reversed. Now it is he who is dizzy from hanging at such an unaccustomed height and looking down from mid-air. Lost and dismayed and stammering, he will be laughed at, not by maidservants or the uneducated—they will not see what is happen-ing—but by everyone whose breeding has been the antithesis of a slave's.

e   Such are the two characters, Theodorus. The one is nursed in freedom and leisure, the philosopher, as you call him. He may be excused if he looks foolish or use-less when faced with some menial task, if he cannot tie up bedclothes into a neat bun-dle or flavour a dish with spices and a speech with flattery. The other is smart in the

176   dispatch of all such services, but has not learnt to wear his cloak like a gentleman, or caught the accent of discourse that will rightly celebrate the true life of happiness for gods and men.

    THEODORUS: If you could convince everyone, Socrates, as you convince me, there would be more peace and fewer evils in the world.

    SOCRATES: Evils, Theodorus, can never be done away with, for the good must al-ways have its contrary; nor have they any place in the divine world; but they must

b   needs haunt this region of our mortal nature. That is why we should make all speed to take flight from this world to the other; and that means becoming like the divine so far as we can, and that again is to become righteous with the help of wisdom. But it is no such easy matter to convince men that the reasons for avoiding wickedness and seek-ing after goodness are not those which the world gives. The right motive is not that one should seem innocent and good—that is no better, to my thinking, than an old wives' tale—but let us state the truth in this way. In the divine there is no shadow of unrighteousness, only the perfection of righteousness; and nothing is more like the divine c than any one of us who becomes as righteous as possible. It is here that a man shows his true spirit and power or lack of spirit and nothingness. For to know this is wisdom and excellence of the genuine sort; not to know it is to be manifestly blind and base. All other forms of seeming power and intelligence in the rulers of society are as mean and vulgar as the mechanic's skill in handicraft. If a man's words and deeds are un- d righteous and profane, he had best not persuade himself that he is a great man because he sticks at nothing, glorying in his shame as such men do when they fancy that others say of them: They are no fools, no useless burdens to the earth, but men of the right sort to weather the storms of public life.

Let the truth be told: they are what they fancy they are not, all the more for deceiving themselves; for they are ignorant of the very thing it most concerns them to know—the penalty of injustice. This is not, as they imagine, stripes and death, which do not always fall on the wrong-doer, but a penalty that cannot be escaped. e

THEODORUS: What penalty is that?

SOCRATES: There are two patterns, my friend, in the unchangeable nature of things, one of divine happiness, the other of godless misery—a truth to which their folly makes them utterly blind, unaware that in doing injustice they are growing less like one of these patterns and more like the other. The penalty they pay is the life they 177 lead, answering to the pattern they resemble. But if we tell them that, unless they rid themselves of their superior cunning, that other region which is free from all evil will not receive them after death, but here on earth they will dwell for all time in some form of life resembling their own and in the society of things as evil as themselves, all this will sound like foolishness to such strong and unscrupulous minds.

THEODORUS: So it will, Socrates.

SOCRATES: I have good reason to know it, my friend. But there is one thing about b them: when you get them alone and make them explain their objections to philosophy, then, if they are men enough to face a long examination without running away, it is odd how they end by finding their own arguments unsatisfying; somehow their flow of eloquency runs dry, and they become as speechless as an infant.

All this, however, is a digression; we must stop now, and dam the flood of topics that threatens to break in and drown our original argument. With your leave, let us go c back to where we were before.

THEODORUS: For my part, I rather prefer listening to your digressions, Socrates; they are easier to follow at my time of life. However, let us go back, if you like.

*   *   *

SOCRATES: . . . Do you accept my description of the process of thinking? 189e

THEAETETUS: How do you describe it?

SOCRATES: As a discourse that the mind carries on with itself about any subject it is considering. You must take this explanation as coming from an ignoramus; but I have a notion that, when the mind is thinking, it is simply talking to itself, asking questions and answering them, and saying Yes or No. When it reaches a decision—which 190 may come slowly or in a sudden rush—when doubt is over and the two voices affirm the same thing, then we call that its "judgment." So I should describe thinking as discourse, and judgment as a statement pronounced, not aloud to someone else, but silently to oneself.

THEAETETUS: I agree.

SOCRATES: It seems, then, that when a person thinks of one thing as another, he is affirming to himself that the one is the other.

* * *

210   SOCRATES: So, apparently, to the question, What is knowledge? our definition will reply: "Correct belief together with knowledge of a differentness," for, according to it, "adding an account" will come to that.

THEAETETUS: So it seems.

SOCRATES: Yes; and when we are inquiring after the nature of knowledge, nothing could be sillier than to say that it is correct belief together with a *knowledge* of differentness or of anything whatever.

So, Theaetetus, neither perception, nor true belief, nor the addition of an "ac-
b   count" to true belief can be knowledge.

THEAETETUS: Apparently not.

SOCRATES: Are we in labour, then, with any further child, my friend, or have we brought to birth all we have to say about knowledge?

THEAETETUS: Indeed we have; and for my part I have already, thanks to you, given utterance to more than I had in me.

SOCRATES: All of which our midwife's skill pronounces to be mere wind eggs and not worth the rearing?

THEAETETUS: Undoubtedly.

SOCRATES: Then supposing you should ever henceforth try to conceive afresh,
c   Theaetetus, if you succeed, your embryo thoughts will be the better as a consequence of today's scrutiny; and if you remain barren, you will be gentler and more agreeable to your companions, having the good sense not to fancy you know what you do not know. For that, and no more, is all that my art can effect; nor have I any of that knowledge possessed by all the great and admirable men of our own day or of the past. But this midwife's art is a gift from heaven; my mother had it for women, and I for young
d   men of a generous spirit and for all in whom beauty dwells.

Now I must go to the portico of the King-Archon to meet the indictment which Meletus has drawn up against me. But tomorrow morning, Theodorus, let us meet here again.

TIMAEUS (in part)

27ᵈ   TIMAEUS: . . . We must, then, in my judgment, first make this distinction. What is that which is always real and has no becoming, and what is that which is always be-
28   coming and is never real? That which is apprehensible by thought with a rational account is the thing that is always unchangeably real; whereas that which is the object of

Plato, *Plato's Cosmology: The Timaeus of Plato* (27d–34b), translated by F.M. Cornford (New York: Macmillan/Library of the Liberal Arts, 1937).

belief together with unreasoning sensation is the thing that becomes and passes away, but never has real being. Again, all that becomes must needs become by the agency of some cause; for without a cause nothing can come to be. Now whenever the maker of anything looks to that which is always unchanging and uses a model of that description   b in fashioning the form and quality of his work, all that he thus accomplishes must be good. If he looks to something that has come to be and uses a generated model, it will not be good.

So concerning the whole Heaven or World—let us call it by whatsoever name may be most acceptable to it—we must ask the question which, it is agreed, must be asked at the outset of inquiry concerning anything: Has it always been, without any source of becoming; or has it come to be, starting from some beginning? It has come to be; for it can be seen and touched and it has body, and all such things are sensible; and, as we saw, sensible things, that are to be apprehended by belief together with sensa-   c tion, are things that become and can be generated. But again, that which becomes, we say, must necessarily become by the agency of some cause. The maker and father of this universe it is a hard task to find, and having found him it would be impossible to declare him to all mankind. Be that as it may, we must go back to this question about the world: After which of the two models did its builder frame it—after that which is always in the same unchanging state, or after its maker is good, clearly he looked to the   29 eternal; on the contrary supposition (which cannot be spoken without blasphemy), to that which has come to be. Everyone, then, must see that he looked to the eternal; for the world is the best of things that have become, and he is the best of causes. Having come to be, then, in this way, the world has been fashioned on the model of that which is comprehensible by rational discourse and understanding and is always in the same state.

Again, these things being so, our world must necessarily be a likeness of some-   b thing. Now in every matter it is of great moment to start at the right point in accordance with the nature of the subject. Concerning a likeness, then, and its model we must make this distinction: an account is of the same order as the things which it sets forth—an account of that which is abiding and stable and discoverable by the aid of reason will itself be abiding and unchangeable (so far as it is possible and it lies in the nature of an account to be incontrovertible and irrefutable, there must be no falling   c short of that); while an account of what is made in the image of that other, but is only a likeness, will itself be but likely, standing to accounts of the former kind in a proportion: as reality is to becoming, so is truth to belief. If then, Socrates, in many respects concerning many things—the gods and the generation of the universe—we prove unable to render an account at all points entirely consistent with itself and exact, you must not be surprised. If we can furnish accounts no less likely than any other, we must   d be content, remembering that I who speak and you my judges are only human, and consequently it is fitting that we should, in these matters, accept the likely story and look for nothing further.

SOCRATES: Excellent, Timaeus; we must certainly accept it as you say. Your prelude we have found exceedingly acceptable; so now go on to develop your main theme.

TIMAEUS: Let us, then, state for what reason becoming and this universe were   e framed by him who framed them. He was good; and in the good no jealousy in any matter can ever arise. So, being without jealousy, he desired that all things should   30 come as near as possible to being like himself. That this is the supremely valid principle of becoming and of the order of the world, we shall most surely be right to accept from men of understanding. Desiring, then, that all things should be good and, so far as might be, nothing imperfect, the god took over all that is visible—not at rest, but in discordant and unordered motion—and brought it from disorder into order, since he judged that order was in every way the better.

Now it was not, nor can it ever be, permitted that the work of the supremely good should be anything but that which is best. Taking thought, therefore, he found that, among things that are by nature visible, no work that is without intelligence will ever be better than one that has intelligence, when each is taken as a whole, and moreover that intelligence cannot be present in anything apart from soul. In virtue of this reasoning, when he framed the universe, he fashioned reason within soul and soul within body, to the end that the work he accomplished might be by nature as excellent and perfect as possible. This, then, is how we must say, according to the likely account, that this world came to be, by the god's providence, in very truth a living creature with soul and reason.

This being premised, we have now to state what follows next: What was the living creature in whose likeness he framed the world? We must not suppose that it was any creature that ranks only as a species; for no copy of that which is incomplete can ever be good. Let us rather say that the world is like, above all things, to that Living Creature of which all other living creatures, severally and in their families, are parts. For that embraces and contains within itself all the intelligible living creatures, just as this world contains ourselves and all other creatures that have been formed as things visible. For the god, wishing to make this world most nearly like that intelligible thing which is best and in every way complete, fashioned it as a single visible living creature, containing within itself all living things whose nature is of the same order.

Have we, then, been right to call it one Heaven, or would it have been true rather to speak of many and indeed of an indefinite number? One we must call it, if we are to hold that it was made according to its pattern. For that which embraces all the intelligible living creatures that there are, cannot be one of a pair; for then there would have to be yet another Living Creature embracing those two, and they would be parts of it; and thus our world would be more truly described as a likeness, not of them, but of that other which would embrace them. Accordingly, to the end that this world may be like the complete Living Creature in respect of its uniqueness, for that reason its maker did not make two worlds nor yet an indefinite number; but this Heaven has come to be and is and shall be hereafter one and unique.

Now that which comes to be must be bodily, and so visible and tangible; and nothing can be visible without fire, or tangible without something solid, and nothing is solid without earth. Hence the god, when he began to put together the body of the universe, set about making it of fire and earth. But two things alone cannot be satisfactorily united without a third; for there must be some bond between them drawing them together. And of all bonds the best is that which makes itself and the terms it connects a unity in the fullest sense; and it is of the nature of a continued geometrical proportion to effect this most perfectly. For whenever, of three numbers, the middle one between any two that are either solids (cubes?) or squares is such that, as the first is to it, so is it to the last, and conversely as the last is to the middle, so is the middle to the first, then since the middle becomes first and last, and again the last and first become middle, in that way all will necessarily come to play the same part towards one another, and by so doing they will all make a unity.

Now if it had been required that the body of the universe should be a plane surface with no depth, a single mean would have been enough to connect its companions and itself; but in fact the world was to be solid in form, and solids are always conjoined, not by one mean, but by two. Accordingly the god set water and air between fire and earth, and made them, so far as was possible, proportional to one another, so that as fire is to air, so is air to water, and as air is to water, so is water to earth, and thus he bound together the frame of a world visible and tangible.

For these reasons and from such constituents, four in number, the body of the   c
universe was brought into being, coming into concord by means of proportion, and from these it acquired Amity, so that coming into unity with itself it became indissoluble by any other save him who bound it together.

Now the frame of the world took up the whole of each of these four; he who put it together made it consist of all the fire and water and air and earth, leaving no part or power of any one of them outside. This was his intent: first, that it might be in the   d
fullest measure a living being whole and complete, of complete parts; next, that it   33
might be single, nothing being left over, out of which such another might come into being; and moreover that it might be free from age and sickness. For he perceived that, if a body be composite, when hot things and cold and all things that have strong powers beset that body and attack it from without, they bring it to untimely dissolution and cause it to waste away by bringing upon it sickness and age. For this reason and so considering, he fashioned it as a single whole consisting of all these wholes, complete   b
and free from age and sickness.

And for shape he gave it that which is fitting and akin to its nature. For the living creature that was to embrace all living creatures within itself, the fitting shape would be the figure that comprehends in itself all the figures there are; accordingly, he turned its shape rounded and spherical, equidistant every way from center to extremity—a figure the most perfect and uniform of all; for he judged uniformity to be immeasurably better than its opposite.

And all round on the outside he made it perfectly smooth, for several reasons. It   c
had no need of eyes, for nothing visible was left outside; nor of hearing, for there was nothing outside to be heard. There was no surrounding air to require breathing, nor yet was it in need of any organ by which to receive food into itself or to discharge it again when drained of its juices. For nothing went out or came into it from anywhere, since there was nothing: it was designed to feed itself on its own waste and to act and be   d
acted upon entirely by itself and within itself; because its framer thought that it would be better self-sufficient, rather than dependent upon anything else.

It had no need of hands to grasp with or to defend itself, nor yet of feet or any-   34
thing that would serve to stand upon; so he saw no need to attach to it these limbs to no purpose. For he assigned to it the motion proper to its bodily form, namely that one of the seven which above all belongs to reason and intelligence; accordingly, he caused it to turn about uniformly in the same place and within its own limits and made it revolve round and round; he took from it all the other six motions and gave it no part in their wanderings. And since for this revolution it needed no feet, he made it without feet or legs.

All this, then, was the plan of the god who is forever for the god who was some-   b
time to be. According to this plan he made it smooth and uniform, everywhere equidistant from its center, a body whole and complete, with complete bodies for its parts. And in the center he set a soul and caused it to extend throughout the whole and further wrapped its body round with soul on the outside; and so he established one world alone, round and revolving in a circle, solitary but able by reason of its excellence to bear itself company, needing no other acquaintance or friend but sufficient to itself. On all these accounts the world which he brought into being was a blessed god.

ARISTOTLE
384–322 B.C.

Aristotle was born in Stagira, on the border of Macedonia. His mother, Phaestis, was from a family of doctors, and his father, Nicomachus, was the court physician to the king of Macedonia. At seventeen, Aristotle was sent to Athens. There he studied in Plato's Academy for two decades, but, as he later wrote, he loved the truth more than he loved Plato, and so he had no mind to remain a mere disciple. In 347 B.C., after Plato's death, he left Athens and spent the next four years conducting zoological investigations on the islands of Assos and Lesbos.

About 343 B.C., he was called to Macedonia by King Philip to tutor the king's son—the future Alexander the Great. Upon Alexander's ascension to the throne seven years later, Aristotle returned to Athens to set up the Lyceum, a rival to the Academy. Aristotle did much of his teaching walking up and down the colonnades with advanced students. As a result, his school and philosophy came to be called by the Greek word for walking around: *peripatetikos*, from which we get our word "peripatetic." Tradition has it that as Alexander the Great moved east, conquering Persia and moving into India, he would send back biological specimens for Aristotle's school. Although most scholars doubt this popular story, it is nevertheless clear that under Alexander's patronage, the Lyceum flourished.

However, the connection to Alexander proved a liability in the end. On Alexander's death in 323 B.C., Athenians went on a rampage against any and all associated with him. Indicted on charges of impiety, Aristotle fled Athens, "lest," as he put it, "the Athenians sin twice against philosophy" (referring, of course, to the unjust trial and death of Socrates). Aristotle died a year later. A popular but again highly questionable story says he drowned investigating marine life.

There is no doubt that after Plato, Aristotle is the most influential philosopher of all time. In the early Middle Ages, his thought was preserved and commented upon by the great Arab philosophers. He dominated later medieval philosophy to such an extent that St. Thomas Aquinas referred to him simply as *philosophus*, the "philosopher." Logic, as taught until about the time of World War II, was essentially Aristotle's logic. His *Poetics* is still a classic of literary criticism, and his dicta on tragedy are widely accepted even today. Criticism of Aristotle's metaphysical and epistemological views has spread ever since Bacon and Descartes inaugurated modern philosophy; but for all that, the problems Aristotle saw, the distinctions he introduced, and the terms he defined are still central in many, if not most, philosophical discussions. His influence and prestige, like Plato's, are international and beyond all schools.

*   *   *

Aristotle found Plato's theory of Forms unacceptable. Like Plato, he wanted to discover universals, but he did not believe they existed apart from particulars. The form of a chair, for instance, can be thought of apart from the matter out of which the chair is made, but the form does not subsist as a separate invisible entity. The universal of "chairness" exists only in particular chairs—there is no other-worldly "Form of Chairness." Accordingly, Aristotle began his philosophy not with reflection on or dialogue about eternal Forms but with observations of particular objects.

In observing the world, Aristotle saw four "causes" responsible for making an object what it is: the material, formal, efficient, and final. In the case of a chair, for example, the chair's material cause is its wood and cloth, its formal cause is the structure or form given in its plan or blueprint, its efficient cause is the worker who made it, and its final cause is sitting. The material cause, then, is that *out of which* a thing is made, the formal cause is that *into which* a thing is made, the efficient cause is that *by which* a thing is made, and the final cause is that *for which* a thing is made. It is the last of these, the final cause, that Aristotle held to be most important, for it determined the other three. The "goal" or "end" (*telos* in Greek), the final cause, of any given substance is the key to its understanding. This means that all nature is to be understood in terms of final causes or purposes. This is known as a "teleological" explanation of reality.

As Aristotle applied these insights to human beings, he asked what the *telos* of a person could be. By observing what is unique to persons and what they, in fact, do seek, Aristotle came to the conclusion that the highest good or end for humans is *eudaimonia*. While this word is generally translated as "happiness," one must be careful to acknowledge that Aristotle's understanding of "happiness" is rather different from ours. *Eudaimonia* happiness is not a feeling of euphoria—in fact, it is not a feeling at all. It is rather "activity in accordance with virtue." Much of the material from the *Nicomachean Ethics* presented here is devoted both to clarifying the word and to discovering how this kind of "happiness" is to be achieved.

*   *   *

Aristotle's extant works lack the literary grace of Plato's. Like Plato, Aristotle is said to have written popular dialogues—the "exoteric" writings intended for those who were not students at the Lyceum—but they have not survived. What we have instead are the difficult "esoteric" works: lecture notes for classes at school. According to some scholars, these are not even Aristotle's notes, but the notes of students collected by editors. In any case, the writings as we have them contain much overlapping, repetition, and apparent contradiction.

The first five chapters of the *Categories*, with which we begin, help clear up a number of questions about Aristotle's conception of substance. Written as a treatise on language, the *Categories* makes clear why Aristotle rejected Plato's approach to knowledge of the Forms.

The brief selection from *On Interpretation (De Interpretatione)* presents Aristotle's philosophy of language. He analyzes the structure of sentences that express propositions and, in Chapter 9, presents a famous puzzle about the present truth-value of propositions concerning future events. This material has been the subject of much recent debate by such thinkers as Heidegger and Derrida. The selections from the *Categories* and *On Interpretation* are both given in J.L. Ackrill's translation.

The *Posterior Analytics*, which deals with the forms of argument and inquiry, is divided into two books. The selection from Book I included here deals with the nature of knowledge, demonstration, and truth and defines several key terms. The material from Book II considers the four possible forms of inquiry and explains how the individual mind comes to know the basic truths. The translation is by G.R.G. Mure.

Book II of the *Physics* deals with some of the main questions of physical science. After defining the term "nature," Aristotle discusses change and necessity. And making a distinction between physics and mathematics, he discusses the four causes. Throughout this text, Aristotle displays his teleological understanding of nature—that is, that natural processes operate for an end or purpose. This work is translated by R.P. Hardie and R.K. Gaye.

The *Metaphysics* probably consists of several independent treatises. Book I (*Alpha*) of this collection develops Aristotle's four causes and reviews the history of philosophy to his time. Book XII (*Lambda*) employs many of the concepts previously introduced, such as substance, actuality, and potency, and then moves to Aristotle's theology of the Unmoved Mover. The work concludes with Aristotle's rejection of Platonic Forms as separate, mathematical entities. Apparently Aristotle was responding to Plato's successors, who emphasized the mathematical nature of the Forms. W.D. Ross is the translator.

The first part of the selection presented from Aristotle's *On the Soul (De Anima)* gives a definition of the soul and distinguishes its faculties. The second part discusses the passive and the active mind. As this selection makes clear, Aristotle rejected Plato's view of a soul separate from the body. The selection is given in the translation by J.A. Smith.

The *Nicomachean Ethics*, is still considered one of the greatest works in ethics. Named for Aristotle's son, Nicomachus, it discusses the nature of the good and of moral and intellectual virtues, as well as investigating specific virtues. The lengthy selection presented here (about one-half of the complete work) reflects this vast range of topics and includes discussions of the subject matter and nature of ethics; of the good for an individual; of moral virtue; of the mean; of the conditions of responsibility for an action; of pride, vanity, humility, and the great-souled man (Aristotle's ideal); of the superiority of loving over being loved; and finally, of human happiness. The translation is Martin Ostwald's.

Our final selection, from various portions of the *Politics* (translated by Benjamin Jowett), gives a sense of Aristotle's political theory. In this work, the implications of his ethics are applied to the community. After dicussing the nature and purpose of the state, Aristotle presents several options for a good state: rule of one (monarchy), rule of a few (aristocracy), or rule of the many (constitutional government). Any of these would be acceptable if it is focused on the common good, for "political society exists for the sake of noble actions." Aristotle concludes that a strong middle class is the best guarantee of a good state.

The marginal page numbers, with their "a" and "b," are those of all scholarly editions—Greek, English, German, French, and others.

*   *   *

Timothy A. Robinson, *Aristotle in Outline* (Indianapolis, IN: Hackett, 1995) provides an excellent short introduction for the beginning student. W.K.C. Guthrie, *A History of Greek Philosophy, VI: Aristotle: An Encounter* (Cambridge: Cambridge University Press, 1981) and the classic W.D. Ross, *Aristotle* (1923; reprinted in New York: Meridian Books, 1959) are more advanced studies. John Herman Randall, Jr., *Aristotle* (New York: Columbia University Press, 1960); Marjorie Grene, *A Portrait of Aristotle* (Chicago: University of Chicago Press, 1963); J.L. Ackrill, *Aristotle the Philosopher* (Oxford: Oxford University Press, 1981); Jonathan Barnes, *Aristotle* (Oxford: Oxford University Press, 1982); Jonathan Lear, *Aristotle: The Desire to Understand* (Cambridge: Cambridge University Press, 1988); Terence Irwin, *Aristotle's First Principles* (Oxford: Oxford University Press, 1988); and Jonathan Barnes, ed., *The Cambridge Companion to Aristotle* (Cambridge: Cambridge University Press, 1995) also provide helpful overviews of Aristotle's life and thought. For general collections of essays, see R. Bambrough, ed., *New Essays on Plato and Aristotle* (London: Routledge & Kegan Paul, 1965); J.M.E. Moravcsik, ed., *Aristotle: A Collection of Critical Essays* (New York: Anchor Doubleday, 1967); J. Barnes, M. Schofield, and R. Sorabji, eds., *Articles on Aristotle*, four volumes. (London: Duckworth, 1979); Terence Irwin, ed., *Aristotle's Ethics, Aristotle: Substance, Form, and Matter* and *Aristotle: Metaphysics, Epistemology, Natural Philosophy* (all three, Hamden, CT: Garland Publishing, 1995); and Cynthia A. Freeland, ed., *Feminist Interpretations of Aristotle* (College Park, PA: Pennsylvania State University Press, 1998). For help with specific works (besides the *Nicomachean Ethics*), see Lindsay Judson, ed., *Aristotle's Physics: A Collection of Essays* (Oxford: Oxford University Press, 1991); Helen S. Lang, *Aristotle's Physics and Its Medieval Varieties* (Albany: SUNY Press, 1992); Martha C. Nussbaum and Amelie O. Rorty, eds., *Essays on Aristotle's De Anima* (Oxford: Oxford University Press, 1992); Michael Durrant, ed., *Aristotle's De Anima in Focus* (Oxford: Routledge, 1993); Michael Davis, *The Politics of Philosophy: A Commentary on Aristotle's Politics,* (Lanham, MD: Rowan & Littlefield, 1996); and Helen S. Lang, *The Order of Nature in Aristotle's Physics* (Cambridge: Cambridge University Press, 1998). The *Nichomachean Ethics* has been such an influential book that many commentaries and essays have been written about it. Among these are H.H. Joachim, *Aristotle: The Nicomachean Ethics*, edited by D.A. Rees (Oxford: Clarendon Press, 1951); W.F.R. Hardie, *Aristotle's Ethical Theory*, 2nd edition (Oxford: Oxford University Press, 1980); Amelie O. Rorty, ed., *Essays on Aristotle's Ethics* (Berkeley: University of California Press, 1980); J.O. Urmson, *Aristotle's*

Ethics (Oxford: Basil Blackwell, 1988); Sarah Brodie, *Ethics with Aristotle* (Oxford: Oxford University Press, 1991); and Francis Sparshott, *Taking Life Seriously: A Study of the Argument of the Nichomachean Ethics* (Toronto: University of Toronto Press, 1994). Alasdair C. MacIntyre's pair of books, *After Virtue: A Study in Moral Theory* (Notre Dame, IN: University of Notre Dame Press, 1981) and *Whose Justice? Which Rationality?* (Notre Dame, IN: University of Notre Dame Press, 1988) are interesting examples of recent attempts to apply Aristotle's ethics to contemporary moral problems.

CATEGORIES (in part)

1^a

1. When things have only a name in common and the definition of being which corresponds to the name is different, they are called *homonymous*. Thus, for example, both a man and a picture are animals. These have only a name in common and the definition of being which corresponds to the name is different; for if one is to say what being an animal is for each of them, one will give two distinct definitions.

5

When things have the name in common and the definition of being which corresponds to the name is the same, they are called *synonymous*. Thus, for example, both a man and an ox are animals. Each of these is called by a common name, "animal," and the definition of being is also the same; for if one is to give the definition of each—what being an animal is for each of them—one will give the same definition.

10

When things get their name from something, with a difference of ending, they are called *paronymous*. Thus, for example, the grammarian gets his name from grammar, the brave get theirs from bravery.

15

2. Of things that are said, some involve combination while others are said without combination. Examples of those involving combination are "man runs," "man wins"; and of those without combination "man," "ox," "runs," "wins."

20

Of things there are: (*a*) some are *said of* a subject but are not in any subject. For example, man is said of a subject, the individual man, but is not in any subject. (*b*) Some are in a subject but are not said of any subject. (By "in a subject" I mean what is in something, not as a part, and cannot exist separately from what it is in.) For example, the individual knowledge-of-grammar is in a subject, the soul, but is not said of any subject; and the individual white is in a subject, the body (for all colour is in a body), but is not said of any subject. (*c*) Some are both said of a subject and in a subject. For example, knowledge is in a subject, the soul, and is also said of a subject, knowledge-of-grammar. (*d*) Some are neither in a subject nor said of a subject, for example, the individual man or individual horse—for nothing of this sort is either in a subject or said of a subject. Things that are individual and numerically one are, without exception, not said of any subject, but there is nothing to prevent some of them from being in a subject—the individual knowledge-of-grammar is one of the things in a subject.

25

1^b

5

Aristotle, *Categories*, Chapters 1–5 from *Aristotle's Categories and De Interpretatione*, translated by J.L. Ackrill (Oxford: Oxford University Press, 1963). Reprinted by permission of Oxford University Press.

Diskobolos, by Myron. A Roman
copy after a bronze original of ca. 450
B.C. Myron's athlete epitomizes the
ideal Olympian goals of godlike
perfection and rational beauty.
(Museo del Terme, Rome)

3. Whenever one thing is predicated of another as of a subject, all things said of what is   10
predicated will be said of the subject also. For example, man is predicated of the individual man, and animal of man; so animal will be predicated of the individual man   15
also—for the individual man is both a man and an animal.

　　The differentiae of genera which are different and not subordinate one to the
other are themselves different in kind. For example, animal and knowledge: footed,
winged, aquatic, two-footed, are differentiae of animal, but none of these is a differen-   20
tia of knowledge; one sort of knowledge does not differ from another by being two-
footed. However, there is nothing to prevent genera subordinate one to the other from
having the same differentiae. For the higher are predicated of the genera below them,
so that all differentiae of the predicated genus will be differentiae of the subject also.

4. Of things said without any combination, each signifies either substance or quantity   25
or qualification or a relative or where or when or being-in-a-position or having or
doing or being-affected. To give a rough idea, examples of substance are man, horse;
of quantity: four-foot, five-foot; of qualification: white, grammatical; of a relative: 2ᵃ

double, half, larger; of where: in the Lyceum, in the market-place; of when: yesterday, last-year; of being-in-a-position: is-lying, is-sitting; of having: has-shoes-on, has-armour-on; of doing: cutting, burning; of being-affected: being-cut, being-burned.

5   None of the above is said just by itself in any affirmation, but by the combination of these with one another an affirmation is produced. For every affirmation, it seems, is either true or false; but of things said without any combination none is either true or 10   false (e.g., "man," "white," "runs," "wins").

5. A *substance*—that which is called a substance most strictly, primarily, and most of 15   all—is that which is neither said of a subject nor in a subject, e.g., the individual man or the individual horse. The species in which the things primarily called substances are, are called *secondary substances*, as also are the genera of these species. For example, the individual man belongs in a species, man, and animal is a genus of the species; so these—both man and animal—are called secondary substances.

It is clear from what has been said that if something is said of a subject both its 20   name and its definition are necessarily predicated of the subject. For example, man is said of a subject, the individual man, and the name is of course predicated (since you will be predicating man of the individual man), and also the definition of man will be 25   predicated of the individual man (since the individual man is also a man). Thus both the name and the definition will be predicated of the subject. But as for things which are in a subject, in most cases neither the name nor the definition is predicated of the 30   subject. In some cases there is nothing to prevent the name from being predicated of the subject, but it is impossible for the definition to be predicated. For example, white, which is in a subject (the body), is predicated of the subject; for a body is called white. But the definition of white will never be predicated of the body.

35   All the other things are either said of the primary substances as subjects or in them as subjects. This is clear from an examination of cases. For example, animal is predicated of man and therefore also of the individual man; for were it predicated of none of the individual men it would not be predicated of man at all. Again, colour is in 2ᵇ   body and therefore also in an individual body; for were it not in some individual body it would not be in body at all. Thus all the other things are either said of the primary 5   substances as subjects or in them as subjects. So if the primary substances did not exist it would be impossible for any of the other things to exist.

Of the secondary substances the species is more a substance than the genus, since it is nearer to the primary substance. For if one is to say of the primary substance 10   what it is, it will be more informative and apt to give the species than the genus. For example, it would be more informative to say of the individual man that he is a man than that he is an animal (since the one is more distinctive of the individual man while the other is more general); and more informative to say of the individual tree that it is a 15   tree than that it is a plant. Further, it is because the primary substances are subjects for all the other things and all the other things are predicated of them or are in them, that they are called substances most of all. But as the primary substances stand to the other 20   things, so the species stands to the genus: the species is a subject for the genus (for the genera are predicated of the species but the species are not predicated reciprocally of the genera). Hence for this reason too the species is more a substance than the genus.

But of the species themselves—those which are not genera—one is no more a substance than another: it is no more apt to say of the individual man that he is a man 25   than to say of the individual horse that it is a horse. And similarly of the primary sub-stances one is no more a substance than another: the individual man is no more a sub-stance than the individual ox.

It is reasonable that, after the primary substances, their species and genera should be the only other things called (secondary) substances. For only they, of things predicated, reveal the primary substance. For if one is to say of the individual man what he is, it will be in place to give the species or the genus (though more informative to give man than animal); but to give any of the other things would be out of place—for example, to say "white" or "runs" or anything like that. So it is reasonable that these should be the only other things called substances. Further, it is because the primary substances are subjects for everything else that they are called substances most strictly. But as the primary substances stand to everything else, so the species and genera of the primary substances stand to all the rest: all the rest are predicated of these. For if you will call the individual man grammatical it follows that you will call both a man and an animal grammatical; and similarly in other cases.

It is a characteristic common to every substance not to be in a subject. For a primary substance is neither said of a subject nor in a subject. And as for secondary substances, it is obvious at once that they are not in a subject. For man is said of the individual man as subject but is not in a subject: man is not *in* the individual man. Similarly, animal also is said of the individual man as subject but animal is not in the individual man. Further, while there is nothing to prevent the name of what is in a subject from being sometimes predicated of the subject, it is impossible for the definition to be predicated. But the definition of the secondary substances, as well as the name, is predicated of the subject: you will predicate the definition of man of the individual man, and also that of animal. No substance, therefore, is in a subject.

This is not, however, peculiar to substance; the differentia also is not in a subject. For footed and two-footed are said of man as subject but are not in a subject; neither two-footed nor footed is in man. Moreover, the definition of the differentia is predicated of that of which the differentia is said. For example, if footed is said of man the definition of footed will also be predicated of man; for man is footed.

We need not be disturbed by any fear that we may be forced to say that the parts of a substance, being in a subject (the whole substance), are not substances. For when we spoke of things *in a subject* we did not mean things belonging in something as *parts*.

It is a characteristic of substances and differentiae that all things called from them are so called synonymously. For all the predicates from them are predicated either of the individuals or of the species. (For from a primary substance there is no predicate, since it is said of no subject; and as for secondary substances, the species is predicated of the individual, the genus both of the species and of the individual. Similarly, differentiae too are predicated both of the species and of the individuals.) And the primary substances admit the definition of the species and of the genera, and the species admits that of the genus; for everything said of what is predicated will be said of the subject also. Similarly, both the species and the individuals admit the definition of the differentiae. But synonymous things were precisely those with both the name in common and the same definition. Hence all the things called from substances and differentiae are so called synonymously.

Every substance seems to signify a certain "this." As regards the primary substances, it is indisputably true that each of them signifies a certain "this"; for the thing revealed is individual and numerically one. But as regards the secondary substances, though it appears from the form of the name—when one speaks of man or animal—that a secondary substance likewise signifies a certain "this," this is not really true; rather, it signifies a certain qualification, for the subject is not, as the primary substance is, one, but man and animal are said of many things. However, it does not signify sim-

20   ply a certain qualification, as white does. White signifies nothing but a qualification, whereas the species and the genus mark off the qualification of substance—they signify substance of a certain qualification. (One draws a wider boundary with the genus than with the species, for in speaking of animal one takes in more than in speaking of man.)

25   Another characteristic of substances is that there is nothing contrary to them. For what would be contrary to a primary substance? For example, there is nothing contrary to an individual man, nor yet is there anything contrary to man or to animal. This, how-ever, is not peculiar to substance but holds of many other things also, for example, of quantity. For there is nothing contrary to four-foot or to ten or to anything of this

30   kind—unless someone were to say that many is contrary to few or large to small; but still there is nothing contrary to any *definite* quantity.

35   Substance, it seems, does not admit of a more and a less. I do not mean that one substance is not more a substance than another (we have said that it is), but that any given substance is not called more, or less, than that which it is. For example, if this substance is a man, it will not be more a man or less a man either than itself or than an-

4ᵃ   other man. For one man is not more a man than another, as one pale thing is more pale than another and one beautiful thing more beautiful than another. Again, a thing is called more, or less, such-and-such than itself; for example, the body that is pale is called more pale now than before, and the one that is hot is called more, or less, hot.

5   Substance, however, is not spoken of thus. For a man is not called more a man now than before, nor is anything else that is a substance. Thus substance does not admit of a more and a less.

10   It seems most distinctive of substance that what is numerically one and the same is able to receive contraries. In no other case could one bring forward anything, numer-ically one, which is able to receive contraries. For example, a colour which is numeri-cally one and the same will not be black and white, nor will numerically one and the

15   same action be bad and good; and similarly with everything else that is not substance. A substance, however, numerically one and the same, is able to receive contraries. For example, an individual man—one and the same—becomes pale at one time and dark at

20   another, and hot and cold, and bad and good.

Nothing like this is to be seen in any other case, unless someone might object and say that statements and beliefs are like this. For the same statement seems to be both true and false. Suppose, for example, that the statement that somebody is sitting is

25   true; after he has got up this same statement will be false. Similarly with beliefs. Sup-pose you believe truly that somebody is sitting; after he has got up you will believe falsely if you hold the same belief about him. However, even if we were to grant this,

30   there is still a difference in the way contraries are received. For in the case of sub-stances it is by themselves changing that they are able to receive contraries. For what has become cold instead of hot, or dark instead of pale, or good instead of bad, has changed (has altered); similarly in other cases too it is by itself undergoing change that

35   each thing is able to receive contraries. Statements and beliefs, on the other hand, themselves remain completely unchangeable in every way; it is because the actual

4ᵇ   thing changes that the contrary comes to belong to them. For the statement that some-body is sitting remains the same; it is because of a change in the actual thing that it comes to be true at one time and false at another. Similarly with beliefs. Hence at least the way in which it is able to receive contraries— through a change in itself—would be distinctive of substance, even if we were to grant that beliefs and statements are able to

5   receive contraries. However, this is not true. For it is not because they themselves re-ceive anything that statements and beliefs are said to be able to receive contraries, but

10   because of what has happened to something else. For it is because the *actual thing* ex-

ists or does not exist that the statement is said to be true or false, not because it is able itself to receive contraries. No statement, in fact, or belief is changed at all by anything. So, since nothing happens in them, they are not able to receive contraries. A substance, on the other hand, is said to be able to receive contraries because it itself receives contraries. For it receives sickness and health, and paleness and darkness; and because it itself receives the various things of this kind it is said to be able to receive contraries. It is, therefore, distinctive of substance that what is numerically one and the same is able to receive contraries. This brings to an end our discussion of substance.

ON INTERPRETATION (in part)

1. First we must settle what a name is and what a verb is, and then what a negation, an affirmation, a statement, and a sentence are.

Now spoken sounds are symbols of affections in the soul, and written marks symbols of spoken sounds. And just as written marks are not the same for all men, neither are spoken sounds. But what these are in the first place signs of—affections of the soul—are the same for all; and what these affections are likenesses of—actual things—are also the same. These matters have been discussed in the work on the soul and do not belong to the present subject.

Just as some thoughts in the soul are neither true nor false while some are necessarily one or the other, so also with spoken sounds. For falsity and truth have to do with combination and separation. Thus names and verbs by themselves—for instance "man" or "white" when nothing further is added—are like the thoughts that are without combination and separation; for so far they are neither true nor false. A sign of this is that even "goat-stag" signifies something but not, as yet, anything true or false—unless "is" or "is not" is added (either simply or with reference to time).

2. A *name* is a spoken sound significant by convention, without time, none of whose parts is significant in separation. For in "Whitfield" the "field" does not signify anything in its own right, as it does in the phrase "white field." Not that it is the same with complex names as with simple ones: in the latter the part is in no way significant, in the former it has some force but is not significant of anything in separation, for example the "boat" in "pirate-boat."

I say "by convention" because no name is a name naturally but only when it has become a symbol. Even inarticulate noises (of beasts, for instance) do indeed reveal something, yet none of them is a name.

"Not man" is not a name, nor is there any correct name for it. It is neither a phrase nor a negation. Let us call it an indefinite name.

"Philo's," "to-Philo," and the like are not names but inflexions of names. The same account holds for them as for names except that an inflexion when combined with "is," "was," or "will be" is not true or false whereas a name always is. Take, for example, "Philo's is" or "Philo's is not"; so far there is nothing either true or false.

Aristotle, *De Interpretatione*, Chapters 1–9 from *Aristotle's Categories and De Interpretatione*, translated by J.L. Ackrill (Oxford: Oxford University Press, 1963). Reprinted by permission of Oxford University Press.

3. A *verb* is what additionally signifies time, no part of it being significant separately; and it is a sign of things said of something else.

It additionally signifies time: "recovery" is a name, but "recovers" is a verb, because it additionally signifies something's holding *now*. And it is always a sign of what 10   holds, that is, holds of a subject.

"Does not recover" and "does not ail" I do not call verbs. For though they additionally signify time and always hold of something, yet there is a difference—for which there is no name. Let us call them indefinite verbs, because they hold indiffer- 15   ently of anything whether existent or non-existent. Similarly, "recovered" and "will-recover" are not verbs but inflexions of verbs. They differ from the verb in that it additionally signifies the present time, they the time outside the present.

When uttered just by itself a verb is a name and signifies something—the 20   speaker arrests his thought and the hearer pauses—but it does not yet signify whether it is or not. For not even "to be" or "not to be" is a sign of the actual thing (nor if you say simply "that which is"); for by itself it is nothing, but it additionally signifies some 25   combination, which cannot be thought of without the components.

4. A *sentence* is a significant spoken sound some part of which is significant in separation—as an expression, not as an affirmation.

I mean that animal, for instance, signifies something, but not that it is or is not 30   (though it will be an affirmation or negation if something is added); the single syllables of "animal," on the other hand, signify nothing. Nor is the "ice" in "mice" significant; here it is simply a spoken sound. In double words, as we said, a part does signify, but not in its own right.

17ᵃ   Every sentence is significant (not as a tool but, as we said, by convention), but not every sentence is a statement-making sentence, but only those in which there is truth or falsity. There is not truth or falsity in all sentences: a prayer is a sentence but is neither true or false. The present investigation deals with the statement making sen- 5   tence; the others we can dismiss, since consideration of them belongs rather to the study of rhetoric or poetry.

5. The first single statement-making sentence is the affirmation, next is the negation. The others are single in virtue of a connective.

10   Every statement-making sentence must contain a verb or an inflexion of a verb. For even the definition of man is not yet a statement-making sentence—unless "is" or "will be" or "was" or something of this sort is added. (To explain why "two-footed land animal" is one thing and not many belongs to a different inquiry; certainly it will 15   not be one simply through being said all together.)

A single statement-making sentence is either one that reveals a single thing or one that is single in virtue of a connective. There are more than one if more things than one are revealed or if connectives are lacking.

(Let us call a name or a verb simply an expression, since by saying it one cannot reveal anything by one's utterance in such a way as to be making a statement, whether one is answering a question or speaking spontaneously.)

20   Of these the one is a simple statement, affirming or denying something of something, the other is compounded of simple statements and is a kind of composite sentence. The simple statement is a significant spoken sound about whether something does or does not hold (in one of the divisions of time).

6. An *affirmation* is a statement affirming something of something, a *negation* is a   25
statement denying something of something.

Now it is possible to state of what does hold that it does not hold, of what does
not hold that it does hold, of what does hold that it does hold, and of what does not   30
hold that it does not hold. Similarly for times outside the present. So it must be possible to deny whatever anyone has affirmed, and to affirm whatever anyone has denied.
Thus it is clear that for every affirmation there is an opposite negation, and for every
negation an opposite affirmation. Let us call an affirmation and a negation which are
opposite a *contradiction*. I speak of statements as opposite when they affirm and deny   35
the same thing of the same thing—not homonymously, together with all other such
conditions that we add to counter the troublesome objections of sophists.

7. Now of actual things some are universal, others particular (I call universal that
which is by its nature predicated of a number of things, and particular that which is
not; man, for instance, is a universal, Callias a particular). So it must sometimes be of a   17[a]
universal that one states that something holds or does not, sometimes of a particular.
Now if one states universally of a universal that something holds or does not, there will
be contrary statements (examples of what I mean by "stating universally of a univer-   5
sal" are: every man is white—no man is white). But when one states something of a
universal but not universally, the statements are not contrary (though what is being revealed may be contrary). Examples of what I mean by "stating of a universal not universally" are: a man is white—a man is not white; man is a universal but it is not used   10
universally in the statement (for "every" does not signify the universal but that it is
taken universally). It is not true to predicate a universal universally of a subject, for
there cannot be an affirmation in which a universal is predicated universally of a sub-   15
ject, for instance: every man is every animal.

I call an affirmation and a negation *contradictory* opposites when what one signifies universally the other signifies not universally, e.g. every man is white—not
every man is white, no man is white—some man is white. But I call the universal affirmation and the universal negation contrary opposites, e.g., every man is just—no man   20
is just. So these cannot be true together, but their opposites may both be true with respect to the same thing, e.g. not every man is white—some man is white.   25

Of contradictory statements about a universal taken universally it is necessary
for one or the other to be true or false; similarly if they are about particulars, e.g.
Socrates is white—Socrates is not white. But if they are about a universal not taken
universally it is not always the case that one is true and the other false. For it is true   30
to say at the same time that a man is white and that a man is not white, or that a man
is noble and a man is not noble (for if base, then not noble; and if something is becoming something, then it is not that thing). This might seem absurd at first sight,   35
because "a man is not white" looks as it if signifies also at the same time that no man
is white; this, however, does not signify the same, nor does it necessarily hold at the
same time.

It is evident that a single affirmation has a single negation. For the negation must
deny the same thing as the affirmation affirmed, and of the same thing, whether a par-   18[a]
ticular or a universal (taken either universally or not universally). I mean, for example,
Socrates is white—Socrates is not white. But if something else is denied, or the same
thing is denied of something else, that will not be the opposite statement, but a different one. The opposite of "every man is white" is "not every man is white"; of "some   5
man is white," "no man is white"; of "a man is white," "a man is not white."

We have explained, then: that a single affirmation has a single negation as its contradictory opposite, and which these are; that contrary statements are different, and which these are; and that not all contradictory pairs are true or false, why this is, and when they are true or false.

8. A single affirmation or negation is one which signifies one thing about one thing (whether about a universal taken universally or not), e.g. every man is white—not every man is white, a man is white—a man is not white, no man is white—some man is white—assuming that "white" signifies one thing.

But if one name is given to two things which do not make up one thing, there is not a single affirmation. Suppose, for example, that one gave the name cloak to horse and man; "a cloak is white" would not be a single affirmation. For to say this is no different from saying a horse and a man is white, and this is no different from saying a horse is white and a man is white. So if this last signifies more than one thing and is more than one affirmation, clearly the first also signifies either more than one thing or nothing (because no man is a horse). Consequently it is not necessary, with these statements either, for one contradictory to be true and the other false.

9. With regard to what is and what has been it is necessary for the affirmation or the negation to be true or false. And with universals taken universally it is always necessary for one to be true and the other false, and with particulars too, as we have said; but with universals not spoken of universally it is not necessary. But with particulars that are going to be it is different.

For if every affirmation or negation is true or false it is necessary for everything either to be the case or not to be the case. For if one person says that something will be and another denies this same thing, it is clearly necessary for one of them to be saying what is true—if every affirmation is true or false; for both will not be the case together under such circumstances. For if it is true to say that it is white or is not white, it is necessary for it to be white or not white; and if it is white or is not white, then it was true to say or deny this. If it is not the case it is false, if it is false it is not the case. So it is necessary for the affirmation or the negation to be true. It follows that nothing either is or is happening, or will be or will not be, by chance or as chance has it, but everything of necessity and not as chance has it (since either he who says or he who denies is saying what is true). For otherwise it might equally well happen or not happen, since what is as chance has it is no more thus than not thus, nor will it be.

Again, if it is white now it was true to say earlier that it would be white; so that it was always true to say of anything that has happened that it would be so. But if it was always true to say that it was so, or would be so, it could not not be so, or not be going to be so. But if something cannot not happen it is impossible for it not to happen; and if it is impossible for something not to happen it is necessary for it to happen. Everything that will be, therefore, happens necessarily. So nothing will come about as chance has it or by chance; for if by chance, not of necessity.

Nor, however, can we say that *neither* is true—that it neither will be nor will not be so. For, firstly, though the affirmation is false the negation is not true, and though the negation is false the affirmation, on this view, is not true. Moreover, if it is true to say that something is white and large, both have to hold of it, and if true that they will hold tomorrow, they will have to hold tomorrow; and if it neither will be nor will not be the case tomorrow, then there is no "as chance has it." Take a sea-battle: it would have neither to happen nor not to happen.

These and others like them are the absurdities that follow if it is necessary for every affirmation and negation either about universals spoken of universally or about particulars, that one of the opposites be true and the other false, and that nothing of what happens is as chance has it, but everything is and happens of necessity. So there would be no need to deliberate or to take trouble (thinking that if we do this, this will happen, but if we do not, it will not). For there is nothing to prevent someone's having said ten thousand years beforehand that this would be the case, and another's having denied it; so that whichever of the two was true to say then, will be the case of necessity. Nor, of course, does it make any difference whether any people made the contradictory statements or not. For clearly this is how the actual things are even if someone did not affirm it and another deny it. For it is not because of the affirming or denying that it will be or will not be the case, nor is it a question of ten thousand years beforehand rather than any other time. Hence, if in the whole of time the state of things was such that one or the other was true, it was necessary for this to happen, and for the state of things always to be such that everything that happens happens of necessity. For what anyone has truly said would be the case cannot not happen; and of what happens it was always true to say that it would be the case.

But what if this is impossible? For we see that what will be has an origin both in deliberation and in action, and that, in general, in things that are not always actual there is the possibility of being and of not being; here both possibilities are open, both being and not being, and consequently, both coming to be and not coming to be. Many things are obviously like this. For example, it is possible for this cloak to be cut up, and yet it will not be cut up but will wear out first. But equally, its not being cut up is also possible, for it would not be the case that it wore out first unless its not being cut up were possible. So it is the same with all other events that are spoken of in terms of this kind of possibility. Clearly, therefore, not everything is or happens of necessity: some things happen as chance has it, and of the affirmation and the negation neither is true rather than the other; with other things it is one rather than the other and as a rule, but still it is possible for the other to happen instead.

What is, necessarily is, when it is; and what is not, necessarily is not, when it is not. But not everything that is, necessarily is; and not everything that is not, necessarily is not. For to say that everything that is, is of necessity, when it is, is not the same as saying unconditionally that it is of necessity. Similarly with what is not. And the same account holds for contradictories: everything necessarily is or is not, and will be or will not be; but one cannot divide and say that one or the other is necessary. I mean, for example: it is necessary for there to be or not to be a sea-battle tomorrow; but it is not necessary for a sea-battle to take place tomorrow, nor for one not to take place— though it is necessary for one to take place or not to take place. So, since statements are true according to how the actual things are, it is clear that wherever these are such as to allow of contraries as chance has it, the same necessarily holds for the contradictories also. This happens with things that are not always so or are not always not so. With these it is necessary for one or the other of the contradictories to be true or false—not, however, this one or that one, but as chance has it; or for one to be true rather than the other, yet not already true or false.

Clearly, then, it is not necessary that of every affirmation and opposite negation one should be true and the other false. For what holds for things that are does not hold for things that are not but may possibly be or not be; with these it is as we have said.

POSTERIOR ANALYTICS (in part)

BOOK I

71ᵃ   1. All instruction given or received by way of argument proceeds from pre-existent knowledge. This becomes evident upon a survey of all the species of such instruction. The mathematical sciences and all other speculative disciplines are acquired in this
5   way, and so are the two forms of dialectical reasoning, *syllogistic* and *inductive;* for each of these latter makes use of old knowledge to impart new, the syllogism assuming an audience that accepts its premisses, induction exhibiting the universal as implicit in
10   the clearly known particular. Again, the persuasion exerted by rhetorical arguments is in principle the same, since they use either example, a kind of induction, or enthymeme, a form of syllogism.

The pre-existent knowledge required is of two kinds. In some cases admission of the fact must be assumed, in others comprehension of the meaning of the term used, and sometimes both assumptions are essential. Thus, we assume that every predicate
15   can be either truly affirmed or truly denied of any subject, and that "triangle" means so and so; as regards "unit" we have to make the double assumption of the meaning of the word and the existence of the thing. The reason is that these several objects are not equally obvious to us. Recognition of a truth may in some cases contain as factors both previous knowledge and also knowledge acquired simultaneously with that recognition-knowledge, this latter, of the particulars actually falling under the universal and therein already virtually known. For example, the student knew beforehand that the an-
20   gles of every triangle are equal to two right angles; but it was only at the actual moment at which he was being led on to recognize this as true in the instance before him that he came to know "this figure inscribed in the semicircle" to be a triangle. For some things (viz. the singulars finally reached which are not predicable of anything else as subject) are only learnt in this way, i.e., there is here no recognition through a middle
25   of a minor term as subject to a major. Before he was led on to recognition or before he actually drew a conclusion, we should perhaps say that in a manner he knew, in a manner not.

If he did not in an unqualified sense of the term *know* the existence of this triangle, how could he *know* without qualification that its angles were equal to two right angles? No: clearly he *knows* not without qualification but only in the sense that he *knows* universally. If this distinction is not drawn, we are faced with the dilemma in the *Meno:* either a man will learn nothing or what he already knows; for we cannot accept
30   the solution which some people offer. A man is asked, "Do you, or do you not, know that every pair is even?" He says he does know it. The questioner then produces a particular pair, of the existence, and so *a fortiori* of the evenness, of which he was unaware. The solution which some people offer is to assert that they do not know that
71ᵇ   every pair is even, but only that everything which they know to be a pair is even: yet what they know to be even is that of which they have demonstrated evenness, i.e. what they made the subject of their premiss, viz. not merely every triangle or number which they know to be such, but any and every number or triangle without reservation. For no

Reprinted from Aristotle's *Posterior Analytics*, Book I, 1–2; Book II, 19, translated by G.R.G. Mure by permission of Oxford University Press.

premiss is ever couched in the form "every number which you know to be such," or "every rectilinear figure which you know to be such": the predicate is always construed   5
as applicable to any and every instance of the thing. On the other hand, I imagine there is nothing to prevent a man in one sense knowing what he is learning, in another not knowing it. The strange thing would be, not if in some sense he knew what he was learning, but if he were to know it in that precise sense and manner in which he was learning it.

2. We suppose ourselves to possess unqualified scientific knowledge of a thing, as opposed to knowing it in the accidental way in which the sophist knows, when we think   10
that we know the cause on which the fact depends, as the cause of that fact and of no other, and, further, that the fact could not be other than it is. Now that scientific know-
ing is something of this sort is evident-witness both those who falsely claim it and those who actually possess it, since the former merely imagine themselves to be, while the latter are also actually, in the condition described. Consequently the proper object   15
of unqualified scientific knowledge is something which cannot be other than it is.

There may be another manner of knowing as well-that will be discussed later. What I now assert is that at all events we do know by demonstration. By demonstration I mean a syllogism productive of scientific knowledge, a syllogism, that is, the grasp of which is *eo ipso* such knowledge. Assuming then that my thesis as to the nature of sci-   20
entific knowing is correct, the premisses of demonstrated knowledge must be true, pri-
mary, immediate, better known than and prior to the conclusion, which is further re-
lated to them as effect to cause. Unless these conditions are satisfied, the basic truths will not be "appropriate" to the conclusion. Syllogism there may indeed be without these conditions, but such syllogism, not being productive of scientific knowledge, will not be demonstration. The premisses must be true: for that which is non-existent can-   25
not be known—we cannot know, e.g., that the diagonal of a square is commensurate with its side. The premisses must be primary and indemonstrable; otherwise they will require demonstration in order to be known, since to have knowledge, if it be not accidental knowledge, of things which are demonstrable, means precisely to have a demonstration of them. The premisses must be the causes of the conclusion, better known than it, and prior to it; its causes, since we possess scientific knowledge of a   30
thing only when we know its cause; prior, in order to be causes; antecedently known, this antecedent knowledge being not our mere understanding of the meaning, but knowledge of the fact as well. Now "prior" and "better known" are ambiguous terms, for there is a difference between what is prior and better known in the order of being and what is prior and better known to man. I mean that objects nearer to sense are prior   72[a]
and better known to man; objects without qualification prior and better known are those further from sense. Now the most universal causes are furthest from sense and particular causes are nearest to sense, and they are thus exactly opposed to one another.   5
In saying that the premisses of demonstrated knowledge must be primary, I mean that they must be the "appropriate" basic truths, for I identify primary premiss and basic truth. A "basic truth" in a demonstration is an immediate proposition. An immediate proposition is one which has no other proposition prior to it. A proposition is either part of an enunciation, i.e. it predicates a single attribute of a single subject. If a proposition is dialectical, it assumes either part indifferently; if it is demonstrative, it lays   10
down one part to the definite exclusion of the other because that part is true. The term "enunciation" denotes either part of a contradiction indifferently. A contradiction is an opposition which of its own nature excludes a middle. The part of a contradiction which conjoins a predicate with a subject is an affirmation; the part disjoining them is

15   a negation. I call an immediate basic truth of syllogism a "thesis" when, though it is not susceptible of proof by the teacher, yet ignorance of it does not constitute a total bar to progress on the part of the pupil: one which the pupil must know if he is to learn anything whatever is an *axiom*. I call it an axiom because there are such truths and we give them the name of axioms *par excellence*. If a thesis assumes one part or the other

20   of an enunciation, i.e., asserts either the existence or the non-existence of a subject, it is a hypothesis; if it does not so assert, it is a definition. Definition *is* a "thesis" or a "laying something down," since the arithmetician lays it down that to be a unit is to be quantitatively indivisible; but it is not a hypothesis, for to define what a unit is is not the same as to affirm its existence.

25   Now since the required ground of our knowledge—i.e., of our conviction—of a fact is the possession of such a syllogism as we call demonstration, and the ground of the syllogism is the facts constituting its premises, we must not only know the primary premises—some if not all of them—beforehand, but know them better than the conclusion: for the cause of an attribute's inherence in a subject always itself inheres in the subject more firmly than that attribute; e.g. the cause of our loving anything is

30   dearer to us than the object of our love. So since the primary premises are the cause of our knowledge—i.e., of our conviction—it follows that we know them better—that is, are more convinced of them—than their consequences, precisely because our knowledge of the latter is the effect of our knowledge of the premises. Now a man cannot believe in anything more than in the things he knows, unless he has either actual

35   knowledge of it or something better than actual knowledge. But we are faced with this paradox if a student whose belief rests on demonstration has not prior knowledge; a man must believe in some, if not in all, of the basic truths more than in the conclusion. Moreover, if a man sets out to acquire the scientific knowledge that comes through demonstration, he must not only have a better knowledge of the basic truths and a firmer conviction of them than of the connexion which is being demonstrated: more

72^b than this, nothing must be more certain or better known to him than these basic truths in their character as contradicting the fundamental premises which lead to the opposed and erroneous conclusion. For indeed the conviction of pure science must be unshakable.

*   *   *

99^{b}15   19. As regards syllogism and demonstration, the definition of, and the conditions required to produce each of them, are now clear, and with that also the definition of, and the conditions required to produce, demonstrative knowledge, since it is the same as demonstration. As to the basic premises, how they become known and what is the developed state of knowledge of them is made clear by raising some preliminary problems.

20   We have already said that scientific knowledge through demonstration is impossible unless a man knows the primary immediate premises. But there are questions which might be raised in respect of the apprehension of these immediate premises: one might not only ask whether it is of the same kind as the apprehension of the conclusions, but also whether there is or is not scientific knowledge of both; or scientific

25   knowledge of the latter, and of the former a different kind of knowledge; and, further, whether the developed states of knowledge are not innate but come to be in us, or are innate but at first unnoticed. Now it is strange if we possess them from birth; for it means that we possess apprehensions more accurate than demonstration and fail to notice them. If on the other hand we acquire them and do not previously possess them,

how could we apprehend and learn without a basis of pre-existence knowledge? For that is impossible, as we used to find in the case of demonstration. So it emerges that neither can we possess them from birth, nor can they come to be in us if we are without knowledge of them to the extent of having no such developed state at all. Therefore we must possess a capacity of some sort, but not such as to rank higher in accuracy than these developed states. And this at least is an obvious characteristic of all animals, for they possess a congenital discriminative capacity which is called sense-perception. But though sense-perception is innate in all animals, in some the sense-impression comes to persist, in others it does not. So animals in which this persistence does not come to be have either no knowledge at all outside the act of perceiving, or no knowledge of objects of which no impression persists; animals in which it does come into being have perception and can continue to retain the sense-impression in the soul: and when such persistence is frequently repeated a further distinction at once arises between those which out of the persistence of such sense-impressions develop a power of systematizing them and those which do not. So out of sense-perception comes to be what we call memory, and out of frequently repeated memories of the same thing develops experience; for a number of memories constitute a single experience. From experience again—i.e., from the universal now stabilized in its entirety within the soul, the one beside the many which is a single identity within them all—originate the skill of the craftsman and the knowledge of the man of science, skill in the sphere of coming to be and science in the sphere of being.

We conclude that these states of knowledge are neither innate in a determinate form, nor developed from other higher states of knowledge, but from sense-perception. It is like a rout in battle stopped by first one man making a stand and then another, until the original formation has been restored. The soul is so constituted as to be capable of this process.

Let us now restate the account given already, though with insufficient clearness. When one of a number of logically indiscriminable particulars has made a stand, the earliest universal is present in the soul: for though the act of sense-perception is of the particular, its content is universal—is man, for example, not the man Callias. A fresh stand is made among these rudimentary universals, and the process does not cease until the indivisible concepts, the true universals, are established: e.g. such and such a species of animal is a step towards the genus animal, which by the same process is a step towards a further generalization.

Thus it is clear that we must get to know the primary premises by induction; for the method by which even sense-perception implants the universal is inductive. Now of the thinking states by which we grasp truth, some are unfailingly true, others admit of error—opinion, for instance, and calculation, whereas scientific knowing and intuition are always true: further, no other kind of thought except intuition is more accurate than scientific knowledge, whereas primary premises are more knowable than demonstrations, and all scientific knowledge is discursive. From these considerations it follows that there will be no scientific knowledge of the primary premises, and since except intuition nothing can be truer than scientific knowledge, it will be intuition that apprehends the primary premises—a result which also follows from the fact that demonstration cannot be the originative source of demonstration, nor, consequently, scientific knowledge of scientific knowledge. If, therefore, it is the only other kind of true thinking except scientific knowing, intuition will be the originative source of scientific knowledge. And the originative source of science grasps the original basic premiss, while science as a whole is similarly related as originative source to the whole body of fact.

PHYSICS (in part)

BOOK II

192^b 1. Of things that exist, some exist by nature, some from other causes. By nature the animals and their parts exist, and the plants and the simple bodies (earth, fire, air, water)—for we say that these and the like exist by nature.

All the things mentioned plainly differ from things which are not constituted by nature. For each of them has within itself a principle of motion and of stationariness (in
15   respect of place, or of growth and decrease, or by way of alteration). On the other hand, a bed and a coat and anything else of that sort, *qua* receiving these designations—i.e., in so far as they are products of art—have no innate impulse to change. But
20   in so far as they happen to be composed of stone or of earth or of a mixture of the two, they do have such an impulse, and just to that extent—which seems to indicate that nature is a principle or cause of being moved and of being at rest in that to which it belongs primarily, in virtue of itself and not accidentally.

I say "not accidentally," because (for instance) a man who is a doctor might himself
25   be a cause of health to himself. Nevertheless it is not in so far as he is a patient that he possesses the art of medicine: it merely has happened that the same man is doctor and patient—and that is why these attributes are not always found together. So it is with all other artificial products. None of them has in itself the principle of its own pro-
30   duction. But while in some cases (for instance houses and the other products of manual labour) that principle is in something else external to the thing, in others—those which may cause a change in themselves accidentally—it lies in the things themselves (but not in virtue of what they are).

Nature then is what has been stated. Things have a nature which have a principle of this kind. Each of them is a substance; for it is a subject, and nature is always in a subject.
35   The term "according to nature" is applied to all these things and also to the attributes which belong to them in virtue of what they are, for instance the property of
193^a fire to be carried upwards—which is not a nature nor has a nature but is by nature or according to nature.

What nature is, then, and the meaning of the terms "by nature" and "according to nature," has been stated. *That* nature exists, it would be absurd to try to prove; for it is obvious that there are many things of this kind, and to prove what is obvious by what is
5   not is the mark of a man who is unable to distinguish what is self-evident from what is not. (This state of mind is clearly possible. A man blind from birth might reason about colours.) Presumably therefore such persons must be talking about words without any thought to correspond.

10   Some identify the nature or substance of a natural object with that immediate constituent of it which taken by itself is without arrangement, e.g., the wood is the nature of the bed, and the bronze the nature of the statue.

As an indication of this Antiphon points out that if you planted a bed and the rotting wood acquired the power of sending up a shoot, it would not be a bed that would

come up, but *wood* which shows that the arrangement in accordance with the rules of   15
the art is merely an accidental attribute, whereas the substance is the other, which, further, persists continuously through the process.

But if the material of each of these objects has itself the same relation to something else, say bronze (or gold) to water, bones (or wood) to earth and so on, *that* (they   20
say) would be their nature and substance. Consequently some assert earth, others fire
or air or water or some or all of these, to be the nature of the things that are. For whatever any one of them supposed to have this character—whether one thing or more than
one thing—this or these he declared to be the whole of substance, all else being its af-   25
fections, states, or dispositions. Every such thing they held to be eternal (for it could
not pass into anything else), but other things to come into being and cease to be times
without number.

This then is one account of nature, namely that it is the primary underlying matter of things which have in themselves a principle of motion or change.

Another account is that nature is the shape or form which is specified in the defi-   30
nition of the thing.

For the word "nature" is applied to what is according to nature and the natural in
the same way as "art" is applied to what is artistic or a work of art. We should not say
in the latter case that there is anything artistic about a thing, if it is a bed only potentially, not yet having the form of a bed; nor should we call it a work of art. The same is   35
true of natural compounds. What is potentially flesh or bone has not yet its own nature,
and does not exist by nature, until it receives the form specified in the definition, which   193^{b}
we name in defining what flesh or bone is. Thus on the second account of nature, it
would be the shape or form (not separable except in statement) of things which have in   5
themselves a principle of motion. (The combination of the two, e.g. man, is not nature
but by nature.)

The form indeed is nature rather than the matter; for a thing is more properly said
to be what it is when it exists in actuality than when it exists potentially. Again man is
born from man but not bed from bed. That is why people say that the shape is not the
nature of a bed, but the wood is—if the bed sprouted, not a bed but wood would come   10
up. But even if the shape *is* art, then on the same principle the shape of man is his nature. For man is born from man.

Again, nature in the sense of a coming-to-be proceeds towards nature. For it is
not like doctoring, which leads not to the art of doctoring but to health. Doctoring must
start from the art, not lead to it. But it is not in this way that nature is related to nature.   15
What grows *qua* growing grows from something into something. Into what then does it
grow? Not into that from which it arose but into that to which it tends. The shape then
is nature.

Shape and nature are used in two ways. For the privation too is in a way form.
But whether in unqualified coming to be there is privation, i.e., a contrary, we must   20
consider later.

2. We have distinguished, then, the different ways in which the term "nature" is used.

The next point to consider is how the mathematician differs from the student of
nature; for natural bodies contain surfaces and volumes, lines and points, and these are
the subject-matter of mathematics.   25

Further, is astronomy different from natural science or a department of it? It seems
absurd that the student of nature should be supposed to know the nature of sun or moon,
but not to know any of their essential attributes, particularly as the writers on nature obviously do discuss their shape and whether the earth and the world are spherical or not.   30

Now the mathematician, though he too treats of these things, nevertheless does not treat of them as the limits of a natural body; nor does he consider the attributes indicated as the attributes of such bodies. That is why he separates them, for in thought they are separable from motion, and it makes no difference, nor does any falsity result, if they are separated. The holders of the theory of Forms do the same, though they are not aware of it; for they separate the objects of natural science, which are less separable than those of mathematics. This becomes plain if one tries to state in each of the two cases the definitions of the things and of their attributes. Odd and even, straight and curved, and likewise number, line, and figure, do not involve motion; not so flesh and bone and man—*these* are defined like snub nose, not like curved.

Similar evidence is supplied by the more natural of the branches of mathematics, such as optics, harmonics, and astronomy. These are in a way the converse of geometry. While geometry investigates natural lines but not *qua* natural, optics investigates mathematical lines, but *qua* natural, not *qua* mathematical.

Since two sorts of thing are called nature, the form and the matter, we must investigate its objects as we would the essence of snubness, that is neither independently of matter nor in terms of matter only. Here too indeed one might raise a difficulty. Since there are two natures, with which is the student of nature concerned? Or should he investigate the combination of the two? But if the combination of the two, then also each severally. Does it belong then to the same or to different sciences to know each severally?

If we look at the ancients, natural science would seem to be concerned with the *matter*. (It was only very slightly that Empedocles and Democritus touched on form and essence.)

But if on the other hand art imitates nature, and it is the part of the same discipline to know the form and the matter up to a point (e.g., the doctor has a knowledge of health and also of bile and phlegm, in which health is realized and the builder both of the form of the house and of the matter, namely that it is bricks and beams, and so forth): if this is so, it would be the part of natural science also to know nature in both its senses.

Again, that for the sake of which, or the end, belongs to the same department of knowledge as the means. But the nature is the end or that for the sake of which. For if a thing undergoes a continuous change toward some end, that last stage is actually that for the sake of which. (That is why the poet was carried away into making an absurd statement when he said "he has the end for the sake of which he was born." For not every stage that is last claims to be an end, but only that which is best.)

For the arts make their material (some simply make it, others make it serviceable), and we use everything as if it was there for our sake. (We also are in a sense an end. "That for the sake of which" may be taken in two ways, as we said in our work *On Philosophy*.) The arts, therefore, which govern the matter and have knowledge are two, namely the art which uses the product and the art which directs the production of it. That is why the using art also is in a sense directive; but it differs in that it knows the form, whereas the art which is directive as being concerned with production knows the matter. For the helmsman knows and prescribes what sort of form a helm should have, the other from what wood it should be made and by means of what operations. In the products of art, however, we make the material with a view to the function, whereas in the products of nature the matter is there all along.

Again, matter is a relative thing—for different forms there is different matter.

How far then must the student of nature know the form or essence? Up to a point, perhaps, as the doctor must know sinew or the smith bronze (i.e., until he understands the purpose of each); and the student of nature is concerned only with things

whose forms are separable indeed, but do not exist apart from matter. Man is begotten by man and by the sun as well. The mode of existence and essence of the separable it is   15
the business of first philosophy to define.

3. Now that we have established these distinctions, we must proceed to consider causes, their character and number. Knowledge is the object of our inquiry, and men do not think they know a thing till they have grasped the "why" of it (which is to grasp   20
its primary cause). So clearly we too must do this as regards both coming to be and passing away and every kind of natural change, in order that, knowing their principles, we may try to refer to these principles each of our problems.

In one way, then, that out of which a thing comes to be and which persists, is called a cause, e.g., the bronze of the statue, the silver of the bowl, and the genera of   25
which the bronze and the silver are species.

In another way, the form or the archetype, i.e., the definition of the essence, and its genera, are called causes (e.g., of the octave the relation of 2:1, and generally number), and the parts in the definition.

Again, the primary source of the change or rest; e.g., the man who deliberated is   30
a cause, the father is cause of the child, and generally what makes of what is made and what changes of what is changed.

Again, in the sense of end or that for the sake of which a thing is done, e.g., health is the cause of walking about. ("Why is he walking about?" We say: "To be healthy," and, having said that, we think we have assigned the cause.) The same is true   35
also of all the intermediate steps which are brought about through the action of something else as means towards the end, e.g., reduction of flesh, purging, drugs, or surgical instruments are means towards health. All these things are for the sake of the end,   195^a
though they differ from one another in that some are activities, others instruments.

This then perhaps exhausts the number of ways in which the term "cause" is used.

As things are called causes in many ways, it follows that there are several causes of the same thing (not merely accidentally), e.g., both the art of the sculptor and the   5
bronze are causes of the statue. These are causes of the statue *qua* statue, not in virtue of anything else that it may be—only not in the same way, the one being the material cause, the other the cause whence the motion comes. Some things cause each other reciprocally, e.g., hard work causes fitness and *vice versa*, but again not in the same way, but the one as end, the other as the principle of motion. Further the same thing is   10
the cause of contrary results. For that which by its presence brings about one result is sometimes blamed for bringing about the contrary by its absence. Thus we ascribe the wreck of a ship to the absence of the pilot whose presence was the cause of its safety.

All the causes now mentioned fall into four familiar divisions. The letters are the causes of syllables, the material of artificial products, fire and the like of bodies, the   15
parts of the whole, and the premises of the conclusion, in the sense of "that from which." Of these pairs the one set are causes in the sense of what underlies, e.g., the parts, the other set in the sense of essence—the whole and the combination and the   20
form. But the seed and the doctor and the deliberator, and generally the maker, are all sources whence the change or stationariness originates, which the others are causes in the sense of the end or the good of the rest; for that for the sake of which tends to be what is best and the end of the things that lead up to it. (Whether we call it good or ap-   25
parently good makes no difference.)

Such then is the number and nature of the kinds of cause.

Now the modes of causation are many, though when brought under heads they too can be reduced in number. For things are called causes in many ways and even

30 within the same kind one may be prior to another: e.g., the doctor and the expert are causes of health, the relation 2:1 and number of the octave, and always what is inclusive to what is particular. Another mode of causation is the accidental and its genera, e.g., in one way Polyclitus, in another a sculptor is the cause of a statue, because being

35 Polyclitus and a sculptor are accidentally conjoined. Also the classes in which the accidental attribute is included; thus a man could be said to be the cause of a statue or, gen-

195^b erally, a living creature. An accidental attribute too may be more or less remote, e.g., suppose that a pale man or a musical man were said to be the cause of the statue.

All causes, both proper and accidental, may be spoken of either as potential or as
5 actual; e.g., the cause of a house being built is either a house-builder or a house-builder building.

Similar distinctions can be made in the things of which the causes are causes, e.g., of this statue or of a statue or of an image generally, of this bronze or of bronze or
10 of material generally. So too with the accidental attributes. Again we may use a complex expression for either and say, e.g., neither "Polyclitus" nor a "sculptor" but "Polyclitus, the sculptor."

All these various uses, however, come to six in number, under each of which again the usage is twofold. It is either what is particular or a genus, or an accidental at-
15 tribute or a genus of that, and these either as a complex or each by itself; and all either as actual or as potential. The difference is this much, that causes which are actually at work and particular exist and cease to exist simultaneously with their effect, e.g., this healing person with this being-healed person and that housebuilding man with that
20 being-built house; but this is not always true of potential causes—the house and the housebuilder do not pass away simultaneously.

In investigating the cause of each thing it is always necessary to seek what is most precise (as also in other things): thus a man builds because he is a builder, and a
25 builder builds in virtue of his art of building. This last cause then is prior; and so generally.

Further, generic effects should be assigned to generic causes, particular effects to particular causes, e.g., statue to sculptor, this statue to this sculptor; and powers are relative to possible effects, actually operating causes to things which are actually being effected.

30 This must suffice for our account of the number of causes and the modes of causation.

4. But chance and spontaneity are also reckoned among causes: many things are said both to be and to come to be as a result of chance and spontaneity. We must inquire
35 therefore in what manner chance and spontaneity are present among the causes enumerated, and whether they are the same or different, and generally what chance and spontaneity are.

Some people even question whether there are such things or not. They say that
196^a nothing happens by chance, but that everything which we ascribe to chance or spontaneity has some definite cause, e.g., coming by chance into the market and finding there a man whom one wanted but did not expect to meet is due to one's wish to go
5 and buy in the market. Similarly, in other so-called cases of chance it is always possible, they maintain, to find something which is the cause; but not chance, for if chance were real, it would seem strange indeed, and the question might be raised, why on
10 earth none of the wise men of old in speaking of the causes of generation and decay took account of chance; whence it would seem that they too did not believe that anything is by chance. But there is a further circumstance that is surprising. Many things

both come to be and are by chance and spontaneity, and although all know that each of them can be ascribed to some cause (as the old argument said which denied chance),   15 nevertheless they all speak of some of these things as happening by chance and others not. For this reason they ought to have at least referred to the matter in some way or other.

Certainly the early physicists found no place for chance among the causes which they recognized—love, strife, mind, fire, or the like. This is strange, whether they supposed that there is no such thing as chance or whether they thought there is but omitted to mention it—and that too when they sometimes used it, as Empedocles does when he   20 says that the air is not always separated into the highest region, but as it may chance. At any rate he says in his cosmogony that "it happened to run that way at that time, but it often ran otherwise." He tells us also that most of the parts of animals came to be by chance.

There are some who actually ascribe this heavenly sphere and all the worlds to   25 spontaneity. They say that the vortex arose spontaneously, i.e., the motion that separated and arranged the universe in its present order. This statement might well cause surprise. For they are asserting that chance is not responsible for the existence or generation of animals and plants, nature or mind or something of the kind being the cause   30 of them (for it is not any chance thing that comes from a given seed but an olive from one kind and a man from another); and yet at the same time they assert that the heavenly sphere and the divinest of visible things arose spontaneously, having no such cause as is assigned to animals and plants. Yet if this is so, it is a fact which deserves to   35 be dwelt upon, and something might well have been said about it. For besides the other absurdities of the statement, it is the more absurd that people should make it when they   196^b see nothing coming to be spontaneously in the heavens, but much happening by chance among the things which as they say are not due to chance; whereas we should have expected exactly the opposite.

Others there are who believe that chance is a cause, but that it is inscrutable to   5 human intelligence, as being a divine thing and full of mystery.

Thus we must inquire what chance and spontaneity are, whether they are the same or different, and how they fit into our division of causes.

5. First then we observe that some things always come to pass in the same way, and   10 others for the most part. It is clearly of neither of these that chance, or the result of chance, is said to be the cause—neither of that which is by necessity and always, nor of that which is for the most part. But as there is a third class of events besides these two—events which all say are by chance—it is plain that there is such a thing as   15 chance and spontaneity; for we know that things of this kind are due to chance and that things due to chance are of this kind.

Of things that come to be, some come to be for the sake of something, others not. Again, some of the former class are in accordance with intention, others not, but both are in the class of things which are for the sake of something. Hence it is clear that even among the things which are outside what is necessary and what is for the most   20 part, there are some in connexion with which the phrase "for the sake of something" is applicable. (Things that are for the sake of something include whatever may be done as a result of thought or of nature.) Things of this kind, then, when they come to pass accidentally are said to be by chance. For just as a thing is something either in virtue of   25 itself or accidentally, so may it be a cause. For instance, the housebuilding faculty is in virtue of itself a cause of a house, whereas the pale or the musical is an accidental cause. That which is per se cause is determinate, but the accidental cause is indeter-

minable; for the possible attributes of an individual are innumerable. As we said, then,
when a thing of this kind comes to pass among events which are for the sake of something, it is said to be spontaneous or by chance. (The distinction between the two must
be made later—for the present it is sufficient if it is plain that both are in the sphere of
things done for the sake of something.)

Example: A man is engaged in collecting subscriptions for a feast. He would
have gone to such and such a place for the purpose of getting the money, if he had
known. He actually went there for another purpose, and it was only accidentally that he
got his money by going there; and this was not due to the fact that he went there as a
rule or necessarily, nor is the end effected (getting the money) a cause present in himself—it belongs to the class of things that are objects of choice and the result of
thought. It is when these conditions are satisfied that the man is said to have gone by
chance. If he had chosen and gone for the sake of this—if he always or normally went
there when he was collecting payments—he would not be said to have gone by chance.

It is clear then that chance is an accidental cause in the sphere of those actions
for the sake of something which involves choice. Thought, then, and chance are in the
same sphere, for choice implies thought.

It is necessary, no doubt, that the causes of what comes to pass by chance be indefinite; and that is why chance is supposed to belong to the class of the indefinite and
to be inscrutable to man, and why it might be thought that, in a way, nothing occurs by
chance. For all these statements are correct, as might be expected. Things *do*, in a way,
occur by chance, for they occur accidentally and chance is an accidental cause. But it is
not the cause without qualification of anything; for instance, a housebuilder is the
cause of a house; accidentally, a fluteplayer may be so.

And the causes of the man's coming and getting the money (when he did not
come for the sake of that) are innumerable. He may have wished to see somebody or
been following somebody or avoiding somebody, or may have gone to see a spectacle.
Thus to say that chance is unaccountable is correct. For an account is of what holds always or for the most part, whereas chance belongs to a third type of event. Hence,
since causes of this kind are indefinite, chance too is indefinite. (Yet in some cases one
might raise the question whether *any* chance fact might be the cause of the chance occurrence, e.g., of health the fresh air or the sun's heat may be the cause, but having had
one's hair cut *cannot*; for some accidental causes are more relevant to the effect than
others.)

Chance is called good when the result is good, evil when it is evil. The terms
"good fortune" and "ill fortune" are used when either result is of considerable magnitude. Thus one who comes within an ace of some great evil or great good is said to be
fortunate or unfortunate. The mind affirms the presence of the attribute, ignoring the
hair's breadth of difference. Further, it is with reason that good fortune is regarded as
unstable; for chance is unstable, as none of the things which result from it can hold always or for the most part.

Both are then, as I have said, accidental causes—both chance and spontaneity—
in the sphere of things which are capable of coming to pass not simply, nor for the
most part and with reference to such of these as might come to pass for the sake of
something.

6. They differ in that spontaneity is the wider. Every result of chance is from what is
spontaneous, but not everything that is from what is spontaneous is from chance.

Chance and what results from chance are appropriate to agents that are capable
of good fortune and of action generally. Therefore necessarily chance is in the sphere

of actions. This is indicated by the fact that good fortune is thought to be the same, or nearly the same, as happiness, and happiness to be a kind of action, since it is well-doing. Hence what is not capable of action cannot do anything by chance. Thus an inanimate thing or a beast or a child cannot do anything by chance, because it is incapable of choice; nor can good fortune or ill fortune be ascribed to them, except metaphorically, as Protarchus, for example, said that the stones of which altars are made are fortunate because they are held in honour, while their fellows are trodden under foot. Even these things, however, can in a way be affected by chance, when one who is dealing with them does something to them by chance, but not otherwise.

The spontaneous on the other hand is found both in the beasts and in many inanimate objects. We say, for example, that the horse came spontaneously, because, though his coming saved him, he did not come for the sake of safety. Again, the tripod fell spontaneously, because, though it stood on its feet so as to serve for a seat, it did not fall so as to serve for a seat.

Hence it is clear that events which belong to the general class of things that may come to pass for the sake of something, when they come to pass not for the sake of what actually results, and have an external cause, may be described by the phrase "from spontaneity." These spontaneous events are said to be from chance if they have the further characteristics of being the objects of choice and happening to agents capable of choice. This is indicated by the phrase "in vain," which is used when one thing which is for the sake of another, does not result in it. For instance, taking a walk is for the sake of evacuation of the bowels; if this does not follow after walking, we say that we have walked in vain and that the walking was vain. This implies that what is naturally for the sake of an end is in vain, when it does not effect the end for the sake of which it was the natural means—for it would be absurd for a man to say that he had bathed in vain because the sun was not eclipsed, since the one was not done for the sake of the other. Thus the spontaneous is even according to its derivation the case in which the thing itself happens in vain. The stone that struck the man did not fall for the sake of striking him; therefore it fell spontaneously, because it might have fallen by the action of an agent and for the sake of striking. The difference between spontaneity and what results by chance is greatest in things that come to be by nature; for when anything comes to be contrary to nature, we do not say that it came to be by chance, but by spontaneity. Yet strictly this too is different from the spontaneous proper; for the cause of the latter is external, that of the former internal.

We have now explained what chance is and what spontaneity is, and in what they differ from each other. Both belong to the mode of causation "source of change," for either some natural or some intelligent agent is always the cause; but in this sort of causation the number of possible causes is infinite.

Spontaneity and chance are causes of effects which, though they might result from intelligence or nature, have in fact been caused by something accidentally. Now since nothing which is accidental is prior to what is *per se*, it is clear that no accidental cause can be prior to a cause *per se*. Spontaneity and chance, therefore, are posterior to intelligence and nature. Hence, however true it may be that the heavens are due to spontaneity, it will still be true that intelligence and nature will be prior causes of this universe and of many things in it besides.

7. It is clear then that there are causes, and that the number of them is what we have stated. The number is the same as that of the things comprehended under the question "why." The "why" is referred ultimately either, in things which do not involve motion, e.g., in mathematics, to the "what" (to the definition of straight line or commensurable

or the like); or to what initiated a motion, e.g., "why did they go to war?—because

20   there had been a raid"; or we are inquiring "for the sake of what?"—"that they may rule"; or in the case of things that come into being, we are looking for the matter. The causes, therefore, are these and so many in number.

Now, the causes being four, it is the business of the student of nature to know about them all, and if he refers his problems back to all of them, he will assign the "why" in the way proper to his science—the matter, the form, the mover, that for the

25   sake of which. The last three often coincide; for the what and that for the sake of which are one, while the primary source of motion is the same in species as these. For man generates man—and so too, in general, with all things which cause movement by being themselves moved; and such as are not of this kind are no longer inside the province of natural science, for they cause motion not by possessing motion or a source of motion in themselves, but being themselves incapable of motion. Hence there are three

30   branches of study, one of things which are incapable of motion, the second of things in motion, but indestructible, the third of destructible things.

The question "why," then, is answered by reference to the matter, to the form, and to the primary moving cause. For in respect of coming to be it is mostly in this last way that causes are investigated—"what comes to be after what? what was the primary

35   agent or patient?" and so at each step of the series.

Now the principles which cause motion in a natural way are two, of which one is

198^b   not natural, as it has no principle of motion in itself. Of this kind is whatever causes movement, not being itself moved, such as that which is completely unchangeable, the primary reality, and the essence of a thing, i.e., the form; for this is the end or that for the sake of which. Hence since nature is for the sake of something, we must know this

5   cause also. We must explain the "why" in all the senses of the term, namely, that from this that will necessarily result ("from this" either without qualification or for the most part); that this must be so if that is to be so (as the conclusion presupposes the premises); that this was the essence of the thing; and because it is better thus (not without qualification, but with reference to the substance in each case).

10   8. We must explain then first why nature belongs to the class of causes which act for the sake of something; and then about the necessary and its place in nature, for all writers ascribe things to this cause, arguing that since the hot and the cold and the like are of such and such a kind, therefore certain things *necessarily* are and come to be—and

15   if they mention any other cause (one friendship and strife, another mind), it is only to touch on it, and then good-bye to it.

A difficulty presents itself: why should not nature work, not for the sake of something, nor because it is better so, but just as the sky rains, not in order to make the corn grow, but of necessity? (What is drawn up must cool, and what has been cooled

20   must become water and descend, the result of this being that the corn grows.) Similarly if a man's crop is spoiled on the threshing-floor, the rain did not fall for the sake of this—in order that the crop might be spoiled—but that result just followed. Why then should it not be the same with the parts in nature, e.g., that our teeth should come up of

25   necessity—the front teeth sharp, fitted for tearing, the molars broad and useful for grinding down the food—since they did not arise for this end, but it was merely a coincident result; and so with all other parts in which we suppose that there is purpose? Wherever then all the parts came about just what they would have been if they had

30   come to be for an end, such things survived, being organized spontaneously in a fitting way; whereas those which grew otherwise perished and continue to perish, as Empedocles says his "man-faced ox-progeny" did.

Such are the arguments (and others of the kind) which may cause difficulty on this point. Yet it is impossible that this should be the true view. For teeth and all other natural things either invariably or for the most part come about in a given way; but of not one of the results of chance or spontaneity is this true. We do not ascribe to chance or mere coincidence the frequency of rain in winter, but frequent rain in summer we do; nor heat in summer but only if we have it in winter. If then, it is agreed that things are either the result of coincidence or for the sake of something, and these cannot be the result of coincidence or spontaneity, it follows that they must be for the sake of something; and that such things are all due to nature even the champions of the theory which is before us would agree. Therefore action for an end is present in things which come to be and are by nature. 35

199a

5

Further, where there is an end, all the preceding steps are for the sake of that. Now surely as in action, so in nature; and as in nature, so it is in each action, if nothing interferes. Now action is for the sake of an end; therefore the nature of things also is so. Thus if a house, e.g. had been a thing made by nature, it would have been made in the same way as it is now by art; and if things made by nature were made not only by nature but also by art, they would come to be in the same way as by nature. The one, then, is for the sake of the other; and generally art in some cases completes what nature cannot bring to a finish, and in others imitates nature. If, therefore, artificial products are for the sake of an end, so clearly also are natural products. The relation of the later to the earlier items is the same in both. 10

15

This is most obvious in the animals other than man: they make things neither by art nor after inquiry or deliberation. That is why people wonder whether it is by intelligence or by some other faculty that these creatures work,—spiders, ants, and the like. By gradual advance in this direction we come to see clearly that in plants too that is produced which is conducive to the end—leaves, e.g. grow to provide shade for the fruit. If then it is both by nature and for an end that the swallow makes its nest and the spider its web, and plants grow leaves for the sake of the fruit and send their roots down (not up) for the sake of nourishment, it is plain that this kind of cause is operative in things which come to be and are by nature. And since nature is twofold, the matter and the form, of which the latter is the end, and since all the rest is for the sake of the end, the form must be the cause in the sense of that for the sake of which. 20

25

30

Now mistakes occur even in the operations of art: the literate man makes a mistake in writing and the doctor pours out the wrong dose. Hence clearly mistakes are possible in the operations of nature also. If then in art there are cases in which what is rightly produced serves a purpose, and if where mistakes occur there was a purpose in what was attempted, only it was not attained, so must it be also in natural products, and monstrosities will be failures in the purposive effort. Thus in the original combinations the "ox-progeny," if they failed to reach a determinate end must have arisen through the corruption of some principle, as happens now when the seed is defective. 199b

5

Further, seed must have come into being first, and not straightway the animals: what was "undifferentiated first" was seed.

Again, in plants too we find that for the sake of which, though the degree of organization is less. Were there then in plants also olive-headed vine-progeny, like the "man-headed ox-progeny," or not? An absurd suggestion; yet there must have been, if there were such things among animals. 10

Moreover, among the seeds anything must come to be at random. But the person who asserts this entirely does away with nature and what exists by nature. For those things are natural which, by a continuous movement originated from an internal principle, arrive at some end: the same end is not reached from every principle; nor any 15 chance end, but always the tendency in each is towards the same end, if there is no impediment.

20   The end and the means towards it may come about by chance. We say, for instance, that a stranger has come by chance, paid the ransom, and gone away, when he does so as if he had come for that purpose, though it was not for that that he came. This is accidental, for chance is an accidental cause, as I remarked before. But when an

25   event takes place always or for the most part, it is not accidental or by chance. In natural products the sequence is invariable, if there is no impediment.

It is absurd to suppose that purpose is not present because we do not observe the agent deliberating. Art does not deliberate. If the ship-building art were in the wood, it would produce the same results by nature. If, therefore, purpose is present in art, it is

30   present also in nature. The best illustration is a doctor doctoring himself: nature is like that.

It is plain then that nature is a cause, a cause that operates for a purpose.

35   9. As regards what is of necessity, we must ask whether the necessity is hypothetical, or simple as well. The current view places what is of necessity in the process of pro-

200ᵃ   duction, just as if one were to suppose that the wall of a house necessarily comes to be because what is heavy is naturally carried downwards and what is light to the top, so that the stones and foundations take the lowest place, with earth above because it is lighter, and wood at the top of all as being the lightest. Whereas, though the wall does

5   not come to be *without* these, it is not *due* to these, except as its material cause: it comes to be for the sake of sheltering and guarding certain things. Similarly in all other things which involve that for the sake of which: the product cannot come to be without things which have a necessary nature, but it is not due to these (except as its material); it comes to be for an end. For instance, why is a saw such as it is? To effect so-and-so and for the

10   sake of so-and-so. This end, however, cannot be realized unless the saw is made of iron. It is, therefore, necessary for it to be of iron, if we are to have a saw and perform the operation of sawing. What is necessary then, is necessary on a hypothesis, not as an end. Necessity is in the matter, while that for the sake of which is in the definition.

15   Necessity in mathematics is in a way similar to necessity in things which come to be through the operation of nature. Since a straight line is what it is, it is necessary that the angles of a triangle should equal two right angles. But not conversely; though if the angles are *not* equal to two right angles, then the straight line is not what it is ei-

20   ther. But in things which come to be for an end, the reverse is true. If the end is to exist or does exist, that also which precedes it will exist or does exist; otherwise just as there, if the conclusion is not true, the principle will not be true, so here the end or that for the sake of which will not exist. For this too is itself a principle, but of the reasoning, not of the action. (In mathematics the principle is the principle of the reasoning

25   only, as there is no action.) If then there is to be a house, such-and-such things must be made or be there already or exist, or generally the matter relative to the end, bricks and stones if it is a house. But the end is not due to these except as the matter, nor will it come to exist because of them. Yet if they do not exist at all, neither will the house, or the saw—the former in the absence of stones, the latter in the absence of iron—just as in the other case the principles will not be true, if the angles of the triangle are not

30   equal to two right angles.

The necessary in nature, then, is plainly what we call by the name of matter, and the changes in it. Both causes must be stated by the student of nature, but especially the end; for that is the cause of the matter, not *vice versa*; and the end is that for the sake of

200ᵇ   which, and the principle starts from the definition or essence: as in artificial products,

since a house is of such-and-such a kind, certain things must necessarily come to be or be there already, or since health is this, these things must *necessarily* come to be or be there already, so too if man is this, then these; if these, then those. Perhaps the necessary is present also in the definition. For if one defines the operation of sawing as being a certain kind of dividing, then this cannot come about unless the saw has teeth of a certain kind; and these cannot be unless it is of iron. For in the definition too there are some parts that stand as matter.

5

METAPHYSICS (in part)

Book I

1. All men by nature desire to know. An indication of this is the delight we take in our senses; for even apart from their usefulness they are loved for themselves; and above all others the sense of sight. For not only with a view to action, but even when we are not going to do anything, we prefer sight to almost everything else. The reason is that this, most of all the senses, makes us know and brings to light many differences between things.

980[a]

25

By nature animals are born with the faculty of sensation, and from sensation memory is produced in some of them, though not in others. And therefore the former are more intelligent and apt at learning than those which cannot remember; those which are incapable of hearing sounds are intelligent though they cannot be taught, e.g., the bee, and any other race of animals that may be like it; and those which besides memory have this sense of hearing, can be taught.

980[b]

25

The animals other than man live by appearances and memories, and have but little of connected experience; but the human race lives also by art and reasonings. And from memory experience is produced in men; for many memories of the same thing produce finally the capacity for a single experience. Experience seems to be very similar to science and art, but really science and art come to men *through* experience; for "experience made art," as Polus says, "but inexperience luck." And art arises, when from many notions gained by experience one universal judgement about similar objects is produced. For to have a judgement that when Callias was ill of this disease this did him good, and similarly in the case of Socrates and in many individual cases, is a matter of experience; but to judge that it has done good to all persons of a certain constitution, marked off in one class, when they were ill of this disease, e.g. to phlegmatic or bilious people when burning with fever,—this is a matter of art.

981[a]

5

10

With a view to action experience seems in no respect inferior to art, and we even see men of experience succeeding more than those who have theory without experience. The reason is that experience is knowledge of individuals, art of universals, and actions and productions are all concerned with the individual; for the physician does

15

Aristotle, *Metaphysics*, Books I and XII, translated by W.D. Ross from *The Works of Aristotle*, translated into English under the editorship of W.D. Ross (Oxford: Clarendon Press, 1908–1952). Reprinted by permission of Oxford University Press.

not cure a man, except in an incidental way, but Callias or Socrates or some other
called by some such individual name, who happens to be a man. If, then, a man has
theory without experience, and knows the universal but does not know the individual
included in this, he will often fail to cure; for it is the individual that is to be cured. But
yet we think that *knowledge* and *understanding* belong to art rather than to experience,
and we suppose artists to be wiser than men of experience (which implies that wisdom
depends in all cases rather on knowledge); and this because the former know the cause,
but the latter do not. For men of experience know that the thing is so, but do not know
why, while the others know the "why" and the cause. Hence we think that the master-
workers in each craft are more honourable and know in a truer sense and are wiser than
the manual workers, because they know the causes of the things that are done (we
think the manual workers are like certain lifeless things which act indeed, but act without knowing what they do, as fire burns,—but while the lifeless things perform each of
their functions by a natural tendency, the labourers perform them through habit); thus
we view them as being wiser not in virtue of being able to act, but of having the theory
for themselves and knowing the causes. And in general it is a sign of the man who
knows, that he can teach, and therefore we think art more truly knowledge than experience is; for artists can teach, and men of mere experience cannot.

Again, we do not regard any of the senses as wisdom; yet surely these give the
most authoritative knowledge of particulars. But they do not tell us the "why" of anything—e.g. why fire is hot; they only say that it is hot.

At first he who invented any art that went beyond the common perceptions of
man was naturally admired by men, not only because there was something useful in the
inventions, but because he was thought wise and superior to the rest. But as more arts
were invented, and some were directed to the necessities of life, others to its recreation,
the inventors of the latter were always regarded as wiser than the inventors of the former, because their branches of knowledge did not aim at utility. Hence when all such
inventions were already established, the sciences which do not aim at giving pleasure
or at the necessities of life were discovered, and first in the places where men first
began to have leisure. This is why the mathematical arts were founded in Egypt; for
there the priestly caste was allowed to be at leisure.

We have said in the *Ethics* what the difference is between art and science and the
other kindred faculties; but the point of our present discussion is this, that all men suppose what is called wisdom to deal with the first causes and the principles of things.
This is why, as has been said before, the man of experience is thought to be wiser than
the possessors of any perception whatever, the artist wiser than the men of experience,
the master-worker than the mechanic, and the theoretical kinds of knowledge to be
more of the nature of wisdom than the productive. Clearly then wisdom is knowledge
about certain causes and principles.

2. Since we are seeking this knowledge, we must inquire of what kind are the causes
and the principles, the knowledge of which is wisdom. If we were to take the notions
we have about the wise man, this might perhaps make the answer more evident. We
suppose first, then, that the wise man knows all things, as far as possible, although he
has not knowledge of each of them individually; secondly, that he who can learn things
that are difficult, and not easy for man to know, is wise (sense-perception is common
to all, and therefore easy and no mark of wisdom); again, he who is more exact and
more capable of teaching the causes is wiser, in every branch of knowledge; and of the
sciences, also, that which is desirable on its own account and for the sake of knowing it
is more of the nature of wisdom than that which is desirable on account of its results,

and the superior science is more of the nature of wisdom than the ancillary; for the wise man must not be ordered but must order, and he must not obey another, but the less wise must obey *him*.

Such and so many are the notions, then, which we have about wisdom and the wise. Now of these characteristics that of knowing all things must belong to him who has in the highest degree universal knowledge; for he knows in a sense all the subordinate objects. And these things, the most universal, are on the whole the hardest for men to know; for they are furthest from the senses. And the most exact of the sciences are those which deal most with first principles; for those which involve fewer principles are more exact than those which involve additional principles, e.g., arithmetic [is more exact than] than geometry. But the science which investigates causes is also more capable of reaching, for the people who teach are those who tell the causes of each thing. And understanding and knowledge pursued for their own sake are found most in the knowledge of that which is most knowable; for he who chooses to know for the sake of knowing will choose most readily that which is most truly knowledge, and such is the knowledge of that which is most knowable; and the first principles and the causes are most knowable; for by reason of these, and from these, all other things are known, but these are not known by means of the things subordinate to them. And the science which knows to what end each thing must be done is the most authoritative of the sciences, and more authoritative than any ancillary science; and this end is the good in each class, and in general the supreme good in the whole of nature. Judged by all the tests we have mentioned, then, the name in question falls to the same science; this must be a science that investigates the first principles and causes; for the good, i.e., that for the sake of which, is one of the causes.

That it is not a science of production is clear even from the history of the earliest philosophers. For it is owing to their wonder that men both now begin and at first began to philosophize; they wondered originally at the obvious difficulties, then advanced little by little and stated difficulties about the greater matters, e.g., about the phenomena of the moon and those of the sun and the stars, and about the genesis of the universe. And a man who is puzzled and wonders thinks himself ignorant (whence even the lover of myth is in a sense a lover of wisdom, for myth is composed of wonders); therefore since they philosophized in order to escape from ignorance, evidently they were pursuing science in order to know, and not for any utilitarian end. And this is confirmed by the facts; for it was when almost all the necessities of life and the things that make for comfort and recreation were present, that such knowledge began to be sought. Evidently then we do not seek it for the sake of any other advantage; but as the man is free, we say, who exists for himself and not for another, so we pursue this as the only free science, for it alone exists for itself.

Hence the possession of it might be justly regarded as beyond human power; for in many ways human nature is in bondage, so that according to Simonides "God alone can have this privilege," and it is unfitting that man should not be content to seek the knowledge that is suited to him. If, then, there is something in what the poets say, and jealousy is natural to the divine power, it would probably occur in this case above all, and all who excelled in this knowledge would be unfortunate. But the divine power cannot be jealous (indeed, according to the proverb, "bards tell many a lie"), nor should any science be thought more honourable than one of this sort. For the most divine science is also most honourable; and this science alone is, in two ways, most divine. For the science which it would be most meet for God to have is a divine science, and so is any science that deals with divine objects; and this science alone has both these qualities; for God is thought to be among the causes of all things and to be a first principle, and such a science either God alone can have, or God above all others. All the sciences, indeed, are more necessary than this, but none is better.

Yet the acquisition of it must in a sense end in something which is the opposite of our original inquiries. For all men begin, as we said, by wondering that the matter is so (as in the case of automatic marionettes or the solstices or the incommensurability of the diagonal of a square with the side; for it seems wonderful to all men who have not yet perceived the explanation that there is a thing which cannot be measured even by the smallest unit). But we must end in the contrary and, according to the proverb, the better state, as is the case in these instances when men learn the cause; for there is nothing which would surprise a geometer so much as if the diagonal turned out to be commensurable.

We have stated, then, what is the nature of the science we are searching for, and what is the mark which our search and our whole investigation must reach.

3. Evidently we have to acquire knowledge of the original causes (for we say we know each thing only when we think we recognize its first cause), and causes are spoken of in four senses. In one of these we mean the substance, i.e., the essence (for the "why" is referred finally to the formula, and the ultimate "why" is a cause and principle); in another the matter or substratum, in a third the source of the change, and in a fourth the cause opposed to this, that for the sake of which and the good (for this is the end of all generation and change). We have studied these causes sufficiently in our work on nature, but yet let us call to our aid those who have attacked the investigation of being and philosophized about reality before us. For obviously they too speak of certain principles and causes; to go over their views, then, will be of profit to the present inquiry, for we shall either find another kind of cause, or be more convinced of the correctness of those which we now maintain.

Of the first philosophers, most thought the principles which were of the nature of matter were the only principles of all things; that of which all things that are consist, and from which they first come to be, and into which they are finally resolved (the substance remaining, but changing in its modifications), this they say is the element and the principle of things, and therefore they think nothing is either generated or destroyed, since this sort of entity is always conserved, as we say Socrates neither comes to be absolutely when he comes to be beautiful or musical, nor ceases to be when he loses these characteristics, because the substratum, Socrates himself, remains. So they say nothing else comes to be or ceases to be; for there must be some entity—either one or more than one—from which all other things come to be, it being conserved.

Yet they do not all agree as to the number and the nature of these principles. Thales, the founder of this school of philosophy, says the principle is water (for which reason he declared that the earth rests on water), getting the notion perhaps from seeing that the nutriment of all things is moist, and that heat itself is generated from the moist and kept alive by it (and that from which they come to be is a principle of all things). He got his notion from this fact, and from the fact that the seeds of all things have a moist nature, and that water is the origin of the nature of moist things.

Some think that the ancients who lived long before the present generation, and first framed accounts of the gods, had a similar view of nature; for they made Ocean and Tethys the parents of creation, and described the oath of the gods as being by water, which they themselves call Styx; for what is oldest is most honourable, and the

most honourable thing is that by which one swears. It may perhaps be uncertain   984ª
whether this opinion about nature is primitive and ancient, but Thales at any rate is
said to have declared himself thus about the first cause. Hippo no one would think fit to
include among these thinkers, because of the paltriness of his thought.

Anaximenes and Diogenes make air prior to water, and the most primary of the   5
simple bodies, while Hippasus of Metapontium and Heraclitus of Ephesus say this of
fire, and Empedocles says it of the four elements, adding a fourth—earth—to those
which have been named; for these, he says, always remain and do not come to be, except that they come to be more or fewer, being aggregated into one and segregated out   10
of one.

Anaxagoras of Clazomenae, who, though older than Empedocles, was later in his
philosophical activity, says the principles are infinite in number; for he says almost all
the things that are homogeneous are generated and destroyed (as water or fire is) only
by aggregation and segregation, and are not in any other sense generated or destroyed,   15
but remain eternally.

From these facts one might think that the only cause is the so-called material
cause; but as men thus advanced, the very facts showed them the way and joined in
forcing them to investigate the subject. However true it may be that all generation
and destruction proceed from some one or more elements, why does this happen and   20
what is the cause? For at least the substratum itself does not make itself change; e.g.,
neither the wood nor the bronze causes the change of either of them, nor does the
wood manufacture a bed and the bronze a statue, but something else is the cause of   25
the change. And to seek this is to seek the second cause, as we should say,—that
from which comes the beginning of movement. Now those who at the very beginning
set themselves to this kind of inquiry, and said the substratum was one, were not at
all dissatisfied with themselves; but some at least of those who maintain it to be
one—as though defeated by this search for the second cause—say the one and nature   30
as a whole is unchangeable not only in respect of generation and destruction (for this
is an ancient belief, and all agreed in it), but also of all other change; and this view is
peculiar to them. Of those who said the universe was one, none succeeded in discov-   984ᵇ
ering a cause of this sort, except perhaps Parmenides, and he only insomuch that he
supposes that there is not only one but in some sense two causes. But for those who
make more elements it is more possible to state the second cause, e.g., for those who   5
make hot and cold, or fire and earth, the elements; for they treat fire as having a nature which fits it to move things, and water and earth and such things they treat in the
contrary way.

When these men and the principles of this kind had had their day, as the latter
were found inadequate to generate the nature of things, men were again forced by the
truth itself, as we said, to inquire into the next kind of cause. For surely it is not likely   10
either that fire or earth or any such element should be the reason why things manifest
goodness and beauty both in their being and in their coming to be, or that those
thinkers should have supposed it was; nor again could it be right to ascribe so great a
matter to spontaneity and luck. When one man said, then, that reason was present—as   15
in animals, so throughout nature—as the cause of the world and of all its order, he
seemed like a sober man in contrast with the random talk of his predecessors. We
know that Anaxagoras certainly adopted these views, but Hermotimus of Clazomenae
is credited with expressing them earlier. Those who thought thus stated that there is a   20
principle of things which is at the same time the cause of beauty, and that sort of cause
from which things acquire movement.

4. One might suspect that Hesiod was the first to look for such a thing—or someone else who put love or desire among existing things as a principle, as Parmenides does; for he, in constructing the genesis of the universe, says:

> Love first of all the Gods she planned.

And Hesiod says:

> First of all things was chaos made, and then
> Broad-breasted earth, and love that foremost is
> Among all the immortals,

which implies that among existing things there must be a cause which will move things and bring them together. How these thinkers should be arranged with regard to priority of discovery let us be allowed to decide later; but since the contraries of the various forms of good were also perceived to be present in nature—not only order and the beautiful, but also disorder and the ugly, and bad things in greater number than good, and ignoble things than beautiful, therefore another thinker introduced friendship and strife, each of the two the cause of one of these two sets of qualities. For if we were to follow out the view of Empedocles, and interpret it according to its meaning and not to its lisping expression, we should find that friendship is the cause of good things, and strife of bad. Therefore, if we said that Empedocles in a sense both mentions, and is the first to mention, the bad and the good as principles, we should perhaps be right, since the cause of all goods is the good itself.

These thinkers, as we say, evidently got hold up to a certain point of two of the causes which we distinguished in our work on nature—the matter and the source of the movement,—vaguely, however, and with no clearness, but as untrained men behave in fights; for they go round their opponents and often strike fine blows, but they do not fight on scientific principles, and so these thinkers do not seem to know what they say; for it is evident that, as a rule, they make no use of their causes except to a small extent. For Anaxagoras uses reason as a *deus ex machina* for the making of the world, and when he is at a loss to tell for what cause something necessarily is, then he drags reason in, but in all other cases ascribes events to anything rather than to reason. And Empedocles, though he uses the causes to a greater extent than this, neither does so sufficiently nor attains consistency in their use. At least, in many cases he makes friendship segregate things, and strife aggregate them. For when the universe is dissolved into its elements by strife, fire is aggregated into one, and so is each of the other elements; but when again under the influence of friendship they come together into one, the parts must again be segregated out of each element.

Empedocles, then, in contrast with his predecessors, was the first to introduce this cause in a divided form, not positing one source of movement, but different and contrary sources. Again, he was the first to speak of four material elements; yet he does not use four, but treats them as two only; he treats fire by itself, and its opposites—earth, air, and water—as one kind of thing. We may learn this by study of his verses.

This philosopher then, as we say, spoke of the principles in this way, and made them of this number. Leucippus and his associate Democritus say that the full and the empty are the elements, calling the one being and the other non-being—the full and solid being, the empty non-being (that is why they say that what is is no more than what is not, because body no more is than the void); and they make these the material causes of things. And as those who make the underlying substance one generate all

other things by its modifications, supposing the rare and the dense to be the sources of the modifications, in the same way these philosophers say the differences in the elements are the causes of all other qualities. These differences, they say, are three—   15
shape and order and position. For they say that what is is differentiated only by "rhythm" and "inter-contact" and "turning"; and of these rhythm is shape, inter-contact is order, and turning is position; for A differs from N in shape, AN from NA in order, Ⅎ from H in position. The question of movement—whence or how it belongs to things—these thinkers, like the others, lazily neglected.   20

Regarding the two causes, then, as we say, the inquiry seems to have been pushed thus far by the early philosophers.

5. Contemporaneously with these philosophers and before them, the Pythagoreans, as they are called, devoted themselves to mathematics; they were the first to advance this study, and having been brought up in it they thought its principles were the principles   25
of all things. Since of these principles numbers are by nature the first, and in numbers they seemed to see many resemblances to the things that exist and come into being—more than in fire and earth and water (such and such a modification of numbers being   30
justice, another being soul and reason, another being opportunity—and similarly almost all other things being numerically expressible); since, again, they saw that the attributes and the ratios of the musical scales were expressible in numbers; since, then, all other things seemed in their whole nature to be modelled after numbers, and num-   986^a
bers seemed to be the first things in the whole of nature, they supposed the elements of numbers to be the elements of all things, and the whole heaven to be a musical scale and a number. And all the properties of numbers and scales which they could show to agree with the attributes and parts and the whole arrangement of the heavens, they col-   5
lected and fitted into their scheme; and if there was a gap anywhere, they readily made additions so as to make their whole theory coherent. E.g. as the number ten is thought to be perfect and to comprise the whole nature of numbers, they say that the bodies   10
which move through the heavens are ten, but as the visible bodies are only nine, to meet this they invent a tenth—the "counter-earth." We have discussed these matters more exactly elsewhere.

But the object of our discussion is that we may learn from these philosophers also what they suppose to be the principles and how these fall under the causes we   15
have named. Evidently, then, these thinkers also consider that number is the principle both as matter for things and as forming their modifications and states, and hold that the elements of number are the even and the odd, and of these the former is unlimited, and the latter limited; and the one proceeds from both of these (for it is both even and   20
odd), and number from the one; and the whole heaven, as has been said, is numbers.

Other members of this same school say there are ten principles, which they arrange in two columns of cognates—limit and unlimited, odd and even, one and plurality, right and left, male and female, resting and moving, straight and curved, light   25
and darkness, good and bad, square and oblong. In this way Alcmaeon of Croton seems also to have conceived the matter, and either he got this view from them or they got it from him; for he expressed himself similarly to them. For he says most human   30
affairs go in pairs, meaning not definite contrarieties such as the Pythagoreans speak of, but any chance contrarieties, e.g. white and black, sweet and bitter, good and bad, great and small. He threw out indefinite suggestions about the other contrarieties, but the Pythagoreans declared both how many and which their contrarieties are.   986^b

From both these schools, then, we can learn this much, that the contraries are the principles of things; and how many these principles are and which they are, we can

learn from one of the two schools. But how these principles can be brought together
under the causes we have named has not been clearly and articulately stated by them;
they seem, however, to range the elements under the head of matter; for out of these as
immanent parts they say substance is composed and moulded.

From these facts we may sufficiently perceive the meaning of the ancients who
said the elements of nature were more than one; but there are some who spoke of the
universe as if it were one entity, though they were not all alike either in the excellence
of their statement or in regard to the nature of the entity. The discussion of them is in
no way appropriate to our present investigation of causes, for they do not, like some of
the natural philosophers, assume what exists to be one and yet generate it out of the
one as out of matter, but they speak in another way; those others add change, since
they generate the universe, but these thinkers say the universe is unchangeable. Yet
this much is appropriate to the present inquiry: Parmenides seems to fasten on that
which is one in formula, Melissus on that which is one in matter, for which reason the
former says that it is limited, the latter that it is unlimited; while Xenophanes, the first
of this school of monists (for Parmenides is said to have been his pupil), gave no clear
statement, nor does he seem to have grasped either of these two kinds of unity, but he
contemplates the whole heaven and says the One is God. Now these thinkers, as we
said, must be neglected for the purposes of the present inquiry—two of them entirely,
as being a little too naive, viz. Xenophanes and Melissus; but Parmenides seems to
speak with somewhat more insight. For, claiming that, besides the existent, nothing
non-existent exists, he thinks that the existent is of necessity one and that nothing else
exists (on this we have spoken more clearly in our work on nature), but being forced to
follow the phenomena, and supposing that what is is one in formula but many according to perception, he now posits two causes and two principles, calling them hot and
cold, i.e. fire and earth; and of these he ranges the hot with the existent, and the other
with the non-existent.

From what has been said, then, and from the wise men who have now sat in
council with us, we have got this much—both from the earliest philosophers, who regard the first principle as corporeal (for water and fire and such things are bodies), and
of whom some suppose that there is one corporeal principle, others that there are more
than one, but both put these under the head of matter; and from some others who posit
both this cause and besides this the source of movement, which is stated by some as
one and by others as two.

Down to the Italian school, then, and apart from it, philosophers have treated
these subjects rather obscurely, except that, as we said, they have used two kinds of
cause, and one of these—the source of movement—some treat as one and others as
two. But the Pythagoreans have said in the same way that there are two principles, but
added this much, which is peculiar to them, that they thought finitude and infinity were
not attributes of certain other things, e.g. of fire or earth or anything else of this kind,
but that infinity itself and unity itself were the substance of the things of which they are
predicated. This is why number was the substance of all things. On this subject, then,
they expressed themselves thus; and regarding the question of essence they began to
make statements and definitions, but treated the matter too simply. For they both defined superficially and thought that the first subject of which a given term would be
predicable, was the substance of the thing, as if one supposed that double and two were
the same, because two is the first thing of which double is predicable. But surely to be
double and to be two are not the same; if they are, one thing will be many—a consequence which they actually drew. From the earlier philosophers, then, and from their
successors we can learn this much.

6. After the systems we have named came the philosophy of Plato, which in most respects followed these thinkers, but had peculiarities that distinguished it from the philosophy of the Italians. For, having in his youth first become familiar with Cratylus and with the Heraclitean doctrines (that all sensible things are ever in a state of flux and there is no knowledge about them), these views he held even in later years. Socrates, however, was busying himself about ethical matters and neglecting the world of nature as a whole but seeking the universal in these ethical matters, and fixed thought for the first time on definitions; Plato accepted his teaching, but held that the problem applied not to any sensible thing but to entities of another kind—for this reason, that the common definition could not be a definition of any sensible thing, as they were always changing. Things of this other sort, then, he called Ideas, and sensible things, he said, were apart from these, and were all called after these; for the multitude of things which have the same name as the Form exist by participation in it. Only the name "participation" was new; for the Pythagoreans say that things exist by imitation of numbers, and Plato says they exist by participation, changing the name. But what the participation or the imitation of the Forms could be they left an open question.

Further, besides sensible things and Forms he says there are the objects of mathematics, which occupy an intermediate position, differing from sensible things in being eternal and unchangeable, from Forms in that there are many alike, while the Form itself is in each case unique.

Since the Forms are the causes of all other things, he thought their elements were the elements of all things. As matter, the great and the small were principles; as substance, the One; for from the great and the small, by participation in the One, come the numbers.

But he agreed with the Pythagoreans in saying that the One is substance and not a predicate of something else; and in saying that the numbers are the causes of the substance of other things, he also agreed with them; but positing a dyad and constructing the infinite out of great and small, instead of treating the infinite as one, is peculiar to him; and so is his view that the numbers exist apart from sensible things, while they say that the things themselves are numbers, and do not place the objects of mathematics between Forms and sensible things. His divergence from the Pythagoreans in making the One and the numbers separate from things, and his introduction of the Forms, were due to his inquiries in the region of definitory formulae (for the earlier thinkers had no tincture of dialectic), and his making the other entity besides the One a dyad was due to the belief that the numbers, except those which were prime, could be neatly produced out of the dyad as out of a plastic material.

Yet what happens is the contrary; the theory is not a reasonable one. For they make many things out of the matter, and the form generates only once, but what we observe is that one table is made from one matter, while the man who applies the form, though he is one, makes many tables. And the relation of the male to the female is similar; for the latter is impregnated by one copulation, but the male impregnates many females; yet these are imitations of those first principles.

Plato, then, declared himself thus on the points in question; it is evident from what has been said that he has used only two causes, that of the essence and the material cause (for the Forms are the cause of the essence of all other things, and the One is the cause of the essence of the Forms); and it is evident what the underlying matter is, of which the Forms are predicated in the case of sensible things, and the One in the case of Forms, viz. that this is a dyad, the great and the small. Further, he has assigned the cause of good and that of evil to the elements, one to each of the two, as we say some of his predecessors sought to do, e.g. Empedocles and Anaxagoras.

7. Our account of those who have spoken about first principles and reality and of the way in which they have spoken, has been concise and summary; but yet we have learnt this much from them, that of those who speak about principle and cause no one has mentioned any principle except those which have been distinguished in our work on nature, but all evidently have some inkling of *them*, though only vaguely. For some speak of the first principle as matter, whether they suppose one or more first principles, and whether they suppose this to be a body or to be incorporeal; e.g. Plato spoke of the great and the small, the Italians of the infinite, Empedocles of fire, earth, water, and air, Anaxagoras of the infinity of homogeneous things. These, then, have all had a notion of this kind of cause, and so have all who speak of air or fire or water, or something denser than fire and rarer than air; for some have said the prime element is of this kind. These thinkers grasped this cause only; but certain others have mentioned the source of movement, e.g. those who make friendship and strife, or reason, or love, a principle.

The essence, i.e. the substance of things, no one has expressed distinctly. It is mentioned chiefly by those who believe in the Forms; for they do not suppose either that the Forms are the matter of sensible things, and the One the matter of the Forms, or that they are the source of movement (for they say these are causes rather of immobility and of being at rest), but they furnish the Forms as the essence of every other thing, and the One as the essence of the Forms.

That for the sake of which actions and changes and movements take place, they assert to be a cause in a way, but not in this way, i.e. not in the way in which it is its *nature* to be a cause. For those who speak of reason or friendship class these causes as goods; they do not speak, however, as if anything that exists either existed or came into being for the sake of these, but as if movements started from these. In the same way those who say the One or the existent is the good, say that it is the cause of substance, but not that substance either is or comes to be for the sake of this. Therefore it turns out that in a sense they both say and do not say the good is a cause; for they do not call it a cause *qua* good but only incidentally.

All these thinkers, then, as they cannot pitch on another cause, seem to testify that we have determined rightly both how many and of what sort the causes are. Besides this it is plain that when the causes are being looked for, either all four must be sought thus or they must be sought in one of these four ways. Let us next discuss the possible difficulties with regard to the way in which each of these thinkers has spoken, and with regard to his views about the first principles.

8. Those, then, who say the universe is one and posit one kind of thing as matter, and as corporeal matter which has spatial magnitude, evidently go astray in many ways. For they posit the elements of bodies only, not of incorporeal things, though there are incorporeal things. And in trying to state the causes of generation and destruction, and in giving an account of the nature of all things, they do away with the cause of movement. Further, they err in not positing the substance, i.e. the essence, as the cause of anything, and besides this in lightly calling any of the simple bodies except earth the first principle, without inquiring how they are produced out of one another,—I mean fire, water, earth, and air. For some things are produced out of others by combination, others by separation, and this makes the greatest difference to their priority and posteriority. For in a way the property of being most elementary of all would seem to belong to the first thing from which they are produced by combination, and *this* property would belong to the most fine-grained and subtle of bodies. Therefore those who make fire the principle would be most in agreement with this argument. But each of the other thinkers agrees that the element of corporeal things is of this sort. At least none of the

later philosophers who said the world was one claimed that earth was the element, evidently because of the coarseness of its grain. (Of the other three elements each has   5
found some judge on its side; for some maintain that fire, others that water, others that
air is the element. Yet why, after all, do they not name earth also, as most men do—for
people say all things are earth. And Hesiod says earth was produced first of corporeal   10
things; so ancient and popular has the opinion been.) According to this argument, then,
no one would be right who either says the first principle is any of the elements other
than fire, or supposes it to be denser than air but rarer than water. But if that which is   15
later in generation is prior in nature, and that which is concocted and compounded is
later in generation, the contrary of what we have been saying must be true,—water
must be prior to air, and earth to water.

Let this suffice, then, as our statement about those who posit one cause such as
we mentioned; but the same is true if we suppose more of these, as Empedocles says   20
the matter of things is four bodies. For he too is confronted by consequences some of
which are the same as have been mentioned, while others are peculiar to him. For we
see these bodies produced from one another, which implies that the same body does
not always remain fire or earth (we have spoken about this in our works on nature); and   25
regarding the moving cause and the question whether we must suppose one or two, he
must be thought to have spoken neither correctly nor altogether plausibly. And in general those who speak in this way must do away with change of quality, for on their
view cold will not come from hot nor hot from cold. For if it did there would be something that accepted those very contraries, and there would be some one entity that became fire and water, which Empedocles denies.   30

As regards Anaxagoras, if one were to suppose that he said there were two elements, the supposition would accord thoroughly with a view which Anaxagoras himself did not state articulately, but which he must have accepted if any one had developed his view. True, to say that in the beginning all things were mixed is absurd both
on other grounds and because it follows that they must have existed before in an unmixed form, and because nature does not allow any chance thing to be mixed with any   989^b
chance thing, and also because on this view modifications and accidents could be separated from substances (for the same things which are mixed can be separated); yet if
one were to follow him up, piecing together what he means, he would perhaps be seen   5
to be somewhat modern in his views. For when nothing was separated out, evidently
nothing could be truly asserted of the substance that then existed. I mean, e.g. that it
was neither white nor black, nor grey nor any other colour, but of necessity colourless;
for if it had been coloured, it would have had one of these colours. And similarly, by   10
this same argument, it was flavourless, nor had it any similar attribute; for it could not
be either of any quality or of any size, nor could it be any definite kind of thing. For if
it were, one of the particular forms would have belonged to it, and this is impossible,
since all were mixed together; for the particular form would necessarily have been already separated out, but he says all were mixed except reason, and this alone was un-   15
mixed and pure. From this it follows, then, that he must say the principles are the One
(for this is simple and unmixed) and the Other, which is of such a nature as we suppose
the indefinite to be before it is defined and partakes of some form. Therefore, while expressing himself neither rightly nor clearly, he means something like what the later   20
thinkers say and what is now more clearly seen to be the case.

But these thinkers are, after all, at home only in arguments about generation and
destruction and movement; for it is practically only of this sort of substance that they
seek the principles and the causes. But those who extend their vision to all things that
exist, and of existing things suppose some to be perceptible and others not perceptible,   25

evidently study both classes, which is all the more reason why one should devote some time to seeing what is good in their views and what bad from the stand-point of the inquiry we have now before us.

30   The "Pythagoreans" use stranger principles and elements than the natural philosophers (the reason is that they got the principles from non-sensible things, for the objects of mathematics, except those of astronomy, are of the class of things without movement); yet their discussions and investigations are all about nature; for they gen-

990ᵃ   erate the heavens, and with regard to their parts and attributes and functions they observe the phenomena, and use up the principles and the causes in explaining these, which implies that they agree with the others, the natural philosophers, that what exists

5   is just all that which is perceptible and contained by the so-called heavens. But the causes and the principles which they mention are, as we said, sufficient to act as steps even up to the higher realms of reality, and are more suited to these than to theories about nature. They do not tell us at all, however, how there can be movement if limit

10   and unlimited and odd and even are the only things assumed, or how without process and change there can be generation and destruction, or how the bodies that move through the heavens can do what they do. Further, if we either granted them that spatial magnitude consists of these elements, or this were proved still how would some bodies

15   be light and others have weight? To judge from what they assume and maintain, they speak no more of mathematical bodies than of perceptible; hence they have said nothing whatever about fire or earth or the other bodies of this sort, I suppose because they have nothing to say which applies *peculiarly* to perceptible things.

Further, how are we to combine the beliefs that the modifications of number, and

20   number itself, are causes of what exists and happens in the heavens both from the beginning and now, and that there is no other number than this number out of which the world is composed? When in one particular region they place opinion and opportunity, and, a little above or below, injustice and sifting or mixture, and allege as proof of this

25   that each one of these is a number, but when there happens to be already in each place a plurality of the extended bodies composed of numbers, because these modifications of number attach to the various groups of places,—this being so, is this number, which we must suppose each of these abstractions to be, the same number which is exhibited

30   in the material universe, or is it another than this? Plato says it is different; yet even he thinks that both these bodies and their causes are numbers, but that the intelligible numbers are causes, while the others are *sensible*.

9. Let us leave the Pythagoreans for the present; for it is enough to have touched on them as much as we have done. But as for those who posit the Ideas as causes, firstly,

990ᵇ   in seeking to grasp the causes of the things around us, they introduced others equal in number to these, as if a man who wanted to count things thought he could not do it while they were few, but tried to count them when he had added to their number. For the Forms are practically equal to or not fewer than the things, in trying to explain

5   which these thinkers proceeded from them to the Forms. For to each set of substances there answers a Form which has the same name and exists apart from the substances, and so also in the case of all other groups in which there is one character common to many things, whether the things are in this changeable world or are eternal.

Further, of the ways in which we prove that the Forms exist, none is convincing;

10   for from some no inference necessarily follows, and from some it follows that there are Forms of things of which we think there are no Forms.

For according to the arguments from the existence of the sciences there will be Forms of all things of which there are sciences, and according to the argument that there is one attribute common to many things there will be Forms even of negations, and according to the argument that there is an object for thought even when the thing has perished, there will be Forms of perishable things; for we can have an image of these.

Further, of the more accurate arguments, some lead to Ideas of relations, of   15
which we say there is no independent class, and others involve the difficulty of the "third man."

And in general the arguments for the Forms destroy the things for whose existence we are more anxious than for the existence of the Ideas; for it follows that not the dyad but number is first, i.e. that the relative is prior to the absolute—besides all the   20
other points on which certain people by following out the opinions held about the Ideas have come into conflict with the principles of the theory.

Further, according to the assumption on which our belief in the Ideas rests, there will be Forms not only of substances but also of many other things (for the concept is single not only in the case of substances but also in the other cases, and there are sci-   25
ences not only of substance but also of other things, and a thousand other such conclusions also follow). But according to the necessities of the case and the opinions held about the Forms, if they can be shared there must be Ideas of substances only. For they are not shared incidentally, but a thing must share in its Form as in something not pred-   30
icated of a subject (e.g. if a thing shares in double itself, it shares also in eternal, but incidentally; for eternal happens to be predicable of the double). Therefore the Forms will be substance; and the same terms indicate substance in this and in the ideal world   991ᵃ
(or what will be the meaning of saying that there is something apart from the particulars—the one over many?). And if the Ideas and the particulars that share them have the same Form, there will be something common to these; for why should two be one and the same in the perishable 2's or in those which are many but eternal, and not the   5
same in the two itself as in the particular 2? But if they have not the same Form, they must have only the name in common, and it is as if one were to call both Callias and a wooden image a man, without observing any community between them.

Above all one might discuss the question what on earth the Forms contribute to sensible things, either to those that are eternal or to those that come into being and cease   10
to be. For they cause neither movement nor any change in them. But again they help in no way towards the *knowledge* of the other things (for they are not even the substance of these, else they would have been in them), nor towards their being, if they are not in the particulars which share in them; though if they were, they might be thought to be causes, as white causes whiteness in that with which it is mixed. But this argument,   15
which first Anaxagoras and later Eudoxus and certain others used, is too easily upset; for it is not difficult to collect many insuperable objections to such a view.

But further all other things cannot come from the Forms in any of the usual   20
senses of "from." And to say that they are patterns and the other things share them is to use empty words and poetical metaphors. For what is it that works, looking to the Ideas? Anything can either be, or become, like another without being copied from it, so that whether Socrates exists or not a man might come to be like Socrates; and evidently   25
this might be so even if Socrates were eternal. And there will be several patterns of the same thing, and therefore several Forms, e.g. animal and two-footed and also man himself will be Forms of man. Again, the Forms are patterns not only of sensible things, but of themselves too, e.g. the Form of genus will be a genus of Forms; therefore the   30
same thing will be pattern and copy.

Again it must be held to be impossible that the substance and that of which it is   991ᵇ
the substance should exist apart; how, therefore, can the Ideas, being the substances of things, exist apart?

In the Phaedo the case is stated in this way—that the Forms are causes both of being and of becoming; yet when the Forms exist, still the things that share in them do not come into being, unless there is some efficient cause; and many other things come into being (e.g. a house or a ring), of which we say there are no Forms. Clearly, therefore, even the other things can both be and come into being owing to such causes as produce the things just mentioned.

Again, if the forms are numbers, how can they be causes? Is it because existing things are other numbers, e.g. one number is man, another is Socrates, another Callias? Why then are the one set of numbers causes of the other set? It will not make any difference even if the former are eternal and the latter are not. But if it is because things in this sensible world (e.g. harmony) are ratios of numbers, evidently there is some one class of things of which they are ratios. If, then, this—the matter—is some definite thing, evidently the numbers themselves too will be ratios of something to something else. E.g. if Callias is a numerical ratio between fire and earth and water and air, his Idea also will be a number of certain other underlying things; and the Idea of man, whether it is a number in a sense or not, will still be a numerical ratio of certain things and not a number proper, nor will it be a number merely because it is a numerical ratio.

Again, from many numbers one number is produced, but how can one Form come from many Forms? And if the number comes not from the many numbers themselves but from the units in them, e.g. in ten thousand, how is it with the units? If they are specifically alike, numerous absurdities will follow, and also if they are not alike (neither the units in the same number being like one another nor those in different numbers being all like to all); for in what will they differ, as they are without quality? This is not a plausible view, nor can it be consistently thought out. Further, they must set up a second kind of number (with which arithmetic deals), and all the objects which are called intermediate by some thinkers; and how do these exist or from what principles do they proceed? Or why must they be intermediate between the things in this sensible world and the things-in-themselves? Further, the units in two must each come from a prior two; but this is impossible. Further, why is a number, when taken all together, one? Again, besides what has been said, if the units are *diverse* they should have spoken like those who say there are four, or two, elements; for each of these thinkers gives the name of element not to that which is common, e.g. to body, but to fire and earth, whether there is something common to them, viz. body, or not. But in fact they speak as if the One were homogeneous like fire or water; and if this is so, the numbers will not be substances. Evidently, if there is a One-in-itself and this is a first principle, "one" is being used in more than one sense; for otherwise the theory is impossible.

When we wish to refer substances to their principles, we state that lines come from the short and long (i.e. from a kind of small and great), and the plane from the broad and narrow, and the solid from the deep and shallow. Yet how then can the plane contain a line, or the solid a line or a plane? For the broad and narrow is a different class of things from the deep and shallow. Therefore, just as number is not present in these, because the many and few are different from these, evidently no other of the higher classes will be present in the lower. But again the broad is not a genus which includes the deep, for then the solid would have been a species of plane. Further, from what principle will the presence of the points in the line be derived? Plato even used to object to this class of things as being a geometrical fiction. He called the indivisible lines the principle of lines—and he used to lay this down often. Yet these must have a limit; therefore the argument from which the existence of the line follows proves also the existence of the point.

In general, though philosophy seeks the cause of perceptible things, we have given this up (for we say nothing of the cause from which change takes its start), but while we fancy we are stating the substance of perceptible things, we assert the existence of a second class of substances, while our account of the way in which they are the substances of perceptible things is empty talk; for sharing, as we said before, means nothing. Nor have the Forms any connexion with that which we see to be the cause in the case of the sciences, and for whose sake mind and nature produce all that they do produce,—with this cause we assert to be one of the first principles; but mathematics has come to be the whole of philosophy for modern thinkers, though they say that it should be studied for the sake of other things. Further, one might suppose that the substance which according to them underlies as matter is too mathematical, and is a predicate and differentia of the substance, i.e. of the matter, rather than the matter itself; i.e. the great and the small are like the rare and the dense which the natural philosophers speak of, calling these the primary differentiae of the substratum; for these are a kind of excess and defect. And regarding movement, if the great and the small are to be movement, evidently the Forms will be moved; but if they are not, whence did movement come? If we cannot answer this the whole study of nature has been annihilated.

And what is thought to be easy—to show that all things are one— is not done; for by "exposition" all things do not come to be one but there comes to be a One-in-itself, if we grant all the assumptions. And not even this follows, if we do not grant that the universal is a class; and this in some cases it cannot be.

Nor can it be explained either how the lines and planes and solids that come after the numbers exist or can exist, or what meaning they have; for these can neither be Forms (for they are not numbers), nor the intermediates (for those are the objects of mathematics), nor the perishable things. This is evidently a distinct fourth class.

In general, if we search for the elements of existing things without distinguishing the many senses in which things are said to exist, we cannot succeed, especially if the search for the elements of which things are made is conducted in this manner. For it is surely impossible to discover what acting or being acted on, or the straight, is made of, but if elements can be discovered at all, it is only the elements of substances; therefore to seek the elements of all existing things or to think one has them is incorrect. And how could we *learn* the elements of all things? Evidently we cannot start by knowing something before. For as he who is learning geometry, though he may know other things before, knows none of the things with which the science deals and about which he is to learn, so is it in all other cases. Therefore if there is a science of all things, as some maintain, he who is learning this will know nothing before. Yet all learning is by means of premises which are (either all or some of them) known before,—whether the learning be by demonstration or by definitions; for the elements of the definition must be known before and be familiar; and learning by induction proceeds similarly. But again, if the science is innate, it is wonderful that we are unaware of our possession of the greatest of sciences. Again, how is one to *know* what all things are made of, and how is this to be made *evident*? This also affords a difficulty; for there might be a conflict of opinion, as there is about certain syllables; some say *za* is made out of *s* and *d* and *a*, while others say it is a distinct sound and none of those that are familiar. Further, how could we know the objects of sense without having the sense in question? Yet we should, if the elements of which all things consist, as complex sounds consist of their proper elements, are the same.

10. It is evident, then, even from what we have said before, that all men seem to seek the causes named in the *Physics*, and that we cannot name any beyond these; but they seek these vaguely; and though in a sense they have all been described before, in a
15   sense they have not been described at all. For the earliest philosophy is, on all subjects, like one who lisps, since in its beginnings it is but a child. For even Empedocles says bone exists by virtue of the ratio in it. Now this is the essence and the substance of the thing. But it is similarly necessary that the ratio should be the substance of flesh and of
20   everything else, or of none; there it is on account of this that flesh and bone and everything else will exist, and not on account of the matter, which *he* names,—fire and earth and water and air. But while he would necessarily have agreed if another had said this, he has not said it clearly.

On such questions our views have been expressed before; but let us return to
25   enumerate the difficulties that might be raised on these same points; for perhaps we may get some help towards our later difficulties.

* * *

BOOK XII

1069ᵃ   1. Substance is the subject of our inquiry; for the principles and the causes we are seeking are those of substances. For if the universe is of the nature of a whole, substance is
20   its first part; and if it coheres by virtue of succession, on this view also substance is first, and is succeeded by quality, and then by quantity. At the same time these latter are not even beings in the unqualified sense, but are quantities and movements—or else even the not-white and the not-straight would be; at least we say even these *are*,
25   e.g. "there is a not-white." Further, none of the others can exist apart. And the old philosophers also in effect testify to this; for it was of substance that they sought the principles and elements and causes. The thinkers of the present day tend to rank universals as substances (for genera are universals, and these they tend to describe as principles and substances, owing to the abstract nature of their inquiry); but the old thinkers ranked particular things as substances, e.g. fire and earth, but not what is common to both, body.
30   There are three kinds of substance—one that is sensible (of which one subdivision is eternal and another is perishable, and which all recognize, as comprising e.g. plants and animals),—of this we must grasp the elements, whether one or many; and another that is immovable, and this certain thinkers assert to be capable of existing
35   apart, some dividing it into two, others combining the Forms and the objects of mathematics into one class, and others believing only in the mathematical part of this class. The former two kinds of substance are the subject of natural science (for they imply
1069ᵇ   movement); but the third kind belongs to another science, if there is no principle common to it and to the other kinds.

Sensible substance is changeable. Now if change proceeds from opposites or
5   from intermediate points, and not from all opposites (for the voice is not-white) but from the contrary, there must be something underlying which changes into the contrary state; for the contraries do not change.

2. Further, something persists, but the contrary does not persist; there is, then, some third thing besides the contraries, viz. the matter. Now since changes are of four kinds—either in respect of the essence or of the quality or of the quantity or of the

place, and change in respect of the "this" is simple generation and destruction, and   10
change in quantity is increase and diminution, and change in respect of an affection is
alteration, and change in place is motion, changes will be from given states into those
contrary to them in these several respects. The matter, then, which changes must be capable of both states. And since things are said to be in two ways, everything changes   15
from that which is potentially to that which is actually, e.g. from the potentially white
to the actually white, and similarly in the case of increase and diminution. Therefore
not only can a thing come to be, incidentally, out of that which is not, but also all
things come to be out of that which is, but is potentially, and is not actually. And this is
the "One" of Anaxagoras; for instead of "all things were together" and the "Mixture"   20
of Empedocles and Anaximander and the account given by Democritus, it is better to
say all things were together potentially but not actually. Therefore these thinkers seem
to have had some notion of matter.

Now all things that change have matter, but different matter; and of eternal   25
things those which are not generable but are movable in space have matter—not matter
for generation, however, but for motion from one place to another.

(One might raise the question from what sort of non-being generation proceeds;
for things are said not to be in three ways.)

If, then, a thing exists potentially, still it is not potentially any and every thing,
but different things come from different things; nor is it satisfactory to say that all
things were together; for they differ in their matter, since otherwise why did an infinity   30
of things come to be, and not one thing? For Reason is one, so that if matter also is
one, that must have come to be in actuality what the matter was in potentiality. The
causes and the principles, then, are three, two being the pair of contraries of which one
is formula and form and the other is privation, and the third being the matter.

3. Next we must observe that neither the matter nor the form comes to be—i.e. the   35
proximate matter and form. For everything that changes is something and is changed
by something and into something. That by which it is changed is the primary mover;   1070ᵃ
that which is changed, the matter; that into which it is changed, the form. The process,
then, will go on to infinity, if not only the bronze comes to be round but also the round
or the bronze comes to be; therefore there must be a stop at some point.

Next we must observe that each substance comes into being out of something
synonymous. (Natural objects and other things are substances.) For things come into   5
being either by art or by nature or by chance or by spontaneity. Now art is a principle
of movement in something other than the thing moved, nature is a principle in the
thing itself (for man begets man), and the other causes are privations of these two.

There are three kinds of substance—the matter, which is a "this" by being perceived (for all things that are characterized by contact and not by organic unity are   10
matter and substratum); the nature, a "this" and a state that it moves towards; and
again, thirdly, the particular substance which is composed of these two, e.g. Socrates
or Callias. Now in some cases the "this" does not exist apart from the composite substance, e.g. the form of house does not so exist, unless the art of building exists apart   15
(nor is there generation and destruction of these forms, but it is in another way that the
house apart from its matter, and health, and all things of art, exist and do not exist); but
if it does it is only in the case of natural objects. And so Plato was not far wrong when
he said that there are as many Forms as there are kinds of natural things (if there are
Forms at all),—though not of such things as fire, flesh, head; for all these are matter,   20
and the last matter is the matter of that which is in the fullest sense substance. The
moving causes exist as things preceding the effects, but causes in the sense of formulae

are simultaneous with their effects. For when a man is healthy, then health also exists; and the shape of a bronze sphere exists at the same time as the bronze sphere. But we must examine whether any form also survives afterwards. For in some cases this may be so, e.g. the soul may be of this sort—not all soul but the reason; for doubtless it is impossible that *all* soul should survive. Evidently then there is no necessity, on this ground at least, for the existence of the Ideas. For man is begotten by man, each individual by an individual; and similarly in the arts; for the medical art is the formula of health.

4. The causes and the principles of different things are in a sense different, but in a sense, if one speaks universally and analogically, they are the same for all. For we might raise the question whether the principles and elements are different or the same for substances and for relatives, and similarly in the case of each of the categories. But it is paradoxical that they should be the same for all. For then from the same elements will proceed relatives and substances. What then will this common element be? For there is nothing common to and distinct from substance and the other things which are predicated; but the element is prior to the things of which it is an element. But again substance is not an element of relatives, nor is any of these an element of substance. Further, how can all things have the same elements? For none of the elements can be the same as that which is composed of the elements, e.g. *b* or *a* cannot be the same as *ba*. (None, therefore, of the intelligibles, e.g. unity or being, is an element; for these are predicable of each of the compounds as well.) None of the elements then would be either a substance or a relative; but it must be one or other. All things then have not the same elements.

Or, as we put it, in a sense they have and in a sense they have not; e.g. perhaps the elements of perceptible bodies are, as *form*, the hot, and in another sense the cold, which is the *privation*; and, as *matter*, that which directly and of itself is potentially these; and both these are substances and also the things composed of these, of which these are the principles (i.e. any unity which is produced out of the hot and the cold, e.g. flesh or bone); for the product must be different from the elements. These things then have the same elements and principles, but different things have different elements; and if we put the matter thus, all things have not the same elements, but analogically they have; i.e. one might say that there are three principles—the form, the privation, and the matter. But each of these is different for each class, e.g. in colour they are white, black, and surface. Again, there is light, darkness, and air; and out of these are produced day and night.

Since not only the elements present in a thing are causes, but also something external, i.e. the moving cause, clearly while principle and element are different both are causes, and principle is divided into these two kinds; and that which moves a thing or makes it rest is a principle and a substance. Therefore analogically there are three elements, and four causes and principles; but the elements are different in different things, and the primary moving cause is different for different things. Health, disease, body; the moving cause is the medical art. Form, disorder of a particular kind, bricks; the moving cause is the building art. And since the moving cause in the case of natural things is, for instance man, and in the products of thought it is the form or its contrary, there are in a sense three causes, while in a sense there are four. For the medical art is in some sense health, and the building art is the form of the house, and man begets man; further, besides these there is that which as first of all things moves all things.

5. Some things can exist apart and some cannot, and it is the former that are substances. And therefore all things have the same causes, because, without substances,

affections and movements do not exist. Further, these causes will probably be soul and body, or reason and desire and body.

And in yet another way, analogically identical things are principles, i.e. actuality and potency; but these also are not only different for different things but also apply in different senses to them. For in some cases the same thing exists at one time actually and at another potentially, e.g. wine or flesh or man does so. (And these too fall under the above-named causes. For the form exists actually, if it can exist apart, and so does the complex of form and matter, and the privation, e.g. darkness or the diseased. But the matter exists potentially; for this is that which can become both the actual things.) But the distinction of actuality and potentiality applies differently to cases where the matter is not the same, in which cases the form also is not the same but different; e.g. the cause of man is the elements in man (viz. fire and earth as matter, and the peculiar form), and the external cause, whatever it is, e.g. the father, and besides these the sun and its oblique course, which are neither matter nor form nor privation nor of the same species with man, but moving causes.

Further, one must observe that some causes can be expressed in universal terms, and some cannot. The primary principles of all things are the actual primary "this" and another thing which exists potentially. The universal causes, then, of which we spoke do not *exist*. For the *individual* is the source of the individuals. For while man is the cause of man universally, there *is* no universal man; but Peleus is the cause of Achilles, and your father of you, and this particular *b* of this particular *ba*, though *b* in general is the cause of *ba* taken without qualification.

Again, if the causes of substances are causes of everything, still different things have different causes and elements, as was said; the causes of things that are not in the same class, e.g. of colours, sounds, substances, and quantities, are different except in an analogical sense; and those of things in the same species are different, not in species, but in the sense that the causes of different individuals are different, your matter and form and moving cause being different from mine, while in their universal formula they are the same. And if we inquire what are the principles or elements of substances and relations and qualities—whether they are the same or different, clearly when the terms "principle" and "element" are used in several senses the principles and elements of all are the same, but when the senses are distinguished the causes are not the same but different, except that in a special sense the causes of all are the same. They are in a special sense the same, i.e. by analogy, because matter, form, privation, and the moving cause are common to all things; and the causes of substances may be treated as causes of all things in this sense, that when they are removed all things are removed; further, that which is first in respect of fulfillment is the cause of all things. But in another sense there are different first causes, viz. all the contraries which are neither stated as classes nor spoken of in several ways; and, further, the matters of different things are different. We have stated, then, what are the principles of sensible things and how many they are, and in what sense they are the same and in what sense different.

6. Since there were three kinds of substance, two of them natural and one unmovable, regarding the latter we must assert that it is necessary that there should be an eternal unmovable substance. For substances are the first of existing things, and if they are all destructible, all things are destructible. But it is impossible that movement should either come into being or cease to be; for it must always have existed. Nor can time come into being or cease to be; for there could not be a before and an after if time did not exist. Movement also is continuous, then, in the sense in which time is; for time is

10   either the same thing as movement or an attribute of movement. And there is no continuous movement except movement in place, and of this only that which is circular is continuous.

But if there is something which is capable of moving things or acting on them, but is not actually doing so, there will not be movement; for that which has a capacity need not exercise it. Nothing, then, is gained even if we suppose eternal substances, as
15   the believers in the Forms do, unless there is to be in them some principle which can cause movement; and even this is not enough, nor is another substance besides the Forms enough; for if it does not *act*, there will be no movement. Further, even if it acts, this will not be enough, if its substance is potentiality; for there will not be *eternal* movement; for that which is potentially may possibly not be. There must, then, be such
20   a principle, whose very substance is actuality. Further, then, these substances must be without matter; for they must be eternal, at least if anything else is eternal. Therefore they must be actuality.

Yet there is a difficulty; for it is thought that everything that acts is able to act, but that not everything that is able to act acts, so that the potentiality is prior. But if
25   this is so, nothing at all will exist; for it is possible for things to be capable of existing but not yet to exist. Yet if we follow the mythologists who generate the world from night, or the natural philosophers who say that all things were together, the same impossible result ensues. For how will there be movement, if there is no actual cause?
30   Matter will surely not move itself—the carpenter's art must act on it; nor will the menstrual fluids nor the earth set themselves in motion, but the seeds and the semen must act on them.

This is why some suppose eternal actuality—e.g. Leucippus and Plato; for they say there is always movement. But why and what this movement is they do not say, nor, if the world moves in this way or that, do they tell us the cause of its doing so.
35   Now nothing is moved at random, but there must always be something present, e.g. as a matter of fact a thing moves in one way by nature, and in another by force or through the influence of thought or something else. Further, what sort of movement is primary? This makes a vast difference. But again Plato, at least, cannot even say what it is that
1072ᵃ   he sometimes supposes to be the source of movement—that which moves itself; for the *soul* is later, and simultaneous with the heavens, according to his account. To suppose potentiality prior to actuality, then, is in a sense right, and in a sense not; and we have specified these senses.
5   That actuality is prior is testified by Anaxagoras (for his thought is actuality) and by Empedocles in his doctrine of love and strife, and by those who say that there is always movement, e.g. Leucippus.

Therefore chaos or night did not exist for any infinite time, but the same things have always existed (either passing through a cycle of changes or in some other way), since actuality is prior to potentiality. If, then, there is a constant cycle, something
10   must always remain, acting in the same way. And if there is to be generation and destruction, there must be something else which is always acting in different ways. This must, then, act in one way in virtue of itself, and in another in virtue of something else—either of a third agent, therefore, or of the first. But it must be in virtue of the first. For otherwise this again causes the motion both of the third agent and of the sec-
15   ond. Therefore it is better to say the first. For it was the cause of eternal movement; and something else is the cause of variety, and evidently both together are the cause of eternal variety. This, accordingly, is the character which the motions actually exhibit. What need then is there to seek for other principles?

7. Since this is a possible account of the matter, and if it were not true, the world would have proceeded out of night and "all things together" and out of non-being, these difficulties may be taken as solved. There is, then, something which is always moved with an unceasing motion, which is motion in a circle; and this is plain not in theory only but in fact. Therefore the first heavens must be eternal. There is therefore also something which moves them. And since that which is moved and moves is intermediate, there is a mover which moves without being moved, being eternal, substance, and actuality. And the object of desire and the object of thought move in this way; they move without being moved. The primary objects of desire and of thought are the same. For the apparent good is the object of appetite, and the real good is the primary object of wish. But desire is consequent on opinion rather than opinion on desire; for the thinking is the starting-point. And thought is moved by the object of thought, and one side of the list of opposites is in itself the object of thought; and in this, substance is first, and in substance, that which is simple and exists actually. (The one and the simple are not the same; for "one" means a measure, but "simple" means that the thing itself has a certain nature.) But the good, also, and that which is in itself desirable are on this same side of the list; and the first in any class is always best, or analogous to the best.

That that for the sake of which is found among the unmovables is shown by making a distinction; for that for the sake of which is both that *for* which and that *towards* which, and of these the one is unmovable and the other is not. Thus it produces motion by being loved, and it moves the other moving things. Now if something is moved it is capable of being otherwise than as it is. Therefore if the actuality of the heavens is primary motion, then in so far as they are in motion, in *this* respect they are capable of being otherwise,—in place, even if not in substance. But since there is something which moves while itself unmoved, existing actually, this can in no way be otherwise than as it is. For motion in space is the first of the kinds of change, and motion in a circle the first kind of spatial motion; and this the first mover *produces*. The first mover, then, of necessity exists; and in so far as it is necessary, it is good, and in this sense a first principle. For the necessary has all these senses—that which is necessary perforce because it is contrary to impulse, that without which the good is impossible, and that which cannot be otherwise but is *absolutely* necessary.

On such a principle, then, depend the heavens and the world of nature. And its life is such as the best which we enjoy, and enjoy for but a short time. For it is ever in this state (which we cannot be), since its actuality is also pleasure. (And therefore waking, perception, and thinking are most pleasant, and hopes and memories are so because of their reference to these.) And thought in itself deals with that which is best in itself, and that which is thought in the fullest sense with that which is best in the fullest sense. And thought thinks itself because it shares the nature of the object of thought; for it becomes an object of thought in coming into contact with and thinking its objects, so that thought and object of thought are the same. For that which is *capable* of receiving the object of thought, i.e. the substance, is thought. And it is active when it *possesses* this object. Therefore the latter rather than the former is the divine element which thought seems to contain, and the act of contemplation is what is most pleasant and best. If, then, God is always in that good state in which we sometimes are, this compels our wonder; and if in a better this compels it yet more. And God *is* in a better state. And life also belongs to God; for the actuality of thought is life, and God is that actuality; and God's essential actuality is life most good and eternal. We say therefore that God is a living being, eternal, most good, so that life and duration continuous and eternal belong to God; for this *is* God.

Those who suppose, as the Pythagoreans and Speusippus do, that supreme beauty and goodness are not present in the beginning, because the beginnings both of plants and of animals are *causes*, but beauty and completeness are in the *effects* of these, are wrong in their opinion. For the seed comes from other individuals which are prior and complete, and the first thing is not seed but the complete being, e.g. we must say that before the seed there is a man,—not the man produced from the seed, but another from whom the seed comes.

1073ᵃ

It is clear then from what has been said that there is a substance which is eternal and unmovable and separate from sensible things. It has been shown also that this substance cannot have any magnitude, but is without parts and indivisible. For it produces movement through infinite time, but nothing finite has infinite power. And, while every magnitude is either infinite or finite, it cannot, for the above reason, have finite magnitude, and it cannot have infinite magnitude because there is no infinite magnitude at all. But it is also clear that it is impassive and unalterable; for all the other changes are posterior to change of place. It is clear, then, why the first mover has these attributes.

8. We must not ignore the question whether we have to suppose one such substance or more than one, and if the latter, how many; we must also mention, regarding the opinions expressed by others, that they have said nothing that can even be clearly stated about the number of the substances. For the theory of Ideas has no special discussion of the subject; for those who believe in Ideas say the Ideas are numbers, and they speak of numbers now as unlimited, now as limited by the number ten; but as for the reason why there should be just so many numbers, nothing is said with any demonstrative exactness.

We however must discuss the subject, starting from the presuppositions and distinctions we have mentioned. The first principle or primary being is not movable either in itself or accidentally, but produces the primary eternal and single movement. And since that which is moved must be moved by something, and the first mover must be in itself unmovable, and eternal movement must be produced by something eternal and a single movement by a single thing, and since we see that besides the simple spatial movement of the universe, which we say the first and unmovable substance produces, there are other spatial movements—those of the planets—which are eternal (for the body which moves in a circle is eternal and unresting; we have proved these points in the *Physics*), each of these movements also must be caused by a substance unmovable in itself and eternal. For the nature of the stars is eternal, being a kind of substance, and the mover is eternal and prior to the moved, and that which is prior to a substance must be a substance. Evidently, then, there must be substances which are of the same number as the movements of the stars, and in their nature eternal, and in themselves unmovable, and without magnitude, for the reason before mentioned.

1073ᵇ

That the movers are substances, then, and that one of these is first and another second according to the same order as the movements of the stars, is evident. But in the number of movements we reach a problem which must be treated from the standpoint of that one of the mathematical sciences which is most akin to philosophy—viz. of astronomy; for this science speculates about substance which is perceptible but eternal, but the other mathematical sciences, i.e. arithmetic and geometry, treat of no substance. That the movements are more numerous than the bodies that are moved, is evident to those who have given even moderate attention to the matter; for each of the planets has more than one movement. But as to the actual number of these movements, we now—to give some notion of the subject—quote what some of the mathematicians say, that our thought may have some definite number to grasp; but, for the rest, we

must partly investigate for ourselves, partly learn from other investigators, and if those   15
who study this subject form an opinion contrary to what we have now stated, we must
esteem both parties indeed, but follow the more accurate.

Eudoxus supposed that the motion of the sun or of the moon involves, in either
case, three spheres, of which the first is the sphere of the fixed stars, and the second
moves in the circle which runs along the middle of the zodiac, and the third in the cir-   20
cle which is inclined across the breadth of the zodiac; but the circle in which the moon
moves is inclined at a greater angle than that in which the sun moves. And the motion
of the planets involves, in each case, four spheres, and of these also the first and second
are the same as the first two mentioned above (for the sphere of the fixed stars is that   25
which moves all the other spheres, and that which is placed beneath this and has its
movement in the circle which bisects the zodiac is common to all), but the *poles* of the
third sphere of each planet are in the circle which bisects the zodiac, and the motion of
the fourth sphere is in the circle which is inclined at an angle to the equator of the third   30
sphere; and the poles of the third spheres are different for the other planets, but those
of Venus and Mercury are the same.

Callippus made the position of the spheres the same as Eudoxus did, but while
he assigned the same number as Eudoxus did to Jupiter and to Saturn, he thought two
more spheres should be added to the sun and two to the moon, if we were to explain   35
the phenomena, and one more to each of the other planets.

But it is necessary, if all the spheres combined are to explain the phenomena,   1074[a]
that for each of the planets there should be other spheres (one fewer than those hitherto
assigned) which counteract those already mentioned and bring back to the same position the first sphere of the star which in each case is situated below the star in question;
for only thus can all the forces at work produce the motion of the planets. Since, then,   5
the spheres by which the planets themselves are moved are eight and twenty-five, and
of these only those by which the lowest-situated planet is moved need not be counteracted, the spheres which counteract those of the first two planets will be six in number,
and the spheres which counteract those of the next four planets will be sixteen, and the   10
number of all the spheres—those which move the planets and those which counteract
these—will be fifty-five. And if one were not to add to the moon and to the sun the
movements we mentioned, all the spheres will be forty-nine in number.

Let this then be taken as the number of the spheres, so that the unmovable sub-   15
stances and principles may reasonably be taken as just so many; the assertion of *necessity* must be left to more powerful thinkers.

If there can be no spatial movement which does not conduce to the moving of a
star, and if further every being and every substance which is immune from change and
in virtue of itself has attained to the best must be considered an end, there can be no   20
other being apart from these we have named, but this must be the number of the substances. For if there are others, they will cause change as being an end of movement;
but there *cannot* be other movements besides those mentioned. And it is reasonable to
infer this from a consideration of the bodies that are moved; for if everything that   25
moves is for the sake of that which is moved, and every movement belongs to something that is moved, no movement can be for the sake of itself or of another movement,
but all movements must be for the sake of the stars. For if a movement is to be for the
sake of a movement, this latter also will have to be for the sake of something else; so
that since there cannot be an infinite regress, the end of every movement will be one of   30
the divine bodies which move through the heaven.

Evidently there is but one heaven. For if there are many heavens as there are
many men, the moving principles, of which each heaven will have one, will be one in

form but in number many. But all things that are many in number have matter. (For one and the same formula applies to *many* things, e.g. the formula of man; but Socrates is *one*.) But the primary essence has not matter; for it is fulfillment. So the unmovable first mover is one both in formula and in number; therefore also that which is moved always and continuously is one alone; therefore there is one heaven alone.

1074ᵇ   Our forefathers in the most remote ages have handed down to us their posterity a tradition, in the form of a myth, that these substances are gods and that the divine encloses the whole of nature. The rest of the tradition has been added later in mythical form with a view to the persuasion of the multitude and to its legal and utilitarian expediency; they say these gods are in the form of men or like some of the other animals, and they say other things consequent on and similar to these which we have mentioned. But if we were to separate the first point from these additions and take it alone—that they thought the first substances to be gods—we must regard this as an inspired utterance, and reflect that, while probably each art and science has often been developed as far as possible and has again perished, these opinions have been preserved like relics until the present. Only thus far, then, is the opinion of our ancestors and our earliest predecessors clear to us.

9. The nature of the divine thought involves certain problems; for while thought is held to be the most divine of phenomena, the question what it must be in order to have that character involves difficulties. For if it thinks nothing, what is there here of dignity? It is just like one who sleeps. And if it thinks, but this depends on something else, then (as that which is its substance is not the act of thinking, but a capacity) it cannot be the best substance; for it is through thinking that its value belongs to it. Further, whether its substance is the faculty of thought or the act of thinking, what does it think? Either itself or something else; and if something else, either the same always or something different. Does it matter, then, or not, whether it thinks the good or any chance thing? Are there not some things about which it is incredible that it should think? Evidently, then, it thinks that which is most divine and precious, and it does not change; for change would be change for the worse, and this would be already a movement. First, then, if it is not the act of thinking but a capacity, it would be reasonable to suppose that the continuity of its thinking is wearisome to it. Secondly, there would evidently be something else more precious than thought, viz. that which is thought. For both thinking and the act of thought will belong even to one who has the worst of thoughts. Therefore if this ought to be avoided (and it ought, for there are even some things which it is better not to see than to see), the act of thinking cannot be the best of things. Therefore it must be itself that thought thinks (since it is the most excellent of things), and its thinking is a thinking on thinking.

But evidently knowledge and perception and opinion and understanding have always something else as their object, and themselves only by the way. Further, if thinking and being thought are different, in respect of which does goodness belong to thought? For being an act of thinking and being an object of thought are not the same. We answer that in some cases the knowledge is the object. In the productive sciences (if we abstract from the matter) the substance in the sense of essence, and in the theoretical sciences the formula or the act of thinking, is the object. As, then, thought and the object of thought are not different in the case of things that have not matter, they will be the same, i.e. the thinking will be one with the object of its thought.

A further question is left—whether the object of the thought is composite; for if it were, thought would change in passing from part to part of the whole. We answer that everything which has not matter is indivisible. As human thought, or rather the

thought of composite objects, is in a certain period of time (for it does not possess the good at this moment or at that, but its best, being something different from it, is attained only in a whole period of time), so throughout eternity is the thought which has   10
itself for its object.

10. We must consider also in which of two ways the nature of the universe contains the good or the highest good, whether as something separate and by itself, or as the order of the parts. Probably in both ways, as an army does. For the good is found both in the order and in the leader, and more in the latter; for he does not depend on the order but   15
it depends on him. And all things are ordered together somehow, but not all alike,— both fishes and fowls and plants; and the world is not such that one thing has nothing to do with another, but they are connected. For all are ordered together to one end. (But it is as in a house, where the freemen are least at liberty to act as they will, but all   20
things or most things are already ordained for them, while the slaves and the beasts do little for the common good, and for the most part live at random; for this is the sort of principle that constitutes the nature of each.) I mean, for instance, that all must at least come to be dissolved into their elements, and there are other functions similarly in which all share for the good of the whole.

We must not fail to observe how many impossible or paradoxical results con-   25
front those who hold different views from our own, and what are the views of the sub-tler thinkers, and which views are attended by fewest difficulties. All make all things out of contraries. But neither "all things" nor "out of contraries" is right; nor do they tell us how the things in which the contraries are present can be made out of the con-   30
traries; for contraries are not affected by one another. Now for us this difficulty is solved naturally by the fact that there is a third factor. These thinkers however make one of the two contraries matter; this is done for instance by those who make the unequal matter for the equal, or the many matter for the one. But this also is refuted in the same way; for the matter which is one is contrary to nothing. Further, all things, except the one, will, on the view we are criticizing, partake of evil; for the bad is itself one of   35
the two elements. But the other school does not treat the good and the bad even as principles; yet in all things the good is in the highest degree a principle. The school we first mentioned is right in saying that it is a principle, but how the good is a principle they   1075^b
do not say—whether as end or as mover or as form.

Empedocles also has a paradoxical view; for he identifies the good with love. But this is a principle both as mover (for it brings things together) and as matter (for it is part of the mixture). Now even if it happens that the same thing is a principle both as   5
matter and as mover, still *being* them is not the same. In which respect then is love a principle? It is paradoxical also that strife should be imperishable; strife is for him the nature of the bad.

Anaxagoras makes the good a motive principle; for thought moves things, but moves them for the sake of something, which must be something other than it, except according to *our* way of stating the case; for the medical art is in a sense health. It is   10
paradoxical also not to suppose a contrary to the good, i.e. to thought. But all who speak of the contraries make no use of the contraries, unless we bring their views into shape. And why some things are perishable and others imperishable, no one tells us; for they make all existing things out of the same principles. Further, some make existing things out of the non-existent; and others to avoid the necessity of this make all   15
things one.

Further, why should there always be becoming, and what is the cause of becoming?—this no one tells us. And those who suppose two principles must suppose another, a superior principle, and so must those who believe in the Forms; for why did things come to participate, or why do they participate, in the Forms? And all other

20   thinkers are confronted by the necessary consequence that there is something contrary to Wisdom, i.e. to the highest knowledge; but we are not. For there is nothing contrary to that which is primary (for all contraries have matter and are potentially); and the ignorance which is contrary would lead us to a contrary object; but what is primary has no contrary.

Again, if besides sensible things no others exist, there will be no first principle,

25   no order, no becoming, no heavenly bodies, but each principle will have a principle before it, as in the accounts of the mythologists and all the natural philosophers. But if the Forms or the numbers are to exist, they will be causes of nothing; or if not that, at least not of movement.

Further, how is extension, i.e. a *continuum*, to be produced out of unextended

30   parts? For number will not, either as mover or as form, produce a *continuum*. But again there cannot be any contrary that is also a productive or moving principle; for it would be possible for it not to be. Or at least its action would be posterior to its capacity. The world then would not be eternal. But it is; one of these premises, then, must be denied. And we have said how this must be done. Further, in virtue of what the numbers, or the

35   soul and the body, or in general the form and the thing, are one of this no one tells us anything; nor can any one tell, unless he says, as we do, that the mover makes them one. And those who say mathematical number is first and go on to generate one kind of

1076ª   substance after another and give different principles for each, make the substance of the universe a series of episodes (for one substance has no influence on another by its existence or non-existence), and they give us many principles; but the world must not be governed badly.

"The rule of many is not good; let there be one ruler."

ON THE SOUL (in part)

BOOK II

412ª   1. Let the foregoing suffice as our account of the views concerning the soul which have been handed on by our predecessors; let us now make as it were a completely fresh

5   start, endeavouring to answer the question, What is soul? i.e. to formulate the most general possible account of it.

We say that substance is one kind of what is, and that in several senses: in the sense of matter or that which in itself is not a this, and in the sense of form or essence, which is that precisely in virtue of which a thing is called a this, and thirdly in the

10   sense of that which is compounded of both. Now matter is potentiality, form actuality; and actuality is of two kinds, one as e.g. knowledge, the other as e.g. reflecting.

Among substances are by general consent reckoned bodies and especially natural bodies; for they are the principles of all other bodies. Of natural bodies some have life in them, others not; by life we mean self-nutrition and growth and decay. It follows   15
that every natural body which has life in it is a substance in the sense of a composite.

Now given that there are bodies of such and such a kind, viz. having life, the soul cannot be a body; for the body is the subject or matter, not what is attributed to it. Hence the soul must be a substance in the sense of the form of a natural body having   20
life potentially within it. But substance is actuality, and thus soul is the actuality of a body as above characterized. Now there are two kinds of actuality corresponding to knowledge and to reflecting. It is obvious that the soul is an actuality like knowledge; for both sleeping and waking presuppose the existence of soul, and of these waking   25
corresponds to reflecting, sleeping to knowledge possessed but not employed, and knowledge of something is temporally prior.

That is why the soul is an actuality of the first kind of a natural body having life potentially in it. The body so described is a body which is organized. The parts of plants   412^b
in spite of their extreme simplicity are organs; e.g. the leaf serves to shelter the pericarp, the pericarp to shelter the fruit, while the roots of plants are analogous to the mouth of animals, both serving for the absorption of food. If, then, we have to give a general formula applicable to all kinds of soul, we must describe it as an actuality of the first kind   5
of a natural organized body. That is why we can dismiss as unnecessary the question whether the soul and the body are one: it is as though we were to ask whether the wax and its shape are one, or generally the matter of a thing and that of which it is the matter. Unity has many senses (as many as "is" has), but the proper one is that of actuality.

We have now given a general answer to the question, What is soul? It is sub-   10
stance in the sense which corresponds to the account of a thing. That means that it is what it is to be for a body of the character just assigned. Suppose that a tool, e.g. an axe, were a natural body, then being an axe would have been its essence, and so its soul; if this disappeared from it, it would have ceased to be an axe, except in name. As   15
it is, it is an axe; for it is not of a body of that sort that what it is to be, i.e. its account, is a soul, but of a natural body of a particular kind, viz. one having in itself the power of setting itself in movement and arresting itself. Next, apply this doctrine in the case of the parts of the living body. Suppose that the eye were an animal—sight would have been its soul, for sight is the substance of the eye which corresponds to the account, the   20
eye being merely the matter of seeing; when seeing is removed the eye is no longer an eye, except in name—no more than the eye of a statue or of a painted figure. We must now extend our consideration from the parts to the whole living body; for what the part is to the part, that the whole faculty of sense is to the whole sensitive body as such.

We must not understand by that which is potentially capable of living what has   25
lost the soul it had, but only what still retains it; but seeds and fruits are bodies which are potentially of that sort. Consequently, while waking is actuality in a sense corresponding to the cutting and the seeing, the soul is actuality in the sense corresponding to sight and the power in the tool; the body corresponds to what is in potentiality; as   413^a
the pupil *plus* the power of sight constitutes the eye, so the soul *plus* the body constitutes the animal.

From this it is clear that the soul is inseparable from its body, or at any rate that certain parts of it are (if it has parts)—for the actuality of some of them is the actuality   5
of the parts themselves. Yet some may be separable because they are not the actualities of any body at all. Further, we have no light on the problem whether the soul may not be the actuality of its body in the sense in which the sailor is the actuality of the ship.

This must suffice as our sketch or outline of the nature of soul.   10

2. Since what is clear and more familiar in account emerges from what in itself is confused but more observable by us, we must reconsider our results from this point of view. For it is not enough for a definitional account to express as most now do the mere fact; it must include and exhibit the cause also. At present definitions are given in a form analogous to the conclusion of an argument; e.g. What is squaring? The construction of an equilateral rectangle equal to a given oblong rectangle. Such a definition is in form equivalent to a conclusion. One that tells us that squaring is the discovery of a mean proportional discloses the cause of what is defined.

We resume our inquiry from a fresh starting-point by calling attention to the fact that what has soul in it differs from what has not in that the former displays life. Now this word has more than one sense, and provided any one alone of these is found in a thing we say that thing is living—viz. thinking or perception or local movement and rest, or movement in the sense of nutrition, decay and growth. Hence we think of plants also as living, for they are observed to possess in themselves an originative power through which they increase or decrease in all spatial directions; they do not grow up but not down—they grow alike in both, indeed in all, directions; and that holds for everything which is constantly nourished and continues to live, so long as it can absorb nutriment.

This power of self-nutrition can be separated from the other powers mentioned, but not they from it—in mortal beings at least. The fact is obvious in plants; for it is the only psychic power they possess.

413^{b} This is the originative power the possession of which leads us to speak of things as *living* at all, but it is the possession of sensation that leads us for the first time to speak of living things as *animals*; for even those beings which possess no power of local movement but do possess the power of sensation we call animals and not merely living things.

The primary form of sense is touch, which belongs to all animals. Just as the power of self-nutrition can be separated from touch and sensation generally, so touch can be separated from all other forms of sense. (By the power of self-nutrition we mean that part of the soul which is common to plants and animals: all animals whatsoever are observed to have the sense of touch.) What the explanation of these two facts is, we must discuss later. At present we must confine ourselves to saying that soul is the source of these phenomena and is characterized by them, viz. by the powers of self-nutrition, sensation, thinking, and movement.

Is each of these a soul or a part of a soul? And if a part, a part merely distinguishable by definition or a part distinct in local situation as well? In the case of certain of these powers, the answers to these questions are easy, in the case of others we are puzzled what to say. Just as in the case of plants which when divided are observed to continue to live though separated from one another (thus showing that in *their* case the soul of each individual plant was actually one, potentially many), so we notice a similar result in other varieties of soul, i.e. in insects which have been cut in two; each of the segments possesses both sensation and local movement; and if sensation, necessarily also imagination and appetition; for, where there is sensation, there is also pleasure and pain, and, where these, necessarily also desire.

We have no evidence as yet about thought or the power of reflexion; it seems to be a different kind of soul, differing as what is eternal from what is perishable; it alone is capable of being separated. All the other parts of soul, it is evident from what we have said, are, in spite of certain statements to the contrary, incapable of separate existence though, of course, distinguishable by definition. If opining is distinct from perceiving, to be capable of opining and to be capable of perceiving must be distinct, and so with all the other forms of living above enumerated. Further, some animals possess all these parts of soul, some certain of them only, others one only (this is what enables us to classify animals); the cause must be considered later. A similar arrangement is found also within the field of the senses; some classes of animals have all the senses, some only certain of them, others only one, the most indispensable, touch. 414ª

Since the expression "that whereby we live and perceive" has two meanings, just like the expression "that whereby we know"—that may mean either knowledge or the soul, for we can speak of knowing by either, and similarly that whereby we are in health may be either health or the body or some part of the body; and since of these knowledge or health is a form, essence, or account, or if we so express it an activity of a recipient matter—knowledge of what is capable of knowing, health of what is capable of being made healthy (for the activity of that which is capable of originating change seems to take place in what is changed or altered); further, since it is the soul by which primarily we live, perceive, and think:—it follows that the soul must be an account and essence, not matter or a subject. For, as we said, the word substance has three meanings—form, matter, and the complex of both—and of these matter is potentiality, form actuality. Since then the complex here is the living thing, the body cannot be the actuality of the soul; it is the soul which is the actuality of a certain kind of body. Hence the rightness of the view that the soul cannot be without a body, while it cannot be a body; it is not a body but something relative to a body. That is why it is in a body, and a body of a definite kind. It was a mistake, therefore, to do as former thinkers did, merely to fit it into a body without adding a definite specification of the kind or character of that body, although evidently one chance thing will not receive another. It comes about as reason requires: the actuality of any given thing can only be realized in what is already potentially that thing, i.e. in a matter of its own appropriate to it. From all this it is plain that soul is an actuality or account of something that possesses a potentiality of being such.

3. Of the psychic powers above enumerated some kinds of living things, as we have said, possess all, some less than all, others one only. Those we have mentioned are the nutritive, the appetitive, the sensory, the locomotive, and the power of thinking. Plants have none but the first, the nutritive, while another order of living things has this plus the sensory. If any order of living things has the sensory, it must also have the appetitive; for appetite is the genus of which desire, passion, and wish are the species; now all animals have one sense at least, viz. touch, and whatever has a sense has the capacity for pleasure and pain and therefore has pleasant and painful objects present to it, and wherever these are present, there is desire, for desire is appetition of what is pleasant. Further, all animals have the sense for food (for touch is the sense for food); the food of all living things consists of what is dry, moist, hot, cold, and these are the qualities apprehended by touch; all other sensible qualities are apprehended by touch only indirectly. Sounds, colours, and odours contribute nothing to nutriment; flavours fall within the field of tangible qualities. Hunger and thirst are forms of desire, hunger a desire for what is dry and hot, thirst a desire for what is cold and moist; flavour is a sort of seasoning added to both. We must later clear up these points, but at present it may be enough to say that all animals that possess the sense of touch have also appetition. The case of imagination is obscure; we must examine it later. Certain kinds of animals possess in addition the power of locomotion, and still others, i.e. man and possibly another order like man or superior to him, the power of thinking and thought. It is now evident that a single definition can be given of soul only in the same sense as one can be given of figure. For, as in that case there is no figure apart from triangle and those

that follow in order, so here there is no soul apart from the forms of soul just enumerated. It is true that a common definition can be given for figure which will fit all figures without expressing the peculiar nature of any figure. So here in the case of soul and its
25   specific forms. Hence it is absurd in this and similar cases to look for a common definition which will not express the peculiar nature of anything that is and will not apply to the approrate indivisible species, while at the same time omitting to look for an account which will. The cases of figure and soul are exactly parallel; for the particulars
30   subsumed under the common name in both cases—figures and living beings—constitute a series, each successive term of which potentially contains its predecessor, e.g. the square the triangle, the sensory power the self-nutritive. Hence we must ask in the case of each order of living things, What is its soul, i.e. What is the soul of plant, man,
415ª   beast? Why the terms are related in this serial way must form the subject of examination. For the power of perception is never found apart from the power of self-nutrition, while—in plants—the latter is found isolated from the former. Again, no sense is
5   found apart from that of touch, while touch *is* found by itself; many animals have neither sight, hearing, nor smell. Again, among living things that possess sense some have the power of locomotion, some not. Lastly, certain living beings—a small minority— possess calculation and thought, for (among mortal beings) those which possess calcu-
10   lation have all the other powers above mentioned, while the converse does not hold— indeed some live by imagination alone, while others have not even imagination. Reflective thought presents a different problem.

It is evident that the way to give the most adequate definition of soul is to seek in the case of *each* of its forms for the most appropriate definition.

*   *   *

BOOK III

*   *   *

429ª   4. Turning now to the part of the soul with which the soul knows and (whether this is separable from the others in definition only, or spatially as well) we have to inquire what differentiates this part, and how thinking can take place.

If thinking is like perceiving, it must be either a process in which the soul is acted upon by what is capable of being thought, or a process different from but analo-
15   gous to that. The thinking part of the soul must therefore be, while impassible, capable of receiving the form of an object; that is, must be potentially identical in character with its object without being the object. Thought must be related to what is thinkable, as sense is to what is sensible.

Therefore, since everything is a possible object of thought, mind in order, as Anaxagoras says, to dominate, that is, to know, must be pure from all admixture; for
20   the co-presence of what is alien to its nature is a hindrance and a block: it follows that it can have no nature of its own, other than that of having a certain capacity. Thus that in the soul which is called thought (by thought I mean that whereby the soul thinks and judges) is, before it thinks, not actually any real thing. For this reason it cannot reason-
25   ably be regarded as blended with the body: if so, it would acquire some quality, e.g. warmth or cold, or even have an organ like the sensitive faculty: as it is, it has none. It was a good idea to call the soul "the place of forms," though this description holds only of the thinking soul, and even this is the forms only potentially, not actually.

Observation of the sense-organs and their employment reveals a distinction be- 30
tween the impassibility of the sensitive faculty and that of the faculty of thought. After
strong stimulation of a sense we are less able to exercise it than before, as e.g. in the
case of a loud sound we cannot hear easily immediately after, or in the case of a bright 429^b
colour or a powerful odour we cannot see or smell, but in the case of thought thinking
about an object that is highly thinkable renders it more and not less able afterwards to
think of objects that are less thinkable: the reason is that while the faculty of sensation
is dependent upon the body, thought is separable from it. 5

When thought has become each thing in the way in which a man who actually
knows is said to do so (this happens when he is now able to exercise the power on his
own initiative), its condition is still one of potentiality, but in a different sense from the
potentiality which preceded the acquisition of knowledge by learning or discovery; and
thought is then able to think of itself.

Since we can distinguish between a magnitude and what it is to be a magnitude, 10
and between water and what it is to be water, and so in many other cases (though not in
all; for in certain cases the thing and its form are identical), flesh and what it is to be
flesh are discriminated either by different faculties, or by the same faculty in two different states; for flesh necessarily involves matter and is like what is snub-nosed, a *this*
in a *this*. Now it is by means of the sensitive faculty that we discriminate the hot and
the cold, i.e. the factors which combined in a certain ratio constitute flesh: the essential 15
character of flesh is apprehended by something different either wholly separate from
the sensitive faculty or related to it as a bent line to the same line when it has been
straightened out.

Again in the case of abstract objects what is straight is analogous to what is
snub-nosed; for it necessarily implies a continuum: its constitutive essence is different,
if we may distinguish between straightness and what is straight: let us take it to be two-
ness. It must be apprehended, therefore, by a different power or by the same power in a 20
different state. To sum up, in so far as the realities it knows are capable of being separated from their matter, so it is also with the powers of thought.

The problem might be suggested: if thinking is a passive affection, then if
thought is simple and impassible and has nothing in common with anything else, as
Anaxagoras says, how can it come to think at all? For interaction between two factors 25
is held to require a precedent community of nature between the factors. Again it might
be asked, is thought a possible object of thought to itself? For if thought is thinkable
per se and what is thinkable is in kind one and the same, then either thought will belong to everything, or it will contain some element common to it with all other realities
which makes them all thinkable.

Have not we already disposed of the difficulty about interaction involving a 30
common element, when we said that thought is in a sense potentially whatever is thinkable, though actually it is nothing until it has thought? What it thinks must be in it just
as characters may be said to be on a writing-table on which as yet nothing actually 430^a
stands written: this is exactly what happens with thought.

Thought is itself thinkable in exactly the same way as its objects are. For in the
case of objects which involve no matter, what thinks and what is thought are identical;
for speculative knowledge and its object are identical. (Why thought is not always 5
thinking we must consider later.) In the case of those which contain matter each of the
objects of thought is only potentially present. It follows that while they will not have
thought in them (for thought is a potentiality of them only in so far as they are capable
of being disengaged from matter) thought may yet be thinkable.

10   5. Since in every class of things, as in nature as a whole, we find two factors involved, a matter which is potentially all the particulars included in the class, a cause which is productive in the sense that it makes them all (the latter standing to the former, as e.g. an art to its material), these distinct elements must likewise be found within the soul.

15   And in fact thought, as we have described it, is what it is by virtue of becoming all things, while there is another which is what it is by virtue of making all things: this is a sort of positive state like light; for in a sense light makes potential colours into actual colours.

Thought in this sense of it is separable, impassible, unmixed, since it is in its essential nature activity (for always the active is superior to the passive factor, the originating force to the matter).

20   Actual knowledge is identical with its object: in the individual, potential knowledge is in time prior to actual knowledge, but absolutely it is not prior even in time. It does not sometimes think and sometimes not think. When separated it is alone just what it is, and this above is immortal and eternal (we do not remember because, while

25   this is impossible, passive thought is perishable); and without this nothing thinks.

NICHOMACHEAN ETHICS (in part)

BOOK I

1094ᵃ   *1. The Good as the Aim of Action:* Every art or applied science and every systematic investigation, and similarly every action and choice, seem to aim at some good; the good, therefore, has been well defined as that at which all things aim.* But it is clear that there is a difference in the ends at which they aim: in some cases the activ-

5   ity is the end, in others the end is some product beyond the activity. In cases where the end lies beyond the action the product is naturally superior to the activity.

Since there are many activities, arts, and sciences, the number of ends is correspondingly large: of medicine the end is health, of shipbuilding a vessel, of strategy, victory, and of household management, wealth. In many instances several such pur-

10   suits are grouped together under a single capacity: the art of bridle-making, for example, and everything else pertaining to the equipment of a horse are grouped together under horsemanship; horsemanship in turn, along with every other military action, is grouped together under strategy; and other pursuits are grouped together under other capacities. In all these cases the ends of the master sciences are preferable to the ends

15   of the subordinate sciences, since the latter are pursued for the sake of the former. This is true whether the ends of the actions lie in the activities themselves or, as is the case in the disciplines just mentioned, in something beyond the activities.

*We do not know who first gave this definition of the good. It is certainly implied in the Platonic dialogues, especially in *Republic,* Book VI; but the most likely candidate for the formulation here is Eudoxus.

Aristotle, *The Nichomachean Ethics,* Books I–II; Book III, 1-5; Book IV, 3; Books VI–VII; Book X, 6–8, translated by Martin Ostwald (New York: Macmillan/Library of the Liberal Arts, 1962).

2. Politics as the Master Science of the Good: Now, if there exists an end in the realm of action which we desire for its own sake, an end which determines all our other desires; if, in other words, we do not make all our choices for the sake of something else—for in this way the process will go on infinitely so that our desire would be   20
futile and pointless—then obviously this end will be the good, that is, the highest good. Will not the knowledge of this good, consequently, be very important to our lives? Would it not better equip us, like archers who have a target to aim at, to hit the proper mark? If so, we must try to comprehend in outline at least what this good is and to   25
which branch of knowledge or to which capacity it belongs.

This good, one should think, belongs to the most sovereign and most comprehensive master science, and politics* clearly fits this description. For it determines which sciences ought to exist in states, what kind of sciences each group of citizens must learn, and what degree of proficiency each must attain. We observe further that the   1094[b]
most honored capacities, such as strategy, household management, and oratory, are contained in politics. Since this science uses the rest of the sciences, and since, moreover, it legislates what people are to do and what they are not to do, its end seems to   5
embrace the ends of the other sciences. Thus it follows that the end of politics is the good for man. For even if the good is the same for the individual and the state, the good of the state clearly is the greater and more perfect thing to attain and to safeguard. The attainment of the good for one man alone is, to be sure, a source of satisfaction;   10
yet to secure it for a nation and for states is nobler and more divine. In short, these are the aims of our investigation, which is in a sense an investigation of social and political matters.

3. The Limitations of Ethics and Politics: Our discussion will be adequate if it achieves clarity within the limits of the subject matter. For precision cannot be expected in the treatment of all subjects alike, any more than it can be expected in all manufactured articles. Problems of what is noble and just, which politics examines, present so much variety and irregularity that some people believe that they exist only   15
by convention and not by nature. The problem of the good, too, presents a similar kind of irregularity, because in many cases good things bring harmful results. There are instances of men ruined by wealth, and others by courage. Therefore, in a discussion of such subjects, which has to start from a basis of this kind, we must be satisfied to indicate the truth with a rough and general sketch: when the subject and the basis of a dis-   20
cussion consist of matters that hold good only as a general rule, but not always, the conclusions reached must be of the same order. The various points that are made must be received in the same spirit. For a well-schooled man is one who searches for that degree of precision in each kind of study which the nature of the subject at hand admits: it is obviously just as foolish to accept arguments of probability from a mathe-   25
matician as to demand strict demonstrations from an orator.

Each man can judge competently the things he knows, and of these he is a good judge. Accordingly, a good judge in each particular field is one who has been trained in   1095[a]
it, and a good judge in general, a man who has received an all-round schooling. For that reason, a young man is not equipped to be a student of politics; for he has no experience in the actions which life demands of him, and these actions form the basis and

---

Politike is the science of the city-state, the *polis,* and its members, not merely in our narrow "political" sense of the word but also in the sense that a civilized human existence is, according to Plato and Aristotle, only possible in the *polis.* Thus *politike* involves not only the science of the state, "politics," but of our concept of "society" as well.

subject matter of the discussion. Moreover, since he follows his emotions, his study will be pointless and unprofitable, for the end of this kind of study is not knowledge but action. Whether he is young in years or immature in character makes no difference; for his deficiency is not a matter of time but of living and of pursuing all his interests under the influence of his emotions. Knowledge brings no benefit to this kind of person, just as it brings none to the morally weak. But those who regulate their desires and actions by a rational principle* will greatly benefit from a knowledge of this subject. So much by way of a preface about the student, the limitations which have to be accepted, and the objective before us.

4. Happiness Is the Good, But Many Views Are Held About It: To resume the discussion: since all knowledge and every choice is directed toward some good, let us discuss what is in our view the aim of politics, i.e., the highest good attainable by action. As far as its name is concerned, most people would probably agree: for both the common run of people and cultivated men call it happiness, and understand by "being happy" the same as "living well" and "doing well." But when it comes to defining what happiness is, they disagree, and the account given by the common run differs from that of the philosophers. The former say it is some clear and obvious good, such as pleasure, wealth, or honor; some say it is one thing and others another, and often the very same person identifies it with different things at different times: when he is sick he thinks it is health, and when he is poor he says it is wealth; and when people are conscious of their own ignorance, they admire those who talk above their heads in accents of greatness. Some thinkers used to believe that there exists over and above these many goods another good, good in itself and by itself, which also is the cause of good in all these things. An examination of all the different opinions would perhaps be a little pointless, and it is sufficient to concentrate on those which are most in evidence or which seem to make some sort of sense.

Nor must we overlook the fact that arguments which proceed from fundamental principles are different from arguments that lead up to them. Plato, too, rightly recognized this as a problem and used to ask whether the discussion was proceeding from or leading up to fundamental principles, just as in a race course there is a difference between running from the judges to the far end of the track and running back again.** Now, we must start with the known. But this term has two connotations: "what is known to us" and "what is known" pure and simple. Therefore, we should start perhaps from what is known to us. For that reason, to be a competent student of what is right and just, and of politics generally, one must first have received a proper upbringing in moral conduct. The acceptance of a fact as a fact is the starting point, and if this is sufficiently clear, there will be no further need to ask why it is so. A man with this kind of background has or can easily acquire the foundations from which he must start. But if he neither has nor can acquire them, let him lend an ear to Hesiod's words:

*The fundamental meaning of *Logos* is "speech," "statement," in the sense of a coherent and rational arrangement of words; but it can apply to a rational principle underlying many things, and may be translated in different contexts by "rational account," "explanation," "argument," "treatise," or "discussion." In Chapters 7 and 13 below, *Logos* is used in a normative sense, describing the human faculty which comprehends and formulates rational principles and thus guides the conduct of a good and reasonable man.

**A Greek race course was U-shaped with the starting line at the open end, which is also where the judges would have their place. The race was run around a marker set up toward the opposite end of the U, and back again to the starting line.

That man is all-best who himself works out every problem. . . .   10
That man, too, is admirable who follows one who speaks well.
He who cannot see the truth for himself, nor, hearing it from others, store it away in his
   mind, that man is utterly useless.

5. Various Views on the Highest Good: But to return to the point from which we
digressed. It is not unreasonable that men should derive their concept of the good and   15
of happiness from the lives which they lead. The common run of people and the most
vulgar identify it with pleasure, and for that reason are satisfied with a life of enjoyment. For the most notable kinds of life are three: the life just mentioned, the political
life, and the contemplative life.

The common run of people, as we saw, betray their utter slavishness in their
preference for a life suitable to cattle; but their views seem plausible because many   20
people in high places share the feelings of Sardanapallus.* Cultivated and active men,
on the other hand, believe the good to be honor, for honor, one might say, is the end of
the political life. But this is clearly too superficial an answer: for honor seems to depend on those who confer it rather than on him who receives it, whereas our guess is   25
that the good is a man's own possession which cannot easily be taken away from him.
Furthermore, men seem to pursue honor to assure themselves of their own worth; at
any rate, they seek to be honored by sensible men and by those who know them, and
they want to be honored on the basis of their virtue or excellence [<aretē>].** Obviously, then, excellence, as far as they are concerned, is better than honor. One might   30
perhaps even go so far as to consider excellence rather than honor as the end of political life. However, even excellence proves to be imperfect as an end: for a man might
possibly possess it while asleep or while being inactive all his life, and while, in addi-   1096ᵃ
tion, undergoing the greatest suffering and misfortune. Nobody would call the life of
such a man happy, except for the sake of maintaining an argument. But enough of this:
the subject has been sufficiently treated in our publications addressed to a wider audience. In the third place there is the contemplative life, which we shall examine later on.   5
As for the money-maker, his life is led under some kind of constraint: clearly, wealth is
not the good which we are trying to find, for it is only useful, i.e., it is a means to
something else. Hence one might rather regard the aforementioned objects as ends,
since they are valued for their own sake. But even they prove not to be the good,
though many words have been wasted to show that they are. Accordingly, we may dis-   10
miss them.

6. Plato's View of the Good: But perhaps we had better examine the universal
good and face the problem of its meaning, although such an inquiry is repugnant, since
those who have introduced the doctrine of Forms*** are dear to us. But in the interest
of truth, one should perhaps think a man, especially if he is a philosopher, had better
give up even [theories that once were] his own and in fact must do so. Both are dear to   15
us, but it is our sacred duty to honor truth more highly [than friends].

---

*Sardanapallus is the Hellenized name of the Assyrian king Ashurbanipal (669–626 B.C.). Many sto-
ries about his sensual excesses were current in antiquity.

**Aretē denotes the functional excellence of any person, animal, or thing—that quality which en-
ables the possessor to perform his own particular function well. Thus the aretai (plural) of man in relation to
other men are his qualities which enable him to function well in society. The translation "virtue" often seems
too narrow, and accordingly "excellence" and "goodness," or a combination of these, will also be used.

***The reference is of course to Plato's theory of eide or ideai and especially the Form of the Good,
which is Aristotle's chief target here.

The proponents of this theory did not make Forms out of those classes within which they recognized an order involving priority and posteriority; for that reason they made no provision, either, for a Form comprising all numbers.* However, the term "good" is used in the categories of substance, of quality, and of relatedness alike; but a
20   thing-as-such, i.e., a substance, is by nature prior to a relation into which it can enter: relatedness is, as it were, an offshoot or logical accident of substance. Consequently, there cannot be a Form common to the good-as-such and the good as a relation.

Secondly, the term "good" has as many meanings as the word "is": it is used to
25   describe substances, e.g., divinity and intelligence are good; qualities, e.g., the virtues are good; quantities, e.g., the proper amount is good; relatedness, e.g., the useful is good; time, e.g., the right moment is good; place, e.g., a place to live is good; and so forth. It is clear, therefore, that the good cannot be something universal, common to all cases, and single; for if it were, it would not be applicable in all categories but only in one.

Thirdly, since the things which are included under one Form are the subject mat-
30   ter of a single science, there should be a single science dealing with all good things. But in actual fact there are many sciences dealing even with the goods that fall into a single category. To take, for example, the right moment: in war it is the proper concern of strategy, whereas in treating a disease it is part of the study of medicine. Or to take the proper amount: in food it is the subject of medicine; in physical training, of gymnastics.

35   One might even [go further and] raise the question what exactly they mean by a
1096^b "thing-as-such"; for the selfsame definition of "man" applies to both "man-as-such" and a particular man. For inasmuch as they refer to "man," there will be no difference between the two; and if this is true, there will be no difference, either, between "good-as-such" and "good," since both are good. Nor indeed will the "good-as-such" be more of a good because it is everlasting: after all, whiteness which lasts for a long time is no whiter than whiteness which lasts only for a day.

5   The argument of the Pythagoreans on this point seems to be more convincing. They give unity a place in the column of goods; and indeed even Speusippus** seems to follow them. But more about this elsewhere.

An objection might be raised against what we have said on the ground that the [Platonic] doctrine does not refer to every kind of good, and that only things which are
10   pursued and loved for their own sake are called "good" by reference to one single Form. That which produces good or somehow guarantees its permanence, [the Platonists argue,] or that which prevents the opposite of a good from asserting itself is called "good" because it is conducive to the intrinsically good and in a different sense. Now, the term "good" has obviously two different meanings: (1) things which are intrinsically good, and (2) things which are good as being conducive to the intrinsically good.
15   Let us, therefore, separate the intrinsically good things from the useful things and examine whether they are called "good" by reference to a single Form.

---

*Since for Plato and his followers the Forms are absolute being, in which there is no room for becoming or any kind of development, they do not recognize a Form of a developing series, in which each successive member implies the preceding members of the same series. But, as Aristotle proceeds to show, the term "good" belongs to such a developing series: if we call a certain quality, e.g., blueness, "good," we have to assume first that there is such a thing as blueness; i.e., we have to predicate it in the category of substance before we can predicate it in the category of quality.

**Speusippus was Plato's nephew and disciple who succeeded him a head of the Academy from 347–339 B.C.

What sort of things could be called intrinsically good? Are they the goods that are pursued without regard to additional benefits, such as thought, sight, certain pleasures and honors? For even if we pursue these also for the sake of something else, one would still classify them among things intrinsically good. Or is nothing good except the Form of Good? If that is the case, the Form will be pointless. But if, on the contrary, thought, sight, etc. also belong to the group of intrinsically good things, the same definition of "good" will have to be manifested in all of them, just as, for example, the definition of whiteness is the same in snow and in white paint. But in actual fact, the definitions of "good" as manifested in honor, thought, and pleasure are different and distinct. The good, therefore, is not some element common to all these things as derived from one Form.

What, then, is the meaning of "good" [in these different things]? Surely, it is not that they merely happen to have the same name. Do we call them "good" because they are derived from a single good, or because they all aim at a single good? Or do we rather call them "good" by analogy, e.g., as sight is good in the body, so intelligence is good in the soul, and so other things are good within their respective fields?

But perhaps this subject should be dismissed for the present, because a detailed discussion of it belongs more properly to a different branch of philosophy, [namely, first philosophy]. The same applies to the Form [of the Good]: for, assuming that there is some single good which different things possess in common, or that there exists a good absolutely in itself and by itself, it evidently is something which cannot be realized in action or attained by man. But the good which we are now seeking must be attainable.

Perhaps one may think that the recognition of an absolute good will be advantageous for the purpose of attaining and realizing in action the goods which can be attained and realized. By treating the absolute good as a pattern, [they might argue,] we shall gain a better knowledge of what things are good for us, and once we know that, we can achieve them. This argument has, no doubt, some plausibility; however, it does not tally with the procedure of the sciences. For while all the sciences aim at some good and seek to fulfill it, they leave the knowledge of the absolute good out of consideration. Yet if this knowledge were such a great help, it would make no sense that all the craftsmen are ignorant of it and do not even attempt to seek it. One might also wonder what benefit a weaver or a carpenter might derive in the practice of his own art from a knowledge of the absolute Good, or in what way a physician who has contemplated the Form of the Good will become more of a physician or a general more of a general. For actually, a physician does not even examine health in this fashion; he examines the health of man, or perhaps better, the health of a particular man, for he practices his medicine on particular cases. So much for this.

7. The Good Is Final and Self-Sufficient; Happiness Is Defined: Let us return again to our investigation into the nature of the good which we are seeking. It is evidently something different in different actions and in each art: it is one thing in medicine, another in strategy, and another again in each of the other arts. What, then, is the good of each? Is it not that for the sake of which everything else is done? That means it is health in the case of medicine, victory in the case of strategy, a house in the case of building, a different thing in the case of different arts, and in all actions and choices it is the end. For it is for the sake of the end that all else is done. Thus, if there is some one end for all that we do, this would be the good attainable by action; if there are several ends, they will be the goods attainable by action.

Our argument has gradually progressed to the same point at which we were before, and we must try to clarify it still further. Since there are evidently several ends, and since we choose some of these—e.g., wealth, flutes, and instruments generally—as a means to something else, it is obvious that not all ends are final. The highest good, on the other hand, must be something final. Thus, if there is only one final end, this will be the good we are seeking; if there are several, it will be the most final and perfect of them. We call that which is pursued as an end in itself more final than an end which is pursued for the sake of something else; and what is never chosen as a means to something else we call more final than that which is chosen both as an end in itself and as a means to something else. What is always chosen as an end in itself and never as a means to something else is called final in an unqualified sense. This description seems to apply to happiness above all else: for we always choose happiness as an end in itself and never for the sake of something else. Honor, pleasure, intelligence, and all virtue we choose partly for themselves—for we would choose each of them even if no further advantage would accrue from them—but we also choose them partly for the sake of happiness, because we assume that it is through them that we will be happy. On the other hand, no one chooses happiness for the sake of honor, pleasure, and the like, nor as a means to anything at all.

We arrive at the same conclusion if we approach the question from the standpoint of self-sufficiency. For the final and perfect good seems to be self-sufficient. However, we define something as self-sufficient not by reference to the "self" alone. We do not mean a man who lives his life in isolation, but a man who also lives with parents, children, a wife, and friends and fellow citizens generally, since man is by nature a social and political being. But some limit must be set to these relationships; for if they are extended to include ancestors, descendants, and friends of friends, they will go on to infinity. However, this point must be reserved for investigation later. For the present we define as "self-sufficient" that which taken by itself makes life something desirable and deficient in nothing. It is happiness, in our opinion, which fits this description. Moreover, happiness is of all things the one most desirable, and it is not counted as one good thing among many others. But if it were counted as one among many others, it is obvious that the addition of even the least of the goods would make it more desirable; for the addition would produce an extra amount of good, and the greater amount of good is always more desirable than the lesser. We see then that happiness is something final and self-sufficient and the end of our actions.

To call happiness the highest good is perhaps a little trite, and a clearer account of what it is, is still required. Perhaps this is best done by first ascertaining the proper function of man. For just as the goodness and performance of a flute player, a sculptor, or any kind of expert, and generally of anyone who fulfills some function or performs some action, are thought to reside in his proper function, so the goodness and performance of man would seem to reside in whatever is his proper function. Is it then possible that while a carpenter and a shoemaker have their own proper functions and spheres of action, man as man has none, but was left by nature a good-for-nothing without a function? Should we not assume that just as the eye, the hand, the foot, and in general each part of the body clearly has its own proper function, so man too has some function over and above the functions of his parts? What can this function possibly be? Simply living? He shares that even with plants, but we are now looking for something peculiar to man. Accordingly, the life of nutrition and growth must be excluded. Next in line there is a life of sense perception. But this, too, man has in common with the horse, the ox, and every animal. There remains then an active life of the rational element. The rational element has two parts: one is rational in that it obeys the rule of reason, the other in that it possesses and conceives rational rules. Since the expression "life of the rational element" also can be used in two senses, we must make it clear that we mean a life determined by the activity, as opposed to the mere possession, of the rational element. For the activity, it seems, has a greater claim to be the function of man.

The proper function of man, then, consists in an activity of the soul in conformity with a rational principle or, at least, not without it. In speaking of the proper function of a given individual we mean that it is the same in kind as the function of an individual who sets high standards for himself: the proper function of a harpist, for example, is the same as the function of a harpist who has set high standards for himself. The same applies to any and every group of individuals: the full attainment of excellence must be added to the mere function. In other words, the function of the harpist is to play the harp; the function of the harpist who has high standards is to play it well. On these assumptions, if we take the proper function of man to be a certain kind of life, and if this kind of life is an activity of the soul and consists in actions performed in conjunction with the rational element, and if a man of high standards is he who performs these actions well and properly, and if a function is well performed when it is performed in accordance with the excellence appropriate to it; we reach the conclusion that the good of man is an activity of the soul in conformity with excellence or virtue, and if there are several virtues, in conformity with the best and most complete.

But we must add "in a complete life." For one swallow does not make a spring, nor does one sunny day; similarly, one day or a short time does not make a man blessed* and happy.

This will suffice as an outline of the good: for perhaps one ought to make a general sketch first and fill in the details afterwards. Once a good outline has been made, anyone, it seems, is capable of developing and completing it in detail, and time is a good inventor or collaborator in such an effort. Advances in the arts, too, have come about in this way, for anyone can fill in gaps. We must also bear in mind what has been said above, namely that one should not require precision in all pursuits alike, but in each field precision varies with the matter under discussion and should be required only to the extent to which it is appropriate to the investigation. A carpenter and a geometrician both want to find a right angle, but they do not want to find it in the same sense: the former wants to find it to the extent to which it is useful for his work, the latter, wanting to see truth, tries to ascertain what it is and what sort of thing it is. We must, likewise, approach other subjects in the same spirit, in order to prevent minor points from assuming a greater importance than the major tasks. Nor should we demand to know a causal explanation in all matters alike; in some instances, e.g., when dealing with fundamental principles, it is sufficient to point out convincingly that such-and-such is in fact the case. The fact here is the primary thing and the fundamental principle. Some fundamental principles can be apprehended by induction, others by sense perception, others again by some sort of habituation,** and others by still other means. We must try to get at each of them in a way naturally appropriate to it, and must be scrupulous in defining it correctly, because it is of great importance for the subsequent course of the discussion. Surely, a good beginning is more than half the whole, and as it comes to light, it sheds light on many problems.

10

15

20

25

30

1098[b]

5

---

*The distinction Aristotle seems to observe between *makarios,* "blessed" or "supremely happy," and *eudaimon,* "happy," is that the former describes happiness insofar as it is god-given, while the latter describes happiness as attained by man through his own efforts.

**This, according to Aristotle, is the way in which the fundamental principles of ethics are learned, and for that reason a person must be mature in order to be able to study ethics properly. Aristotle is not trying to persuade his listener of the truth of these principles, but takes it for granted that the listener has learned them at home.

8. Popular Views About Happiness Confirm Our Position: We must examine the fundamental principle with which we are concerned, [happiness,] not only on the basis of the logical conclusion we have reached and on the basis of the elements which make
10   up its definition, but also on the basis of the views commonly expressed about it. For in a true statement, all the facts are in harmony; in a false statement, truth soon introduces a discordant note.

Good things are commonly divided into three classes: (1) external goods, (2) goods of the soul, and (3) goods of the body. Of these, we call the goods pertaining to the soul goods in the highest and fullest sense. But in speaking of "soul," we refer to
15   our soul's actions and activities. Thus, our definition tallies with this opinion which has been current for a long time and to which philosophers subscribe. We are also right in defining the end as consisting of actions and activities; for in this way the end is included among the goods of the soul and not among external goods.

20   Also the view that a happy man lives well and fares well fits in with our definition: for we have all but defined happiness as a kind of good life and well-being.

Moreover, the characteristics which one looks for in happiness are all included in our definition. For some people think that happiness is virtue, others that it is practical wisdom, others that it is some kind of theoretical wisdom; others again believe it to be
25   all or some of these accompanied by, or not devoid of, pleasure; and some people also include external prosperity in its definition.* Some of these views are expressed by many people and have come down from antiquity, some by a few men of high prestige, and it is not reasonable to assume that both groups are altogether wrong; the presumption is rather that they are right in at least one or even in most respects.

Now, in our definition we are in agreement with those who describe happiness as
30   virtue or as some particular virtue, for our term "activity in conformity with virtue" implies virtue. But it does doubtless make a considerable difference whether we think of the highest good as consisting in the possession or in the practice of virtue, viz., as being a characteristic or an activity. For a characteristic may exist without producing
1099ᵃ   any good result, as for example, in a man who is asleep or incapacitated in some other respect. An activity, on the other hand, must produce a result: [an active person] will necessarily act and act well. Just as the crown at the Olympic Games is not awarded to the most beautiful and the strongest but to the participants in the contests—for it is
5   among them that the victors are found—so the good and noble things in life are won by those who act rightly.

The life of men active in this sense is also pleasant in itself. For the sensation of pleasure belongs to the soul, and each man derives pleasure from what he is said to love: a lover of horses from horses, a lover of the theater from plays, and in the same
10   way a lover of justice from just acts, and a lover of virtue in general from virtuous acts. In most men, pleasant acts conflict with one another because they are not pleasant by nature, but men who love what is noble derive pleasure from what is naturally pleasant. Actions which conform to virtue are naturally pleasant, and, as a result, such ac-
15   tions are not only pleasant for those who love the noble but also pleasant in themselves. The life of such men has no further need of pleasure as an added attraction, but it contains pleasure within itself. We may even go so far as to state that the man who

---

*The view that virtue alone constitutes happiness was espoused by Antisthenes and the Cynics (and later by the Stoics); the doctrine that all virtues are forms of *phronesis* or "practical wisdom" is attributed to Socrates; theoretical wisdom as virtue may perhaps be attributed to Anaxagoras and his doctrine of *Nous;* the view that pleasure must be added to virtue and wisdom is that of Plato; and the ancient commentators on this passage identify Xenocrates, Plato's pupil and later head of the Academy, as regarding external goods as essential for the good life.

does not enjoy performing noble actions is not a good man at all. Nobody would call a man just who does not enjoy acting justly, nor generous who does not enjoy generous actions, and so on. If this is true, actions performed in conformity with virtue are in themselves pleasant.

Of course it goes without saying that such actions are good as well as noble, and they are both in the highest degree, if the man of high moral standards displays any right judgment about them at all; and his judgment corresponds to our description. So we see that happiness is at once the best, noblest, and most pleasant thing, and these qualities are not separate, as the inscription at Delos makes out:

> The most just is most noble, but health is the best, and to win what one loves is pleasantest.

For the best activities encompass all these attributes, and it is in these, or in the best one of them, that we maintain happiness consists.

Still, happiness, as we have said, needs external goods as well. For it is impossible or at least not easy to perform noble actions if one lacks the wherewithal. Many actions can only be performed with the help of instruments, as it were: friends, wealth, and political power. And there are some external goods the absence of which spoils supreme happiness, e.g., good birth, good children, and beauty: for a man who is very ugly in appearance or ill-born or who lives all by himself and has no children cannot be classified as altogether happy; even less happy perhaps is a man whose children and friends are worthless, or one who has lost good children and friends through death. Thus, as we have said, happiness also requires well-being of this kind, and that is the reason why some classify good fortune with happiness, while others link it to virtue.

9. How Happiness Is Acquired: This also explains why there is a problem whether happiness is acquired by learning, by discipline, or by some other kind of training, or whether we attain it by reason of some divine dispensation or even by chance. Now, if there is anything at all which comes to men as a gift from the gods, it is reasonable to suppose that happiness above all else is god-given; and of all things human it is the most likely to be god-given, inasmuch as it is the best. But although this subject is perhaps more appropriate to a different field of study, it is clear that happiness is one of the most divine things, even if it is not god-sent but attained through virtue and some kind of learning or training. For the prize and end of excellence and virtue is the best thing of all, and it is something divine and blessed. Moreover, if happiness depends on excellence, it will be shared by many people; for study and effort will make it accessible to anyone whose capacity for virtue is unimpaired. And if it is better that happiness is acquired in this way rather than by chance, it is reasonable to assume that this is the way in which it is acquired. For, in the realm of nature, things are naturally arranged in the best way possible—and the same is also true of the products of art and of any kind of causation, especially the highest. To leave the greatest and noblest of things to chance would hardly be right.

A solution of this question is also suggested by our earlier definition, according to which the good of man, happiness, is some kind of activity of the soul in conformity with virtue. All the other goods are either necessary prerequisites for happiness, or are by nature co-workers with it and useful instruments for attaining it. Our results also tally with what we said at the outset: for we stated that the end of politics is the best of ends; and the main concern of politics is to engender a certain character in the citizens and to make them good and disposed to perform noble actions.

1100ᵃ
We are right, then, when we call neither a horse nor an ox nor any other animal happy, for none of them is capable of participating in an activity of this kind. For the same reason, a child is not happy, either; for, because of his age, he cannot yet perform such actions. When we do call a child happy, we do so by reason of the hopes we have for his future. Happiness, as we have said, requires completeness in virtue as well as a

5
complete lifetime. Many changes and all kinds of contingencies befall a man in the course of his life, and it is possible that the most prosperous man will encounter great misfortune in his old age, as the Trojan legends tell about Priam. When a man has met a fate such as his and has come to a wretched end, no one calls him happy.

10
10. Can a Man Be Called "Happy" During His Lifetime?: Must we, then, apply the term "happy" to no man at all as long as he is alive? Must we, as Solon would have us do, wait to see his end?* And, on this assumption, is it also true that a man is actually happy after he is dead? Is this not simply absurd, especially for us who define happiness as a kind of activity? Suppose we do not call a dead man happy, and interpret

15
Solon's words to mean that only when a man is dead can we safely say that he has been happy, since he is now beyond the reach of evil and misfortune—this view, too, is open to objection. For it seems that to some extent good and evil really exist for a dead man, just as they may exist for a man who lives without being conscious of them,

20
for example, honors and disgraces, and generally the successes and failures of his children and descendants. This presents a further problem. A man who has lived happily to his old age and has died as happily as he lived may have many vicissitudes befall his descendants: some of them may be good and may be granted the kind of life which

25
they deserve, and others may not. It is, further, obvious that the descendants may conceivably be removed from their ancestors by various degrees. Under such circumstances, it would be odd if the dead man would share in the vicissitudes of his descendants and be happy at one time and wretched at another. But it would also be

30
odd if the fortunes of their descendants did not affect the ancestors at all, not even for a short time.

But we must return to the problem raised earlier, for through it our present problem perhaps may be solved. If one must look to the end and praise a man not as being happy but as having been happy in the past, is it not paradoxical that at a time when a

35
man actually is happy this attribute, though true, cannot be applied to him? We are un-

1100ᵇ
willing to call the living happy because changes may befall them and because we believe that happiness has permanence and is not amenable to changes under any circumstances, whereas fortunes revolve many times in one person's lifetime. For obviously,

5
if we are to keep pace with a man's fortune, we shall frequently have to call the same man happy at one time and wretched at another and demonstrate that the happy man is a kind of chameleon, and that the foundations [of his life] are unsure. Or is it quite wrong to make our judgment depend on fortune? Yes, it is wrong, for fortune does not determine whether we fare well or ill, but is, as we said, merely an accessory to human

10
life; activities in conformity with virtue constitute happiness, and the opposite activities constitute its opposite.

The question which we have just discussed further confirms our definition. For no function of man possesses as much stability as do activities in conformity with virtue: these seem to be even more durable than scientific knowledge. And the higher

15
the virtuous activities, the more durable they are, because men who are supremely

---

*This is one of the main points made by Solon, Athenian statesman and poet of the early sixth century B.C., in his conversation with the Lydian king, Croesus.

happy spend their lives in these activities most intensely and most continuously, and this seems to be the reason why such activities cannot be forgotten.

The happy man will have the attribute of permanence which we are discussing, and he will remain happy throughout his life. For he will always or to the highest degree both do and contemplate what is in conformity with virtue; he will bear the vicissitudes of fortune most nobly and with perfect decorum under all circumstances, inasmuch as he is truly good and "four-square beyond reproach." 20

But fortune brings many things to pass, some great and some small. Minor instances of good and likewise of bad luck obviously do not decisively tip the scales of 25 life, but a number of major successes will make life more perfectly happy; for, in the first place, by their very nature they help to make life attractive, and secondly, they afford the opportunity for noble and good actions. On the other hand, frequent reverses can crush and mar supreme happiness in that they inflict pain and thwart many activities. Still, nobility shines through even in such circumstances, when a man bears many 30 great misfortunes with good grace not because he is insensitive to pain but because he is noble and high-minded.

If, as we said, the activities determine a man's life, no supremely happy man can ever become miserable, for he will never do what is hateful and base. For in our opin- 35 ion, the man who is truly good and wise will bear with dignity whatever fortune may 1101ᵃ bring, and will always act as nobly as circumstances permit, just as a good general makes the most strategic use of the troops at his disposal, and a good shoemaker makes the best shoe he can from the leather available, and so on with experts in all other 5 fields. If this is true, a happy man will never become miserable; but even so, supreme happiness will not be his if a fate such as Priam's befalls him. And yet, he will not be fickle and changeable; he will not be dislodged from his happiness easily by any mis- 10 fortune that comes along, but only by great and numerous disasters such as will make it impossible for him to become happy again in a short time; if he recovers his happiness at all, it will be only after a long period of time, in which he has won great distinctions.

Is there anything to prevent us, then, from defining the happy man as one whose activities are an expression of complete virtue, and who is sufficiently equipped with 15 external goods, not simply at a given moment but to the end of his life? Or should we add that he must die as well as live in the manner which we have defined? For we cannot foresee the future, and happiness, we maintain, is an end which is absolutely final and complete in every respect. If this be granted, we shall define as "supremely happy" those living men who fulfill and continue to fulfill these requirements, but blissful only 20 as human beings. So much for this question.

11. Do the Fortunes of the Living Affect the Dead?: That the fortunes of his descendants and of all those near and dear to him do not affect the happiness of a dead man at all, seems too unfeeling a view and contrary to the prevailing opinions. Many and different in kind are the accidents that can befall us, and some hit home more closely than others. It would, therefore, seem to be a long and endless task to make de- 25 tailed distinctions, and perhaps a general outline will be sufficient. Just as one's own misfortunes are sometimes momentous and decisive for one's life and sometimes seem comparatively less important, so the misfortunes of our various friends affect us to 30 varying degrees. In each case it makes a considerable difference whether those who are affected by an event are living or dead; much more so than it matters in a tragedy whether the crimes and horrors have been perpetrated before the opening of the play or are part of the plot. This difference, too, must be taken into account and perhaps still

35   more the problem whether the dead participate in any good or evil. These considera-
1101ᵇ tions suggest that even if any good or evil reaches them at all, it must be something
weak and negligible (either intrinsically or in relation to them), or at least something
too small and insignificant to make the unhappy happy or to deprive the happy of their
5   bliss. The good as well as the bad fortunes of their friends seem, then, to have some effect upon the dead, but the nature and magnitude of the effect is such as not to make
the happy unhappy or to produce any similar changes.

10   *12. The Praise Accorded to Happiness:* Now that we have settled these questions, let us consider whether happiness is to be classified among the things which we
praise or rather among those which we honor; for it is clear that it is not a potential [but
an actual good].

     The grounds on which we bestow praise on anything evidently are its quality and
the relation in which it stands to other things. In other words, we praise a just man, a
15   courageous man, and in general any good man, and also his virtue or excellence, on the
basis of his actions and achievements; moreover, we praise a strong man, a swift runner, and so forth, because he possesses a certain natural quality and stands in a certain
relation to something good and worth while. Our feelings about praising the gods provide a further illustration of this point. For it is ridiculous to refer the gods to our stan-
20   dards; but this is precisely what praising them amounts to, since praise, as we said, en-
tails a reference to something else. But if praise is appropriate only for relative things,
it is clear that the best things do not call for praise but for something greater and better,
as indeed is generally recognized: for we call the gods "blessed" and "happy" and use
25   these terms also for the most godlike man. The same is true of good things: no one
praises happiness in the same sense in which he praises justice, but he exalts its bliss as
something better and more nearly divine.

     Eudoxus, too, seems to have used the right method for advocating that pleasure
is the most excellent, for he took the fact that pleasure, though a good, is not praised as
30   an indication of its superiority to the things that are praised, as god and the good are,
for they are the standards to which we refer everything else.

     Praise is proper to virtue or excellence, because it is excellence that makes men
capable of performing noble deeds. Eulogies, on the other hand, are appropriate for
achievements of the body as well as of the mind. However, a detailed analysis of this
subject is perhaps rather the business of those who have made a study of eulogies. For
35   our present purposes, we may draw the conclusion from the preceding argument that
1102ᵃ happiness is one of the goods that are worthy of honor and are final. This again seems
to be due to the fact that it is a starting point or fundamental principle, since for its sake
all of us do everything else. And the source and cause of all good things we consider as
something worthy of honor and as divine.

5   *13. The Psychological Foundations of the Virtues:* Since happiness is a certain
activity of the soul in conformity with perfect virtue, we must now examine what
virtue or excellence is. For such an inquiry will perhaps better enable us to discover the
nature of happiness. Moreover, the man who is truly concerned about politics seems to
devote special attention to excellence, since it is his aim to make the citizens good and
10   law-abiding. We have an example of this in the lawgivers of Crete and Sparta and in
other great legislators. If an examination of virtue is part of politics, this question
clearly fits into the pattern of our original plan.

     There can be no doubt that the virtue which we have to study is human virtue.
15   For the good which we have been seeking is a human good and the happiness a human

happiness. By human virtue we do not mean the excellence of the body, but that of the soul, and we define happiness as an activity of the soul. If this is true, the student of politics must obviously have some knowledge of the workings of the soul, just as the man who is to heal eyes must know something about the whole body. In fact, knowledge is all the more important for the former, inasmuch as politics is better and more valuable than medicine, and cultivated physicians devote much time and trouble to gain knowledge about the body. Thus, the student of politics must study the soul, but he must do so with his own aim in view, and only to the extent that the objects of his inquiry demand: to go into it in greater detail would perhaps be more laborious than his purposes require.

Some things that are said about the soul in our less technical discussions are adequate enough to be used here, for instance, that the soul consists of two elements, one irrational and one rational. Whether these two elements are separate, like the parts of the body or any other divisible thing, or whether they are only logically separable though in reality indivisible, as convex and concave are in the circumference of a circle, is irrelevant for our present purposes.

Of the irrational element, again, one part seems to be common to all living things and vegetative in nature: I mean that part which is responsible for nurture and growth. We must assume that some such capacity of the soul exists in everything that takes nourishment, in the embryonic stage as well as when the organism is fully developed; for this makes more sense than to assume the existence of some different capacity at the latter stage. The excellence of this part of the soul is, therefore, shown to be common to all living things and is not exclusively human. This very part and this capacity seem to be most active in sleep. For in sleep the difference between a good man and a bad is least apparent—whence the saying that for half their lives the happy are no better off than the wretched. This is just what we would expect, for sleep is an inactivity of the soul in that it ceases to do things which cause it to be called good or bad. However, to a small extent some bodily movements do penetrate to the soul in sleep, and in this sense the dreams of honest men are better than those of average people. But enough of this subject: we may pass by the nutritive part, since it has no natural share in human excellence or virtue.

In addition to this, there seems to be another integral element of the soul which, though irrational, still does partake of reason in some way. In morally strong and morally weak men we praise the reason that guides them and the rational element of the soul, because it exhorts them to follow the right path and to do what is best. Yet we see in them also another natural strain different from the rational, which fights and resists the guidance of reason. The soul behaves in precisely same manner as do the paralyzed limbs of the body. When we intend to move the limbs to the right, they turn to the left, and similarly, the impulses of morally weak persons turn in the direction opposite to that in which reason leads them. However, while the aberration of the body is visible, that of the soul is not. But perhaps we must accept it as a fact, nevertheless, that there is something in the soul besides the rational element, which opposes and reacts against it. In what way the two are distinct need not concern us here. But, as we have stated, it too seems to partake of reason; at any rate, in a morally strong man it accepts the leadership of reason, and is perhaps more obedient still in a self-controlled and courageous man, since in him everything is in harmony with the voice of reason.

Thus we see that the irrational element of the soul has two parts: the one is vegetative and has no share in reason at all, the other is the seat of the appetites and of desire in general and partakes of reason insofar as it complies with reason and accepts its leadership; it possesses reason in the sense that we say it is "reasonable" to accept the advice of a father and of friends, not in the sense that we have a "rational" understanding of mathematical propositions. That the irrational element can be persuaded by the rational is shown by the fact that admonition and all manner of rebuke and exhortation are possible. If it is correct to say that the appetitive part, too, has reason, it follows that the rational element of the soul has two subdivisions: the one possesses reason in the strict sense, contained within itself, and the other possesses reason in the sense that it listens to reason as one would listen to a father.

Virtue, too, is differentiated in line with this division of the soul. We call some virtues "intellectual" and others "moral": theoretical wisdom, understanding, and practical wisdom are intellectual virtues, generosity and self-control moral virtues. In speaking of a man's character, we do not describe him as wise or understanding, but as gentle or self-controlled; but we praise the wise man, too, for his characteristic, and praiseworthy characteristics are what we call virtues.

BOOK II

1. Moral Virtue as the Result of Habits: Virtue, as we have seen, consists of two-kinds, intellectual virtue and moral virtue. Intellectual virtue or excellence owes its origin and development chiefly to teaching, and for that reason requires experience and time. Moral virtue, on the other hand, is formed by habit, *ethos,* and its name, *ethike,* is therefore derived, by a slight variation, from *ethos.* This shows, too, that none of the moral virtues is implanted in us by nature, for nothing which exists by nature can be changed by habit. For example, it is impossible for a stone, which has a natural downward movement, to become habituated to moving upward, even if one should try ten thousand times to inculcate the habit by throwing it in the air; nor can fire be made to move downward, nor can the direction of any nature-given tendency be changed by habituation. Thus, the virtues are implanted in us neither by nature nor contrary to nature: we are by nature equipped with the ability to receive them, and habit brings this ability to completion and fulfillment.

Furthermore, of all the qualities with which we are endowed by nature, we are provided with the capacity first, and display the activity afterward. That this is true is shown by the senses: it is not by frequent seeing or frequent hearing that we acquired our senses, but on the contrary we first possess and then use them; we do not acquire them by use. The virtues, on the other hand, we acquire by first having put them into action, and the same is also true of the arts. For the things which we have to learn before we can do them we learn by doing: men become builders by building houses, and harpists by playing the harp. Similarly, we become just by the practice of just actions, self-controlled by exercising self-control, and courageous by performing acts of courage.

This is corroborated by what happens in states. Lawgivers make the citizens good by inculcating [good] habits in them, and this is the aim of every lawgiver; if he does not succeed in doing that, his legislation is a failure. It is in this that a good constitution differs from a bad one.

Moreover, the same causes and the same means that produce any excellence or virtue can also destroy it, and this is also true of every art. It is by playing the harp that men become both good and bad harpists, and correspondingly with builders and all the other craftsmen: a man who builds well will be a good builder, one who builds badly a bad one. For if this were not so, there would be no need for an instructor, but everybody would be born as a good or a bad craftsman. The same holds true of the virtues: in our transactions with other men it is by action that some become just and others unjust, and it is by acting in the face of danger and by developing the habit of feeling fear or confidence that some become brave men and others cowards. The same applies to the appetites and feelings of anger: by reacting in one way or in another to given circumstances some people become self-controlled and gentle, and others self-indulgent and short-tempered. In a word, characteristics develop from corresponding activities. For that reason, we must see to it that our activities are of a certain kind, since any variations in them will be reflected in our characteristics. Hence it is no small matter whether one habit or another is inculcated in us from early childhood; on the contrary, it makes a considerable difference, or, rather, all the difference.

2. Method in the Practical Sciences: The purpose of the present study is not, as it is in other inquiries, the attainment of theoretical knowledge: we are not conducting this inquiry in order to know what virtue is, but in order to become good, else there would be no advantage in studying it. For that reason, it becomes necessary to examine the problem of actions, and to ask how they are to be performed. For, as we have said, the actions determine what kind of characteristics are developed.

That we must act according to right reason is generally conceded and may be assumed as the basis of our discussion. We shall speak about it later and discuss what right reason is and examine its relation to the other virtues. But let us first agree that any discussion on matters of action cannot be more than an outline and is bound to lack precision; for as we stated at the outset, one can demand of a discussion only what the subject matter permits, and there are no fixed data in matters concerning action and questions of what is beneficial, any more than there are in matters of health. And if this is true of our general discussion, our treatment of particular problems will be even less precise, since these do not come under the head of any art which can be transmitted by precept, but the agent must consider on each different occasion what the situation demands, just as in medicine and in navigation. But although such is the kind of discussion in which we are engaged, we must do our best.

First of all, it must be observed that the nature of moral qualities is such that they are destroyed by defect and by excess. We see the same thing happen in the case of strength and of health, to illustrate, as we must, the invisible by means of visible examples: excess as well as deficiency of physical exercise destroys our strength, and similarly, too much and too little food and drink destroys our health; the proportionate amount, however, produces, increases, and preserves it. The same applies to self-control, courage, and the other virtues: the man who shuns and fears everything and never stands his ground becomes a coward, whereas a man who knows no fear at all and goes to meet every danger becomes reckless. Similarly, a man who revels in every pleasure and abstains from none becomes self-indulgent, while he who avoids every pleasure like a boor becomes what might be called insensitive. Thus we see that self-control and courage are destroyed by excess and by deficiency and are preserved by the mean.

Not only are the same actions which are responsible for and instrumental in the origin and development of the virtues also the causes and means of their destruction, but they will also be manifested in the active exercise of the virtues. We can see the truth of this in the case of other more visible qualities, e.g., strength. Strength is produced by consuming plenty of food and by enduring much hard work, and it is the strong man who is best able to do these things. The same is also true of the virtues: by abstaining from pleasures we become self-controlled, and once we are self-controlled

1104^b we are best able to abstain from pleasures. So also with courage: by becoming habituated to despise and to endure terrors we become courageous, and once we have become courageous we will best be able to endure terror.

3. *Pleasure and Pain as the Test of Virtue:* An index to our characteristics is
5   provided by the pleasure or pain which follows upon the tasks we have achieved. A
man who abstains from bodily pleasures and enjoys doing so is self-controlled; if he
finds abstinence troublesome, he is self-indulgent; a man who endures danger with joy,
or at least without pain, is courageous; if he endures it with pain, he is a coward. For
10   moral excellence is concerned with pleasure and pain; it is pleasure that makes us do
base actions and pain that prevents us from doing noble actions. For that reason, as
Plato says, men must be brought up from childhood to feel pleasure and pain at the
proper things; for this is correct education.

Furthermore, since the virtues have to do with actions and emotions, and since
15   pleasure and pain are a consequence of every emotion and of every action, it follows
from this point of view, too, that virtue has to do with pleasure and pain. This is further
indicated by the fact that punishment is inflicted by means of pain. For punishment is a
kind of medical treatment and it is the nature of medical treatments to take effect
through the introduction of the opposite of the disease.* Again, as we said just now,
20   every characteristic of the soul shows its true nature in its relation to and its concern
with those factors which naturally make it better or worse. But it is through pleasures
and pains that men are corrupted, i.e., through pursuing and avoiding pleasures and
pains either of the wrong kind or at the wrong time or in the wrong manner, or by
going wrong in some other definable respect. For that reason some people define the
virtues as states of freedom from emotion and of quietude. However, they make the
25   mistake of using these terms absolutely and without adding such qualifications as "in
the right manner," "at the right or wrong time," and so forth. We may, therefore, assume as the basis of our discussion that virtue, being concerned with pleasure and pain
in the way we have described, makes us act in the best way in matters revolving pleasure and pain, and that vice does the opposite.

The following considerations may further illustrate that virtue is concerned with
30   pleasure and pain. There are three factors that determine choice and three that determine avoidance: the noble, the beneficial, and the pleasurable, on the one hand, and on
the other their opposites: the base, the harmful, and the painful. Now a good man will
go right and a bad man will go wrong when any of these, and especially when pleasure
35   is involved. For pleasure is not only common to man and the animals, but also accom-
1105^a panies all objects of choice: in fact, the noble and the beneficial seem pleasant to us.
Moreover, a love of pleasure has grown up with all of us from infancy. Therefore, this
emotion has come to be ingrained in our lives and is difficult to erase. Even in our ac-
5   tions we use, to a greater or smaller extent, pleasure and pain as a criterion. For this
reason, this entire study is necessarily concerned with pleasure and pain; for it is not
unimportant for our actions whether we feel joy and pain in the right or the wrong way.
Again, it is harder to fight against pleasure than against anger, as Heraclitus says; and
both virtue and art are always concerned with what is harder, for success is better when
10   it is hard to achieve. Thus, for this reason also, every study both of virtue and of politics must deal with pleasures and pains, for if a man has the right attitude to them, he
will be good; if the wrong attitude, he will be bad.

*The idea here evidently is that the pleasure of wrongdoing must be cured by applying its opposite,
i.e., pain.

We have now established that virtue or excellence is concerned with pleasures and pains; that the actions which produce it also develop it and, if differently per-   15 formed, destroy it; and that it actualizes itself fully in those activities to which it owes its origin.

4. Virtuous Action and Virtue: However, the question may be raised what we mean by saying that men become just by performing just actions and self-controlled by practicing self-control. For if they perform just actions and exercise self-control, they are already just and self-controlled, in the same way as they are literate and musical if   20 they write correctly and practice music.

But is this objection really valid, even as regards the arts? No, for it is possible for a man to write a piece correctly by chance or at the prompting of another: but he will be literate only if he produces a piece of writing in a literate way, and that means doing it in accordance with the skill of literate composition which he has in   25 himself.

Moreover, the factors involved in the arts and in the virtues are not the same. In the arts, excellence lies in the result itself, so that it is sufficient if it is of a certain kind. But in the case of the virtues an act is not performed justly or with self-control if the act itself is of a certain kind, but only if in addition the agent has certain characteristics   30 as he performs it: first of all, he must know what he is doing; secondly, he must choose to act the way he does, and he must choose it for its own sake; and in the third place, the act must spring from a firm and unchangeable character. With the exception of knowing what one is about, these considerations do not enter into the mastery of the   1105ᵇ arts; for the mastery of the virtues, however, knowledge is of little or no importance, whereas the other two conditions count not for a little but are all-decisive, since re- peated acts of justice and self-control result in the possession of these virtues. In other words, acts are called just and self-controlled when they are the kind of acts which a   5 just or self-controlled man would perform; but the just and self-controlled man is not he who performs these acts, but he who also performs them in the way just and self- controlled men do.

Thus our assertion that a man becomes just by performing just acts and self- controlled by performing acts of self-control is correct; without performing them, no-   10 body could even be on the way to becoming good. Yet most men do not perform such acts, but by taking refuge in argument they think that they are engaged in philosophy and that they will become good in this way. In so doing, they act like sick men who lis-   15 ten attentively to what the doctor says, but fail to do any of the things he prescribes. That kind of philosophical activity will not bring health to the soul any more than this sort of treatment will produce a healthy body.

5. Virtue Defined: The Genus: The next point to consider is the definition of virtue or excellence. As there are three kinds of things found in the soul: (1) emotions,   20 (2) capacities, and (3) characteristics, virtue must be one of these. By "emotions" I mean appetite, anger, fear, confidence, envy, joy, affection, hatred, longing, emulation, pity, and in general anything that is followed by pleasure or pain; by "capacities" I mean that by virtue of which we are said to be affected by these emotions, for example, the capacity which enables us to feel anger, pain, or pity; and by "characteristics" I   25 mean the condition, either good or bad, in which we are, in relation to the emotions: for example, our condition in relation to anger is bad, if our anger is too violent or not violent enough, but if it is moderate, our condition is good; and similarly with our con- dition in relation to the other emotions.

Now the virtues and vices cannot be emotions, because we are not called good or bad
30   on the basis of our emotions, but on the basis of our virtues and vices. Also, we are neither praised nor blamed for our emotions: a man does not receive praise for being
frightened or angry, nor blame for being angry pure and simple, but for being angry in
1106ᵃ   a certain way. Yet we are praised or blamed for our virtues and vices. Furthermore, no
choice is involved when we experience anger or fear, while the virtues are some kind
of choice or at least involve choice. Moreover, with regard to our emotions we are said
5   to be "moved," but with regard to our virtues and vices we are not said to be "moved"
but to be "disposed" in a certain way.

For the same reason, the virtues cannot be capacities, either, for we are neither
called good or bad nor praised or blamed simply because we are capable of being affected. Further, our capacities have been given to us by nature, but we do not by nature
10   develop into good or bad men. We have discussed this subject before. Thus, if the
virtues are neither emotions nor capacities, the only remaining alternative is that they
are characteristics. So much for the genus of virtue.

6. Virtue Defined: The Differentia: It is not sufficient, however, merely to define
15   virtue in general terms as a characteristic: we must also specify what kind of characteristic it is. It must, then, be remarked that every virtue or excellence (1) renders good
the thing itself of which it is the excellence, and (2) causes it to perform its function
well. For example, the excellence of the eye makes both the eye and its function good,
for good sight is due to the excellence of the eye. Likewise, the excellence of a horse
20   makes it both good as a horse and good at running, at carrying its rider, and at facing
the enemy. Now, if this is true of all things, the virtue or excellence of man, too, will
be a characteristic which makes him a good man, and which causes him to perform his
25   own function well. To some extent we have already stated how this will be true; the
rest will become clear if we study what the nature of virtue is.

Of every continuous entity that is divisible into parts it is possible to take the
larger, the smaller, or an equal part, and these parts may be larger, smaller, or equal either in relation to the entity itself, or in relation to us. The "equal" part is something
median between excess and deficiency. By the median of an entity I understand a point
30   equidistant from both extremes, and this point is one and the same for everybody. By
the median relative to us I understand an amount neither too large nor too small, and
this is neither one nor the same for everybody. To take an example: if ten is many and
two is few, six is taken as the median in relation to the entity, for it exceeds and is ex-
35   ceeded by the same amount, and is thus the median in terms of arithmetical proportion.
1106ᵇ   But the median relative to us cannot be determined in this manner: if ten pounds of
food is much for a man to eat and two pounds little, it does not follow that the trainer
will prescribe six pounds, for this may in turn be much or little for him to eat; it may be
little for Milo* and much for someone who has just begun to take up athletics. The
5   same applies to running and wrestling. Thus we see that an expert in any field avoids
excess and deficiency, but seeks the median and chooses it—not the median of the object but the median relative to us.

If this, then, is the way in which every science perfects its work, by looking to
the median and by bringing its work up to that point—and this is the reason why it is
10   usually said of a successful piece of work that it is impossible to detract from it or to
add to it, the implication being that excess and deficiency destroy success while the

---

*Milo of Croton, said to have lived in the second half of the sixth century B.C., was a wrestler famous
for his remarkable strength.

mean safeguards it (good craftsmen, we say, look toward this standard in the performance of their work)—and if virtue, like nature, is more precise and better than any art, we must conclude that virtue aims at the median. I am referring to moral virtue: for   15
it is moral virtue that is concerned with emotions and actions, and it is in emotions and actions that excess, deficiency, and the median are found. Thus we can experience fear, confidence, desire, anger, pity, and generally any kind of pleasure and pain either too   20
much or too little, and in either case not properly. But to experience all this at the right time, toward the right objects, toward the right people, for the right reason, and in the right manner—that is the median and the best course, the course that is a mark of virtue.

Similarly, excess, deficiency, and the median can also be found in actions. Now virtue is concerned with emotions and actions; and in emotions and actions excess and   25
deficiency miss the mark, whereas the median is praised and constitutes success. But both praise and success are signs of virtue or excellence. Consequently, virtue is a mean in the sense that it aims at the median. This is corroborated by the fact that there are many ways of going wrong, but only one way which is right—for evil belongs to the indeterminate, as the Pythagoreans imagined, but good to the determinate. This, by the way, is also the reason why the one is easy and the other hard: it is easy to miss the   30
target but hard to hit it. Here, then, is an additional proof that excess and deficiency characterize vice, while the mean characterizes virtue: for "bad men have many ways, good men but one."   35

We may thus conclude that virtue or excellence is a characteristic involving choice, and that it consists in observing the mean relative to us, a mean which is defined by a rational principle, such as a man of practical wisdom would use to determine   1107ᵃ
it. It is the mean by reference to two vices: the one of excess and the other of deficiency. It is, moreover, a mean because some vices exceed and others fall short of what   5

According to Aristotle, virtue or excellence "is the mean by reference to two vices: the one of excess and the other of deficiency." For example, in this drawing the person on the left has an excess of confidence and hence is reckless. The person on the right is deficient in confidence and so is cowardly. In terms of fear, the person on the left has a defect and the person on the right has an excess. In both these cases we should seek to rationally choose the "Golden Mean" of the person in the middle: courage.

is required in emotion and in action, whereas virtue finds and chooses the median. Hence, in respect of its essence and the definition of its essential nature virtue is a mean, but in regard to goodness and excellence it is an extreme.

Not every action nor every emotion admits of a mean. There are some actions
10 and emotions whose very names connote baseness, e.g., spite, shamelessness, envy; and among actions, adultery, theft, and murder. These and similar emotions and actions imply by their very names that they are bad; it is not their excess nor their defi-
15 ciency which is called bad. It is, therefore, impossible ever to do right in performing them: to perform them is always to do wrong. In cases of this sort, let us say adultery, rightness and wrongness do not depend on committing it with the right woman at the right time and in the right manner, but the mere fact of committing such action at all is to do wrong. It would be just as absurd to suppose that there is a mean, an excess, and a deficiency in an unjust or a cowardly or a self-indulgent act. For if there were, we would
20 have a mean of excess and a mean of deficiency, and an excess of excess and a deficiency of deficiency. Just as there cannot be an excess and a deficiency of self-control and courage—because the intermediate is, in a sense, an extreme—so there cannot be a mean, excess, and deficiency in their respective opposites: their opposites are wrong
25 regardless of how they are performed; for, in general, there is no such thing as the mean of an excess or a deficiency, or the excess and deficiency of a mean.

7. Examples of the Mean in Particular Virtues: However, this general statement
30 is not enough; we must also show that it fits particular instances. For in a discussion of moral actions, although general statements have a wider range of application, statements on particular points have more truth in them: actions are concerned with particulars and our statements must harmonize with them. Let us now take particular virtues and vices from the following table.

In feelings of fear and confidence courage is the mean. As for the excesses, there
1107ᵇ is no name that describes a man who exceeds in fearlessness—many virtues and vices have no name; but a man who exceeds in confidence is reckless, and a man who exceeds in fear and is deficient in confidence is cowardly.

In regard to pleasures and pains—not all of them and to a lesser degree in the
5 case of pains—the mean is self-control and the excess self-indulgence. Men deficient in regard to pleasure are not often found, and there is therefore no name for them, but let us call them "insensitive."

In giving and taking money, the mean is generosity, the excess and deficiency
10 are extravagance and stinginess. In these vices excess and deficiency work in opposite ways: an extravagant man exceeds in spending and is deficient in taking, while a stingy man exceeds in taking and is deficient in spending. For our present purposes, we may
15 rest content with an outline and a summary, but we shall later define these qualities more precisely.

There are also some other dispositions in regard to money: magnificence is a mean (for there is a difference between a magnificent and a generous man in that the former operates on a large scale, the latter on a small); gaudiness and vulgarity are ex-
20 cesses, and niggardliness a deficiency. These vices differ from the vices opposed to generosity. But we shall postpone until later a discussion of the way in which they differ.

As regards honor and dishonor, the mean is high-mindedness, the excess is what we might call vanity, and the deficiency small-mindedness. The same relation which, as we said, exists between magnificence and generosity, the one being distinguished
25 from the other in that it operates on a small scale, exists also between high-mindedness and another virtue: as the former deals with great, so the latter deals with small honors.

For it is possible to desire honor as one should or more than one should or less than one should: a man who exceeds in his desires is called ambitious, a man who is deficient unambitious, but there is no name to describe the man in the middle. There are likewise no names for the corresponding dispositions except for the disposition of an ambitious man which is called ambition. As a result, the men who occupy the extremes lay claim to the middle position. We ourselves, in fact, sometimes call the middle person ambitious and sometimes unambitious; sometimes we praise an ambitious and at other times an unambitious man. The reason why we do that will be discussed in the sequel; for the present, let us discuss the rest of the virtues and vices along the lines we have indicated.

In regard to anger also there exists an excess, a deficiency, and a mean. Although there really are no names for them, we might call the mean gentleness, since we call a man who occupies the middle position gentle. Of the extremes, let the man who exceeds be called short-tempered and his vice a short temper, and the deficient man apathetic and his vice apathy.

There are, further, three other means which have a certain similarity with one another, but differ nonetheless one from the other. They are all concerned with human relations in speech and action, but they differ in that one of them is concerned with truth in speech and action and the other two with pleasantness: *(a)* pleasantness in amusement and *(b)* pleasantness in all our daily life. We must include these, too, in our discussion, in order to see more clearly that the mean is to be praised in all things and that the extremes are neither praiseworthy nor right, but worthy of blame. Here, too, most of the virtues and vices have no name, but for the sake of clarity and easier comprehension we must try to coin names for them, as we did in earlier instances.

To come to the point; in regard to truth, let us call the man in the middle position truthful and the mean truthfulness. Pretense in the form of exaggeration is boastfulness and its possessor boastful, while pretense in the form of understatement is self-depreciation and its possessor a self-depreciator.

Concerning pleasantness in amusement, the man in the middle position is witty and his disposition wittiness; the excess is called buffoonery and its possessor a buffoon; and the deficient man a kind of boor and the corresponding characteristic boorishness.

As far as the other kind of pleasantness is concerned, pleasantness in our daily life, a man who is as pleasant as he should be is friendly and the mean is friendliness. A man who exceeds is called obsequious if he has no particular purpose in being pleasant, but if he is acting for his own material advantage, he is a flatterer. And a man who is deficient and unpleasant in every respect is a quarrelsome and grouchy kind of person.

A mean can also be found in our emotional experiences and in our emotions. Thus, while a sense of shame is not a virtue, a bashful or modest man is praised. For even in these matters we speak of one kind of person as intermediate and of another as exceeding if he is terror-stricken and abashed at everything. On the other hand, a man who is deficient in shame or has none at all is called shameless, whereas the intermediate man is bashful or modest.

Righteous indignation is the mean between envy and spite, all of these being concerned with the pain and pleasure which we feel in regard to the fortunes of our neighbors. The righteously indignant man feels pain when someone prospers undeservedly; an envious man exceeds him in that he is pained when he sees anyone prosper; and a spiteful man is so deficient in feeling pain that he even rejoices [when someone suffers undeservedly].

But we shall have an opportunity to deal with these matters again elsewhere. After that, we shall discuss justice; since it has more than one meaning, we shall distin-
10   guish the two kinds of justice and show in what way each is a mean.

8. The Relation Between the Mean and Its Extremes: There are, then, three kinds of disposition: two are vices (one marked by excess and one by deficiency), and one, virtue, the mean. Now, each of these dispositions is, in a sense, opposed to both the others: the extremes are opposites to the middle as well as to one another, and the middle is opposed to the extremes. Just as an equal amount is larger in relation to a smaller
15   and smaller in relation to a larger amount, so, in the case both of emotions and of actions, the middle characteristics exceed in relation to the deficiencies and are deficient in relation to the excesses. For example, a brave man seems reckless in relation to a
20   coward, but in relation to a reckless man he seems cowardly. Similarly, a self-controlled man seems self-indulgent in relation to an insensitive man and insensitive in relation to a self-indulgent man, and a generous man extravagant in relation to a stingy man and stingy in relation to an extravagant man. This is the reason why people at the extremes each push the man in the middle over to the other extreme: a coward calls a brave man
25   reckless and a reckless man calls a brave man a coward, and similarly with the other qualities.

However, while these three dispositions are thus opposed to one another, the extremes are more opposed to one another than each is to the median; for they are further apart from one another than each is from the median, just as the large is further re-
30   moved from the small and the small from the large than either one is from the equal. Moreover, there appears to be a certain similarity between some extremes and their median, e.g., recklessness resembles courage and extravagance generosity; but there is a very great dissimilarity between the extremes. But things that are furthest removed
35   from one another are defined as opposites, and that means that the further things are removed from one another the more opposite they are.

1109ª   In some cases it is the deficiency and in others the excess that is more opposed to the median. For example, it is not the excess, recklessness, which is more opposed to courage, but the deficiency, cowardice; while in the case of self-control it is not the defect, insensitivity, but the excess, self-indulgence which is more opposite. There are
5   two causes for this. One arises from the nature of the thing itself: when one of the extremes is closer and more similar to the median, we do not treat it but rather the other extreme as the opposite of the median. For instance, since recklessness is believed to be more similar and closer to courage, and cowardice less similar, it is cowardice
10   rather than recklessness which we treat as the opposite of courage. For what is further removed from the middle is regarded as being more opposite. So much for the first cause which arises from the thing itself. The second reason is found in ourselves: the more we are naturally attracted to anything, the more opposed to the median does this
15   thing appear to be. For example, since we are naturally more attracted to pleasure we incline more easily to self-indulgence than to a disciplined kind of life. We describe as more opposed to the mean those things toward which our tendency is stronger; and for that reason the excess, self-indulgence, is more opposed to self-control than is its corresponding deficiency.

9. How to Attain the Mean: Our discussion has sufficiently established (1) that
20   moral virtue is a mean and in what sense it is a mean; (2) that it is a mean between two vices, one of which is marked by excess and the other by deficiency; and (3) that it is a mean in the sense that it aims at the median in the emotions and in actions. That is why

it is a hard task to be good; in every case it is a task to find the median: for instance, not   25
everyone can find the middle of a circle, but only a man who has the proper knowledge. Similarly, anyone can get angry—that is easy—or can give away money or
spend it; but to do all this to the right person, to the right extent, at the right time, for
the right reason, and in the right way is no longer something easy that anyone can do.
It is for this reason that good conduct is rare, praiseworthy, and noble.

The first concern of a man who aims at the median should, therefore, be to avoid   30
the extreme which is more opposed to it, as Calypso advises: "Keep clear your ship of
yonder spray and surf." For one of the two extremes is more in error than the other,
and since it is extremely difficult to hit the mean, we must, as the saying has it, sail in   35
the second best way and take the lesser evil; and we can best do that in the manner we   1109[b]
have described.

Moreover, we must watch the errors which have the greatest attraction for us
personally. For the natural inclination of one man differs from that of another, and we
each come to recognize our own by observing the pleasure and pain produced in us [by
the different extremes]. We must then draw ourselves away in the opposite direction,
for by pulling away from error we shall reach the middle, as men do when they   5
straighten warped timber. In every case we must be especially on our guard against
pleasure and what is pleasant, for when it comes to pleasure we cannot act as unbiased
judges. Our attitude toward pleasure should be the same as that of the Trojan elders   10
was toward Helen, and we should repeat on every occasion the words they addressed
to her. For if we dismiss pleasure as they dismissed her, we shall make fewer mistakes.

In summary, then, it is by acting in this way that we shall best be able to hit the
median. But this is no doubt difficult, especially when particular cases are concerned.
For it is not easy to determine in what manner, with what person, on what occasion,   15
and for how long a time one ought to be angry. There are times when we praise those
who are deficient in anger and call them gentle, and other times when we praise violently angry persons and call them manly. However, we do not blame a man for
slightly deviating from the course of goodness, whether he strays toward excess or toward deficiency, but we do blame him if his deviation is great and cannot pass unno-   20
ticed. It is not easy to determine by a formula at what point and for how great a divergence a man deserves blame; but this difficulty is, after all, true of all objects of sense
perception: determinations of this kind depend upon particular circumstances, and the
decision rests with our [moral] sense.

This much, at any rate, is clear: that the median characteristic is in all fields the
one that deserves praise, and that it is sometimes necessary to incline toward the excess   25
and sometimes toward the deficiency. For it is in this way that we will most easily hit
upon the median, which is the point of excellence.

BOOK III

1. Actions Voluntary and Involuntary: Virtue or excellence is, as we have seen,   30
concerned with emotions and actions. When these are voluntary we receive praise and
blame; when involuntary, we are pardoned and sometimes even pitied. Therefore, it is,
I dare say, indispensable for a student of virtue to differentiate between voluntary and
involuntary actions, and useful also for lawgivers, to help them in meting out honors
and punishments.

35
1110ª   It is of course generally recognized that actions done under constraint or due to ignorance are involuntary. An act is done under constraint when the initiative or source of motion comes from without. It is the kind of act in which the agent or the person acted upon contributes nothing. For example, a wind might carry a person somewhere he did not want to go, or men may do so who have him in their power. But a problem arises in regard to actions that are done through fear of a greater evil or for some noble

5   purpose, for instance, if a tyrant were to use a man's parents or children as hostages in ordering him to commit a base deed, making their survival or death depend on his compliance or refusal. Are actions of this kind voluntary or involuntary? A similar problem also arises when a cargo is jettisoned in a storm. Considering the action itself,

10   nobody would voluntarily throw away property; but when it is a matter of saving one's own life and that of his fellow passengers, any sensible man would do so. Actions of this kind are, then, of a mixed nature, although they come closer to being voluntary than to being involuntary actions. For they are desirable at the moment of action; and the end for which an action is performed depends on the time at which it is done. Thus the terms "voluntary" and "involuntary" are to be used with reference to the moment

15   of action. In the cases just mentioned, the agent acts voluntarily, because the initiative in moving the parts of the body which act as instruments rests with the agent himself; and where the source of motion is within oneself, it is in one's power to act or not to act. Such actions, then, are voluntary, although in themselves they are perhaps involuntary, since nobody would choose to do any one of them for its own sake.

[That actions of this kind are considered as voluntary is also shown by the fact

20   that] sometimes people are even praised for doing them, for example, if they endure shameful or painful treatment in return for great and noble objectives. If the opposite is the case, reproach is heaped upon them, for only a worthless man would endure utter disgrace for no good or reasonable purpose. There are some instances in which such

25   actions elicit forgiveness rather than praise, for example, when a man acts improperly under a strain greater than human nature can bear and which no one could endure. Yet there are perhaps also acts which no man can possibly be compelled to do, but rather than do them he should accept the most terrible sufferings and death. Thus, the circumstances that compel Alcmaeon in Euripides' play to kill his own mother are patently absurd.* In making a choice, it is sometimes hard to decide what advantages and dis-

30   advantages should be weighed against one another, and what losses we should endure to gain what we want; but it is even harder to abide by a decision once it is made. For as a rule, what we look forward to is painful and what we are forced to do is base. It is because of this difficulty that praise or blame depends on whether or not a man successfully resists compulsion.

1110ᵇ   What kind of actions can we say, then, are done under constraint? To state the matter without qualification, are all actions done under constraint of which the cause is external and to which the agent contributes nothing? On the other hand, actions which are in themselves involuntary, yet chosen under given circumstances in return for certain benefits and performed on the initiative of the agent—although such actions are involuntary considered in themselves, they are nonetheless voluntary under the circum-

*Euripides' play has not come down to us. According to the myth, Alcmaeon killed his mother, Eriphyle, to avenge the death of his father, Amphiaraus. Amphiaraus, foreknowing through his gift of prophecy that he would be doomed if he joined the expedition of the Seven against Thebes, refused to join it until compelled to do so by his wife, who had been bribed by the gift of a necklace to make him join. An ancient commentator on this passage tells us that Alcmaeon's motive for killing his mother in Euripides' play was to escape the curse of his father.

stances, and because benefits are expected in return. In fact, they have a greater resem- 5
blance to voluntary actions. For actions belong among particulars, and the particular
act is here performed voluntarily. But it is not easy to lay down rules how, in making a
choice, two alternatives are to be balanced against one another; there are many differences in the case of particulars.

[There is a conceivable objection to this definition of "voluntary."] Suppose
someone were to assert that pleasant and noble acts are performed under constraint because the pleasant and the noble are external to us and have a compelling power. But 10
on this view, all actions would be done under constraint: for every man is motivated by
what is pleasant and noble in everything he does. Furthermore, it is painful to act under
constraint and involuntarily, but the performance of pleasant and noble acts brings
pleasure. Finally, it is absurd to blame external circumstances rather than oneself for
falling an easy prey to such attractions, and to hold oneself responsible for noble
deeds, while pleasure is held responsible for one's base deeds. 15

It appears, thus, that an act done under constraint is one in which the initiative or
source of motion comes from without, and to which the person compelled contributes
nothing.

Turning now to acts due to ignorance, we may say that all of them are non-voluntary, but they are involuntary only when they bring sorrow and regret in their train: a
man who has acted due to ignorance and feels no compunction whatsoever for what he
has done was not a voluntary agent, since he did not know what he was doing, nor yet 20
was he involuntary, inasmuch as he feels no sorrow. There are, therefore, two distinct
types of acts due to ignorance: a man who regrets what he has done is considered an
involuntary agent, and a man who does not may be called a non-voluntary agent; for as
the two cases are different, it is better to give each its own name.

There also seems to be a difference between actions *due to* ignorance and acting 25
in ignorance. A man's action is not considered to be due to ignorance when he is drunk
or angry, but due to intoxication and anger, although he does not know what he is
doing and is in fact acting in ignorance.

Now every wicked man is in a state of ignorance as to what he ought to do and
what he should refrain from doing, and it is due to this kind of error that men become
unjust and, in general, immoral. But an act can hardly be called involuntary if the agent 30
is ignorant of what is beneficial. Ignorance in moral choice does not make an act involuntary—it makes it wicked; nor does ignorance of the universal, for that invites reproach; rather, it is ignorance of the particulars* which constitute the circumstances
and the issues involved in the action. It is on these that pity and pardon depend, for a 1111ᵃ
person who acts in ignorance of a particular circumstance acts involuntarily.

It might, therefore, not be a bad idea to distinguish and enumerate these circumstances. They are: ignorance of (1) who the agent is, (2) what he is doing, (3) what
thing or person is affected, and sometimes also (4) the means he is using, e.g., some

---

*A few remarks ought to be made about the practical syllogism involved in this passage. Reasoning
on matters of conduct involves two premises, one major and one minor. The major premise is always universal, e.g., "to remove by stealth another person's property is stealing," and the minor premise particular, e.g.,
"this horse is another person's property," so that the conclusion would be: "To remove this horse by stealth
is stealing." What Aristotle says here is that ignorance of the major premise produces an immoral act, while
ignorance of the minor premise produces an involuntary act which may be pitied or pardoned. Thus it is a
moral defect for a man not to know that to remove by stealth another person's property is stealing. In an involuntary act, on the other hand, the agent does know the universal premise, but is ignorant of the particular,
i.e., that this horse is the property of another. We shall hear more about the practical syllogism later, especially in VII, 3.

5   tool, (5) the result intended by his action, e.g., saving a life, and (6) the manner in which he acts, e.g., gently or violently.

Now no one except a madman would be ignorant of all these factors, nor can he obviously be ignorant of (1) the agent; for how could a man not know his own identity? But a person might be ignorant of (2) what he is doing. For example, he might plead that something slipped out of his mouth, or that he did not know that he was di-
10   vulging a secret, as Aeschylus said when he was accused of divulging the Mysteries;* or again, as a man might do who discharges a catapult, he might allege that it went off accidentally while he only wanted to show it. Moreover, (3) someone might, like Merope, mistake a son for an enemy;** or (4) he might mistake a pointed spear for a foil, or a heavy stone for a pumice stone. Again, (5) someone might, in trying to save a
15   man by giving him something to drink, in fact kill him; or, (6) as in sparring, a man might intend merely to touch, and actually strike a blow.

As ignorance is possible with regard to all these factors which constitute an action, a man who acts in ignorance of any one of them is considered as acting involuntarily, especially if he is ignorant of the most important factors. The most important factors are the thing or person affected by the action and the result. An action upon this
20   kind of ignorance is called involuntary, provided that it brings also sorrow and regret in its train.

Since an action is involuntary when it is performed under constraint or through ignorance, a voluntary action would seem to be one in which the initiative lies with the agent who knows the particular circumstances in which the action is performed.

[This implies that acts due to passion and appetite are voluntary.] For it is per-
25   haps wrong to call involuntary those acts which are due to passion and appetite. For on that assumption we would, in the first place, deny that animals or even children are capable of acting voluntarily. In the second place, do we perform none of the actions that are motivated by appetite and passion voluntarily? Or do we perform noble acts voluntarily and base acts involuntarily? The latter alternative is ridiculous, since the cause in both cases is one and the same. But it is no doubt also absurd to call those things which
30   we ought to desire "involuntary." For in some cases we should be angry and there are some things for which we should have an appetite, as for example, health and learning. Moreover, we think of involuntary actions as painful, while actions that satisfy our appetite are pleasant. And finally, what difference is there, as far as involuntariness is concerned, between a wrong committed after calculation and a wrong committed in a
1111ᵇ   fit of passion? Both are to be avoided; but the irrational emotions are considered no less a part of human beings than reasoning is, and hence, the actions of a man which spring from passion and appetite [are equally a part of him]. It would be absurd, then, to count them as involuntary.

2. Choice: After this definition of voluntary and involuntary actions, our next
5   task is to discuss choice. For choice seems to be very closely related to virtue and to be a more reliable criterion for judging character than actions are.

Choice clearly seems to be something voluntary, but it is not the same as voluntariness; voluntariness is a wider term. For even children and animals have a share in

---

*The Mysteries were a secret form of religious worship whose doctrines and rites were revealed only to the initiated; Aeschylus was accused before the Areopagus of having divulged some of the secrets of the Eleusinian Mysteries. Aeschylus pleaded that he had not known the matter was secret and was acquitted.
**In a lost play of Euripides, Merope was about to slay her son Cresphontes, believing him to be an enemy.

the voluntary, but not in choice. Also, we can describe an act done on the spur of the moment as a voluntary act, but not the result of choice. 10

It seems to be a mistake to identify choice, as some people do, with appetite, passion, wish, or some form of opinion. For choice is not shared by irrational creatures, whereas appetite and passion are. Moreover, the acts of a morally weak person are accompanied by appetite, but not by choice, while a morally strong person acts from choice, but not from appetite. Also, appetite can be opposed to choice, but not appetite 15 to appetite. Again, appetite deals with what is pleasant and painful, while choice deals neither with the pleasant nor with the painful. The resemblance between choice and passion is even slighter. For an act due to passion hardly seems to be based on choice.

Choice is not even the same as wish, although the two seem to be close to one another. For choice does not have the impossible as its object, and if anyone were to 20 assert that he was *choosing* the impossible, he would be considered a fool. But wish can be for the impossible, e.g., immortality.* Wish has as its objects also those things which cannot possibly be attained through our own agency. We might, for instance, wish for the victory of a particular actor or a particular athlete. But no one chooses 25 such things, for we choose only what we believe might be attained through our own agency. Furthermore, wish is directed at the end rather than the means, but choice at the means which are conducive to a given end. For example, we *wish* to be healthy and *choose* the things that will give us health. Similarly, we say that we *wish* to be happy and describe this as our wish, but it would not be fitting to say that we *choose* to be happy. In general, choice seems to be concerned with the things that lie within our 30 power.

Again, choice cannot be identified with opinion. For opinion may refer to any matter, the eternal and the impossible no less than things within our power. Also, opinions are characterized by their truth or falsity, not by their moral goodness or badness, as choices are.

Now, perhaps no one identifies choice with opinion in general; but it would not even be correct to identify it with some particular opinion. For our character is deter- 1112ª mined by our choosing good or evil, not by the opinions we hold. We choose to take or avoid a good or an evil, but we hold opinions as to what a thing is, whom it will benefit, or how: but [the decision] to take or avoid is by no means an opinion. Also, a 5 choice is praised for being directed to the proper object or for being correctly made, but opinions are praised for being true. Moreover, we make a choice of things which we definitely know to be good, whereas we form opinions about what we do not quite know. Nor does it seem that the same people make the best choices and also hold the best opinions: some hold rather good opinions, but because of a moral depravity they 10 do not make the right choice. Whether opinion precedes or follows choice is immaterial; for we are not concerned with this problem, but only whether choice is to be identified with some form of opinion.

Since choice, then, is none of the things mentioned, what is it or what kind of thing? As we have said, it clearly seems to be something voluntary, but not everything voluntary is the object of choice. Could it be the result of preceding deliberation? [This 15 is probably correct,] for choice involves reason and thought. The very name "choice" seems to suggest that it is something "chosen before" other things.

---

*This statement should not be regarded as a rejection on Aristotle's part of a doctrine of immortality. What he is asserting here is merely a reflection of the common Greek distinction between "mortal" men and "immortal" gods: it is impossible to choose to live forever, but it is possible to wish it.

3. Deliberation: [To turn to deliberation:] do people deliberate about everything? And is everything an object of deliberation? Or are there some things about which one cannot deliberate? Perhaps we ought to say that an object of deliberation is what a sensible man would deliberate about, but not a fool or madman. Now, nobody deliberates about the eternal, such as the order of the universe or the incommensurability of the diagonal and the side of the square. Nor, on the other hand, do we deliberate about things that are in motion if they always occur in the same way, whether by sheer necessity, by nature, or by some other cause: for example, we do not deliberate about solstices and sunrises. Neither do we deliberate about irregular occurrences, such as drought or rain, nor about chance events, such as the discovery of a treasure. We do not even deliberate about anything and everything that concerns man: no Spartan deliberates about what form of government would be best for the Scythians. For none of these things can happen through our agency.

But what we do deliberate about are things that are in our power and can be realized in action; in fact, these are the only things that remain to be considered. For in addition to nature, necessity, and chance, we regard as causal principles intelligence and anything done through human agency. But of course different groups of people deliberate only about what is attainable by their own actions. Also, there can be no deliberation in any science that is exact and self-contained, such as writing the letters of the alphabet: we have no differences of opinion as to how they are to be written. Rather, we deliberate about matters which are done through our own agency, though not always in the same manner, e.g., about questions of medicine or of acquiring wealth. We deliberate more about navigation than about physical training, because navigation is less exact as a discipline. The same principle can also be applied to the other branches of knowledge. But we deliberate more about the arts than about the sciences, since we have more differences of opinion about them. Deliberation, then, operates in matters that hold good as a general rule, but whose outcome is unpredictable, and in cases in which an indeterminate element is involved. When great issues are at stake, we distrust our own abilities as insufficient to decide the matter and call in others to join us in our deliberations.

We deliberate not about ends but about the means to attain ends: no physician deliberates whether he should cure, no orator whether he should be convincing, no statesman whether he should establish law and order, nor does any expert deliberate about the end of his profession. We take the end for granted, and then consider in what manner and by what means it can be realized. If it becomes apparent that there is more than one means by which it can be attained, we look for the easiest and best; if it can be realized by one means only, we consider in what manner it can be realized by that means, and how that means can be achieved in its turn. We continue that process until we come to the first link in the chain of causation, which is the last step in order of discovery. For when a man deliberates, he seems to be seeking something and to be analyzing his problem in the manner described, as he would a geometrical figure: the last step in the analysis is at once the first in constructing the figure. (By the way, it seems that not all investigation is deliberation—mathematical investigation is not—though every deliberation is an investigation.) Moreover, if in the process of investigation we encounter an insurmountable obstacle, for example, if we need money and none can be procured, we abandon our investigation; but if it turns out to be possible, we begin to act. By "possible" I mean those things which can be realized through our own agency: for even what our friends do for us is, in a way, done through our own agency, since the initiative is our own. Sometimes the object of our investigation is to find the instruments we need and sometimes to discover how to use them. The same is true of other

matters, too: sometimes we have to find what the means are, and sometimes how they 30
are to be used or through whom they can be acquired. To sum up our conclusions: (1)
man is the source of his actions; (2) deliberation is concerned with things attainable by
human action; and (3) actions aim at ends other than themselves. For we cannot deliberate about ends but about the means by which ends can be attained. Nor can we deliberate about particular facts, e.g., whether this is a loaf of bread or whether this loaf of   1113ᵃ
bread has been properly baked: such facts are the object of sense perception. And if we
continue deliberating each point in turn, we shall have to go on to infinity.

The object of deliberation and the object of choice are identical, except that the
object of choice has already been determined, since it has been decided upon on the
basis of deliberation. For every man stops inquiring how he is to act when he has   5
traced the initiative of action back to himself and to the dominant part of himself: it is
this part that exercises choice. This may be illustrated by the ancient political systems
represented in Homer, where the kings would make a choice and then proclaim it to the
people.

Since, then, the object of choice is something within our power which we desire
as a result of deliberation, we may define choice as a deliberate desire for things that   10
are within our power: we arrive at a decision on the basis of deliberation, and then let
the deliberation guide our desire. So much for an outline of choice, its objects, and the
fact that it is concerned with means rather than ends.

4. Wish: That wish is concerned with the end has already been stated. Now, some   15
people think that its object is the good, and others think that it is what seems good.
Those who maintain that it is the good are faced with the conclusion that a man who
makes a wrong choice does not really wish what he wishes: for if it is the object of his
wish it must be good, while in the case in question it is actually bad. On the other hand,
those who assert that the object of wish is what seems good must conclude that nothing   20
is by nature the object of wish, but only what seems good to a particular individual. Yet
different, and in many instances opposite things seem good to different individuals.

If these consequences are unacceptable, must we not admit that in an unqualified
sense and from the standpoint of truth the object of wish is the good, but that for each
individual it is whatever seems good to him? [This distinction solves the problem.]
Thus, what seems good to a man of high moral standards is truly the object of wish,
whereas a worthless man wishes anything that strikes his fancy. It is the same with the   25
human body: people whose constitution is good find those things wholesome which really are so, while other things are wholesome for invalids, and similarly their opinions
will vary as to what is bitter, sweet, hot, heavy, and so forth. [Just as a healthy man
judges these matters correctly, so in moral questions] a man whose standards are high
judges correctly, and in each case what is truly good will appear to him to be so. Thus,   30
what is good and pleasant differs with different characteristics or conditions, and perhaps the chief distinction of a man of high moral standards is his ability to see the truth
in each particular moral question, since he is, as it were, the standard and measure for
such questions. The common run of people, however, are misled by pleasure. For
though it is not the good, it seems to be, so that they choose the pleasant in the belief   1113ᵇ
that it is good and avoid pain thinking that it is evil.

5. Man as Responsible Agent: Now, since the end is the object of wish, and
since the means to the end are the objects of deliberation and choice, it follows that actions concerned with means are based on choice and are voluntary actions. And the ac-   5
tivities in which the virtues find their expression deal with means. Consequently, virtue

or excellence depends on ourselves, and so does vice. For where it is in our power to act, it is also in our power not to act, and where we can say "no," we can also say "yes." Therefore, if we have the power to act where it is noble to act, we also have the power not to act where not to act is base; and conversely, if we have the power not to act where inaction is noble, we also have the power to act where action is base. But if we have the power to act nobly or basely, and likewise the power not to act, and if such action or inaction constitutes our being good and evil, we must conclude that it depends on us whether we are decent or worthless individuals. The saying, "No one is voluntarily wicked nor involuntarily happy," seems to be partly false and partly true. That no one is involuntarily happy is true, but wickedness is voluntary. If we do not accept that, we must contradict the conclusions at which we have just arrived, and must deny that man is the source and begetter of his actions as a father is of his children. But if our conclusions are accepted, and if we cannot trace back our actions to starting points other than those within ourselves, then all actions in which the initiative lies in ourselves are in our power and are voluntary actions.

These conclusions are corroborated by the judgment of private individuals and by the practice of lawgivers. They chastise and punish evildoers, except those who have acted under constraint or due to some ignorance for which they are not responsible, but honor those who act nobly; their intention seems to be to encourage the latter and to deter the former. Yet nobody encourages us to perform what is not within our power and what is not voluntary: there would be no point in trying to stop by persuasion a man from feeling hot, in pain, or hungry, and so forth, because we will go on feeling these conditions no less for that.

Even ignorance is in itself no protection against punishment if a person is thought to be responsible for his ignorance. For example, the penalty is twice as high if the offender acted in a state of drunkenness, because the initiative is his own: he had the power not to get drunk, and drunkenness was responsible for his ignorance. Moreover, punishment is inflicted for offenses committed in ignorance of such provisions of the law as the offender ought to have known or might easily have known. It is also inflicted in other cases in which ignorance seems to be due to negligence: it was in the offender's power not to be ignorant, it is argued, and he could have made sure had he wanted to.

But, it might be objected, carelessness may be part of a man's character. We counter, however, by asserting that a man is himself responsible for becoming careless, because he lives in a loose and carefree manner; he is likewise responsible for being unjust or self-indulgent, if he keeps on doing mischief or spending his time in drinking and the like. For a given kind of activity produces a corresponding character. This is shown by the way in which people train themselves for any kind of contest or performance: they keep on practicing for it. Thus, only a man who is utterly insensitive can be ignorant of the fact that moral characteristics are formed by actively engaging in particular actions.

Moreover, it is unreasonable to maintain that a man who acts unjustly or self-indulgently does not wish to be unjust or self-indulgent. If a man is not ignorant of what he is doing when he performs acts which will make him unjust, he will of course become unjust voluntarily; nor again, can wishing any more make him stop being unjust and become just than it can make a sick man healthy. Let us assume the case of a man who becomes ill voluntarily through living a dissolute life and disobeying doctors' orders. In the beginning, before he let his health slip away, he could have avoided becoming ill: but once you have thrown a stone and let it go, you can no longer recall it, even though the power to throw it was yours, for the initiative was within you. Simi-

larly, since an unjust or a self-indulgent man initially had the possibility not to become   20
unjust or self-indulgent, he has acquired these traits voluntarily; but once he has acquired them it is no longer possible for him not to be what he is.

There are some cases in which not only the vices of the soul, but also those of the
body are voluntary and are accordingly criticized. Nobody blames a man for being
ugly by nature; but we do blame those who become ugly through lack of exercise and
through taking no care of their person. The same applies to infirmities and physical   25
handicaps: every one would pity rather than reproach a man who was blind by nature
or whose blindness is due to disease or accident, but all would blame him if it were
caused by drunkenness or some other form of self-indulgence. In other words, those
bodily vices which depend on ourselves are blamed and those which do not are not
blamed. This being so, we may conclude that other kinds of vice for which we are   30
blamed also depend upon ourselves.

But someone might argue as follows: "All men seek what appears good to them,
but they have no control over how things appear to them; the end appears different to   1114^b
different men." If, we reply, the individual is somehow responsible for his own characteristics, he is similarly responsible for what appears to him [to be good]. But if he
is not so responsible, no one is responsible for his own wrongdoing, but everyone
does wrong through ignorance of the proper end, since he believes that his actions
will bring him the greatest good. However, the aim we take for the end is not deter-   5
mined by the choice of the individual himself, but by a natural gift of vision, as it
were, which enables him to make correct judgments and to choose what is truly good:
to be well endowed by nature means to have this natural gift. For to be well and properly provided by nature with the greatest and noblest of gifts, a gift which can be got
or learned from no one else, but which is one's possession in the form in which nature   10
has given it: that is the meaning of being well endowed by nature in the full and true
sense of the word.

But if this theory is true, how will virtue be any more voluntary than vice? The
end has been determined for, and appears to, a good man and a bad man alike by nature or something of that sort; and both will use the end thus determined as the stan-   15
dard for any actions they may undertake. Thus, whether the end that appears [to be
good] to a particular person, whatever it may be, is not simply given to him by nature
but is to some extent due to himself; or whether, though the end is given by nature,
virtue is voluntary in the sense that a man of high moral standards performs the actions
that lead up to the end voluntarily: in either case vice, too, is bound to be no less voluntary than virtue. For, like the good man, the bad man has the requisite ability to per-   20
form actions through his own agency, even if not to formulate his own ends. If, then,
our assertion is correct, viz., that the virtues are voluntary because we share in some
way the responsibility for our own characteristics and because the ends we set up for
ourselves are determined by the kind of persons we are, it follows that the vices, too,   25
are voluntary; for the same is true of them.

To sum up: we have described the virtues in general and have given an outline of
the genus to which they belong, i.e., that they are means and that they are characteristics. We have stated that they spontaneously tend to produce the same kind of actions
as those to which they owe their existence; that they are in our power and voluntary;
and that they follow the dictates of right reason. However, our actions and our charac-   30
teristics are not voluntary in the same sense: we are in control of our actions from beginning to end, insofar as we know the particular circumstances surrounding them. But
we control only the beginning of our characteristics: the particular steps in their devel-   1115^a
opment are imperceptible, just as they are in the spread of a disease; yet since the

power to behave or not to behave in a given way was ours in the first place, our characteristics are voluntary.

*   *   *

BOOK IV

*   *   *

1123ᵃ   *3. High-Mindedness, Pettiness, and Vanity:* High-mindedness, as its very name suggests, seems to be concerned with great and lofty matters. Let us take the nature of
1123ᵇ   these matters as the first point of our discussion. It makes no difference whether we investigate the characteristic or the man who is characterized by it. A man is regarded as high-minded when he thinks he deserves great things and actually deserves them; one who thinks he deserves them but does not is a fool, and no man, insofar as he is virtuous, is either foolish or senseless. This then is the description of a high-minded
5   man. A person who deserves little and thinks he deserves little is not high-minded, but is a man who knows his limitations. For high-mindedness implies greatness, just as beauty implies stature in body: small people may have charm and proportion but not beauty. A man who thinks he deserves great things but does not deserve them is
10   vain, though not everybody who overestimates himself is vain. One who underestimates himself is small-minded regardless of whether his actual worth is great or moderate, or whether it is small and he thinks that it is smaller still. A man of great deserts, it would seem, is most [liable to be small-minded,] for what would he do if his deserts were not as great as they are? Thus, measured by the standard of greatness, the high-minded man is an extreme, but by the standard of what is right he occupies
15   the median; for his claims correspond to his deserts, whereas the others exceed or fall short.

Accordingly, if a high-minded man thinks he deserves and actually does deserve great things, especially the greatest, there is one matter that will be his major concern. "Deserts" is a relative term that refers to external goods; and as the greatest external good, we may posit that which we pay as a tribute to the gods, for which eminent people strive most, and which is the prize for the noblest achievements. Honor fits that de-
20   scription, for it is the greatest of external goods. Consequently, it is in matters of honor and dishonor that a high-minded man has the right attitude. It is an obvious fact, and need not be argued, that the high-minded are concerned with honor. For they regard themselves as worthy of honor above all else, but of an honor that they deserve. A small-minded man falls short both in view of his own deserts and in relation to the
25   claims of a high-minded person, while a vain man exceeds his own deserts but does not exceed the high-minded.

This means that the high-minded man, inasmuch as he deserves what is greatest, is the best. For the deserts of the better man are always greater, and those of the best man the greatest. It follows that a truly high-minded man must be good. And what is
30   great in each virtue would seem to be the mark of a high-minded person. It would be quite out of character for him to run away in battle with arms swinging or to do wrong to anyone. For what motive does he have to act basely, he to whom nothing is great? If we were to examine [his qualities] one by one, we should see the utter absurdity of thinking of a high-minded man as being anything but good. If he were base, he would
35   not even deserve honor, for honor is the prize of excellence and virtue, and it is re-
1124ᵃ   served as a tribute to the good. High-mindedness thus is the crown, as it were, of the

virtues: it magnifies them and it cannot exist without them. Therefore, it is hard to be truly high-minded and, in fact, impossible without goodness and nobility.

A high-minded man is, then, primarily concerned with honor and dishonor. From   5 great honors and those that good men confer upon him he will derive a moderate amount of pleasure, convinced that he is only getting what is properly his or even less. For no honor can be worthy of perfect virtue. Yet he will accept it, because they have no greater tribute to pay to him. But he will utterly despise honors conferred by ordinary people and on trivial grounds, for that is not what he deserves. Similarly, he will   10 despise dishonor, for no dishonor can be justified in his case. A high-minded man, as we have stated, is concerned primarily with honors. But he will of course also have a moderate attitude toward wealth, power, and every manner of good or bad luck that may befall him. He will not be overjoyed when his luck is good, nor will bad luck be   15 very painful to him. For even toward honor, his attitude is that it is not of the greatest moment. Power and wealth are desirable for the honor they bring; at any rate, those who have them wish to gain honor through them. But a person who attaches little importance even to honor will also attach little importance to power and wealth. As a result, he is regarded as haughty.

Gifts of fortune, it is believed, also contribute to high-mindedness. Men of noble   20 birth, of power, or of wealth are regarded as worthy of honor, since they occupy a superior position, and whatever is superior in goodness is held in greater honor. That is why the gifts of fortune make men more high-minded, for they are honored by some people [for having them]. But in truth it is the good man alone that ought to be honored,   25 though a man who has both excellence and good fortune is regarded as still more worthy of honor. Whoever possesses the goods of fortune without possessing excellence or virtue is not justified in claiming great deserts for himself, nor is it correct to call him high-minded, for neither is possible without perfect virtue. Their good fortune notwithstanding, such people become haughty and arrogant, for without virtue it is not   30 easy to bear the gifts of fortune gracefully. Unable to bear them and considering them-   1124^b selves superior, they look down upon others, while they themselves do whatever they please. They imitate the high-minded man wherever they can, but they are not really like him. Thus, they look down upon others, but they do not act in conformity with excellence. A high-minded person is justified in looking down upon others for he has the   5 right opinion of them, but the common run of people do so without rhyme or reason.

A high-minded man does not take small risks and, since there are only a few things which he honors, he is not even fond of risks. But he will face great risks, and in the midst of them he will not spare his life, aware that life at any cost is not worth having. He is the kind of man who will do good, but who is ashamed to accept a good turn, because the former marks a man as superior, the latter as inferior. Moreover, he will re-   10 quite good with a greater good, for in this way he will not only repay the original benefactor but put him in his debt at the same time by making him the recipient of an added benefit. The high-minded also seem to remember the good turns they have done, but not those they have received. For the recipient is inferior to the benefactor, whereas a high-minded man wishes to be superior. They listen with pleasure to what good they have done, but with displeasure to what good they have received. That is apparently   15 why Thetis does not mention the good turns she had done to Zeus,* and why the Spartans did not mention theirs to the Athenians, but only the good they had received. It is, further, typical of a high-minded man not to ask for any favors, or only reluctantly, but

*The reference is to Thetis' interception with Zeus to help avenge the wrong done her son Achilles by Agamemnon.

to offer aid readily. He will show his stature in his relations with men of eminence and fortune, but will be unassuming toward those of moderate means. For to be superior to the former is difficult and dignified, but superiority over the latter is easy. Furthermore, there is nothing ignoble in asserting one's dignity among the great, but to do so among the lower classes is just as crude as to assert one's strength against an invalid. He will not go in for pursuits that the common people value, nor for those in which the first place belongs to others. He is slow to act and procrastinates, except when some great honor or achievement is at stake. His actions are few, but they are great and distinguished. He must be open in hate and open in love, for to hide one's feelings and to care more for the opinion of others than for truth is a sign of timidity. He speaks and acts openly: since he looks down upon others his speech is free and truthful, except when he deliberately depreciates himself in addressing the common run of people. He cannot adjust his life to another, except a friend, for to do so is slavish. That is, [by the way,] why all flatterers are servile and people from the lower classes are flatterers. He is not given to admiration, for nothing is great to him. He bears no grudges, for it is not typical of a high-minded man to have a long memory, especially for wrongs, but rather to overlook them. He is not a gossip, for he will talk neither about himself nor about others, since he is not interested in hearing himself praised or others run down. Nor again is he given to praise; and for the same reason he does not speak evil of others, not even of his enemies, except to scorn them. When he encounters misfortunes that are unavoidable or insignificant, he will not lament and ask for help. That kind of attitude belongs to someone who takes such matters seriously. He is a person who will rather possess beautiful and profitless objects than objects which are profitable and useful, for they mark him more as self-sufficient.

Further, we think of a slow gait as characteristic of a high-minded man, a deep voice, and a deliberate way of speaking. For a man who takes few things seriously is unlikely to be in a hurry, and a person who regards nothing as great is not one to be excitable. But a shrill voice and a swift gait are due to hurry and excitement.

Such, then, is the high-minded man. A man who falls short is small-minded, and one who exceeds is vain. Now here, too, these people are not considered to be bad— for they are not evildoers—but only mistaken. For a small-minded man deprives himself of the good he deserves. What seems to be bad about him is due to the fact that he does not think he deserves good things and that he does not know himself; if he did, he would desire what he deserves, especially since it is good. It is not that such people are regarded as foolish, but rather [that they are looked upon] as retiring. However, a reputation of this sort seems to make them even worse. For while any given kind of man strives to get what he deserves, these people keep aloof even from noble actions and pursuits and from external goods as well, because they consider themselves undeserving.

Vain people, on the other hand, are fools and do not know themselves, and they show it openly. They take in hand honorable enterprises of which they are not worthy, and then they are found out. They deck themselves out with clothes and showy gear and that sort of thing, and wish to publicize what fortune has given them. They talk about their good fortune in the belief that that will bring them honor.

Small-mindedness is more opposed to high-mindedness than vanity is, for it occurs more frequently and is worse. Thus, as we have said, high-mindedness is concerned with high honors.

*   *   *

BOOK VI

1. Moral and Intellectual Excellence; the Psychological Foundations of Intellectual Excellence: We stated earlier that we must choose the median, and not excess or   1138ᵇ
deficiency, and that the median is what right reason dictates. Let us now analyze this   20
second point.

In all the characteristics we have discussed, as in all others, there is some target
on which a rational man keeps his eye as he bends and relaxes his efforts to attain it.
There is also a standard that determines the several means which, as we claim, lie between excess and deficiency, and which are fixed by right reason. But this statement,   25
true though it is, lacks clarity. In all other fields of endeavor in which scientific knowledge is possible, it is indeed true to say that we must exert ourselves or relax neither
too much nor too little, but to an intermediate extent and as right reason demands. But
if this is the only thing a person knows, he will be none the wiser: he will, for example,   30
not know what kind of medicines to apply to his body, if he is merely told to apply
whatever medical science prescribes and in a manner in which a medical expert applies
them. Accordingly, in discussing the characteristics of the soul, too, it is not enough
that the statement we have made be true. We must also have a definition of what right
reason is and what standard determines it.

In analyzing the virtues of the soul we said that some are virtues of character and   35
others excellence of thought or understanding. We have now discussed the moral   1139ᵃ
virtues, [i.e., the virtues of character]. In what follows, we will deal with the others,
[i.e., the intellectual virtues,] beginning with some prefatory remarks about the soul.
We said in our earlier discussion that the soul consists of two parts, one rational and
one irrational. We must now make a similar distinction in regard to the rational part.   5
Let it be assumed that there are two rational elements: with one of these we apprehend
the realities whose fundamental principles do not admit of being other than they are,
and with the other we apprehend things which do admit of being other. For if we grant
that knowledge presupposes a certain likeness and kinship of subject and object, there   10
will be a generically different part of the soul naturally corresponding to each of two
different kinds of object. Let us call one the scientific and the other the calculative element. Deliberating and calculating are the same thing, and no one deliberates about objects that cannot be other than they are. This means that the calculative constitutes one
element of the rational part of the soul. Accordingly, we must now take up the question   15
which is the best characteristic of each element, since that constitutes the excellence or
virtue of each. But the virtue of a thing is relative to its proper function.

2. The Two Kinds of Intellectual Excellence and Their Objects: Now, there are
three elements in the soul which control action and truth: sense perception, intelligence, and desire. Of these sense perception does not initiate any action. We can see
this from the fact that animals have sense perception but have no share in action.*   20
What affirmation and negation are in the realm of thought, pursuit and avoidance are in
the realm of desire. Therefore, since moral virtue is a characteristic involving choice,
and since choice is a deliberate desire, it follows that, if the choice is to be good, the
reasoning must be true and the desire correct; that is, reasoning must affirm what de-   25
sire pursues. This then is the kind of thought and the kind of truth that is practical and

---

*Throughout the *Ethics,* Aristotle uses *praxis* ("action") as equivalent to "moral action," "conduct,"
and assumes animals are not capable of this.

concerned with action. On the other hand, in the kind of thought involved in theoretical knowledge and not in action or production, the good and the bad state are, respectively, truth and falsehood; in fact, the attainment of truth is the function of the intellectual faculty as a whole. But in intellectual activity concerned with action, the good state is
30   truth in harmony with correct desire.

Choice is the starting point of action: it is the source of motion but not the end for the sake of which we act, i.e., the final cause. The starting point of choice, however, is desire and reasoning directed toward some end. That is why there cannot be choice either without intelligence and thought or without some moral characteristic; for good
35   and bad action in human conduct are not possible without thought and character. Now thought alone moves nothing; only thought which is directed to some end and con-
1139ᵇ   cerned with action can do so. And it is this kind of thought also which initiates production. For whoever produces something produces it for an end. The product he makes is not an end in an unqualified sense, but an end only in a particular relation and of a particular operation. Only the goal of action is an end in the unqualified sense: for the good life is an end, and desire is directed toward this. Therefore, choice is either intelligence motivated by desire or desire operating through thought, and it is as a combina-
5   tion of these two that man is a starting point of action.

(No object of choice belongs to the past: no one chooses to have sacked Troy. For deliberation does not refer to the past but only to the future and to what is possible; and it is not possible that what is past should not have happened. Therefore, Agathon is
10   right when he says:

> One thing alone is denied even to god:
> to make undone the deeds which have been done.*)

As we have seen, truth is the function of both intellectual parts [of the soul]. Therefore, those characteristics which permit each part to be as truthful as possible will be the virtues of the two parts.

3. The Qualities by Which Truth Is Attained: (a) Pure Science or Knowledge: So let us make a fresh beginning and discuss these characteristics once again. Let us take
15   for granted that the faculties by which the soul expresses truth by way of affirmation or denial are five in number: art, science, practical wisdom, theoretical wisdom, and intelligence. Conviction and opinion do not belong here, for they may be false.

What pure science or scientific knowledge is—in the precise sense of the word and not in any of its wider uses based on mere similarity—will become clear in the fol-
20   lowing. We are all convinced that what we *know* scientifically cannot be otherwise than it is; but of facts which can possibly be other than they are we do not know whether or not they continue to be true when removed from our observation. Therefore, an object of scientific knowledge exists of necessity, and is, consequently, eternal. For everything that exists of necessity in an unqualified sense is eternal, and what is eternal is ungenerated and imperishable [and hence cannot be otherwise].
25   Moreover, all scientific knowledge is held to be teachable, and what is scientifically knowable is capable of being learned. All teaching is based on what is already known, as we have stated in the *Analytics;* some teaching proceeds by induction and some by syllogism. Now, induction is the starting point [for knowledge] of the univer-

---

*Agathon was a tragic poet who flourished in the last quarter of the fifth century B.C. Plato's *Symposium* is set in his house.

sal as well [as the particular], while syllogism proceeds *from* universals. Consequently, there are starting points or principles from which a syllogism proceeds and which are 30 themselves not arrived at by a syllogism. It is, therefore, induction that attains them. Accordingly, scientific knowledge is a capacity for demonstration and has, in addition, all the other qualities which we have specified in the *Analytics*. When a man believes something in the way there specified, and when the starting points or principles on which his beliefs rest are known to him, then he has scientific knowledge; unless he knows the starting points or principles better than the conclusion, he will have scientific knowledge only incidentally. So much for our definition of scientific knowledge 35 or pure science.

4. *(b) Art or Applied Science:* Things which admit of being other than they are 1140ª include both things made and things done. Production is different from action—for that point we can rely even on our less technical discussions. Hence, the characteristic of acting rationally is different from the characteristic of producing rationally. It also 5 follows that one does not include the other, for action is not production nor production action. Now, building is an art or applied science, and it is essentially a characteristic or trained ability of rationally producing. In fact, there is no art that is not a characteristic or trained ability of rationally producing, nor is there a characteristic of rationally producing that is not an art. It follows that art is identical with the characteristic of 10 producing under the guidance of true reason. All art is concerned with the realm of coming-to-be, i.e., with contriving and studying how something which is capable both of being and of not being may come into existence, a thing whose starting point or source is in the producer and not in the thing produced. For art is concerned neither with things which exist or come into being by necessity, nor with things produced by nature: these have their source of motion within themselves. 15

Since production and action are different, it follows that art deals with production and not with action. In a certain sense, fortune and art are concerned with the same things, as Agathon says: "Fortune loves art and art fortune." So, as we have said, art is a characteristic of producing under the guidance of true reason, and lack of art, on the 20 contrary, is a characteristic of producing under the guidance of false reason; and both of them deal with what admits of being other than it is.

5. *(c) Practical Wisdom:* We may approach the subject of practical wisdom by studying the persons to whom we attribute it. Now, the capacity of deliberating well 25 about what is good and advantageous for oneself is regarded as typical of a man of practical wisdom—not deliberating well about what is good and advantageous in a partial sense, for example, what contributes to health or strength, but what sort of thing contributes to the good life in general. This is shown by the fact that we speak of men as having practical wisdom in a particular respect, i.e., not in an unqualified sense, 30 when they calculate well with respect to some worthwhile end, one that cannot be attained by an applied science or art. It follows that, in general, a man of practical wisdom is he who has the ability to deliberate.

Now no one deliberates about things that cannot be other than they are or about actions that he cannot possibly perform. Since, as we saw, pure science involves demonstration, while things whose starting points or first causes can be other than they 35 are do not admit of demonstration—for such things too and not merely their first causes can all be other than they are—and since it is impossible to deliberate about what exists by necessity, we may conclude that practical wisdom is neither a pure sci- 1140ᵇ ence nor an art. It is not a pure science, because matters of action admit of being other than they are, and it is not an applied science or art, because action and production are generically different.

What remains, then, is that it is a truthful characteristic of acting rationally in matters good and bad for man. For production has an end other than itself, but action does not: good action is itself an end. That is why we think that Pericles* and men like him have practical wisdom. They have the capacity of seeing what is good for themselves and for mankind, and these are, we believe, the qualities of men capable of managing households and states.

This also explains why we call "self-control" *sophrosyne:* it "preserves" our "practical wisdom." What it preserves is the kind of conviction we have described. For the pleasant and the painful do not destroy and pervert every conviction we hold—not, for example, our conviction that a triangle has or does not have the sum of its angles equal to two right angles—but only the convictions we hold concerning how we should act. In matters of action, the principles or initiating motives are the ends at which our actions are aimed. But as soon as a man becomes corrupted by pleasure or pain, the goal no longer appears to him as a motivating principle: he no longer sees that he should choose and act in every case for the sake of and because of this end. For vice tends to destroy the principle or initiating motive of action.

Necessarily, then, practical wisdom is a truthful rational characteristic of acting in matters involving what is good for man. Furthermore, whereas there exists such a thing as excellence in art, it does not exist in practical wisdom.** Also, in art a man who makes a mistake voluntarily is preferable to one who makes it involuntarily; but in practical wisdom, as in every virtue or excellence, such a man is less desirable. Thus it is clear that practical wisdom is an excellence or virtue and not an art. Since there are two parts of the soul that contain a rational element, it must be the virtue of one of them, namely of the part that forms opinions.*** For opinion as well as practical wisdom deals with things that can be other than they are. However, it is not merely a rational characteristic or trained ability. An indication that it is something more may be seen in the fact that a trained ability of that kind can be forgotten, whereas practical wisdom cannot.

6. (d) Intelligence: Since pure science or scientific knowledge is a basic conviction concerning universal and necessary truths, and since everything demonstrable and all pure science begins from fundamental principles (for science proceeds rationally), the fundamental principle or starting point for scientific knowledge cannot itself be the object either of science, of art, or of practical wisdom. For what is known scientifically is demonstrable, whereas art and practical wisdom are concerned with things that can be other than they are. Nor are these fundamental principles the objects of theoretical wisdom: for it is the task of a man of theoretical wisdom to have a demonstration for certain truths.† Now, if scientific knowledge, practical wisdom, theoretical wisdom, and intelligence are the faculties by which we attain truth and by which we are never deceived both in matters which can and in those matters which cannot be other than they are; and if three of these—I am referring to practical wisdom, scientific knowl-

---

*The name of Pericles (ca. 495–429 B.C.) is almost synonymous with the Athenian democracy.

**Because practical wisdom is itself a complete virtue or excellence, while the excellence of art depends on the goodness or badness of its product.

***"Opinion" here corresponds to the "calculative element" in Chapter 1: both are defined by reference to contingent facts, those which may be otherwise than they are.

†In other words, the undemonstrable first or fundamental principles cannot be the proper and complete object of theoretical wisdom: as the next chapter shows, they are included within its sphere.

edge, and theoretical wisdom—cannot be the faculty in question, we are left with the conclusion that it is intelligence that apprehends fundamental principles.

7. (e) Theoretical Wisdom: We attribute "wisdom" in the arts to the most precise and perfect masters of their skills: we attribute it to Phidias as a sculptor in marble and to Polycletus as a sculptor in bronze. In this sense we signify by "wisdom" nothing but excellence of art or craftsmanship. However, we regard some men as being wise in general, not in any partial sense or in some other particular respect, as Homer says in the *Margites:*   10

The gods let him not be a digger or a ploughman nor wise at anything.   15

It is, therefore, clear, that wisdom must be the most precise and perfect form of knowledge. Consequently, a wise man must not only know what follows from fundamental principles, but he must also have true knowledge of the fundamental principles themselves. Accordingly, theoretical wisdom must comprise both intelligence and scientific knowledge. It is science in its consummation, as it were, the science of the things that are valued most highly.   20

For it would be strange to regard politics or practical wisdom as the highest kind of knowledge, when in fact man is not the best thing in the universe. Surely, if "healthy" and "good" mean one thing for men and another for fishes, whereas "white" and "straight" always mean the same, "wise" must mean the same for everyone, but "practically wise" will be different. For each particular being ascribes practical wisdom in matters relating to itself to that thing which observes its interests well, and it will entrust itself to that thing. That is the reason why people attribute practical wisdom even to some animals—to all those which display a capacity of forethought in matters relating to their own life.   25

It is also evident that theoretical wisdom is not the same as politics. If we are to call "theoretical wisdom" the knowledge of what is helpful to us, there will be many kinds of wisdom. There is no single science that deals with what is good for all living things any more than there is a single art of medicine dealing with everything that is, but a different science deals with each particular good. The argument that man is the best of living things makes no difference. There are other things whose nature is much more divine than man's: to take the most visible example only, the constituent parts of the universe.   30   1141[b]

Our discussion has shown that theoretical wisdom comprises both scientific knowledge and [apprehension by the] intelligence of things which by their nature are valued most highly. That is why it is said that men like Anaxagoras and Thales have theoretical but not practical wisdom: when we see that they do not know what is advantageous to them, we admit that they know extraordinary, wonderful, difficult, and superhuman things, but call their knowledge useless because the good they are seeking is not human.   5

Practical wisdom, on the other hand, is concerned with human affairs and with matters about which deliberation is possible. As we have said, the most characteristic function of a man of practical wisdom is to deliberate well: no one deliberates about things that cannot be other than they are, nor about things that are not directed to some end, an end that is a good attainable by action. In an unqualified sense, that man is good at deliberating who, by reasoning, can aim at and hit the best thing attainable to man by action.   10

Nor does practical wisdom deal only with universals. It must also be familiar with particulars, since it is concerned with action and action has to do with particulars.   15

This explains why some men who have no scientific knowledge are more adept in practical matters, especially if they have experience, than those who do have scientific knowledge. For if a person were to know that light meat is easily digested, and hence wholesome, but did not know what sort of meat is light, he will not produce health, 20   whereas someone who knows that poultry is light and wholesome is more likely to produce health.*

Now, practical wisdom is concerned with action. That means that a person should have both [knowledge of universals and knowledge of particulars] or knowledge of particulars rather [than knowledge of universals]. But here, too, it seems, there is a supreme and comprehensive science involved, [i.e., politics].

8. Practical Wisdom and Politics: Political wisdom and practical wisdom are both the same characteristic, but their essential aspect is not the same. There are two 25   kinds of wisdom concerning the state: the one, which acts as practical wisdom supreme and comprehensive, is the art of legislation; the other, which is practical wisdom as dealing with particular facts, bears the name which, [in everyday speech,] is common to both kinds, politics, and it is concerned with action and deliberation. For a decree, [unlike a law, which lays down general principles,] is a matter for action, inasmuch as it is the last step [in the deliberative process]. That is why only those who make decrees are said to engage in politics, for they alone, like workmen, "do" things.**

It is also commonly held that practical wisdom is primarily concerned with one's 30   own person, i.e., with the individual, and it is this kind that bears the name "practical wisdom," which properly belongs to others as well. The other kinds are called household management, legislation, and politics, the last of which is subdivided into deliberative and judicial.***

Now, knowing what is good for oneself is, to be sure, one kind of knowledge; 1142ª   but it is very different from the other kinds. A man who knows and concerns himself with his own interests is regarded as a man of practical wisdom, while men whose concern is politics are looked upon as busybodies. Euripides' words are in this vein:

5   How can I be called "wise," who might have filled a common soldier's place, free from all care, sharing an equal lot . . . ? For those who reach too high and are too active. . . .

For people seek their own good and think that this is what they should do. This opinion has given rise to the view that it is such men who have practical wisdom. And yet, surely one's own good cannot exist without household management nor without a po- 10   litical system. Moreover, the problem of how to manage one's own affairs properly needs clarification and remains to be examined.

An indication that what we have said is correct is the following common observation. While young men do indeed become good geometricians and mathematicians and attain theoretical wisdom in such matters, they apparently do not attain practical

*The point here is that, in practical matters, a man who knows by experience that poultry is wholesome is likely to be more successful than a man who only has the scientific knowledge that light meat is digestible and therefore wholesome, without knowing the particular fact that poultry is light meat.

**I.e., lawgivers and other men who are concerned with political wisdom in the supreme and comprehensive sense are not generally regarded as being engaged in politics. The analogy to workmen represents of course not Aristotle's view, which vigorously distinguishes action from production, but rather reflects a widespread attitude toward politics.

***In Athens, "deliberative" politics referred to matters debated in the Council and the Popular Assembly, and "judicial" politics to matters argued in the lawcourts.

wisdom. The reason is that practical wisdom is concerned with particulars as well [as with universals], and knowledge of particulars comes from experience. But a young man has no experience, for experience is the product of a long time. In fact, one might also raise the question why it is that a boy may become a mathematician but not a philosopher or a natural scientist. The answer may be that the objects of mathematics are the result of abstraction, whereas the fundamental principles of philosophy and natural science come from experience. Young men can assert philosophical and scientific principles but can have no genuine convictions about them, whereas there is no obscurity about the essential definitions in mathematics.

Moreover, in our deliberations error is possible as regards either the universal principle or the particular fact: we may be unaware either that all heavy water is bad, or that the particular water we are faced with is heavy.

That practical wisdom is not scientific knowledge is [therefore] evident. As we stated, it is concerned with ultimate particulars, since the actions to be performed are ultimate particulars. This means that it is at the opposite pole from intelligence. For the intelligence grasps limiting terms and definitions that cannot be attained by reasoning, while practical wisdom has as its object the ultimate particular fact, of which there is perception but no scientific knowledge. This perception is not the kind with which [each of our five senses apprehends] its proper object, but the kind with which we perceive that in mathematics the triangle is the ultimate figure. For in this direction, too, we shall have to reach a stop. But this [type of mathematical cognition] is more truly perception than practical wisdom, and it is different in kind from the other [type of perception which deals with the objects proper to the various senses].

9. Practical Wisdom and Excellence in Deliberation: There is a difference between investigating and deliberating: to deliberate is to investigate a particular kind of object. We must also try to grasp what excellence in deliberation is: whether it is some sort of scientific knowledge, opinion, shrewd guessing, or something generically different from any of these.

Now, scientific knowledge it is certainly not:* people do not investigate matters they already know. But good deliberation is a kind of deliberation, and when a person deliberates he is engaged in investigating and calculating [things not yet decided]. Nor yet is it shrewd guessing. For shrewd guessing involves no reasoning and proceeds quickly, whereas deliberation takes a long time. As the saying goes, the action which follows deliberation should be quick, but deliberation itself should be slow. Furthermore, quickness of mind is not the same as excellence in deliberation: quickness of mind is a kind of shrewd guessing. Nor again is excellence in deliberation any form of opinion at all. But since a person who deliberates badly makes mistakes, while he who deliberates well deliberates correctly, it clearly follows that excellence in deliberation is some kind of correctness. But it is correctness neither of scientific knowledge nor of opinion. There cannot be correctness of scientific knowledge any more than there can be error of scientific knowledge; and correctness of opinion is truth. Moreover, anything that is an object of opinion is already fixed and determined, while deliberation deals with objects which remain to be determined. Still, excellence in deliberation does involve reasoning, and we are, consequently, left with the alternative that it is correctness of a process of thought; for thinking is not yet an affirmation. For while opinion is no longer a process of investigation but has reached the point of affirmation, a person

25

30

1142ᵇ

5

10

---

*Here, as in most of the following paragraph, Aristotle seems to be taking issue with Plato, who had identified the two, e.g., in *Republic,* Book IV, 428b.

15   who deliberates, whether he does so well or badly, is still engaged in investigating and calculating something [not yet determined].

Good deliberation is a kind of correctness of deliberation. We must, therefore, first investigate what deliberation is and with what objects it is concerned. Since the term "correctness" is used in several different senses, it is clear that not every kind of correctness in deliberation [is excellence in deliberation]. For (1) a morally weak or a bad man will, as a result of calculation, attain the goal which he has proposed to himself as the right goal to attain. He will, therefore, have deliberated correctly, but what
20   he will get out of it will be a very bad thing. But the result of good deliberation is generally regarded as a good thing. It is this kind of correctness of deliberation which is good deliberation, a correctness that attains what is good.

But (2) it is also possible to attain something good by a false syllogism, i.e., to arrive at the right action, but to arrive at it by the wrong means when the middle term is false. Accordingly, this process, which makes us attain the right goal but not by the
25   right means, is still not good deliberation.

Moreover, (3) it is possible that one man attains his goal by deliberating for a long time, while another does so quickly. Now, long deliberation, too, is not as such good deliberation: excellence in deliberation is correctness in assessing what is beneficial, i.e., correctness in assessing the goal, the manner, and the time.

Again, (4) it is possible for a person to have deliberated well either in general, in an unqualified sense, or in relation to some particular end. Good deliberation in the un-
30   qualified sense of course brings success in relation to what is, in an unqualified sense, the end, [i.e., in relation to the good life]. Excellence in deliberation as directed toward some particular end, however, brings success in the attainment of some particular end.

Thus we may conclude that, since it is a mark of men of practical wisdom to have deliberated well, excellence in deliberation will be correctness in assessing what is conducive to the end, concerning which practical wisdom gives a true conviction.

10. Practical Wisdom and Understanding: Understanding, i.e., excellence in un-
1143ᵃ   derstanding, the quality which makes us call certain people "men of understanding" and "men of good understanding," is in general not identical with scientific knowledge or with opinion. For [if it were opinion,] everyone would be a man of understanding, [since everyone forms opinions]. Nor is it one of the particular branches of science, in the sense in which medicine, for example, is the science of matters pertaining to health, or geometry the science which deals with magnitudes. For understanding is concerned neither with eternal and unchangeable truth nor with anything and everything that
5   comes into being [and passes away again]. It deals with matters concerning which doubt and deliberation are possible. Accordingly, though its sphere is the same as that of practical wisdom, understanding and practical wisdom are not the same. Practical wisdom issues commands: its end is to tell us what we ought to do and what we ought not to do. Understanding, on the other hand, only passes judgment. [There is no difference between understanding and excellence in understanding:] for excellence in under-
10   standing is the same as understanding, and men of understanding are men of good understanding.

Thus understanding is neither possession nor acquisition of practical wisdom. Just as learning is called "understanding" when a man makes use of his faculty of knowledge, so [we speak of "understanding"] when it implies the use of one's faculty of opinion in judging statements made by another person about matters which belong
15   to the realm of practical wisdom—and in judging such statements rightly, for *good* understanding means that the judgment is right. It is from this act of learning or under-

standing [what someone else says] that the term "understanding" as predicated of "men of good understanding" is derived. For we frequently use the words "learning" and "understanding" synonymously.

11. Practical Wisdom and Good Sense: As for what is called "good sense," the quality which makes us say of a person that he has the sense to forgive others, [i.e., sympathetic understanding], and that he has good sense, this is a correct judgment of   20
what is fair or equitable. This is indicated by the fact that we attribute to an equitable man especially sympathetic understanding and that we say that it is fair, in certain cases, to have the sense to forgive. Sympathetic understanding is a correct critical sense or judgment of what is fair; and a correct judgment is a true one.

All these characteristics, as one would expect, tend toward the same goal. We at-   25
tribute good sense, understanding, practical wisdom, and intelligence to the same persons, and in saying that they have good sense, we imply at the same time that they have a mature intelligence and that they are men of practical wisdom and understanding. For what these capacities [have in common is that they are] all concerned with ultimate particular facts. To say that a person has good judgment in matters of practical   30
wisdom implies that he is understanding and has good sense or that he has sympathetic understanding; for equitable acts are common to all good men in their relation with someone else. Now, all matters of action are in the sphere of the particulars and ultimates. Not only must a man of practical wisdom take cognizance of particulars, but understanding and good sense, too, deal with matters of action, and matters of action are ultimates. As for intelligence, it deals with ultimates at both ends of the scale. It is intelligence, not reasoning, that has as its objects primary terms and definitions as well as ultimate particulars. Intelligence grasps, on the one hand, the unchangeable, primary   1143^b
terms and concepts for demonstrations; on the other hand, in questions of action, it grasps the ultimate, contingent fact and the minor premise. For it is particular facts that form the starting points or principles for [our knowledge of] the goal of action: universals arise out of particulars. Hence one must have perception of particular facts, and   5
this perception is intelligence.* Intelligence is, therefore, both starting point and end; for demonstrations start with ultimate terms and have ultimate facts as their objects.

That is why these characteristics are regarded as natural endowments and, although no one is provided with theoretical wisdom by nature, we do think that men have good sense, understanding, and intelligence by nature. An indication of this is that we think of these characteristics as depending on different stages of life, and that at a given stage of life a person acquires intelligence and good sense: the implication is that [human] nature is the cause. Therefore, we ought to pay as much attention to the sayings and opinions, undemonstrated though they are, of wise and experienced older men as we do to demonstrated truths. For experience has given such men an eye with   10
which they can see correctly.**

We have now completed our discussion of what practical and theoretical wisdom are; we have described the sphere in which each operates, and we have shown that   15
each is the excellence of a different part of the soul.

12. The Use of Theoretical and Practical Wisdom: One might raise some questions about the usefulness of these two virtues. Theoretical wisdom, [as we have de-

---

*I.e., we can attain the end—happiness—only by discovering the general rules of moral conduct, and these, in turn, rest on the immediate apprehension by intelligence of particular moral facts.

**The "eye given by experience" is of course *nous,* "intelligence."

scribed it,] will study none of the things that make a man happy, for it is not at all con-
20   cerned with the sphere of coming-to-be [but only with unchanging realities]. Practical
wisdom, on the other hand, *is* concerned with this sphere, but for what purpose do we
need it? (1) It is true that practical wisdom deals with what is just, noble, and good for
man; and it is doing such things that characterizes a man as good. But our ability to
perform such actions is in no way enhanced by knowing them, since the virtues are
characteristics, [that is to say, fixed capacities for action, acquired by habit]. The same
25   also applies, after all, to matters of health and well-being (not in the sense of "producing health and well-being" but in the sense of "being healthy and well" as the manifes-
tation of a physical condition or a characteristic): our ability to perform actions [which
show that we are healthy and well] is in no way enhanced by a mastery of the science
of medicine or of physical training.

(2) But if we are to say that the purpose of practical wisdom is not to *know* what
is just, noble, and good, but to *become* just, noble, and good, it would be of no use at
all to a man who is already good. Moreover, it is of no use to those who do not have
30   virtue, for it makes no difference whether they have practical wisdom themselves or
listen to others who have it. It is quite sufficient to take the same attitude as we take toward health: we want to be healthy, yet we do not study medicine.

(3) In addition, it would seem strange if practical wisdom, though [intrinsically]
inferior to theoretical wisdom, should surpass it in authority, because that which pro-
35   duces a thing rules and directs it.

These, then, are the questions we must discuss: so far we have only stated them
as problems.

1144ª   First of all, then, we should insist that both theoretical and practical wisdom are
necessarily desirable in themselves, even if neither of them produces anything. For
each one of them is the virtue of a different part of the soul.

Secondly, they do in fact produce something: theoretical wisdom produces happiness, not as medicine produces health, but as health itself makes a person healthy.
5   For since theoretical wisdom is one portion of virtue in its entirety, possessing and ac-
tualizing it makes a man happy. [For happiness, as we have seen (Book I, 7) consists in
the activity of virtue.]

In the third place, a man fulfills his proper function only by way of practical wisdom and moral excellence or virtue: virtue makes us aim at the right target, and practical wisdom makes us use the right means. The fourth part of the soul, the nutritive,
10   does not have a virtue [which makes man fulfill his proper function,] since it does not
play any role in the decision to act or not to act.

Finally, the argument has to be met that our ability to perform noble and just
acts is in no way enhanced by practical wisdom. We have to begin a little further
back and take the following as our starting point. It is our contention that people may
perform just acts without actually being just men, as in the case of people who do
15   what has been laid down by the laws but do so either involuntarily or through ignorance or for an ulterior motive, and not for the sake of performing just acts. [Such
persons are not just men] despite the fact that they act the way they should, and perform all the actions which a morally good man ought to perform. On the other hand,
it seems that it is possible for a man to be of such a character that he performs each
particular act in such a way as to make him a good man—I mean that his acts are due
20   to choice and are performed for the sake of the acts themselves. Now, it is virtue
which makes our choice right. It is not virtue, however, but a different capacity,
which determines the steps which, in the nature of the case, must be taken to implement this choice.

We must stop for a moment to make this point clearer. There exists a capacity called "cleverness," which is the power to perform those steps which are conducive to   25
a goal we have set for ourselves and to attain that goal. If the goal is noble, cleverness deserves praise; if the goal is base, cleverness is knavery. That is why men of practical wisdom are often described as "clever" and "knavish." But in fact this capacity [alone] is not practical wisdom, although practical wisdom does not exist without it. Without virtue or excellence, this eye of the soul, [intelligence,] does not acquire the character-   30
istic of practical wisdom: that is what we have just stated and it is obvious. For the syllogisms which express the principles initiating action run: "Since the end, or the highest good, is such-and-such . . ."—whatever it may be; what it really is does not matter for our present argument. But whatever the true end may be, only a good man can judge it correctly. For wickedness distorts and causes us to be completely mistaken   35
about the fundamental principles of action. Hence it is clear that a man cannot have practical wisdom unless he is good.

13. Practical Wisdom and Moral Virtue: Accordingly, we must also re-examine   1144^b
virtue or excellence. Virtue offers a close analogy to the relation that exists between practical wisdom and cleverness. Just as these two qualities are not identical but similar, so we find the same relation between natural virtue and virtue in the full sense. It seems that the various kinds of character inhere in all of us, somehow or other, by nature. We tend to be just, capable of self-control, and to show all our other character   5
traits from the time of our birth. Yet we still seek something more, the good in a fuller sense, and the possession of these traits in another way. For it is true that children and beasts are endowed with natural qualities or characteristics, but it is evident that without intelligence these are harmful. This much, to be sure, we do seem to notice: as in the case of a mighty body which, when it moves without vision, comes down with a   10
mighty fall because it cannot see, so it is in the matter under discussion. If a man acts blindly, i.e., using his natural virtue alone, he will fail; but once he acquires intelligence, it makes a great difference in his action. At that point, the natural characteristic will become that virtue in the full sense which it previously resembled.

Consequently, just as there exist two kinds of quality, cleverness and practical wisdom, in that part of us which forms opinions, [i.e., in the calculative element,] so   15
also there are two kinds of quality in the moral part of us, natural virtue and virtue in the full sense. Now virtue in the full sense cannot be attained without practical wisdom. That is why some people maintain that all the virtues are forms of practical wisdom, and why Socrates' approach to the subject was partly right and partly wrong. He was wrong in believing that all the virtues are forms of wisdom, but right in saying that   20
there is no virtue without wisdom. This is indicated by the fact that all the current definitions of virtue,* after naming the characteristic and its objects, add that it is a characteristic "guided by right reason." Now right reason is that which is determined by practical wisdom. So we see that these thinkers all have some inkling that virtue is a characteristic of this kind, namely, a characteristic guided by practical wisdom.   25

But we must go a little beyond that. Virtue or excellence is not only a characteristic which is guided by right reason, but also a characteristic which is united with right reason; and right reason in moral matters is practical wisdom.** In other words, while Socrates believed that the virtues *are* rational principles—he said that all of them are

*The reference is to the doctrines of Plato's successors in the Academy.
**I.e., right reason is not only an external standard of action, but it also lives in us and makes us virtuous.

Lapith and Centaur, Metope from Parthenon, 477–438 B.C. According to a Greek myth, the Lapiths invited the Centaurs to the wedding feast of their king, Peirthon, as a gesture of goodwill. Upon seeing the beauty of the Lapiety bride, the Centaurs succumbed to their animal instincts of lust and drunkenness and turned the feast into an abduction attempt and brawl. The Lapith warriors, under the cool wisdom of Apollo, brought a sense of calm to the chaos. The image is a symbolic lesson in its appeal for human reason and order over the lower animal instinct of passion—a lesson also taught by Aristotle in the *Nichomachean Ethics.* (*British Museum, London, Great Britain*)

30   forms of knowledge—we, on the other hand, think that they are *united with* a rational principle.

Our discussion, then, has made it clear that it is impossible to be good in the full sense of the word without practical wisdom or to be a man of practical wisdom without moral excellence or virtue. Moreover, in this way we can also refute the dialectical argument which might be used to prove that the virtues exist independently of one another. The same individual, it might be argued, is not equally well-endowed by nature

35   for all the virtues, with the result that at a given point he will have acquired one virtue but not yet another. In the case of the natural virtues this may be true, but it cannot

1145ª   happen in the case of those virtues which entitle a man to be called good in an unqualified sense. For in the latter case, as soon as he possesses this single virtue of practical wisdom, he will also possess all the rest.

It is now clear that we should still need practical wisdom, even if it had no bearing on action, because it is the virtue of a part of our soul. But it is also clear that [it does have an important bearing on action, since] no choice will be right without practical wisdom and virtue. For virtue determines the end, and practical wisdom makes us   5
do what is conducive to the end.

Still, practical wisdom has no authority over theoretical wisdom or the better part of our soul* any more than the art of medicine has authority over health. [Just as medicine does not use health but makes the provisions to secure it, so] practical wisdom does not use theoretical wisdom but makes the provisions to secure it. It issues commands to attain it, but it does not issue them to wisdom itself. To say the contrary   10
would be like asserting that politics governs the gods, because it issues commands about everything in the state, [including public worship].

Book VII

1. Moral Strength and Moral Weakness: Their Relation to Virtue and Vice and Current Beliefs About Them: We have to make a fresh start now by pointing out that   15
the qualities of character to be avoided are three in kind: vice, moral weakness, and brutishness. The opposites of two of these are obvious: one is called virtue or excellence and the other moral strength. The most fitting description of the opposite of brutishness would be to say that it is superhuman virtue, a kind of heroic and divine excellence; just   20
as Homer has Priam say about Hector that he was of surpassing excellence:

for he did not seem like one who was child of a mortal man, but of god.

Therefore, if, as is said, an excess of virtue can change a man into a god, the characteristic opposed to brutishness must evidently be something of this sort. For just as vice   25
and virtue do not exist in brute beasts, no more can they exist in a god. The quality of gods is something more worthy of honor than [human] virtue or excellence, and the quality of a brute is generically different from [human] vice.

If it is rare to find a man who is divine—as the Spartans, for example, customarily use the attribute "divine man" to express an exceptionally high degree of admiration for a person—it is just as rare that a brute is found among men. It does happen,   30
particularly among barbarians, but in some cases disease and physical disability can make a man brutish. "Brutishness" is also used as a term of opprobrium for those who exceed all other men in vice.

But we must defer until later some mention of this kind of disposition, and vice has already been discussed. We must now discuss moral weakness, softness, and ef-   35
feminacy, also moral strength and tenacity. We will do so on the assumption that each of these two sets of characteristics is neither identical with virtue or with wickedness   1145^b

*That is, the scientific or cognitive part in the soul, the rational element which grasps necessary and permanent truths.

nor generically different from it, but different species respectively of the covering genera, [namely, qualities to be sought and qualities to be avoided].

   The proper procedure will be the one we have followed in our treatment of other subjects: we must present phenomena, [that is, the observed facts of moral life and the current beliefs about them,] and, after first stating the problems inherent in these, we
5 must, if possible, demonstrate the validity of all the beliefs about these matters,* and, if not, the validity of most of them or of the most authoritative. For if the difficulties are resolved and current beliefs are left intact, we shall have proved their validity sufficiently.

   Now the current beliefs are as follows: (1) Moral strength and tenacity are qualities of great moral value and deserve praise, while moral weakness and softness are
10 base and deserve blame. (2) A man who is morally strong tends to abide by the results of his calculation, and a morally weak man tends to abandon them. (3) A morally weak man does, on the basis of emotion, what he knows to be base, whereas a morally strong man, knowing that certain appetites are base, refuses to follow them and accepts the guidance of reason. (4) Though a self-controlled man is called morally strong and tena-
15 cious, some people affirm and others deny [the converse, namely,] that a morally strong person is self-controlled in every respect; likewise, some people call a self-indulgent person "morally weak" and a morally weak person "self-indulgent" without discriminating between the two, while others say that they are different. (5) Sometimes it is said that a man of practical wisdom cannot possibly be morally weak, and sometimes people who have practical wisdom and who are clever are said to be morally weak. (6) Finally, it is said that moral weakness is shown even in anger and in the pur-
20 suit of honor and profit. These, then, are the opinions commonly heard.

   2. Problems in the Current Beliefs About Moral Strength and Moral Weakness:
The problems we might raise are these. [As to (3):] how can a man be morally weak in his actions, when his basic assumption is correct [as to what he should do]? Some people claim that it is impossible for him to be morally weak if he has knowledge [of what he ought to do]. Socrates, for example, believed that it would be strange if, when a man
25 possesses knowledge, something else should overpower it and drag it about like a slave. In fact, Socrates was completely opposed to the view [that a man may know what is right but do what is wrong], and did not believe that moral weakness exists. He claimed that no one acts contrary to what is best in the conviction [that what he is doing is bad], but through [ignorance of the fact that it is bad].

   Now this theory is plainly at variance with the observed facts, and one ought to investigate the emotion [involved in the acts of a morally weak man]: if it comes about through ignorance, what manner of ignorance is it? For evidently a man who is morally weak in his actions does not think [that he ought to act the way he does] before he is in
30 the grip of emotion.

   There are some people** who accept only certain points of Socrates' theory, but reject others. They agree that nothing is better or more powerful than *knowledge,* but they do not agree that no one acts contrary to what he *thought* was the better thing to do. Therefore, they say, a [morally weak person] does not have knowledge but opinion
35 when he is overpowered by pleasures.

---

*"Matters" here translates the Greek word *pathos,* which we usually render as "emotion" or "affect." Here, however, it is used in a loose and general sense to include the whole class of moral phenomena. In other words, Aristotle does not mean to deny here that the qualities enumerated above are lasting characteristics.
   **I.e., Plato's followers in the Academy.

However, if it really is opinion and not knowledge, if, in other words, the basic conviction which resists [the emotion] is not strong but weak, as it is when people are in doubt, we can forgive a man for not sticking to his opinions in the face of strong appetites. But we do not forgive wickedness or anything else that deserves blame [as moral weakness does. Hence it must be something stronger than opinion which is over-powered]. But does that mean that it is practical wisdom* which resists [the appetite]? This, after all, is the strongest [kind of conviction]. But that would be absurd: for it would mean that the same man will have practical wisdom and be morally weak at the same time, and there is no one who would assert that it is the mark of a man of practical wisdom to perform voluntarily the basest actions. In addition, it has been shown before that a man of practical wisdom is a man of action he is concerned with ultimate particulars that he possesses the other virtues.

Furthermore, [as regards (4)]: if being a morally strong person involves having strong and base appetites, a self-controlled man will not be morally strong nor a morally strong man self-controlled. It is out of character for a self-controlled person to have excessive or base appetites. Yet a morally strong man certainly must have such appetites: for if the appetites are good, the characteristic which prevents him from following them is bad, and that would mean that moral strength is not always morally good. If, on the other hand, our appetites are weak and not base, there is nothing extra-ordinary in resisting them, nor is it a great achievement if they are base and weak.

Again, [to take (1) and (2),] if moral strength makes a person abide by any and every opinion, it is a bad thing; for example, if it makes him persist in a false opinion. And if moral weakness makes a man abandon any and every opinion, moral weakness will occasionally be morally good, as, for example, in the case of Neoptolemus in Sophocles' *Philoctetes.* Neoptolemus deserves praise when he does not abide by the resolution which Odysseus had persuaded him to adopt, because it gives him pain to tell a lie.

Further, [concerning (1) and (3),] the sophistic argument presents a problem. The Sophists want to refute their opponents by leading them to conclusions which contradict generally accepted facts. Their purpose is to have success bring them the reputation of being clever, and the syllogism which results only becomes a problem or quandary [for their opponents]. For the mind is in chains when, because it is dissatisfied with the conclusion it has reached, it wishes not to stand still, while on the other hand its inability to resolve the argument makes forward movement impossible. Now, they have one argument which leads to the conclusion that folly combined with moral weakness is virtue. This is the way it runs: [if a man is both foolish and morally weak,] he acts contrary to his conviction because of his moral weakness; but [because of his folly,] his conviction is that good things are bad and that he ought not to do them. Therefore, [acting contrary to his conviction,] he will do what is good and not what is bad.

A further problem [arises from (2) and (4)]. A person who, in his actions, pursues, and prefers what is pleasant, convinced or persuaded [that it is good],** would seem to be better than one who acts the same way not on the basis of calculation, but because of moral weakness. For since he may be persuaded to change his mind, he can be cured more easily. To a morally weak man, on the other hand, applies the proverb, "When water chokes you, what can you wash it down with?" For if he had been per-

1146ᵃ

5

10

15

20

25

30

35

*The point is this: if the kind of conviction a morally weak man has is neither knowledge nor a weak conviction, it must be a strong conviction, and practical wisdom is such a conviction.
**I.e., a self-indulgent person.

1146^b suaded to act the way he does, he would have stopped acting that way when persuaded to change his mind. But as it is, though persuaded that he ought to do one thing, he nevertheless does another.

Finally, if everything is the province of moral weakness and moral strength, who would be morally weak in the unqualified sense of the word? No one has every form of
5   moral weakness, but we do say of some people that they are morally weak in an unqualified sense.

These are the sort of problems that arise. Some of the conflicting opinions must be removed and others must be left intact. For the solution of a problem is the discovery [of truth].

3. Some Problems Solved: Moral Weakness and Knowledge: Our first step is, then, to examine (1) whether morally weak people act knowingly or not, and, if knowingly, in what sense. Secondly, (2) we must establish the kind of questions with which
10   a morally weak and a morally strong man are concerned. I mean, are they concerned with all pleasure and pain or only with certain distinct kinds of them? Is a morally strong person the same as a tenacious person or are they different? Similar questions must also be asked about all other matters germane to this study.

The starting point of our investigation is the question *(a)* whether the morally
15   strong man and the morally weak man have their distinguishing features in the situations with which they are concerned or in their manner [of reacting to the situation]. What I mean is this: does a morally weak person owe his character to certain situations to [which he reacts], or to the manner [in which he reacts], or to both? Our second question *(b)* is whether or not moral weakness and moral strength are concerned with all [situations and feelings. The answer to both these questions is that] a man who is
20   morally weak in the unqualified sense is not [so described because of his reaction] to every situation, but only to those situations in which also a self-indulgent man may get involved. Nor is he morally weak because of the mere fact of his relationship to these situations, [namely, that he yields to temptation]. In that case moral weakness would be the same as self-indulgence. Instead, his moral weakness is defined by the manner [in which he yields]. For a self-indulgent person is led on by his own choice, since he believes that he should always pursue the pleasure of the moment. A morally weak man, on the other hand, does not think he should, but pursues it, nonetheless.

(1) The contention that it is true opinion rather than knowledge which a morally
25   weak man violates in his actions has no bearing on our argument. For some people have no doubts when they hold an opinion, and think they have exact knowledge. Accordingly, if we are going to say that the weakness of their belief is the reason why those who hold opinion will be more liable to act against their conviction than those who have knowledge, we shall find that there is no difference between knowledge and
30   opinion. For some people are no less firmly convinced of what they believe than others are of what they know: Heraclitus is a case in point.* *(a)* But the verb "to know" has two meanings: a man is said to "know" both when he does not use the knowledge he has and when he does use it. Accordingly, when a man does wrong it will make a difference whether he is not exercising the knowledge he has, [viz., that it is wrong to do what he is doing,] or whether he is exercising it. In the latter case, we would be baffled,
35   but not if he acted without exercising his knowledge.

---

*The reference is not to any specific utterance of Heraclitus, but to the tone of intense conviction with which he asserted all his doctrines, some of which Aristotle finds patently false, and hence examples of opinion rather than knowledge.

Moreover, *(b)* since there are two kinds of premise,* [namely, universal and particular,] it may well happen that a man knows both [major and minor premise of a   1147ᵃ
practical syllogism] and yet acts against his knowledge, because the [minor] premise
which he uses is universal rather than particular. [In that case, he cannot apply his
knowledge to his action,] for the actions to be performed are particulars. Also, there
are two kinds of universal term to be distinguished: one applies to *(i)* the agent, and the   5
other *(ii)* to the thing. For example, when a person knows that dry food is good for all
men, [he may also know] *(i)* that he is a man, or *(ii)* that this kind of food is dry. But
whether the particular food before him is of this kind is something of which a morally
weak man either does not have the knowledge or does not exercise it. So we see that
there will be a tremendous difference between these two ways of knowing. We do not
regard it as at all strange that a morally weak person "knows" in the latter sense [with
one term nonspecific], but it would be surprising if he "knew" in the other sense,
[namely with both terms apprehended as concrete particulars].

There is *(c)* another way besides those we have so far described, in which it is   10
possible for men to have knowledge. When a person has knowledge but does not use it,
we see that "having" a characteristic has different meanings. There is a sense in which
a person both has and does not have knowledge, for example, when he is asleep, mad,
or drunk. But this is precisely the condition of people who are in the grip of the emo-   15
tions. Fits of passion, sexual appetites, and some other such passions actually cause
palpable changes in the body, and in some cases even produce madness. Now it is clear
that we must attribute to the morally weak a condition similar to that of men who are
asleep, mad, or drunk. That the words they utter spring from knowledge [as to what is
good] is no evidence to the contrary. People can repeat geometrical demonstrations
and verses of Empedocles even when affected by sleep, madness, and drink; and be-   20
ginning students can reel off the words they have heard, but they do not yet know the
subject. The subject must grow to be part of them, and that takes time. We must, therefore, assume that a man who displays moral weakness repeats the formulae [of moral
knowledge] in the same way as an actor speaks his lines.

Further, *(d)* we may also look at the cause [of moral weakness] from the view-
point of the science of human nature, in the following way. [In the practical syllogism,]
one of the premises, the universal, is a current belief, while the other involves particu-   25
lar facts which fall within the domain of sense perception. When two premises are
combined into one, [i.e., when the universal rule is realized in a particular case,] the
soul is thereupon bound to affirm the conclusion, and if the premises involve action,
the soul is bound to perform this act at once. For example, if [the premises are]:
"Everything sweet ought to be tasted" and "This thing before me is sweet" ("this   30
thing" perceived as an individual particular object), a man who is able [to taste] and is
not prevented is bound to act accordingly at once.

---

*What is involved in this paragraph is the practical syllogism which was briefly explained in the
footnote on p. 389. However, a refinement is added here, which requires further explanation. A major
premise, Aristotle says, may contain two kinds of universal, e.g., the premise that "dry food is good for all
men" makes a universal statement about (*i*) men and (*ii*) about dry food. Accordingly, two kinds of syllogism can be developed from this major premise. The first: "dry food is good for all men"; "I am a man";
therefore, "dry food is good for me" is here neglected by Aristotle, because the agent is obviously always
aware of being a person. But the second possible syllogism: "dry food is good for all men"; "this kind of
food is dry"; therefore, "this kind of food is good for me," leaves the agent only with the general knowledge
that, for example, cereals are good, but the individual will not yet know whether this barley is a cereal.
"Knowledge" of this sort will obviously not serve to check a healthy appetite faced with an attractive bowl
of porridge.

Now, suppose that there is within us one universal opinion forbidding us to taste [things of this kind], and another [universal] opinion which tells us that everything sweet is pleasant, and also [a concrete perception], determining our activity, that the particular thing before us is sweet; and suppose further that the appetite [for pleasure] happens to be present. [The result is that] one opinion tells us to avoid that thing, while
35   appetite, capable as it is of setting in motion each part of our body, drives us to it. [This is the case we have been looking for, the defeat of reason in moral weakness.] Thus it turns out that a morally weak man acts under the influence of some kind of reasoning
1147ᵇ   and opinion, an opinion which is not intrinsically but only incidentally opposed to right reason; for it is not opinion but appetite that is opposed to right reason.* And this explains why animals cannot be morally weak: they do not have conceptions of univer-
5   sals, but have only the power to form mental images and memory of particulars.

How is the [temporary] ignorance of a morally weak person dispelled and how does he regain his [active] knowledge [of what is good]? The explanation is the same as it is for drunkenness and sleep, and it is not peculiar to the affect of moral weakness. To get it we have to go to the students of natural science.
10   The final premise, consisting as it does in an opinion about an object perceived by the senses, determines our action. When in the grip of emotion, a morally weak man either does not have this premise, or he has it not in the sense of knowing it, but in the sense of uttering it as a drunken man may utter verses of Empedocles. [Because he is not in active possession of this premise,] and because the final [concrete] term of his reasoning is not a universal and does not seem to be an object of scientific knowledge in the same way that a universal is, [for both these reasons] we seem to be led to the
15   conclusion which Socrates sought to establish. Moral weakness does not occur in the presence of knowledge in the strict sense, and it is sensory knowledge, not science, which is dragged about by emotion.

This completes our discussion of the question whether a morally weak person acts with knowledge or without knowledge, and in what sense it is possible for him to act knowingly.

4. More Problems Solved: The Sphere in Which Moral Weakness Operates: (2)
20   The next point we have to discuss is whether it is possible for a man to be morally weak in the unqualified sense, or whether the moral weakness of all who have it is concerned with particular situations. If the former is the case, we shall have to see with what kind of situations he is concerned.

Now, it is clearly in their attitude to pleasures and pains that men are morally strong and tenacious and morally weak and soft. There are two sources of pleasure: some are necessary, and others are desirable in themselves but admit of excess. The
25   necessary kind are those concerned with the body: I mean sources of pleasure such as food and drink and sexual intercourse, in short, the kind of bodily pleasures which we assigned to the sphere of self-indulgence and self-control.** By sources of pleasure

---

*The point is this: there is a kind of reasoning involved in the actions of a morally weak person: such a person starts out with the opinion that everything sweet is pleasant, finds a particular sweet thing, and knows that the thing is pleasant. But this person also has right reason, which warns not to taste everything sweet. However, the appetite for pleasure, taking hold of the opinion that everything sweet is pleasant, transforms this opinion into the action of tasting. What is contrary to right reason (i.e., contrary to the knowledge that not everything sweet should be tasted) is not the person's opinion (that sweet things are pleasant) but rather the person's appetite for pleasure.

**I.e., the sensual pleasures of taste and touch.

which are not necessary but desirable in themselves, I mean, for example, victory, 30
honor, wealth, and similar good and pleasant things. Now, *(a)* those who violate the
right reason that they possess by excessive indulgence in the second type of pleasures,
are not called morally weak in the unqualified sense, but only with a qualification: we
call them "morally weak in regard to material goods," or profit, or honor, or anger, but
not "morally weak" pure and simple. They are different from the morally weak in the
unqualified sense and share the same name only by analogy, as in our example of the   35
man called Man, who won an Olympic victory. In his case there is not much difference   1148ᵃ
between the general definition of man and the definition proper to him alone, and yet
there was a difference. [That there is similarly a difference between the two senses of
morally weak] is shown by the fact that we blame moral weakness—regardless of
whether it is moral weakness in the unqualified sense or moral weakness concerning
some particular bodily pleasure—not only as an error, but also as a kind of vice. But   5
we do not blame as vicious those [who are morally weak in matters of material goods,
profit, ambition, anger, and so forth].

(b) We now come to those bodily enjoyments which, we say, are the sphere of
the self-controlled and the self-indulgent. Here a man who pursues the excesses of
things pleasant and avoids excesses of things painful (of hunger, thirst, heat, cold, and
of anything we feel by touch or taste), and does so not by choice but against his choice
and thinking, is called "morally weak" without the addition of "in regard to such-and-   10
such," e.g., "in regard to feelings of anger," but simply morally weak without qualification. The truth of this is proved by the fact that persons who indulge in bodily pleasures are called "soft," but not persons who indulge in feelings of anger and so forth.
For this reason, we class the morally weak man with the self-indulgent, and the
morally strong with the self-controlled. But we do not include [in the same category]
those who indulge in feelings of anger, because moral weakness and self-indulgence
are, in a way, concerned with the same pleasures and pains. That is, they are concerned   15
with the same pleasures and pains but not in the same way. Self-indulgent men pursue
the excess by choice, but the morally weak do not exercise choice.

That is why we are probably more justified in calling a person self-indulgent
who shows little or no appetite in pursuing an excess of pleasures and in avoiding
moderate pains, than a person who is driven by strong appetite [to pursue pleasure   20
and to avoid pain]. For what would the former do, if, in addition, he had the vigorous appetite of youth and felt strong pain at lacking the objects necessary for his
pleasure?

Some appetites and desires are generically noble and worth while—[let us re-
member] our earlier distinction of pleasant things into those which are by nature desir-   25
able, the opposite of these, and those which are intermediate between the two—for example, material goods, profit, victory, and honor. Now, people are not blamed for
being affected by all these and similar objects of pleasure and by those of the intermediate kind, nor are they blamed for having an appetite or a liking for them; they are
blamed only for the manner in which they do so, if they do so to excess. This, by the
way, is why [we do not regard as wicked] all those who, contrary to right reason, are
overpowered by something that is noble and good by nature, or who pursue it—those,
for example, who devote themselves to the pursuit of honor or to their children and   30
parents more than they should. All these things are good, and those who devote themselves to them are praised. And yet even here there is an element of excess, if, like
Niobe, one were to fight against the gods [for the sake of one's children], or if one
showed the same excessively foolish devotion to his father as did Satyros, nicknamed   1148ᵇ

"the filial."* So we see that there cannot be any wickedness in this area, because, as we stated, each of these things is in itself naturally desirable. But excess in one's attachment to them is base and must be avoided.

Similarly, there cannot be moral weakness in this area [of things naturally desirable]. Moral weakness is not only something to be avoided, but it is also something that deserves blame. Still, because there is a similarity in the affect, people do call it "moral weakness," but they add "in regard to [such-and-such]," in the same way as they speak of a "bad" doctor or a "bad" actor without meaning to imply that the person is bad in the unqualified sense. So just as in the case of the doctor and the actor [we do not speak of "badness" in the unqualified sense], because their badness is not vice but only something similar to vice by analogy, so it is clear that, in the other case, we must understand by "moral weakness" and "moral strength" only that which operates in the same sphere as self-control and self-indulgence. When we use these terms of anger, we do so only in an analogous sense. Therefore, we add a qualification and say "morally weak in regard to anger," just as we say "morally weak in regard to honor or profit."

5. Moral Weakness and Brutishness: (1) Some things are pleasant by nature, partly *(a)* without qualification, and partly *(b)* pleasant for different classes of animals and humans. Then (2) there are things which are not pleasant by nature, but which come to be pleasant *(a)* through physical disability, *(b)* through habit, or *(c)* through an [innate] depravity of nature. We can observe characteristics corresponding to each of the latter group (2), just as [we did in discussing (1), things pleasant by nature]. I mean (2c) characteristics of brutishness, for instance, the female who is said to rip open pregnant women and devour the infants; or what is related about some of the savage tribes near the Black Sea, that they delight in eating raw meat or human flesh, and that some of them lend each other their children for a feast; or the story told about Phalaris.**

These are characteristics of brutishness. Another set of characteristics (2a) develops through disease and occasionally through insanity, as, for example, in the case of the man who offered his mother as a sacrifice to the gods and ate of her, or the case of the slave who ate the liver of his fellow slave. Other characteristics are the result of disease or (2b) of habit, e.g., plucking out one's hair, gnawing one's fingernails, or even chewing coal or earth, and also sexual relations between males. These practices are, in some cases, due to nature, but in other cases they are the result of habit, when, for example, someone has been sexually abused from childhood.

When nature is responsible, no one would call the persons affected morally weak any more than one would call women morally weak, because they are passive and not active in sexual intercourse. Nor would we apply the term to persons in a morbid condition as a result of habit. To have one of these characteristics means to be outside the limits of vice, just as brutishness, too, lies outside the limits of vice. To have such characteristics and to master them or be mastered by them does not constitute moral

---

*Niobe boasted that, with her six (or in some versions, seven) sons and an equal number of daughters, she was at least equal to the goddess Leto, who only had two children, the twins Apollo and Artemis. Apollo and Artemis thereupon killed all her children, and Niobe was turned into stone. Who exactly Satyros was, we do not know. Ancient commentators tell us that he committed suicide when his father died, or that he called his father a god.

**Phalaris, tyrant of Acragas in the second quarter of the sixth century B.C., was said to have built a hollow brazen bull, in which he roasted his victims alive, presumably to eat them afterwards. There were several other stories current in antiquity about his brutality.

[strength or] weakness in an unqualified sense but only by analogy, just as a person is not to be called morally weak without qualification when he cannot master his anger, but only morally weak in regard to the emotion involved.

For all excessive folly, cowardice, self-indulgence, and ill-temper is either brutish   5
or morbid. When someone is by nature the kind of person who fears everything, even the rustling of a mouse, his cowardice is brutish, while the man's fear of the weasel was due to disease. In the case of folly, those who are irrational by nature and live only by their senses, as do some distant barbarian tribes, are brutish, whereas those whose irra-   10
tionality is due to a disease, such as epilepsy, or to insanity, are morbid.

Sometimes it happens that a person merely possesses one of these characteristics without being mastered by it—I mean, for example, if a Phalaris had restrained his ap-petite so as not to eat the flesh of a child or so as not to indulge in some perverse form of sexual pleasure. But it also happens that a man not only has the characteristic but is   15
mastered by it. Thus, just as the term "wickedness" refers in its unqualified sense to man alone, while in another sense it is qualified by the addition of "brutish" or "mor-bid," in precisely the same way it is plain that there is a brutish and a morbid kind of moral weakness [i.e., being mastered by brutishness or disease], but in its unqualified sense the term "moral weakness" refers only to human self-indulgence.   20

It is, accordingly, clear that moral weakness and moral strength operate only in the same sphere as do self-indulgence and self-control, and that the moral weakness which operates in any other sphere is different in kind, and is called "moral weakness" only by extension, not in an unqualified sense.

6. Moral Weakness in Anger: At this point we may observe that moral weakness   25
in anger is less base than moral weakness in regard to the appetites. For (1) in a way, anger seems to listen to reason, but to hear wrong, like hasty servants, who run off be-fore they have heard everything their master tells them, and fail to do what they were ordered, or like dogs, which bark as soon as there is a knock without waiting to see if   30
the visitor is a friend. In the same way, the heat and swiftness of its nature make anger hear but not listen to an order, before rushing off to take revenge. For reason and imag-ination indicate that an insult or a slight has been received, and anger, drawing the con-clusion, as it were, that it must fight against this sort of tiring, simply flares up at once. Appetite, on the other hand, is no sooner told by reason and perception that something   35
is pleasant than it rushes off to enjoy it. Consequently, while anger somehow follows   1149ᵇ
reason, appetite does not. Hence appetite is baser [than anger]. For when a person is morally weak in anger, he is in a sense overcome by reason, but the other is not over-come by reason but by appetite.

Further, (2) it is more excusable to follow one's natural desires, inasmuch as we are also more inclined to pardon such appetites as are common to all men and to the   5
extent that they are common to all. Now anger and ill temper are more natural than are the appetites which make us strive for excess and for what is not necessary. Take the example of the man who was defending himself against the charge of beating his father with the words: "Yes, I did it: my father, too, used to beat his father, and he beat his, and"—pointing to his little boy—"he will beat me when he grows up to be a man. It   10
runs in the family." And the story goes that the man who was being dragged out of the house by his son asked him to stop at the door, on the grounds that he himself had not dragged his father any further than that.

Moreover, (3) the more underhanded a person is, the more unjust he is. Now, a hot-tempered man is not underhanded; nor is anger: it is open. But appetite has the   15
same attribute as Aphrodite, who is called "weaver of guile on Cyprus born," and as

her "pattern-pierced zone," of which Homer says: "endearment that steals the heart away even from the thoughtful." Therefore, since moral weakness of this type [which involves the appetite] is more unjust and baser than moral weakness concerning anger, it is this type which constitutes moral weakness in the unqualified sense and is even a kind of vice.*

20   Again, (4) no one feels pain when insulting another without provocation, whereas everyone who acts in a fit of anger acts with pain. On the contrary, whoever unprovoked insults another, feels pleasure. If, then, acts which justify outbursts of anger are more unjust than others, it follows that moral weakness caused by appetite [is more unjust than moral weakness caused by anger], for anger does not involve unprovoked insult.

It is now clear that moral weakness in regard to the appetites is more disgraceful than moral weakness displayed in anger, and also that moral strength and weakness op-
25   erate in the sphere of the bodily appetites and pleasures. But we must still grasp the distinctions to be made within bodily appetites and pleasures. For, as we stated at the beginning, some pleasures are human, i.e., natural in kind as well as in degree, while others are brutish, and others again are due to physical disability and disease. It is only
30   with the first group of these, [i.e., the human pleasures,] that self-control and self-indulgence are concerned. For that reason, we do not call beasts either self-controlled or self-indulgent; if we do so, we do it only metaphorically, in cases where a general distinction can be drawn between one class of animals and another on the basis of wantonness, destructiveness, and indiscriminate voracity. [This use is only metaphorical] because beasts are incapable of choice and calculation, but [animals of this type] stand
35   outside the pale of their nature, just as madmen do among humans.
1150ᵃ   Brutishness is a lesser evil than vice, but it is more horrifying. For [in a beast] the better element cannot be perverted, as it can be in man, since it is lacking. [To compare a brute beast and a brutish man] is like comparing an inanimate with an animate being to see which is more evil. For the depravity of a being which does not possess the source that initiates its own motion is always less destructive [than the depravity of
5   a being that possesses this source], and intelligence is such a source. A similar comparison can be made between injustice [as such] and an unjust man: each is in some sense worse than the other, for a bad man can do ten thousand times as much harm as a beast.

7. Moral Strength and Moral Weakness: Tenacity and Softness: As regards the pleasures, pains, appetites, and aversions that come to us through touch and taste, and
10   which we defined earlier as the sphere of self-indulgence and self-control, it is possible to be the kind of person who is overcome even by those which most people master; but it is also possible to master those by which most people are overcome. Those who are overcome by pleasure or master it are, respectively, morally weak and morally strong; and in the case of pain, they are, respectively, soft and tenacious. The disposition
15   which characterizes the majority of men lies between these two, although they tend more to the inferior characteristics.

Some pleasures are necessary, up to a certain point, and others are not, whereas neither excesses nor deficiencies of pleasure are necessary. The same is also true of appetites and pains. From all this it follows that a man is self-indulgent when he pursues
20   excesses of pleasant things, or when he [pursues necessary pleasures] to excess, by choice, for their own sakes, and not for an ulterior result. A man of this kind inevitably feels no regret, and is as a result incorrigible. For a person who feels no regret is incor-

---

*But it is not vice in the unqualified sense, for that would involve choice.

rigible. A person deficient [in his pursuit of the necessary pleasures] is the opposite [of self-indulgent], and the man who occupies the middle position is self-controlled. In the same way, a man who avoids bodily pain [is self-indulgent], provided he does so by choice and not because he is overcome by them.

A choice is not exercised either by a person who is driven by pleasure, or by a   25
person who is avoiding the pain of [unsatisfied] appetite. There is, accordingly, a difference between indulging by choice and not by choice. Everyone would think worse of a man who would perform some disgraceful act actuated only slightly or not at all by appetite, than of a person who was actuated by a strong appetite. And we would regard as worse a man who feels no anger as he beats another man, than someone who does so in anger. For what would he do, if he were in the grip of emotion when acting?   30
Hence a self-indulgent man is worse than one who is morally weak.

So we see that one of the characteristics described, [viz., the deliberate avoidance of pain,] constitutes rather a kind of softness, while a person possessing the other, [viz., the deliberate pursuit of excessive pleasures,] is self-indulgent.

A morally strong is opposed to a morally weak man, and a tenacious to a soft man. For being tenacious consists in offering resistance, while moral strength consists in mastering. Resistance and mastery are two different things, just as not being de-   35
feated differs from winning a victory. Hence, moral strength is more desirable than tenacity. A man who is deficient [in his resistance to pains] which most people with-   1150^b
stand successfully is soft and effeminate. For effeminacy is a form of softness. A man of this kind lets his cloak trail, in order to save himself the pain of lifting it up, and plays the invalid without believing himself to be involved in the misery which a true   5
invalid suffers.

The situation is similar in the case of moral strength and moral weakness. If a person is overcome by powerful and excessive pleasures or pains, we are not surprised. In fact, we find it pardonable if he is overcome while offering resistance, as, for example, Theodectes' Philoctetes* does when bitten by the snake, or as Cercyon in Carcinus' *Alope,*** or as people who try to restrain their laughter burst out in one great guf-   10
faw, as actually happened to Xenophantus.*** But we are surprised if a man is overcome by and unable to withstand those [pleasures and pains] which most people resist successfully, unless his disposition is congenital or caused by disease, as among the kings of Scythia, for example, in whom softness is congenital,† and as softness dis-   15
tinguishes the female from the male.

A man who loves amusement is also commonly regarded as being self-indulgent, but he is actually soft. For amusement is relaxation, inasmuch as it is respite from work, and a lover of amusement is a person who goes in for relaxation to excess.

---

*Theodectes (ca. 375–334 B.C.) spent most of his life at Athens. He studied under Plato, Isocrates, and Aristotle, and in addition to writing tragedies, won a considerable reputation as an orator. An ancient note on this passage tells us that, in Theodectes' tragedy, Philoctetes, after repressing his pain for a long time, finally bursts out: "Cut off my hand!"

**Carcinus was a fourth-century B.C. Athenian tragic poet. According to an ancient commentator, "Cercyon had a daughter Alope. Upon learning that his daughter Alope had committed adultery, he asked her who had perpetrated the deed, and said: 'If you tell me, I will not be grieved at all.' When Alope told him who the adulterer was, Cercyon was so overcome with grief that he could no longer stand life and renounced living."

***The occasion is not known. Xenophantus is said to have been a musician at the court of Alexander the Great (356–323 B.C.). Seneca tells us that when Xenophantus sang, Alexander was so stirred that he seized his weapons in his hands.

†According to the Hippocratic treatise *On Airs, Waters, and Places* 22, horseback riding caused softness among the Scythian aristocracy.

One kind of moral weakness is impetuosity and another is a lack of strength.
People of the latter kind deliberate but do not abide by the results of their deliberation,
20   because they are overcome by emotion, while the impetuous are driven on by emotion,
because they do not deliberate. [If they deliberated, they would not be driven on so
easily,] for as those who have just been tickled are immune to being tickled again, so
some people are not overcome by emotion, whether pleasant or painful, when they feel
and see it coming and have roused themselves and their power of reasoning in good
time. Keen and excitable persons are the most prone to the impetuous kind of moral
25   weakness. Swiftness prevents the keen and vehemence the excitable from waiting for
reason to guide them, since they tend to be led by their imagination.

8. Moral Weakness and Self-Indulgence: A self-indulgent man, as we stated, is
30   one who feels no regret, since he abides by the choice he has made. A morally weak
person, on the other hand, always feels regret. Therefore, the formulation of the problem, as we posed it above, does not correspond to the facts: it is a self-indulgent man
who cannot be cured, but a morally weak man is curable. For wickedness is like a disease such as dropsy or consumption, while moral weakness resembles epilepsy: the
former is chronic, the latter intermittent. All in all, moral weakness and vice are generically different from each other. A vicious man is not aware of his vice, but a morally
35   weak man knows his weakness.

Among the morally weak, those who lose themselves in [emotion, i.e., the im-
1151ᵃ   petuous,] are better than those who have a rational principle but do not abide by it,
[i.e., those who lack strength]. For they are overcome by a lesser emotion and do not
yield without previous deliberation, as the impetuous do. A man who has this kind of
moral weakness resembles those who get drunk quickly and on little wine, or on less
wine than most people do.
5   That moral weakness is not a vice [in the strict sense] is now evident, though in a
certain sense it is perhaps one. For moral weakness violates choice, whereas vice is in
accordance with choice. Nevertheless, they are similar in the actions to which they
lead, just as Demodocus said of the Milesians:

The Milesians are no stupid crew, except that they do what the stupid do.*

10   Similarly, the morally weak are not unjust, but they will act like unjust men.

A morally weak man is the kind of person who pursues bodily pleasures to excess and contrary to right reason, though he is not persuaded [that he ought to do so];
the self-indulgent, on the other hand, is persuaded to pursue them because he is the
kind of man who does so. This means that it is the former who is easily persuaded to
change his mind, but the latter is not. For virtue or excellence preserves and wicked-
15   ness destroys the initiating motive or first cause [of action], and in actions the initiating
motive or first cause is the end at which we aim, as the hypotheses are in mathematics.
For neither in mathematics nor in moral matters does reasoning teach us the principles
or starting points; it is virtue, whether natural or habitual, that inculcates right opinion
about the principle or first premise. A man who has this right opinion is self-controlled,
20   and his opposite is self-indulgent.

But there exists a kind of person who loses himself under the impact of emotion
and violates right reason, a person whom emotion so overpowers that he does not act
according to the dictates of right reason, but not sufficiently to make him the kind of

*Demodocus wrote lampooning epigrams in the sixth century B.C.

man who is persuaded that he must abandon himself completely to the pursuit of such pleasures. This is the morally weak man: he is better than the self-indulgent, and he is   25
not bad in the unqualified sense of the word. For the best thing in him is saved: the principle or premise [as to how he should act]. Opposed to him is another kind of man, who remains steadfast and does not lose himself, at least not under the impact of emotion. These considerations make it clear that moral strength is a characteristic of great moral worth, while moral weakness is bad.

9. Steadfastness in Moral Strength and Moral Weakness: Is a man morally strong when he abides by any and every dictate of reason and choice, or only when he abides by the right choice? And is a man morally weak when he does not abide by every choice   30
and dictate of reason, or only when he fails to abide by the rational dictate which is not false and the choice which is right? This is the problem we stated earlier. Or is it true reason and right choice as such, but any other kind of choice incidentally, to which the   35
one remains steadfast and the other does not? [This seems to be the correct answer,] for if a person chooses and pursues the attainment of *a* by means of *b,* his pursuit and   1151^b
choice are for *a* as such but for *b* incidentally. And by "as such" we mean "in the unqualified sense." Therefore, there is a sense in which the one abides by and the other abandons any and every kind of opinion, but in the unqualified sense, only true opinion.

There are those who remain steadfast to their opinion and are called "obstinate."   5
They are hard to convince and are not easily persuaded to change their mind. They bear a certain resemblance to a morally strong person, just as an extravagant man resembles one who is generous, and a reckless man resembles one who is confident. But they are, in fact, different in many respects. The one, the morally strong, will be a person who does not change under the influence of emotion and appetite, but on occasion   10
he will be persuaded [by argument]. Obstinate men, on the other hand, are not easily persuaded by rational argument; but to appetites they are amenable, and in many cases are driven on by pleasures. The various kinds of obstinate people are the opinionated, the ignorant, and the boorish. The opinionated let themselves be influenced by pleasure and pain: they feel the joy of victory, when someone fails to persuade them to change   15
their mind, and they feel pain when their views are overruled, like decrees that are declared null and void. As a result, they bear a greater resemblance to the morally weak than to the morally strong.

Then there are those who do not abide by their decisions for reasons other than moral weakness, as, for example, Neoptolemus in Sophocles' *Philoctetes.* Granted it was under the influence of pleasure that he did not remain steadfast, but it was a noble pleasure: it was noble in his eyes to be truthful, but he was persuaded by Odysseus to tell a lie. For not anybody who acts under the influence of pleasure is self-indulgent,   20
bad, or morally weak, but only those who do so under the influence of a base pleasure.

There is also a type who feels less joy than he should at the things of the body and, therefore, does not abide by the dictates of reason. The median between this type and the morally weak man is the man of moral strength. For a morally weak person   25
does not abide by the dictates of reason, because he feels more joy than he should [in bodily things], but the man under discussion feels less joy than he should. But a morally strong man remains steadfast and does not change on either account. Since moral strength is good, it follows that both characteristics opposed to it are bad, as they in fact turn out to be. But since one of the two opposites is in evidence only in a few   30
people and on few occasions, moral strength is generally regarded as being the only opposite of moral weakness, just as self-control is thought to be opposed only to self-indulgence.

Since many terms are used in an analogical sense, we have come to speak analogically of the "moral strength" of a self-controlled man. [There is a resemblance between the two] since a morally strong man is the kind of person who does nothing contrary to the dictates of reason under the influence of bodily pleasures, and the same is true of a self-controlled man. But while a morally strong man has base appetites, a self-controlled man does not and is, moreover, a person who finds no pleasure in anything that violates the dictates of reason. A morally strong man, on the other hand, does find pleasure in such things, but he is not driven by them. There is also a similarity between the morally weak and the self-indulgent in that both pursue things pleasant to the body; but they are different in that a self-indulgent man thinks he ought to pursue them, while the morally weak thinks he should not.

10. Moral Weakness and Practical Wisdom: It is not possible for the same person to have practical wisdom and be morally weak at the same time, for it has been shown that a man of practical wisdom is *ipso facto* a man of good character. Moreover, to be a man of practical wisdom, one must not only know [what one ought to do], but he must also be able to act accordingly. But a morally weak man is not able so to act. However, there is no reason why a clever man could not be morally weak. That is why occasionally people are regarded as possessing practical wisdom, but as being morally weak at the same time; it is because cleverness differs from practical wisdom in the way we have described in our first discussion of the subject. They are closely related in that both follow the guidance of reason, but they differ in that [practical wisdom alone] involves moral choice.

Furthermore, a morally weak man does not act like a man who has knowledge and exercises it, but like a man asleep or drunk. Also, even though he acts voluntarily—for he knows in a sense what he is doing and what end he is aiming at—he is not wicked, because his moral choice is good,* and that makes him only half-wicked. He is not unjust, either, for he is no underhanded plotter. [For plotting implies deliberation,] whereas one type of morally weak man does not abide by the results of his deliberation, while the other, the excitable type, does not even deliberate. So we see that a morally weak person is like a state which enacts all the right decrees and has laws of a high moral standard, but does not apply them, a situation which Anaxandrides made fun of: "Thus wills the state, that cares not for its laws."** A wicked man, on the other hand, resembles a state which does apply its laws, but the laws are bad.

In relation to the characteristics possessed by most people, moral weakness and moral strength lie at the extremes. For a morally strong person remains more steadfast and a morally weak person less steadfast than the capacity of most men permits.

The kind of moral weakness displayed by excitable people is more easily cured than the moral weakness of those who deliberate but do not abide by their decisions; and those who are morally weak through habituation are more curable than those who are morally weak by nature. For it is easier to change habit than to change nature. Even habit is hard to change, precisely because it resembles nature, as Euenus says:

A habit, friend, is of long practice born,
and practice ends in fashioning man's nature.***

---

*I.e., his basic moral purpose is good, even though it is eventually vitiated by appetite.

**Anaxandrides (fl. 382–349 B.C.) migrated from his native Rhodes (or Colophon) to Athens, where he gained fame as a poet of the Middle Comedy.

***Euenus of Paros was a famous Sophist, who lived in the late fifth century B.C.

We have now completed our definitions of moral strength, moral weakness, tenacity, and softness, and stated how these characteristics are related to one another.   35

11. Pleasure: Some Current Views: It is the role of a political philosopher to   1152^b
study pleasure and pain. For he is the supreme craftsman of the end to which we look when we call one particular thing bad and another good in the unqualified sense. Moreover, an examination of this subject is one of the tasks we must logically undertake,   5
since we established that virtue and vice of character are concerned with pains and pleasures, and most people claim that happiness involves pleasure. That is why the word "blessed" is derived from the word "enjoy."

Now, (1) some people believe that no pleasure is good, either in itself or incidentally, since the good and pleasure are not the same thing.* (2) Others hold that, though   10
some pleasures are good, most of them are bad.** (3) Then there is a third view, according to which it is impossible for pleasure to be the highest good, even if all pleasures are good.***

[The following arguments are advanced to support (1) the contention that] pleasure is not a good at all: *(a)* All pleasure is a process or coming-to-be leading to the natural state [of the subject] and perceived [by the subject]; but no process is of the same order as its ends, e.g., the building process is not of the same order as a house. Further, *(b)* a self-controlled man avoids pleasures. Again, *(c)* a man of practical wis-   15
dom does not pursue the pleasant, but what is free from pain.† Moreover, *(d)* pleasures are an obstacle to good sense: the greater the joy one feels, e.g., in sexual intercourse, the greater the obstacle; for no one is capable of rational insight while enjoying sexual relations.‡ Also, *(e)* there is no art of pleasure; yet every good is the result of an art. Finally, *(f)* children and beasts pursue pleasures, whereas they do not know what is good.

[The arguments for the view (2) that] not all pleasures are good are: *(a)* Some   20
pleasures are disgraceful and cause for reproach; and *(b)* some pleasures are harmful, for there are pleasant things that may cause disease.

[And the argument in favor of (3), the contention that] pleasure is not the highest good, is that it is not an end but a process or coming-to-be. These are roughly the views put forward.

12. The Views Discussed: (1) Is Pleasure a Good Thing?: But the following considerations will show that the arguments we have enumerated do not lead us to the   25
conclusion that (1) pleasure is not a good, or (3) that it is not the highest good. In the first place, [to answer argument (1a) and (3),] we use the word "good" in two senses: a thing may be good in the unqualified sense, or "good" for a particular person. Hence the term has also two meanings when applied to natural states and characteristics [of persons], and consequently also when applied to their motions and processes. This

---

*This view seems to have been propounded by Speusippus, Plato's nephew and disciple, who succeeded him as head of the Academy from 347–339 B.C. A similar view had been espoused by Antisthenes (ca. 455–ca. 360 B.C.), the friend of Socrates and precursor of the Cynic School.

**This is probably a reference to the view stated by Plato in *Philebus* 13b.

***No particular proponents of this view can be identified, but they are also discussed in Plato's *Philebus* 53c–55c.

†Arguments *(b)* and *(c)* had probably been used by Speusippus and before him perhaps by Antisthenes.

‡This argument may come from Archytas, a Pythagorean philosopher, mathematician, ruler of Tarentum, and friend of Plato, in the first half of the fourth century B.C.

means that motions and processes which are generally held to be bad are partly bad
without qualification, but not bad for a particular person, and even desirable for him;
and partly not even desirable for a particular person except on occasion and for a short
time, though they are not desirable in an unqualified sense. Others again are not even
pleasures, but only appear to be, for example, all processes accompanied by pain and
undergone for remedial purposes, such as the processes to which the sick are subjected.

Secondly, the good has two aspects: it is both an activity and a characteristic.
Now, the processes which restore us to our natural characteristic condition are only incidentally pleasant; but the activity which is at work when our appetites [want to see us
restored] is the activity of that part of our characteristic condition and natural state
which has been left unimpaired. For that matter, there are pleasures which do not involve pain and appetite (e.g., the activity of studying) and we experience them when
there is nothing deficient in our natural state. [That processes of restoration are only incidentally pleasant] is shown by the fact that the pleasant things which give us joy
while our natural state is being replenished are not the same as those which give us joy
once it has been restored. Once restored, we feel joy at what is pleasant in the unqualified sense, but while the replenishment goes on, we enjoy even its opposite: for instance, we enjoy sharp and bitter things, none of which are pleasant either by nature or
in the unqualified sense. Consequently, the pleasures [derived from them, too, are not
pleasant either by nature or in the unqualified sense], for the difference that exists between various pleasant things is the same as that which is found between the pleasures
derived from them.

In the third place, there is no need to believe that there exists something better
than pleasure which is different from it, just as, according to some, the end is better
than the process which leads to it. For pleasures are not processes, nor do all pleasures
involve processes: they are activities and an end, and they result not from the process
of development we undergo, but from the use we make of the powers we have. Nor do
all pleasures have an end other than themselves; that is only true of the pleasures of
those who are being led to the perfection of their natural states. For that reason, it is not
correct, either, to say that pleasure is a process perceived [by the subject]: one should
rather call it an "activity of our characteristic condition as determined by our natural
state," and instead of "perceived" we should call it "unobstructed." (There are some
who believe pleasure to be process on the ground that it is good in the true sense of the
word, for they think that activity is process, but it is, as a matter of fact, different.)

The argument (2b) that pleasures [are bad, because] some pleasant things may
cause disease, is like arguing that wholesome things are bad, because some of them are
bad for making money. Both pleasant and wholesome things are bad in the relative
senses mentioned, but that does not make them bad in themselves: even studying is occasionally harmful to health.

Also, (1d) neither practical wisdom nor any characteristic is obstructed by the
pleasure arising from it, but only by alien pleasures extraneous to it. The pleasures
arising from study and learning will only intensify study and learning, [but they will
never obstruct it].

The argument (1e) that no pleasure is the result of an art makes good sense. For
art never produces any activity at all: it produces the capacity for the activity. Nevertheless, the arts of perfume-making as well as of cooking are generally regarded as arts
of pleasure.

The arguments (1b) that a self-controlled person avoids pleasure, (1c) that a man
of practical wisdom pursues a life free from pain, and (1f) that children and beasts pursue pleasure, are all refuted by the same consideration. We have stated in what sense

pleasures are good without qualification and in what sense not all pleasures are good.   30
These last mentioned are the pleasures which beasts and children pursue, while a man
of practical wisdom wants to be free from the pain which they imply. They are the
pleasures that involve appetite and pain, i.e., the bodily pleasures—for they are of this
sort—and their excesses, in terms of which a self-indulgent man is self-indulgent. That   35
is why a self-controlled man avoids these pleasures. But there are pleasures even for
the self-controlled.

13. The Views Discussed: (3) Is Pleasure the Highest Good?: To continue: there
is general agreement that pain is bad and must be avoided. One kind of pain is bad in   1153^b
the unqualified sense, and another kind is bad, because in some way or other it ob-
structs us. Now, the opposite of a thing to be avoided—in the sense that it must be
avoided and is bad—is good. It follows, therefore, necessarily that pleasure is a good.
Speusippus tried to solve the question by saying that, just as the greater is opposed   5
both to the less and to the equal, [so pleasure is opposed both to pain and to the good].
But this solution does not come out correctly: surely, he would not say that pleasure is
essentially a species of evil.

But (2a) even if some pleasures are bad, it does not mean that the highest good
cannot be some sort of pleasure, just as the highest good may be some sort of knowledge, even though some kinds of knowledge are bad. Perhaps we must even draw the
necessary conclusion that it is; for since each characteristic has its unobstructed activities, the activity of all characteristics or of one of them—depending on whether the for-   10
mer or the latter constitutes happiness—if unobstructed, must be the most desirable of
all. And this activity is pleasure. Therefore, the highest good is some sort of pleasure,
despite the fact that most pleasures are bad and, if you like, bad in the unqualified
sense of the word. It is for this reason that everyone thinks that the happy life is a
pleasant life, and links pleasure with happiness. And it makes good sense this way: for   15
no activity is complete and perfect as long as it is obstructed, and happiness is a complete and perfect thing. This is why a happy man also needs the goods of the body, external goods, and the goods of fortune, in order not to be obstructed by their absence.

But those who assert* that a man is happy even on the rack and even when great
misfortunes befall him, provided that he is good, are talking nonsense, whether they   20
know it or not. Since happiness also needs fortune, some people regard good fortune as
identical with happiness. But that is not true, for even good fortune, if excessive, can
be an obstruction; perhaps we are, in that case, no longer justified in calling it "good
fortune," for its definition is determined by its relation to happiness.

Also, the fact that all beasts and all men pursue pleasure is some indication that it   25
is, in a sense, the highest good:

> There is no talk that ever quite dies down,
> if spread by many men. . . .

But since no single nature and no single characteristic condition is, or is regarded, as the
best [for all], people do not all pursue the same pleasure, yet all pursue pleasure. Perhaps   30
they do not even pursue the pleasure which they think or would say they pursue, but they
all pursue the same [thing], pleasure. For everything has by nature something divine
about it. But the bodily pleasures have arrogated the name "pleasure" unto themselves as
their own private possession, because everyone tends to follow them and participates in

*The Cynics are probably meant.

35 them more frequently than in any others. Accordingly, since these are the only pleasures with which they are familiar, people think they are the only ones that exist.

1154ᵃ   It is also evident that if pleasure, i.e., the activity [of our faculties], is not good, it will be impossible for a happy man to live pleasantly. For to what purpose would he need pleasure, if it were not a good and if it is possible that a happy man's life is one of

5   pain? For if pain is neither good nor bad, pleasure is not, either: so why should he avoid it? Surely, the life of a morally good man is no pleasanter [than that of anyone else], if his activities are not more pleasant.

14. The Views Discussed: (2) Are Most Pleasures Bad?: The subject of the pleasures of the body demands the attention of the proponents of the view that, though some pleasures—for instance, the noble pleasures—are highly desirable, the pleasures

10 of the body—that is, the pleasures which are the concern of the self-indulgent man— are not. If that is true, why then are the pains opposed to them bad? For bad has good as its opposite. Is it that the necessary pleasures are good in the sense in which anything not bad is good? Or are they good up to a certain point? For all characteristics and motions which cannot have an excess of good cannot have an excess of pleasure,

15 either; but those which can have an excess of good can also have an excess of pleasure. Now, excess is possible in the case of the goods of the body, and it is the pursuit of excess, but not the pursuit of necessary pleasures, that makes a man bad. For all men get some kind of enjoyment from good food, wine, and sexual relations, but not everyone enjoys these things in the proper way. The reverse is true of pain: a bad person does not avoid an excess of it, but he avoids it altogether. For the opposite of an excess is

20 pain only for the man who pursues the excess.

        It is our task not only to say what is true, but also to state what causes error, since that helps carry conviction. For when we can give a reasoned explanation why something which appears to be true is, in fact, not true, it makes us give greater credence to

25 what is true. Accordingly, we must now explain why the pleasures of the body appear to be more desirable.

        The first reason, then, is that pleasure drives out pain. When men experience an excess of pain, they pursue excessive pleasure and bodily pleasure in general, in the belief that it will remedy the pain. These remedial [pleasures] become very intense—

30 and that is the very reason why they are pursued—because they are experienced in contrast with their opposite.

        As a matter of fact, these two reasons which we have stated also explain why pleasure is not regarded as having any moral value: some pleasures are the actions that spring from a bad natural state—either congenitally bad, as in the case of a beast, or bad by habit, as in the case of a bad man—while other pleasures are remedial and indicate a deficient natural state, and to be in one's natural state is better than to be moving

1154ᵇ toward it. But since the remedial pleasures only arise in the process of reaching the perfected state, they are morally good only incidentally.

        The second reason is that the pleasures of the body are pursued because of their intensity by those incapable of enjoying other pleasures. Take, for example, those who induce themselves to be thirsty. There is no objection to this practice, if the pleasures are harmless; but if they are harmful, it is bad. For many people have nothing else to

5   give them joy, and because of their nature, it is painful for them to feel neither [pleasure nor pain]. Actually, animal nature is under a constant strain, as the students of natural science attest when they say that seeing and hearing are painful, but [we do not

10 feel the pain because,] as they assert, we have become accustomed to it. Similarly, whereas the growing process [we go through] in our youth puts us into the same [exhil-

arated] state as that of a drunken man, and [makes] youth the age of pleasure, excitable natures, on the other hand, always need remedial action: as a result of [the excess of black bile in their] constitutional blend, their bodies are exposed to constant gnawing sensations, and they are always in a state of vehement desire. Now, since pain is driven out by the pleasure opposed to it or by any strong pleasure at all, excitable people be-   15
come self-indulgent and bad.

Pleasures unattended by pain do not admit of excess. The objects of these pleasures are what is pleasant by nature and not what is incidentally pleasant. By "things incidentally pleasant" I mean those that act as remedies. For since it is through some action of that part of us which has remained sound that a cure is effected, the remedy is regarded as being pleasant. But [pleasant by nature it is not]: pleasant by nature are those things which produce the action of an unimpaired natural state.   20

There is no single object that continues to be pleasant forever, because our nature is not simple but contains another natural element, which makes us subject to decay. Consequently, whenever one element does something, it runs counter to the nature of the other; and whenever the two elements are in a state of equilibrium, the act per-   25
formed seems neither painful nor pleasant. If there is a being with a simple nature, the same action will always be the most pleasant to him. That is why the divinity always enjoys one single and simple pleasure: for there is not only an activity of motion but also an activity of immobility, and pleasure consists in rest rather than in motion. But "change in all things is pleasant," as the poet has it, because of some evil in us. For just as a man who changes easily is bad, so also is a nature that needs to change. The rea-   30
son is that such a nature is not simple and not [entirely] good.

This completes our discussion of moral strength and moral weakness, and of pleasure and pain. We have stated what each of them is and in what sense some of them are good and some bad. It now remains to talk about friendship.

*   *   *

Book X

*   *   *

6. Happiness and Activity: Now that we have completed our discussion of the   1176ᵃ
virtues, and of the different kinds of friendship and pleasure, it remains to sketch an   30
outline of happiness, since, as we assert, it is the end or goal of human [aspirations]. Our account will be more concise if we recapitulate what we have said so far.

We stated, then, that happiness is not a characteristic; if it were, a person who passes his whole life in sleep, vegetating like a plant, or someone who experiences the   35
greatest misfortunes could possess it. If, then, such a conclusion is unacceptable, we must, in accordance with our earlier discussion, classify happiness as some sort of ac-   1176ᵇ
tivity. Now, some activities are necessary and desirable only for the sake of something else, while others are desirable in themselves. Obviously, happiness must be classed as an activity desirable in itself and not for the sake of something else. For happiness   5
lacks nothing and is self-sufficient. Activities desirable in themselves are those from which we seek to derive nothing beyond the actual exercise of the activity. Actions in conformity with virtue evidently constitute such activities; for to perform noble and good deeds is something desirable for its own sake.

Pleasant amusements, too, [are desirable for their own sake]. We do not choose them for the sake of something else, since they lead to harm rather than good when we   10 become neglectful of our bodies and our property. But most of those who are considered happy find an escape in pastimes of this sort, and this is why people who are well versed in such pastimes find favor at the courts of tyrants; they make themselves pleasant by providing what the tyrants are after, and what they want is amusement. Accordingly, such amusements are regarded as being conducive to happiness, because men who are in positions of power devote their leisure to them. But perhaps such persons cannot be [regarded as] evidence. For virtue and intelligence, which are the sources of morally good activities, do not consist in wielding power. Also, if these men, who have never tasted pure and generous pleasure, find an escape in the pleasures of the body, this is no sufficient reason for thinking that such pleasures are in fact more desirable. For children, too, think that what they value is actually the best. It is, therefore, not surprising that as children apparently do not attach value to the same things as do adults, so bad men do not attach value to the same things as do good men. Accordingly, as we have stated repeatedly, what is valuable and pleasant to a morally good man actually is valuable and pleasant. Each individual considers that activity most desirable which corresponds to his own proper characteristic condition, and a morally good man, of course, so considers activity in conformity with virtue.

Consequently, happiness does not consist in amusement. In fact, it would be strange if our end were amusement, and if we were to labor and suffer hardships all our life long merely to amuse ourselves. For, one might say, we choose everything for the sake of something else—except happiness; for happiness is an end. Obviously, it is foolish and all too childish to exert serious efforts and toil for purposes of amusement. Anacharsis* seems to be right when he advises to play in order to be serious; for amusement is a form of rest, and since we cannot work continuously we need rest. Thus rest is not an end, for we take it for the sake of [further] activity. The happy life is regarded as a life in conformity with virtue. It is a life which involves effort and is not spent in amusement.

Moreover, we say that what is morally good is better than what is ridiculous and brings amusement, and the better the organ or man—whichever may be involved in a particular case—the greater the moral value of the activity. But the activity of the better organ or the better man is in itself superior and more conducive to happiness.

Furthermore, any person at all, even a slave, can enjoy bodily pleasures no less than the best of men. But no one would grant that a slave has a share in happiness any more than that he lives a life of his own. For happiness does not consist in pastimes of this sort, but in activities that conform with virtue, as we have stated earlier.

7. Happiness, Intelligence, and the Contemplative Life: Now, if happiness is activity in conformity with virtue, it is to be expected that it should conform with the highest virtue, and that is the virtue of the best part of us. Whether this is intelligence or something else which, it is thought, by its very nature rules and guides us and which gives us our notions of what is noble and divine; whether it is itself divine or the most divine thing in us; it is the activity of this part [when operating] in conformity with the excellence or virtue proper to it that will be complete happiness. That it is an activity concerned with theoretical knowledge or contemplation has already been stated.

This would seem to be consistent with our earlier statements as well as the truth. For this activity is not only the highest—for intelligence is the highest possession we

---

*Anacharsis, who is said to have lived early in the sixth century B.C., was a Scythian whose travels all over the Greek world brought him a reputation for wisdom. He allegedly met Solon at Athens and was numbered in some ancient traditions among the Seven Wise Men.

have in us, and the objects which are the concern of intelligence are the highest objects of knowledge—but also the most continuous: we are able to study continuously more easily than to perform any kind of action. Furthermore, we think of pleasure as a necessary ingredient in happiness. Now everyone agrees that of all the activities that conform with virtue activity in conformity with theoretical wisdom is the most pleasant. At any rate, it seems that [the pursuit of wisdom or] philosophy holds pleasures marvelous in purity and certainty, and it is not surprising that time spent in knowledge is more pleasant than time spent in research. Moreover, what is usually called "self-sufficiency" will be found in the highest degree in the activity which is concerned with theoretical knowledge. Like a just man and any other virtuous man, a wise man requires the necessities of life; once these have been adequately provided, a just man still needs people toward whom and in company with whom to act justly, and the same is true of a self-controlled man, a courageous man, and all the rest. But a wise man is able to study even by himself, and the wiser he is the more is he able to do it. Perhaps he could do it better if he had colleagues to work with him, but he still is the most self-sufficient of all. Again, study seems to be the only activity which is loved for its own sake. For while we derive a greater or a smaller advantage from practical pursuits beyond the action itself, from study we derive nothing beyond the activity of studying. Also, we regard happiness as depending on leisure; for our purpose in being busy is to have leisure, and we wage war in order to have peace. Now, the practical virtues are activated in political and military pursuits, but the actions involved in these pursuits seem to be unleisurely. This is completely true of military pursuits, since no one chooses to wage war or foments war for the sake of war; he would have to be utterly bloodthirsty if he were to make enemies of his friends simply in order to have battle and slaughter. But the activity of the statesman, too, has no leisure. It attempts to gain advantages beyond political action, advantages such as political power, prestige, or at least happiness for the statesman himself and his fellow citizens, and that is something other than political activity: after all, the very fact that we investigate politics shows that it is not the same [as happiness]. Therefore, if we take as established (1) that political and military actions surpass all other actions that conform with virtue in nobility and grandeur; (2) that they are unleisurely, aim at an end, and are not chosen for their own sake; (3) that the activity of our intelligence, inasmuch as it is an activity concerned with theoretical knowledge, is thought to be of greater value than the others, aims at no end beyond itself, and has a pleasure proper to itself—and pleasure increases activity; and (4) that the qualities of this activity evidently are self-sufficiency, leisure, as much freedom from fatigue as a human being can have, and whatever else falls to the lot of a supremely happy man; it follows that the activity of our intelligence constitutes the complete happiness of man, provided that it encompasses a complete span of life; for nothing connected with happiness must be incomplete.

However, such a life would be more than human. A man who would live it would do so not insofar as he is human, but because there is a divine element within him. This divine element is as far above our composite nature* as its activity is above the active exercise of the other, [i.e., practical,] kind of virtue. So if it is true that intelligence is divine in comparison with man, then a life guided by intelligence is divine in comparison with human life. We must not follow those who advise us to have human thoughts, since we are [only] men, and mortal thoughts, as mortals should; on the contrary, we should try to become immortal as far as that is possible and do our utmost to

25

30

1177^b

5

10

15

20

25

30

---

*Human beings, consisting of soul and body, i.e., of form and matter, are composite beings, whereas the divine, being all intelligence, is not.

1178ᵃ live in accordance with what is highest in us. For though this is a small portion [of our nature], it far surpasses everything else in power and value. One might even regard it as each man's true self, since it is the controlling and better part. It would, therefore, be strange if a man chose not to live his own life but someone else's.

5   Moreover, what we stated before will apply here, too: what is by nature proper to each thing will be at once the best and the most pleasant for it. In other words, a life guided by intelligence is the best and most pleasant for man, inasmuch as intelligence, above all else, is man. Consequently, this kind of life is the happiest.

8. The Advantages of the Contemplative Life: A life guided by the other kind of virtue, [the practical,] is happy in a secondary sense, since its active exercise is confined to man. It is in our dealings with one another that we perform just, courageous, 10 and other virtuous acts, when we observe the proper kind of behavior toward each man in private transactions, in meeting his needs, in all manner of actions, and in our emotions, and all of these are, as we see, peculiarly human. Moreover, some moral acts seem to be determined by our bodily condition, and virtue or excellence of character seems in many ways closely related to the emotions. There is also a close mutual con-15 nection between practical wisdom and excellence of character, since the fundamental principles of practical wisdom are determined by the virtues of character, while practical wisdom determines the right standard for the moral virtues. The fact that these virtues are also bound up with the emotions indicates that they belong to our composite 20 nature, and the virtues of our composite nature are human virtues; consequently, a life guided by these virtues and the happiness [that goes with it are likewise human]. The happiness of the intelligence, however, is quite separate [from that kind of happiness]. That is all we shall say about it here, for a more detailed treatment lies beyond the scope of our present task.

It also seems that such happiness has little need of external trimmings, or less 25 need than moral virtue has. Even if we grant that both stand in equal need of the necessities of life, and even if the labors of a statesman are more concerned with the needs of our body and things of that sort—in that respect the difference between them may be small—yet, in what they need for the exercise of their activities, their difference will be great. A generous man will need money to perform generous acts, and a just 30 man will need it to meet his obligations. For the mere wish to perform such acts is inscrutable, and even an unjust man can pretend that he wishes to act justly. And a courageous man will need strength if he is to accomplish an act that conforms with his virtue, and a man of self-control the possibility of indulgence. How else can he or any 35 other virtuous man make manifest his excellence? Also, it is debatable whether the moral purpose or the action is the more decisive element in virtue, since virtue depends 1178ᵇ on both. It is clear of course that completeness depends on both. But many things are needed for the performance of actions, and the greater and nobler the actions the more is needed. But a man engaged in study has no need of any of these things, at least not for the active exercise of studying; in fact one might even go so far as to say that they 5 are a hindrance to study. But insofar as he is human and lives in the society of his fellow men, he chooses to act as virtue demands, and accordingly, he will need externals for living as a human being.

A further indication that complete happiness consists in some kind of contemplative activity is this. We assume that the gods are in the highest degree blessed and 10 happy. But what kind of actions are we to attribute to them? Acts of justice? Will they not look ridiculous making contracts with one another, returning deposits, and so forth? Perhaps acts of courage—withstanding terror and taking risks, because it is

noble to do so? Or generous actions? But to whom will they give? It would be strange to think that they actually have currency or something of the sort. Acts of self-control?   15
What would they be? Surely, it would be in poor taste to praise them for not having bad appetites. If we went through the whole list we would see that a concern with actions is petty and unworthy of the gods. Nevertheless, we all assume that the gods exist and, consequently, that they are active; for surely we do not assume them to be always asleep like Endymion.* Now, if we take away action from a living being, to say noth-   20
ing of production, what is left except contemplation? Therefore, the activity of the divinity which surpasses all others in bliss must be a contemplative activity, and the human activity which is most closely akin to it is, therefore, most conducive to happiness.

This is further shown by the fact that no other living being has a share in happiness, since they all are completely denied this kind of activity. The gods enjoy a life   25
blessed in its entirety; men enjoy it to the extent that they attain something resembling the divine activity; but none of the other living beings can be happy, because they have no share at all in contemplation or study. So happiness is coextensive with study, and the greater the opportunity for studying, the greater the happiness, not as an incidental   30
effect but as inherent in study; for study is in itself worthy of honor. Consequently, happiness is some kind of study or contemplation.

But we shall also need external well-being, since we are only human. Our nature is not self-sufficient for engaging in study: our body must be healthy and we must have   35
food and generally be cared for. Nevertheless, if it is not possible for a man to be supremely happy without external goods, we must not think that his needs will be great and many in order to be happy; for self-sufficiency and moral action do not consist in   1179ᵃ
an excess [of possessions]. It is possible to perform noble actions even without being ruler of land and sea; a man's actions can be guided by virtue also if his means are   5
moderate. That this is so can be clearly seen in the fact that private individuals evidently do not act less honorably but even more honorably than powerful rulers. It is enough to have moderate means at one's disposal, for the life of a man whose activity is guided by virtue will be happy.

Solon certainly gave a good description of a happy man, when he said that he is a   10
man moderately supplied with external goods, who had performed what he, Solon, thought were the noblest actions, and who had lived with self-control. For it is possible to do what one should even with moderate possessions. Also Anaxagoras, it seems, did not assume that a happy man had to be rich and powerful. He said that he would not be surprised if a happy man would strike the common run of people as strange, since they   15
judge by externals and perceive nothing but externals. So it seems that our account is in harmony with the opinion of the wise.

Now, though such considerations carry some conviction, in the field of moral action truth is judged by the actual facts of life, for it is in them that the decisive element lies. So we must examine the conclusions we have reached so far by applying them to   20
the actual facts of life: if they are in harmony with the facts we must accept them, and if they clash we must assume that they are mere words.

A man whose activity is guided by intelligence, who cultivates his intelligence and keeps it in the best condition, seems to be most beloved by the gods. For if the gods have any concern for human affairs—and they seem to have—it is to be expected   25
that they rejoice in what is best and most akin to them, and that is our intelligence; it is

*Supposedly the most beautiful of men, Endymion was loved by the Moon, who cast him into a perpetual sleep that she might descend and embrace him each night.

also to be expected that they requite with good those who most love and honor intelligence, as being men who care for what is dear to the gods and who act rightly and nobly. That a wise man, more than any other, has all these qualities is perfectly clear.

30   Consequently, he is the most beloved by the gods, and as such he is, presumably, also the happiest. Therefore, we have here a further indication that a wise man attains a higher degree of happiness than anyone.

POLITICS (in part)

Book I

1252ᵃ   1. Every state is a community of some kind, and every community is established with a view to some good; for everyone always acts in order to obtain that which they think good. But, if all communities aim at some good, the state or political community,

5   which is the highest of all, and which embraces all the rest, aims at good in a greater degree than any other, and at the highest good.

Some people think that the qualifications of a statesman, king, householder, and master are the same, and that they differ, not in kind, but only in the number of their

10   subjects. For example, the ruler over a few is called a master; over more, the manager of a household; over a still larger number, a statesman or king, as if there were no difference between a great household and a small state. The distinction which is made be-

15   tween the king and the statesman is as follows: When the government is personal, the ruler is a king; when, according to the rules of the political science, the citizens rule and are ruled in turn, then he is called a statesman.

But all this is a mistake, as will be evident to any one who considers the matter

20   according to the method which has hitherto guided us. As in other departments of science, so in politics, the compound should always be resolved into the simple elements or least parts of the whole. We must therefore look at the elements of which the state is composed, in order that we may see in what the different kinds of rule differ from one another, and whether any scientific result can be attained about each one of them.

25   2. He who thus considers things in their first growth and origin, whether a state or anything else, will obtain the clearest view of them. In the first place there must be a union of those who cannot exist without each other; namely, of male and female, that the race may continue (and this is a union which is formed, not of choice, but because, in com-

30   mon with other animals and with plants, mankind have a natural desire to leave behind them an image of themselves), and of natural ruler and subject, that both may be preserved. For that which can foresee by the exercise of mind is by nature lord and master, and that which can with its body give effect to such foresight is a subject, and by nature a slave; hence master and slave have the same interest. Now nature has distin-

1252ᵇ   guished between the female and the slave. For she is not niggardly, like the smith who fashions the Delphian knife for many uses; she makes each thing for a single use, and

Aristotle, *Politics*, (I, 1–2; III, 6–9; IV, 11–12; VII, 3b–4, 9), translated by Benjamin Jowett.

every instrument is best made when intended for one and not for many uses. But
among barbarians no distinction is made between women and slaves, because there is   5
no natural ruler among them: they are a community of slaves, male and female. That is
why the poets say,

> It is meet that Hellenes should rule over barbarians;

as if they thought that the barbarian and the slave were by nature one.

Out of these two relationships the first thing to arise is the family, and Hesiod is   10
right when he says,

> First house and wife and an ox for the plough,

for the ox is the poor man's slave. The family is the association established by nature
for the supply of men's everyday wants, and the members of it are called by Charondas, "companions of the cupboard," and by Epimenides the Cretan, "companions of
the manger." But when several families are united, and the association aims at some-   15
thing more than the supply of daily needs, the first society to be formed is the village.
And the most natural form of the village appears to be that of a colony from the family,
composed of the children and grandchildren, who are said to be, suckled with the same
milk." And this is the reason why Hellenic states were originally governed by kings;
because the Hellenes were under royal rule before they came together, as the barbar-   20
ians still are. Every family is ruled by the eldest, and therefore in the colonies of the
family the kingly form of government prevailed because they were of the same blood.
As Homer says:

> Each one gives law to his children and to his wives.

For they lived dispersedly, as was the manner in ancient times. That is why men say
that the Gods have a king, because they themselves either are or were in ancient times   25
under the rule of a king. For they imagine not only the forms of the Gods but their
ways of life to be like their own.

When several villages are united in a single complete community, large enough
to be nearly or quite self-sufficing, the state comes into existence, originating in the
bare needs of life, and continuing in existence for the sake of a good life. And there-   30
fore, if the earlier forms of society are natural, so is the state, for it is the end of them,
and the nature of a thing is its end. For what each thing is when fully developed, we
call its nature, whether we are speaking of a man, a horse, or a family. Besides, the
final cause and end of a thing is the best, and to be self-sufficing is the end and the   1253^a
best.

Hence it is evident that the state is a creation of nature, and that man is by nature
a political animal. And he who by nature and not by mere accident is without a state, is
either a bad man or above humanity; he is like the

> Tribeless, lawless, hearthless one,   5

whom Homer denounces—the natural outcast is forthwith a lover of war; he may be
compared to an isolated piece at draughts.

Now, that man is more of a political animal than bees or any other gregarious animals is evident. Nature, as we often say, makes nothing in vain, and man is the only

10 animal who has the gift of speech. And whereas mere voice is but an indication of pleasure or pain, and is therefore found in other animals (for their nature attains to the perception of pleasure and pain and the intimation of them to one another, and no further), the power of speech is intended to set forth the expedient and inexpedient, and therefore likewise the just and the unjust. And it is a characteristic of man that he alone

15 has any sense of good and evil, of just and unjust, and the like, and the association of living beings who have this sense makes a family and a state.

Further, the state is by nature clearly prior to the family and to the individual,

20 since the whole is of necessity prior to the part; for example, if the whole body be destroyed, there will be no foot or hand, except in an equivocal sense, as we might speak of a stone hand; for when destroyed the hand will be no better than that. But things are defined by their function and power; and we ought not to say that they are the same when they no longer have their proper quality, but only that they have the same name.

25 The proof that the state is a creation of nature and prior to the individual is that the individual, when isolated, is not self-sufficing; and therefore he is like a part in relation to the whole. But he who is unable to live in society, or who has no need because he is sufficient for himself, must be either a beast or a god: he is no part of a state. A social

30 instinct is implanted in all men by nature, and yet he who first founded the state was the greatest of benefactors. For man, when perfected, is the best of animals, but, when separated from law and justice, he is the worst of all; since armed injustice is the more dangerous, and he is equipped at birth with arms, meant to be used by intelligence and excellence, which he may use for the worst ends. That is why, if he has not excellence,

35 he is the most unholy and the most savage of animals, and the most full of lust and gluttony. But justice is the bond of men in states; for the administration of justice, which is the determination of what is just, is the principle of order in political society.

* * *

BOOK III

1278^b 6. Having determined these questions, we have next to consider whether there is only one form of government or many, and if many, what they are, and how many, and what are the differences between them.

10 A constitution is the arrangement of magistracies in a state, especially of the highest of all. The government is everywhere sovereign in the state, and the constitution is in fact the government. For example, in democracies the people are supreme, but in oligarchies, the few; and, therefore, we say that these two constitutions also are different: and so in other cases.

15 First, let us consider what is the purpose of a state, and how many forms of rule there are by which human society is regulated. We have already said, in the first part of this treatise, when discussing household management and the rule of a master, that

20 man is by nature a political animal. And therefore, men, even when they do not require one another's help, desire to live together; not but that they are also brought together by their common interests in so far as they each attain to any measure of well-being. This is certainly the chief end, both of individuals and of states. And mankind meet together and maintain the political community also for the sake of mere life (in which

25 there is possibly some noble element so long as the evils of existence do not greatly overbalance the good). And we all see that men cling to life even at the cost of enduring great misfortune, seeming to find in life a natural sweetness and happiness.

There is no difficulty in distinguishing the various kinds of rule; they have been 30
often defined already in our popular discussions. The rule of a master, although the slave
by nature and the master by nature have in reality the same interests, is nevertheless exercised primarily with a view to the interest of the master, but accidentally considers the 35
slave, since, if the slave perish, the rule of the master perishes with him. On the other
hand, the government of a wife and children and of a household, which we have called
household management, is exercised in the first instance for the good of the governed or
for the common good of both parties, but essentially for the good of the governed, as we 40
see to be the case in medicine, gymnastic, and the arts in general, which are only acciden- 1279[a]
tally concerned with the good of the artists themselves. For there is no reason why the
trainer may not sometimes practise gymnastics, and the helmsman is always one of the
crew. The trainer or the helmsman considers the good of those committed to his care. But,
when he is one of the persons taken care of, he accidentally participates in the advantage, 5
for the helmsman is also a sailor, and the trainer becomes one of those in training. And so
in politics: when the state is framed upon the principle of equality and likeness, the citizens think that they ought to hold office by turns. Formerly, as is natural, everyone would 10
take his turn of service; and then again, somebody else would look after his interest, just as
he, while in office, had looked after theirs. But nowadays, for the sake of the advantage
which is to be gained from the public revenues and from office, men want to be always in
office. One might imagine that the rulers, being sickly, were only kept in health while they 15
continued in office; in that case we may be sure that they would be hunting after places.
The conclusion is evident: that governments which have a regard to the common interest
are constituted in accordance with strict principles of justice, and are therefore true forms;
but those which regard only the interest of the rulers are all defective and perverted forms, 20
for they are despotic, whereas a state is a community of freemen.

7. Having determined these points, we have next to consider how many forms of government there are, and what they are; and in the first place what are the true forms, for 25
when they are determined the perversions of them will at once be apparent. The words
constitution and government have the same meaning, and the government, which is the
supreme authority in states, must be in the hands of one, or of a few, or of the many.
The true forms of government, therefore, are those in which the one, or the few, or the
many, govern with a view to the common interest; but governments which rule with a 30
view to the private interest, whether of the one, or of the few, or of the many, are perversions. For the members of a state, if they are truly citizens, ought to participate in its
advantages. Of forms of government in which one rules, we call that which regards the
common interest, kingship; that in which more than one, but not many, rule, aristocracy; and it is so called, either because the rulers are the best men, or because they have 35
at heart the best interests of the state and of the citizens. But when the many administer
the state for the common interest, the government is called by the generic name—a
constitution. And there is a reason for this use of language. One man or a few may
excel in excellence; but as the number increases it becomes more difficult for them to 40
attain perfection in every kind of excellence, though they may in military excellence, 1279[b]
for this is found in the masses. Hence in a constitutional government the fighting-men
have the supreme power, and those who possess arms are the citizens.

Of the above-mentioned forms, the perversions are as follows:—of kingship,
tyranny; of aristocracy, oligarchy; of constitutional government, democracy. For 5
tyranny is a kind of monarchy which has in view the interest of the monarch only; oligarchy has in view the interest of the wealthy; democracy, of the needy: none of them
the common good of all. 10

8. But there are difficulties about these forms of government, and it will therefore be necessary to state a little more at length the nature of each of them. For he who would make a philosophical study of the various sciences, and is not only concerned with practice, ought not to overlook or omit anything, but to set forth the truth in every particular. Tyranny, as I was saying, is monarchy exercising the rule of a master over the political society; oligarchy is when men of property have the government in their hands; democracy, the opposite, when the indigent, and not the men of property, are the rulers. And here arises the first of our difficulties, and it relates to the distinction just drawn. For democracy is said to be the government of the many. But what if the many are men of property and have the power in their hands? In like manner oligarchy is said to be the government of the few; but what if the poor are fewer than the rich, and have the power in their hands because they are stronger? In these cases the distinction which we have drawn between these different forms of government would no longer hold good.

Suppose, once more, that we add wealth to the few and poverty to the many, and name the governments accordingly—an oligarchy is said to be that in which the few and the wealthy, and a democracy that in which the many and the poor are the rulers— there will still be a difficulty. For, if the only forms of government are the ones already mentioned, how shall we describe those other governments also just mentioned by us, in which the rich are the more numerous and the poor are the fewer, and both govern in their respective states?

The argument seems to show that, whether in oligarchies or in democracies, the number of the governing body, whether the greater number, as in a democracy, or the smaller number, as in an oligarchy, is an accident due to the fact that the rich everywhere are few, and the poor numerous. But if so, there is a misapprehension of the causes of the difference between them. For the real difference between democracy and oligarchy is poverty and wealth. Wherever men rule by reason of their wealth, whether they be few or many, that is an oligarchy, and where the poor rule, that is a democracy. But in fact the rich are few and the poor many; for few are well-to-do, whereas freedom is enjoyed by all, and wealth and freedom are the grounds on which the two parties claim power in the state.

9. Let us begin by considering the common definitions of oligarchy and democracy, and what is oligarchical and democratic justice. For all men cling to justice of some kind, but their conceptions are imperfect and they do not express the whole idea. For example, justice is thought by them to be, and is, equality-not, however, for all, but only for equals. And inequality is thought to be, and is, justice; neither is this for all, but only for unequals. When the persons are omitted, then men judge erroneously. The reason is that they are passing judgement on themselves, and most people are bad judges in their own case. And whereas justice implies a relation to persons as well as to things, and a just distribution, as I have already said in the *Ethics,* implies the same ratio between the persons and between the things, they agree about the equality of the things, but dispute about the equality of the persons, chiefly for the reason which I have just given—because they are bad judges in their own affairs; and secondly, because both the parties to the argument are speaking of a limited and partial justice, but imagine themselves to be speaking of absolute justice. For the one party, if they are unequal in one respect, for example wealth, consider themselves to be unequal in all; and the other party, if they are equal in one respect, for example free birth, consider themselves to be equal in all. But they leave out the capital point. For if men met and associated out of regard to wealth only, their share in the state

would be proportioned to their property, and the oligarchical doctrine would then seem to carry the day. It would not be just that he who paid one mina should have the same share of a hundred minae, whether of the principal or of the profits, as he who paid the remaining ninety-nine. But a state exists for the sake of a good life, and not for the sake of life only: if life only were the object, slaves and brute animals might form a state, but they cannot, for they have no share in happiness or in a life based on choice. Nor does a state exist for the sake of alliance and security from injustice, nor yet for the sake of exchange and mutual intercourse; for then the Tyrrhenians and the Carthaginians, and all who have commercial treaties with one another, would be the citizens of one state. True, they have agreements about imports, and engagements that they will do no wrong to one another, and written articles of alliance. But there are no magistracies common to the contracting parties; different states have each their own magistracies. Nor does one state take care that the citizens of the other are such as they ought to be, nor see that those who come under the terms of the treaty do no wrong or wickedness at all, but only that they do no injustice to one another. Whereas, those who care for good government take into consideration political excellence and defect. Whence it may be further inferred that excellence must be the care of a state which is truly so called, and not merely enjoys the name: for without this end the community becomes a mere alliance which differs only in place from alliances of which the members live apart; and law is only a convention, "a surety to one another of justice," as the sophist Lycophron says, and has no real power to make the citizens good and just.

This is obvious; for suppose distinct places, such as Corinth and Megara, to be brought together so that their walls touched, still they would not be one city, not even if the citizens had the right to intermarry, which is one of the rights peculiarly characteristic of states. Again, if men dwelt at a distance from one another, but not so far off as to have no intercourse, and there were laws among them that they should not wrong each other in their exchanges, neither would this be a state. Let us suppose that one man is a carpenter, another a farmer, another a shoemaker, and so on, and that their number is ten thousand: nevertheless, if they have nothing in common but exchange, alliance, and the like, that would not constitute a state. Why is this? Surely not because they are at a distance from one another; for even supposing that such a community were to meet in one place, but that each man had a house of his own, which was in a manner his state, and that they made alliance with one another, but only against evildoers; still an accurate thinker would not deem this to be a state, if their intercourse with one another was of the same character after as before their union. It is clear then that a state is not a mere society, having a common place, established for the prevention of mutual crime and for the sake of exchange. These are conditions without which a state cannot exist; but all of them together do not constitute a state, which is a community of families and aggregations of families in well-being, for the sake of a perfect and self–sufficing life. Such a community can only be established among those who live in the same place and intermarry. Hence there arise in cities family connexions, brotherhoods, common sacrifices, amusements which draw men together. But these are created by friendship, for to choose to live together is friendship. The end of the state is the good life, and these are the means towards it. And the state is the union of families and villages in a perfect and self-sufficing life, by which we mean a happy and honourable life.

Our conclusion, then, is that political society exists for the sake of noble actions, and not of living together. Hence they who contribute most to such a society have a greater share in it than those who have the same or a greater freedom or nobility of birth but are inferior to them in political virtue; or than those who exceed them in wealth but are surpassed by them in virtue.

From what has been said it will be clearly seen that all the partisans of different forms of government speak of a part of justice only.

*   *   *

BOOK IV

1295ᵃ   11. We have now to inquire what is the best constitution for most states, and the best life for most men, neither assuming a standard of virtue which is above ordinary persons, nor an education which is exceptionally favoured by nature and circumstances, nor yet an ideal state which is an aspiration only, but having regard to the life in which the majority are able to share, and to the form of government which states in general can attain. As to those aristocracies, as they are called, of which we were just now speaking, they either lie beyond the possibilities of the greater number of states, or they approximate to the so-called constitutional government, and therefore need no separate discussion. And in fact the conclusion at which we arrive respecting all these forms rests upon the same grounds. For if what was said in the *Ethics* is true, that the happy life is the life according to excellence lived without impediment, and that excellence is a mean, then the life which is in a mean, and in a mean attainable by everyone, must be the best. And the same principles of excellence and badness are characteristic of cities and of constitutions; for the constitution is so to speak the life of the city.

Now in all states there are three elements: one class is very rich, another very poor, and a third in a mean. It is admitted that moderation and the mean are best, and therefore it will clearly be best to possess the gifts of fortune in moderation; for in that condition of life men are most ready to follow rational principle. But he who greatly excels in beauty, strength, birth, or wealth, or on the other hand who is very poor, or very weak, or of very low status, finds it difficult to follow rational principle. Of these two the one sort grow into violent and great criminals, the others into rogues and petty rascals. And two sorts of offences correspond to them, the one committed from violence, the other from roguery [Again, the middle class is least likely to shrink from rule, or to be over-ambitious for it], both of which are injuries to the state. Again, those who have too much of the goods of fortune, strength, wealth, friends, and the like, are neither willing nor able to submit to authority. The evil begins at home; for when they are boys, by reason of the luxury in which they are brought up, they never learn, even at school, the habit of obedience. On the other hand, the very poor, who are in the opposite extreme, are too degraded. So that the one class cannot obey, and can only rule despotically; the other knows not how to command and must be ruled like slaves. Thus arises a city, not of freemen, but of masters and slaves, the one despising, the other envying; and nothing can be more fatal to friendship and good fellowship in states than this: for good fellowship springs from friendship; when men are at enmity with one another, they would rather not even share the same path. But a city ought to be composed, as far as possible, of equals and similars; and these are generally the middle classes. Wherefore the city which is composed of middle-class citizens is necessarily best constituted in respect of the elements of which we say the fabric of the state naturally consists. And this is the class of citizens which is most secure in a state, for they do not, like the poor, covet other men's goods; nor do others covet theirs, as the poor covet the goods of the rich; and as they neither plot against others, nor are themselves plotted against, they pass through life safely. Wisely then did Phocylides pray—"Many things are best in the mean; I desire to be of a middle condition in my city."

Thus it is manifest that the best political community is formed by citizens of the 35 middle class, and that those states are likely to be well-administered in which the middle class is large, and stronger if possible than both the other classes, or at any rate than either singly; for the addition of the middle class turns the scale, and prevents either of the extremes from being dominant. Great then is the good fortune of a state in which the cit- 40 izens have a moderate and sufficient property; for where some possess much, and the 1296ª others nothing, there may arise an extreme democracy, or a pure oligarchy; or a tyranny may grow out of either extreme—either out of the most rampant democracy, or out of an oligarchy; but it is not so likely to arise out of the middle constitutions and those akin to them. I will explain the reason for this hereafter, when I speak of the revolutions of 5 states. The mean condition of states is clearly best, for no other is free from faction; and where the middle class is large, there are least likely to be factions and dissensions. For a similar reason large states are less liable to faction than small ones, because in them 10 the middle class is large; whereas in small states it is easy to divide all the citizens into two classes who are either rich or poor, and to leave nothing in the middle. And democracies are safer and more permanent than oligarchies, because they have a middle class 15 which is more numerous and has a greater share in the government; for when there is no middle class, and the poor are excessive in number, troubles arise, and the state soon comes to an end. A proof of the superiority of the middle class is that the best legislators have been of a middle condition; for example, Solon, as his own verses testify; and Ly- 20 curgus, for he was not a king; and Charondas, and almost all legislators.

These considerations will help us to understand why most governments are either democratic or oligarchical. The reason is that the middle class is seldom numerous in them, and whichever party, whether the rich or the common people, transgresses the 25 mean and predominates, draws the constitution its own way, and thus arises either oligarchy or democracy. There is another reason—the poor and the rich quarrel with one another, and whichever side gets the better, instead of establishing a just or popular 30 government, regards political supremacy as the prize of victory, and the one party sets up a democracy and the other an oligarchy. Further, both the parties which had the supremacy in Greece looked only to the interest of their own form of government, and established in states, the one, democracies, and the other, oligarchies; they thought of 35 their own advantage, and of the advantage of the other states not at all. For these reasons the middle form of government has rarely, if ever, existed, and among a very few only. One man alone of all who ever ruled in Greece was induced to give this middle constitution to states. But it has now become a habit among the citizens of states not 40 even to care about equality; all men are seeking for dominion, or, if conquered, are 1296ᵇ willing to submit.

What then is the best form of government, and what makes it the best, is evident; and of other constitutions, since we say that there are many kinds of democracy and many of oligarchy, it is not difficult to see which has the first and which the second or 5 any other place in the order of excellence, now that we have determined which is the best. For that which is nearest to the best must of necessity be better, and that which is further from the mean worse, if we are judging absolutely and not relatively to given conditions: I say "relatively to given conditions," since a particular government may 10 be preferable, but another form may be better for some people.

12. We have now to consider what and what kind of government is suitable to what and what kind of men. I may begin by assuming, as a general principle common to all 15

governments, that the portion of the state which desires the permanence of the constitution ought to be stronger than that which desires the reverse. Now every city is com-
20   posed of quality and quantity. By quality I mean freedom, wealth, education, good birth, and by quantity, superiority of numbers. Quality may exist in one of the classes which make up the state, and quantity in the other. For example, the meanly-born may be more in number than the well-born, or the poor than the rich, yet they may not so much exceed in quantity as they fall short in quality; and therefore there must be a
25   comparison of quantity and quality. Where the number of the poor exceeds a given proportion, there will naturally be a democracy, varying in form with the sort of people who compose it in each case. If, for example, the farmers exceed in number, the first
30   form of democracy will then arise; if the artisans and labouring class, the last; and so with the intermediate forms. But where the rich and the notables exceed in quality more than they fall short in quantity, there oligarchy arises, similarly assuming various forms according to the kind of superiority possessed by the oligarchs.

35   The legislator should always include the middle class in his government; if he makes his laws oligarchical, let him look to the middle class; if he makes them democratic, he should equally by his laws try to attach this class to the state. There only can
40   the government ever be stable where the middle class exceeds one or both of the oth-
1297ᵃ ers, and in that case there will be no fear that the rich will unite with the poor against the rulers. For neither of them will ever be willing to serve the other, and if they look for some form of government more suitable to both, they will find none better than this, for the rich and the poor will never consent to rule in turn, because they mistrust
5   one another. The arbiter is always the one most trusted, and he who is in the middle is an arbiter. The more perfect the admixture of the political elements, the more lasting will be the constitution. Many even of those who desire to form aristocratic governments make a mistake, not only in giving too much power to the rich, but in attempting
10   to cheat the people. There comes a time when out of a false good there arises a true evil, since the encroachments of the rich are more destructive to the constitution than those of the people.

*   *   *

Book VII

1325ᵇ 3. . . . If we are right in our view, and happiness is assumed to be acting well, the active life will be the best, both for every city collectively, and for individuals. Not that a life of action must necessarily have relation to others, as some persons think, nor are those ideas only to be regarded as practical which are pursued for the sake of practical re-
20   sults, but much more the thoughts and contemplations which are independent and complete in themselves; since acting well, and therefore a certain kind of action, is an end, and even in the case of external actions the directing mind is most truly said to act. Neither, again, is it necessary that states which are cut off from others and choose to
25   live alone should be inactive; for activity, as well as other things, may take place by sections; there are many ways in which the sections of a state act upon one another. The same thing is equally true of every individual. If this were otherwise, the gods and the universe, who have no external actions over and above their own energies, would
30   be far enough from perfection. Hence it is evident that the same life is best for each individual, and for states and for mankind collectively.

4. Thus far by way of introduction. In what has preceded I have discussed other forms of government; in what remains the first point to be considered is what should be the conditions of the ideal or perfect state; for the perfect state cannot exist without a due supply of the means of life. And therefore we must presuppose many purely imaginary conditions, but nothing impossible. There will be a certain number of citizens, a country in which to place them, and the like. As the weaver or shipbuilder or any other artisan must have the material proper for his work (and in proportion as this is better prepared, so will the result of his art be nobler), so the statesman or legislator must also have the materials suited to him.

First among the materials required by the statesman is population: he will consider what should be the number and character of the citizens, and then what should be the size and character of the country. Most persons think that a state in order to be happy ought to be large; but even if they are right, they have no idea what is a large and what a small state. For they judge of the size of the city by the number of the inhabitants; whereas they ought to regard, not their number, but their power. A city too, like an individual, has a work to do; and that city which is best adapted to the fulfilment of its work is to be deemed greatest, in the same sense of the word great in which Hippocrates might be called greater, not as a man, but as a physician, than some one else who was taller. And even if we reckon greatness by numbers, we ought not to include everybody, for, there must always be in cities a multitude of slaves and resident aliens and foreigners; but we should include those only who are members of the state, and who form an essential part of it. The number of the latter is a proof of the greatness of a city; but a city which produces numerous artisans and comparatively few soldiers cannot be great, for a great city is not the same as a populous one. Moreover, experience shows that a very populous city can rarely, if ever, be well governed; since all cities which have a reputation for good government have a limit of population. We may argue on grounds of reason, and the same result will follow. For law is order, and good law is good order; but a very great multitude cannot be orderly: to introduce order into the unlimited is the work of a divine power—of such a power as holds together the universe. Beauty is realized in number and magnitude, and the state which combines magnitude with good order must necessarily be the most beautiful. To the size of states there is a limit, as there is to other things, plants, animals, implements; for none of these retain their natural power when they are too large or too small, but they either wholly lose their nature, or are spoiled. For example, a ship which is only a span long will not be a ship at all, nor a ship a quarter of a mile long; yet there may be a ship of a certain size, either too large or too small, which will still be a ship, but bad for sailing. In like manner a state when composed of too few is not, as a state ought to be, self-sufficient; when of too many, though self-sufficient in all mere necessaries, as a nation may be, it is not a state, being almost incapable of constitutional government. For who can be the general of such a vast multitude, or who the herald, unless he have the voice of a Stentor?

A state, then, only begins to exist when it has attained a population sufficient for a good life in the political community: it may indeed, if it somewhat exceeds this number, be a greater state. But, as I was saying, there must be a limit. What the limit should be will be easily ascertained by experience. For both governors and governed have duties to perform; the special functions of a governor are to command and to judge. But if the citizens of a state are to judge and to distribute offices according to merit, then they must know each other's characters; where they do not possess this knowledge, both the election to offices arid the decision of lawsuits will go wrong. When the population is

20   very large they are manifestly settled at haphazard, which clearly ought not to be. Besides, in an over-populous state foreigners and resident aliens will readily acquire the rights of citizens, for who will find them out? Clearly then the best limit of the population of a state is the largest number which suffices for the purposes of life, and can be

25   taken in at a single view.

*   *   *

1328ᵇ   9. . . . Since we are here speaking of the best form of government, i.e. that under which the state will be most happy (and happiness, as has been already said, cannot exist without excellence), it clearly follows that in the state which is best governed and possesses men who are just absolutely, and not merely relatively to the principle of the

40   constitution, the citizens must not lead the life of artisans or tradesmen, for such a life is ignoble and inimical to excellence. Neither must they be farmers, since leisure is

1329ᵃ   necessary both for the development of excellence and the performance of political duties.

Again, there is in a state a class of warriors, and another of councillors, who ad-

5   vise about the expedient and determine matters of law, and these seem in an especial manner parts of a state. Now, should these two classes be distinguished, or are both functions to be assigned to the same persons? Here again there is no difficulty in seeing that both functions will in one way belong to the same, in another, to different persons. To different persons in so far as these employments are suited to different primes of life, for the one requires wisdom and the other strength. But on the other hand, since

10   it is an impossible thing that those who are able to use or to resist force should be willing to remain always in subjection, from this point of view the persons are the same; for those who carry arms can always determine the fate of the constitution. It remains therefore that both functions should be entrusted by the ideal constitution to the same

15   persons, not, however, at the same time, but in the order prescribed by nature, who has given to young men strength and to older men wisdom. Such a distribution of duties will be expedient and also just, and is founded upon a principle of conformity to merit. Besides, the ruling class should be the owners of property, for they are citizens, and the

20   citizens of a state should be in good circumstances; whereas artisans or any other class which is not a producer of excellence have no share in the state. This follows from our first principle, for happiness cannot exist without excellence, and a city is not to be termed happy in regard to a portion of the citizens, but in regard to them all. And

25   clearly property should be in their hands, since the farmers will of necessity be slaves or barbarian country people.

Of the classes enumerated there remain only the priests, and the manner in which their office is to be regulated is obvious. No farmer or artisan should be appointed to it;

30   for the gods should receive honour from the citizens only. Now since the body of the citizens is divided into two classes, the warriors and the councillors, and it is fitting that the worship of the gods should be duly performed, and also a rest provided in their service for those who from age have given up active life, to the old men of these two classes should be assigned the duties of the priesthood.

35   We have shown what are the necessary conditions, and what the parts of a state: farmers, artisans, and labourers of all kinds are necessary to the existence of states, but the parts of the state are the warriors and councillors. And these are distinguished severally from one another, the distinction being in some cases permanent, in others not.

HELLENISTIC AND ROMAN PHILOSOPHY

———◀◯▶———

Following the death of Alexander the Great in 323 B.C., three of his generals, Ptolemy, Seleucus, and Antigonus, carved up the empire he had created. For the next three centuries, descendants of these three men ruled the eastern Mediterranean world. By 30 B.C., with the Roman Emperor Octavian's defeat of Anthony and Cleopatra and the annexation of Egypt, the period of Greek rule (known as the "Hellenistic" period from the word <hellen>, meaning "Greek") was over. Real power in the area had shifted westward to emerging Rome.

This shift from Greek to Roman authority did not happen without social and political turmoil, and the philosophies that developed during this period reflect that turmoil. The emphasis now was not on complete systems of thought, such as those proposed by Plato and Aristotle. In their place were theories focusing on the practical questions of the good life for individuals. In a world that seemed more and more chaotic and uncontrollable, philosophers began to seek personal salvation more than comprehensive theories. Even the Platonic Academy and the Aristotelian Lyceum, which continued for centuries, moved from the constructive doctrines of their founders to more narrowly defined critical issues.

Reprinted in this section are selections from the three major Hellenistic schools—the Stoic, the Epicurean, and the Skeptical. All three of these schools continued into the Roman period and were adapted and modified by their Roman adherents. In order to understand these Hellenistic schools, we must return to Socrates, for all three schools had roots in his life and teaching.

The roots of the Stoic school can be traced back to Socrates' follower Antisthenes. Antisthenes, a rhetorician with an Athenian father and a Phrygian, non-Greek mother, had been a teacher before he met Socrates, who made a profound impression on him. It seems to have been Socrates' character—his self-control and self-sufficiency, his indifference to winter cold (see the *Symposium*), his serenely ironic superiority in every experience, and the opinions of others (see the *Apology*)—that struck Antisthenes with the force of revelation. What he learned from Socrates was neither a metaphysic nor even a philosophic method but, as he put it, "to live with myself." When he disposed of his possessions, keeping only a ragged old coat, Socrates is said to have taunted him: "I see your vanity through the holes of your coat." Antisthenes founded a school whose members acquired the nickname of "Cynics" <*kynikos*>, Greek for "doglike." The Cynics slept on the ground, neglected their clothes, let their beards grow to unusual lengths, and despised the conventions of society, insisting that virtue and happiness consist in self-control and independence. They believed that human dignity was independent of human laws and customs.

Of Antisthenes' Cynic disciples, none was more famous than Diogenes, who went about carrying a lantern in daylight and, when asked why, would reply, "I am looking for an honest man." He made his home in a tub. His eccentric behavior attracted the attention of even Alexander the Great, who, on visiting him, asked whether there was anything at all that he could do to please him. Diogenes replied: "Yes, get out of my sunlight."

Emphasizing self-control and independence, and locating human dignity outside law and convention, the Cynicism of Antisthenes and Diogenes flowed like a tributary into Stoicism. Stoicism, in turn, became the dominant philosophy of the Roman Empire.

Another early Socratic school, the Cyrenaics, was founded by one of Socrates' associates and admirers, Aristippus of Cyrene, from Libya, in northern Africa.

Laocoön, second century B.C., by Hagesandros, Polydoros, and Athenodoros, all of Rhodes. The Trojan priest Laocoön protested against bringing the Greeks' wooden horse into the city. According to one version of the legend, he was punished for his interference when Apollo sent two serpents to kill him and his sons. The Hellenistic philosophers sought relief from tortured emotions such as this work depicts. (*Hirmer Fotoarchiv*)

The Cyrenaics disparaged speculative philosophy and extolled the pleasure of the moment. But, following Aristippus, they maintained that the purest pleasure derives from self-mastery and the philosophic life. Only philosophy can protect human beings from passion, which inevitably brings suffering. While despising popular opinion, the Cyrenaics did believe that custom, law, and altruism contributed to long-range pleasure. The Cyrenaic philosophy, with its understanding of the good life as enjoyment of stable pleasures, led to the development of the Epicurean school.

A third Hellenistic school of philosophy, Skepticism, also had its roots in Socrates' teachings: specifically, in Socrates' repeated claim that he did not know anything. Based on the work of Pyrrho of Elis (ca. 360–270 B.C.), this movement stressed the contradictory nature of knowledge and advocated suspending judgment and achieving an attitude of detachment.

Reviewing the development of Greek philosophy from the Pre-Socratics to the Stoics, Epicureans, and Skeptics, one is struck by the overwhelming concern in the later schools with peace of mind. There is, as a consequence, one quality that preclassical and classical Greeks possessed preeminently and that Stoics, Epicureans, and Skeptics preeminently lacked: enthusiasm. But there was another movement developing in the ancient world—one that abounded in enthusiasm and changed the course of Western philosophy: Christianity. Though the dates of this movement overlap the dates of the philosophers in this volume, the Christian story appears in Volume II as an introduction to medieval philosophy.

The last great movement of Greek philosophy was Neoplatonism. The leader of this return to Platonic concepts, Plotinus (A.D. 204–270), did not lack enthusiasm, but he was, nevertheless, more remote from classical Greek attitudes than were the Hellenistic philosophers. He extolled the spirit to the point of saying he was ashamed to have a body; his fervor was entirely mystical, and he longed, to cite his famous words, to attain "the flight of the Alone to the Alone." Thus he perfected the less classical tendencies of Plato's thought, merging those tendencies with Neopythagoreanism and with Oriental notions such as the emanations from the One.

In A.D. 529, Plato's Academy was closed by Emperor Justinian, bringing to an end a millennium of Greek philosophy.

*   *   *

For clear, concise introductions to the Hellenistic and Roman philosophers, see Frederick Copleston, "Post-Aristotelian Philosophy," in his *A History of Philosophy: Volume I, Greece & Rome, Part II* (Garden City, NY: Image Books, 1962); D.W. Hamlyn, "Greek Philosophy after Aristotle," in D.J. O'Connor, ed., *A Critical History of Western Philosophy* (New York: The Free Press, 1964); John Dillon, *The Middle Platonists, 80 B.C. to A.D. 220* (Ithaca, NY: Cornell University Press, 1996); and David Furley, *Routledge History of Philosophy, Volume II: From Aristotle to Augustine* (New York: Routledge, 1999). Eduard Zeller, *The Stoics, Epicureans, and Sceptics,* translated by Oswald J. Reichel (New York: Russell & Russell, 1962); Émile Bréhier, *The Hellenistic and Roman Age,* translated by Wade Baskin (Chicago: University of Chicago Press, 1965); A.A. Long, *Hellenistic Philosophy: Stoics, Epicureans, Sceptics* (New York: Scribners, 1974); and R.W. Sharples, *Stoics, Epicureans and Sceptics* (Oxford: Routledge, 1996), are all solid histories of the period. A.A. Long and

D.N. Sedley, eds., *The Hellenistic Philosophers,* two volumes. (Cambridge: Cambridge University Press, 1987), provide source material and discussions, while Jacques Brunschwig, *Papers in Hellenistic Philosophy,* translated by Janet Lloyd (Cambridge: Cambridge University Press, 1994) and Terence Irwin, ed., *Hellenistic Philosophy* (Hamden, CT: Garland Publishing, 1995) give technical expositions of a number of important issues. For primary sources and helpful introductions, see Whitney J. Oates, ed., *The Stoic and Epicurean Philosophers: The Complete Extant Writings of Epicurus, Epictetus, Lucretius, Marcus Aurelius* (New York: Random House, 1940).

EPICURUS
341–270 B.C.

Like Pythagoras, Epicurus was born on the Greek island of Samos. At eighteen he went to Athens for a year, then joined his father in Colophon, the city where Xenophanes had been born. He studied the writings of Democritus and eventually set up his own school on the island of Lesbos. From there he moved to the Hellespont and, finally, to Athens in 307 B.C. As he moved from place to place, many of his students followed him. In Athens he established a community known as the "Garden," where he spent the rest of his life teaching and writing.

Epicurus's community welcomed people of all classes and of both sexes. The school required no fee from students, accepting what each individual was able and willing to pay. Epicurus himself was almost worshiped by his disciples, and members of his group had to swear an oath: "I will be faithful to Epicurus in accordance with whom I have made it my choice to live."* Among the later followers of Epicurus's thought, the Roman poet Lucretius (98–55 B.C.) considered him to be a god. Yet Epicurus was not overbearing or authoritarian. According to all accounts, he was kind and generous, treating his followers as friends, not subordinates. While dying in agony from a urinary obstruction, Epicurus wrote a letter that illustrates his gracious spirit. The extant portion includes these words to his friend Idomeneus: "I have a bulwark against all this pain from the joy in my soul at the memory of our conversations together."**

Epicurus wrote over three hundred volumes, but all that has survived are some fragments, three complete letters, and a short treatise summarizing his

*Reported in J.V. Luce, *Introduction to Greek Philosophy* (New York: Thames and Hudson, 1992), p. 140.
**Ibid.

views. These surviving works provide an understanding of Epicurus's physics and ethics and give some sense of his psychology and theory of knowledge. Epicurus's first letter, To Herodotus, explains his atomistic theory. Like Democritus, Epicurus asserts that reality is composed of atoms and the void. But unlike Democritus, whose atomism is deterministic, Epicurus broaches the notion that atoms sometimes inexplicably "swerve." As atoms "fell downward" through the void, some of them swerved from their paths and collided with other atoms, setting off a chain reaction that eventually led to the world as we know it. Epicurus goes on to explore the implications of this theory for perception and knowledge.

The second letter, *To Pythocles,* on astronomy and meteorology, is of questionable origin and adds little to our understanding of Epicurus's thought. But the third letter, *To Menoeceus,* together with the short work *Principle Doctrines* explains his central ethical theory. Epicurus declares that pleasure is the highest good, though some pleasures are unnatural and unnecessary. In contrast to the modern understanding of the word "epicurean," Epicurus opposed exotic meals and profuse consumption. Such indulgences never bring permanent pleasure and frequently lead to its opposite: pain. Instead Epicurus advocates enjoying only the "natural" pleasures—those most likely to lead to contentment and repose.

The surviving complete works were incorporated by Diogenes Laertius in his *Lives of Eminent Philosophers.* Using the Russel M. Geer translations, all but the second letter are given here.

*   *   *

The classic secondary work on Epicurus is Cyril Bailey, *The Greek Atomists and Epicurus* (Oxford: Clarendon Press, 1928). Norman Wentworth De Witt, *Epicurus and His Philosophy* (Minneapolis: University of Minnesota Press, 1954), provides an interesting interpretation—one which John M. Rist, *Epicurus: An Introduction* (Cambridge: Cambridge University Press, 1972), contests. A.E. Taylor, *Epicurus* (1911; reprinted New York: Books for Libraries Press, 1969); G.K. Stradach, *The Philosophy of Epicurus* (Evanston, IL: Northwestern University Press, 1963); and Diskin Clay, *Lucretius and Epicurus* (Ithaca, NY: Cornell University Press, 1983), give helpful overviews. A.J. Festugière, *Epicurus and His Gods,* translated by C.W. Chilton (1955; reprinted London: Russell, 1969), and James H. Nichols, Jr., *Epicurean Political Philosophy* (Ithaca, NY: Cornell University Press, 1976), deal with specific topics.

LETTER TO HERODOTUS

I. INTRODUCTION

A. REASONS FOR THE LETTER

This letter presents a brief compendium of the physics to refresh the memories of those already familiar with the theories.

Epicurus to Herodotus, greeting.

Some, Herodotus, are not able to study carefully all my works on natural science or to examine closely the longer treatises. For them I have already written an epitome of the whole system so that they may acquire a fair grasp of at least the general principles and thereby have confidence in themselves on the chief points whenever they take up the study of physics. Those, too, who have acquired a reasonably complete view of all the parts ought to keep in mind an outline of the principles of the whole; for such a comprehensive grasp is often required, the details not so often. You must continually return to these primary principles and memorize them thoroughly enough to secure a grasp of the essential parts of the system. Accurate knowledge of the details will follow if once you have understood and memorized the outline of the whole. Even for the thoroughly trained student this is the most important result of his accurate knowledge: he is able to make immediate use of the things he perceives and of the resulting concepts by assigning them to the simple classes and calling them by their own names; for it is not possible for anyone to hold in mind in condensed form the whole interrelated system unless he is able to comprehend by means of short formulas all that might be expressed in detail. Therefore, since such a course is useful to all who are engaged with natural science, I, who recommend continuous activity in this field and am myself gaining peaceful happiness from just this life, have composed for you such a brief compendium of the chief principles of my teaching as a whole.

B. METHODS OF PROOF

Words must be used in their natural meanings. All natural science rests on the evidence of the senses.

First, Herodotus, we must understand the meanings of words in order that by expressing our opinions, investigations, and problems in exact terms, we may reach judgments and not use empty phrases, leaving matters undecided although we argue endlessly. We must accept without further explanation the first mental image brought up by each word if we are to have any standard to which to refer a particular inquiry, problem, or opinion.

Epicurus, *Letters, Principal Doctrines, and Vatican Sayings,* translated by Russel M. Geer (New York: Macmillan/Library of the Liberal Arts, 1964).

Next, we must use our sensations as the foundation of all our investigations; that is, we must base investigations on the mental apprehensions,* upon the purposeful use of the several senses that furnish us with knowledge, and upon our immediate feelings.** In these ways we can form judgments on those matters that can be confirmed by the senses and also on those beyond their reach.

II. The Universe

A. Basic Principles

Matter can be neither created nor destroyed. The universe as a whole is unchanging.

Now that this has been established we must consider the phenomena that cannot be perceived by the senses. The first principle is that nothing can be created from the non-existent; for otherwise anything would be formed from any thing without the need of seed. If all that disappears were destroyed into the non-existent, all matter would be destroyed, since that into which it would be dissolved has no existence. Truly this universe has always been such as it now is, and so it shall always be; for there is nothing into which it can change, and there is nothing outside the universe that can enter into it and bring about a change.

B. Atoms and the Void

The universe consists of matter, recognized by the senses, and void, in which matter moves. Other conceivable things are "accidents" or "properties" of these. Sensible objects are composed of atoms, which themselves are indestructible.

Moreover, the universe consists of material bodies and void. That the bodies exist is made clear to all by sensation itself, on which reason must base its judgment in regard to what is imperceptible, as I have said above. If that which we call "void" and "space" and "the untouchable" did not exist, the particles of matter would have no place in which to exist or through which to move, as it is clear they do move.

In addition to these two, there is nothing that we can grasp in the mind, either through concepts or through analogy with concepts,*** that has real existence and is not referred to merely as a property or an accident of material things or of the void.

Of material things, some are compounds, others are the simple particles from which the compounds are formed. The particles are indivisible and unchangeable, as is necessary if all is not to be dissolved to nothing, but something strong is to remain after the dissolution of the compounds, something solid, which cannot be destroyed in

---

*That is, upon the apprehension by the mind of the mental concepts that are themselves the result of repeated sensations.

**The feelings are concerned with ethical matters only.

***That is, either through mental images formed by emanations received by the senses or directly by the mind from material things, or through mental combinations of these images.

any way. Therefore, it is necessary that the first beginnings be indivisible particles of matter.

C. THE INFINITY OF THE UNIVERSE

i. The universe is infinite, for there is nothing to bound it, and each of its elements is also infinite.

Moreover, the universe as a whole is infinite, for whatever is limited has an outermost edge to limit it, and such an edge is defined by something beyond. Since the universe does not have an edge, it has no limit; and since it lacks a limit, it is infinite and unbounded. Moreover, the universe is infinite both in the number of its atoms and in the extent of its void. If, on the one hand, the void were infinite and matter finite, the atoms would not remain anywhere but would be carried away and scattered through the infinite void, since there would be no atoms from without to support them and hold them together by striking them. If, on the other hand, the void were finite, there would not be room in it for an infinite number of atoms.

ii. To account for the differences in sensible objects, the atoms must exist in many forms, the number of different forms being inconceivably great but not infinite, while the number of atoms of each form is infinite.

In addition, the indivisible, solid particles of matter, from which composite bodies are formed and into which such bodies are dissolved, exist in so many different shapes that the mind cannot grasp their number; for it would not be possible for visible objects to exhibit such great variation in form and quality if they were made by repeated use of atoms of conceivable variety. The number of atoms of each shape is infinite; but the number of varieties cannot be infinite, only inconceivably great.

D. THE MOTION OF THE ATOMS

The atoms move continuously, both freely in space, and with more limited motion forming gases, liquids, and solids. This motion had no beginning.

The atoms move without interruption through all time. Some of them fall in a straight line; some swerve from their courses; and others move back and forth as the result of collisions. These last make up the objects that our senses recognize. Some of those that move in this way after collisions separate far from each other; the others maintain a vibrating motion, either closely entangled with each other or confined by other atoms that have become entangled. There are two reasons for this continued vibration. The nature of the void that separates each of the atoms from the next permits it, for the void is not able to offer any resistance; and the elasticity that is characteristic of the atoms causes them to rebound after each collision. The degree of entanglement of the atoms determines the extent of the recoil from the collision. These motions had no beginning, for the atoms and the void have always existed.

If all these things are remembered, a statement as brief as this provides a sufficient outline for our understanding of the nature of that which exists.

E. THE INFINITE NUMBER OF WORLDS

Because atoms and space are infinite, the number of worlds, like or unlike ours, is also infinite.

Finally, the number of worlds, some like ours and some unlike, is also infinite. For the atoms are infinite in number, as has been shown above, and they move through the greatest distances. The atoms suited for the creation and maintenance of a world have not been used up in the formation of a single world or of a limited number of them, whether like our world or different from it. There is nothing therefore that will stand in the way of there being an infinite number of worlds.

III. SENSE PERCEPTION

A. SIGHT

i. Thin films, which we call "idols," are constantly given off by objects, retaining the form and color of the object.

Moreover, there are images of the same shape as the solid bodies from which they come but in thinness far surpassing anything that the senses can perceive. It is not impossible that emanations of this sort are formed in the air that surrounds a body, that there are opportunities for the creation of these thin, hollow films, and that the particles composing them retain as they flow from the solid object the same position and relative order* that they had while on its surface. Such images we call "idols."

ii. Because their unsurpassed fineness frees them from internal and external collisions, the idols move with almost atomic speed.

Nothing in nature as we see it prevents our believing that the idols are of a texture unsurpassed in fineness. For this reason, their velocity is also unsurpassed, since they always find a proper passage, and since moreover their course is retarded by few if any collisions, while a body made up of an inconceivably large number of atoms suffers many collisions as soon as it begins to move.

iii. These films, which are replaced by new matter as soon as they leave the surfaces of bodies, usually retain their forms; but sometimes a new idol is formed in midair.

Moreover, there is nothing to prevent our believing that the creation of idols is as swift as thought. They flow from the surfaces of a body in a constant stream, but this is not made evident by any decrease in the size of the body since other atoms are flooding in. For a long time the idols keep their atoms in the same relative position and order that they occupied on the surface of the solid, although sometimes the idols do become confused, and sometimes they combine in the air. This combination takes place quickly since there is no need of filling up their substance within. There are also some other ways in which idols come into being. No one of these statements is contradicted

---

*By keeping the same position (orientation), they retain the color of the object; by keeping the same relative order, its shape.

by sensation if we examine the ways in which sensation brings us clear visions of external objects and of the relations between them.

iv. Both thought and sight are due to idols coming from objects to us.

We must suppose that we see or think of the outer form of a thing when something comes to us from its surface. We could not as readily perceive the color and shape of external objects by means of impressions made on the air that lies between us and them, or by means of rays or beams of some sort sent from us to them, as we can when outlines of some kind, like the objects in color and shape and of the proper size to affect either our eyes or our minds, come to us from the objects. Since these move in rapid succession they present a single uninterrupted image; and they maintain a quality in harmony with their source because their energy, which has been imparted to them by the vibrations of the atoms in the depths of the solid object, is itself proportionate to the energy of that source.

v. The mental picture from the intent look or the concentrated thought is true. Error results when opinion adds something.

When, by the purposeful use of our mind or of our organs or sense, we receive a mental picture of the shape of an object or of its concomitant qualities, this picture is true, since it is created by the continuous impact of the idols or by an impression left by one of them. Whatever is false and erroneous is due to what opinion adds to an image that is waiting to be confirmed, or at least not to be contradicted, by further evidence of the senses, and which then fails to be so confirmed or is contradicted. The mental pictures that we receive in the images that either come to our minds in sleep or are formed by the purposeful use of the mind or of the other instruments of judgment would not have such similarity to those things that exist and that we call true if there were not some such material effluence actually coming to us from the objects; and the errors would not occur if we did not permit in ourselves some other activity similar to the purposeful apprehension of mental images but yet different. From this other activity error results if its conclusions are not confirmed by further evidence or are contradicted, but truth if they are so confirmed or are not contradicted. Therefore, we must do our best to hold opinion in check in order that we may neither destroy the criteria of judgment, which depend on the clear view, nor confuse everything by placing erroneous opinion on an equality with firmly established truth.

B. HEARING

An effluence from the source of sound, splitting up into particles each like the whole, which come in sequence to the ear, causes hearing.

Moreover, we hear when a kind of stream is carried to our ears from a person who speaks or from an object that makes a sound or noise or in any way whatever arouses in us the sense of hearing. This stream divides into particles, each of which is of the same nature as the whole, and these particles preserve a common relationship to each other and a peculiar continuity that extends back to the source of the sound and usually arouses comprehension in the hearer; or if it fails to do this, it at least makes clear that there is something outside. Without some common relationship extending out from the source, there would not be such awareness. We must not suppose that the air itself receives an impression from the spoken word or sound, for indeed the air is far from admitting any such thing. Rather, the force that is created in us when we speak causes such a displacement of particles, capable of forming a breathlike stream, that it produces in the person to whom we are speaking the sensation of hearing.

C. Smell

Effluences likewise rouse the sense of smell.

We must also suppose that, like sounds, smells could not produce any sensation if there were not carried from the object certain particles of a nature proper to stir the organ of this sense. Some of these are disorderly and unpleasant; some are gentle and agreeable.

IV. The Atoms

A. Properties of the Atoms

i. The unchanging atoms possess no qualities save size, mass, and shape. Other qualities result from atomic position or motion.

We must suppose that the atoms possess none of the qualities of visible things except shape, mass, and size, and whatever is a necessary concomitant of shape.* For every quality changes; but the atoms do not change in any way, since in the dissolution of composite things something hard and indestructible must survive that will make changes possible—not changes into nothingness and from nothingness, but changes brought about by alterations in the positions of some atoms and by the addition or removal of some. It is necessary that the particles that alter their positions and come and go be indestructible, not sharing in the nature of the visible things that are changed, but having their own peculiar shapes and masses; for this much must be unalterable. Even among sensible things, we see that those that are altered by the loss of matter on all sides still retain shape; but the other qualities do not survive in the changing object, as shape survives, but are removed from the whole body. These properties that remain are enough to cause the differences in composite things, since it is necessary that something survive and be not utterly destroyed.

ii. The atoms vary in size, but are not of every size, for if they were, some would be visible.

We must not think that there are atoms of every size lest the visible world prove us wrong; yet we must suppose that there are some differences in size. If there are some differences, it will be easier to explain our feelings and sensations. But the atoms need not be of every size in order to account for the differences in qualities; and if they were of every size, some would necessarily be large enough for us to see. It is clear that this is not the case, and it is impossible to think how an atom might become visible.

---

*For example, roughness or smoothness.

B. The Parts of the Atom

i. We cannot assume matter to be infinitely divisible. A thing containing infinite material parts, no matter how small they were, would itself be infinitely large.

Next, we cannot suppose that in a finite body the parts, no matter how small, are infinite in number. Therefore, not only must we exclude infinite division into smaller and smaller parts lest we make everything weak, and in our conception of the parts that compose a whole be compelled to make them less and less, finally reducing real things to nothingness; but also in dealing with finite things we must not accept as possible an infinite progression to parts each smaller than the last. For if once you say that in a finite thing there are parts infinite in number even if of the least possible size, you cannot think how this can be. For how can a thing containing infinite parts be finite in size? It is clear that the infinite parts are each of some size, and however small they may be, the whole must be infinite in magnitude.

ii. As in a visible thing there is a smallest part recognizable by the eye, which cannot be seen by itself and the total number of these smallest parts measures the whole, so in the atom there is also a least part recognizable by the mind, which cannot exist by itself, and the total number of these parts measures the atom.

Again, if in the finite body there is a part that can just be distinguished by the eye even if it is not visible by itself, we must believe that there is an adjacent part similar to this, and that if one went on in this way in his mind from one point to the next, he could not continue without end. We must suppose that the smallest perceptible part is not like those bodies that are large enough that we can move our eyes from one part to another, nor yet is it wholly unlike such bodies. Although it has some similarity to them,* it does not admit division into parts. But if because of this similarity we think to mark off mentally a separate portion of the part on this side or that, we find that we are looking at the similar part adjacent to it. If, starting out from the first of these parts and not dwelling on the same one, we inspect them one after another, we find that they do not touch each other part against part,** but by their own one special characteristic they measure magnitude, there being many of them in large bodies, few in small.*** We must suppose that the least part of the atom has the same relation to the whole as the least perceptible part has to the whole visible object. It is clear that the least part of the atom is smaller than the least perceptible part, but it has the same relationship to the whole of which it is a part. We have already stated from its relationship to sensible bodies that the atom has size, although far inferior to them in this respect. Furthermore, the uncompounded least parts of the atoms must be regarded as fixed units, which offer themselves to us in our mental survey of the invisible as a means for the measurement of the atoms, both greater and smaller.† The similarity between the least parts of atoms

---

*That is, it is like them in that it has extension, which a geometrical point lacks.

**A peculiar but logical idea. Ordinarily, when two bodies are in contact, the left part of one, let us say, touches the right part of the other. But these smallest visible parts are so small that they themselves have no visible parts. They therefore appear to us to touch each other, not part against part, but whole against whole.

***Their special characteristic is that they have extension but lack parts. They are therefore suitable units of measurement, since every visible body will consist of a whole number of such parts with no fractions remaining.

†As each sensible body must consist of a given number of the least visible parts, so each atom must consist of a given whole number of these atomic least parts.

and the least perceptible parts of sensible things is sufficient to justify our reasoning up to this point; but it is not possible that the least parts of atoms ever moved individually and came together.

C. The Motion of the Atoms

i. Although there can be neither top nor bottom in infinite space, the terms up and down have meaning with respect to ourselves.

Next, we cannot predicate up or down of infinite space as if there were a highest or lowest. Yet if it were possible to draw a line from the point where we are standing upward to infinity in the space above our heads, neither this line nor one drawn downward from the observer to infinity would appear to be at the same time both up and down with reference to the same spot, for this would be nonsense. Thus it is possible to think of one motion extending to infinity in the direction that we call up and one extending down, even if what moves from us into the spaces above our heads comes a thousand times to the feet of those above us and what moves downward comes to the heads of those below; for one of the motions is nonetheless regarded as extending as a whole to infinity in one direction, and the other motion in the other direction.

ii. The atoms, always moving in the void, always possess equal velocity, whether their motion be caused by collision or by weight. If unchecked, an atom will cross any conceivable distance in an inconceivably short time.

Moreover, it is necessary that the atoms possess equal velocity whenever they are moving through the void and nothing collides with them. For heavy bodies will not be carried more quickly than small, light ones when nothing at all opposes them, nor do the small bodies, because they all find suitable passages, excel the large ones, provided the latter are not obstructed. This is equally true of the atoms' motions upwards or to the side because of collisions and of their downward motion because of their own weight. The atom will traverse space with the speed of thought as long as the motion caused in either of these ways maintains itself; that is, until the atom is deflected either by some external force, or by its own weight which counteracts the force of the earlier collision. Moreover, since the motion through the void takes place without any interference from colliding particles, any conceivable distance is completed in an inconceivably brief time. For it is the occurrence or nonoccurrence of collisions that gives the appearance of slow or rapid motion.

iii. At any point of time the atoms of a compound body are moving in all directions with atomic speed, but because of their constant collisions and changes of direction, the motion of the body as a whole in any appreciable time may be brought within the reach of our senses.

Although all atoms have the same velocity, it will be said that in the case of compounds some atoms move faster than others. Men will say this because even in the shortest continuous period of time the compound and the atoms in it do move in one direction. However, in points of time recognized only by the reason, the atoms are not in motion in one direction but are constantly colliding with each other until the motion as a continuous whole comes within the reach of our senses. For what opinion adds about what the senses cannot perceive, namely that in times perceptible only by the reason there will be a continuity of motion, is not true in the case of the atoms. What is grasped by the purposeful use of the senses or by the mental apprehension of concepts contains the whole truth. We must not suppose that in times perceptible by the reason the whole moving compound moves in various directions, for this is unthinkable; and if this were true, when the body arrived in a perceptible time from any quarter whatever, the direction from which we observe its motion would not be that from which it originally started. The visible motion of the body will be the result of the internal collisions, even if below the visible level we leave the velocity of the atoms unaffected by the collisions. An understanding of this principle will be useful.

V. The Soul

A. Composition of the Soul

The soul is material, composed of finely divided particles, some like breath, some like fire, and some of a third, unnamed kind.
Next, referring to the sensations and the feelings as the most certain foundation for belief, we must see that, in general terms, the soul is a finely divided, material thing, scattered through the whole aggregation of atoms that make up the body, most similar to breath with a certain admixture of heat,* in some ways resembling the one, in some ways the other. But there is also a part of the soul that goes beyond even these two in fineness, and for this reason it is more ready to share in the feelings of the body. All this is made evident to us by the powers of the soul, that is, by its feelings, its rapidity of action, its rational faculties, and its possession of those things whose loss brings death to us.

B. The Soul and the Body in Sensation

The soul experiences sensation only when enclosed in the body; and the body receives from the soul a share in this sensation. Sensation may survive the loss of parts of the body, but it ceases with the destruction of the soul or of the whole body.
Next, we must conclude that the primary cause of sensation is in the soul; yet it would not have acquired sensation if it had not been in some way enclosed by the rest of the body. But the rest of the body, having given the soul the proper setting for experiencing sensation, has itself also gained from the soul a certain share in this capacity. Yet it does not fully share with the soul, and for this reason when the soul departs, the body no longer experiences sensation; for the body did not have this capacity in itself but made sensation possible for that other that had come into existence along with it, namely the soul. The soul, thanks to the power perfected in it by the motions of the body, at once bringing to completion its own power to experience sensation, returned a share of this power to the body because of their close contact and common feelings, as I have said. For this reason, sensation is never lost while the soul remains, even though other parts of the body have been destroyed. Indeed, even if a portion of the soul is lost with the loss in whole or in part of that portion of the body that enclosed it, if any part at all of the soul survives, it will still experience sensation; but when the rest of the

---

*Epicurus believed heat was a material substance.

body survives both as a whole and part by part, it has no sensation if that collection of atoms, small though it be, that makes up the soul has been lost. However, if the whole body is destroyed, the soul is scattered and no longer enjoys the same powers and motions; and as a result, it no longer possesses sensation. Whenever that in which the soul has existed is no longer able to confine and hold it in, we cannot think of the soul as still enjoying sensation, since it would no longer be within its proper system and would no longer have the use of the appropriate motions.

C. Material Nature of the Soul

The term "incorporeal" is properly applied only to the void, which cannot act or be acted on. Since the soul can act and be acted upon, it is not incorporeal.

Moreover, we must clearly observe this also, that the word "incorporeal" in its common use is applied only to that which we can think of as existing by itself.* Now there is no incorporeal thing that we can think of as existing by itself except the void. The void can neither act nor be acted upon; it only gives to corporeal things a space through which to move. Therefore, those who say that the soul is incorporeal are talking nonsense; for in that case the soul would be unable to act or be acted upon, and we clearly see that the soul is capable of both.

D. Conclusion

If you refer all this discussion about the soul to your feelings and sensations, remembering what was said at the beginning of the discussion, you will find enough embraced in this outline to enable you, starting from it, to work out the details with certainty.

VI. Properties and Accidents

A. Properties

Shape, mass, etc., are properties of things. They cannot exist by themselves; they are not separable parts of the things to which they belong; without them the things could not be perceived.

In the next place, shapes, colors, sizes, mass, and all other things that are spoken of as belonging to a body must be thought of as properties either of bodies in general or of bodies that are perceptible and are recognized by our perception of these properties.** These properties are not to be regarded as having existence by themselves, for we cannot think of them apart from things of which they are properties; nor are they wholly without existence. They are not some kind of immaterial thing attached to the body, nor are they parts of the body; but from all of them together the body as a whole

---

*That is, we do not apply the term to attributes or properties.
**Shape, size, and mass are properties of all bodies; color, of visible bodies only.

receives its permanent character. We do not mean that these properties come together and form the body as happens when a large body is formed from its separate parts, either from the primary parts or from large parts that are smaller than the whole, whatever it is; we merely mean, as I have said, that the whole body receives its own permanent character from the presence in it of these properties. Each of the properties of a body has its own appropriate way of being perceived and distinguished; and the body as a whole is perceived along with its properties, not separately from them, and is identified by this composite recognition.

B. ACCIDENTS

i. Like properties, accidents can be recognized only in connection with bodies; but they are not permanent attributes as are the properties.

It also often happens that there are qualities that do not permanently accompany bodies. They, too, do not exist by themselves, yet they are not wholly without being. They do not belong to the class that is below the level of perception, nor are they incorporeal. In applying to them the term "accidents" in its commonest meaning, we make it clear that they have neither the nature of the whole that we comprehend as a composite and call "body," nor the nature of the permanent properties without which a body cannot be thought of. By the appropriate senses each of them can be recognized in company with the composite body to which it belongs; but we see a particular accident only when it is present with the body, since accidents are not unchanging attendants. We must not deny the reality of this clear vision of the accidents on the ground that they neither possess the nature of the whole which they accompany and which we call body, nor share in its permanent properties; and we must not think that they exist by themselves, since this is not conceivable for the accidents or for the properties. They must all be accepted as what they appear to be, namely accidents belonging to bodies, not permanent properties nor things having any place by themselves in nature; but they are seen to have just the character that our senses ascribe to them.

ii. Time presents a special problem. We cannot visualize it, and we can recognize it only as an accident of an event, which is itself an accident.

Before turning from this subject, we must carefully consider one more matter. Time is not to be sought for like other things that we seek in an underlying object by comparing them with the mental images that we look for in our own minds,* but we must consider the clear data of experience by virtue of which we distinguish between a long time and a short one, regarding the empirical data as closely allied to the concept of time. We need not search for better descriptions of time, but we must use the very ones that are at hand; nor need we assert that something else is of the same nature as this unique entity, as some indeed do; but we should take into consideration as of chief importance only the things with which we associate time and the ways in which we measure it. This requires no elaborate demonstration, only a review of the facts. We associate time with days and nights and their parts, and in the same way with changes in our own feelings and with motion and rest, recognizing that the very thing that we call time is in its turn a special sort of accident of these accidents.

---

*One can visualize an object or even a property or an accident in connection with an object, but one cannot visualize time.

VII. THE WORLDS

A. THE CREATION OF WORLDS

Each world was formed by being separated from its own whirling mass, and will be dissolved again.

In addition to what we have said, it is necessary to believe that the worlds* and every limited complex that has a continuous similarity to the visible world have been formed from the infinite, each of them, greater and smaller, separating out from its own whirling mass. We must suppose also that these will all be dissolved again, some more quickly and some more slowly, some afflicted by one calamity and others by another.

One must not suppose that because of necessity worlds in a single pattern were created, or in every possible pattern. . . .

B. FORMS OF LIFE IN THE WORLDS

We may assume animal and vegetable life in the other worlds similar to that on ours.

. . . Moreover, we may believe that in all the worlds there are animals, plants, and the other things we see; for no one can show that the seeds from which grow animals, plants, and the other things we see might or might not have been included in one particular world and that in another kind of world this was impossible.

VIII. THE DEVELOPMENT OF CIVILIZATION

A. THE ARTS AND CRAFTS

Instinct led men to the first developments, which reason then improved upon.

Moreover, we may assume that by the conditions that surround them, men were taught or forced by instinct to do many things of many kinds, but reason later elaborated on what had been begun by instinct and introduced new inventions. In some fields, great progress was made, in others, less; and in some times and ages reason had more success in freeing men from their fears of the powers above than in others.

B. LANGUAGE

Language was a natural development, differing in different tribes. Later, speech was clarified by deliberate selection.

So too we may suppose that in the beginning words did not receive meaning by design. The natural characters of men who underwent different experiences and re-

---

*Each world consists of an earth and the heavenly bodies associated with it. (Epicurus stated above that the number of worlds is infinite.)

ceived different impressions according to their tribes, caused them to emit air from their lips formed in harmony with each of the experiences and impressions, the men of each tribe differing in their own separate ways as the tribes differed because of their differing environments. But later in each race, by common agreement, men assigned particular meanings to particular sounds so that what they said to each other might be less ambiguous and the meaning be more quickly made clear. When men who had known them introduced certain things not previously seen, they assigned names to them, sometimes being forced instinctively to utter the word, but sometimes making their meaning clear by logically selecting the sound in accordance with the general usage.*

IX. THE PHENOMENA OF THE HEAVENS

A. CAUSES OF CELESTIAL PHENOMENA

No divinity directs the heavenly bodies, for this is inconsistent with divine happiness; nor are they themselves divine.

Now as to celestial phenomena, we must believe that these motions, periods, eclipses, risings, settings, and the like do not take place because there is some divinity in charge of them, who so arranges them in order and will maintain them in that order, and who at the same time enjoys both perfect happiness and immortality; for activity and anxiety, anger and kindness are not in harmony with blessedness, but are found along with weakness, fear, and dependence on one's neighbors. We must also avoid the belief that masses of concentrated fire have attained a state of divine blessedness and undertaken these motions of their own free will. In all the terms with which we set forth our conceptions of such blessedness, we must preserve due reverence lest from irreverent words there grow opinions that deny this majesty. If we fail, this contradiction will cause the greatest confusion in our souls. Therefore we must believe that, at the time of the first formation of these bodies at the creation of the world, the law of their motions was fully ordained.

B. PURPOSES OF, AND LIMITATIONS ON, THE STUDY OF CELESTIAL PHENOMENA

i. While knowledge of the general principles governing these matters is essential to our happiness, the study of the details is vain. We must accept the possibility of multiple causes.

Now we must accept the following beliefs: that to acquire exact knowledge about basic causes is the task of natural philosophy; that, as far as the heavenly bodies are concerned, our happiness depends on this basic knowledge and upon knowing the general nature of the visible phenomena of the heavens and whatever is necessary for certainty up to this point; that in these first principles there is neither multiformity nor any possibility of variation; and that in the immortal and blessed nature there is

---

*That is, by giving a name suggested by the similarity of the new thing to something that had already been named.

absolutely nothing that causes doubt and confusion. That these statements are true without qualification we can ascertain by reason. But we must also know that whatever belongs to the investigations of settings and risings, periods and eclipses, and the like—that this is of no import for the happiness that comes from knowledge; and that those who have learned these things but are ignorant of the original nature and the basic causes are subject to fears as great as if they knew nothing, or perhaps to even greater fears because the amazement that follows the study of these phenomena is not able to solve the problem of their relation to the essential principles.* Therefore, if we find that there are many possible causes for periods, settings, risings, eclipses, and the like, just as we found many possible causes in our investigation of details, we need not think that our investigation of these matters has not reached a certainty sufficient to secure for us peace of mind and happiness. We must search for the causes of celestial phenomena and in general of that which cannot be clearly perceived by first finding in how many ways similar phenomena are produced within the range of our senses; and we must pay no heed to those who, in the case of phenomena that can only be seen from a distance, fail to distinguish between that which is and remains single and that which may happen in many different ways,** and who do not know under what conditions it is possible and under what conditions impossible to achieve peace of mind. If we know this, that phenomena may take place in many ways, we shall be as little disturbed if we merely think it possible that a particular phenomenon happens in some particular way as we would be if we knew this as an absolute fact.

ii. Men imagine that the celestial bodies are divine yet ascribe to them purposes inconsistent with divinity; and they anticipate eternal suffering after death. Peace of mind follows freedom from such fears, and will be gained if we trust to our immediate feelings and sensations.

In addition to these general matters, we must observe this also, that there are three things that account for the major disturbances in men's minds. First, they assume that the celestial bodies are blessed and eternal yet have impulses, actions, and purposes quite inconsistent with divinity. Next, they anticipate and foresee eternal suffering as depicted in the myths, or even fear the very lack of consciousness that comes with death as if this could be of concern to them. Finally, they suffer all this, not as a result of reasonable conjecture, but through some sort of unreasoning imagination; and since in imagination they set no limit to suffering, they are beset by turmoil as great as if there were a reasonable basis for their dread, or even greater. But it is peace of mind to have been freed from all this and to have constantly in memory the essential principles of the whole system of belief. We must therefore turn our minds to immediate feelings and sensations***—in matters of general concern to the common feelings and sensations of mankind, in personal matters, to our own—and to every immediate evidence from each of the means of judgment. If we heed these, we shall rightly track down the sources of disturbance and fear, and when we have learned the causes of celestial phenomena and of the other occasional happenings, we shall be free from what other men most dread.

---

*Epicurus has in mind astrology and its effect upon its devotees.

**That is, between the basic principle (the atomic system), which is fixed and unalterable, and such observed phenomena as eclipses, which may be caused in different ways at different times and in different worlds.

***Our sensations lead to knowledge of what a thing is; our feelings, chiefly in terms of pleasure and pain, tell us what to seek and what to avoid, that is, what is good and what is evil.

X. CONCLUSION

This summary will be useful both for the beginner and also, as an easily remembered outline, for the more proficient.

Here then, Herodotus, you have the most important points in regard to natural science set down in such condensed form that this discourse may be accurately held in mind. I think that one who masters this, even if he does not progress to all the parts of a detailed study, will have very great strength compared with other men. He will also be able of himself to make clear many detailed points in regard to our system as a whole, and these general principles themselves will constantly aid him if he but hold them in memory. For these points are such that those who have made considerable progress and even those who are proficient in the detailed study, by solving their problems with reference to this survey, will make the greatest advances in the knowledge of the whole; and some of those who have made less progress toward perfect knowledge can, hastily and without oral instruction, run through the matters of most importance for peace of mind.

LETTER TO MENOECEUS

I. INTRODUCTION

Epicurus to Menoeceus, greeting.

Let no young man delay the study of philosophy, and let no old man become weary of it; for it is never too early nor too late to care for the well-being of the soul. The man who says that the season for this study has not yet come or is already past is like the man who says it is too early or too late for happiness. Therefore, both the young and the old should study philosophy, the former so that as he grows old he may still retain the happiness of youth in his pleasant memories of the past, the latter so that although he is old he may at the same time be young by virtue of his fearlessness of the future. We must therefore study the means of securing happiness, since if we have it we have everything, but if we lack it we do everything in order to gain it.

II. BASIC TEACHINGS

A. THE GODS

The gods exist; but it is impious to accept the common beliefs about them. They have no concern with men.

Epicurus, *Letters, Principal Doctrines, and Vatican Sayings,* translated by Russel M. Geer (New York: Macmillan/Library of the Liberal Arts, 1964).

Practice and study without ceasing that which I was always teaching you, being assured that these are the first principles of the good life. After accepting god as the immortal and blessed being depicted by popular opinion, do not ascribe to him anything in addition that is alien to immortality or foreign to blessedness, but rather believe about him whatever can uphold his blessed immortality. The gods do indeed exist, for our perception of them is clear; but they are not such as the crowd imagines them to be, for most men do not retain the picture of the gods that they first receive. It is not the man who destroys the gods of popular belief who is impious, but he who describes the gods in the terms accepted by the many. For the opinions of the many about the gods are not perceptions but false suppositions. According to these popular suppositions, the gods send great evils to the wicked, great blessings to the righteous, for they, being always well disposed to their own virtues, approve those who are like themselves, regarding as foreign all that is different.*

B. DEATH

Philosophy, showing that death is the end of all consciousness, relieves us of all fear of death. A life that is happy is better than one that is merely long.

Accustom yourself to the belief that death is of no concern to us, since all good and evil lie in sensation and sensation ends with death. Therefore the true belief that death is nothing to us makes a mortal life happy, not by adding to it an infinite time, but by taking away the desire for immortality. For there is no reason why the man who is thoroughly assured that there is nothing to fear in death should find anything to fear in life. So, too, he is foolish who says that he fears death, not because it will be painful when it comes, but because the anticipation of it is painful; for that which is no burden when it is present gives pain to no purpose when it is anticipated. Death, the most dreaded of evils, is therefore of no concern to us; for while we exist death is not present, and when death is present we no longer exist. It is therefore nothing either to the living or to the dead since it is not present to the living, and the dead no longer are.

But men in general sometimes flee death as the greatest of evils, sometimes long for it as a relief from the evils of life.

The wise man neither renounces life nor fears its end; for living does not offend him, nor does he suppose that not to live is in any way an evil. As he does not choose the food that is most in quantity but that which is most pleasant, so he does not seek the enjoyment of the longest life but of the happiest.

He who advises the young man to live well, the old man to die well, is foolish, not only because life is desirable, but also because the art of living well and the art of dying well are one. Yet much worse is he who says that it is well not to have been born, but once born, be swift to pass through Hades' gates.

If a man says this and really believes it, why does he not depart from life? Certainly the means are at hand for doing so if this really be his firm conviction. If he says it in mockery, he is regarded as a fool among those who do not accept his teaching.

Remember that the future is neither ours nor wholly not ours, so that we may neither count on it as sure to come nor abandon hope of it as certain not to be.

---

*The ambiguous rendition of the last part of this sentence is intentional. "They" may be the gods, who approve men like themselves, or men, who approve gods.

III. THE MORAL THEORY

A. PLEASURE AS THE MOTIVE

*The necessary desires are for health of body and peace of mind; if these are sat-
isfied, that is enough for the happy life.*

You must consider that of the desires some are natural, some are vain, and of
those that are natural, some are necessary, others only natural. Of the necessary desires, some are necessary for happiness, some for the ease of the body, some for life itself. The man who has a perfect knowledge of this will know how to make his every
choice or rejection tend toward gaining health of body and peace of mind, since this is
the final end of the blessed life. For to gain this end, namely freedom from pain and
fear, we do everything. When once this condition is reached, all the storm of the soul is
stilled, since the creature need make no move in search of anything that is lacking, nor
seek after anything else to make complete the welfare of the soul and the body. For we
only feel the lack of pleasure when from its absence we suffer pain; but when we do
not suffer pain, we no longer are in need of pleasure. For this reason we say that pleasure is the beginning and the end of the blessed life. We recognize pleasure as the first
and natural good; starting from pleasure we accept or reject; and we return to this as
we judge every good thing, trusting this feeling of pleasure as our guide.

B. PLEASURES AND PAINS

*Pleasure is the greatest good; but some pleasures bring pain, and in choosing,
we must consider this.*

For the very reason that pleasure is the chief and the natural good, we do not
choose every pleasure, but there are times when we pass by pleasures if they are outweighed by the hardships that follow; and many pains we think better than pleasures
when a greater pleasure will come to us once we have undergone the long-continued
pains. Every pleasure is a good since it has a nature akin to ours; nevertheless, not
every pleasure is to be chosen. Just so, every pain is an evil, yet not every pain is of a
nature to be avoided on all occasions. By measuring and by looking at advantages and
disadvantages, it is proper to decide all these things; for under certain circumstances
we treat the good as evil, and again, the evil as good.

C. SELF-SUFFICIENCY

The truly wise man is the one who can be happy with a little.

We regard self-sufficiency as a great good, not so that we may enjoy only a few
things, but so that, if we do not have many, we may be satisfied with the few, being
firmly persuaded that they take the greatest pleasure in luxury who regard it as least
needed, and that everything that is natural is easily provided, while vain pleasures are
hard to obtain. Indeed, simple sauces bring a pleasure equal to that of lavish banquets
if once the pain due to need is removed; and bread and water give the greatest pleasure
when one who is in need consumes them. To be accustomed to simple and plain living
is conducive to health and makes a man ready for the necessary tasks of life. It also

makes us more ready for the enjoyment of luxury if at intervals we chance to meet with it, and it renders us fearless against fortune.

D. TRUE PLEASURE

The truest happiness does not come from enjoyment of physical pleasures but from a simple life, free from anxiety, with the normal physical needs satisfied.

When we say that pleasure is the end, we do not mean the pleasure of the profligate or that which depends on physical enjoyment—as some think who do not understand our teachings, disagree with them, or give them an evil interpretation—but by pleasure we mean the state wherein the body is free from pain and the mind from anxiety. Neither continual drinking and dancing, nor sexual love, nor the enjoyment of fish and whatever else the luxurious table offers brings about the pleasant life; rather, it is produced by the reason which is sober, which examines the motive for every choice and rejection, and which drives away all those opinions through which the greatest tumult lays hold of the mind.

E. PRUDENCE

Prudence or practical wisdom should be our guide.

Of all this the beginning and the chief good is prudence. For this reason prudence is more precious than philosophy itself. All the other virtues spring from it. It teaches that it is not possible to live pleasantly without at the same time living prudently, nobly, and justly, nor to live prudently, nobly, and justly without living pleasantly; for the virtues have grown up in close union with the pleasant life, and the pleasant life cannot be separated from the virtues.

IV. CONCLUSION

A. PANEGYRIC* ON THE PRUDENT MAN

Whom then do you believe to be superior to the prudent man: he who has reverent opinions about the gods, who is wholly without fear of death, who has discovered what is the highest good in life and understands that the highest point in what is good is easy to reach and hold and that the extreme of evil is limited either in time or in suffering, and who laughs at that which some have set up as the ruler of all things, Necessity? He thinks that the chief power of decision lies within us, although some things come about by necessity, some by chance, and some by our own wills; for he sees that necessity is irresponsible and chance uncertain, but that our actions are subject to no power. It is for this reason that our actions merit praise or blame. It would be better to accept the myth about the gods than to be a slave to the determinism of the physicists; for the myth hints at a hope for grace through honors paid to the gods,

*[Formal praise for a festival]

but the necessity of determinism is inescapable. Since the prudent man does not, as do many, regard chance as a god for the gods do nothing in disorderly fashion or as an unstable cause of all things, he believes that chance does not give man good and evil to make his life happy or miserable, but that it does provide opportunities for great good or evil. Finally, he thinks it better to meet misfortune while acting with reason than to happen upon good fortune while acting senselessly; for it is better that what has been well-planned in our actions should fail than that what has been ill-planned should gain success by chance.

B. FINAL WORDS TO MENOECEUS

Meditate on these and like precepts, by day and by night, alone or with a like-minded friend. Then never, either awake or asleep, will you be dismayed; but you will live like a god among men; for life amid immortal blessings is in no way like the life of a mere mortal.

PRINCIPAL DOCTRINES

I. That which is blessed and immortal is not troubled itself, nor does it cause trouble to another. As a result, it is not affected by anger or favor, for these belong to weakness.

II. Death is nothing to us; for what has been dissolved has no sensation, and what has no sensation is nothing to us.

III. The removal of all that causes pain marks the boundary of pleasure. Wherever pleasure is present and as long as it continues, there is neither suffering nor grieving nor both together.

IV. Continuous bodily suffering does not last long. Intense pain is very brief, and even pain that barely outweighs physical pleasure does not last many days. Long illnesses permit physical pleasures that are greater than the pain.

V. It is impossible to live pleasantly without living prudently, well, and justly, and to live prudently, well, and justly without living pleasantly. Even though a man live well and justly, it is not possible for him to live pleasantly if he lacks that from which stems the prudent life.

VI. Any device whatever by which one frees himself from the fear of others is a natural good.

VII. Some, thinking thus to make themselves safe from men, wished to become famous and renowned. They won a natural good if they made their lives secure; but if their lives were not secure, they did not have that for which, following the rule of nature, they first sought.

VIII. No pleasure is evil in itself; but the means by which certain pleasures are gained bring pains many times greater than the pleasures.

Epicurus, *Letters, Principal Doctrines, and Vatican Sayings,* translated by Russel M. Geer (New York: Macmillan/Library of the Liberal Arts, 1964).

IX. If every pleasure were cumulative, and if this were the case both in time and in regard to the whole or the most important parts of our nature, then pleasures would not differ from each other.

X. If the things that produce the pleasures of the dissolute were able to drive away from their minds their fears about what is above them and about death and pain, and to teach them the limit of desires, we would have no reason to find fault with the dissolute; for they would fill themselves with pleasure from every source and would be free from pain and sorrow, which are evil.

XI. If our dread of the phenomena above us, our fear lest death concern us, and our inability to discern the limits of pains and desires were not vexatious to us, we would have no need of the natural sciences.

XII. It is not possible for one to rid himself of his fears about the most important things if he does not understand the nature of the universe but dreads some of the things he has learned in the myths. Therefore, it is not possible to gain unmixed happiness without natural science.

XIII. It is of no avail to prepare security against other men while things above us and beneath the earth and in the whole infinite universe in general are still dreaded.

XIV. When reasonable security from men has been attained, then the security that comes from peace of mind and withdrawal from the crowd is present, sufficient in strength and most unmixed in well-being.

XV. Natural wealth is limited and easily obtained; the wealth defined by vain fancies is always beyond reach.

XVI. Fortune seldom troubles the wise man. Reason has controlled his greatest and most important affairs, controls them throughout his life, and will continue to control them.

XVII. The just man is least disturbed; the unjust man is filled with the greatest turmoil.

XVIII. When once the pain caused by need has been removed, bodily pleasure will not be increased in amount but only varied in quality. The mind attains its utmost pleasure in reflecting on the very things that used to cause the greatest mental fears and on things like them.

XIX. Time that is unlimited and time that is limited afford equal pleasure if one measures pleasure's extent by reason.

XX. The flesh believes that pleasure is limitless and that it requires unlimited time; but the mind, understanding the end and limit of the flesh and ridding itself of fears of the future, secures a complete life and has no longer any need for unlimited time. It does not, however, avoid pleasure; and when circumstances bring on the end of life, it does not depart as if it still lacked any portion of the good life.

XXI. The man who understands the limits of living knows that it is easy to obtain that which removes the pain caused by want and that which perfects the whole life. Therefore, he has no need of things that involve struggle.

XXII. It is necessary to take into account the real purpose of knowledge and all the evidence of that clear perception to which we refer our opinions. If we do not, all will be full of bad judgment and confusion.

XXIII. If you struggle against all your sensations, you will have no standard of comparison by which to measure even the sensations you judge false.

XXIV. If you reject any sensation, and if you fail to distinguish between conjecture based upon that which awaits confirmation and evidence given by the senses, by the feelings, and by the mental examinations of confirmed concepts, you will confuse the other sensations with unfounded conjecture and thus destroy the whole basis for judgment. If among all opinions you accept as equally valid both those that await confirmation and those that have been confirmed, you will not free yourself from error, since you will have preserved all the uncertainty about every judgment of what is true and what is not true.

XXV. If you do not at all times refer each of your actions to the natural end,* but fall short of this and turn aside to something else in choosing and avoiding, your deeds will not agree with your words.

XXVI. Those desires that do not bring pain if they are not satisfied are not necessary; and they are easily thrust aside whenever to satisfy them appears difficult or likely to cause injury.

XXVII. Of the things that wisdom prepares for insuring lifelong happiness, by far the greatest is the possession of friends.

XXVIII. The same wisdom that permits us to be confident that no evil is eternal or even of long duration also recognizes that in our limited state the security that can be most perfectly gained is that of friendship.

XXIX. Of the desires, some are natural and necessary; some are natural but not necessary; and others are neither natural nor necessary but arise from empty opinion.

XXX. Among the bodily desires, those rest on empty opinion that are eagerly pursued although if unsatisfied they bring no pain. That they are not got rid of is because of man's empty opinion, not because of their own nature.

XXXI. Natural justice is a compact resulting from expediency by which men seek to prevent one man from injuring others and to protect him from being injured by them.

XXXII. There is no such thing as justice or injustice among those beasts that cannot make agreements not to injure or be injured. This is also true of those tribes that are unable or unwilling to make agreements not to injure or be injured.

XXXIII. There is no such thing as justice in the abstract; it is merely a compact between men in their various relations with each other, in whatever circumstances they may be, that they will neither injure nor be injured.

XXXIV. Injustice is not evil in itself, but only in the fear and apprehension that one will not escape those who have been set up to punish the offense.

XXXV. If a man has secretly violated any of the terms of the mutual compact not to injure or be injured, he cannot feel confident that he will be undetected in the future even if he has escaped ten thousand times in the past; for until his death it will remain uncertain whether he will escape.

XXXVI. In general, justice is the same for all, a thing found useful by men in their relations with each other; but it does not follow that it is the same for all in each individual place and circumstance.

XXXVII. Among the things commonly held just, that which has proved itself useful in men's mutual relationships has the stamp of justice whether or not it be the same for all; if anyone makes a law and it does not prove useful in men's relationships with each other, it is no longer just in its essence. If, however, the law's usefulness in the matter of justice should change and it should meet men's expectations only for a short time, nonetheless during that short time it was just in the eyes of those who look simply at facts and do not confuse themselves with empty words.

*That is, to pleasure.

XXXVIII. If, although no new circumstances have arisen, those things that were commonly held just in these matters did not in their actual effects correspond with that conception, they were not just. Whenever, as a result of new circumstances, the same things that had been regarded as just were no longer useful, they were just at the time when they were useful for the relations of citizens to each other; but afterwards, when they were no longer useful, they were no longer just.

XXXIX. He who has best controlled his lack of confidence in the face of external forces has, as far as possible, treated these externals as akin to himself or, when that was impossible, at least as not alien. Where he was not able to do even this, he kept to himself and avoided whatever it was best to avoid.

XL. Those who were best able to prepare security for themselves in relation to their neighbors* lived most pleasantly with their neighbors since they had the most perfect assurance; and enjoying the most complete intimacy, they did not lament the death of one who died before his time as if it were an occasion for sorrow.

---

*That is, those who were most self-sufficient and least dependent upon others

The Early Stoa:

ZENO OF CITIUM
ca. 336–ca. 265 B.C.

CLEANTHES
ca. 331–ca. 233 B.C.

Zeno was born in the small town of Citium on the island of Cyprus. As a young man he moved to Athens, where, it is said, he discovered philosophy by reading Xenophon's description of Socrates, the *Memorabilia*. Socrates being long dead, Zeno attached himself for some time to the Cynics. Zeno agreed with the Cynics that self-control over emotions was essential to a virtuous life. Zeno was also attracted to the teachings of Heraclitus—particularly to the Heraclitean notion of an eternal fire or *Logos* that controls the universe. Sometime around 300 B.C., Zeno set up a school of philosophy in the Painted Porch <*stoa poikile*>, a school that came to be known as "Stoic." His Stoic school may have been established specifically to counter the philosophy of Epicurus. At any rate, he argued that virtue, not pleasure, was the only good, and that natural law, not the random swerving of atoms, was the key principle of the universe. While teaching at his school, Zeno read widely and was greatly respected for his learning, his character, and the simplicity of his life. A severe and austere man, he was, like some of the Pre-Socratics, a sage as well as a philosopher. Zeno believed strongly in divine signs. He is said to have committed suicide after breaking his toe on a rock, believing the incident to be a sign of God's will.

Like Epicurus before him, Zeno divided philosophy into logic (including the theory of knowledge), physics, and ethics. In their discussions of logic, Zeno and his followers examined at great length the relationships among words, their meanings, and the objects to which they refer. They developed several subtle distinctions that are still examined and discussed today (see the suggested readings). They also developed an understanding of sensory knowledge based on impressions that was similar to the theories of Epicurus.

In physics, Zeno developed an elaborate cosmology that includes both a passive and an active principle. The passive principle is matter, while the active principle is the "fiery breath" *<pneuma>*, known by such names as god, mind, fate, Zeus, and *Logos*. This active principle is not separate from the world, but permeates it, molding passive matter into an ordered universe. Permeating everything, god/mind directs the course of affairs and connects all parts into one whole, like a giant organism. The key to ethics for Zeno and his disciples is to live in harmony with this active principle. This requires both the wisdom to know what part we are to play and the "apathy" *<apatheia>*, or avoidance of strong emotions, to accept what we cannot change. Happiness, or more accurately, contentment, is possible in any condition. In fact, among prominent later Stoics, Epictetus was born a slave, whereas Marcus Aurelius was a Roman emperor.

The selection here is from Diogenes Laertius's *Lives of Eminent Philosophers,* in which Laertius summarizes Stoic ethics and physics. It should be noted that Laertius refers not only to Zeno and Cleanthes, but also to Chrysippus, Cleanthes' successor at the Stoa, and to the later Stoics Archedemus and Posidonius. The translation is that of R.D. Hicks.

Cleanthes was born in Assos and raised in Athens. He too studied first with the Cynics before becoming a disciple of Zeno at the Stoa. Following Zeno's death, Cleanthes became head of the Stoic school. Unlike his master, Cleanthes was known as a gentle man with great patience. He was like his master in another respect, however—he too is reported to have killed himself. Cleanthes is best known for his "Hymn to Zeus," a strong tribute to nature's orderliness and benevolence. The translation is that of James Adam.

*   *   *

For general introductions to the Stoics, see E. Vernon Arnold, *Roman Stoicism* (1911; reprinted New York: Humanities Press, 1958); L. Edelstein, *The Meaning of Stoicism* (Cambridge, MA: Harvard University Press, 1966); John M. Rist, *Stoic Philosophy* (Cambridge: Cambridge University Press, 1969); F.H. Sandbach, *The Stoics* (New York: Norton, 1975); and Margaret E. Reeser, *The Nature of Man in Early Stoic Philosophy* (New York: St. Martin's Press, 1989). For comparisons between Stoicism and other Hellenistic schools, see R.M. Wenley, *Stoicism and Its Influence* (1924; reprinted New York: Cooper Square, 1963); Edwin R. Bevan, *Stoics and Sceptics* (Oxford: Clarendon Press, 1913); and R.D. Hicks, *Stoic and Epicurean* (1910; reprinted New York: Russell and Russell, 1962). For collections of essays consult A.A. Long, ed., *Problems in Stoicism* (London: Athlone Press, 1971); J.M. Rist, ed., *The Stoics* (Berkeley: University of California Press, 1978); and A.A. Long, ed., *Stoic Studies* (Cambridge: Cambridge University Press, 1996). For specialized studies, consult Benson Mates, *Stoic Logic* (Berkeley: University of California Press, 1953); Samuel Sambursky, *Physics of the Stoics* (London: Russell, 1959); and Gerard Watson, *The Stoic Theory of Knowledge* (Belfast: Queen's University, 1966).

ZENO OF CITIUM (selections from Diogenes Laertius)

ETHICS

An animal's first impulse, say the Stoics, is to self-preservation, because nature from the outset endears it to itself, as Chrysippus affirms in the first book of his work *On Ends:* his words are, "The dearest thing to every animal is its own constitution and its consciousness thereof"; for it was not likely that nature should estrange the living thing from itself or that she should leave the creature she has made without either estrangement from or affection for its own constitution. We are forced then to conclude that nature in constituting the animal made it near and dear to itself; for so it comes to repel all that is injurious and give free access to all that is serviceable or akin to it.

As for the assertion made by some people that pleasure is the object to which the first impulse of animals is directed, it is shown by the Stoics to be false. For pleasure, if it is really felt, they declare to be a by-product, which never comes until nature by itself has sought and found the means suitable to the animal's existence or constitution; it is an aftermath comparable to the condition of animals thriving and plants in full bloom. And nature, they say, made no difference originally between plants and animals, for she regulates the life of plants too, in their case without impulse and sensation, just as also certain processes go on of a vegetative kind in us. But when in the case of animals impulse has been superadded, whereby they are enabled to go in quest of their proper aliment, for them, say the Stoics, Nature's rule is to follow the direction of impulse. But when reason by way of a more perfect leadership has been bestowed on the beings we call rational, for them life according to reason rightly becomes the natural life. For reason supervenes to shape impulse scientifically.

This is why Zeno was the first (in his treatise *On the Nature of Man*) to designate as the end "life in agreement with nature" (or living agreeably to nature), which is the same as a virtuous life, virtue being the goal towards which nature guides us. So too Cleanthes in his treatise *On Pleasure,* as also Posidonius, and Hecato in his work *On Ends.* Again, living virtuously is equivalent to living in accordance with experience of the actual course of nature, as Chrysippus says in the first book of his *De finibus;* for our individual natures are parts of the nature of the whole universe. And this is why the end may be defined as life in accordance with nature, or, in other words, in accordance with our own human nature as well as that of the universe, a life in which we refrain from every action forbidden by the law common to all things, that is to say, the right reason which pervades all things, and is identical with this Zeus, lord and ruler of all that is. And this very thing constitutes the virtue of the happy man and the smooth current of life, when all actions promote the harmony of the spirit dwelling in the individual man with the will of him who orders the universe. Diogenes then expressly declares the end to be to act with good reason in the selection of what is natural. Archedemus says the end is to live in the performance of all befitting actions.

Reprinted by permission of the publishers and the Loeb Classical Library from Diogenes Laertius, *Lives of Eminent Philosophers,* Volume II, translated by R.D. Hicks (Cambridge, MA: Harvard University Press, 1925). Copyright © 1925 by Harvard University Press.

Stoa Poikile, or the Painted Porch, where Zeno of Citrium first taught (as reconstructed). *(American School of Classical Studies)*

By the nature with which our life ought to be in accord, Chrysippus understands both universal nature and more particularly the nature of man, whereas Cleanthes takes the nature of the universe alone as that which should be followed, without adding the nature of the individual.

And virtue, he holds, is a harmonious disposition, choice-worthy for its own sake and not from hope or fear or any external motive. Moreover, it is in virtue that happiness consists; for virtue is the state of mind which tends to make the whole of life harmonious. When a rational being is perverted, this is due to the deceptiveness of external pursuits or sometimes to the influence of associates. For the starting-points of nature are never perverse.

*   *   *

They hold the emotions to be judgements, as is stated by Chrysippus in his treatise *On the Passions:* avarice being a supposition that money is a good, while the case is similar with drunkenness and profligacy and all the other emotions.

And grief or pain they hold to be an irrational mental contraction. Its species are pity, envy, jealousy, rivalry, heaviness, annoyance, distress, anguish, distraction. Pity is grief felt at undeserved suffering; envy, grief at others' prosperity; jealousy, grief at the possession by another of that which one desires for oneself; rivalry, pain at the possession by another of what one has oneself. Heaviness or vexation is grief which weighs us down, annoyance that which coops us up and straitens us for want of room, distress a pain brought on by anxious thought that lasts and increases, anguish painful grief, distraction irrational grief, rasping and hindering us from viewing the situation as a whole.

Fear is an expectation of evil. Under fear are ranged the following emotions: terror, nervous shrinking, shame, consternation, panic, mental agony. Terror is a fear which produces fright; shame is fear of disgrace; nervous shrinking is a fear that one will have to act; consternation is fear due to a presentation of some unusual occurrence; panic is fear with pressure exercised by sound; mental agony is fear felt when some issue is still in suspense.

Desire or craving is irrational appetency, and under it are ranged the following states: want, hatred, contentiousness, anger, love, wrath, resentment. Want, then, is a craving when it is baulked and, as it were, cut off from its object, but kept at full stretch and attracted towards it in vain. Hatred is a growing and lasting desire or craving that it should go ill with somebody. Contentiousness is a craving or desire connected with partisanship; anger a craving or desire to punish one who is thought to have done you an undeserved injury. The passion of love is a craving from which good men are free; for it is an effort to win affection due to the visible presence of beauty. Wrath is anger which has long rankled and has become malicious, waiting for its opportunity, as is illustrated by the lines:

> Even though for the one day he swallow his anger, yet doth he still keep his displeasure thereafter in his heart, till he accomplish it.*

Resentment is anger in an early stage.

Pleasure is an irrational elation at the accruing of what seems to be choiceworthy; and under it are ranged ravishment, malevolent joy, delight, transport. Ravishment is pleasure which charms the ear. Malevolent joy is pleasure at another's ills. Delight is the mind's propulsion to weakness, its name in Greek <terpsis> being akin to <trepsis> or turning. To be in transports of delight is the melting away of virtue.

And as there are said to be certain infirmities in the body, as for instance gout and arthritic disorders, so too there is in the soul love of fame, love of pleasure, and the like. By infirmity is meant disease accompanied by weakness; and by disease is meant a fond imagining of something that seems desirable. And as in the body there are tendencies to certain maladies such as colds and diarrhea, so it is with the soul, there are tendencies like enviousness, pitifulness, quarrelsomeness, and the like.

Also they say that there are three emotional states which are good, namely, joy, caution, and wishing. Joy, the counterpart of pleasure, is rational elation; caution, the counterpart of fear, rational avoidance; for though the wise man will never feel fear, he will yet use caution. And they make wishing the counterpart of desire (or craving), inasmuch as it is rational appetency. And accordingly, as under the primary passions are classed certain others subordinate to them, so too is it with the primary eupathies or good emotional states. Thus under wishing they bring well-wishing or benevolence, friendliness, respect, affection; under caution, reverence and modesty; under joy, delight, mirth, cheerfulness.

Now they say that the wise man is passionless, because he is not prone to fall into such infirmity. But they add that in another sense the term apathy is applied to the bad man, when, that is, it means that he is callous and relentless. Further, the wise man is said to be free from vanity; for he is indifferent to good or evil report. However, he

*Iliad, I. 81, 82.

is not alone in this, there being another who is also free from vanity, he who is ranged among the rash, and that is the bad man. Again, they tell us that all good men are austere or harsh, because they neither have dealings with pleasure themselves nor tolerate those who have. The term harsh is applied, however, to others as well, and in much the same sense as a wine is said to be harsh when it is employed medicinally and not for drinking at all.

Again, the good are genuinely in earnest and vigilant for their own improvement, using a manner of life which banishes evil out of sight and makes what good there is in things appear. At the same time they are free from pretence; for they have stripped off all pretence or "make-up" whether in voice or in look. Free too are they from all business cares, declining to do anything which conflicts with duty. They will take wine, but not get drunk. Nay more, they will not be liable to madness either; not but what there will at times occur to the good man strange impressions due to melancholy or delirium, ideas not determined by the principle of what is choice-worthy but contrary to nature. Nor indeed will the wise man ever feel grief; seeing that grief is irrational contraction of the soul, as Apollodorus says in his *Ethics*.

*　*　*

It is also their doctrine that amongst the wise there should be a community of wives with free choice of partners, as Zeno says in his Republic and Chrysippus in his treatise *On Government* [and not only they, but also Diogenes the Cynic and Plato]. Under such circumstances we shall feel paternal affection for all the children alike, and there will be an end of the jealousies arising from adultery. The best form of government they hold to be a mixture of democracy, kingship, and aristocracy (or the rule of the best).

Such, then, are the statements they make in their ethical doctrines, with much more besides, together with their proper proofs: let this, however, suffice for a statement of them in a summary and elementary form.

PHYSICS

Their physical doctrine they divide into sections (1) about bodies; (2) about principles; (3) about elements; (4) about the gods; (5) about bounding surfaces and space whether filled or empty. This is a division into species; but the generic division is into three parts, dealing with (i) the universe; (ii) the elements; (iii) the subject of causation.

The part dealing with the universe admits, they say, of division into two: for with one aspect of it the mathematicians also are concerned, in so far as they treat questions relating to the fixed stars and the planets, *e.g.* whether the sun is not just so large as it appears to be, and the same about the moon, the question of their revolutions, and other inquiries of the same sort. But there is another aspect or field of cosmological inquiry, which belongs to the physicists alone: this includes such questions as what the substance of the universe is, whether the sun and the stars are made up of forms and matter, whether the world has had a beginning in time or not, whether it is animate or inanimate, whether it is destructible or indestructible, whether it is governed by providence, and all the rest. The part concerned with causation, again, is itself subdivided into two. And in one of its aspects medical inquiries have a share in it, in so far as it involves investigation of the ruling principle of the soul and the phenomena of soul, seeds, and the like. Whereas the other part is claimed by the mathematicians also, *e.g.* how vision is to be explained, what causes the image on the mirror, what is the origin of clouds, thunder, rainbows, halos, comets, and the like.

They hold that there are two principles in the universe, the active principle and the passive. The passive principle, then, is a substance without quality, *i.e.* matter, whereas the active is the reason inherent in this substance, that is God. For he is everlasting and is the artificer of each several thing throughout the whole extent of matter. This doctrine is laid down by Zeno of Citium in his treatise *On Existence,* Cleanthes in his work *On Atoms,* Chrysippus in the first book of his *Physics* towards the end, Archedemus in his treatise *On Elements,* and Posidonius in the second book of his *Physical Exposition.* There is a difference, according to them, between principles and elements; the former being without generation or destruction, whereas the elements are destroyed when all things are resolved into fire. Moreover, the principles are incorporeal and destitute of form, while the elements have been endowed with form.

Body is defined by Apollodorus in his *Physics* as that which is extended in three dimensions, length, breadth, and depth. This is also called solid body. But surface is the extremity of a solid body, or that which has length and breadth only without depth. That surface exists not only in our thought but also in reality is maintained by Posidonius in the third book of his *Celestial Phenomena.* A line is the extremity of a surface or length without breadth, or that which has length alone. A point is the extremity of a line, the smallest possible mark or dot.

God is one and the same with Reason, Fate, and Zeus; he is also called by many other names. In the beginning he was by himself; he transformed the whole of substance through air into water, and just as in animal generation the seed has a moist vehicle, so in cosmic moisture God, who is the seminal reason of the universe, remains behind in the moisture as such an agent, adapting matter to himself with a view to the next stage of creation. Thereupon he created first of all the four elements, fire, water, air, earth. They are discussed by Zeno in his treatise *On the Whole,* by Chrysippus in the first book of his *Physics,* and by Archedemus in a work *On Elements.* An element is defined as that from which particular things first come to be at their birth and into which they are finally resolved. The four elements together constitute unqualified substance or matter. Fire is the hot element, water the moist, air the cold, earth the dry. Not but what the quality of dryness is also found in the air. Fire has the uppermost place; it is also called aether, and in it the sphere of the fixed stars is first created; then comes the sphere of the planets, next to that the air, then the water, and lowest of all the earth, which is at the centre of all things.

The term universe or cosmos is used by them in three senses: (1) of God himself, the individual being whose quality is derived from the whole of substance; he is indestructible and ingenerable, being the artificer of this orderly arrangement, who at stated periods of time absorbs into himself the whole of substance and again creates it from himself. (2) Again, they give the name of cosmos to the orderly arrangement of the heavenly bodies in itself as such; and (3) in the third place to that whole of which these two are parts. Again, the cosmos is defined as the individual being qualifying the whole of substance, or, in the words of Posidonius in his elementary treatise on *Celestial Phenomena,* a system made up of heaven and earth and the natures in them, or, again, as a system constituted by gods and men and all things created for their sake. By heaven is meant the extreme circumference or ring in which the deity has his seat.

The world, in their view, is ordered by reason and providence: so says Chrysippus in the fifth book of his treatise *On Providence* and Posidonius in his work *On the*

Gods, book iii—inasmuch as reason pervades every part of it, just as does the soul in us. Only there is a difference of degree; in some parts there is more of it, in others less. For through some parts it passes as a "hold" or containing force, as is the case with our bones and sinews; while through others it passes as intelligence, as in the ruling part of the soul. Thus, then, the whole world is a living being, endowed with soul and reason, and having aether for its ruling principle: so says Antipater of Tyre in the eighth book of his treatise *On the Cosmos.* Chrysippus in the first book of his work *On Providence* and Posidonius in his book *On the Gods* say that the heaven, but Cleanthes that the sun, is the ruling power of the world. Chrysippus, however, in the course of the same work gives a somewhat different account, namely, that it is the purer part of the aether; the same which they declare to be preeminently God and always to have, as it were in sensible fashion, pervaded all that is in the air, all animals and plants, and also the earth itself, as a principle of cohesion.

The world, they say, is one and finite, having a spherical shape, such a shape being the most suitable for motion, as Posidonius says in the fifth book of his *Physical Discourse* and the disciples of Antipater in their works on the Cosmos. Outside of the world is diffused the infinite void, which is incorporeal. By incorporeal is meant that which, though capable of being occupied by body, is not so occupied. The world has no empty space within it, but forms one united whole. This is a necessary result of the sympathy and tension which binds together things in heaven and earth. Chrysippus discusses the void in his work *On Void* and in the first book of his *Physical Sciences;* so too Apollophanes in his *Physics,* Apollodorus, and Posidonius in his *Physical Discourse,* book ii. But these, it is added [*i.e.* sympathy and tension], are likewise bodies.

Time too is incorporeal, being the measure of the world's motion. And time past and time future are infinite, but time present is finite. They hold that the world must come to an end, inasmuch as it had a beginning, on the analogy of those things which are understood by the senses. And that of which the parts are perishable is perishable as a whole. Now the parts of the world are perishable, seeing that they are transformed one into the other. Therefore the world itself is doomed to perish. Moreover, anything is destructible if it admits of deterioration; therefore the world is so, for it is first evaporated and again dissolved into water.

The world, they hold, comes into being when its substance has first been converted from fire through air into moisture and then the coarser part of the moisture has condensed as earth, while that whose particles are fine has been turned into air, and this process of rarefaction goes on increasing till it generates fire. Thereupon out of these elements animals and plants and all other natural kinds are formed by their mixture. The generation and the destruction of the world are discussed by Zeno in his treatise *On the Whole,* by Chrysippus in the first book of his *Physics,* by Posidonius in the first book of his work *On the Cosmos,* by Cleanthes, and by Antipater in his tenth book *On the Cosmos.* Panaetius, however, maintained that the world is indestructible.

The doctrine that the world is a living being, rational, animate, and intelligent, is laid down by Chrysippus in the first book of his treatise *On Providence,* by Apollodorus in his *Physics,* and by Posidonius. It is a living thing in the sense of an animate substance endowed with sensation; for animal is better than non-animal, and nothing is better than the world, ergo the world is a living being. And it is endowed with soul, as is clear from our several souls being each a fragment of it. Boëthus, however, denies that the world is a living thing. The unity of the world is maintained by Zeno in his treatise *On the Whole,* by Chrysippus, by Apollodorus in his *Physics,* and by Posidonius in the first book of his *Physical Discourse.* By the totality of things, the All, is meant, according to Apollodorus, (1) the world, and in another sense (2) the system composed of the world and the void outside it. The world then is finite, the void infinite.

Of the stars some are fixed, and are carried round with the whole heaven; others, the wandering stars or planets, have their special motions. The sun travels in an oblique path through the zodiac. Similarly the moon travels in a spiral path. The sun is pure fire: so Posidonius in the seventh book of his *Celestial Phenomena.* And it is larger than the earth, as the same author says in the sixth book of his *Physical Discourse.* Moreover it is spherical in shape like the world itself according to this same author and his school. That it is fire is proved by its producing all the effects of fire; that it is larger than the earth by the fact that all the earth is illuminated by it; nay more, the heaven beside. The fact too that the earth casts a conical shadow proves that the sun is greater than it. And it is because of its great size that it is seen from every part of the earth.

The moon, however, is of a more earthy composition, since it is nearer to the earth. These fiery bodies and the stars generally derive their nutriment, the sun from the wide ocean, being a fiery kindling, though intelligent; the moon from fresh waters, with an admixture of air, close to the earth as it is: thus Posidonius in the sixth book of his *Physics;* the other heavenly bodies being nourished from the earth. They hold that the stars are spherical in shape and that the earth too is so and is at rest; and that the moon does not shine by her own light, but by the borrowed light of the sun when he shines upon her.

An eclipse of the sun takes place when the moon passes in front of it on the side towards us, as shown by Zeno with a diagram in his treatise *On the Whole.* For the moon is seen approaching at conjunctions and occulting it and then again receding from it. This can best be observed when they are mirrored in a basin of water. The moon is eclipsed when she falls into the earth's shadow: for which reason it is only at the full moon that an eclipse happens [and not always then], although she is in opposition to the sun every month; because the moon moves in an oblique orbit, diverging in latitude relatively to the orbit of the sun, and she accordingly goes farther to the north or to the south. When, however, the moon's motion in latitude has brought her into the sun's path through the zodiac, and she thus comes diametrically opposite to the sun, there is an eclipse. Now the moon is in latitude right on the zodiac, when she is in the constellations of Cancer, Scorpio, Aries and Taurus: so Posidonius and his followers tell us.

The deity, say they, is a living being, immortal, rational, perfect or intelligent in happiness, admitting nothing evil [into him], taking providential care of the world and all that therein is, but he is not of human shape. He is, however, the artificer of the universe and, as it were, the father of all, both in general and in that particular part of him which is all-pervading, and which is called many names according to its various powers. They give the name Dia <*Dia*> because all things are due to <*dia*> him; Zeus <*Zana*> in so far as he is the cause of life <*zan*> or pervades all life; the name Athena is given, because the ruling part of the divinity extends to the aether; the name Hera marks its extension to the air; he is called Hephaestus since it spreads to the creative fire; Poseidon, since it stretches to the sea; Demeter, since it reaches to the earth. Similarly men have given the deity his other titles, fastening, as best they can, on some one or other of his peculiar attributes.

The substance of God is declared by Zeno to be the whole world and the heaven, as well as by Chrysippus in his first book *Of the Gods,* and by Posidonius in his first book with the same title. Again, Antipater in the seventh book of his work *On the Cosmos* says that the substance of God is akin to air, while Boëthus in his work *On Nature* speaks of the sphere of the fixed stars as the substance of God. Now the term Nature is used by them to mean sometimes that which holds the world together, sometimes that which causes terrestrial things to spring up. Nature defined as a force moving of itself, producing and preserving in being its offspring in accordance with seminal principles within definite periods, and effecting results homogeneous with their sources. Nature, they hold, aims both at utility and at pleasure, as is clear from the analogy of human craftsmanship. That all things happen by fate or destiny is maintained by Chrysippus in his treatise *De fato,* by Posidonius in his *De fato,* book ii, by Zeno and by Boëthus in his *De fato,* book i. Fate is defined as an endless chain of causation, whereby things are, or as the reason or formula by which the world goes on. What is more, they say that divination in all its forms is a real and substantial fact, if there is really Providence. And they prove it to be actually a science on the evidence of certain results: so Zeno, Chrysippus in the second book of his *De divinatione,* Athenodorus, and Posidonius in the second book of his *Physical Discourse* and the fifth book of his *De divinatione.* But Panaetius denies that divination has any real existence.

The primary matter they make the substratum of all things: so Chrysippus in the first book of his *Physics,* and Zeno. By matter is meant that out of which anything whatsoever is produced. Both substance and matter are terms used in a twofold sense according as they signify (1) universal or (2) particular substance or matter. The former neither increases nor diminishes, while the matter of particular things both increases and diminishes. Body according to them is substance which is finite: so Antipater in his second book *On Substance,* and Apollodorus in his *Physics.* Matter can also be acted upon, as the same author says, for if it were immutable, the things which are produced would never have been produced out of it. Hence the further doctrine that matter is divisible *ad infinitum.* Chrysippus says that the division is not *ad infinitum,* but itself infinite; for there is nothing infinitely small to which the division can extend. But nevertheless the division goes on without ceasing.

Hence, again, their explanation of the mixture of two substances is, according to Chrysippus in the third book of his *Physics,* that they permeate each other through and through, and that the particles of the one do not merely surround those of the other or lie beside them. Thus, if a little drop of wine be thrown into the sea, it will be equally diffused over the whole sea for a while and then will be blended with it.

Also they hold that there are daemons *<daimones>* who are in sympathy with mankind and watch over human affairs. They believe too in heroes, that is, the souls of the righteous that have survived their bodies.

Of the changes which go on in the air, they describe winter as the cooling of the air above the earth due to the sun's departure to a distance from the earth; spring as the right temperature of the air consequent upon his approach to us; summer as the heating of the air above the earth when he travels to the north; while autumn they attribute to the receding of the sun from us. As for the winds, they are streams of air, differently named according to the localities from which they blow. And the cause of their production is the sun through the evaporation of the clouds. The rainbow is explained as the reflection of the sun's rays from watery clouds or, as Posidonius says in his *Meteorology,* an image of a segment of the sun or moon in a cloud suffused with dew, which is hollow and visible without intermission, the image showing itself as if in a mirror in the form of a circular arch. Comets, bearded stars, and meteors are fires which arise when dense air is carried up to the region of aether. A shooting star is the sudden kindling of a mass of fire in rapid motion through the air, which leaves a trail behind it presenting an appearance of length. Rain is the transformation of cloud into water, when moisture drawn up by the sun from land or sea has been only partially evaporated. If this is cooled down, it is called hoar-frost. Hail is frozen cloud, crumbled by a wind; while snow is moist matter from a cloud which has congealed: so Posidonius in the eighth book of his *Physical Discourse.* Lightning is a kindling of clouds from being rubbed together or being rent by wind, as Zeno says in his treatise *On the Whole;* thunder the noise these clouds make when they rub against each other or burst. Thunderbolt is the term used when the fire is violently kindled and hurled to the ground with great force as the clouds grind against each other or are torn by the wind. Others say that it is a compression of fiery air descending with great force. A typhoon is a great and violent thunderstorm whirlwind-like, or a whirlwind of smoke from a cloud that has burst. A "prester" is a cloud rent all round by the force of fire and wind. Earthquakes, say they, happen when the wind finds its way into, or is imprisoned in, the hollow parts of the earth: so Posidonius in his eighth book; and some of them are tremblings, others openings of the earth, others again lateral displacements, and yet others vertical displacements.

They maintain that the parts of the world are arranged thus. The earth is in the middle answering to a centre; next comes the water, which is shaped like a sphere all round it, concentric with the earth, so that the earth is in water. After the water comes a spherical layer of air. There are five celestial circles: first, the arctic circle, which is always visible; second, the summer tropic; third, the circle of the equinox; fourth, the winter tropic; and fifth, the antarctic, which is invisible to us. They are called parallel, because they do not incline towards one another; yet they are described round the same centre. The zodiac is an oblique circle, as it crosses the parallel circles. And there are five terrestrial zones: first, the northern zone which is beyond the arctic circle, uninhabitable because of the cold; second, a temperate zone; a third, uninhabitable because of great heats, called the torrid zone; fourth, a counter-temperate zone; fifth, the southern zone, uninhabitable because of its cold.

Nature in their view is an artistically working fire, going on its way to create; which is equivalent to a fiery, creative, or fashioning breath. And the soul is a nature capable of perception. And they regard it as the breath of life, congenital with us; from which they infer first that it is a body and secondly that it survives death. Yet it is perishable, though the soul of the universe, of which the individual souls of animals are parts, is indestructible. Zeno of Citium and Antipater, in their treatises *De anima,* and Posidonius define the soul as a warm breath; for by this we become animate and this enables us to move. Cleanthes indeed holds that all souls continue to exist until the general conflagration; but Chrysippus says that only the souls of the wise do so.

They count eight parts of the soul: the five senses, the generative power in us, our power of speech, and that of reasoning. They hold that we see when the light between the visual organ and the object stretches in the form of a cone: so Chrysippus in the second book of his *Physics* and Apollodorus. The apex of the cone in the air is at the eye, the base at the object seen. Thus the thing seen is reported to us by the medium of the air stretching out towards it, as if by a stick.

We hear when the air between the sonant body and the organ of hearing suffers concussion, a vibration which spreads spherically and then forms waves and strikes upon the ears, just as the water in a reservoir forms wavy circles when a stone is thrown into it. Sleep is caused, they say, by the slackening of the tension in our senses, which affects the ruling part of the soul. They consider that the passions are caused by the variations of the vital breath.

Semen is by them defined as that which is capable of generating offspring like the parent. And the human semen which is emitted by a human parent in a moist vehicle is mingled with parts of the soul, blended in the same ratio in which they are present in the parent. Chrysippus in the second book of his *Physics* declares it to be in substance identical with vital breath or spirit. This, he thinks, can be seen from the seeds cast into the earth, which, if kept till they are old, do not germinate, plainly because their fertility has evaporated. Sphaerus and his followers also maintain that semen derives its origin from the whole of the body; at all events every part of the body can be reproduced from it. That of the female is according to them sterile, being, as Sphaerus says, without tension, scanty, and watery. By ruling part of the soul is meant that which is most truly soul proper, in which arise presentations and impulses and from which issues rational speech. And it has its seat in the heart.

Such is the summary of their Physics which I have deemed adequate.

HYMN TO ZEUS

O God most glorious, called by many a name,
Nature's great King, through endless years the same;
Omnipotence, who by thy just decree
Controllest all, hail, Zeus, for unto thee
Behooves thy creatures in all lands to call.
We are thy children, we alone, of all
On earth's broad ways that wander to and fro,
Bearing thine image whereso'er we go.
Wherefore with songs of praise thy power I will forth show
Lo! yonder Heaven, that round the earth is wheeled,
Follows thy guidance, still to thee doth yield
Glad homage; thine unconquerable hand
Such flaming minister, the levin brand,
Wieldeth, a sword two-edged, whose deathless might
Pulsates through all that Nature brings to light;
Vehicle of the universal Word, that flows
Through all, and in the light celestial glows
Of stars both great and small. A King of Kings
Through ceaseless ages, God, whose purpose brings
To birth, whate'er on land or in the sea
Is wrought, or in high heaven's immensity;
Save what the sinner works infatuate.
Nay, but thou knowest to make crooked straight:
Chaos to thee in order: in thine eyes
The unloved is lovely, who didst harmonize
Things evil with things good, that there should be
One Word through all things everlastingly.
One Word—whose voice alas! the wicked spurn;
Insatiate for the good their spirits yearn:
Yet seeing see not, neither hearing hear
God's universal law, which those revere,
By reason guided, happiness who win.

"The Hymn of Cleanthes" from James Adams, *The Vitality of Platonism* (Cambridge: Cambridge University Press, 1911). Reprinted by permission.

The rest, unreasoning, diverse shapes of sin
Self-prompted follow: for an idle name
Vainly they wrestle in the lists of fame:
Others inordinately riches woo,
Or dissolute, the joys of flesh pursue.
Now here, now there they wander, fruitless still,
Forever seeking good and finding ill.
Zeus the all-bountiful, whom darkness shrouds,
Whose lightning lightens in the thunder-clouds;
Thy children save from error's deadly away:
Turn thou the darkness from their souls sway:
Vouchsafe that unto knowledge they attain;
For thou by knowledge art made strong to reign
O'er all, and all things rulest righteously.
So by thee honoured, we will honour thee,
Praising thy works continually with songs,
As mortals should; nor higher meed belongs
E'en to the gods, than justly to adore
The universal law for evermore.

EPICTETUS
ca. A.D. 50–ca. A.D. 130

Epictetus was born a slave in Hierapolis, a small town in Phrygia, Asia Minor (in present-day Turkey). His master was Epaphroditus, a member of Emperor Nero's personal staff in Rome. As was often done at that time, Epaphroditus saw to it that Epictetus had a good education, sending him to study with the Roman Stoic, Rufus. Epictetus gained his freedom sometime after the death of the emperor in A.D. 68 and began to teach philosophy in Rome. In A.D. 89 or 93 Emperor Domitian expelled all philosophers from Rome. Domitian seems to have been especially angry with the Stoics for teaching that sovereignty comes from God and is for the benefit of the people. (Epictetus's reported claim that he had the same regard for the emperor as for his water-pot could not have helped.) Epictetus moved to Nicropolis in Epirus (northwestern Greece), where he established a thriving Stoic school and lived a simple life with few material goods. As an old man, he married so that he could adopt a child who otherwise would have been "exposed," that is, left to die. Those whom he taught described him as a humble, charitable man of great moral and religious devotion.

Epictetus never wrote anything, but one of his admiring students, Arrian, composed eight *Discourses* based on Epictetus's lectures, along with a summary of the great man's thought, the *Encheiridion* (or *Manual*). The *Encheiridion*, given here complete in the W.A. Oldfather translation, builds on the early Stoa's concept of *Logos*. Since the *Logos* or natural law permeates everything, it provides us with moral intuition, so all persons have the capacity for virtue. But in order to live the moral life, one must apply these intuitions to specific cases. Education is necessary if we are to learn how to properly connect moral insights with life. We must begin by recognizing the fact that we cannot change events that happen to us, but we can change our attitude toward those events. To accomplish this and achieve the good life, we must go through three stages. First, we must order our desires and overcome our fears. Next, we must perform our duties—in whatever role fate has given us. Finally, we must think clearly and judge accurately. Only then will we gain inner tranquillity.

Despite Emperor Domitian's condemnation, Stoicism had a special appeal to the Roman mind. The Romans were not much interested in the speculative and theoretical content of Zeno's early Stoa. Instead, in the austere moral emphasis of Epictetus, with his concomitant stress on self-control and superiority to pain, the Romans found an ideal for the wise man, whereas the Stoic description of natural law provided a basis for Roman law. One might say that the pillars of republican Rome tended to be Stoical, even if some Romans had never heard of Stoicism.

*   *   *

For works on the Stoics in general, which include Epictetus, see the introductory material on the Early Stoa on page 474. For a volume specifically on Epictetus, see John Bonforte, *The Philosophy of Epictetus* (New York: Philosophical Library, 1955). Iason Xenakis, *Epictetus: Philosopher-Therapist* (The Hague, Netherlands: Martinus Nijhoff, 1969), makes an interesting application of Epictetus; while W.A. Oldfather, *Contributions Towards a Bibliography of Epictetus* (Urbana: University of Illinois Press, 1927; supplement, 1952), furnishes a bibliography. For a study of Epictetus's star pupil, see Philip A. Stadter, *Arrian of Nicomedia* (Chapel Hill: University of North Carolina Press, 1980).

ENCHEIRIDION (Manual)

1. Some things are under our control, while others are not under our control. Under our control are conception, choice, desire, aversion, and in a word, everything that is our own doing; not under our control are our body, our property, reputation, office and, in a word, everything that is not our own doing. Furthermore, the things under our control are by nature free, unhindered, and unimpeded; while the things not under our control are weak, servile, subject to hindrance, and not our own. Remember, therefore, that if what is naturally slavish you think to be free, and what is not your own to be your own, you will be hampered, will grieve, will be in turmoil, and will blame both gods and men; while if you think only what is your own to be your own, and what is not your own to be, as it really is, not your own, then no one will ever be able to exert compulsion upon you, no one will hinder you, you will blame no one, will find fault with no one, will do absolutely nothing against your will, you will have no personal enemy, no one will harm you, for neither is there any harm that can touch you.

With such high aims, therefore, remember that you must bestir yourself with no slight effort to lay hold of them, but you will have to give up some things entirely, and defer others for the time being. But if you wish for these things also, and at the same time for both office and wealth, it may be that you will not get even these latter, because you aim also at the former, and certainly you will fail to get the former, which alone bring freedom and happiness.

Make it, therefore, your study at the very outset to say to every harsh external impression, "You are an external impression and not at all what you appear to be." After that examine it and test it by these rules which you have, the first and most important of which is this: Whether the impression has to do with the things which are under our control, or with those which are not under our control; and, if it has to do with some one of the things not under our control, have ready to hand the answer, "It is nothing to me."

2. Remember that the promise of desire is the attainment of what you desire, that of aversion is not to fall into what is avoided, and that he who fails in his desire is unfortunate, while he who falls into what he would avoid experiences misfortune. If, then, you avoid only what is unnatural among those things which are under your control, you will fall into none of the things which you avoid; but if you try to avoid disease, or death, or poverty, you will experience misfortune. Withdraw, therefore, your aversion from all the matters that are not under our control, and transfer it to what is unnatural among those which are under our control. But for the time being remove utterly your desire; for if you desire some one of the things that are not under our control you are bound to be unfortunate; and, at the same time, not one of the things that are under our control, which it would be excellent for you to desire, is within your grasp. But employ only choice and refusal, and these too but lightly, and with reservations, and without straining.

3. With everything which entertains you, is useful, or of which you are fond, remember to say to yourself, beginning with the very least things, "What is its nature?" If you are fond of a jug, say, "I am fond of a jug"; for when it is broken you will not be disturbed. If you kiss your own child or wife, say to yourself that you are kissing a human being; for when it dies you will not be disturbed.

4. When you are on the point of putting your hand to some undertaking, remind yourself what the nature of that undertaking is. If you are going out of the house to bathe, put before your mind what happens at a public bath—those who splash you with water, those who jostle against you, those who vilify you and rob you. And thus you will set about your undertaking more securely if at the outset you say to yourself, "I want to take a bath, and, at the same time, to keep my moral purpose in harmony with nature." And so do in every undertaking. For thus, if anything happens to hinder you in your bathing, you will be ready to say, "Oh, well, this was not the only thing that I wanted, but I wanted also to keep your moral purpose in harmony with nature; and I shall not so keep it if I am vexed at what is going on."

5. It is not the things themselves that disturb men, but their judgements about these things. For example, death is nothing dreadful, or else Socrates too would have thought so, but the judgement that death is dreadful, *this* is the dreadful thing. When, therefore, we are hindered, or disturbed, or grieved, let us never blame anyone but ourselves, that means, our own judgements. It is the part of an uneducated person to blame others where he himself fares ill; to blame himself is the part of one whose education has begun; to blame neither another nor his own self is the part of one whose education is already complete.

6. Be not elated at any excellence which is not your own. If the horse in his elation were to say, "I am beautiful," it could be endured; but when you say in your elation, "I have a beautiful horse," rest assured that you are elated at something good which belongs to a horse. What then, is your own? The use of external impressions. Therefore, when you are in harmony with nature in the use of external impressions, then be elated; for then it will be some good of your own at which you will be elated.

7. Just as on a voyage, when your ship has anchored, if you should go on shore to get fresh water, you may pick up a small shell-fish or little bulb on the way, but you have to keep your attention fixed on the ship, and turn about frequently for fear lest the captain should call; and if he calls, you must give up all these things, if you would escape being thrown on board all tied up like the sheep. So it is also in life: If there be given you, instead of a little bulb and a small shell-fish, a little wife and child, there will be no objection to that; only, if the Captain calls, give up all these things and run to the ship, without even turning around to look back. And if you are an old man, never even get very far away from the ship, for fear that when He calls you may be missing.

8. Do not seek to have everything that happens happen as you wish, but wish for everything to happen as it actually does happen, and your life will be serene.

9. Disease is an impediment to the body, but not to the moral purpose, unless that consents. Lameness is an impediment to the leg, but not to the moral purpose. And say this to yourself at each thing that befalls you; for you will find the thing to be an impediment to something else, but not to yourself.

10. In the case of everything that befalls you, remember to turn to yourself and see what faculty you have to deal with it. If you see a handsome lad or woman, you will find continence the faculty to employ here; if hard labour is laid upon you, you will find endurance; in this fashion, your external impressions will not run away with you.

11. Never say about anything, "I have lost it," but only "I have given it back." Is your child dead? It has been given back. Is your wife dead? She has been given back. "I have had my farm taken away." Very well, this too has been given back. "Yet it was a rascal who took it away." But what concern is it of yours by whose instrumentality the Giver called for its return? So long as He gives it to you, take care of it as of a thing that is not your own, as travellers treat their inn.

12. If you wish to make progress, dismiss all reasoning of this sort: "If I neglect my affairs, I shall have nothing to live on." "If I do not punish my slave-boy he will turn out bad." For it is better to die of hunger, but in a state of freedom from grief and fear, than to live in plenty, but troubled in mind. And it is better for your slave-boy to be bad than for you to be unhappy. Begin, therefore, with the little things. Your paltry oil gets spilled, your miserable wine stolen; say to yourself, "This is the price paid for a calm spirit, this the price for peace of mind." Nothing is got without a price. And when you call your slave-boy, bear in mind that it is possible he may not heed you, and again, that even if he does heed, he may not do what you want done. But he is not in so happy a condition that your peace of mind depends upon him.

13. If you wish to make progress, then be content to appear senseless and foolish in externals, do not make it your wish to give the appearance of knowing anything; and if some people think you to be an important personage, distrust yourself. For be assured that it is no easy matter to keep your moral purpose in a state of conformity with nature, and, at the same time, to keep externals; but the man who devotes his attention to one of these two things must inevitably neglect the other.

14. If you make it your will that your children and your wife and your friends should live forever, you are silly; for you are making it your will that things not under

Theater at Ephesus, Turkey, built A.D. 41–117. In theaters like this, with a capacity for
more than eighteen thousand spectators, Greek playwrights presented all-day festivals of
drama on every phase of Greek life from the tragic to the comic. It is not surprising that
Epictetus uses the image of the play and the playwright to make his point. *(Gian Berto
Vanni/Art Resource)*

your control should be under your control, and that what is not your own should be
your own. In the same way, too, if you make it your will that your slave-boy be free
from faults, you are a fool; for you are making it your will that vice be not vice, but
something else. If, however, it is your will not to fail in what you desire, this is in your
power. Wherefore, exercise yourself in that which is in your power. Each man's master
is the person who has the authority over what the man wishes or does not wish, so as to
secure it, or take it away. Whoever, therefore, wants to be free, let him neither wish for
anything, nor avoid anything, that is under the control of others; or else he is necessarily a slave.

15. Remember that you ought to behave in life as you would at a banquet. As
something is being passed around it comes to you; stretch out your hand and take a
portion of it politely. It passes on; do not detain it. Or it has not come to you yet; do not
project your desire to meet it, but wait until it comes in front of you. So act toward
children, so toward a wife, so toward office, so toward wealth; and then some day you
will be worthy of the banquets of the gods. But if you do not take these things even
when they are set before you, but despise them, then you will not only share the banquet of the gods, but share also their rule. For it was by so doing that Diogenes and
Heracleitus, and men like them, were deservedly divine and deservedly so called.

16. When you see someone weeping in sorrow, either because a child has gone
on a journey, or because he has lost his property, beware that you be not carried away
by the impression that the man is in the midst of external ills, but straightway keep be-

fore you this thought: "It is not what has happened that distresses this man (for it does not distress another), but his judgement about it." Do not, however, hesitate to sympathize with him so far as words go, and, if occasion offers, even to groan with him; but be careful not to groan also in the centre of your being.

17. Remember that you are an actor in a play, the character of which is determined by the Playwright: if He wishes the play to be short, it is short; if long, it is long; if He wishes you to play the part of a beggar, remember to act even this role adroitly; and so if your role be that of a cripple, an official, or a layman. For this is your business, to play admirably the role assigned you; but the selection of that role is Another's.

18. When a raven croaks inauspiciously, let not the external impression carry you away, but straightway draw a distinction in your own mind, and say, "None of these portents are for me, but either for my paltry body, or my paltry estate, or my paltry opinion, or my children, or my wife. But for me every portent is favourable, if I so wish; for whatever be the outcome, it is within my power to derive benefit from it."

19. You can be invincible if you never enter a contest in which victory is not under your control. Beware lest, when you see some person preferred to you in honour, or possessing great power, or otherwise enjoying high repute, you are ever carried away by the external impression, and deem him happy. For if the true nature of the good is one of the things that are under our control, there is no place for either envy or jealousy; and you yourself will not wish to be a praetor, or a senator, or a consul, but a free man. Now there is but one way that leads to this, and that is to despise the things that are not under our control.

20. Bear in mind that it is not the man who reviles or strikes you that insults you, but it is your judgement that these men are insulting you. Therefore, when someone irritates you, be assured that it is your own opinion which has irritated you. And so make it your first endeavour not to be carried away by the external impression; for if once you gain time and delay, you will more easily become master of yourself.

21. Keep before your eyes day by day death and exile, and everything that seems terrible, but most of all death; and then you will never have any abject thought, nor will you yearn for anything beyond measure.

22. If you yearn for philosophy, prepare at once to be met with ridicule, to have many people jeer at you, and say, "Here he is again, turned philosopher all of a sudden," and "Where do you suppose he got that high brow?" But do you not put on a high brow, and do you so hold fast to the things which to you seem best, as a man who has been assigned by God to this post; and remember that if you abide by the same principles, those who formerly used to laugh at you will later come to admire you, but if you are worsted by them, you will get the laugh on yourself twice.

23. If it should ever happen to you that you turn to externals with a view to pleasing someone, rest assured that you have lost your plan of life. Be content, therefore, in everything to be a philosopher, and if you wish also to be taken for one, show to yourself that you are one, and you will be able to accomplish it.

24. Let not these reflections oppress you: "I shall live without honour, and be nobody anywhere." For, if lack of honour is an evil, you cannot be in evil through the instrumentality of some other person, any more than you can be in shame. It is not your business, is it, to get office, or to be invited to a dinner-party? Certainly not. How, then, can this be any longer a lack of honour? And how is it that you will be "nobody anywhere," when you ought to be somebody only in those things which are under your control, wherein you are privileged to be a man of the very greatest honour? But your friends will be without assistance? What do you mean by being "without assistance"?

They will not have paltry coin from you, and you will not make them Roman citizens. Well, who told you that these are some of the matters under our control, and not rather things which others do? And who is able to give another what he does not himself have? "Get money, then," says some friend, "in order that we too may have it." If I can get money and at the same time keep myself self-respecting, and faithful, and high-minded, show me the way and I will get it. But if you require me to lose the good things that belong to me, in order that you may acquire the things that are not good, you can see for yourselves how unfair and inconsiderate you are. And which do you really prefer? Money, or a faithful and self-respecting friend? Help me, therefore, rather to this end, and do not require me to do those things which will make me lose these qualities.

"But my country," says he, "so far as lies in me, will be without assistance." Again I ask, what kind of assistance do you mean? It will not have loggias or baths of your providing. And what does that signify? For neither does it have shoes provided by the blacksmith, nor has it arms provided by the cobbler; but it is sufficient if each man fulfil his own proper function. And if you secured for it another faithful and self-respecting citizen, would you not be doing it any good? "Yes." Very well, and then you also would not be useless to it. "What place, then, shall I have in the State?" says he. Whatever place you can have, and at the same time maintain the man of fidelity and self-respect that is in you. But if, through your desire to help the State, you lose these qualities, of what good would you become to it, when in the end you turned out to be shameless and unfaithful?

25. Has someone been honoured above you at a dinner-party, or in salutation, or in being called in to give advice? Now if these matters are good, you ought to be happy that he got them; but if evil, be not distressed because you did not get them; and bear in mind that, if you do not act the same way that others do, with a view to getting things which are not under our control, you cannot be considered worthy to receive an equal share with others. Why, how is it possible for a person who does not haunt some man's door, to have equal shares with the man who does? For the man who does not do escort duty, with the man who does? For the man who does not praise, with the man who does? You will be unjust, therefore, and insatiable, if, while refusing to pay the price for which such things are bought, you want to obtain them for nothing. Well, what is the price for heads of lettuce? An obol, perhaps. If, then, somebody gives up his obol and gets his heads of lettuce, while you do not give your obol, and do not get them, do not imagine that you are worse off than the man who gets his lettuce. For as he has his heads of lettuce, so you have your obol which you have not given away.

Now it is the same way also in life. You have not been invited to somebody's dinner-party? Of course not; for you didn't give the host the price at which he sells his dinner. He sells it for praise; he sells it for personal attention. Give him the price, then, for which it is sold, if it is to your interest. But if you wish both not to give up the one and yet to get the other, you are insatiable and a simpleton. Have you, then, nothing in place of the dinner? Indeed you have; you have not had to praise the man you did not want to praise; you have not had to put up with the insolence of his doorkeepers.

26. What the will of nature is may be learned from a consideration of the points in which we do not differ from one another. For example, when some other person's slave-boy breaks his drinking-cup, you are instantly ready to say. "That's one of the things which happen." Rest assured, then, that when your own drinking-cup gets broken, you ought to behave in the same way that you do when the other man's cup is broken. Apply now the same principle to the matters of greater importance. Some other person's child or wife has died; no one but would say, "Such is the fate of man." Yet

when a man's own child dies, immediately the cry is, "Alas! Woe is me!" But we ought to remember how we feel when we hear of the same misfortune befalling others.

27. Just as a mark is not set up in order to be missed, so neither does the nature of evil arise in the universe.

28. If someone handed over your body to any person who met you, you would be vexed; but that you hand over your mind to any person that comes along, so that, if he reviles you, it is disturbed and troubled—are you not ashamed of that?

29. In each separate thing that you do, consider the matters which come first and those which follow after, and only then approach the thing itself. Otherwise, at the start you will come to it enthusiastically, because you have never reflected upon any of the subsequent steps, but later on, when some difficulties appear, you will give up disgracefully. Do you wish to win an Olympic victory? So do I, by the gods! for it is a fine thing. But consider the matters which come before that, and those which follow after, and only when you have done that, put your hand to the task. You have to submit to discipline, follow a strict diet, give up sweet cakes, train under compulsion, at a fixed hour, in heat or in cold; you must not drink cold water, nor wine just whenever you feel like it; you must have turned yourself over to your trainer precisely as you would to a physician. Then when the contest comes on, you have to "dig in" beside your opponent, and sometimes dislocate your wrist, sprain your ankle, swallow quantities of sand, sometimes take a scourging, and along with all that get beaten. After you have considered all these points, go on into the games, if you still wish to do so; otherwise, you will be turning back like children. Sometimes they play wrestlers, again gladiators, again they blow trumpets, and then act a play. So you too are now an athlete, now a gladiator, then a rhetorician, then a philosopher, yet with your whole soul nothing; but like an ape you imitate whatever you see, and one thing after another strikes your fancy. For you have never gone out after anything with circumspection, nor after you had examined it all over, but you act haphazard and half-heartedly.

In the same way, when some people have seen a philosopher and have heard someone speaking like Euphrates (though, indeed, who can speak like him?), they wish to be philosophers themselves. Man, consider first the nature of the business, and then learn your own natural ability, if you are able to bear it. Do you wish to be a contender in the pentathlon, or a wrestler? Look to your arms, your thighs, see what your loins are like. For one man has a natural talent for one thing, another for another. Do you suppose that you can eat in the same fashion, drink in the same fashion, give way to impulse and to irritation, just as you do now? You must keep vigils, work hard, abandon your own people, be despised by a paltry slave, be laughed to scorn by those who meet you, in everything get the worst of it, in honour, in office, in court, in every paltry affair. Look these drawbacks over carefully, if you are willing at the price of these things to secure tranquillity, freedom, and calm. Otherwise, do not approach philosophy; don't act like a child—now a philosopher, later on a tax-gatherer, then a rhetorician, then a procurator of Caesar. These things do not go together. You must be one person, either good or bad; you must labour to improve either your own government principle or externals; you must work hard either on the inner man, or on things outside; that is, play either the rôle of a philosopher or else that of a layman.

30. Our duties are in general measured by our social relationships. He is a father. One is called upon to take care of him, to give way to him in all things, to submit when he reviles or strikes you. "But he is a bad father." Did nature, then, bring you into relationship with a *good* father? No, but simply with a father. "My brother does me wrong." Very well, then, maintain the relation that you have toward him; and do not

consider what he is doing, but what you will have to do, if your moral purpose is to be in harmony with nature. For no one will harm you without your consent; you will have been harmed only when you think you are harmed. In this way, therefore, you will discover what duty to expect of your neighbour, your citizen, your commanding officer, if you acquire the habit of looking at your social relations with them.

31. In piety towards the gods, I would have you know, the chief element is this, to have right opinions about them—as existing and as administering the universe well and justly—and to have set yourself to obey them and to submit to everything that happens, and to follow it voluntarily, in the belief that it is being fulfilled by the highest intelligence. For if you act in this way, you will never blame the gods, nor find fault with them for neglecting you. But this result cannot be secured in any other way than by withdrawing your idea of the good and the evil from the things which are not under our control, and placing it in those which are under our control, and in those alone. Because, if you think any of those former things to be good or evil, then, when you fail to get what you want and fall into what you do not want, it is altogether inevitable that you will blame and hate those who are responsible for these results. For this is the nature of every living creature, to flee from and to turn aside from the things that appear harmful, and all that produces them, and to pursue after and to admire the things that are helpful, and all that produces them. Therefore, it is impossible for a man who thinks that he is being hurt to take pleasure in that which he thinks is hurting him, just as it is also impossible for him to take pleasure in the hurt itself. Hence it follows that even a father is reviled by a son when he does not give his child some share in the things that seem to be good; and this it was which made Polyneices and Eteocles enemies of one another, the thought that the royal power was a good thing. That is why the farmer reviles the gods, and so also the sailor, and the merchant, and those who have lost their wives and their children. For where a man's interest lies, there is also his piety. Wherefore, whoever is careful to exercise desire and aversion as he should, is at the same time careful also about piety. But it is always appropriate to make libations, and sacrifices, and to give of the firstfruits after the manner of our fathers, and to do all this with purity, and not in a slovenly or careless fashion, nor, indeed, in a miserly way, nor yet beyond our means.

32. When you have recourse to divination, remember that you do not know what the issue is going to be, but that you have come in order to find this out from the diviner; yet if you are indeed a philosopher, you know, when you arrive, what the nature of it is. For if it is one of the things which are not under our control, it is altogether necessary that what is going to take place is neither good nor evil. Do not, therefore, bring to the diviner desire or aversion, and do not approach him with trembling, but having first made up your mind that every issue is indifferent and nothing to you, but that, whatever it may be, it will be possible for you to turn it to good use, and that no one will prevent this. Go, then, with confidence to the gods as to counsellors; and after that, when some counsel has been given you, remember whom you have taken as counsellors, and whom you will be disregarding if you disobey. But go to divination as Socrates thought that men should go, that is, in cases where the whole inquiry has reference to the outcome, and where neither from reason nor from any other technical art are means vouchsafed for discovering the matter in question. Hence, when it is your duty to share the danger of a friend or of your country, do not ask of the diviner whether you ought to share that danger. For if the diviner forewarns you that the omens of sacrifice have been unfavourable, it is clear that death is portended, or the injury of some member of your body, or exile; yet reason requires that even at this risk you are to stand by your friend, and share the danger with your country. Wherefore, give heed

to the greater diviner, the Pythian Apollo, who cast out of his temple the man who had not helped his friend when he was being murdered.

33. Lay down for yourself, at the outset, a certain stamp and type of character for yourself, which you are to maintain whether you are by yourself or are meeting with people. And be silent for the most part, or else make only the most necessary remarks, and express these in few words. But rarely, and when occasion requires you to talk, talk, indeed, but about no ordinary topics. Do not talk about gladiators, or horse-races, or athletes, or things to eat or drink—topics that arise on all occasions; but above all, do not talk about people, either blaming, or praising, or comparing them. If, then, you can, by your own conversation bring over that of your companions to what is seemly. But if you happen to be left alone in the presence of aliens, keep silence.

Do not laugh much, nor at many things, nor boisterously.

Refuse, if you can, to take an oath at all, but if that is impossible, refuse as far as circumstances allow.

Avoid entertainments given by outsiders and by persons ignorant of philosophy; but if an appropriate occasion arises for you to attend, be on the alert to avoid lapsing into the behaviour of such laymen. For you may rest assured, that, if a man's companion be dirty, the person who keeps close company with him must of necessity get a share of his dirt, even though he himself happens to be clean.

In things that pertain to the body take only as much as your bare need requires, I mean such things as food, drink, clothing, shelter, and household slaves; but cut down everything which is for outward show or luxury.

In your sex-life preserve purity, as far as you can, before marriage, and, if you indulge, take only those privileges which are lawful. However, do not make yourself offensive, or censorious, to those who do indulge, and do not make frequent mention of the fact that you do not yourself indulge.

If someone brings you word that So-and-so is speaking ill of you, do not defend yourself against what has been said, but answer, "Yes, indeed, for he did not know the rest of the faults that attach to me; if he had, these would not have been the only ones he mentioned."

It is not necessary, for the most part, to go to the public shows. If, however, a suitable occasion ever arises, show that your principal concern is for none other than yourself, which means, wish only for that to happen which does happen, and for him only to win who does win; for so you will suffer no hindrance. But refrain utterly from shouting, or laughter at anyone, or great excitement. And after you have left, do not talk a great deal about what took place, except in so far as it contributes to your own improvement; for such behaviour indicates that the spectacle has aroused your admiration.

Do not go rashly or readily to people's public reading, but when you do go, maintain your own dignity and gravity, and at the same time be careful not to make yourself disagreeable.

When you are about to meet somebody, in particular when it is one of those men who are held in very high esteem, propose to yourself the question, "What would Socrates or Zeno have done under these circumstances?" and then you will not be at a loss to make proper use of the occasion. When you go to see one of those men who have great power, propose to yourself the thought that you will not find him at home, that you will be shut out, that the door will be slammed in your face, that he will pay no attention to you. And if, despite all this, it is your duty to go, go and take what comes, and never say to yourself, "It was not worth all the trouble." For this is characteristic of the layman, that is, a man who is vexed at externals.

In your conversation avoid making mention at great length and excessively of your own deeds or dangers, because it is not as pleasant for others to hear about your adventures, as it is for you to call to mind your own dangers.

Avoid also raising a laugh, for this is a kind of behaviour that slips easily into vulgarity, and at the same time is calculated to lessen the respect which your neighbours have of you. It is dangerous also to lapse into foul language. When, therefore, anything of the sort occurs, if the occasion be suitable, go even so far as to reprove the person who has made such a lapse; if, however, the occasion does not arise, at all events show by keeping silence, and blushing, and frowning, that you are displeased by what has been said.

34. When you get an external impression of some pleasure, guard yourself, as with impressions in general, against being carried away by it; nay, let the matter wait upon your leisure, and give yourself a little delay. Next think of the two periods of time, first, that in which you will enjoy your pleasure, and second, that in which, after the enjoyment is over, you will later repent and revile your own self; and set over against these two periods of time how much joy and self-satisfaction you will get if you refrain. However, if you feel that a suitable occasion has arisen to do the deed, be careful not to allow its enticement, and sweetness, and attractiveness to overcome you; but set over against all this the thought, how much better is the consciousness of having won a victory over it.

35. When you do a thing which you have made up your mind ought to be done, never try not to be seen doing it, even though most people are likely to think unfavourably about it. If, however, what you are doing is not right, avoid the deed itself altogether; but if it is right, why fear those who are going to rebuke you wrongly?

36. Just as the propositions, "It is day," and "it is night," are full of meaning when separated, but meaningless if united; so also, granted that for you to take the larger share at a dinner is good for your body, still, it is bad for the maintenance of the proper kind of social feeling. When, therefore, you are eating with another person, remember to regard, not merely the value for your body of what lies before you, but also to maintain your respect for your host.

37. If you undertake a role which is beyond your powers, you both disgrace yourself in that one, and at the same time neglect the role which you might have filled with success.

38. Just as you are careful, in walking about, not to step on a nail or to sprain your ankle, so be careful also not to hurt your governing principle. And if we observe this rule in every action, we shall be more secure in setting about it.

39. Each man's body is a measure for his property, just as the foot is a measure for his shoe. If, then, you abide by this principle, you will maintain the proper measure, but if you go beyond it, you cannot help but fall headlong over a precipice, as it were, in the end. So also in the case of your shoe; if once you go beyond the foot, you get first a gilded shoe, then a purple one, then an embroidered one. For once you go beyond the measure there is no limit.

40. Immediately after they are fourteen, women are called "ladies" by men. And so when they see that they have nothing else but only to be the bedfellows of men, they begin to beautify themselves, and put all their hopes in that. It is worthwhile for us to take pains, therefore, to make them understand that they are honoured for nothing else but only for appearing modest and self-respecting.

41. It is a mark of an ungifted man to spend a great deal of time in what concerns his body, as in much exercise, much eating, much drinking, much evacuating of the

bowels, much copulating. But these things are to be done in passing; and let your whole attention be devoted to the mind.

42. When someone treats you ill or speaks ill of you, remember that he acts or speaks thus because he thinks it is incumbent upon him. That being the case, it is impossible for him to follow what appears good to you, but what appears good to himself; whence it follows that, if he gets a wrong view of things, the man that suffers is the man that has been deceived. For if a person thinks a true composite judgement to be false, the composite judgement does not suffer, but the person who has been deceived. If, therefore, you start from this point of view, you will be gentle with the man who reviles you. For you should say on each occasion, "He thought that way about it."

43. Everything has two handles, by one of which it ought to be carried and by the other not. If your brother wrongs you, do not lay hold of the matter by the handle of the wrong that he is doing, because this is the handle by which the matter ought not to be carried; but rather by the other handle—that he is your brother, that you were brought up together, and then you will be laying hold of the matter by the handle by which it ought to be carried.

44. The following statements constitute a *non sequitur:* "I am richer than you are, therefore I am superior to you"; or, "I am more eloquent than you are, therefore I am superior to you." But the following conclusions are better: "I am richer than you are, therefore my property is superior to yours"; or, "I am more eloquent than you are, therefore my elocution is superior to yours." But *you* are neither property nor elocution.

45. Somebody is hasty about bathing; do not say that he bathes badly, but that he is hasty about bathing. Somebody drinks a good deal of wine; do not say that he drinks badly, but that he drinks a good deal. For until you have decided what judgement prompts him, how do you know that what he is doing is bad? And thus the final result will not be that you receive convincing sense-impressions of some things, but give your assent to others.

46. On no occasion call yourself a philosopher, and do not, for the most part, talk among laymen about your philosophic principles, but do what follows from your principles. For example, at a banquet do not say how people ought to eat, but eat as a man ought. For remember how Socrates had so completely eliminated the thought of ostentation, that people came to him when they wanted him to introduce them to philosophers, and he used to bring them along. So well did he submit to being overlooked. And if talk about some philosophic principle arises among laymen, keep silence for the most part for there is great danger that you will spew up immediately what you have not digested. So when a man tells you that you know nothing, and you, like Socrates, are not hurt, then rest assured that you are making a beginning with the business you have undertaken. For sheep, too, do not bring their fodder to the shepherds and show how much they have eaten, but they digest their food within them, and on the outside produce wool and milk. And so do you, therefore, make no display to the laymen of your philosophical principles, but let them see the results which come from these principles when digested.

47. When you have become adjusted to simple living in regard to your bodily wants, do not preen yourself about the accomplishment; and so likewise, if you are a water-drinker, do not on every occasion say that you are a water-drinker. And if ever you want to train to develop physical endurance, do it by yourself and not for outsiders to behold; do not throw your arms around statues, but on occasion, when you are very thirsty, take cold water into your mouth, and then spit it out, without telling anybody.

48. This is the position and character of a layman: He never looks for either help or harm from himself, but only from externals. This is the position and character of the philosopher: He looks for all his help or harm from himself.

Signs of one who is making progress are: He censures no one, praises no one, blames no one, finds fault with no one, says nothing about himself as though he were somebody or knew something. When he is hampered or prevented, he blames himself. And if anyone compliments him, he smiles to himself at the person complimenting; while if anyone censures him, he makes no defence. He goes about like an invalid, being careful not to disturb, before it has grown firm, any part which is getting well. He has put away from himself his every desire, and has transferred his aversion to those things only, of what is under our control, which are contrary to nature. He exercises no pronounced choice in regard to anything. If he gives the appearance of being foolish or ignorant he does not care. In a word, he keeps guard against himself as though he were his own enemy lying in wait.

49. When a person gives himself airs because he can understand and interpret the books of Chrysippus, say to yourself, "If Chrysippus had not written obscurely, this man would have nothing about which to give himself airs."

But what is it I want? To learn nature and to follow her. I seek, therefore, someone to interpret her; and having heard that Chrysippus does so, I go to him. But I do not understand what he has written; I seek, therefore, the person who interprets Chrysippus. And down to this point there is nothing to justify pride. But when I find the interpreter, what remains is to put his precepts into practice; this is the only thing to be proud about. If, however, I admire the mere act of interpretation, what have I done but turned into a grammarian instead of a philosopher? The only difference, indeed, is that I interpret Chrysippus instead of Homer. Far from being proud, therefore, when somebody says to me, "Read me Chrysippus," I blush the rather, when I am unable to show him such deeds as match and harmonize with his words.

50. Whatever principles are set before you, stand fast by these like laws, feeling that it would be impiety for you to transgress them. But pay no attention to what somebody says about you, for this is, at length, not under your control.

51. How long will you still wait to think yourself worthy of the best things, and in nothing to transgress against the distinctions set up by the reason? You have received the philosophical principles which you ought to accept, and you have accepted them. What sort of a teacher, then, do you still wait for, that you should put off reforming yourself until he arrives? You are no longer a lad, but already a full-grown man. If you are now neglectful and easy-going, and always making one delay after another, and fixing first one day and then another, after which you will pay attention to yourself, then without realizing it you will make no progress, but, living and dying, will continue to be a layman throughout. Make up your mind, therefore, before it is too late, that the fitting thing for you to do is to live as a mature man who is making progress, and let everything which seems to you to be best be for you a law that must not be transgressed. And if you meet anything that is laborious, or sweet, or held in high repute, or in no repute, remember that now is the contest, and here before you are the Olympic games, and that it is impossible to delay any longer, and that it depends on a single day and a single action, whether progress is lost or saved. This is the way Socrates became what he was, by paying attention to nothing but his reason in everything that he encountered. And even if you are not yet a Socrates, still you ought to live as one who wishes to be a Socrates.

52. The first and most necessary division in philosophy is that which has to do with the application of the principles, as, for example, Do not lie. The second deals

with the demonstrations, as, for example, How comes it that we ought not to lie? The third confirms and discriminates between these processes, as, for example, How does it come that this is a proof? For what is a proof, what is logical consequence, what contradiction, what truth, what falsehood? Therefore, the third division is necessary because of the second, and the second because of the first; while the most necessary of all, and the one in which we ought to rest, is the first. But we do the opposite; for we spend our time in the third division, and all our zeal is devoted to it, while we utterly neglect the first. Wherefore, we lie, indeed, but are ready with the arguments which prove that one ought not to lie.

53. Upon every occasion we ought to have the following thoughts at our command:

Lead thou me on, O Zeus, and Destiny,
To that goal long ago to me assigned.
I'll follow and not falter; if my will
Prove weak and craven, still I'll follow on.

Cleanthes

Whoso has rightly with necessity complied, We count him wise, and skilled in things divine.

Euripides

Well, O Crito, if so it is pleasing to the gods, so let it be.

Socrates [Crito, 43D]

Anytus and Meletus can kill me, but they cannot hurt me.

Socrates [Apology, 30C]

LUCRETIUS
ca. 99–55 B.C.

Virtually nothing is known of Titus Lucretius Carus except his famous poem, *On the Nature of Things* (*De Rerum Natura*). According to a secondhand report, he was driven insane by a love potion and eventually committed suicide. Apart from this story, our knowledge of his life can be gained only from his poem. From internal evidence, it seems he came from a wealthy Roman family and that he did some traveling. He also seems to have intentionally avoided the social and political upheavals of his day.

In his poem, Lucretius embraces and expounds the philosophy of Epicurus. In particular, he develops his master's atomistic materialism. Lucretius holds that in all nature there are only atoms moving in a void. (Actually, Lucretius wrote in Latin and did not use the Greek word *atom;* his word was *primordia,* "first-beginnings.") As these atoms fall downward in empty space, some swerve from their course and collide with others. These collisions lead to the world as we experience it.

Lucretius uses this theory to explain human activity as well. The human soul is made up of very fine atoms, and free will is simply the result of a "swerve" of atoms. Sensation occurs when thin films or "idols" (i.e., images) are thrown off from objects and, entering through our sense organs, jostle the atoms of the mind. Consciousness is also explained atomistically as the motion of our soul atoms.

In our selection from Book Two of *On the Nature of Things,* reprinted here in the Martin Ferguson Smith translation, Lucretius describes this atomic swerve. Book Three from the same work, excerpted here, presents Lucretius's claim that death is simply the cessation of sensation and consciousness. As he explains,

". . . death is nothing to us, it matters not one jot, ... when we shall no longer be, when the parting shall have come about between body and spirit from which we are compacted into one whole, then sure enough nothing at all will be able to happen to us, who will then no longer be. . . ." There is no afterlife to fear, no immortality to be sought: Death awaits everyone and is final.

* * *

On the Nature of Things is noted as much for its literary qualities as for its philosophy, and numerous books have been written about Lucretius's hexameter verse. George Santayana, *Three Philosophical Poets: Lucretius, Dante, and Goethe* (Cambridge, MA: Harvard University Press, 1910) and Henri Bergson, *The Philosophy of Poetry: The Genius of Lucretius,* translated by Wade Baskin (New York: Philosophical Library, 1959), consider Lucretius as both philosopher and poet. For a general explication of Lucretius's philosophy, see John Masson, *Lucretius, Epicurean and Poet* (London: Murray, 1907); George Depue Hadzsits, *Lucretius and His Influence* (New York: Cooper Square Publishers, 1963); E.J. Kenney, *Lucretius* (Oxford: Oxford University Press, 1977); and Diskin Clay, *Lucretius and Epicurus* (Ithaca, NY: Cornell University Press, 1983). David Konstan, *Some Aspects of Epicurean Psychology* (Leiden, Netherlands: Brill, 1973), and James H. Nichols, Jr., *Epicurean Political Philosophy: The De Rerum Natura of Lucretius* (Ithaca, NY: Cornell University Press, 1976) are specialized studies; while Cosmo Alexander Gordon, *A Bibliography of Lucretius* (London: Rupert Hart-Davis, 1962) provides a bibliography.

ON THE NATURE OF THINGS (in part)

BOOK TWO

* * *

[216] One further point in this matter I desire you to understand: that while the first bodies are being carried downwards by their own weight in a straight line through the void, at times quite uncertain and uncertain places, they swerve a little from their course, just so much as you might call a change of motion. For if they were not apt to incline, all would fall downwards like raindrops through the profound void, no collision would take place and no blow would be caused amongst the first-beginnings: thus nature would never have produced anything.

[225] But if by chance anyone believes it to be possible that heavier elements, being carried more quickly straight through the void, fall from above on the lighter,

Reprinted by permission of the publishers and the Loeb Classical Library from Lucretius, *De Rerum Natura,* translated by W.H.D. Rouse, revised by Martin Ferguson Smith (Cambridge, MA: Harvard University Press, 1975). Copyright © 1975 by Harvard University Press.

and so deal blows which can produce generative motions, he is astray and departs far from true reasoning. For whatever things fall through water and through fine air, these must speed their fall in accordance with their weights, because the body of water and the thin nature of air cannot delay each thing equally, but yield sooner overcome by the heavier; but contrariwise empty void cannot offer any support to anything anywhere or at any time. But it must give way continually, as its nature demands: therefore they must all be carried with equal speed, although not of equal weight, through the unresisting void. So the heavier bodies will never be able to fall from above on the lighter, nor deal blows of themselves so as to produce the various motions by which nature carries on her processes. Therefore again and again I say, the bodies must incline a little; and not more than the least possible, or we shall seem to assume oblique movements, and thus be refuted by the facts. For this we see to be manifest and plain, that weights, as far as in them lies, cannot travel obliquely, when they drop straight from above, as far as one can perceive; but who is there who can perceive that they never swerve ever so little from the straight undeviating course?

[251] Again, if all motion is always one long chain, and new motion arises out of the old in order invariable, and if the first-beginnings do not make by swerving a beginning of motion such as to break the decrees of fate, that cause may not follow cause from infinity, whence comes this free will in living creatures all over the earth, whence I say is this will wrested from the fates by which we proceed whither pleasure leads each, swerving also our motions not at fixed times and fixed places, but just where our mind has taken us? For undoubtedly it is his own will in each that begins these things, and from the will movements go rippling through the limbs.

[263] Do you not see also, when the cells are thrown open at a given moment, that nevertheless the eager force of the horses cannot burst forth so suddenly as the mind itself craves? For all the mass of matter must be stirred up together through the whole body, in order that thus stirred up together it may all with one combined effort follow the passion of the mind; thus you may see that the beginning of motion is made by the intelligence, and the action moves on first from the will of the mind, then to be passed onwards through the whole body and limbs.

[272] Nor is this the same as when we move forwards impelled by a blow from the strength and mighty effort of another; for then it is clear that all the matter of the whole body moves and is hurried against our will, until the will has curbed it back through the limbs. In this case do you see then that, although an external force propels many men and forces them often to move on against their will and to be hurried headlong, yet there is in our breast something strong enough to fight against it and to resist? by the arbitrament of which, also, the mass of matter is compelled at times to be turned throughout body and limbs, and, when thrust forward, is curbed back and settles back steadily.

[284] Therefore you must admit that the same exists in the seeds also, that motions have some cause other than blows and weights, from which this power is born in us, since we see that nothing can be produced from nothing. For it is weight that prevents all things from being caused through blows by a sort of external force; but what keeps the mind itself from having necessity within it in all actions, and from being as it were mastered and forced to endure and to suffer, is the minute swerving of the first beginnings at no fixed place and at no fixed time.

*   *   *

BOOK THREE

O you [Epicurus] who first amid so great a darkness were able to raise aloft a light so clear, illumining the blessings of life, you I follow, O glory of the Grecian race, and now on the marks you have left I plant my own footsteps firm, not so much desiring to be your rival, as for love, because I yearn to copy you: for why should a swallow vie with swans, or what could a kid with its shaking limbs do in running to match himself with the strong horse's vigour? You are our father, the discoverer of truths, you supply us with a father's precepts, from your pages, illustrious man, as bees in the flowery glades sip all the sweets, so we likewise feed on all your golden words, your words of gold, ever most worthy of life eternal. For as soon as your reasoning begins to proclaim the nature of things revealed by your divine mind, away flee the mind's terrors, the walls of the world open out, I see action going on throughout the whole void: before me appear the gods in their majesty, and their peaceful abodes, which no winds ever shake nor clouds besprinkle with rain, which no snow congealed by the bitter frost mars with its white fall, but the air ever cloudless encompasses them and laughs with its light spread wide abroad. There moreover nature supplies everything, and nothing at any time impairs their peace of mind. But contrariwise nowhere appear the regions of Acheron; yet the earth is no hindrance to all being clearly seen, whatsoever goes on below under our feet throughout the void. Thereupon from all these things a sort of divine delight gets hold upon me and a shuddering, because nature thus by your power has been so manifestly laid open and uncovered in every part.

[31] And since I have shown of what kind are the beginnings of all things, and in how varying and different shapes they fly of their own accord driven in everlasting motion, and how all things can be produced from these, following next upon this the nature of mind and spirit must now clearly be explained in my verses, and that fear of Acheron be sent packing which troubles the life of man from its deepest depths, suffuses all with the blackness of death, and leaves no delight clean and pure. For when men often declare that disease and a life of infamy are more to be feared than the bottomless Pit of death, and that they know the nature of the soul to be that of blood or even air if their whim so direct, and that they have no need of our reasoning, what follows will show you that they make all these boasts in vainglory rather than because the fact itself is established. These same men, driven from their native land and banished far from the sight of men, stained with some disgraceful charge, in short afflicted with all tribulations, yet live; and in spite of all, wherever the wretches go they sacrifice to their ancestors, and slay black cattle, and send down oblations to the departed ghosts, and in their bitter days direct their minds far more eagerly to superstition. Thus it is more useful to scrutinize a man in danger or peril, and to discern in adversity what manner of man he is: for only then are the words of truth drawn up from the very heart, the mask is torn off, the reality remains.

[59] Moreover, avarice and the blind lust of distinction, which drive wretched men to transgress the bounds of law, and sometimes by sharing and scheming crime to strive night and day with exceeding toil to climb the pinnacle of power, these sores of life in no small degree are fed by the fear of death. For in general degrading scorn and bitter need are seen to be far removed from sweetness and stability of life, and a lingering as it were before the gates of death; from which men desiring to escape afar and to remove themselves far away, driven by false terror, amass wealth by civil bloodshed and greedily multiply riches, piling murder upon murder; cruelly they rejoice at the mournful death of a brother, they hate and they fear a kinsman's hospitality.

[74] In like manner and through the same fear, they are often consumed with envy that before their very eyes he is clothed in power, he is the sight of the town, who parades in shining pomp, while they complain that they themselves are wallowing in darkness and mire. Some wear out their lives for the sake of a statue and a name. And often it goes so far, that for fear of death men are seized by hatred of life and of seeing the light, so that with sorrowing heart they devise their own death, forgetting that this fear is the fountain of their cares: it induces one man to violate honour, another to break the bonds of friendship, and in a word to overthrow all natural feeling; for often before now men have betrayed fatherland or beloved parents in seeking to avoid the regions of Acheron. For as children tremble and fear everything in the blind darkness, so we in the light sometimes fear what is no more to be feared than the things that children in the dark hold in terror and imagine will come true. This terror, therefore, and darkness of the mind must be dispersed, not by rays of the sun nor the bright shafts of daylight, but by the aspect and law of nature.

[94] First I say that the mind, which we often call the intelligence, in which is situated the understanding and the government of life, is a part of man, no less than hands and feet and eyes are parts of the whole living being.

[98] [However, some philosophers have thought] that the feeling of the mind is not situated in any fixed part, but that it is a sort of vital condition of the body, called harmony by the Greeks, which makes us live endowed with feeling, although the intelligence is not situated in any part; as when the body is often said to have good health, and yet this health is no part of the healthy creature. Thus they do not place the feeling of the mind in any fixed part; and in this they seem to me to wander very far astray. For indeed the body which we can see plain before us is often sick, although we are yet happy in the other part which lies hidden; and again it often happens that the contrary is true in its turn, when one wretched in mind is happy in all his body, not otherwise than if the sick man's foot gives him pain when there is no pain meanwhile in the head. Besides, when the frame is given over to soft sleep, and the body lies outspread heavy and without sensation, there is yet something in us which at that time is agitated in many ways, and admits into itself all the motions of joy and cares of the heart, which have no meaning.

[117] Next, that you may recognize that the spirit also lies within the frame and that it is not harmony that causes the body to feel, firstly it happens that if a great part of the body be taken away, yet life often remains in our frame; and again when a few particles of heat have dispersed abroad and air is driven out through the mouth, the same life in a moment deserts the veins and leaves the bones; so that from this you may recognize that not all particles have a like function or support life equally, but rather that those which are seeds of wind and warming heat see to it that life lingers in the frame. There is therefore within the body itself a heat and a vital wind which deserts our frame on the point of death.

[130] Therefore, since the nature of the mind and spirit has been found to be in some way a part of the man, give back the name of harmony, brought down to musicians from high Helicon, or perhaps the musicians themselves drew it from some other source and applied it to that which then lacked a name of its own. Be that how it may, let them keep it; do you now learn what else I have to say.

[136] Next, I say that mind and spirit are held in conjunction together and compound one nature in common, but that the head so to speak and lord over the whole body is the understanding which we call mind and intelligence. And this has its abiding place in the middle region of the breast. For in this place throbs terror and fear, hereabouts is melting joy: here therefore is the intelligence and the mind. The rest of the

spirit, dispersed abroad through the whole body, obeys and is moved according to the will and working of the intelligence. This alone by itself has sense, alone for itself rejoices, when nothing affects either spirit or body at the same time. And just as when head or eye is hurt by an attack of pain in us we are not tormented in the whole of our body, so the mind sometimes is hurt by itself, and is eager with joy, when the rest of the spirit throughout the limbs and frame is not stirred by any new sensation. But when the intelligence is moved by more vehement fear, we see the whole spirit throughout the frame share in the feeling: sweatings and pallor hence arise over the whole body, the speech falters, the voice dies away, blackness comes before the eyes, a sounding is in the ears, the limbs give way beneath; in a word we often see men fall to the ground for mental terror; so that everyone may easily recognize from this that the spirit is conjoined with the mind, and when this has been smitten by the mind's power, straightway it strikes and drives forward the body.

[161] This same reasoning teaches that the nature of mind and spirit is bodily; for when it is seen to drive forward the limbs, to arouse the body from sleep, to change the countenance, to guide and steer the whole man, and we see that none of these things can be done without touch, and further that there is no touch without body, must we not confess that mind and spirit have a bodily nature? Besides you perceive the mind to suffer along with the body, and to share our feeling in the body. If the grim force of a weapon driven deep to the dividing of bones and sinews fails to hit the life, yet a languor follows and a blissful fall to the ground, and upon the ground a turmoil that comes about in the mind, and sometimes a kind of hesitating desire to rise. Therefore the nature of the mind must be bodily, since it suffers by bodily weapons and blows.

[177] Now I shall go on to explain to you, of what kind of body this mind is, and of what it is formed. First I say that it is exceedingly delicate and formed of exceedingly minute particles. That this is so, you may consider the following points to convince you. Nothing is seen to be done so swiftly as the mind determines it to be done and does its own first act; therefore the mind bestirs itself more quickly than any of these things which are seen plain before our eyes. But that which is so readily moved must consist of seeds exceedingly rounded and exceedingly minute, that they may be moved when touched by a small moving power. For water moves and flows with so very small a moving power because it is made of small rolling shapes. But on the other hand the nature of honey has more cohesion, its fluid is more sluggish, and its movement more tardy; for the whole mass of its matter coheres more closely, assuredly because it is not made of bodies so smooth or so delicate and round. For a checked and light breath of air can make, as you may see, a high heap of poppy-seed slip down from the top; but contrariwise it cannot stir a pile of stones or wheat-ears. So, according as bodies are extremely small and smooth, they have power of motion; but contrariwise, whatever is found to be more weighty and rough is by so much the more stable. Now, therefore, since the nature of the mind has been found to be moved with unusual ease, it must consist of bodies exceedingly small and smooth and round. If this be known to you, my good friend, it will be found of advantage in many ways, and you will call it useful.

[208] Another thing also makes clear of how fine a texture it is, and in how small a space it might be contained if it could be gathered together; namely that as soon as death's peaceful calm has taken possession of a man, when mind and spirit have departed, you could not perceive any jot or tittle to be diminished from the body whether in look or in weight: death presents all, except vital sense and warming heat. Accordingly the whole spirit must consist of very small seeds, being interlaced through veins,

flesh, and sinews, since, when the whole has already departed from all the body, never-theless the outward contour of the limbs presents itself undiminished, nor is one jot of the weight lacking; just as happens when the bouquet of wine has vanished, or when the sweet breath of ointment has dispersed into the air, or when the flavour has passed from a substance, and yet the thing itself does not seem any smaller to the eye for all that, nor is anything lost in the weight, because assuredly many minute seeds compose the flavour and the smell in the whole substance of the things. Therefore again and again I say, we may understand the substance of mind and spirit to be made of very minute seeds, since in departing it takes nothing from the weight.

[231] But we must not believe this nature to be single. For a kind of thin breath mixed with heat leaves the dying, and the heat, moreover, draws air with it. Nor is there any heat which is not mixed with air; for since its nature is rarefied, many first-beginnings of air must be moving through it. Already, therefore, the nature of the mind is found to be threefold; yet all these three together are not enough to produce feeling, since the mind cannot admit that any of these can produce sense-bringing motions and the thoughts which a man revolves in his mind. A fourth nature must therefore be added to these; this is entirely without name; nothing exists more easily moved and more thin than this, or made of elements smaller and smoother; and this first distributes the sense-giving motions through the limbs. For this is first set in motion, being com-posed of small shapes; after that, heat takes on the movement, and the unseen power of wind, then the air; after which all is set in movement, the blood is agitated, the flesh is all thrilled through with feeling, last is communicated to bone and marrow it may be: the pleasure, it may be the opposite excitement. Nor is it easy for pain to soak through thus far, or any violent mischief, without throwing all into so great a riot that no place is left for life, and the particles of spirit flee abroad through all the pores of the body. But usually there is an end to the movement almost at the surface of the body; on this account we are strong enough to retain life.

[258] Now when I long to explain how these things are intermingled and in what ways they are arranged so as to be active, I am drawn away against my will by the poverty of our mother tongue; but notwithstanding I will touch upon the chief points, so far as I can.

[262] The first-beginnings of the elements so interpenetrate one another in their motions that no single element can be separated off nor can its power act divided from the rest by space, but they are, as it were, the many forces of a single body. Just as in the flesh of any living creature there is a scent and a certain heat and flavour, and yet from all these is made one body grown complete: so heat and air and the unseen power of wind commingled form one nature along with that quickly moving force, which from itself distributes amongst them the beginning of motion, whence first the sense-bringing motion arises spreading through the flesh. For this nature lies deep down, hid-den in the most secret recess, and there is nothing in our body more deeply seated than this; and it is itself furthermore the spirit of the whole spirit. Just as commingled in our frame and in all our body the force of mind and the power of spirit lies hidden, because it is composed of small and scanty elements: so, I tell you, this force without name composed of minute particles lies hid, and is furthermore itself as it were spirit of the whole spirit and lords it in all the body. In like manner it is necessary that wind and air and heat interact commingled throughout the frame, one element yielding place to an-other or rising pre-eminent in such a way that a unity be seen to be made of all, or else heat and wind apart and the power of air apart would destroy and dissipate the sensa-tion by being separated.

Roman Construction
The Romans were masters of practical construction. Many of their greatest architectural
feats were devoted to transportation, commerce, and amusement (not unlike today).
a. The Roman Forum. Artist's Reconstruction. The Forum was the primary market and
meeting place in Rome. (*Library of Congress/Instructional Resources Corp.*)
b. Appian Way. The Romans built excellent roads to places as far away as Britain. The
roads were constructed of six inches of lava on top of twelve inches of gravel on top of nine
inches of small stones on top of ten to twenty inches of large stones. The result was a solid
thoroughfare that the army could use in all weather. (*Italian Tourist Office*)
c. Aqueduct. Aqueducts were used to bring water into the cities of the Empire. This one, in
Spain, is still in use. (*Joelle Burrows*)
d. Circus Flaminius. Huge stadiums such as this one allowed for chariot races, horse races,
and other spectacles. Admission was free and over 100,000 people would often attend.
(*Pearson Education/PH College*)

[288] The mind has also that heat, which it takes on when it boils in wrath and
fire flashes more fiercely from the eyes; it has also abundance of that cold wind, fear's
comrade, which makes the limbs shiver and stirs the frame; it has too that quietude of
calm air which comes about when the heart is tranquil and the countenance serene. But
there is more of the hot in those creatures whose bitter hearts and angry minds easily
boil up in wrath. A notable instance of this is the violent fury of the lion, which so

often bursts his breast with roaring and growling, nor can he find room in his heart for the storm of passion. But the cold mind of the stag has more of wind, and more speedily sends currents of cold breath through his flesh, which cause a tremulous movement to pervade the limbs. But the nature of the cow lives more by the peaceful air; never overmuch excited by the smoky torch of wrath which when applied spreads a shade of blinding darkness around, never pierced and frozen with cold shafts of fear: she stands between the two, stags and wild lions.

[307] So also is it in the race of men: although training may bring some to an equal outside polish, yet it leaves there those original traces of the character of each mind. And we must not suppose that faults can be torn up by the roots, so that one man will not too readily run into bitter anger, another be attacked somewhat too soon by fear, a third put up with an affront more meekly than he should. And in many other respects the various natures of men must differ, and the habits that follow from them; I cannot now set forth the hidden causes of these, nor find names enough to fit the shapes assumed by the first-beginnings from which arises this variety in things. One thing I see that I can affirm in this regard is this: so trivial are the traces of different natures that remain, beyond reason's power to expel, that nothing hinders our living a life worthy of gods.

[323] This nature then is contained by the whole body, and is itself the body's guardian and source of its existence, for they cling together with common roots, and manifestly they cannot be torn asunder without destruction. Just as it is not easy to tear out the scent from lumps of frankincense, without its very nature being destroyed: so it is not easy to draw out mind and spirit from the whole body, without the dissolution of all. So interwoven are their elements from their first origin in the life which they live together; and we see that neither body nor mind has the power to feel singly without the other's help, but by common motions proceeding from both conjointly sensation is kindled for us in our flesh.

[337] Besides, a body is never born by itself, nor grows by itself, nor is it seen to last long after death. For it is not as when the liquid of water often throws off the heat which has been given to it, and yet is not itself torn to pieces for that reason, but remains uninjured; not thus, I say, can the frame endure disruption apart from the spirit which has left it; but it is utterly undone, torn to pieces, and rots away. From the first moment of life, the interdependent contacts of body and spirit, while yet laid away in the mother's body and womb, so learn the vital motions, that disruption apart cannot be without their ruin and damage; so that you may see that, since conjunction is necessary to their existence, so also theirs must be a joint nature.

[350] Furthermore, if anyone denies that body can feel, and believes that it is the spirit mingled throughout with the body that takes on that motion which we name feeling, he fights against things that are quite manifest and true. For who will ever explain what it is for the body to feel, unless it be what experience has openly shown and taught us? "But the spirit gone, the body lacks feeling in every part." Yes, for it loses that which in life was not its own property; as there are many other things that it loses when it is driven from life.

[359] Moreover, to say that the eyes can discern nothing, but that the mind looks out through them as through open portals, is difficult, when their own feeling leads us to the opposite conclusion; for it is their feeling that draws us and pushes us on to the very eyeballs; especially since we are often unable to perceive glaring objects because our bright eyes are hindered by the brightness, which never happens with portals; for an open door through which we look out ourselves never receives any annoyance. Be-

sides, if our eyes act as portals, why then take the eyes away, and it is obvious that the mind should perceive things all the better with doors, posts and all, removed.

[370] There is another thing, laid down by the revered judgement of the great Democritus, to which you could never assent: that the first-beginnings of body and of soul are placed one beside one alternately in pairs, and so link the frame together. For, as the elements of spirit are much smaller than those which compose our body and flesh, so they are fewer also in number and are dispersed at rare intervals through the frame; so that at least you may safely say that the first-beginnings of spirit lie at such intervals apart as equal the smallest things which falling upon us are able to awaken sense-bringing motions in our body. For sometimes we do not feel dust clinging to the body, or chalk* shaken on us settling on our limbs, nor do we feel the impact of a mist by night, or a spider's gossamer threads when we are caught in their net as we go along, nor the flimsy vesture of the same creature falling upon our head, nor birds' feathers or flying thistle-down, which are so exceeding light that they usually find it a heavy task to fall, nor the progress of every creeping thing, nor each of the footsteps that gnats and suchlike place on our body: so true is it that many particles must be moved in us, before the seeds of spirit mingled with our bodies throughout our frame begin to feel that the first-beginnings** have been struck, and before they can go buffeting over such great intervals, run together, meet together, and leap apart in turn.

[396] And the mind is more potent in holding fast the barriers of life, and has more dominance over life, than the spirit's force. For without the mind and intelligence no particle of the spirit can abide in the frame for an instant, but readily follows after it, and departs into the air, and leaves the limbs cold in the chill of death. But he remains in life to whom the mind and intelligence remains. He may be a mutilated trunk dismembered all about, the spirit removed all around and separated from the limbs, yet he lives and breathes the vital air. Deprived of a great part of the spirit, if not of all, yet he lingers and clings to life; just as when the eye is lacerated all round, if the pupil remains unhurt, there abides the lively power of seeing, provided you do not mangle the whole eyeball and cut round the pupil and leave that isolated; for that will not be done without destroying them both. But if that tiny spot in the middle of the eye is eaten through, in a trice the light is out and darkness follows, even though the radiant orb is otherwise unharmed. Such is the alliance by which spirit and mind are forever bound.

[417] Listen now: that you may be able to recognize that the minds and light spirits of living creatures are born and are mortal, I shall proceed to set forth verses worthy of your character, long sought out and found with delightful toil. Be so good as to apply both these names to one thing; and when for example I speak of spirit, showing it to be mortal, believe me to speak also of mind, inasmuch as it is one thing and a combined nature.

[425] First of all, since I have shown it to be delicate and composed of minute particles and elements much smaller than the flowing liquid of water or cloud or smoke—for it surpasses these far in quickness, and moves if touched by a more delicate cause, inasmuch as it is moved by images of smoke and mist, as for example when sunk in sleep we perceive altars exhale their steam on high and send up smoke (for without doubt these are images borne to us)—now, therefore, since, when vessels are shattered, you perceive the water flowing out on all sides and the liquid dispersing, and since mist and smoke disperse abroad into the air, believe that the spirit also is spread

---

*[Chalk was used as a cosmetic and for bleaching clothes.]
**[The body-atoms.]

abroad and passes away far more quickly, and is more speedily dissolved into its first bodies, as soon as it has departed withdrawn from the limbs of a man. In fact if the body, which is in a way its vessel, cannot contain it, when once broken up by any cause and rarefied by the withdrawal of blood from the veins, how could you believe that it could be contained by any air, which is a more porous container than our body?

[445] Besides, we feel that the mind is begotten along with the body, and grows up with it, and with it grows old. For as toddling children have a body infirm and tender, so a weak intelligence goes with it. Next, when their age has grown up into robust strength, the understanding too and the power of the mind is enlarged. Afterwards, when the body is now wrecked with the mighty strength of time, and the frame has succumbed with blunted strength, the intellect limps, the tongue babbles, the intelligence totters, all is wanting and fails at the same time. It follows therefore that the whole nature of the spirit is dissolved abroad, like smoke, into the high winds of the air, since we see it begotten along with the body, and growing up along with it, and as I have shown, falling to pieces at the same time worn out with age.

[459] Add to this that, just as the body itself is liable to awful diseases and harsh pain, so we see the mind liable to anxious care and grief and fear; therefore it follows that the mind also partakes of death.

[463] Moreover, in bodily diseases the mind often wanders astray; for it is demented and talks deliriously, and at times is carried by heavy lethargy into the deep everlasting sleep with eyes drooping and dejected head, from which it can neither catch the voices nor recognize the looks of those who stand round calling it back to life, their faces and cheeks bedewed with tears. Therefore you must confess that the mind also is dissolved, since the contagion of disease penetrates within it; for both pain and disease are makers of death, as we have been well taught by the perishing of many before now.

[476] Moreover, when the piercing power of wine has penetrated into a man, and its fire has been dispersed abroad, spreading through the veins, why does heaviness come upon the limbs, why are his legs impeded, why does he stagger, his tongue grow tardy, his mind soaked, his eyes swim, noise and hiccups and brawls burst out, and all the rest of such things follow, why is this, I say, unless it be that the vehement fury of wine is accustomed to confuse the spirit while yet in the body? But if anything can be confused and impeded, this indicates that, if some cause a little more compelling should penetrate, the thing would perish, and be robbed of its future life.

[487] Moreover, we have often seen someone constrained on a sudden by the violence of disease, who, as if struck by a thunderbolt, falls to the ground, foams at the mouth, groans and shudders, raves, grows rigid, twists, pants irregularly, outwearies himself with contortions; assuredly because the spirit, torn asunder by the violence of the disease throughout the frame, is in turmoil and foams, just as in the salt sea the waves boil under the mighty strength of the winds. Further, groans are forced out, because the limbs are afflicted with pain, and in general because seeds of voice are ejected and rush forth from the mouth in a mass, where they have been, as it were, accustomed to pass, where is the established highroad. There is raving, because the strength of mind and spirit is set in a turmoil and, as I have shown, divided apart and separated up and drawn asunder by that same poison. Next, when the cause of the disease has already turned back, and the corroding humour of the diseased body has returned to its secret haunts, then first, staggering as it were, the man rises, and by degrees comes back to his full senses and receives back his spirit. Since, therefore, the mind and spirit are tossed about by so great diseases in the very body itself, and are

miserably torn asunder and distressed, why do you believe that the same without body, in the open air, amidst mighty winds, are able to live?

[510] And since we see that the mind, like a sick body, can be healed and changed by medicine, this also foreshows that the mind has a mortal life. For it is necessary to add parts or transpose them or draw away at least some tittle from the whole, whenever anyone attempts and begins to alter the mind or indeed to change any other nature whatever. But that which is immortal does not permit its parts to be transposed, or anything to be added, or one jot to ebb away; for whatever by being changed passes outside its own boundaries, at once that is death for that which was before. Therefore, if the mind is sick, it gives indications of mortality, as I have shown, or if it is changed by medicine: so completely is the truth seen to combat false reasoning, and to cut off its retreat as it flies, and to convict falsehood by a double refutation.

[526] Furthermore, we often see a man pass away by degrees, and limb by limb lose the sensation of life: first the toes of the feet grow livid, and the nails, next die feet and legs, afterwards over the other limbs go creeping the cold footsteps of death. Since in this case the substance of the spirit is divided and passes away and does not issue forth whole at one time, it must be held to be mortal. But if by any chance you think that it can of its own accord pull itself inwards through the limbs and draw together its portions into one place, and that is how it withdraws sensation from all the limbs, then the place into which all that quantity of spirit is gathered together ought to seem more sensitive; but since this place is nowhere to be found, undoubtedly, as I said before, the spirit is torn to pieces and dispersed abroad, perishes therefore. Moreover, if I had the whim after all to concede a falsehood, and to grant you that the spirit might be concentrated in the body of those who are leaving the daylight by dying piecemeal, yet you must confess the spirit to be mortal, for it does not matter whether it passes away dispersed abroad through the air, or draws in its parts upon itself and grows dull, seeing that more and more sensation leaves the whole man on all sides, and on all sides less and less of life remains.

[548] And since the mind is one part of a man, which abides planted in a fixed place, just as eyes and ears are and all the other organs of sense that govern life; and just as hand or eye or nose separated from us can neither feel nor be, but rather are soon dissolved in putrefaction, so the mind cannot be by itself without body or without the man himself, which body seems to be a kind of vessel for it or any other similitude you may choose for a closer conjunction, since in fact the body does cling closely to it.

[558] Furthermore, the quickened power of body and mind have vigour and enjoy life only in close conjunction together; for neither can the nature of the mind show vital motions alone by itself without the body, nor again deprived of the spirit can the body endure and use the senses. To be sure, just as the eye torn from its roots cannot by itself distinguish anything apart from the whole body, so it is seen that mind and spirit can do nothing alone. Undoubtedly because their first-beginnings are held in by the whole body, commingled throughout veins and flesh, sinews and bones, and cannot leap freely apart through wide intervals: for this reason, when shut in together, they make those sense-giving motions, which they cannot make outside the body when cast forth into the winds of the air after death, because they are not held in as before. For air will be a body and a living creature, if the spirit shall be able to keep itself together, and to confine itself to those motions which before it used to make in the sinews and in the body itself. Therefore again and again I say, when all the covering of the body is broken up, and the breath of life is cast forth out, you must confess that the sensations of the mind are dissolved, and the spirit too, since the two exist by union.

[580] Again, since the body cannot endure tearing apart from the spirit without putrefying with a loathsome stench, why do you doubt that the strength of the spirit, after gathering together from its depths and inmost recesses, has oozed out already dispersed abroad like smoke, and that the reason why the body changing and crumbling in such ruin has collapsed altogether, is that its foundations to their inmost recesses have been moved from their place while the spirit was oozing out all through the limbs and through all the meandering passages and pores that are in the body? So that in many ways you may learn that the spirit was scattered abroad when it went out through the limbs, and had been torn all apart within the body itself, before it glided out and swam into the winds of the air. Moreover, while the spirit still moves about within the bounds of life, nevertheless, when weakened by some cause or other, it often appears to wish to depart and to be released from the whole body, and the countenance appears to grow languid as at the last hour, and all the limbs to relax and droop from the bloodless body. This is what happens when the phrase is used "the mind fails" or "the spirit faints": when all is trepidation, and all those present desire to pull back again the last bond of life. For at that time the intelligence and all the power of the spirit are shaken altogether, and these fail together with the body itself, so that a slightly more serious cause could dissolve them. Why then after all do you doubt that, when driven without the body, weak, outside, in the open, without a covering, the spirit could not only not endure through all time, but could not last even for the smallest space?

[607] It is evident that no one in dying feels his soul go forth from the whole body intact, nor rise first to the throat and then pass up to the gullet; rather he feels it fail in the particular region where it is located, as he knows his other senses to be dispersing abroad each in its own part. But if our intelligence were immortal, in dying it would not so much complain of dispersing abroad, but rather of passing out and quitting its [skin], like a snake.

[615] Again, why are the mind's intelligence and understanding never produced in the head or feet or hands, but abide in one sole position and fixed region in all men, if not because fixed positions are assigned to each thing for its birth and a place where it may endure when made, with its manifold limbs being arranged in such a way that their order is never reversed? So surely one thing follows another; neither is flame accustomed to be produced from streams, nor frost in fire.

[624] Besides, if the nature of the spirit is immortal and can feel when separated from our body, we must, I think, assume that it is endowed with the five senses; in no other way can we imagine the spirits below to be wandering in Acheron. Painters therefore, and the earlier generations of writers, have introduced the spirits thus provided with senses. But apart from the body there can never be either eyes or nose or hand by itself for the spirit, nor tongue apart from the body, nor ears; therefore spirits by themselves cannot either have sensation or exist.

[634] And since we feel that vital sense inheres in the whole body, and see that it is the whole that is animated, if suddenly some force with a swift blow shall cut the body through the middle so as to sever the two parts asunder, there is no doubt that the spirit also will be sundered apart and cleft apart and cut apart with the body. But that which is cleft and divided into parts assuredly renounces all claim to be everlasting.

[642] They tell how scythed chariots,* reeking with indiscriminate slaughter, often shear off a limb so suddenly that it is seen to quiver on the ground when it falls shorn from the trunk, although the man's mind and strength can feel no pain, from the swiftness of the blow, and at the same time because the mind is absorbed in the ardour

*[War-chariots with scythes (blades) attached to the wheels.]

of battle; with what is left of his body he pursues battle and blood, and does not observe that his left arm, it may be, with its shield has been carried off amidst the horses by the wheels and their ravening scythes, or another that his right arm has fallen while he climbs and presses on. Then another essays to rise with a leg lost, while the dying foot hard by on the ground twitches its toes. Even the head shorn off from the hot and living trunk retains on the ground the look of life and its open eyes, until it has rendered up all that is left of the spirit.

[657] Moreover, when you see a serpent with flickering tongue, menacing tail, long body, if it please you to cut up both parts with your steel into many pieces, you will see all the parts cut away writhing separately while the wound is fresh, and bespattering the earth with gore, and the fore part turning back and seeking to gnaw itself, that by its bite it may assuage the burning pain of the wound which struck it. Shall we say then that there is a whole spirit in each of these fractions? But in that way it will follow that one living creature had many spirits in its body. Therefore that spirit which was one has been divided apart together with the body; and so each must be considered mortal, since each alike is cut asunder into many parts.

[670] Besides, if the nature of the spirit is immortal and creeps into the body as we are born, why can we not remember also the time that has passed before, and why do we keep no traces of things done? For if the power of the mind has been so greatly changed that it has lost all recollection of things done, that, I think, is not far removed from death. Therefore you must confess that the spirit that was before has perished, and that which now is has now been made.

[679] Besides, if the body is already complete when the quickened power of the mind is accustomed to be introduced into us, at the moment when we are born and when we enter the threshold of life, it ought not so to live that it should be seen to grow with the body and together with the frame in the very blood, but it should live alone by itself as it might be in a cage, while nevertheless all the body should be full of streams of sensation. Therefore again and again I say that spirits must not be considered to be without beginning or free from the law of death. For we must not believe that they could have been so closely connected with our bodies if they had been introduced from without, when experience manifestly proves the clean contrary; for the spirit is so closely connected with the body through all the veins, flesh, sinews, and bones that even the teeth feel like the rest, as their aching proves, and the twinge of cold water, and the crunching of rough grit, when it has got into them out of bread; and since they are so closely connected, it is clear that they are not able to emerge intact and loosen themselves away whole from all the sinews and bones and joints.

[698] But if by any chance you think that the spirit is accustomed to creep in from without and so to ooze through our frame, so much the more will it perish, being interfused with the body; for that which permeates is dissolved, perishes therefore. The spirit is distributed through all the pores of the body; just as food, while it is being dispersed into all the members and limbs, perishes and supplies, another nature from its substance, so spirit and mind, even though they enter whole into a new body, yet in permeating it are dissolved, while the particles are being dispersed through all the pores, as we may call them, into the limbs, those particles that compose this mind which now lords it in our body, born of that mind which perished at the time when it was distributed through the limbs. Therefore the spirit is seen to be neither without a birthday nor without death.

[713] Again, do any seeds of spirit remain or not in the lifeless body? Now if any are left and are in it, it will be impossible rightly to consider the spirit immortal, since it has gone away diminished by the loss of some parts. But if it has departed and fled

forth with its component parts so intact that it has left in the body no particles of itself, how do corpses exhale worms from flesh already grown putrid,* whence comes all the great mass of living creatures, boneless and bloodless, that surge through the swelling limbs? Now if you believe by any chance that spirits can creep into the worms from without and come one by one into the bodies, if you do not ponder why many thousands of spirits gather together where one has gone away, here is a question that it seems worthwhile to ask and to bring under examination, whether in fact the spirits go a hunting for all the seeds of little worms and themselves make them a habitation, or whether they creep as it were into bodies already formed. But there is no answer to the question why they should make bodies themselves, or why they should take that trouble. For, when they are without bodies, they are not plagued with disease as they fly about, or with cold and hunger; for it is the body rather that is troubled through susceptibility to these infirmities, and the mind suffers many maladies by contact with it. Grant, however, that it be as useful as you will that these make them a body to enter: but how they can, there is no way to be seen. Spirits therefore do not make themselves bodies and limbs. Nor is there any possibility that they creep into bodies already made; for they will not be able to conjoin themselves closely together with these, nor will harmony be established through community of sensation.

[741] Furthermore, why does bitter fury go with the sullen breed of lions, why craft with foxes, why is the instinct of flight transmitted to deer from their fathers, the father's timidity impelling their limbs, why are all other qualities of this sort generated in the body and the character from the beginnings of life, if not because in each seed and breed its own fixed power of mind grows along with each body? But if it were immortal, and accustomed to pass from body to body, living creatures would show confused habits: the dog of Hyrcanian breed** would often flee before the horned stag's onset; the hawk would tremble, flying through the air from the advancing dove; men would lack reason, the wild generations of wild beasts would have it.

[754] For it is based on false reasoning to say that an immortal spirit is altered by a change of body; for that which changes is dissolved, therefore perishes. The parts of the spirit are transposed, and move from their position; therefore they must be capable of being dissolved also through the frame, to perish at last one and all with the body.

[760] But if they say that the spirits of men always pass into men's bodies, I will still ask why a foolish spirit can be made of a wise one, why no child is ever prudent, and no foal ever so accomplished as the horse of powerful strength. No doubt they will take refuge in saying that in a tender body the mind becomes tender. But even if this is so, you must confess that the spirit is mortal, since being changed so completely throughout the body it loses its former life and feeling.

[769] Or how will the power of the mind be able to grow strong together with any given body and attain the longed-for flowering of life, unless it shall be its partner in the first origin? Or why does it wish to issue forth from a frame grown old? Does it fear to remain imprisoned in a putrefying corpse, fear lest its house, worn out with the long lapse of years, fall in upon it? But there are no dangers for the immortal.

[776] Again, to suppose that spirits stand ready for the amours and the parturition of wild beasts is plainly too ridiculous—immortal spirits awaiting mortal frames

---

*[Lucretius is reflecting the popular belief of his time that worms are spontaneously generated from dead flesh.]

**[The dogs of Hyrcania, on the southeast shore of the Caspian Sea, were noted for their ferocity.]

in number numberless, and struggling together in hot haste which first and foremost shall creep in unless perhaps the spirits have contracts so arranged, that the spirit which comes flying up first may creep in first, and they need not come to blows one whit.

[784] Again, a tree cannot grow in the sky, nor clouds be in the deep sea, nor fish live in the fields, nor can blood be in sticks nor sap in rocks. It is fixed and arranged where each thing is to grow and have its being. So the nature of the mind cannot arise alone without body, nor exist far from sinews and blood. But if it could do this, the power of the mind itself could much more easily be in the head or shoulders or the heels of the feet, and be born in any part, and at least remain in the same man, the same vessel. But since even in our body there is seen to be a fixed rule and ordinance in what place mind and spirit may exist and grow apart, so much the more must we deny that they can endure and be produced wholly outside the body. Therefore, when the body has perished, you must confess that the spirit has passed away, torn to pieces throughout the body.

[800] In fact, to yoke mortal with immortal, and to think that they can be partners in feeling and act upon each other, is folly; for what can be considered more discordant, more contradictory or inconsistent, than that what is mortal can be yoked together in combination with immortal and imperishable, to weather furious storms!

[808] Besides, whatever bodies abide everlasting must, either, being of solid structure, reject blows and allow nothing to penetrate them that could dissever asunder the close-joined parts within, as the particles of matter are, the nature of which we have shown before; or else the reason why they can endure through all time must be that they are free from assaults, as the void is, which remains untouched and is not a whit affected by blows; or again because there is no extent of space around into which things can as it were disperse and dissolve, as the sum of all sums* is eternal, and there is no place without it into which its elements may escape, nor bodies to fall upon it and dissolve it asunder with a strong blow.

[819] But if possibly the reason why the spirit is to be held immortal is rather this, that it is sheltered and protected by the forces of life, either because nothing comes at all that is hostile to its existence, or because all that does come goes back, in some way repulsed before we can perceive what harm it does, [experience manifestly shows that this cannot be true.] For not to mention that it sickens along with bodily disease, something often comes that torments it about the future, keeps it miserable in fear, wearies it with anxiety, and, when there has been evil done in the past, its sins bring remorse. Add madness which is peculiar to the mind, and forgetfulness of all things, add that it is drowned in the black waters of lethargy.

[830] Therefore death is nothing to us, it matters not one jot, since the nature of the mind is understood to be mortal; and as in time past we felt no distress, while from all quarters the Carthaginians were coming to the conflict, when the whole world, shaken by the terrifying tumult of war, shivered and quaked under the lofty and breezy heaven, and was in doubt under which domination all men were destined to fall by land and sea;** so, when we shall no longer be, when the parting shall have come about between body and spirit from which we are compacted into one whole, then sure enough nothing at all will be able to happen to us, who will then no longer be, or to make us feel, not if earth be commingled with sea and sea with sky.

*[The universe.]
**[Referring to the Second Punic War, 218–201 B.C.]

MARCUS AURELIUS
A.D. 121–180

Marcus Aurelius was born to a patrician family of Rome. Following the death of his parents, he was raised by his grandfather and eventually adopted by the future emperor, Aurelius Antonius. While still a boy, he became a Stoic, giving himself fully to the study and practice of Stoicism. Following the death of Aurelius Antonius in 161, Marcus Aurelius became emperor of Rome. By nature a gentle and peace-loving man, he nevertheless spent most of his reign fighting in campaigns against the barbarians on the borders of the empire. He was also forced to deal with an epidemic of the plague, a revolt by one of his generals, the death of four of his five sons, and a perceived threat from a new religion, Christianity. Yet as eighteenth-century historian Edward Gibbon explains in *The Decline and Fall of the Roman Empire:*

> His life was the noblest commentary on the precepts of Zeno [of Citium—founder of Stoicism]. He was severe to himself, indulgent to the imperfections of others, just and beneficent to all mankind. He regretted that Avidius Cassius, who excited a rebellion in Syria, had disappointed him, by a voluntary death, of the pleasure of converting an enemy into a friend; and he justified the sincerity of that sentiment, by moderating the zeal of the senate against the adherents of the traitor. War he detested, as the disgrace and calamity of human nature, but when the necessity of a just defence called upon him to take up arms, he readily exposed his person to eight winter campaigns on the frozen banks of the Danube, the severity of which was at last fatal [he died in A.D. 180] to the weakness of his constitution. His memory was revered by a grateful posterity, and above a century after his death, many persons preserved the image of Marcus [Aurelius], among those of their household gods.

516

While on his miliary campaigns, Marcus Aurelius wrote a book of disconnected reflections on life known as the *Meditations*. These *Meditations* reflect a
Stoic acceptance of nature and of the need for self-control in the face of adversity. As a practical Roman, Marcus Aurelius was not interested in the metaphysical materialism of the early Stoa. Instead, he stressed the need for active benevolence and the acceptance of divine providence, or fate. Touching on several
topics, the passage here, translated by George Long, includes Marcus Aurelius's
claim that apparent evil is actually a part of the overall good of the universe. As
Alexander Pope (*Essay on Man*) said fifteen hundred years later:

> All Nature is but Art, unknown to thee;
> All Chance, Direction, which thou canst not see;
> All Discord, Harmony, not understood;
> All partial Evil, universal Good:
> And, spite of Pride, in erring Reason's spite,
> One truth is clear, "Whatever IS, is RIGHT."

*   *   *

A.S.L. Farquharson, *Marcus Aurelius: His Life and His World,* edited by D.A.
Rees (Oxford: Basil Blackwell, 1951), provides a helpful general study of Marcus Aurelius. E.R. Dodds, *Pagan and Christian in an Age of Anxiety* (Cam-
bridge: Cambridge University Press, 1965), examines the culture in which Mar-
cus Aurelius lived and wrote; while Henry D. Sedgwick, *Marcus Aurelius* (New
Haven, CT: Yale University Press, 1922), and Anthony Richard Birley, *Marcus
Aurelius: A Biography* (New Haven, CT: Yale University Press, 1987), provide
general biographies. For commentaries on the *Meditations* see the classic, A.S.L.
Farquharson, ed., *The Meditations of the Emperor Marcus Antonius* (Oxford:
Clarendon Press, 1944), and the more recent, but difficult, R.B. Rutherford, *The
Meditations of Marcus Aurelius: A Study* (Oxford: Oxford University Press,
1989).

MEDITATIONS (in part)

BOOK IV

The attitude of that which rules within us towards outside events, if it is in accord with
nature, is ever to adapt itself easily to what is possible in the given circumstances. It
does not direct its affection upon any particular set of circumstances to work upon, but
it starts out toward its objects with reservations, and converts any obstacle into material for its own action, as fire does when it overpowers what is thrown upon it. A small

Marcus Aurelius Antonius, *Meditations,* translated by G.M.A. Grube (New York: Macmillan, Library of the
Liberal Arts, 1963).

Dying Gaul, a Roman copy after a bronze original of ca. 225 B.C. While the original statue depicts a casualty inflicted by the troops of Attalus I of Pergamon (241–197 B.C.), Marcus Aurelius, despite his pacifist philosophy, also led his troops against the barbarian Gauls. (*Alinari-Scala/Art Resource*)

flame might be quenched by it, but a bright fire very rapidly appropriates to itself whatever is put upon it, consumes it and rises higher because of these obstacles.

2. Let no action be done at random, or in any other way than in accordance with the principle which perfects the art.

3. Men seek retreats for themselves in country places, on beaches and mountains, and you yourself are wont to long for such retreats, but that is altogether unenlightened when it is possible at any hour you please to find a retreat within yourself. For nowhere can a man withdraw to a more untroubled quietude than in his own soul, especially a man who has within him things of which the contemplation will at once put him perfectly at ease, and by ease I mean nothing other than orderly conduct. Grant yourself this withdrawal continually, and refresh yourself. Let these be brief and elemental doctrines which when present will suffice to overwhelm all sorrows and to send you back no longer resentful of the things to which you return.

For what is it you resent? The wickedness of men? Reflect on the conclusion that rational beings are born for the sake of each other, that tolerance is a part of righteousness, and that men do not sin on purpose. Consider how many men have been hostile and suspicious, have hated and waged war, and then been laid out for burial or reduced to ashes. Desist then. Do you resent the portions received from the whole? Consider the alternatives afresh, namely "Providence or atoms," and how many proofs there are that the universe is like a city community. Are you still affected by the things of the body? Reflect that the mind, once it has freed itself and come to know its own capacities, is no longer involved in the movements of animal life, whether these be smooth or tumultuous. For the rest, recall all you have heard about pain and pleasure, to which you have given assent.

Does paltry fame disturb you? Look how swift is the forgetting of all things in the chaos of infinite time before and after, how empty is noisy applause, how liable to change and uncritical are those who seem to speak well of us, how narrow the boundaries within which fame is confined. The whole earth is but a point in the universe, and how small a part of the earth is the corner in which you live. And how many are those who there will praise you, and what sort of men are they?

From now on keep in mind the retreat into this little territory within yourself. Avoid spasms and tensions above all: be free and look at your troubles like a man, a citizen and a mortal creature. Among the foremost things which you will look into are these two: first, that external matters do not affect the soul but stand quietly outside it, while true disturbances come from the inner judgment; second, that everything you see has all but changed already and is no more. Keep constantly in mind in how many things you yourself have witnessed changes already. The universe is change, life is understanding.

4. If we have intelligence in common, so we have reason which makes us reasoning beings, and that practical reason which orders what we must or must not do; then the law too is common to us and, if so, we are citizens; if so, we share a common government; if so, the universe is, as it were, a city—for what other common government could one say is shared by all mankind?

From this, the common city, we derive our intelligence, our reason and our law—from what else? Just as the dry earth-element in me has been portioned off from earth somewhere, and the water in me from the other element, the air or breath from some other source and the dry and fiery from a source of its own (for nothing comes from what does not exist or returns to it), so also then the intelligence comes from somewhere.

5. Death, like birth, is a mystery of nature. The one is a joining together of the same elements into which the other is a dissolving. In any case, it is nothing of which one should be ashamed, for it is not incompatible with the nature of a rational being or the logic of its composition.

6. Their nature inevitably required that they behave in this way. He who wants this not to be wants a fig tree not to produce its acrid juice. In any case remember this: within a very short time both you and he will have died, and soon not even your name will survive.

7. Discard the thought of injury, and the words "I have been injured" are gone; discard the words "I have been injured," and the injury is gone.

8. What does not make a man worse does not make his life worse, and does him no injury, external or internal.

9. The nature of the universally beneficial has inevitably brought this about.

10. "Everything which happens, is right." Examine this saying carefully and you will find it so. I do not mean right merely in the sense that it fits the pattern of events, but in the sense of just, as if someone were giving each his due. Examine this then as you have begun to do, and, whatever you do, do it as a good man should, as the word good is properly understood. Safeguard this goodness in your every action.

11. Do not think the thoughts of an insolent man or those he wishes you to think, but see things as they truly are.

12. You should always be ready for two things, first, to do only what reason, as embodied in the arts of kingship and legislation, perceives to be to the benefit of mankind; second, to change your course if one be present to put you right and make

you abandon a certain opinion. Such change, however, should always result from being convinced of what is just and for the common good, and what you choose to do must be of that nature, not because pleasure or fame may result from it.

13. "You are endowed with reason." "I am." "Then why not use it, for, if it fulfills its proper function, what more do you want?"

14. You exist as a part of the Whole. You will disappear into the Whole which created you, or rather you will be taken up into the creative Reason when the change comes.

15. Many grains of incense on the same altar; one was cast earlier, the other later, but it makes no difference.

16. Within ten days you will seem a god to the same men who now think you a beast or an ape, if you go back to your principles and the worship of Reason.

17. Live not as if you had ten thousand years before you. Necessity is upon you. While you live, while you may, become good.

18. How much ease he gains who does not look at what his neighbor says or does or thinks, but only at what he himself is doing in order that his own action may be just, pious, and good. Do not glance aside at another's black character but run the straight course to the finishing line, without being diverted.

19. The man who thrills at the thought of later fame fails to realize that every one of those who remember him will very shortly die, as well as himself. So will their successors, until all memory of him is quenched as it travels through the minds of men, the flame of whose life is lit and then put out. But suppose those who will remember you to be immortal and the memory of you everlasting; even so, what is it to you? And I do not mean that praise is nothing to you when dead, but what is it to you while you live, except insofar as it affects your management of affairs? For now you inopportunely neglect nature's gift of virtue while you cling to some other concern.

20. All that has any beauty at all owes this to itself, and is complete in itself, but praise is no part of it. Nothing becomes either better or worse for being praised, and I mean this to apply also to things more commonly called beautiful, such as works of nature or works of art. As for the truly beautiful, it has no need of anything further, any more than does law, or truth, or kindness or reverence. Which of these things is made beautiful by praise or destroyed by censure? Does an emerald become less beautiful if it is not praised? What of gold, ivory, purple, a lyre, a dagger, a little flower or a bush?

21. If souls live on, how has the air of heaven made room for them through eternity? How has the earth made room for such a long time for the bodies of those who are buried in it? Just as on earth, after these bodies have persisted for a while, their change and decomposition makes room for other bodies, so with the souls which have migrated into the upper air. After they have remained there for a certain time, they change and are dissolved and turned to fire as they are absorbed into the creative Reason, and in this way make room for those additional souls who come to share their dwelling place. Thus might one answer on the assumption that souls live on.

One should not, however, consider only the multitude of bodies that are buried thus, but also take into account the multitude of animals eaten every day by us and by other animals, how great is the number thus consumed and in a manner buried in the bodies of those who eat them. Yet there is room for them nevertheless because they are transformed into blood and changed into air and fire.

Where lies the investigation of the truth in this matter? In distinguishing between the matter and the cause.

22. Do not wander aimlessly, but give every impulse its just due, and in every sensation preserve the power of comprehension.

23. Everything which is in tune with you, O Universe, is in tune with me. Nothing which happens at the right time for you is early or late for me. Everything, O Nature, which your seasons produce is fruit to me. All things come from you, exist in you, and will return to you. If he could say: "Beloved city of Cecrops," will you not say: "Beloved city of Zeus"?

24. "Do but little, if you would have contentment." Surely it is better to do what is necessary, as much as the reason of one who is by nature a social creature demands, and in the manner reason requires it to be done. This will not only bring the contentment derived from right conduct, but also that of doing little, since most of our words and actions are unnecessary and whoever eliminates these will have more leisure and be less disturbed. Hence one should on each occasion remind oneself: "Surely this is not one of the necessary actions?" One should eliminate not only unnecessary actions but also unnecessary imaginings, for then no irrelevant actions will follow.

25. Make trial of how the life of the good man turns out for you, of the man who is glad of the share he receives from the Whole and satisfied if his own action be just and his own disposition kindly.

26. You have seen those things; look also at these: do not disturb yourself, achieve simplicity in yourself. Someone does wrong? The wrong is to himself. Something has happened to you? It is well. From the beginning all that happens has been ordained and fated for you as your part of the Whole. In a word, life is short; we must therefore derive benefit from the present circumstances with prudence and with justice. Be sober and relaxed.

27. Either a universe with order and purpose or a medley thrown together by chance, but that too has order. Or can there be order of a kind in your inner world, but no order in the Whole, especially as all things are distinguished from one another, yet intermingle, and respond to each other?

28. A character that is black, effeminate, obstinate, beast-like, subhuman, childish, stupid, repulsive, vulgar, money-grubbing, tyrannical.

29. If the man who does not understand the truths embodied in the universe is a stranger in it, no less a stranger is he who does not understand what happens in the world of sense. An exile is he who flees from social principle; blind, who keeps the eye of his mind closed; a beggar, who has need of another and does not possess within himself all that is of use in life. A tumor on the universe is he who cuts himself off in rebellion against the logic of our common nature because he is dissatisfied with his lot, for it is that nature which brought it about, as it also brought you about. He is but a splinter off the community who separates his own soul from that of all rational beings, which is one.

30. One man practices philosophy though he has no tunic, another, though he has no book. Yet another man is half naked: "I have no bread," says he, "but I stay on the path of Reason." I have the nurture provided by learning, but I do not stay on that path.

31. Treasure what little you have learnt and find refreshment in it. Go through what remains of your life as one who has wholeheartedly entrusted all that is his to the gods and has not made himself either despot or slave to any man.

32. Consider, for the sake of argument, the times of Vespasian; you will see all the same things: men marrying, begetting children, being ill, dying, fighting wars, feasting, trading, farming, flattering, asserting themselves, suspecting, plotting, praying for the death of others, grumbling at their present lot, falling in love, hoarding, longing for consulships and kingships. But the life of those men no longer exists, anywhere. Then turn to the times of Trajan; again, everything is the same; and that life too is dead. Contemplate and observe in the same way the records of the other periods of

time, indeed of whole nations: how many men have struggled eagerly and then, after a little while, fell and were resolved into their elements. But above all call to mind those whom you yourself have witnessed vainly struggling because they would not act in accord with their own nature and cling to it, and be satisfied with it. It is necessary thus to remind ourselves that every action requires the attention we give it to be measured according to its value, for if you do not dwell more than is fitting upon things of lesser importance, you will not impatiently give up the struggle.

33. Words of old in common usage now sound strange; so the names of men much sung of old are strange today. Camilius, Caeso, Volesus, Dentatus, a little later Scipio and Cato, too, then even Augustus, then even Hadrian and Antoninus. For all things fade and quickly become legend, soon to be lost in total forgetting. This I say of those who shone in wondrous glory; as for other men, they are no sooner dead than "unknown, unheard of." But in any case, what is eternal remembrance? It is altogether vain.

What is it which should earnestly concern us? This only: a just mind, actions for the common good, speech which never lies, and a disposition which welcomes all that happens as necessary and comprehensible, as flowing from a like origin and source.

34. Surrender yourself willingly to Clotho to help her spin whatever fate she will.

35. All is ephemeral, the one remembering and the one remembered.

36. Observe continually all that is born through change, and accustom yourself to reflect that the nature of the Whole loves nothing so much as to change existing things and to make similar new things. All that exists is in a sense the seed of what will be born from it, but you regard as seeds only those which are cast into the earth or the womb. But that is too unenlightened.

37. You will now soon be dead, but you are not yet simple, nor undisturbed, nor free of the suspicion that harm may come to you from outside, nor gracious to all, nor convinced that the only wisdom lies in righteous action.

38. Look to their directing minds, observe the wise: what they avoid and what they pursue.

39. Whether a thing is bad for you does not depend upon another man's directing mind, nor upon any turn or change in your environment. Upon what then? Upon that part of you which judges what is bad. Let it make no such judgment and all is well. Even when that which is closest to it, your body, is cut, burnt, suppurating or festering, let the judging part of you keep calm. That is, let it judge that anything which happens equally to a bad and a good man cannot be either bad or good; for that which happens both to the man who lives in disaccord with nature and to the man who lives in accord with it cannot itself be either in accord with nature or contrary to it.

40. One should continually think of the universe as one living being, with one substance and one soul—how all it contains falls under its one unitary perception, how all its actions derive from one impulse, how all things together cause all that happens, and the nature of the resulting web and pattern of events.

41. You are a little soul carrying a corpse, as Epictetus says.

42. There is no evil in things in process of change, nor any good in things resulting from change.

43. Time is a river of things that become, with a strong current. No sooner is a thing seen than it has been swept away, and something else is being carried past, and still another thing will follow.

44. Everything that happens is as customary and understandable as the rose in springtime or the fruit in summer. The same is true of disease, death, slander and conspiracy, and all the things which delight or pain foolish men.

45. What happens next is always intimately related to what went before. It is not a question of merely adding up disparate things connected by inevitable succession, but events are logically interdependent. Just as the realities are established in tune with one another, so, in the world of sense, phenomena do not occur merely in succession, but they display an amazing affinity with one another.

46. Always remember the words of Heraclitus that "the death of earth becomes water and the death of water becomes air, and that of air, fire, and so back again." Remember also what he says about the man who has forgotten whither the road leads. And "men are at odds with that with which they are in most constant touch, namely the Reason" which governs all; and again, "those things seem strange to them which they meet every day"; and "we must not act and speak as if asleep," for even then we seem to act and speak. And that one should not accept things "like children from parents" simply because they have been handed down to us.

47. If a god were to tell you that you will die tomorrow, or at any rate the day after, you would not make much of the difference between the day after and tomorrow—not unless you were altogether ignoble, for how short is the time between!

So now consider that the difference between the last possible year and tomorrow is no great matter.

48. Think continually how many doctors have died who often knit their brows over their dying patients, how many astrologers who had foretold the deaths of others as a matter of importance, how many philosophers who had discoursed at great length on death and immortality, how many heroic warriors who had killed many men, how many tyrants who had used their power over men's lives with terrible brutality, as if immortal themselves. How often have not whole cities died, if I may use the phrase, Helike, Pompeii, Herculaneum, and innumerable others. Go over in your mind the dead whom you have known, one after the other: one paid the last rites to a friend and was himself laid out for burial by a third, who also died; and all in a short time. Altogether, human affairs must be regarded as ephemeral, and of little worth: yesterday sperm, tomorrow a mummy or ashes.

Journey then through this moment of time in accord with nature, and graciously depart, as a ripened olive might fall, praising the earth which produced it, grateful to the tree that made it grow.

49. Be like a rock against which the waves of the sea break unceasingly. It stands unmoved, and the feverish waters around it are stilled.

"I am unfortunate because this has happened to me." No indeed, but I am fortunate because I endure what has happened without grief, neither shaken by the present nor afraid of the future. Something of this sort could happen to any man, but not every man can endure it without grieving. Why then is this more unfortunate than that is fortunate? Would you call anything a misfortune which is not incompatible with man's nature, or call incompatible with the nature of man that which is not contrary to his nature's purpose? You have learned to know that purpose. What has happened can then in no way prevent you from being just, great-hearted, chaste, wise, steadfast, truthful, self-respecting and free, or prevent you from possessing those other qualities in the presence of which man's nature finds its own fulfillment. Remember in the future, when something happens which tends to make you grieve, to cling to this doctrine: this is no misfortune, but to endure it nobly is good fortune.

50. It is simple but effective in helping you despise death to go over the list of those who clung to life a long time. What advantage have they over those who died prematurely? Anyway, wherever are they? Caedicianus, Fabius, Julianus, Lepidus, and any other there may be. They assisted at the burial of many and then were buried them-

selves. In any case, the difference in time is short; among what great troubles we endure it to the end, in what poor company, in how puny a body! Is it not rather a burden? See the abyss of past time behind you and another infinity of time in front. In that context, what difference is there between one who lives three days and a Nestor who lives for three generations?

51. Hasten always along the short road—the road in accord with nature is short—so that you always say and do what is most wholesome. To keep this aim before one frees a man from the wearisome troubles of military service, management of all kinds of affairs, and affectation.

PYRRHO
ca. 360–ca. 270 B.C.

SEXTUS EMPIRICUS
A.D. third century

Pyrrho was born in the town of Elis on the Greek Peloponnesus. He joined the expedition of Alexander the Great to India and there met several of the learned magi of the East. Following Alexander's death in 323 B.C., Pyrrho returned to Elis and spent the rest of his life teaching there.

Pyrrho was greatly influenced by the Democritean notion that the world is not as our sense perceptions would lead us to believe. According to Pyrrho, we can know only appearances relative to each person—there is no way we can know things as they really are. This means that any statement we might make about reality can be opposed by an equally valid statement that contradicts it. Given this inability to know which assertion is true, Pyrrho said we should develop an attitude of "suspended judgment" <*epoche*> and thus gradually attain "unperturbedness" or "quietude" <*ataraxia*>. This claimed inability to know came to be called "Skepticism."

Pyrrho left no writings, but his philosophy is well represented by the works of the third-century A.D. author Sextus Empiricus. Little is known about this writer other than that he was apparently a Greek physician, that he was the head of a Skeptical school in some major city, and that he wrote the Outlines of Pyrrhonism. The selection reprinted here, in the R.G. Bury translation, begins by dividing philosophers into three categories: "Dogmatists," who claim to know the truth; those inheritors of Plato's Academy, such as Carneades, who made the opposite dogmatic claim that no truth is possible; and the Pyrrhoist skeptics, who suspend judgment while looking for the truth. Sextus Empiricus goes on to explain the nature of such a suspension of judgment and concludes with a discussion of how this suspension leads to "quietude." In the process of his explication,

Sextus avoids self-refutation by explaining that he is not describing what is really true (which would be dogmatism), but only how things *appear* to him to be.

As for its impact, elements of Pyrrhoist skepticism are echoed in Hegel's concept of the dialectic (with the claim that every statement can be contradicted by its opposite) and in Husserl's use of <*epoche*>. Thinkers such as Montaigne, Hume, and Santayana have used skepticism to attack the dogmatic philosophies of their day. While it has rarely been an established school of thought, skepticism has raised questions for all systematic philosophers since the time of Pyrrho.

*   *   *

For general accounts of Greek skepticism, see Mary Mills Patrick, *The Greek Skeptics* (New York: Columbia University Press, 1929); Charlotte L. Stough, *Greek Skepticism: A Study in Epistemology* (Berkeley: University of California Press, 1969); Leo Groarke, *Greek Scepticism: Anti-Realist Trends in Ancient Thought* (Montreal: McGill-Queen's University Press, 1990); R.J. Hankinson, *The Skeptics* (Oxford: Routledge, 1995); Myles Burnyest and Michael Frede, *The Original Sceptics* (Indianapolis, IN: Hackett, 1996); and a collection of essays, Malcolm Schofield, Myles Burnyeat, and Jonathan Barnes, eds., *Doubt and Dogmatism: Studies in Hellenistic Epistemology* (Oxford: Clarendon Press, 1979). For works specifically on Sextus Empiricus, see Mary Mills Patrick, *Sextus Empiricus and Greek Scepticism* (Cambridge: D. Bell, 1899) and Benson Mates, *The Skeptic Way: Sextus Empiricus's Outlines of Pyrrhonism* (Oxford: Oxford University Press, 1995). Edwyn Robert Bevan, *Stoics and Skeptics* (Oxford: Clarendon Press, 1913), provides a comparison with the Stoics; while Benson Mates, *Stoic Logic* (Berkeley: University of California Press, 1953), includes an explanation of Sextus Empiricus's contribution to the field of logic.

OUTLINES OF PYRRHONISM (in part)

BOOK I

1. *Of the Main Difference Between Philosophic Systems.* The natural result of any investigation is that the investigators either discover the object of their search or deny that it is discoverable and confess it to be inapprehensible or persist in their search. So, too, with regard to the objects investigated by philosophy, this is probably why some have claimed to have discovered the truth, others have asserted that it cannot be apprehended, while others again go on inquiring. Those who believe they have discovered it

are the "Dogmatists," specially so called—Aristotle, for example, and Epicurus and the Stoics and certain others; Cleitomachus and Carneades and other Academics treat it as inapprehensible; the Sceptics keep on searching. Hence it seems reasonable to hold that the main types of philosophy are three—the Dogmatic, the Academic, and the Sceptic. Of the other systems it will best become others to speak: our task at present is to describe in outline the Sceptic doctrine, first premising that of none of our future statements do we positively affirm that the fact is exactly as we state it, but we simply record each fact, like a chronicler, as it appears to us at the moment.

2. *Of the Arguments of Scepticism.* Of the Sceptic philosophy one argument (or branch of exposition) is called "general," the other "special." In the general argument we set forth the distinctive features of Scepticism, stating its purport and principles, its logical methods, criterion, and end or aim; the "Tropes," also, or "Modes," which lead to suspension of judgment, and in what sense we adopt the Sceptic formulae, and the distinction between Scepticism and the philosophies which stand next to it. In the special argument we state our objections regarding the several divisions of so-called philosophy. Let us, then, deal first with the general argument, beginning our description with the names given to the Sceptic School.

3. *Of the Nomenclature of Scepticism.* The Sceptic School, then, is also called "Zetetic" from its activity in investigation and inquiry, and "Ephectic" or Suspensive from the state of mind produced in the inquirer after his search, and "Aporetic" or Dubitative either from its habit of doubting and seeking, as some say, or from its indecision as regards assent and denial, and "Pyrrhonean" from the fact that Pyrrho appears to us to have applied himself to Scepticism more thoroughly and more conspicuously than his predecessors.

4. *What Scepticism Is.* Scepticism is an ability, or mental attitude, which opposes appearances to judgements in any way whatsoever, with the result that, owing to the equipollence of the objects and reasons thus opposed, we are brought firstly to a state of mental suspense and next to a state of "unperturbedness" or quietude. Now we call it an "ability" not in any subtle sense, but simply in respect of its "being able." By "appearances" we now mean the objects of sense-perception, whence we contrast them with the objects of thought or "judgements." The phrase "in any way whatsoever" can be connected either with the word "ability," to make us take the word "ability," as we said, in its simple sense, or with the phrase "opposing appearances to judgements"; for inasmuch as we oppose these in a variety of ways—appearances to appearances, or judgements to judgements, or *alternando* appearances to judgements,—in order to ensure the inclusion of all these antitheses we employ the phrase "in any way whatsoever." Or, again, we join "in any way whatsoever" to "appearances and judgements" in order that we may not have to inquire how the appearances appear or how the thought-objects are judged, but may take these terms in the simple sense. The phrase "opposed judgements" we do not employ in the sense of negations and affirmations only but simply as equivalent to "conflicting judgements." "Equipollence" we use of equality in respect of probability and improbability, to indicate that no one of the conflicting judgements takes precedence of any other as being more probable. "Suspense" is a state of mental rest owing to which we neither deny nor affirm anything. "Quietude" is an untroubled and tranquil condition of soul. And how quietude enters the soul along with suspension of judgement we shall explain in our chapter [12] "What Is the End of Scepticism."

5. *Of the Sceptic.* In the definition of the Sceptic system there is also implicitly included that of the Pyrrhonean philosopher: he is the man who participates in this "ability."

6. *Of the Principles of Scepticism.* The originating cause of Scepticism is, we say, the hope of attaining quietude. Men of talent, who were perturbed by the contradictions in things and in doubt as to which of the alternatives they ought to accept, were led on to inquire what is true in things and what false, hoping by the settlement of the question to attain quietude. The main basic principle of the Sceptic system is that of opposing to every proposition an equal proposition; for we believe that as a consequence of this we end by ceasing to dogmatize.

7. *Does the Sceptic Dogmatize?* When we say that the Sceptic refrains from dogmatizing we do not use the term "dogma," as some do, in the broader sense of "approval of a thing" (for the Sceptic gives assent to the feelings which are the necessary results of sense-impressions, and he would not, for example, say when feeling hot or cold "I believe that I am not hot or cold"); but we say that "he does not dogmatize" using "dogma" in the sense, which some give it, of "assent to one of the non-evident objects of scientific inquiry"; for the Pyrrhonean philosopher assents to nothing that is non-evident. Moreover, even in the act of enunciating the Sceptic formulae concerning things non-evident—such as the formula "No more (one thing than another)," or the formula "I determine nothing," or any of the others which we shall presently mention,—he does not dogmatize. For whereas the dogmatizer posits the things about which he is said to be dogmatizing as really existent, the Sceptic does not posit these formulae in any absolute sense; for he conceives that, just as the formula "All things are false" asserts the falsity of itself as well as of everything else, as does the formula "Nothing is true," so also the formula "No more" asserts that itself like all the rest, is "No more this than that," and thus cancels itself along with the rest. And of the other formulae we say the same. If then, while the dogmatizer posits the matter of his dogma as substantial truth, the Sceptic enunciates his formulae so that they are virtually canceled by themselves, he should not be said to dogmatize in his enunciation of them. And, most important of all, in his enunciation of these formulae he states what appears to himself and announces his own impression in an undogmatic way, without making any positive assertion regarding the external realities.

8. *Has the Sceptic a Doctrinal Rule?* We follow the same lines in replying to the question "Has the Sceptic a doctrinal rule?" For if one defines a "doctrinal rule" as "adherence to a number of dogmas which are dependent both on one another and on appearances," and defines "dogma" as "assent to a non-evident proposition," then we shall say that he has not a doctrinal rule. But if one defines "doctrinal rule" as "procedure which, in accordance with appearance, follows a certain line of reasoning, that reasoning indicating how it is possible to seem to live rightly (the word 'rightly' being taken, not as referring to virtue only, but in a wider sense) and tending to enable one to suspend judgement," then we say that he has a doctrinal rule. For we follow a line of reasoning which, in accordance with appearances, points us to a life conformable to the customs of our country and its laws and institutions, and to our own instinctive feelings.

9. *Does the Sceptic Deal with Physics?* We make a similar reply also to the question "Should the Sceptic deal with physical problems?" For while, on the one hand, so far as regards making firm and positive assertions about any of the matters dogmatically treated in physical theory, we do not deal with physics; yet, on the other hand, in respect of our mode of opposing to every proposition an equal proposition and of our theory of quietude we do treat of physics. This, too, is the way in which we approach the logical and ethical branches of so-called "philosophy."

10. *Do the Sceptics Abolish Appearances?* Those who say that "the Sceptics abolish appearances," or phenomena, seem to me to be unacquainted with the state-

ments of our School. For, as we said above, we do not overthrow the affective sense-impressions which induce our assent involuntarily; and these impressions are "the appearances." And when we question whether the underlying object is such as it appears, we grant the fact that it appears, and our doubt does not concern the appearance itself but the account given of the appearance,—and that is a different thing from questioning the appearance itself. For example, honey appears to us to be sweet (and this we grant, for we perceive sweetness through the senses), but whether it is also sweet in its essence is for us a matter of doubt, since this is not an appearance but a judgement regarding the appearance. And even if we do actually argue against the appearances, we do not propound such arguments with the intention of abolishing appearances, but by way of pointing out the rashness of the Dogmatists; for if reason is such a trickster as to all but snatch away the appearances from under our very eyes, surely we should view it with suspicion in the case of things non-evident so as not to display rashness by following it.

11. *Of the Criterion of Scepticism.* That we adhere to appearances is plain from what we say about the Criterion of the Sceptic School. The word "Criterion" is used in two senses: in the one it means "the standard regulating belief in reality or unreality," (and this we shall discuss in our refutation); in the other it denotes the standard of action by conforming to which in the conduct of life we perform some actions and abstain from others; and it is of the latter that we are now speaking. The criterion, then, of the Sceptic School is, we say, the appearance, giving this name to what is virtually the sense-presentation. For since this lies in feeling and involuntary affection, it is not open to question. Consequently, no one, I suppose, disputes that the underlying object has this or that appearance; the point in dispute is whether the object is in reality such as it appears to be.

Adhering, then, to appearances we live in accordance with the normal rules of life, undogmatically, seeing that we cannot remain wholly inactive. And it would seem that this regulation of life is fourfold, and that one part of it lies in the guidance of Nature, another in the constraint of the passions, another in the tradition of laws and customs, another in the instruction of the arts. Nature's guidance is that by which we are naturally capable of sensation and thought; constraint of the passions is that whereby hunger drives us to food and thirst to drink; tradition of customs and laws, that whereby we regard piety in the conduct of life as good, but impiety as evil; instruction of the arts, that whereby we are not inactive in such arts as we adopt. But we make all these statements undogmatically.

12. *What Is the End of Scepticism?* Our next subject will be the End of the Sceptic system. Now an "End" is "that for which all actions or reasonings are undertaken, while it exists for the sake of none"; or, otherwise, "the ultimate object of appetency." We assert still that the Sceptic's End is quietude in respect of matters of opinion and moderate feeling in respect of things unavoidable. For the Sceptic, having set out to philosophize with the object of passing judgement on the sense-impressions and ascertaining which of them are true and which false, so as to attain quietude thereby, found himself involved in contradictions of equal weight, and being unable to decide between them suspended judgement; and as he was thus in suspense there followed, as it happened, the state of quietude in respect of matters of opinion. For the man who opines that anything is by nature good or bad is forever being disquieted: when he is without the things which he deems good he believes himself to be tormented by things naturally bad and he pursues after the things which are, as he thinks, good; which when he has obtained he keeps falling into still more perturbations because of his irrational and immoderate elation, and in his dread of a change of fortune he uses every endeav-

our to avoid losing the things which he deems good. On the other hand, the man who determines nothing as to what is naturally good or bad neither shuns nor pursues anything eagerly; and, in consequence, he is unperturbed.

The Sceptic, in fact, had the same experience which is said to have befallen the painter Apelles. Once, they say, when he was painting a horse and wished to represent in the painting the horse's foam, he was so unsuccessful that he gave up the attempt and flung at the picture the sponge on which he used to wipe the paints off his brush, and the mark of the sponge produced the effect of a horse's foam. So, too, the Sceptics were in hopes of gaining quietude by means of a decision regarding the disparity of the objects of sense and of thought, and being unable to effect this they suspended judgement; and they found that quietude, as if by chance, followed upon their suspense, even as a shadow follows its substance. We do not, however, suppose that the Sceptic is wholly untroubled; but we say that he is troubled by things unavoidable; for we grant that he is old at times and thirsty, and suffers various affections of that kind. But even in these cases, whereas ordinary people are afflicted by two circumstances,—namely, by the affections themselves and in no less a degree, by the belief that these conditions are evil by nature,—the Sceptic, by his rejection of the added belief in the natural badness of all these conditions, escapes here too with less discomfort. Hence we say that, while in regard to matters of opinion the Sceptic's End is quietude, in regard to things unavoidable it is "moderate affection." But some notable Sceptics have added the further definition "suspension of judgement in investigations."

13. *Of the General Modes Leading to Suspension of Judgement.* Now that we have been saying that tranquillity follows on suspension of judgement, it will be our next task to explain how we arrive at this suspension. Speaking generally, one may say that it is the result of setting things in opposition. We oppose either appearances to appearances or objects of thought to objects of thought or *alternando.* For instance, we oppose appearances when we say "The same tower appears round from a distance, but square from close at hand"; and thoughts to thoughts, when in answer to him who argues the existence of Providence from the order of the heavenly bodies we oppose the fact that often the good fare ill and the bad fare well, and draw from this the inference that Providence does not exist. And thoughts we oppose to appearances, as when Anaxagoras countered the notion that snow is white with the argument, "Snow is frozen water, and water is black; therefore snow also is black." With a different idea we oppose things present sometimes to things present, as in the foregoing examples, and sometimes to things past or future, as, for instance, when someone propounds to us a theory which we are unable to refute, we say to him in reply, "Just as, before the birth of the founder of the School to which you belong, the theory it holds was not as yet apparent as a sound theory, although it was really in existence, so likewise it is possible that the opposite theory to that which you now propound is already really existent, though not yet apparent to us, so that we ought not as yet to yield assent to this theory which at the moment seems to be valid."

But in order that we may have a more exact understanding of these antitheses I will describe the Modes by which suspension of judgement is brought about, but without making any positive assertion regarding either their number or their validity; for it is possible that they may be unsound or there may be more of them than I shall enumerate.

14. *Concerning the Ten Modes.* The usual tradition amongst the older Sceptics is that the "modes" by which "suspension" is supposed to be brought about are ten in number; and they also give them the synonymous names of "arguments" and "positions." They are these: the first, based on the variety in animals; the second, on the dif-

ferences in human beings; the third, on the different structures of the organs of sense; the fourth, on the circumstantial conditions; the fifth, on positions and intervals and locations; the sixth, on intermixtures; the seventh, on the quantities and formations of the underlying objects; the eighth, on the fact of relativity; the ninth, on the frequency or rarity of occurrence; the tenth, on the disciplines and customs and laws, the legendary beliefs and the dogmatic convictions. This order, however, we adopt without prejudice.

*   *   *

15. *Of the Five Modes.* The later Sceptics hand down Five Modes leading to suspension, namely these: the first based on discrepancy, the second on regress *ad infinitum,* the third on relativity, the fourth on hypothesis, the fifth on circular reasoning. That based on discrepancy leads us to find that with regard to the object presented there has arisen both amongst ordinary people and amongst the philosophers an interminable conflict because of which we are unable either to choose a thing or reject it, and so fall back on suspension. The Mode based upon regress *ad infinitum* is that whereby we assert that the thing adduced as a proof of the matter proposed needs a further proof, and this again another, and so on *ad infinitum,* so that the consequence is suspension, as we possess no starting-point for our argument. The Mode based upon relativity, as we have already said, is that whereby the object has such or such an appearance in relation to the subject judging and to the concomitant percepts, but as to its real nature we suspend judgement. We have the Mode based on hypothesis when the Dogmatists, being forced to recede *ad infinitum,* take as their starting-point something which they do not establish by argument but claim to assume as granted simply and without demonstration. The Mode of circular reasoning is the form used when the proof itself which ought to establish the matter of inquiry requires confirmation derived from that matter; in this case, being unable to assume either in order to establish the other, we suspend judgement about both.

That every matter of inquiry admits of being brought under these Modes we shall show briefly in this way. The matter proposed is either a sense-object or a thought-object, but whichever it is, it is an object of controversy; for some say that only sensibles are true, others only intelligibles, others that some sensible and some intelligible objects are true. Will they then assert that the controversy can or cannot be decided? If they say it cannot, we have it granted that we must suspend judgement; for concerning matters of dispute which admit of no decision it is impossible to make an assertion. But if they say that it can be decided, we ask by what is it to be decided. For example, in the case of the sense-object (for we shall base our argument on it first), is it to be decided by a sense-object or a thought-object? For if they say by a sense-object, since we are inquiring about sensibles that object itself also will require another to confirm it; and if that too is to be a sense-object, it likewise will require another for its confirmation, and so on *ad infinitum.* And if the sense-object shall have to be decided by a thought-object, then, since thought-objects also are controverted, this being an object of thought will need examination and confirmation. Whence then will it gain confirmation? If from an intelligible object, it will suffer a similar regress *ad infinitum;* and if from a sensible object, since an intelligible was adduced to establish the sensible and a sensible to establish the intelligible, the Mode of circular reasoning is brought in.

If, however, our disputant, by way of escape from this conclusion, should claim to assume as granted and without demonstration some postulate for the demonstration of the next steps of his argument, then the Mode of hypothesis will be brought in, which allows no escape. For if the author of the hypothesis is worthy of credence, we shall be no less worthy of credence every time that we make the opposite hypothesis. Moreover, if the author of the hypothesis assumes what is true he causes it to be suspected by assuming it by hypothesis rather than after proof; while if it is false, the foundation of his argument will be rotten. Further, if hypothesis conduces at all to proof, let the subject of inquiry itself be assumed and not some other thing which is merely a means to establish the actual subject of the argument; but if it is absurd to assume the subject of inquiry, it will also be absurd to assume that upon which it depends.

It is also plain that all sensibles are relative; for they are relative to those who have the sensations. Therefore it is apparent that whatever sensible object is presented can easily be referred to one of the Five Modes. And concerning the intelligible object we argue similarly. For if it should be said that it is a matter of unsettled controversy, the necessity of our suspending judgement will be granted. And if, on the other hand, the controversy admits of decision, then if the decision rests on an intelligible object we shall be driven to the regress *ad infinitum,* and to circular reasoning if it rests on a sensible; for since the sensible again is controverted and cannot be decided by means of itself because of the regress *ad infinitum,* it will require the intelligible object, just as also the intelligible will require the sensible. For these reasons, again, he who assumes anything by hypothesis will be acting illogically. Moreover, objects of thought, or intelligibles, are relative; for they are so named on account of their relation to the person thinking, and if they had really possessed the nature they are said to possess, there would have been no controversy about them. Thus the intelligible also is referred to the Five Modes, so that in all cases we are compelled to suspend judgement concerning the object presented.

Such then are the Five Modes handed down amongst the later Sceptics; but they propound these not by way of superseding the Ten Modes, but in order to expose the rashness of the Dogmatists with more variety and completeness by means of the Five in conjunction with the Ten.

PLOTINUS
ca. A.D. 204–270

The last great school of Greek philosophy was Neoplatonism, and its most famous representative was Plotinus, born in Lykopolis, Egypt, in A.D. 204. In his late-twenties, Plotinus began to study in Alexandria with Ammonius Saccas, a shadowy figure who was also the teacher of the theologian Origen. After eleven years with Ammonius, Plotinus joined an expedition to Persia to learn Persian and Indian wisdom. The trek proved unsuccessful and Plotinus moved to Rome. There he established a school of philosophy and a friendship with the emperor Gallenius. At one point, he sought permission to found a city based on Plato's *Republic,* but the plan came to naught. He stayed in Rome, teaching and writing, until the death of the emperor in 268. He then moved to the home of a friend where he died in 270, apparently from leprosy.

Developing Plato's dualistic understanding of reality, Plotinus taught that true reality lies "beyond" the physical world. This "reality beyond reality" has no limits and so cannot be described by words, since words invariably have limits. Plotinus, again borrowing from Plato, calls this ultra-reality the "Good" or the "One." The One/Good has no limits and is so supremely rich that it overflows or "emanates" to produce "Intellectual-Principle" or "Divine Mind" <*nous*>. This Intellectual-Principle, in turn, overflows and "Divine-Soul" emanates from it. This process continues as Divine-Soul generates the material world. The lowest level of emanation, at the furthest extreme from the One/Good, is the utter formlessness and unreality of matter.

The goal of philosophy is to awaken individuals to the reality beyond the material world. But philosophy alone cannot take a person to the highest reality of the One. Only mystical experience can unite an individual with the One. Plotinus himself claimed to have achieved such a union four times during his life.

Plotinus's writings were edited by one of his pupils, Porphyry, in the form of six groups of nine "Tractates" (treatises), published as the so-called *Enneads* (from the Greek word for "nine"). The selections given here, in the A.H. Armstrong translation, begin with the Treatise on Beauty. This Tractate explains how the ascent of the soul to the One/Good is dependent on the beauty of soul, a god-like disposition. Plotinus' description parallels the ascending dialectic in Plato's *Symposium* (210a). The second selection discusses the three "hypostases," or stages—the One/Good, the Intellectual-Principle, and the World-Soul—explaining how each is generated from the one above. The final selection is thought to have been written late in Plotinus's life and gives a detailed description of the soul's ascent to ecstatic union. At the end of this tractate, Plotinus, in order to represent the One/Good, borrows Plato's image of the sun from the Myth of the Cave.

Neoplatonism, with its emphasis on the otherworldly and the need for escape from the physical world, was the perfect philosophy for the chaotic final days of the Roman Empire. Plotinus' thought had a profound influence on Christian thought, especially on St. Augustine. Indeed, if St. Thomas is considered an Aristotelian, St. Augustine may be called a Neoplatonist. Many later thinkers, such as Eckhart, Nicolas of Cusa, Comenius, Boehme, Hegel, and Schelling, also had their philosophy molded by Neoplatonist doctrines.

* * *

Joseph Katz, *Plotinus' Search for the Good* (New York: King's Crown Press, 1950); Émile Bréhier, *The Philosophy of Plotinus,* translated by Joseph Thomas (Chicago: University of Chicago Press, 1958); and Lloyd P. Gerson, *Plotinus* (Oxford: Routledge, 1994) are good introductions to the study of Plotinus. For more advanced studies, see A.H. Armstrong, *The Architecture of the Intelligible Universe in the Philosophy of Plotinus* (Cambridge: Cambridge University Press, 1940); J.M. Rist, *Plotinus: The Road to Reality* (Cambridge: Cambridge University Press, 1967); and Lloyd P. Gerson, ed., *The Cambridge Companion to Plotinus* (Cambridge: Cambridge University Press, 1996). E.R. Dodds, *Select Passages Illustrating Neoplatonism,* translated by E.R. Dodds (New York: Macmillan, 1923), and Dominic J. O'Meara, *Plotinus: An Introduction to the Enneads* (Oxford: Oxford University Press, 1993), provide anthologies of the *Enneads* with discussions of important passages. For discussions of Neoplatonism as a school, see Thomas Whittaker, *The Neo-Platonists* (Cambridge: Cambridge University Press, 1918); Arthur O. Lovejoy's influential book, *The Great Chain of Being* (Cambridge, MA: Harvard University Press, 1936); R.T. Wallis, *Neoplatonism* (London: Duckworth, 1972); and the collection of essays, R. Baine Harris, ed., *The Structure of Being: A Neoplatonic Approach* (Norfolk, VA: International Society for Neoplatonic Studies, 1982). John Dillon, *The Middle Platonists* (Ithaca, NY: Cornell University press, 1996) provides an overview of Platonism in the period leading up to Plotinus.

ENNEADS (in part)

ENNEAD I, TRACTATE 6: BEAUTY

1. Beauty is mostly in sight, but it is to be found too in things we hear, in combinations of words and also in music, and in all music [not only in songs]; for tunes and rhythms are certainly beautiful: and for those who are advancing upwards from sense-perception ways of life and actions and characters and intellectual activities are beautiful, and there is the beauty of virtue. If there is any beauty prior to these, this discussion will reveal it.

Very well then, what is it which makes us imagine that bodies are beautiful and attracts our hearing to sounds because of their beauty? And how are all the things which depend on soul beautiful? Are they all made beautiful by one and the same beauty or is there one beautifulness in bodies and a different one in other things? And what are they, or what is it? Some things, bodies for instance, are not beautiful from the nature of the objects themselves, but by participation, others are beauties themselves, like the nature of virtue. The same bodies appear sometimes beautiful, sometimes not beautiful, so that their being bodies is one thing, their being beautiful another. What is this principle, then, which is present in bodies? We ought to consider this first. What is it that attracts the gaze of those who look at something, and turns and draws them to it and makes them enjoy the sight? If we find this perhaps we can use it as a stepping-stone and get a sight of the rest. Nearly everyone says that it is good proportion of the parts to each other and to the whole, with the addition of good colour, which produces visible beauty, and that with the objects of sight and generally with everything else, being beautiful is being well-proportioned and measured. On this theory nothing single and simple but only a composite thing will have any beauty. It will be the whole which is beautiful, and the parts will not have the property of beauty by themselves, but will contribute to the beauty of the whole. But if the whole is beautiful the parts must be beautiful too; a beautiful whole can certainly not be composed of ugly parts; all the parts must have beauty. For these people, too, beautiful colours, and the light of the sun as well, since they are simple and do not derive their beautifulness from good proportion, will be excluded from beauty. And how do they think gold manages to be beautiful? And what makes lightning in the night and stars beautiful to see? And in sounds in the same way the simple will be banished, though often in a composition which is beautiful as a whole each separate sound is beautiful. And when, though the same good proportion is there all the time, the same face sometimes appears beautiful and sometimes does not, surely we must say that being beautiful is something else over and above good proportion, and good proportion is beautiful because of something else? But if when these people pass on to ways of life and beautiful expressions of thought they allege good proportion as the cause of beauty in these too, what can be meant by good proportion in beautiful ways of life or laws or studies or branches of knowledge? How can speculations be well-proportioned in relation to each other? If it is because they agree, there can be concord and agreement between bad ideas. The statement that "righteousness is a fine sort of silliness" agrees with and is in tune with the saying that "morality is stupidity"; the two fit perfectly. Again, every sort of virtue is a beauty of the soul, a truer beauty than those mentioned before; but how is virtue well-proportioned? Not like magnitudes or a number. We grant that the soul has several parts, but what is the formula for the composition or mixture in the soul of parts or speculations? And what [on this theory], will the beauty of the intellect alone by itself be?

2. So let us go back to the beginning and state what the primary beauty in bodies really is. It is something which we become aware of even at the first glance; the soul speaks of it as if it understood it, recognises and welcomes it and as it were adapts itself to it. But when it encounters the ugly it shrinks back and rejects it and turns away from it and is out of tune and alienated from it. Our explanation of this is that the soul, since it is by nature what it is and is related to the higher kind of reality in the realm of being, when it sees something akin to it or a trace of its kindred reality, is delighted and thrilled and returns to itself and remembers itself and its own possessions. What likeness, then, is there between beautiful things here and There? If there is a likeness, let us agree that they are alike. But how are both the things in that world and the things in this beautiful? We maintain that the things in this world are beautiful by participating in form; for every shapeless thing which is naturally capable of receiving shape and form is ugly and outside the divine formative power as long as it has no share in formative power and form. This is absolute ugliness. But a thing is also ugly when it is not completely dominated by shape and formative power, since its matter has not submitted to be completely shaped according to the form. The form, then, approaches and composes that which is to come into being from many parts into a single ordered whole; it brings it into a completed unity and makes it one by agreement of its parts; for since it is one itself, that which is shaped by it must also be one as far as a thing can be which is composed of many parts. So beauty rests upon the material thing when it has been brought into unity, and gives itself to parts and wholes alike. When it comes upon something that is one and composed of like parts it gives the same gift to the whole; as sometimes art gives beauty to a whole house with its parts, and sometimes nature gives beauty to a single stone. So then the beautiful body comes into being by sharing in a formative power which comes from the divine forms.

3. The power ordained for the purpose recognises this, and there is nothing more effective for judging its own subject-matter, when the rest of the soul judges along with it; or perhaps the rest of the soul too pronounces the judgement by fitting the beautiful body to the form in itself and using this for judging beauty as we use a ruler for judging straightness. But how does the bodily agree with that which is before body? How does the architect declare the house outside beautiful by fitting it to the form of house within him? The reason is that the house outside, apart from the stones, is the inner form divided by the external mass of matter, without parts but appearing in many parts. When sense-perception, then, sees the form in bodies binding and mastering the nature opposed to it, which is shapeless, and shape riding gloriously upon other shapes, it gathers into one that which appears dispersed and brings it back and takes it in, now without parts, to the soul's interior and presents it to that which is within as something in tune with it and fitting it and dear to it; just as when a good man sees a trace of virtue in the young, which is in tune with his own inner truth, the sight delights him. And the simple beauty of colour comes about by shape and the mastery of the darkness in matter by the presence of light which is incorporeal and formative power and form. This is why fire itself is more beautiful than all other bodies, because it has the rank of form in relation to the other elements; it is above them in place and is the

finest and subtlest of all bodies, being close to the incorporeal. It alone does not admit the others; but the others admit it for it warms them but is not cooled itself; it has colour primarily and all other things take the form of colour from it. So it shines and glitters as if it was a form. The inferior thing which becomes faint and dull by the fire's light, is not beautiful any more, as not participating in the whole form of colour. The melodies in sounds, too, the imperceptible ones which make the perceptible ones, make the soul conscious of beauty in the same way, showing the same thing in another medium. It is proper to sensible melodies to be measured by numbers, not according to any and every sort of formula but one which serves for the production of form so that it may dominate. So much, then, for the beauties in the realm of sense, images and shadows which, so to speak, sally out and come into matter and adorn it and excite us when they appear.

4. But about the beauties beyond, which it is no more the part of sense to see, but the soul sees them and speaks of them without instruments—we must go up to them and contemplate them and leave sense to stay down below. Just as in the case of the beauties of sense it is impossible for those who have not seen them or grasped their beauty—those born blind, for instance,—to speak about them, in the same way only those can speak about the beauty of ways of life who have accepted the beauty of ways of life and kinds of knowledge and everything else of the sort; and people cannot speak about the splendour of virtue who have never even imagined how fair is the face of justice and moral order; "neither the evening nor the morning star are as fair." But there must be those who see this beauty by that with which the soul sees things of this sort, and when they see it they must be delighted and overwhelmed and excited much more than by those beauties we spoke of before, since now it is true beauty they are grasping. These experiences must occur whenever there is contact with any sort of beautiful thing, wonder and a shock of delight and longing and passion and a happy excitement. One can have these experiences by contact with invisible beauties, and souls do have them, practically all, but particularly those who are more passionately in love with the invisible, just as with bodies all see them, but all are not stung as sharply, but some, who are called lovers, are most of all.

5. Then we must ask the lovers of that which is outside sense "What do you feel about beautiful ways of life, as we call them, and beautiful habits and well-ordered characters and in general about virtuous activities and dispositions and the beauty of souls? What do you feel when you see your own inward beauty? How are you stirred to wild exultation, and long to be with yourselves, gathering your selves together away from your bodies?" For this is what true lovers feel. But what is it which makes them feel like this? Not shape or colour or any size, but soul, without colour itself and possessing a moral order without colour and possessing all the other light of the virtues; you feel like this when you see, in yourself or in someone else, greatness of soul, a righteous life, a pure morality, courage with its noble look, and dignity and modesty advancing in a fearless, calm and unperturbed disposition, and the godlike light of intellect shining upon all this. We love and delight in these qualities, but why do we call them beautiful? They exist and appear to us and he who sees them cannot possibly say anything else except that they are what really exists. What does "really exists" mean? That they exist as beauties. But the argument still requires us to explain why real beings make the soul lovable. What is this kind of glorifying light on all the virtues? Would you like to take the opposites, the uglinesses in soul, and contrast them with the beauties? Perhaps a consideration of what ugliness is and why it appears so will help us to find what we are looking for. Suppose, then, an ugly soul, dissolute and unjust, full of all lusts, and all disturbance, sunk in fears by its cowardice and jealousies by its

pettiness, thinking mean and mortal thoughts as far as it thinks at all, altogether distorted, loving impure pleasures, living a life which consists of bodily sensations and finding delight in its ugliness. Shall we not say that its ugliness came to it as a "beauty" brought in from outside, injuring it and making it impure and "mixed with a great deal of evil," with its life and perceptions no longer pure, but by the admixture of evil living a dim life and diluted with a great deal of death, no longer seeing what a soul ought to see, no longer left in peace in itself because it keeps on being dragged out, and down, and to the dark? Impure, I think, and dragged in every direction towards the objects of sense, with a great deal of bodily stuff mixed into it, consorting much with matter and receiving a form other than its own it has changed by a mixture which makes it worse; just as if anyone gets into mud or filth he does not show any more the beauty which he had what is seen is what he wiped off on himself from the mud and filth; his ugliness has come from an addition of alien matter, and his business, if he is to be beautiful again, is to wash and clean himself and so be again what he was before. So we shall be right in saying that the soul becomes ugly by mixture and dilution and inclination towards the body and matter. This is the soul's ugliness, not being pure and unmixed, like gold, but full of earthiness; if anyone takes the earthy stuff away the gold is left, and is beautiful, when it is singled out from other things and is alone by itself. In the same way the soul too, when it is separated from the lusts which it has through the body with which it consorted too much, and freed from its other affections, purged of what it gets from being embodied, when it abides alone has put away all the ugliness which came from the other nature.

6. For, as was said in old times, self-control, and courage and every virtue, is a purification, and so is even wisdom itself. This is why the mysteries are right when they say riddlingly that the man who has not been purified will lie in mud when he goes to Hades, because the impure is fond of mud by reason of its badness; just as pigs, with their unclean bodies, like that sort of thing. For what can true self-control be except not keeping company with bodily pleasures, but avoiding them as impure and belonging to something impure? Courage, too, is not being afraid of death. And death is the separation of body and soul; and a man does not fear this if he welcomes the prospect of being alone. Again, greatness of soul is despising the things here and wisdom is an intellectual activity which turns away from the things below and leads the soul to those above. So the soul when it is purified becomes form and formative power, altogether bodiless and intellectual and entirely belonging to the divine, whence beauty springs and all that is akin to it. Soul, then, when it is raised to the level of intellect increases in beauty. Intellect and the things of intellect are its beauty, its own beauty and not another's, since only then [when it is perfectly conformed to intellect] is it truly soul. For this reason it is right to say that the soul's becoming something good and beautiful is its being made like to God, because from Him come beauty and all else which falls to the lot of real beings. Or rather, beautifulness is reality, and the other kind of thing is the ugly, and this same is the primary evil; so for God the qualities of goodness and beauty are the same, or the realities, the good and the beautiful. So we must follow the same line of enquiry to discover beauty and goodness, and ugliness and evil. And first we must posit beauty which is also the good; from this immediately comes intellect, which is beauty; and soul is given beauty by intellect. Everything else is beautiful by the shaping of soul, the beauties in actions and in ways of life. And soul makes beautiful the bodies which are spoken of as beautiful; for since it is a divine thing and a kind of part of beauty, it makes everything it grasps and masters beautiful, as far as they are capable of participation.

7. So we must ascend again to the good, which every soul desires. Anyone who has seen it knows what I mean when I say that it is beautiful. It is desired as good, and the desire for it is directed to good, and the attainment of it is for those who go up to the higher world and are converted and strip off what we put on in our descent; (just as for those who go up to the celebrations of sacred rites there are purifications, and strippings off of the clothes they wore before, and going up naked) until, passing in the ascent all that is alien to the God, one sees with one's self alone That alone, simple, single and pure, from which all depends and to which all look and are and live and think for it is the cause of life and mind and being. If anyone sees it, what passion will he feel, what longing in his desire to be united with it, what a shock of delight! The man who has not seen it may desire it as good, but he who has seen it glories in its beauty and is full of wonder and delight, enduring a shock which causes no hurt, loving with true passion and piercing longing; he laughs at all other loves and despises what he thought beautiful before; it is like the experience of those who have met appearances of gods or spirits and do not any more appreciate as they did the beauty of other bodies. "What then are we to think, if anyone contemplates the absolute beauty which exists pure by itself, uncontaminated by flesh or body, not in earth or heaven, that it may keep its purity?" All these other things are external additions and mixtures and not primary, but derived from it. If then one sees That which provides for all and remains by itself and gives to all but receives nothing into itself, if he abides in the contemplation of this kind of beauty and rejoices in being made like it, how can he need any other beauty? For this, since it is beauty most of all, and primary beauty, makes its lovers beautiful and lovable. Here the greatest, the ultimate contest is set before our souls; all our toil and trouble is for this, not to be left without a share in the best of visions. The man who attains this is blessed in seeing that "blessed sight," and he who fails to attain it has failed utterly. A man has not failed if he fails to win beauty of colours or bodies, or power or office or kingship even, but if he fails to win this and only this. For this he should give up the attainment of kingship and of rule over all earth and sea and sky, if only by leaving and overlooking them he can turn to That and see.

8. But how shall we find the way? What method can we devise? How can one see the "inconceivable beauty" which stays within in the holy sanctuary and does not come out where the profane may see it? Let him who can, follow and come within, and leave outside the sight of his eyes and not turn back to the bodily splendours which he saw before. When he sees the beauty in bodies he must not run after them; we must know that they are images, traces, shadows, and hurry away to that which they image. For if a man runs to the image and wants to seize it as if it was the reality (like a beautiful reflection playing on the water, which some story somewhere, I think, said riddlingly a man wanted to catch and sank down into the stream and disappeared) then this man who clings to beautiful bodies and will not let them go, will, like the man in the story, but in soul, not in body, sink down into the dark depths where intellect has no delight, and stay blind in Hades, consorting with shadows there and here. This would be truer advice "Let us fly to our dear country." What then is our way of escape, and how are we to find it? We shall put out to sea, as Odysseus did, from the witch Circe or Calypso—as the poet says (I think with a hidden meaning)— and was not content to stay though he had delights of the eyes and lived among much beauty of sense. Our country from which we came is there, our Father is there. How shall we travel to it, where is our way of escape? We cannot get there on foot; for our feet only carry us everywhere in this world, from one country to another. You must not get ready a carriage, either, or a boat. Let all these things go, and do not look. Shut

your eyes, and change to and wake another way of seeing, which everyone has but few use.

9. And what does this inner sight see? When it is just awakened it is not at all able to look at the brilliance before it. So that the soul must be trained, first of all to look at beautiful ways of life then at beautiful works, not those which the arts produce, but the works of men who have a name for goodness: then look at the souls of the people who produce the beautiful works. How then can you see the sort of beauty a good soul has? Go back into yourself and look; and if you do not yet see yourself beautiful, then, just as someone making a statue which has to be beautiful cuts away here and polishes there and makes one part smooth and clears another till he has given his statue a beautiful face, so you too must cut away excess and straighten the crooked and clear the dark and make it bright, and never stop "working on your statue" till the divine glory of virtue shines out on you, till you see "self-mastery enthroned upon its holy seat." If you have become this, and see it, and are at home with yourself in purity, with nothing hindering you from becoming in this way one, with no inward mixture of anything else, but wholly yourself, nothing but true light, not measured by dimensions, or bounded by shape into littleness, or expanded to size by unboundedness, but everywhere unmeasured, because greater than all measure and superior to all quantity; when you see that you have become this, then you have become sight; you can trust yourself then; you have already ascended and need no one to show you; concentrate your gaze and see. This alone is the eye that sees the great beauty. But if anyone comes to the sight bleary-eyed with wickedness, and unpurified, or weak and by his cowardice unable to look at what is very bright, he sees nothing, even if someone shows him what is there and possible to see. For one must come to the sight with a seeing power made akin and like to what is seen. No eye ever saw the sun without becoming sunlike, nor can a soul see beauty without becoming beautiful. You must become first all godlike and all beautiful if you intend to see God and beauty. First the soul will come in its ascent to intellect and there will know the Forms, all beautiful, and will affirm that these, the Ideas, are beauty; for all things are beautiful by these, by the products and essence of intellect. That which is beyond this we call the nature of the Good, which holds beauty as a screen before it. So in a loose and general way of speaking the Good is the primary beauty; but if one distinguishes the intelligibles [from the Good] one will say that the place of the Forms is the intelligible beauty, but the Good is That which is beyond, the "spring and origin" of beauty; or one will place the Good and the primal beauty on the same level. In any case, however, beauty is in the intelligible world.

*   *   *

ENNEAD V, TRACTATE 1:
ON THE THREE PRIMARY HYPOSTASES

1. What is it, then, which has made the souls forget their father, God, and be ignorant of themselves and him, even though they are parts which come from his higher world and altogether belong to it? The beginning of evil for them was audacity and coming to birth and the first otherness and the wishing to belong to themselves. Since they were clearly delighted with their own independence, and made great use of self-movement, running the opposite course and getting as far away as possible, they were ignorant even that they themselves came from that world; just as children who are immediately torn from their parents and brought up far away do not know who they themselves or

their parents are. Since they do not any more see their father or themselves, they despise themselves through ignorance of their birth and honour other things, admiring everything rather than themselves, and, astonished and delighted by and dependent on these [earthly] things, they broke themselves loose as far as they could in contempt of that from which they turned away; so that their honour for these things here and their contempt for themselves is the cause of their utter ignorance of God. For what pursues and admires something else admits at the same time its own inferiority; but by making itself inferior to things which come into being and perish and considering itself the most contemptible and the most liable to death of all the things which it admires it could not possibly have any idea of the nature and power of God. One must therefore speak in two ways to men who are in this state of mind, if one is going to turn them round to what lies in the opposite direction and is primary, and to lead them up to that which is highest, one, and first. What, then, are these two ways? One shows how contemptible are the things now honoured by the soul, and this we shall develop more amply elsewhere, but the other teaches and reminds the soul how high its birth and value are, and this is prior to the other one and when it is clarified will also make the other obvious. This is what we must speak about now; it is close to the subject of our investigation and will be useful for that other discourse. For that which investigates is the soul, and it should know what it is as an investigating soul, so that it may learn first about itself, whether it has the power to investigate things of this kind, and if it has an eye of the right kind to see them, and if the investigation is suitable for it. For if the objects are alien, what is the point? But if they are akin, the investigation is suitable and discovery is possible.

2. Let every soul, then, first consider this, that it made all living things itself, breathing life into them, those that the earth feeds and those that are nourished by the sea, and the divine stars in the sky; it made the sun itself, and this great heaven, and adorned it itself, and drives it round itself, in orderly movement; it is a nature other than the things which it adorns and moves and makes live; and it must necessarily be more honourable than they, for they come into being or pass away when the soul leaves them or grants life to them, but soul itself exists for ever because "it does not depart from itself." This is how soul should reason about the manner in which it grants life in the whole universe and in individual things. Let it look at the great soul, being itself another soul which is no small one, which has become worthy to look by being freed from deceit and the things that have bewitched the other souls, and is established in quietude. Let not only its encompassing body and the body's raging sea be quiet, but all its environment: the earth quiet, and the sea and air quiet, and the heaven itself at peace. Into this heaven at rest let it imagine soul as if flowing in from outside, pouring in and entering it everywhere and illuminating it: as the rays of the sun light up a dark cloud, and make it shine and give it a golden look, so soul entering into the body of heaven gives it life and gives it immortality and wakes what lies inert. And heaven, moved with an everlasting motion by the wise guidance of soul, becomes a "fortunate living being" and gains its value by the indwelling of soul; before soul it was a dead body, earth and water, or rather the darkness of matter and non-existence, and "what the gods hate," as a poet says. The power and nature of soul will become still clearer and more obvious if one considers here how it encompasses the heaven and drives it by its own acts of will. For soul has given itself to the whole magnitude of heaven, as far as it extends, and every stretch of space both great and small, is ensouled; one body lies in one place and one in another, and one is here and another there; some are separated by being in opposite parts of the universe, and others in other ways. But soul is not like this and it is not by being cut up that it gives life, by a part of itself for each in-

dividual thing, but all things live by the whole, and all soul is present everywhere, made like to the father who begat it in its unity and its universality. And by its power the heaven is one, though it is multiple with one part in one place and one in another, and our universe is a god by the agency of this soul. And the sun also is a god because it is ensouled, and the other heavenly bodies, and we, if we are in any way divine, are so for this reason: for "corpses are more throwable away than dung." But that which is for the gods the cause of their being gods must necessarily be a divinity senior to them. But our soul is of the same kind, and when you look at it without its accretions and take it in its purified state you will find that very same honourable thing which [we said] was soul, more honourable than everything which is body. For all bodily things are earth; and even if they are fire, what would its burning principle be [but soul]? And the same is true of all things compounded of these, even if you add water to them, and air as well. But if the bodily is worth pursuing because it is ensouled, why does one let oneself go and pursue another? But by admiring the soul in another, you admire yourself.

3. Since the soul is so honourable and divine a thing, be sure already that you can attain God by reason of its being of this kind, and with this as your motive ascend to him: in all certainty you will not look far; and the stages between are not many. Grasp then the soul's upper neighbour, more divine than this divine thing, after which and from which the soul comes. For, although it is a thing of the kind which our discussion has shown it to be, it is an image of Intellect; just as a thought in its utterance is an image of the thought in soul, so soul itself is the expressed thought of Intellect, and its whole activity, and the life which it sends out to establish another reality; as fire has the heat which remains with it and the heat which it gives. But one must understand that the activity on the level of Intellect does not flow out of it, but the external activity comes into existence as something distinct. Since then its existence derives from Intellect soul is intellectual, and its intellect is in discursive reasonings, and its perfection comes from Intellect, like a father who brings to maturity a son whom he begat imperfect in comparison with himself. Soul's establishment in reality, then, comes from Intellect and its thought becomes actual in its seeing of Intellect. For when it looks into Intellect, it has within it and as its own what it thinks in its active actuality. And we should call these alone activities of the soul, all it does intellectually and which spring from its own home; its inferior activities come from elsewhere and belong to a soul of this inferior kind. Intellect therefore makes soul still more divine by being its father and by being present to it; for there is nothing between but the fact that they are different, soul as next in order and as the recipient, Intellect as the form; and even the matter of Intellect is beautiful, since it has the form of Intellect and is simple. But what Intellect is like is clear from this very fact that it is superior to soul which is of such great excellence.

4. But one might see this also from what follows: if someone admires this perceptible universe, observing its size and beauty and the order of its everlasting course, and the gods in it, some of whom are seen and some are invisible, and the spirits, and all animals and plants, let him ascend to its archetypal and truer reality and there see them all intelligible and eternal in it, in its own understanding and life; and let him see pure Intellect presiding over them, and immense wisdom, and the true life of Kronos, a god who is fullness and intellect. For he encompasses in himself all things immortal, every intellect, every god, every soul, all for ever unmoving. For why should it seek to change when all is well with it? Where should it seek to go away to when it has everything in itself? But it does not even seek to increase, since it is most perfect. Therefore all things in it are perfect, that it may be altogether perfect, having nothing which is not

so, having nothing in itself which does not think; but it thinks not by seeking but by having. Its blessedness is not something acquired, but all things are in eternity, and the true eternity, which time copies, running round the soul, letting some things go and attending to others. For around Soul things come one after another: now Socrates, now a horse, always some one particular reality; but Intellect is all things. It has therefore everything at rest in the same place, and it only is, and its "is" is for ever, and there is no place for the future for then too it is—or for the past—for nothing there has passed away—but all things remain stationary for ever, since they are the same, as if they were satisfied with themselves for being so.

But each of them is Intellect and Being, and the whole is universal Intellect and Being, Intellect making Being exist in thinking it, and Being giving Intellect thinking and existence by being thought. But the cause of thinking is something else, which is also cause of being; they both therefore have a cause other than themselves. For they are simultaneous and exist together and one does not abandon the other, but this one is two things, Intellect and Being and thinking and thought, Intellect as thinking and Being as thought. For there could not be thinking without otherness, and also sameness. These then are primary, Intellect, Being, Otherness, Sameness; but one must also include Motion and Rest. One must include movement if there is thought, and rest that it may think the same; and otherness, that there may be thinker and thought; or else, if you take away otherness, it will become one and keep silent; and the objects of thought, also, must have otherness in relation to each other. But one must include sameness, because it is one with itself, and all have some common unity; and the distinctive quality of each is otherness. The fact that there are several of these primaries makes number and quantity; and the particularity of each makes quality, and from these as principles everything else comes.

5. This god, then, which is over the soul, is multiple; and soul exists among the intelligible realities in close unity with them, unless it wills to desert them. When it has come near then to him and, in a way, become one with him, it lives for ever. Who is it, then, who begat this god? The simple god, the one who is prior to this kind of multiplicity, the cause of this one's existence and multiplicity, the maker of number. For number is not primary: the One is prior to the dyad, but the dyad is secondary and, originating from the One, has it as definer, but is itself of its own nature indefinite; but when it is defined, it is already a number, but a number as substance; and soul too is a number. For masses and magnitudes are not primary: these things which have thickness come afterwards, and sense-perception thinks they are realities. Even in seeds it is not the moisture which is honourable, but what is unseen: and this is number and rational principle. Therefore what is called number in the intelligible world and the dyad are rational principles and Intellect; but the dyad is indefinite when one forms an idea of it by what may be called the substrate, but each and every number which comes from it and the One is a form, as if Intellect was shaped by the numbers which came to exist in it; but it is shaped in one way by the One and in another by itself, like sight in its actuality; for intellection is seeing sight, and both are one.

6. How then does it see, and whom does it see? And how did it come into existence at all and arise from the One so as to be able to see? For the soul now knows that these things must be, but longs to answer the question repeatedly discussed also by the ancient philosophers, how from the One, if it is such as we say it is, anything else, whether a multiplicity or a dyad or a number, came into existence, and why it did not on the contrary remain by itself, but such a great multiplicity flowed from it as that which is seen to exist in beings, but which we think it right to refer back to the One. Let us speak of it in this way, first invoking God himself, not in spoken words, but

stretching ourselves out with our soul into prayer to him, able in this way to pray alone to him alone. The contemplator, then, since God exists by himself as if inside the temple, remaining quiet beyond all things, must contemplate what correspond to the images already standing outside the temple, or rather that one image which appeared first; and this is the way in which it appeared: everything which is moved must have some end to which it moves. The One has no such end, so we must not consider that it moves. If anything comes into being after it, we must think that it necessarily does so while the One remains continually turned towards itself. When we are discussing eternal realities we must not let coming into being in time be an obstacle to our thought; in the discussion we apply the word "becoming" to them in attributing to them causal connection and order, and must therefore state that what comes into being from the One does so without the One being moved: for if anything came into being as a result of the One's being moved, it would be the third starting from the One, not the second, since it would come after the movement. So if there is a second after the One it must have come to be without the One moving at all, without any inclination or act of will or any sort of activity on its part. How did it come to be then, and what are we to think of as surrounding the One in its repose? It must be a radiation from it while it remains unchanged, like the bright light of the sun which, so to speak, runs round it, springing from it continually while it remains unchanged. All things which exist, as long as they remain in being, necessarily produce from their own substances, in dependence on their present power, a surrounding reality directed to what is outside them, a kind of image of the archetypes from which it was produced: fire produces the heat which comes from it; snow does not only keep its cold inside itself. Perfumed things show this particularly clearly. As long as they exist, something is diffused from themselves around them, and what is near them enjoys their existence. And all things when they come to perfection produce; the One is always perfect and therefore produces everlastingly; and its product is less than itself. What then must we say about the most perfect? Nothing can come from it except that which is next greatest after it. Intellect is next to it in greatness and second to it: for Intellect sees it and needs it alone; but it has no need of Intellect; and that which derives from something greater than Intellect is intellect, which is greater than all things, because the other things come after it: as Soul is an expression and a kind of activity of Intellect, just as Intellect is of the One. But soul's expression is obscure—for it is a ghost of Intellect—and for this reason it has to look to Intellect; but Intellect in the same way has to look to that god, in order to be Intellect. But it sees him, not as separated from him, but because it comes next after him, and there is nothing between, as also there is not anything between soul and Intellect. Everything longs for its parent and loves it, especially when parent and offspring are alone; but when the parent is the highest good, the offspring is necessarily with him and separate from him only in otherness.

7. But we say that Intellect is an image of that Good; for we must speak more plainly; first of all we must say that what has come into being must be in a way that Good, and retain much of it and be a likeness of it, as light is of the sun. But Intellect is not that Good. How then does it generate Intellect? Because by its return to it it sees: and this seeing is Intellect. For that which apprehends something else is either sense-perception or intellect; (sense-perception is a line etc.) but the circle is of a kind which can be divided; but this [intellectual apprehension] is not so. There is One here also, but the One is the productive power of all things. The things, then, of which it is the productive power are those which Intellect observes, in a way cutting itself off from the power; otherwise it would not be Intellect. For Intellect also has of itself a kind of intimate perception of its power, that it has power to produce substantial reality. Intel-

lect, certainly, by its own means even defines its being for itself by the power which comes from the One, and because its substance is a kind of single part of what belongs to the One and comes from the One, it is strengthened by the One and made perfect in substantial existence by and from it. But Intellect sees, by means of itself, like something divided proceeding from the undivided, that life and thought and all things come from the One, because that God is not one of all things; for this is how all things come from him, because he is not confined by any shape; that One is one alone: if he was all things, he would be numbered among beings. For this reason that One is none of the things in Intellect, but all things come from him. This is why they are substances; for they are already defined and each has a kind of shape. Being must not fluctuate, so to speak, in the indefinite, but must be fixed by limit and stability; and stability in the intelligible world is limitation and shape, and it is by these that it receives existence. "Of this lineage" is this Intellect of which we are speaking, a lineage worthy of the purest Intellect, that it should spring from nowhere else but the first principle, and when it has come into existence should generate all realities along with itself, all the beauty of the Ideas and all the intelligible gods; and it is full of the beings which it has generated and as it were swallows them up again, by keeping them in itself and because they do not fall out into matter and are not brought up in the house of Rhea; as the mysteries and the myths about the gods say riddlingly that Kronos, the wisest god, before the birth of Zeus took back and kept within himself all that he begat, and in this way is full and is Intellect in satiety; and after this they say he begat Zeus who is then his Koros [that is, boy and satiety]; for Intellect generates soul, since it is perfect Intellect. For since it was perfect it had to generate, and not be without offspring when it was so great a power. But its offspring could not be better than it (this is not so even here below) but had to be a lesser image of it, and in the same way indefinite, but defined by its parent and, so to speak, given a form. And the offspring of Intellect is a rational form and an existing being, that which thinks discursively; it is this which moves round Intellect and is light and trace of Intellect and dependent on it, united to it on one side and so filled with it and enjoying it and sharing in it and thinking, but, on the other side, in touch with the things which came after it, or rather itself generating what must necessarily be worse than soul; about these we must speak later. This is as far as the divine realities extend.

8. This is the reason why Plato says that all things are threefold "about the king of all"—he means the primary realities—and "the second about the second and the third about the third." But he also says that there is a "father of the cause," meaning Intellect by "the cause": for Intellect is his craftsman; and he says that it makes Soul in that "mixing-bowl" he speaks of. And the father of Intellect which is the cause he calls the Good and that which is beyond Intellect and "beyond being." And he also often calls Being and Intellect Idea: so Plato knew that Intellect comes from the Good and Soul from Intellect. And [it follows] that these statements of ours are not new; they do not belong to the present time, but were made long ago, not explicitly, and what we have said in this discussion has been an interpretation of them, relying on Plato's own writings for evidence that these views are ancient. And Parmenides also, before Plato, touched on a view like this, in that he identified Being and Intellect and that it was not among things perceived by the senses that he placed Being, when he said "Thinking and Being are the same." And he says that this Being is unmoved—though he does attach thinking to it—taking all bodily movement from it that it may remain always in the same state, and likening it to "the mass of a sphere," because it holds all things in its circumference and because its thinking is not external, but in itself. But when he said it was one, in his own works, he was open to criticism because this one of his was

The School of Plato, Roman Mosaic, n.d. The Platonism of late antiquity (and the Middle
Ages) was strongly influenced by Plotinus's development and modification of Plato's
thought. (*Scala/Art Resource, N.Y.*)

discovered to be many. But Parmenides in Plato speaks more accurately, and distinguishes from each other the first One, which is more properly called One, and the second which he calls "One-Many" and the third, "One and Many." In this way he too
agrees with the doctrine of the three natures.

9. And Anaxagoras also, when he says that Intellect is pure and unmixed, posits
that the first principle is simple and that the One is separate, but he neglects to give an
accurate account because of his antiquity. Heraclitus also knows that the one is eternal
and intelligible: for bodies are always coming into being and flowing away. And for
Empedocles Strife divides, but Love is the One—he too makes it incorporeal—and the
elements serve as matter. Later, Aristotle makes the first principle separate and intelligible, but when he says that it knows itself, he goes back again and does not make it
the first principle; and by making many other intelligible realities, as many as the heav-

enly spheres, that each particular intelligible may move one particular sphere, he describes the intelligible world in a different way from Plato, making a probable assumption which has no philosophical necessity. But one might doubt whether it is even probable: for it would be more probable that all the spheres, contributing their several movements to a single system, should look to one principle, the first. And one might enquire whether Aristotle thinks that the many intelligibles derive from one, the first, or whether there are many primary principles in the intelligible world; and if they derive from one, the situation will clearly be analogous to that of the heavenly spheres in the sense-world, where each contains the other and one, the outermost, dominates; so that there too the first would contain the others and there will be an intelligible universe; and, just as here in the sense-world the spheres are not empty, but the first is full of heavenly bodies and the others have heavenly bodies in them, so there also the moving principles will have many realities in them, and the realities there will be truer. But if each is primary principle, the primary principles will be a random assembly; and why will they be a community and in agreement on one work, the harmony of the whole universe? And how can the perceptible beings in heaven be equal in number to the intelligible movers? And how can the intelligibles even be many, when they are incorporeal, as they are, and matter does not divide them? For these reasons those of the ancient philosophers who took up positions closest to those of Pythagoras and his successors (and Pherecydes) held closely to this nature; but some of them worked out the idea fully in their own writings, others did not do so in written works but in unwritten group discussions, or left it altogether alone.

10. It has been shown that we ought to think that this is how things are, that there is the One beyond being, of such a kind as our argument wanted to show, so far as demonstration was possible in these matters, and next in order there is Being and Intellect, and the nature of Soul in the third place. And just as in nature there are these three of which we have spoken, so we ought to think that they are present also in ourselves. I do not mean in [ourselves as] beings of the sense-world—for these three are separate from the things of sense—but in [ourselves as] beings outside the realm of sense-perception; "outside" here is used in the same sense as those realities are also said to be "outside" the whole universe: so the corresponding realities in man are said to be "outside," as Plato speaks of the "inner man." Our soul then also is a divine thing and of a nature different [from the things of sense], like the universal nature of soul; and the human soul is perfect when it has intellect; and intellect is of two kinds, the one which reasons and the one which makes it possible to reason. Now this reasoning part of the soul, which needs no bodily instrument for its reasoning, but preserves its activity in purity in order that it may be able to engage in pure reasoning, one could without mistake place, as separate and unmixed with body, in the primary intelligible realm. I or we should not look for a place in which to put it, but make it exist outside all place. For this is how it is by itself and outside and immaterial, when it is alone and retains nothing from the nature of body. This is the reason why Plato says of the universe also that the craftsman wrapped the soul round it "from outside," indicating the part of the soul which remains in the intelligible; and he said obscurely about us that the soul is "on top in the head." And his exhortation to separate ourselves is not meant in a spatial sense—this [higher part] of soul is naturally separated—but refers to our not inclining to the body, and to our not having mental images, and our alienation from the body—if by any chance one could make the remaining form of soul ascend, and take along with us to the heights that of it which is established here below, which alone is the craftsman and modeller of the body and is actively concerned with it.

11. Since, then, there exists soul which reasons about what is right and good, and discursive reasoning which enquires about the rightness and goodness of this or that particular thing, there must be some further permanent rightness from which arises the discursive reasoning in the realm of soul. Or how else would it manage to reason? And if soul sometimes reasons about the right and good and sometimes does not, there must be in us Intellect which does not reason discursively but always possesses the right, and there must be also the principle and cause and God of Intellect. He is not divided, but abides, and as he does not abide in place he is contemplated in many beings, in each and every one of those capable of receiving him as another self, just as the centre of a circle exists by itself, but every one of the radii in the circle has its point in the centre and the lines bring their individuality to it. For it is with something of this sort in ourselves that we are in contact with god and are with him and depend upon him; and those of us who converge towards him are firmly established in him.

12. Why then, when we have such great possessions, do we not consciously grasp them, but are mostly inactive in these ways, and some of us are never active at all? They are always occupied in their own activities, Intellect, and that which is before Intellect, always in itself, and soul, which is in this sense "ever-moving." For not everything which is in the soul is immediately perceptible, but it reaches us when it enters into perception; but when a particular active power does not give a share in its activity to the perceiving power, that activity has not yet pervaded the whole soul. We do not therefore yet know it, since we are accompanied by the perceptive power and are not a part of soul but the whole soul. And further, each soul-part, since it is always living, always exercises its own activity by itself; but the discovery of it comes when sharing with the perceptive power and conscious awareness takes place. If then there is to be conscious apprehension of the powers which are present in this way, we must turn our power of apprehension inwards, and make it attend to what is there. It is as if someone was expecting to hear a voice which he wanted to hear and withdrew from other sounds and roused his power of hearing to catch what, when it comes, is the best of all sounds which can be heard; so here also we must let perceptible sounds go (except in so far as we must listen to them) and keep the soul's power of apprehension pure and ready to hear the voices from on high.

* * *

ENNEAD V, TRACTATE 3: ON THE KNOWING HYPOSTASES AND THAT WHICH IS BEYOND

[12. cont.] But the One, as it is beyond Intellect, so is beyond knowledge, and as it does not in any way need anything, so it does not even need knowing; but knowing has its place in the second nature. For knowing is one thing; but that is one without the thing; for if it is one thing it would not be the absolute One: for "absolute" comes before "something."

13. It is, therefore, truly ineffable: for whatever you say about it, you will always be speaking of a "something." But "beyond all things and beyond the supreme majesty of Intellect" is the only one of all the ways of speaking of it which is true; it is not its name, but says that it is not one of all things and "has no name," because we can say nothing of it: we only try, as far as possible, to make signs to ourselves about it. But when we raise the difficulty "Then it has no perception of itself and is not even conscious of itself and does not even know itself," we should consider that by saying this

we are turning ourselves round and going in the opposite direction. I or we are making it many when we make it object of knowledge and knowledge, and by attributing thought to it we make it need thought: even if thought goes intimately with it, thought will be superfluous to it. I or in general thought seems to be an intimate consciousness of the whole when many parts come together in the same thing; [this is so] when a thing knows itself, which is knowing in the proper sense: each single part is just itself and seeks nothing; but if the thinking is of what is outside, the thoughts will be deficient, and not thought in the proper sense. But that which is altogether simple and self-sufficient needs nothing; but what is self-sufficient in the second degree, but needs itself, this is what needs to think itself; and that which is deficient in relation to itself achieves self-sufficiency by being a whole, with an adequacy deriving from all its parts, intimately present to itself and inclining to itself. For intimate self-consciousness is a consciousness of something which is many: even the name bears witness to this. And thinking, which is prior, turns inward to Intellect which is obviously multiple; for even if it only says this, "I am existent," it says it as a discovery, and says it plausibly, for existence is multiple: since if it concentrated its gaze on itself as something simple and said "I am existent," it could not attain either itself or existence. For it does not mean something like a stone by existence, when it is speaking the truth, but says many things in one word. For this being—which is meant to be real being and not what has a trace of being, which would not even be called being because of this trace, but is as image to archetype—contains many things. Well, then, will not each of these many things be thought? Now if you want to grasp the "isolated and alone," you will not think; but absolute being is multiple in itself, and if you speak of something else, being contains it. But if this is so, if anything is the simplest of all, it will not possess thought of itself: for if it is to possess it, it will possess it by being multiple. It is not therefore thought, nor is there any thinking about it.

14. How then do we ourselves speak about it? We do indeed say something about it, but we certainly do not speak it, and we have neither knowledge or thought of it. But if we do not have it in knowledge, do we not have it at all? But we have it in such a way that we speak about it, but do not speak it. For we say what it is not, but we do not say what it is: so that we speak about it from what comes after it. But we are not prevented from having it, even if we do not speak it. But just as those who have a god within them and are in the grip of divine possession may know this much, that they have something greater within them, even if they do not know what, and from the ways in which they are moved and the things they say get a certain awareness of the god who moves them, though these are not the same as the mover; so we seem to be disposed towards the One, divining, when we have our intellect pure, that this is the inner intellect, which gives substance and everything else which belongs to this level, but that he is not only of a kind not to be these, but something higher than what we call "being," but is more and greater than anything said about him, because he is higher than speech and thought and awareness; he gives us these, but he is not these himself.

15. But how does he give them? By having them, or by not having them? But how did he give what he does not have? But if he has them, he is not simple; if he does not have them, how does the multiplicity come from him? One might perhaps grant that he gives one simple thing from himself—yet there would be room for enquiry how this could come from the absolute One; but all the same one can speak of the radiance from him, as from a light—but how can he give many things? Now what comes from him could not be the same as himself. If then it is not the same, it cannot of course be better: for what could be better than the One or in any way transcend him? It must then be worse; and this means more deficient. What then is more deficient than the One?

That which is not one; it is therefore many; but all the same it aspires to the One: so it is a one—many. For all that is not one is kept in being by the one, and is what it is by this "one": for if it had not become one, even though it is composed of many parts, it is not yet what one would call "itself." And if it is possible to say of each individual part what it is, one says it because each of them is one and it is it because of this very fact. But that which does not already have many parts in itself is not one by participation in the One, but is the One itself, not the "one" predicated of something else but because it is this One from which, somehow, the others derive their oneness, some [in a greater degree] because they are near and others [in a lesser degree] because they are far away. For that which comes immediately after it shows clearly that it is immediately after it because its multiplicity is a one-everywhere; for although it is a multiplicity it is at the same time identical with itself and there is no way in which you could divide it, because "all things are together"; for each of the things also which come from it, as long as it participates in life, is a one—many: for it cannot reveal itself as a one—all. But [Intellect] does reveal itself as a one—all, because it comes after the origin: for its origin is really one and truly one. But that which comes after the origin is, somehow, under the pressure of the One, all things by its participation in the One, and each and every part of it is both all and one. What then are "all things"? All things of which that One is the principle. But how is that One the principle of all things? Is it because as principle it keeps them in being, making each one of them exist? Yes, and because it brought them into existence. But how did it do so? By possessing them beforehand. But it has been said that in this way it will be a multiplicity. But it had them in such a way as not to be distinct: they are distinguished on the second level, in the rational form. For this is already actuality; but the One is the potency of all things. But in what way is it the potency? Not in the way in which matter is said to be in potency, because it receives: for matter is passive; but this [material] way of being a potency is at the opposite extreme to making. How then does the One make what it does not have? It does not do it casually, nor reflecting on what it will make, but all the same it will make. Now it has been said that, if anything comes from the One, it must be something different from it; and in being different, it is not one: for if it was, it would be that One. But if it is not one, but two, it must necessarily also be many: for it is already the same and different and qualified and all the rest. And that what comes from the One is certainly not one, may be taken as demonstrated; but it is worth querying the proposition that it is a multiplicity, and a multiplicity of the sort which is observed in what comes after it; and the necessity of there being anything after the One remains to be enquired into.

16. It has been said elsewhere that there must be something after the first, and in a general way that it is power, and overwhelming power; and the point has also been made that this is to be believed on the evidence of all other things, because there is nothing, even among the things on the lowest level, which does not have power to produce. But we now have to add this further point, that, since in things which are generated it is not possible to go upwards but only to go downwards and move further towards multiplicity, the principle of each group of things is simpler than they are themselves. Therefore that which makes the world of sense could not be a world of sense itself, but must be an intellect and an intelligible world; and that which is before this and generates it could not be intellect or an intelligible world, but simpler than intellect and simpler than an intelligible world. For many does not come from many, but this [intelligible] many comes from what is not many: for this would not be the principle if it was also many itself, but something else before it. There must therefore be a concentration into a real one outside all multiplicity and any ordinary sort of simplicity, if it is to be really simple. But how is what comes from it a multiple and universal

rational form, when it is obviously not a rational form? And if it is not this why does rational form come not from rational form [but something else]? And how does what is like the Good come from the Good? What does it have from the Good in virtue of which it is called "like the Good"? Is it unchanging stability? What has this to do with the Good? For we seek stability because it is one of the goods. We seek that before stability from which it will not be necessary to depart, because it is the Good; but if it was not the Good, it would be necessary to go away from it. Is it then having a stable life and abiding willingly with it [which is "desirable"]? If then its life is satisfactory to it, it is clear that it seeks nothing; so its stability seems to be for this reason, that what is there present to it is sufficient for it. But its life is satisfactory because all things are present to it, and present in such a way that they are not other than it. But if it has all life, and a clear and perfect life, then every soul and every intellect is in it, and no part of life or intellect is absent from it. It is sufficient then for itself and seeks nothing; but if it seeks nothing, it has in itself what it would have sought, if it was not present. Therefore it has in itself the Good, which is either something of the sort which we called life and intellect, or something else which is an incidental accompaniment of these. But if this is the Good, there would be nothing beyond life and intellect. But if there is that something beyond, it is clear that the life of this other is directed to that and dependent on that, and has its existence from that and lives towards that; for that is its principle. That, therefore, must be better than life and intellect; thus the other will turn towards it both the life which is in it, a kind of image of the life in that in so far as this lives, and the intellect in it, a kind of representation of what is in that, whatever this may be.

17. What then is better than the wisest life, without fault or mistake, and than Intellect which contains all things, and than universal life and universal Intellect? If we say "That which made them"—well, how did it make them? And, in case something better may appear, our train of thought will not go on to something else but will stop at Intellect. But there are many reasons for going higher, particularly the fact that the self-sufficiency of Intellect which results from its being composed of all things is something which comes to it from outside: each of the things of which it is composed is obviously insufficient; and because each of them has participated in the absolute One and continues to participate in it, it is not the One itself. What then is that in which it participates, which makes it exist, and all things along with it? If it makes each individual thing exist, and it is by the presence of the One that the multitude of individual things in Intellect, and Intellect itself, is self-sufficient, it is clear that it, since it is the cause of existence and self-sufficiency, is not itself existence but beyond it and beyond self-sufficiency.

Is that enough? Can we end the discussion by saying this? No, my soul is still in even stronger labour. Perhaps she is now at the point when she must bring forth, having reached the fullness of her birth-pangs in her eager longing for the One. But we must sing another charm to her, if we can find one anywhere to allay her pangs. Perhaps there might be one in what we have said already, if we sang it over and over again. And what other charm can we find which has a sort of newness about it? The soul runs over all truths, and all the same shuns the truths we know if someone tries to express them in words and discursive thought; for discursive thought, in order to express anything in words, has to consider one thing after another: this is the method of description; but how can one describe the absolutely simple? But it is enough if the intellect comes into contact with it; but when it has done so, while the contact lasts, it is absolutely impossible, nor has it time, to speak; but it is afterwards that it is able to reason about it. One must believe one has seen, when the soul suddenly takes light: for this is from him and he is it; we must think that he is present when, like another god whom someone called to his house, he comes and brings light to us: for if he had not come, he would not have brought the light. So the unenlightened soul does not have him as god; but when it is enlightened it has what it sought, and this is the soul's true end, to touch that light and see it by itself, not by another light, but by the light which is also its means of seeing. It must see that light by which it is enlightened: for we do not see the sun by another light than his own. How then can this happen? Take away everything!